The Handbook of
Global Companies

Handbook of Global Policy Series

Series Editor
David Held
Master of University College and Professor of Politics and International Relations at Durham University

The Handbook of Global Policy series presents a comprehensive collection of the most recent scholarship and knowledge about global policy and governance. Each Handbook draws together newly commissioned essays by leading scholars and is presented in a style which is sophisticated but accessible to undergraduate and advanced students, as well as scholars, practitioners, and others interested in global policy. Available in print and online, these volumes expertly assess the issues, concepts, theories, methodologies, and emerging policy proposals in the field.

Published

The Handbook of Global Climate and Environment Policy
Robert Falkner

The Handbook of Global Energy Policy
Andreas Goldthau

The Handbook of Global Companies
John Mikler

The Handbook of Global Companies

Edited by

John Mikler

WILEY-BLACKWELL

A John Wiley & Sons, Ltd., Publication

This edition first published 2013
© 2013 John Wiley and Sons Ltd.

Wiley-Blackwell is an imprint of John Wiley & Sons, formed by the merger of Wiley's global Scientific, Technical and Medical business with Blackwell Publishing.

Registered Office
John Wiley & Sons Ltd, The Atrium, Southern Gate, Chichester, West Sussex, PO19 8SQ, UK

Editorial Offices
350 Main Street, Malden, MA 02148-5020, USA
9600 Garsington Road, Oxford, OX4 2DQ, UK
The Atrium, Southern Gate, Chichester, West Sussex, PO19 8SQ, UK

For details of our global editorial offices, for customer services, and for information about how to apply for permission to reuse the copyright material in this book please see our website at www.wiley.com/wiley-blackwell.

The right of John Mikler to be identified as the author of the editorial material in this work has been asserted in accordance with the UK Copyright, Designs and Patents Act 1988.

Wiley also publishes its books in a variety of electronic formats. Some content that appears in print may not be available in electronic books.

Designations used by companies to distinguish their products are often claimed as trademarks. All brand names and product names used in this book are trade names, service marks, trademarks or registered trademarks of their respective owners. The publisher is not associated with any product or vendor mentioned in this book. This publication is designed to provide accurate and authoritative information in regard to the subject matter covered. It is sold on the understanding that the publisher is not engaged in rendering professional services. If professional advice or other expert assistance is required, the services of a competent professional should be sought.

Library of Congress Cataloging-in-Publication Data

The handbook of global companies / edited by John Mikler.
   pages cm.
  Includes bibliographical references and index.
  ISBN 978-0-470-67323-2 (cloth)
  1. International business enterprises–Political aspects.   2. Business and politics.
3. International relations.   I. Mikler, John.
   HD2755.5.H368 2013
   322′.3–dc23

                                                           2012047270

A catalogue record for this book is available from the British Library.

Cover image: Singapore cityscape at sunset © Jason Ho / Shutterstock
Cover design by Design Deluxe

Set in 10/12.5pt Sabon by Aptara Inc., New Delhi, India
Printed in Malaysia by Ho Printing (M) Sdn Bhd

1   2013

For Kara, Annika, and Erin

Contents

List of Illustrations

Figures

Tables

Notes on Contributors

Caner Bakir is Assistant Professor in the International Relations Department at Koc University, Istanbul, Turkey. He has worked as an Assistant Lecturer in the Accounting and Finance Department at Monash University, Melbourne. Prior to this, he worked as a banking specialist. His areas of research include institutional analysis, public policy, globalization, and governance. His work has been published in a number of leading journals including *Governance* and *Public Administration* and he has published a book with Bilgi University Press. His researches have been supported by the Scientific & Technological Research Council of Turkey (TUBITAK) and COST ACTION ISO905 (European Cooperation in Science and Technology). Bakir received the Incentive Award in Political Science awarded by TUBITAK in 2010.

Stephen Bell is Professor and former Head of the School of Political Science and International Studies at the University of Queensland. He is a Fellow of the Academy of Social Sciences in Australia. His recent books include *The Rise of the People's Bank of China: The Institutional Development of China's Financial and Monetary System* and *Rethinking Governance: The Centrality of the State in Modern Society*. He is currently working on two Australian Research Council funded projects, one on banking reform in China and the other on the performance of banks in the global financial crisis.

Patrick Bernhagen is Professor of Political Science at Zeppelin University, Germany, and Senior Lecturer in Politics and International Relations at the University of Aberdeen, United Kingdom. His main research interests are the political participation of citizens and firms as well as their strategies and success in gaining political influence. He is the author of *The Political Power of Business: Structure and Information in Public Policymaking* (2007) and co-editor (with Christian Haerpfer, Ronald Inglehart, and Chris Welzel) of *Democratization* (2009).

Pamela Blackmon is Assistant Professor, Department of Political Science at Penn State Altoona. Her research focuses on the policies of the international financial institutions, and she is currently examining the role of export credit agencies in international trade and finance. Her articles have been published in *International Studies Review*, *Women's Studies*, and *Central Asian Survey*, in addition to various book chapters including a review essay in volume VI of the *International Studies Encyclopedia*. Her first book, *In the Shadow of Russia: Reform in Kazakhstan and Uzbekistan*, was published in 2011.

Frank Boons is Associate Professor in the Department of Public Administration at Erasmus University Rotterdam, The Netherlands, and Director of the off-campus PhD program on Cleaner Production, Cleaner Products, Industrial Ecology and Sustainability. He is subject editor, Governance of Material and Energy Flows, of the *Journal of Cleaner Production*.

Sherri Brown has a PhD in Political Science from McMaster University, and was a 2007–2011 Trudeau Foundation Doctoral Scholar and SSHRC Canada Graduate Scholar, with a research specialization in political economy and global health policy. She is currently a postdoctoral fellow at the University of California–San Francisco, with the Center for Tobacco Control Research and Education and the Cardiovascular Research Institute. Her current research explores the roles and impacts of tobacco, food and beverage, and alcohol companies in health policy processes in low- and middle-income countries.

Tanja Brühl is Professor of Political Science at Goethe–University Frankfurt, focusing on international institutions and peace processes. Her main areas of research include global governance; peace and conflict studies; and international environmental politics. Notable publications are, inter alia: *Nichtregierungsorganisationen als Akteure internationaler Umweltverhandlungen* (2003), and "Representing the People? NGOs in International Negotiations," in Kristina Hahn and Jens Steffek (eds), *Evaluating Transnational NGOs: Legitimacy, Accountability, Representation* (2010).

Cantay Caliskan is a graduate student in the Department of International Relations at Koc University, Istanbul, Turkey. His main research interests are political economy, the politics of Cyprus, and renewable energy.

Hevina S. Dashwood is Associate Professor of Political Science at Brock University, Canada. Dashwood's broad research interests encompass private global governance, corporate social responsibility (CSR), and international development. Dashwood's current research program is concerned with CSR adoption in the global mining sector, the dissemination of global standards specific to mining and the translation of global CSR standards at the local level in the developing country context. Dashwood has numerous book chapters and articles in peer-review journals related to CSR and mining, including *Canadian Journal of Political Science*, *Canadian Journal of Development Studies*, *Business and Society Review*, and *Business and Society* (forthcoming). Dashwood's recent book is *The Rise of Global Corporate Social Responsibility: Mining and the Spread of Global Norms* (2012).

Deborah Elms is Head, Temasek Foundation Centre for Trade and Negotiations and Senior Fellow of International Political Economy at the S. Rajaratnam School of International Studies at Nanyang Technological University, Singapore. Dr Elms participates in teaching, research, and networking. Her research interests are negotiations and decision-making, particularly in trade. She also conducts a range of teaching and training for government officials from around Asia, for members of parliament, for business leaders, and for graduate students. She has provided consulting to the governments of Abu Dhabi, Sri Lanka, Cambodia, Taiwan, and Singapore on a range of trade issues. Dr Elms received a PhD in political science from the University of Washington, an MA in International Relations from the University of Southern California, and a BA and BS from Boston University in international relations and journalism.

Matthias Finger holds a PhD in Political Science and a PhD in Adult Education from the University of Geneva. He has been an Assistant Professor at Syracuse University (New York), an Associate Professor at Columbia University (New York), and a Full Professor of Management of Public Enterprises at the Swiss Federal Institute of Public Administration. Since 2002, he holds the Chair of Management of Network Industries at the Ecole Polytechnique Fédérale in Lausanne, Switzerland. Since 2010 he has also been a part-time Professor at the European University Institute in Florence, Italy, where he directs the Florence School of Regulation's Transport Area. His main research interest is on the liberalization, re-regulation, and governance of infrastructures in the transport, energy, and communications sectors. He is the co-editor-in-chief of the journal *Competition and Regulation in Network Industries*.

Ann Florini is Professor of Public Policy, School of Social Sciences, Singapore Management University. She is also Non-resident Senior Fellow in the Foreign Policy Studies Program at the Brookings Institution in Washington, DC. She is internationally recognized as an authority on new approaches to global governance, focusing on the roles of information flows, civil society, and the private sector in addressing global issues. Her books include *China Experiments: From Local Innovation to National Reform* (with Hairong Lai and Yeling Tan, 2012); *The Right to Know: Transparency for an Open World* (2007); *The Coming Democracy: New Rules for Running a New World* (2003; 2005); and *The Third Force: The Rise of Transnational Civil Society* (2000). She has published numerous scholarly and policy articles in such journals as *Energy Policy*, *Global Governance*, *Global Policy*, *International Security*, *International Studies Quarterly*, and *Foreign Policy*. Dr Florini received her PhD in Political Science from UCLA and a Masters in Public Affairs from Princeton University.

Luc Fransen is Assistant Professor at the Institute for Public Administration at Leiden University and Jean Monnet Fellow at the European University Institute. He recently published his monograph *Corporate Social Responsibility and Global Labor Standards* (2012) and has published research articles in amongst others *Socio-Economic Review*, *Governance*, *Organization*, and *Review of International Political Economy*. His research focuses on the transnational governance of social and environmental standards, international labor policy, corporate social responsibility, and the strategies of civil society organizations.

Doris Fuchs is Professor of International Relations and Development at the University of Muenster, Germany. Her primary areas of research are corporate structural and discursive power, private governance, sustainable development/consumption, and food politics and policy. Among her publications are *Business Power in Global Governance* and *An Institutional Basis for Environmental Stewardship*, as well as articles in peer-reviewed journals such as *Millennium, Global Environmental Politics, Business and Politics, International Interactions, Journal on Consumer Policy, Agriculture and Human Values, Food Policy*, and *Energy Policy.*

Andrea Goldstein is the Senior Economic Affairs Officer at the Office for East and Northeast Asia of the UN Economic and Social Commission for Asia and the Pacific. He is on leave from the OECD, where he served in various capacities, including as Deputy Director of the Heiligendamm L'Aquila Process (the G8–G5 political dialogue) Support Unit. Andrea also worked at the World Bank Group and studied at Bocconi, Columbia, and Sussex Universities. He has published widely on emerging economies – including *BRIC* (2011), emerging multinationals, including *Multinational Companies from Emerging Economies: Composition, Conceptualization and Direction in the Global Economy* (2007, 2009) – and the impact of the emergence of China and India on other developing countries. He has published in refereed journals, including the *Asian Development Review, Business History, Cambridge Journal of Economics, CEPAL Review, Industrial and Corporate Change, Journal of Chinese Economic and Business Studies, Journal of World Business, Transnational Corporations*, and *The World Economy.* He has also published op-eds in the *Financial Times, Helsingin Sanomat, Le Monde, South China Morning Post, La Repubblica*, and *Corriere della Sera.* He is a frequent contributor to www.lavoce.info.

Matthias Hofferberth is Assistant Professor for International Relations at the University of Texas, San Antonio. His research and teaching interests lie in the fields of global governance and multinational enterprises, as well as in international relations theory and norms. His recent publication is "The Binding Dynamics of Non-Binding Governance Arrangements: The Voluntary Principles on Security and Human Rights and the Cases of BP and Chevron," *Business and Politics*, 13 (4), 2011.

Sung-Young Kim is Lecturer in the Department of Political Studies at the University of Auckland, New Zealand. His expertise is industry strategy in East Asia and his work has been published in a number of prestigious journals including *Review of International Political Economy* and *New Political Economy.* He is currently working on a book project entitled *Telecommunications Inc.: Korea's Challenge to Qualcomm*, while also undertaking research on Green Growth strategies in East Asia.

Nina Kolleck is a postdoctoral researcher and lecturer for sustainability governance at the Departments of Political and Educational Sciences and Psychology at the Freie Universität Berlin in Germany. She studied Political Science, Economics, and Public Law in Potsdam (Germany), Caen (France), and Quito (Ecuador) and holds a PhD in Political Science from the Freie Universität Berlin.

Sarianna M. Lundan holds the Chair in International Management and Governance at the University of Bremen in Germany. She received her PhD from Rutgers University (United States), and has held prior appointments at the University of Reading (United Kingdom), and at Maastricht University (The Netherlands). She is an

Associate Research Fellow at the Research Institute of the Finnish Economy (ETLA) in Helsinki, and a founding member of the Center for Transnational Studies (Zen-Tra), a joint initiative of the Universities of Bremen and Oldenburg. She has published widely in journals and books, and has co-authored with John H. Dunning the second edition of *Multinational Enterprises and the Global Economy*, which has become an influential reference work in the field of international business. She has also participated extensively in the work of UNCTAD in connection with the World Investment Reports and the Investment Policy Reviews. She is an elected Fellow of the European International Business Academy (EIBA), and serves on several editorial boards, including the *Journal of International Business Studies*, *Multinational Business Review*, and the *Global Strategy Journal*. Her current research interests focus on the co-evolution of multinational enterprises and the institutional environment in which they operate.

Kate Macdonald is a Lecturer at the University of Melbourne, having held previous positions at the London School of Economics and Political Science, the Australian National University, and Oxford University. Her research focuses on the politics of transnational production and business, with a particular focus on social, labor, and human rights regulation of global business.

John A. Mathews is Professor of Strategic Management at Macquarie Graduate School of Management, Macquarie University, Sydney. He is concurrently Eni Chair of Competitive Dynamics and Global Strategy at LUISS Guido Carli University, Rome. He is the author of several books including *Strategizing, Disequilibrium and Profit* (2006), *Dragon Multinational: A New Model of Global Growth* (2002), and *Tiger Technology: The Creation of a Semiconductor Industry in East Asia* (2000), this latter appearing in a Chinese translation. His most recent contribution to the debate over future directions for strategy and entrepreneurship studies is his paper "Lachmannian Insights into Strategic Entrepreneurship: Resources, Activities and Routines in a Disequilibrium World," published in the journal *Organization Studies* in February 2010. Professor Mathews' research has increasingly focused on the interrelated topics of low-carbon economy, renewable energy and the industrial dynamics of transition away from fossil-fueled systems; on industrial clusters and networked development; and on the rise of China in the global economy. Papers addressing these topics recently published include "China's Moves towards Adopting a Circular Economy" in *Journal of Industrial Ecology*; and "Mobilizing Private Financing to Drive an Energy Industrial Revolution" in *Energy Policy*. A book-length treatment of the *Next Great Transformation: The Greening of Capitalism*, is currently under review. Prior to this latest emphasis, his research focused on the internationalization of firms from the periphery, taking advantage of opportunities created by globalization, and expounded in such publications as those related to "Dragon Multinationals," and on patterns of technological learning in the newly industrializing countries of East Asia, with emphasis first on high-tech industries like semiconductors and flat panel displays, and latterly on renewable energies and solar photovoltaic systems.

John Mikler is Senior Lecturer in the Department of Government and International Relations at the University of Sydney. His research interests are primarily focused on the role of transnational economic actors, particularly multinational corporations, and the interaction between them and states, international organizations, and civil society. He is the author of *Greening the Car Industry: Varieties of Capitalism and Climate Change* (2009), and has published widely in journals including *Business and Politics, Regulation and Governance, Global Society, Policy and Society, Cambridge Journal of Regions, Economy and Society,* and *New Political Economy*.

Terry O'Callaghan is a Senior Lecturer at the University of South Australia. His research focuses on political risk in mining and infrastructure sectors, primarily in the Asia-Pacific region. He is Director of the Centre for International Risk at UniSA and has an interest in the study of multinational corporations. He is currently finishing a book on reputation risk.

Tony Porter is Professor of Political Science at McMaster University in Hamilton, Canada. His books include *Globalization and Finance* (2005), *Technology, Governance and Political Conflict in International Industries* (2002), *Private Authority in International Affairs* (1999), co-edited, with A. Claire Cutler and Virginia Haufler, and *The Challenges of Global Business Authority: Democratic Renewal, Stalemate, or Decay?* (2010), co-edited with Karsten Ronit. He is currently co-authoring, with Heather McKeen-Edwards, *Transnational Financial Associations and the Governance of Global Finance: Assembling Power and Wealth*.

Denis Saint-Martin is an expert in public administration and policy. Since 2008, he has been the director of the European Union Centre of Excellence at the Université de Montréal and McGill University. His research interests deal with the regulation of ethics in politics, continuity and institutional change, new public management, and the politics of expertise. In 2005, he was a Fulbright scholar at the Kennedy School of Government and before that was a policy advisor in the Office of the Prime Minister of Canada.

Shana M. Starobin is a PhD candidate at the Nicholas School of the Environment and a Graduate Fellow at the Kenan Institute for Ethics at Duke University. Her most recent publication, "The Search for Credible Information in Social and Environmental Global Governance: The Kosher Label,"appears in the journal *Business and Politics*. Her current research interests include the transnational regulation of food and agriculture and its implications for rural livelihoods and the environment. She received her A.B. *magna cum laude* from Harvard College, and she completed a joint Masters in Public Policy and Environmental Management at Duke.

Marianne Thissen-Smits is a PhD candidate in Politics and International Relations at the University of Aberdeen, United Kingdom. Her research focuses on corporate social responsibility of transnational firms in a cross-country perspective. Prior to her PhD studies she worked as an Inspector for Health, Safety, and the Environment for the Dutch Mining Authorities and as a consultant for UNICEF (Kazakhstan), Shell (Oman), and Delta Environmental Logistics (Nigeria).

Vlado Vivoda is a Research Fellow at Griffith Asia Institute, Griffith University, in Brisbane, Australia. He has published widely on the topics related to the international political economy of extractive industries. His current research focus is on the political economy of mining and energy sectors, and on energy security in the Asia-Pacific region.

Hinrich Voss is a Roberts Academic Research Fellow at the Centre for International Business University of Leeds (CIBUL). He is interested in the international business strategies of multinational enterprises (MNEs) from developed and developing countries. Within this context he researches the internationalization and the international competitiveness of mainland Chinese companies. This research strand incorporates the influence of China's institutions on the international investment behavior of Chinese firms. He is also interested in how emerging market MNEs are affected by climate change policies and the institutional objectives to move towards. His research has been published in the *Journal of International Business Studies*, *Management International Review*, *International Business Review*, and the Chinese Academy of Social Science journal *China & World Economy*. In 2011, he published his monograph "The Determinants of Chinese Outward Investment." Dr Voss has been involved in research projects for UK Trade and Investment (China's Regional Cities) and Nestlé and received external research and travel funding from the EU, the British Economic and Social Research Council, the Sino-British Fellowship Trust, and the Worldwide Universities Network. Before joining CIBUL, he was a Postdoctoral Research Fellow at the White Rose East Asia Centre/National Institute for Chinese Studies. Dr Voss has been Visiting Researcher at the universities of Nanjing and Sydney. He is the Academic Leader of the Worldwide University Network Contemporary China Center (WUN CCC), Head of the advisory board of the NetImpact Chapter of LUBS, and ad hoc expert for the Europe China Research and Advice Network (ECRAN) and the EU SME Center, Beijing.

Stephen Wilks is Professor of Politics and former Deputy Vice Chancellor at the University of Exeter. He was a member of the UK Competition Commission and is currently a member of the UK Competition Appeal Tribunal. He has written extensively on government–industry relations and competition policy. His latest book is *The Political Power of the Business Corporation* forthcoming in 2013.

Cornelia Woll is Research Professor at Sciences Po Paris and co-directs the Max Planck Sciences Po Center for Coping with Instability in Market Societies (MaxPo) and the Interdisciplinary Center for the Evaluation of Public Policy (LIEPP). Her research focuses on international and comparative political economy, in particular business-government relations, trade, financial regulation, and European politics. She is the author of *Firm Interests: How Governments Shape Business Lobbying on Global Trade* (2008) and co-editor with Ben Clift of *Economic Patriotism in Open Economics* (2012). Her current book manuscript analyzes the recent bank bailouts in the United States and the European Union.

Shiufai Wong is Associate Professor at Macao Polytechnic Institute. He was Visiting Assistant Professor at Oklahoma State University and Senior Research Associate at City University of Hong Kong after receiving his PhD in Government and International Relations from the University of Sydney. He also has a decade-long experience in China and Asian markets, working for a German infrastructure consortium in its dealings with central and local governments. He has published more than a dozen articles on the state and governance.

Simon Zadek is writing in his independent capacity, and is Senior Fellow at the Global Green Growth Institute, and Senior Advisor at the International Institute for Sustainable Development. He is the founder and was the Chief Executive of AccountAbility, and until recently a non-resident Senior Fellow at Harvard's J.F. Kennedy School for Government. His book, *The Civil Corporation*, was awarded the Academy of Management's Social Issues in Management Award in 2006.

Preface

Policy is not something that is exclusively a matter for nation states. Nor is global policy purely a matter of concern for the international and intergovernmental organizations to which they belong. Each volume of the handbooks in this series of Handbooks of Global Policy focuses on particular policy areas (such as global trade, global social policy, and global health policy) or on issues (such as global inequality and poverty, and global migration), and all focus on institutions and governance. However, this Handbook explicitly focuses on perhaps the most important non-state actors that impact on and drive global policy processes and outcomes: global companies.

As they have grown and become increasingly multinational in their operations, global companies have taken on the mantle of central organizers of the global economy in addition to national economies. They control global markets and industry sectors, and are determiners of "who gets what" and therefore of social outcomes. The relationship that they have with the governments of nations and their citizens is central to any study of global policy. How odd it is then, that aside from studies of international business and management they remain relatively under-studied by comparison to the state and society. In particular, in the fields of international relations and comparative politics, and their related sub-fields, it is notable that studying global companies as complex and purposive political and social actors, in addition to economic ones, is still a relatively "cutting edge" endeavor. As I have noted elsewhere, while states and social movements are relatively well drawn, it remains the case that global companies are too often sketched as economic mechanisms of profit maximization, responding to market imperatives and regulations, and sometimes seeking to modify both, given their power to do so.

Global companies are so much more complex than this though. The authors of the chapters in this Handbook see them as political, social, and cultural, as well as economic entities, and examine their centrality in debates about global policy in this light. Some of the authors are emerging scholars. Others are well-established names in their fields. I am flattered to have been given the opportunity to approach them and to find myself in their company, and I thank them unreservedly for their excellent contributions. While there were several senior colleagues who warned me that taking on such an endeavor would be both time consuming and stressful, in truth thanks to the quality and timeliness of the chapters contributed it has largely been a delight.

As is always the case in any such project, there are many others who deserve mention. Inevitably, I am bound to leave someone out, and I hope they will forgive their unintended omission. My greatest thanks go to David Held, General Editor for the Handbooks of Global Policy series, for his helpful advice and guidance. I am particularly appreciative of the constructive, positive, and timely manner in which this has been offered – his kind words of encouragement and support have helped make the whole endeavor easier. For their support and advice on how to bring the whole Handbook together, and strategies for managing the processes involved, I also thank Ariadne Vromen, Diarmuid Maguire, Graeme Gill, Rodney Smith, and David Schlosberg. For both their words of encouragement and advice on potential contributors, I would particularly like to thank Linda Weiss, Susan Sell, Sol Picciotto, Natalia Nikolova, Miranda Schreurs, Jennifer Clapp, Claudio Radaelli, Kelly Kollman, Aseem Prakash, Michael Edwards, and Robert Wade. I also wish to thank the staff of Wiley-Blackwell for all their support and advice, particularly Ben Thatcher, Justin Vaughan, Sally Cooper, and Karen Raith. As always, I thank my wife, Kara, for her seemingly limitless understanding, much appreciated suggestions, and patience.

The opportunity in editing this Handbook was to present contemporary thought and analysis on the rise of companies that are more global than national, or are substantially transnational in their operations, with this in the context of a wide-ranging set of volumes on specific aspects of global policy and governance. In the process I have been given the chance to approach those whose work I have long admired, and to become acquainted with those whose research marks them as new and important voices in the field. I can think of no greater pleasure, and I hope that the readers of the Handbook will find it as useful and informative as I have enjoyed editing it.

John Mikler
University of Sydney, Australia

Chapter 1

Global Companies as Actors in Global Policy and Governance

John Mikler

Introduction

Globalization is the master concept of our time, invoked to describe the way in which the vast transborder flows of capital, goods, ideas, and people are transforming society, politics, and economics. However, it is unfortunately the case that the centrality of global companies as actors in this process of transformation, and a complex understanding of the role they play in respect of it, remains more a matter of *a priori* assumptions in much of the globalization literature. In assuming corporations are primarily "mechanisms" for profit maximization, from a policy and governance perspective anything they do beyond this is usually seen as resulting from threats to their financial performance via penalties for non-compliance with regulations, or taxing their products so that changes in market forces present them with no alternative but to change what they offer consumers. Alternatively, incentives are required such as subsidies for new products (e.g. research and development tax breaks), or new opportunities stemming from market mechanisms (e.g. emissions trading schemes). This is made more difficult in a global context, given the structural power of global companies that undermines national efforts to regulate them in the public interest.

Depending on the issues and the circumstances, this may all be true to a greater or lesser extent, but such a simplistic rendering of global companies does not convey enough about their underlying motivations. As their role as agents of globalization has come to be better understood, their motivations are increasingly the subject of much deeper and complex analysis. In particular, many scholars, including the contributors to this Handbook, are now addressing their relative under-construction by comparison to studies of the state and society. They analyze them as not just purely economic, but as political and social actors, and not just for the impacts they have, but the outcomes they drive.

The Handbook of Global Companies, First Edition. Edited by John Mikler.
© 2013 John Wiley & Sons, Ltd. Published 2013 by John Wiley & Sons, Ltd.

The intention in this introductory chapter is to lay some initial foundations and set the scene for the contributions by these scholars in the chapters to follow. Where global companies are located in the waves of theorizing globalization is considered initially, before considering how global companies matter as actors in global policy and governance. With a sense of them in this respect, just who and what they are that they matter in this regard is then outlined in order to set the scene for an overview of the parts and chapters to follow.

The State Is Not Yet Dead and the Market Is Not "in Charge"

Much of the early globalization debates revolved around the manner in which impersonal market forces, rather than states, were increasingly "in charge." As the redoubtable Susan Strange put it, "where states were once the masters of markets, now it is markets which, on many crucial issues, are the masters over the governments of states" (Strange 1996: 4). In the aftermath of the Cold War, this was seen as an inevitable result of the irresistible "forces" of globalization by authors such as Fukuyama (1992) and Ohmae (1990) who saw a world of *laissez faire* capitalism and the "inevitability" of neoliberal market deregulation and privatization that went with it. The view of these hyperglobalists, as they are now often called, was popularized by Friedman's (1999: 87) declaration that all states had no alternative but to don their "golden straightjackets" in recognition that globalization means "your economy grows and your politics shrinks." They could try to put on other "clothes," but not only would they be unfashionable, they would suffer the consequences as the market chastised them for so doing with all the economic, social, and political pain that would be inflicted as a result. As such, many commentators actually foresaw the death of the state. Those on the left of the political spectrum despaired of the prospect, while those on the right celebrated it, but in between the extremes there was a growing acceptance of the proposition that states would increasingly function (rather than rule) in a passive, facilitative role as the places where global market imperatives were played out, and in this respect they would serve as "merely the handmaidens of firms" (Strange 1997: 184; see also Crouch 2004).

What a load of "globaloney" retorted others (Hay and Marsh 2000: 6)![1] Skeptics, such as Hirst and Thompson (1996) and Weiss (1998) who famously dismissed the "myth of the powerless state," subsequently attacked the hyperglobalists' zeal for the inevitability of free market capitalism writ large on the world. Their skepticism was not so much ideological, as it was based on a critique of what seemed a much too sweeping and disembodied account of globalization. In particular, they pointed out that the governments of nations remain very much drivers of the processes and outcomes of governance, as did those who followed them (e.g. see Bell and Hindmoor 2009; Drezner 2007; Weiss 2003). While many stressed the way the marketization of all aspects of society and state functions has produced a neoliberal form of the state, scholars in this vein stressed the way that states have embraced markets as a policy choice rather than having it thrust upon them (e.g. see Tiberghien 2007; Thatcher 2007). Indeed, there has been a vast literature since Vogel's (1996) *Freer Markets More Rules* that examines the marketization of the functions of the state as a process of reregulation rather than deregulation.

As for the ideological aspects underpinning globalization, many scholars have recognized the power of the idea, and the political impact of leaders who enthusiastically embraced the neoliberal market reforms that sprang from it. For example, Margaret Thatcher did her best to institutionalize this view given her much cited "TINA" principle: There Is No Alternative to the free market. Ronald Reagan agreed, as did world leaders of more left-leaning political persuasions who followed, such as Bill Clinton whose 1992 presidential campaign was marked by the phrase "it's the economy stupid" to excuse his administration's likely impotence in the face of global market forces. In a similar vein, on taking office as Britain's new Labour Prime Minister in 1997 Tony Blair said that "the determining context of economic policy is the new global market," which Ralston Saul (1997: 21) cheekily translated as "don't worry, I won't be able to do much." Even so, they were skeptical that there was anything particularly new about globalization. As Wade (1996) pointed out, those predisposed to embrace the inevitability of the market being in charge and the demise of the state have been predicting this for at least the last two hundred years. For example, writers of the early to mid-nineteenth century envisaged "a single, more or less standardized world where all governments would acknowledge the truths of political economy and liberalism would be carried throughout the world" (Hobsbawm 1977, quoted in Wade 1996: 61).

Where are corporations in this debate? As authors such as Culpepper (2011) and Fuchs (2005) note, too often they go missing in what amounts to a states-versus-markets account, with more focus on the states and *a priori* assumptions about the markets. The politics of global capitalism is more complex than this, and the reality is that as key agents of global integration, global companies are central to an understanding of the transformations underway in the policy process and new forms of governance that are the outcome of the increasingly globalized world in which we live. After all, the complex independence that underlies the concept of globalization calls for a study of the continually evolving relationship between state and non-state actors, rather than claiming the loss of sovereignty by states to "markets." Therefore, focusing on global companies as the dominant private actors driving the processes of globalization grounds the debate as it re-embodies the forces for change as opposed to the shrill pronouncements of those who declared the inevitable death of the state on the altar of global forces that are "out there" beyond their control.

Considering global companies also shifts the focus to the processes by which global politics is being transformed. Globalization is a dynamic concept. As the term implies, it is a set of processes not an outcome. It is not an "ism" but a process of "ization." Seen in this light, authors such as Held *et al.* (1999), Dicken (2007), Hay and Marsh (2000), and contributions to be found in collections such as Held and McGrew (2003) are emblematic of those who embrace a contemporary transformationalist perspective on the concept of globalization. They reject the epochal change prophesized by the hyperglobalists, but while sharing the concerns of the skeptics they have a dynamic perspective on the question of state sovereignty, in the sense that they see states' political agency as increasingly relying on them sharing sovereignty with each other in order to retain it, as well as with non-state actors such as global companies that are themselves agents of the transformation underway. Theirs is an institutional and relational conception of globalization through which political agency is being reconstructed as a result of the processes of transformation driven by the actors involved. As such, an actor-centered basis for analysis serves us best in understanding this as it is not that disembodied market "forces" have taken over, but that in a more interdependent world there are more actors involved, and global companies are central among these.

The Dominance of Global Companies

The myth that markets are and should be in charge has long been propounded by those who would attack the state. The "father of liberalism," Adam Smith, was among the first to lead such an attack with his reference to the governing power of the market's invisible hand. The invisible hand he referred to was an allegorical one, but it came to be accepted as real and inevitable. In Mikler (2012) I have argued that the veracity of "the market" as a concept for understanding global economic relations should be more widely debated than it often is. This is because rather than being buffeted by the competitive forces of global markets that the hyperglobalists asserted were now in charge, the reality is that the global economy is highly concentrated and oligopolistic. All the world's major industrialized sectors are now controlled by five multinational corporations (MNCs) at most, while 28% have one corporation that accounts for more than 40% of global sales (Harrod 2006: 25; see also Fuchs 2007).

A basic measure of the size and power of these corporations is given by their annual sales revenues in comparison to the national incomes and expenditures of states. Data from UNCTAD (2011) and the IMF (2011) indicates that in 2008 the top 20 non-financial corporations' sales were worth US$4.3 trillion, equivalent to the combined national expenditure of the bottom 163 states, and greater than the combined gross domestic product (GDP) of the bottom 137 states. These are astonishing figures, given that there are currently 192 states in total. On the basis of GDP, many of the top 20 corporations are as large as middle-income or emerging states such as Chile, Algeria, and the Philippines. On the basis of national expenditure, they are as large as many of the top 30 high income states. Only the world's largest and most influential economic powerhouses, such as the United States, Germany, Japan, and (relatively recently) China may be said to rival them.[2] It may also be noted that in 2008 the United Nations had a budget of just US$4.2 billion (United Nations 2007), and perhaps more pertinently, given that it describes itself as "the only global international organization dealing with the rules of trade between nations" (WTO n.d.a), the World Trade Organization (WTO) had a budget of just US$171 million (WTO n.d.b).[3] These global companies are much larger than not only many of the world's most powerful nations, but also the international organizations to which they belong that are supposed to make "rules for the world" (Barnett and Finnemore 2004).

Global companies are therefore vast conglomerates that underpin not just whole national economies, but the world economy. The decisions they make have flow-on effects to other industries and industrial sectors. For example, 5 of the world's top 30 non-financial corporations are car firms. They dominate the automotive sector which accounts for 4% to 8% of GDP and 2 to 4% of the labor force in OECD countries. The industry's importance is then further magnified in particular states and regions. In the United States, car manufacturing employs 14 million people either directly or indirectly in component suppliers and related industries, contributes 6% to private sector GDP overall and as much as 20% in some regions. In the EU, the car industry accounts for 9% of manufacturing value added and directly or indirectly employs over 12 million. In Japan, 7.1 million people are employed by the industry directly or indirectly, and it accounts for 11% of total manufacturing output (UNEP and ACEA 2002; see also UNEP 2002). Market forces are not in charge on the basis of the disembodied laws of Smith's invisible hand, but the embodied interests of global companies such as these.

The same may be said of Ricardian comparative advantage, because it has long been recognized that the majority of trade between developed countries is intra-firm rather than inter-state in nature (e.g. see Karliner 1997; Grubel and Lloyd 1975). Already by the 1990s, as much as 60 to 70% of trade in manufactured goods between OECD countries was intra-firm (Bonturi and Fukasaku 1993; see also Bardhan and Jaffee 2005; Strange 1996).[4] The reality is that trade data are less a reflection of national comparative advantage, and more of the internal corporate strategies of a handful of global companies and the global supply chains they control. No wonder the Director General of the WTO, Pascal Lamy, recently enjoined corporate leaders to assist in maintaining and crafting future rules for international trade and investment in the following terms:

> It no longer suffices that you trade while relying on governments to craft the regulatory framework for you in the WTO through which your trade relations would take place. You must provide the "evidence," through your trade experience, of what is actually happening on the ground, and must guide us in how to make things better. (WTO 2011)

According to authors such as Sell (2003), they have already taken up his offer. In the context of her analysis of the manner in which the WTO's Trade Related Aspects of International Property Rights agreement was largely fashioned by, and in the interests of, the world's major corporations, she quotes James Enyart, former Director of International Affairs for Monsanto, as saying that "the rules of international commerce are far too important to leave up to government bureaucrats" (Sell 2003: 96).

Scratching the surface, and in so doing removing the veneer of abstractions such as "markets" and "competition" in them, the implications of a global economy dominated by large, powerful, multinational corporations is that rather than Smith's invisible hand of the market, a visible handful of global companies straddle the globe "freed . . . from the restraints of classical competition" (Harrod 2006: 25).

The Geopolitics of Global Companies

Just as power is not globally diffuse in markets, nor is it the case that global companies themselves are everywhere and nowhere. Despite over sixty years of a supposedly global liberal agenda, it remains the case that rich, industrialized countries still account for 80% of world output, 70% of international trade and make up to 90% of foreign direct investments (Chang 2008: 32). But to be more accurate, it is the corporations from these countries that do so. The FT Global 500 companies[5] are responsible for 30% of world output, 70% of international trade and at least 80% of the world's stock of foreign direct investment, and they are not placeless entities.

A third of them are headquartered in the United States, and the top 10 states by headquarters account for 79% of them. They are (in order) the United States, China, Japan, the United Kingdom, France, Canada, Germany, India, Switzerland, and Australia (Financial Times 2011; see also Rugman 2000; Bryant and Bailey 1997).

Those still adhering to the hyperglobalization perspective will be keen to point out even so there is an inevitable process of transnationalization underway, but this is only true up to a point. First, the change so far has been extremely gradual. The United Nations Conference on Trade and Development's (UNCTAD) transnationality index (TNI) is a measurement of corporations' transnationality, and is a simple composite average of foreign assets, sales and employment to total assets, sales and employment. The average TNI for the world's top 100 MNCs grew from 52 to 59 between 1993 and 2008 (UNCTAD 2011; Dicken 2007),[6] so that at this rate it will be another 30 to 40 years before their average TNI reaches 75%. Secondly, such global trends mask national specificities. For example, the average TNIs of US, German, and Japanese firms in the top 100 MNCs are just 51, 55 and 52 respectively (UNCTAD 2011), so that on average the largest corporations headquartered in the world's major industrialized nations retain half their sales, assets, and employment at home. Thirdly, it is by no means certain that the gradual long-term trend towards greater corporate transnationality is irreversible. Corporations have certainly constructed elaborate supply chains to benefit from the weaker standards, lower wages, more "flexible" conditions and general financial benefits of internationalizing their operations. However, as the opportunities for efficiencies shrink with the development of the states in which these companies have invested, such as China and India, and as the rising cost of oil and carbon emissions must ultimately be factored into corporate strategic decision-making, local rather than global strategies may become increasingly attractive (e.g. see Economist 2011). Even if this does not involve a wholesale rush back to corporations' home bases, it may produce a rationalization of their supply chains.

This raises the point that it is not just the location of existing global companies that is important, but the states and regions from which new ones are emerging. Chinese and Indian companies in particular are moving rapidly to take their place on the world stage, and this mirrors the rapid emergence of China and India as economic powers. It is no longer as true to say that "a statistical profile for the current corporation indicates that it is predominantly Anglo-American" (Harrod, 2006: 27–28), but it remains the case that the home bases of the world's largest corporations are like a map of global economic power, both established and emerging. Global companies emerge from, and have their headquarters in, distinct territories from which they then impact on others, and just where these places are is also undergoing transformation.

This is certainly true of ownership and control, which has long been recognized as remaining very much national rather than multinational or global. This is illustrated by considering the car industry. Despite often being taken as "a paradigm case of a globalised industry" (Paterson 2000: 264) because it is dominated by global companies that manufacture and distribute products on an integrated global scale, Deutsch Bank's (2004) overview of it demonstrates that mergers, takeovers, and cross-shareholdings mean that it is controlled by a shrinking handful of companies of predominantly North American, European, and East Asian nationality. Furthermore, one notable aspect of the ongoing aftermath of the global financial crisis is that in times of trouble the boards of corporations seek support from their home countries' governments, as for example General Motors did of the Obama administration. Rather than the notion of the global company as a placeless entity driven by global market imperatives, the reality is that where corporations are based, where they hold their assets, where they employ their workers, where they generate their sales revenue, and where they make their key strategic decisions matters a great deal.

Given that this is the case, institutional considerations may be at least as important as the material aspects. Ultimately, regardless of where a corporation decides to locate its manufacturing operations or where its employees are located, Dicken (2003, 234; echoing earlier arguments made by authors such as Boyer 1996) notes that corporations "are 'produced' through an intricate process of embedding in which the cognitive, cultural, social, political and economic characteristics of the national home base play a dominant part." Organizational and individual behavior within firms, including global companies, are a consequence not just of internal strategies, but of the national institutional contexts in which they remain embedded. Authors such as Rugman (2005), Doremus *et al.* (1999), and Hampden-Turner and Trompenaars (1993) have long noted that corporations retain distinct national and regional characteristics, as has the comparative capitalism literature (e.g. see Whitley 2002; Hall and Soskice 2001, and the extensive debate around their Varieties of Capitalism approach outlined in Hancke 2009).

Haufler (2006: 89) observes that only with Adam Smith's *Wealth of Nations* "does a separation between public and private economic affairs start to be widely discussed." If we conceive global companies as distinct from states and somehow "outside" of international relations, we miss the reality that, as per the transformationalists' perspective in theorizing globalization, it is the way they wield their power relationally with other state and non-state actors, as well as among themselves, that should be the subject of study. As the boundary between what is public versus private becomes increasingly blurred, sovereignty is not necessarily being lost by states, nor authority therefore gained by market actors, as the exercise of it is being transformed. Sometimes policy outcomes remain significantly driven by states, while in others global companies appear more in the driver's seat. Sometimes, states benefit as a result, while in others global companies are the beneficiaries. What can be said is that rather than one or the other definitively being the case, it is virtually impossible to disentangle the interests of the two in developing policies and the outcomes that are delivered. The process is distinct from the outcome (who benefits, who is empowered, who increases their control and so on). The former *always* involves shared sovereignty/authority, and this is distinct from the question of whether sovereignty is enhanced, diminished, or altered as a result. Therefore, and increasingly, global companies are always involved.

Global Companies as Relational Actors

There is far too much analysis not of the role of global companies in globalization debates, but instead of the role of *markets* versus the state, the power of *capital* versus democratically elected representatives, the way corporate *interests* are served rather than those of citizens and so on. A deep and complex understanding of the construction of corporations as social, economic, and political *actors* in policy terms often goes missing. This is surprising, because we have long been told that business is now the "most powerful institution on the planet" and therefore perhaps even the "dominant institution in... society" (Korten 1996). Statements such as these suggest that global companies, which embody business interests, will increasingly "rule" the world as their operations increase in size and scope. Yet there remains a relative dearth of contemporary analysis on what is meant by corporations "ruling" in a policy and governance sense.

The preceding discussion is by way of underlining the point that global companies do not unproblematically override the capacity of states to regulate them. In the face of industry sectors dominated by a visible handful of corporations, it is more efficient for states to reach agreement on rules for their operations rather than seeking to curtail these – i.e. new forms of *re-regulation* rather than deregulation. Braithwaite (2008: 4) explains it thus:

> The corporatization of the world is both a product of regulation and the key driver of regulatory growth... The reciprocal relationship between corporatization and regulation creates a world in which there is more governance of all kinds.

In a similar vein, Amoore (2006: 55; see also Porter 2011) observes that "if IPE[7] persists in its view of the corporation as a unitary agent whose private authority stands outside of the public authority of the state, then, in effect, it will miss the multiple ways in which corporations are authorized to act on behalf of the state." To this we might add international organizations and society. The point that she makes is that there are large, powerful corporations and large, powerful states that act together, and analytically untangling the two is almost impossible.

One obvious response to this would be that states' power to drive policy processes and to govern within their territories as well as in global affairs is being undermined by the very fact of them having to share sovereignty with such powerful transnational non-state actors. After all, it is often pointed out that global companies with international interests and operations can potentially "escape" taxation, shift aspects of their operations to other states where conditions and standards are weaker, but financial incentives are greater, and therefore play states off against one another. This is true even as they retain distinct home bases and seek the support of their home state governments. The power of these governments to embody and reflect the interests of their citizens is undermined in the process. The result is a democratic deficit wrought by the demise of states whose sovereignty is universally attacked, leading to the undermining of citizenship and a splintering of collective communities into individuals, with these individuals increasingly little more than consumers (e.g. see the contributions in Cahill, Stillwell, and Edwards 2012).

This is based on the largely unstated assumption in much of the globalization literature that from a political economy perspective the world is comprised of liberal democratic nation states, with their sovereignty defined in terms of the legitimacy they derive from their ability to express the will of their citizens. Of course, this is not the reality. For example, Diamond (2002: 26) suggests that less than 40% of all countries may be regarded as liberal democracies. Yet, these are the countries on which much of the globalization literature, and the debates in it regarding the endurance of the nation state and its sovereignty, focuses. It is largely the same for the contributions in this issue, and this should not be surprising. Given that the rich, industrialized countries which dominate world politics are liberal democracies, and those that are emerging are (albeit arguably) becoming thus, and that these are where global companies have their home bases, exploring the ways in which sovereignty is shared with market actors in these contexts to achieve policy outcomes necessitates a focus on them. Therefore, although developing countries and states that may be thought of as other than liberal democracies feature in some of the contributions, nevertheless the world's wealthy, industrialized, liberal democratic nations and their corporations feature in all of the contributions to this Handbook.

What should be stressed in respect of these states is that they have long been "modest nation states" Mann (1997: 477). Rather than the sovereign-*ruled* states of centuries past, the modern, democratically sovereign state is not one that seeks an empire by conquering others, is less prone to authoritarianism, governs in the interests of its citizens and is restricted to ruling, at least overtly, over its own territory and not that of others.[8] A legitimate state is seen as one that exercises primarily soft, rather than hard, power. It is in this context that states are reconstructing the ways they share their sovereignty with non-state actors such as global companies, as well as each other, so that the reconstruction of such states' political agency is more qualitative than quantitative, with the "quantity" of their sovereignty having been diminished not just as a result of the "forces" of globalization, markets, or indeed global companies themselves, but over a longer period of time since the Treaty of Westphalia and, more recently, a political choice of governments subsequent to the destruction wrought by the two world wars of the twentieth century. It is not so much a matter of whether sovereignty is diminished by comparison to some state of affairs that has long ceased to exist, let alone been seen as desirable. Instead it is more one of qualitatively understanding the shifting dimensions within which states share their sovereignty to achieve policy outcomes.

The implications of this are quite fascinating. One of these is that although there is a theme in much of the (especially earlier) globalization literature of the inevitability of the neoliberal state, with this involving a ceding of state sovereignty via a process of deregulation and privatization, it is little acknowledged that the corollary of this is a "publicization" of the role of corporations as they assume the mantle of responsibility for performing functions that were once seen as the preserve of the state. The hybrid forms of authority produced in the process mean that Friedman's (1970) dictum that "the business of business is business" seems to have been replaced with one that the "business of business is government" as powerful states effectively outsource their functions, especially in respect of their citizens, while often maintaining the power to determine what these are. In this way, they have "hijacked" the agendas of corporations as much as the converse is the case, and this is why they have not "faded away" into irrelevance (e.g. see Parker 2002). The relationship between states and corporations is what matters, rather than a belief in some artificial boundary between the two that demarcates one as a market actor and the other as a political actor.

Another implication is that these large, powerful market actors should more accurately be seen not just as economic, but also as political and social entities. This is why it makes sense to speak of them exercising authority. It is not "just" that global companies exercise their power in respect of, or over states, but that they possess the ability to make and drive policy outcomes in their own right. At the same time as the transformationalist wave was building in the globalization literature, there has been a growing literature on private authority in world affairs that stresses this (see especially Cutler, Haufler, and Porter 1999; Haufler 2001; Cutler 2003; Sell 2003; Hall and Biersteker 2002). The two literatures "speak" to each other, and how they do so offers opportunities for opening up debates on the extent to which politics is globally transformed. Private actors form relationships with each other, with governments, and directly with society, and in so doing "construct a rich variety of institutional arrangements that structure their behaviour" (Cutler, Haufler, and Porter 1999: 333). These arrangements may take the form of informal industry norms and practices; the advice and recommendations of coordination services firms (e.g. credit ratings agencies); production alliances and subcontractor relationships; business associations; and private regimes (e.g. the International Organization for Standardization).

Through such arrangements, private market actors "govern themselves and others, both domestically and internationally" (Cutler, Haufler, and Porter 1999: 367), and they deploy and exert private authority as a form of governance over states or in concert with them. And sometimes they do so directly with society. For example, global companies wielding private authority appear to be increasingly taking responsibility for the social and environmental effects of their actions. In addition to formal regulations, the relationship between society and business therefore suggests the potential for informal forms of non-state environmental governance (e.g. see Florini 2003; Prakash 2000). In respect of the environment specifically, Wapner (1996: 65) notes that society can "sting" corporations into taking environmental action and that "this sting is a type of governance." Today, the idea of corporations bearing environmental and social responsibility for their actions has become so widely accepted that authors such as Vogel (2006) find corporations to be embracing the "market for virtue." For example, it may be argued that global companies are actually taking over and driving, rather than responding to, debates on sustainability (e.g. see Dauvergne 2012). Such developments are reflected in a burgeoning corporate social responsibility literature (e.g see Crane *et al.* 2009), as corporations have come to realize that their "reputations are valuable commodities that need protection" (O'Callaghan 2007: 98). The result is that social groups, and social concerns, potentially promote or undermine corporate reputations, leading companies to constrain the socially negative aspects of corporate behavior while promoting socially desirable outcomes. The business of business is not just government, but *governance*, as companies claim responsibility for outcomes that were once seen as the preserve of the state.

Therefore, policy outcomes need to be understood in terms of the sharing of sovereignty (on the part of states) and authority (on the part of private market actors), in the dominant national, regional, and international contexts in which this happens. Governance continues to evolve as a function of power relations between public and private actors, and it no longer makes as much sense to talk about the interests of states versus markets/business/corporations, nor of social versus corporate interests, so much as it does to study the way in which identities and functions are becoming merged.

The Organization of This Handbook

This Handbook is organized around six parts the purpose of which is to tease out the implications of global companies as central actors in respect of global policy and governance. The first two parts have contributions from authors who define and spatially locate global companies in a globalizing world and conceptualize the power they wield. The subsequent parts focus on the relations global companies have with the state, international organizations, and society. The final part considers the extent to which global companies may be *loci* of private governance in their own right. In the process, themes such as environmental sustainability and social responsibility are covered, as are cases from particular industrial sectors and individual companies.

In the first part Hinrich Voss, Stephen Wilks, and Andrea Goldstein consider the ways in which global companies act at the global, regional, and national level to drive policy and governance processes. They demonstrate that while global companies exert influence at the global level, it is not the case that the power they wield is diffuse in global "markets" so much as it is embodied in them as key actors on the world stage. As it is embodied in them, it is therefore located somewhere, but in a world characterized by complex interdependence the central point they make is that they drive policy and governance processes at a variety of levels and in the process have global impacts.

While the first part establishes what and where global companies are, the emphasis in the second part is on theorizing the power they wield at the global, regional, and national levels. In this part, Doris Fuchs, Tony Porter, Sherri Brown, Stephen Bell, and Nina Kolleck demonstrate that their interests are not simply and narrowly defined in terms of instrumental action designed to produce material returns. They are not simply economic instruments of profit maximization, but are more complex agents of political and social change. As such, the power they possess and wield is complex, and needs to be understood in its various dimensions. The power wielded by corporations is not only relational, but structural and discursive, and as it is wielded by them it impacts on social and environmental outcomes.

The next three parts consider the relations global companies have with other actors. In Part III, the manner in which states share sovereignty with global companies is considered, and from global companies' perspective the way they in turn share their authority with states. This is especially the case for global companies that have operations and interests in many states and territories. The role played by global companies versus states in the policy process, and the way the two share authority to effect new forms of governance, is the focus of this part, with contributions by Terry O'Callaghan, Vlado Vivoda, Denis Saint-Martin, Sung-Young Kim, Shiufai Wong, Caner Bakir, and Cantay Caliskan.

The globalization of world politics is said to necessitate global governance, if not global government. International organizations are the vehicles for this. Their membership is comprised of states, but increasingly global companies are key players in the drafting of international agreements. If this is not always via their membership of international organizations, it is said to be the case through their ability to influence or even drive negotiations in them. In the fourth part, Sarianna Lundan, Cornelia Woll, Deborah Elms, Matthias Finger, Pamela Blackmon, Marianne Thissen-Smits, and Patrick Bernhagen examine the ways in which they do this, focusing in particular on the extent to which the goals and activities of international organizations may be said to be synonymous with those of global companies.

Capitalist relations of production are social, and it has long been recognized that corporations are socially embedded in the societies in which they are located. Through their activities, they impact on society in both negative and positive ways, and they are increasingly keen to be seen to be proactively doing the latter. Contributions by Ann Florini, Tanja Brühl, Matthias Hofferberth, Kate Macdonald, and Frank Boons in Part V examine the interactions between, and mutual embeddedness of, global companies and society at the national, regional, and global levels, and the potential for "governance without government" as a result.

If global companies are central actors in global, regional, and national policy processes, what outcomes can they be expected to deliver? Finally, in Part VI the question of the current and future potential for global companies as drivers of global private governance, as well as the benefits and drawbacks of this, are considered by Shana Starobin, John Mathews, Luc Fransen, Hevina Dashwood, and Simon Zadek.

By bringing together the work of established and emerging scholars who treat global companies as the subject, rather than object, of analysis in global policy and governance, I hope that readers of this Handbook will have a better appreciation of them as actors in the processes of global policy and governance. Rather than studying global companies for the effect they have *on* states and societies, the authors of the following chapters study them as purposive actors that drive policy processes and deliver outcomes *in their own right*. In doing so, they address a relative deficit in the globalization literature that sees states, international organizations, and global civil society as reasonably well "drawn," while firms are more simply "sketched" as instrumental profit seekers with the power and influence they wield then analyzed in these terms.

The Handbook will therefore be a platform for gathering the insight and work of scholars on the cutting-edge of theory and empirical analysis who tease out the general issues and theories surrounding institutions and governance in respect of global companies, and do so explicitly from the perspective of them as actors not just impacting on, but increasingly proactively driving the policy process. Rather than a state-centric basis for analysis, as in much of the international relations literature, or a focus on the purely business aspects, as in much of the international business and management literature, the result is a fresh perspective on global companies as key agents of global transformation.

Notes

1 They in turn point out that it is a term that has entered common usage to the point where the identity of whoever first coined the term is now unclear.

2 It might also be noted that a list which included financial corporations would have also included banking and insurance companies such as ING Group (revenues of US$198 billion, similar in size to Romania) and AXA Group (revenues of US$152 billion, similar in size to Hungary). The reason they were not included in this list is because they do not strictly make sales in the same manner as non-financial corporations. Instead, they generate revenues. Therefore while some lists include them together, such as the Forbes Global 2000, they are not strictly comparable on the same basis.

3 This is based on a 2008 consolidated budget of CHF184,891,500 converted at a yearly average for 2008 using the exchange rate calculator at http://www.oanda.com/currency/average. Accessed December 19, 2012.

4 Bardhan and Jaffe (2005) more conservatively estimate that the figure for the United States is more conservatively around 50%, but overall the point made by Strange (1996: 47) is that "by 1990 the goods and services sold by foreign affiliates of TNCs were almost double world exports, if intra-firm trade is excluded to avoid double counting."

5 The world's top 500 companies on the basis of their stock-market capitalization.

6 These calculations treat the top 100 corporations as a group, calculating their transnationality based on the sum of their assets, sales, and employment.

7 International political economy.

8 This is why he says "the original backbone of the nation state is turning to jelly" (Mann 1997: 492).

References

Amoore, Louise. 2006. "Making the Modern Multinational." In *Global Corporate Power*, ed. Christopher May, 47–64. Boulder: Lynne Rienner.

Bardhan, Ashok and Jaffee, Dwight. 2005. "On Intra-Firm Trade and Manufacturing Outsourcing and Offshoring." In *Multinationals and Foreign Investment in Economic Development*, ed. Edward Graham, 26–41. Basingstoke: Palgrave Macmillan.

Barnett, Michael and Finnemore, Martha. 2004. *Rules for the World: International Organizations in Global Politics*. Ithaca: Cornell University Press.

Bell, Stephen and Hindmoor, Andrew. 2009. *Rethinking Governance: The Centrality of the State in Modern Society*. Cambridge: Cambridge University Press.

Bonturi, Marcos and Fukasaku, Kiichiro. 1993. "Globalisation and Intra-firm Trade: An Empirical Note." *OECD Economic Studies*, 20 (Spring): 145–159.

Boyer, Robert. 1996. "The Convergence Hypothesis Revisited: Globalization but Still the Century of Nations?" In *National Diversity and Global Capitalism*, ed. Suzanne Berger and Robert Dore, 29–59. Ithaca: Cornell University Press.

Braithwaite, John. 2008. *Regulatory Capitalism: How It Works, Ideas for Making It Work Better*. Cheltenham: Edward Elgar.

Bryant, Raymond and Bailey, Sinéad. 1997. *Third World Political Ecology*. London: Routledge.

Chang, Ha-Joon. 2008. *Bad Samaritans: The Myth of Free Trade and the Secret History of Capitalism*. New York: Bloomsbury.

Crane, Andrew, McWilliams, Abagail, Matten, Dirk, Moon, Jeremy, and Siegel, Donald, eds. 2009. *The Oxford Handbook of Corporate Social Responsibility*. Oxford: Oxford University Press.

Crouch, Colin. 2004. *Post Democracy*. Cambridge: Polity Press.

Culpepper, Pepper. 2011. *Quiet Politics and Business Power: Corporate Control in Europe and Japan*. Cambridge: Cambridge University Press.

Cutler, A. Claire. 2003. *Private Power and Global Authority: Transnational Merchant Law in the Global Political Economy*. Cambridge: Cambridge University Press.

Cutler, A. Claire, Haufler, Virginia, and Porter, Tony, eds. 1999. *Private Authority and International Affairs*. Albany: State University of New York Press.

Dauvergne, Peter, and Lister, Jane. 2012. *Eco-Business: A Big Brand Takeover of Sustainability?* Cambridge, MA: MIT Press.

Deutsche Bank. 2004. *The Drivers: How to Navigate the Auto Industry*. Frankfurt am Main: Deutsche Bank AG.

Diamond, Larry. 2002. "Thinking about Hybrid Regimes." *Journal of Democracy*, 13 (2): 21–35.

Dicken, Peter. 2003. *Global Shift: Transforming the World Economy*, 4th edn. London: Sage Publications.

Dicken, Peter. 2007. *Global Shift: Mapping the Changing Contours of the World Economy*, 5th edn. London: Sage Publications.

Doremus, Paul, Keller, William, Pauly, Louis, and Reich, Simon. 1999. *The Myth of the Global Corporation*. Princeton: Princeton University Press.

Drezner, Daniel. 2007. *All Politics Is Global: Explaining International Regulatory Regimes*. Princeton: Princeton University Press.

Economist. 2011. The Dwindling Allure of Building Factories Offshore, May 12, http://www .economist.com/node/18682182?story_id=18682182. Accessed December 1, 2012.

Financial Times. 2011. *FT Global 500 2010*, http://www.ft.com/reports/ft500-2010. Accessed December 1, 2012.

Florini, Ann. 2003. *The Coming Democracy: New Rules for Running a New World*. Washington, DC: Island Press.

Friedman, Milton. 1970. "The Social Responsibility of Business Is to Increase Profits." *New York Times Magazine*, September 13.

Friedman, Thomas. 1999. *The Lexus and the Olive Tree*. London: Harper Collins.

Fuchs, Doris. 2005. "Commanding Heights? The Strength and Fragility of Business Power in Global Politics." *Millennium*, 33: 771–801.

Fuchs, Doris. 2007. *Business Power in Global Governance*. Boulder: Lynne Rienner.

Fukuyama, Francis. 1992. *The End of History and the Last Man*. New York: Avon Books.

Grubel, Herbert and Lloyd, Peter. 1975. *Intra-Industry Trade: Theory and Measurement of International Trade in Differentiated Products*. London: Macmillan.

Hall, Peter and Soskice, David, eds. 2001. *Varieties of Capitalism: The Institutional Foundations of Comparative Advantage*. Oxford: Oxford University Press.

Hall, Rodney and Biersteker, Thomas, eds. 2002. *The Emergence of Private Authority in Global Governance*. Cambridge: Cambridge University Press.

Hampden-Turner, Charles and Trompenaars, Alfons. 1993. *The Seven Cultures of Capitalism: Value Systems for Creating Wealth in the United States, Japan, Germany, France, Britain, Sweden and the Netherlands*. New York: Currency Doubleday.

Hancké, Bob, ed. 2009. *Debating Varieties of Capitalism: A Reader*. Oxford: Oxford University Press.

Harrod, Jeff. 2006. "The Century of the Corporation." In *Global Corporate Power*, ed. Christopher May, 23–46. Boulder: Lynne Rienner.

Haufler, Virginia. 2001. *A Public Role for the Private Sector: Industry Self-Regulation in a Global Economy*. Washington, DC: Carnegie Endowment for International Peace.

Haufler, Virginia. 2006. "Global Governance and the Private Sector." In *Global Corporate Power*, ed. Christopher May, 85–103. Boulder: Lynne Rienner.

Hay, Colin and David Marsh, David, eds. 2000. *Demystifying Globalization*. Houndmills, Basingstoke: Palgrave Macmillan.

Held, David and McGrew, Anthony, eds. 2003. *The Global Transformations Reader: An Introduction to the Globalization Debate*, 2nd edn. Cambridge: Polity Press.

Held, David, McGrew, Anthony, Goldblatt, David, and Perraton, Jonathan. 1999. *Global Transformations: Politics, Economics and Culture*. Stanford: Stanford University Press.

Hirst, Paul and Thompson, Grahame. 1996. *Globalization in Question*. Cambridge: Polity Press.

Hobsbawm, Eric. 1977. *The Age of Capital*. London: Weidenfeld and Nicolson.

IMF. 2011. *World Economic Outlook Database: April 2011 Edition*, http://www.imf.org/ external/pubs/ft/weo/2011/01/weodata/index.aspx. Accessed December 1, 2012.

Karliner, Joshua. 1997. *The Corporate Planet: Ecology and Politics in the Age of Globalization*. San Francisco: Sierra Club.

Korten, David. 1996. Limits to the Social Responsibility of Business, *The People-Centred Development Forum*, 19, June 1, http://livingeconomiesforum.org/1996/19korten. Accessed June 23, 2012.

Mann, Michael. 1997. "Has Globalisation Ended the Rise and Rise of the Nation-State?" *Review of International Political Economy*, 4 (3): 472–496.

Mikler, John. 2012. "The Illusion of the Power of Markets." *Journal of Australian Political Economy*, 68: 41–61.

O'Callaghan, Terry. 2007. "Disciplining Multinational Enterprises: The Regulatory Power of Reputation Risk." *Global Society*, 21 (1): 95–117.

Ohmae, Kenichi. 1990. *The Borderless World: Power and Strategy in the Interlinked Economy*. London: Collins.

Parker, Christine. 2002. *The Open Corporation*. Cambridge: Cambridge University Press.

Paterson, Matthew. 2000. "Car Culture and Global Environmental Politics." *Review of International Studies*, 26 (2): 253–270.

Porter, Tony. 2011. "Public and Private Authority in the Transnational Response to the 2008 Financial Crisis." *Policy and Society*, 30 (3): 175–184.

Prakash, Aseem. 2000. *Greening the Firm: The Politics of Corporate Environmentalism*. Cambridge: Cambridge University Press.

Ralston Saul, John. 1997. *The Unconscious Civilization*. Maryborough Victoria: Penguin Books.

Rugman, Alan. 2005. *The Regional Multinationals: MNEs and "Global" Strategic Management*. Cambridge: Cambridge University Press.

Rugman, Alan. 2000. *The End of Globalization*, London: Random House Business Books.

Sell, Susan. 2003. *Private Power, Public Law: The Globalization of Intellectual Property Rights*. Cambridge: Cambridge University Press.

Stillwell, Frank, Cahill, Damien, and Edwards, Belinda, eds. 2012. *Neoliberalism: Beyond the Free Market*. Cheltenham; Northampton, MA: Edward Elgar.

Strange, Susan. 1996. *The Retreat of the State: The Diffusion of Power in the World Economy*. Cambridge: Cambridge University Press.

Strange, Susan. 1997. "The Future of Global Capitalism; Or Will Divergence Persist Forever?" In *Political Economy of Modern Capitalism: Mapping Convergence and Diversity*, ed. Colin Crouch and Wolfgang Streeck, 182–191. London: Sage Publications.

Thatcher, Mark. 2007. *Internationalisation and Economic Institutions: Comparing European Experiences*. Oxford: Oxford University Press.

Tiberghien, Yves. 2007. *Entrepreneurial States: Reforming Corporate Governance in France, Japan and Korea*. Ithaca and London: Cornell University Press.

UNCTAD. 2011. "The World's Top 100 Non-Financial TNCs, Ranked by Foreign Assets, 2008." In *Largest Transnational Corporations*, UNCTAD/Erasmus University database, http://www.unctad.org/Templates/Page.asp?intItemID=2443&lang=1. Accessed December 1, 2012.

UNEP. 2002. Industry as a Partner for Sustainable Development – 10 Years After Rio: The UNEP Assessment, http://www.uneptie.org/Outreach/wssd/contributions/publications/pub_global.htm. Accessed December 1, 2012.

UNEP and ACEA. 2002. Industry as a Partner for Sustainable Development: Automotive, http://www.unepti.e.org/outreach/wssd/docs/sectors/final/automotive.pdf. Accessed May 14, 2003.

United Nations. 2007. UN Secretary-General Welcomes Adoption of UN Budget for 2010–2011. *United Nations News Centre*, December 23, http://www.un.org/apps/news/story.asp?NewsID=25159&Cr=Assembly&Cr1=budget. Accessed December 1, 2012.

Vogel, David. 2006. *The Market for Virtue: The Potential and Limits of Corporate Social Responsibility*. Washington, DC: Brookings Institution Press.

Vogel, Steven. 1996. *Freer Markets More Rules: Regulatory Reform in Advanced Industrialized Countries*. Ithaca: Cornell University Press.

Wade, Robert. 1996. "Globalization and Its Limits: Reports of the Death of the National Economy are Greatly Exaggerated." In *National Diversity and Global Capitalism*, ed. Suzanne Berger and Robert Dore, 60–88. Ithaca: Cornell University Press.

Wapner, Paul. 1996. *Environmental Activism and World Civic Politics*. Albany, NY: State University of New York Press.

Weiss, Linda. 1998. *The Myth of the Powerless State*. Cambridge: Polity Press.

Weiss, Linda. 2003. "Introduction: Bringing Domestic Institutions Back In." In *States in the Global Economy: Bringing Domestic Institutions Back In*, ed. Linda Weiss, 1–33. Cambridge: Cambridge University Press.

Whitley, Richard, ed. 2002. *Competing Capitalisms: Institutions and Economies*. Cheltenham: Edward Elgar.

WTO. 2011. As Trade Changes Rapidly, You Must Help Guide WTO, Lamy tells Global Business. *WTO News: Speeches: DG Pascal Lamy*, May 12, http://www.wto.org/english/news_e/sppl_e/sppl192_e.htm. Accessed December 1, 2012.

WTO. n.d.a. What Is the WTO?, http://www.wto.org/english/thewto_e/whatis_e/whatis_e.htm. Accessed December 1, 2012.

WTO. n.d.b. WTO Secretariat Budget for 2008. *The WTO: Secretariat and Budget*, http://www.wto.org/english/thewto_e/secre_e/budget08_e.htm. Accessed December 1, 2012.

Part I   Locating Global Companies

Chapter 2

The Global Company

Hinrich Voss

Introduction

There are plenty of company rankings that refer to "global corporations" or "global brands." Rankings such as Fortune Global 500, Interband's Best Global Brands and Best Global Green Brands or Brand Finance's Top 500 most valuable global brands, Platts Top 250 Global Energy Company Rankings, Corporate Knights Magazine's Global 100 Most Sustainable Companies, Forbes Global 2000, Industry Week's World's 1000 largest manufacturers to name but a few. At the same time, there is talk of "global mindsets," "global strategies" and "global management" (e.g., Yip 2002; Gupta and Govindarajan 2004; Gupta, Govindarajan, and Wang 2008; Ghemawat 2007). While it is true that firms have been engaged in international trading and investments for centuries (Moore and Lewis 1999), it is less clear what a globalized corporation is. It is important to understand the concepts and determinants of global companies because businesses with a strong international presence are often either perceived as saviors or exploiters of, inter alia, economic underdevelopment and institutional differences. A greater understanding of the extent to which firms are international will inform the general discourse about the benefits firms can bring.

The current discourse on global companies has been stimulated by a visible increase in international business activities and the subsequent deepening of globalization. After a period of contraction and the erection of barriers against international business activities, international initiatives to open and liberalize access to markets internationally, have supported international business transactions and they have steadily and significantly increased since the 1970s. Two measures that are typically used to illustrate this are exports and foreign direct investments (FDI). Worldwide exports increased from US$317 billion in 1970 to US$15,254 billion in 2010 (WTO 2012). Over the same period annual FDI outflows rose from

The Handbook of Global Companies, First Edition. Edited by John Mikler.
© 2013 John Wiley & Sons, Ltd. Published 2013 by John Wiley & Sons, Ltd.

US$14 billion to US$1,323 billion, thus increasing the stock of outward FDI from US$548 billion in 1980 to US$20,408 billion in 2010 (UNCTAD 2011a). The sheer size of these numbers indicates the success of the liberalization policies and suggests an increase in the economic and political reach of businesses that are operating globally. In 2010 there were more than 100,000 parent companies that together owned and controlled in excess of 850,000 foreign affiliates with productive assets overseas (UNCTAD 2011b).

Although the aggregate macro-data are impressive, companies have not globalized to equal degrees. Thus, it is contested whether globally well-known brands such as Wal-Mart or Goldman Sachs are really global companies. Lesser known companies like Baader or Galanz might rather be regarded as global companies instead. These statements hold depending on the definition and research context. Wal-Mart and Goldman Sachs are among the largest companies globally and are reported about across the world. Wal-Mart employs the vast majority of its employees in the United States and generates most of its sales in the United States. The share of foreign assets, sales, or employees is skewed in the case of Wal-Mart towards the United States. Goldman Sachs, on the other hand, has offices in a very small number of markets only and therefore a small geographic spread of its affiliations so that it can hardly be labeled as global from this perspective. It can therefore be argued that both firms are not global companies because they do not globally access and manage directly resources at an even level. The German small and medium-sized enterprise (SME) Baader and the Chinese firm Galanz control more than 80% of their respective global markets of food processing machinery and microwaves (Simon 2007; Zeng and Williamson 2005). This certainly demonstrates that these firms compete globally and are critical for their industry worldwide. Baader and Galanz can therefore be classified as global companies because they dominate their sector globally. However, the market share was acquired with little or no physical global presence and the firms operate in niche markets. Thus this statement does not hold anymore if we define a global company by the extent of its foreign assets, employment numbers, and sales, that is, through indicators that are related to the FDI a firm has carried out. Following these indicators Baader and Galanz would not be global companies; the same may be true for Wal-Mart and Goldman Sachs.

Firms are not only internationally active through FDI or trade, non-equity modes of internationalization today play a crucial role in international business. International business activities span a wider range of actions than direct investments. Besides this equity based mode of internationalization, companies adopt a number of non-equity based methods. The former describes direct investment activities and these therefore circumscribe multinational enterprises. A multinational enterprise (MNE) is defined as a company that owns productive assets in at least two countries (Buckley and Casson 1976). The non-equity mode of internationalization comprises, inter alia, exporting, licensing, franchising, contractual agreements such as outsourcing, and service management. This highlights that focusing on one particular mode of international business activities leads to skewed observations on the degree of globalization a firm has achieved and its impact deduced from this. Firms, and MNEs in particular, pursue equity and non-equity internationalization often simultaneously and in the same country. The result is a significant degree of intra-firm trading and licensing (Bernard, Jensen, and Schott 2005). Taking these into consideration, that is, international contractual arrangements such as outsourcing, a different picture emerges for companies such as Wal-Mart which have outsourced large parts of their production to suppliers. Through these arrangements, firms can globally influence other businesses and disseminate business practices and standards. Arguably, therefore, they are global companies.

These examples show that the nature of a global company is difficult to pin down and depends on the definition used. The objective behind any definition of a global company is an attempt to quantify the size, reach, performance, competitiveness, and/or influence and political power of businesses. Depending on the specific objective and the field of study conclusions are then drawn on how successful, beneficial, or threatening corporations are for the home and host country. Often, such investigations focus on the MNE because these businesses have the most visible and easily quantifiable international footprint. This focus does not answer the question whether a global company needs a presence, organizational or operational, in every single market or, at least, continent, in order to be labeled as such? Or if a presence in the markets that account for over 75% of the world's economic activities or 75% of the world's population would be sufficient? Would it be sufficient if global trends and changes in direction were stimulated by a firm?

In order to understand the evolution and reach of global companies, it is pertinent to understand the different types of internationalization and their implications. The remainder of this chapter attempts to do this from an international business perspective. We look first at the different kinds of equity-based international business activities a firm can pursue to get an understanding of the various types, the extent to which they have been used and what potential impact they carry with them. The impact is, in particular, related to the size of businesses. In relation to this, we use the Transnationality Index developed by the United Nations Conference on Trade and Development (UNCTAD) to characterize and describe global companies. This index is critically assessed with regard to its explanatory power and usefulness. Building on the criticism, we introduce non-equity modes of international business activities. Having discussed equity and non-equity modes, a typology is introduced to support the analysis of global companies. This is followed by a reflection on the rise of global companies from emerging markets and the related changing business and political dynamics before this chapter concludes.

Globalized Businesses?

Firms can globalize their business activities in different ways. A foreign direct investment (FDI) is *the* most visible mode of internationalization a firm can embark on to enter into a foreign market. Investments in a foreign country are classified as FDI, in contrast to portfolio investments, when the investing company holds a long-term interest of 10% or more in the invested entity (UNCTAD 2011b). This foreign market entry mode generally signifies a strong and long-term commitment to engage in business interactions in the host country. It brings with it considerable control over the foreign operation and its strategies such as the type of technologies that are employed and transferred, the kind of business activities that are undertaken. The increase of FDI as shown above, prima facie, indicates that businesses have strongly internationalized and increased their control over operations overseas. Portfolio investments, in contrast, are those investments in a foreign entity that remain under the 10% threshold. They tend to indicate a pure financial interest in the firm without any direct influence on the management or the firm's strategy.

The degree of control over the foreign business entity varies with the equity-based entry mode chosen. Minority-owned joint ventures, where the foreign firm holds less than 50%, provide in theory the least power over the business. In majority-owned joint ventures, equity shares above 50% are held; significantly more control can be exerted while full control is ensured when the foreign operation is wholly owned. We further need to differentiate between greenfield and brownfield investments. These terms describe the establishment of a new business (that is, "on an untouched green field" hence greenfield investment) and the merger with or the acquisition of (M&As) an existing business (that is, "the field has already been used," hence brownfield investment). Brownfield investments bring with them a transfer of ownership and control from the previous owner to the investing foreign owner. Of the different types of FDI a firm can carry out, the acquisition of a foreign enterprise is a commonly employed type. M&As accounted on average for 38% of global FDI flows (ranging between 11% and 73%) over the twenty years 1990 to 2010. Global M&A and non-M&A cross-border activities have continuously risen since the 1990s from about US$250 billion in 1990 to peak at nearly US$2,250 billion in 2007. The strong positive development has seen only temporary setbacks caused by the dot.com crises in 2000/01 and the financial and economic crises that started in 2007 (UNCTAD 2011a).

The growth in cross-border investments and the economic influence that comes with it often instigates an assessment of the power these companies develop. Power is here understood as the firm's ability to influence political decisions, economic development, industry structures, and/or technological developments. One commonly employed method to proximate and illustrate the power of companies is the comparison of the companies' annual international turnover or sales with the gross domestic product (GDP) of countries using the Fortune Global 500 ranking and data published by the World Bank (see Table 2.1). According to this comparison MNEs account for eleven of the largest fifty economic entities globally in 2010. If the largest 500 American firms were one economic unit, they alone would have had a cumulative turnover of US$10.8 and US$11.8 trillion in 2010 and 2011, respectively. This would place them second to the United States which recorded GDP of US$14.5 and US$15.1 trillion in these years. For the years 2000 to 2011, these American firms would rank as the world's second-biggest economy (Fortune 2012a). When we consider the largest listed firms globally, the economic size of firms is even more starkly illustrated. In 2010 they generated a cumulative turnover of US$26 trillion – which exceeds the combined GDP of the three largest economies United States, China, and Japan (Fortune 2011). From these comparisons it is deduced that these organizations have greater economic power than most countries and, in consequence, power to influence business environments home or away.

It should be noted that the Fortune Global 500 ranking includes publicly listed businesses only. If it were to include private businesses that are owned by individuals or families, the commodities trading Vitol Group, for example, would be included with a turnover of US$206 billion in 2010 making it the fifth-largest company and securing a place in the top 50 economic organizations (Vitol 2012). Also, this

Table 2.1   The ten economically largest countries and enterprises, 2010.

Country	GDP (US$ billion)	MNE	Sales (US$ billion)	TNI
USA	14,582	Wal-Mart (USA)	408	34.0
China	5878	Royal Dutch Shell (UK/Netherlands)	285	77.1
Japan	5497	ExxonMobil (USA)	285	67.1
Germany	3309	BP (UK)	246	83.7
France	2560	Toyota (Japan)	204	53.1
UK	2246	Japan Post Holdings (Japan)	202	n.a.
Brazil	2087	Sinopec (China)	188	n.a.
Italy	2051	StateGrid (China)	184	n.a.
India	1729	Axa (France)	175	n.a.
Canada	1574	China National Petroleum Corp. (China)	165	2.7

Sources: World Bank (2011), Fortune (2011), and UNCTAD (2011a).

comparison is only indicative of the businesses' activities and does not reveal the real international size and reach of the businesses. Turnover and sales generated globally exclude the reach these organizations have through outsourced, subcontracted and procured activities. The economic size of an organization therefore reveals little about its actual international presence and discloses also only little about its influence. Indeed, four of the ten largest businesses are not included in the Transnationality Index (TNI) by the United Nations Conference on Trade and Development (UNCTAD) (see Table 2.1, column TNI) due to missing international business activities.

UNCTAD has published annually since 1990 the *World Investment Report* which evaluates and comments on the major developments and trends in international business, in particular with regard to FDI and the political environment related to FDI. The country-level FDI data is presented and assessed with regard to who is investing where. This is complemented by micro-level analysis and data (i.e. firm-level data) such as the rankings of the most internationalized, or transnationalized, in UNCTAD speech, firms. The ranking captures the level of foreign and domestic assets, sales, and employment. These are key measurements for assessing the degree of internationalization of a firm (Sullivan 1994; Hassel *et al.* 2003). A recent update of the ranking also takes into consideration the geographic spread of firms through counting the number of foreign affiliates it operates in various countries. These data are used to calculate the TNI. A higher index score suggests that a greater amount of business activities is conducted outside the firm's home country. Royal Dutch Shell and BP, the oil and gas MNEs that are both headquartered in the United Kingdom and the Netherlands, illustrate this well. The home countries are poorly endowed with gas and oil resources. Both countries have therefore extensive operations in North America, Africa, and the Middle East, which is reflected in a high TNI score.

The outflows of FDI have grown steadily over the period 1990 to 2010 as indicated earlier. Over the same period, the average TNI for all companies ranked by UNCTAD has not increased at the same rate. Although an increase is generally observable, it has been a modest one for firms from industrialized countries from the low 50s in the early 1990s to the mid-60s by 2008. A different picture emerges for the companies from developing countries, the so-called late-comer MNEs. Their average TNI has more than doubled from 20 in 1993 to more than 50 in 2009 (UNCTAD various World Investment Reports). Although they still lag behind their industrialized country counterparts by some degree, it illustrates the very impressive internationalization catch-up these firms have achieved within a fairly short time. Unlike the development of FDI, the internationalization progress indicated by the TNI has not been abated by the crises in 2000/1 and 2007 onwards.

The improvement on the TNI scores can be partly attributed to the success of China in attracting FDI since 1992. China has attracted FDI from all major industrialized countries, but in particular from other Asian countries, with Hong Kong and Taiwan-based firms at the forefront. This is reflected in the change in the industry representation among the top ten firms. While end-consumer oriented sectors dominated the rankings for developing countries, this has shifted to manufacturers of electronic equipment who take advantage of lower labor costs in China. As a consequence, Asian businesses are today much more prominently represented in the TNI ranking and record high TNI scores. Indeed, the ten most internationalized developing country firms record a higher average TNI score (94) than the developed countries' top ten (90) (Tables 2.2 and 2.3). This would indicate that the top developing country businesses have become more globalized over the 15-year period. If the degree of transnationality equals power, these firms should also have increased their international influence.

Although the TNI cannot reveal any real power the firms might possess, it suggests which firms might be in a position to have an influence at the micro- and macro-level. The larger degree of international activities indicates that the firm is less reliant on the home country for its business undertakings. This can be interpreted as a greater chance of being a "footloose" company that could fairly easily relocate its operations. This is especially the case when the share of employees overseas is high, that is, the firm benefits from preferential labor conditions elsewhere. A higher TNI score also indicates that the firm has a greater network of international business relations. This, in turn, will support the firm in impact elsewhere. Companies like Nestlé, Nokia, and Unilever are renowned for their levels of innovation and global leadership in their industries. Nestlé and Unilever have also been involved in community development and local specific innovations in developing countries where they have overall made a positive impact (Clay 2005). Of the developing country firms, Flextronics is a Singapore-based contract manufacturer that is seeking locations with lower labor costs in order to strengthen its competitiveness and secure contracts from HP, Lenovo, Microsoft, and others. It therefore has a proportionally high degree of employees overseas and is an example of a potentially footloose company.

The Transnationality Index is an interesting indicator of how much equity-based activities a firm possesses outside its home country. It fails, however, in illuminating to what degree the operations of a company are globalized and to what extent there is a causal relationship between the degree of internationalization and a company's success. The TNI for developing-country firms is a good example to illustrate this. The ten firms are based in Hong Kong, Kuwait, Singapore, and Taiwan. These are countries with very small domestic markets. These markets provide, therefore, relatively little expansion potential and cheap labor supply. In addition, Hong Kong and Taiwan firms are known for their extensive investments in China since it embarked

Table 2.2   The ten most internationalized developed country MNEs, 1995 and 2010.

A. 1995

	Company	Industry	Country	TNI
1	Nestlé SA	Food, beverages, and tobacco	Switzerland	94.0
2	Thomson Corporation	Publishing	Canada	93.3
3	Holderbank Financiere	Construction	Switzerland	92.1
4	Seagram Company Ltd	Food, beverages, and tobacco	Canada	89.7
5	Solvay SA	Chemicals	Belgium	89.6
6	ABB Asea Brown Boveri Ltd	Electrical and electronic equipment	Switzerland	88.6
7	Electrolux AB	Electrical and electronic equipment	Sweden	88.3
8	Unilever PLC	Food, beverages and tobacco	UK/Netherlands	87.1
9	Philips Electronics N.V.	Electrical and electronic equipment	Netherlands	85.4
10	Roche Holding AG	Pharmaceuticals	Switzerland	85.1

B. 2010

	Company	Industry	Country	TNI
1	Nestlé SA	Food, beverages, and tobacco	Switzerland	96.8
2	Anglo American plc	Mining and quarrying	UK	92.5
3	Anheuser-Busch InBev NV	Food, beverages, and tobacco	Belgium	91.5
4	Pernod-Ricard SA	Food, beverages, and tobacco	France	89.6
5	Nokia OYJ	Electrical and electronic equipment	Finland	89.5
6	Linde AG	Chemicals	Germany	88.9
7	WPP PLC	Business services	UK	88.5
8	Xstrata PLC	Mining and quarrying	Switzerland	88.3
9	Unilever PLC	Diversified	UK/Netherlands	88.3
10	Schneider Electric SA	Electricity, gas, and water	France	87.6

Source: UNCTAD (1997; 2007; 2011b).

on its economic opening and reform course in 1978. These firms can therefore relatively easily report a high degree of transnationality by relocating factories from
Taiwan or Hong Kong across the border to China while retaining the headquarters in the homeland. Hong Kong-based Galaxy has its core business operations in
Macau where it is involved in casino gambling. Lee & Man Paper Manufacturing is
listed at the Hong Kong stock exchange and is therefore regarded as a Hong Kong
firm. It has, however, its main operations in China and is actually headquartered
in China. Thus, assets and employment ratios are skewed towards showing greater
internationality while it is indeed a two-country operation.

The TNI is not an indicator that develops alongside the growth and success of
a firm. The Asian electrical & electronic equipment companies Lenovo (China) and
Samsung Electronics (Korea) highlight the apparent disconnect. Lenovo came into
the international spotlight with the acquisition of IBM's PC business in 2005. This
was the first major cross-border acquisition by a mainland Chinese firm and heralded

Table 2.3 The ten most internationalized developing country MNEs, 1995 and 2009.

A. 1995

	Company	Industry	Country	TNI
1	Panamerican Beverages Inc.	Food, beverages, and tobacco	Mexico	75.0
2	First Pacific Company Ltd	Electrical and electronic equipment	HK	72.6
3	Gruma S.A. De C.V.	Food, beverages, and tobacco	Mexico	72.3
4	Creative Technology Ltd	Electrical and electronic equipment	Singapore	69.3
5	Guangdong Investment Ltd	Miscellaneous	HK	65.6
6	Fraser & Neave Ltd	Food, beverages, and tobacco	Singapore	56.7
7	Jardine Matheson Holdings Ltd	Diversified	Bermuda	55.5
8	Cemex SA	Construction	Mexico	49.5
9	Daewoo Corporation	Diversified/trading	Korea	48.4
10	Dairy Farm International Holdings Ltd	Retailing	HK	48.4

B. 2009

	Company	Industry	Country	TNI
1	Noble Group Ltd	Wholesale trade	HK	99.4
2	First Pacific Company Ltd	Electrical and electronic equipment	HK	99.1
3	Flextronics International Ltd	Electrical and electronic equipment	Singapore	98.4
4	Lee & Man Paper Manufacturing Ltd	Wood and paper products	HK	98.3
5	Galaxy Entertainment Group Ltd	Other consumer services	HK	95.3
6	Zain	Telecommunications	Kuwait	92.1
7	Shangri-La Asia Ltd	Other consumer services	HK	92.1
8	Li & Fung Ltd	Wholesale trade	HK	91.1
9	Asia Food & Properties Ltd	Food, beverages, and tobacco	Singapore	89.7
10	Pou Chen Corp	Other consumer goods	Taiwan	89.0

Source: UNCTAD (1997; 2007; 2011b).

the internationalization of Chinese companies. The acquisition catapulted Lenovo into global rankings: it appeared for the first time in the top 10 global PC manu- facturers and in UNCTAD's rankings of the largest developing country MNEs by foreign assets. Despite the successful establishment among the most important PC manufacturers, its degree of internationalization has since decreased not increased. UNCTAD (2007, 2011b) reports a TNI score of 51% in 2005 but of only 40% in 2009. In particular the contributions of assets and sales to Lenovo's degree of inter- nationalization have fallen significantly, suggesting a greater focus on the domestic market. Samsung, on the other hand, has steadily expanded its international busi- ness operations. First listed amongst the largest MNEs from developing countries in 1995 with a TNI of 14%, it is reported to have a TNI of 55% in 2009. The internationalization of Samsung is accounted for by a greater global diversification of its assets, sales, and workforce.

Building on the above criticism that the TNI is likely to make businesses appear more internationalized than they actually are, Alan M. Rugman and colleagues contest the notion of the global company. They portray companies as generally being regional players. The region comprises their home region and, potentially, a second and at times third other region. In a range of empirical studies based on the world's largest firms, as published in the Fortune Global 500, they show that a very significant proportion of the firms' assets and operations are located in their home region and, at times, in a second region. In rare occasions, a third region gains noteworthy importance (Rugman 2005; Rugman, Kudina, and Yip 2007; Rugman and Girod 2003; Rugman and Collinson 2004). While earlier studies focused on firms from industrialized countries, Rugman and Li (2007) indicate that the findings might hold for developing country MNEs as well because their findings show a regional trend for large Chinese firms.

Neither Rugman *et al.*'s work nor the TNI capture the international business activities of small and medium-sized businesses or of privately-held firms. Both groups of businesses include global industry leaders and household names such as Bosch, Cargill, Mars, PricewaterhouseCoopers or the Vitol Group. Cargill and Vitol would be represented amongst the world's largest companies if they were publicly listed given their turnover of more than US$200 billion. As these businesses are not assessed on their internationalization, the findings by Rugman *et al.* and the TNI hold only for a very particular subset of companies.

Moreover, both sets of studies focus on publicly listed companies and easily recordable and therefore readily available data such as employment, assets and sales. Naturally this does not capture any non-equity based modes of globalization and thus fails to capture the real extent to which a firm's business is globalized.

Globalizing through Non-Equity Modes

FDI data and data on the international operations of firms capture what is happening within the hierarchical structure of one company. It does not reveal any activity beyond the company's boundaries and how businesses have globalized different parts of their value chain and established international production networks – that they control but do not necessarily own. Such production networks have become increasingly important for businesses and were estimated by the United Nations Conference on Trade and Development to be worth in excess of US$4 trillion in 2010 (UNCTAD 2011b). Indeed, some globally recognized MNEs such as Apple or Nike have built their businesses around an internationally spread production network which they control but do not own. The relationships in these networks involve multiple corporate actors which are based on non-equity modes of international businesses. Contract manufacturing, contract farming, services outsourcing, franchising and licensing are examples of such modes (UNCTAD 2011b). Through contractual agreements, the network partner executes clearly specified tasks for the benefit of the contractor. To fulfil these tasks, the contractor directs the independent partner to "make capital expenditures, change processes, adopt new procedures" specifically for its own purposes (UNCTAD 2011b: 127). All these modes therefore increase the global footprint of a firm without it being physically present in the country or region. Below we look at some of these to exhibit why and how they matter for an assessment of a global company.

Contract manufacturing or service outsourcing describes the process whereby a firm stops executing a business operation and contracts another firm (or firms) with the operation. Any operation from services to manufacturing can be outsourced. The most common one tends to be partial or wholly outsourcing of manufacturing related activities. Apple and Nike do not produce any of the products they sell but companies like Taiwan-based Foxconn do this for them, often in China-based operations. German car assemblers have outsourced the production of particular models to firms like Magna Steyr (Austria) or Valmet Automotive (Finland). The advantage of outsourcing for firms like Apple and Nike is that they can focus on higher value-added activities that carry greater profit margins with them while reducing their international production footprint. They, as well as the car manufacturer, therefore also profit from greater flexibility. Flexibility arises with regard to product and product variety expansion and the location of the production. Both can, fairly quickly, be adjusted when market demands or institutional changes require this. The potential negative effects of the adjustments are not borne by them but by the contracting firms, the actual manufacturer. An outcome of the outsourcing trend is the establishment of large businesses that are MNEs in their own right and orchestrate their own international production network. The most famous ones in the electronics sector are Flextronics (Singapore) and Foxconn (Taiwan). These firms have been contracted over the years by Apple, HP, Microsoft, Sony, and others to produce laptops, desktops, game consoles, mobile phones, and other electronic goods. Galanz, the Chinese microwave producer, produced up to 80% of the global microwaves at a time without most people knowing about the company (Zeng and Williamson 2005).

The anonymity and lack of transparency of international production networks to outsiders is a major drawback in the assessment of these networks and their impact. Some companies have undertaken efforts to work against this. Within the textile industry, the outdoor apparel company, Patagonia, has started to communicate the locations where the design, assembly, sourcing, and distribution for individual products take place. On Patagonia's website it is possible to identify these locations and get an idea of the international business connections relevant for the production of each product. Nike and Adidas have followed a somewhat different path. After being heavily criticized in the 1990s for taking advantage of labor standards in Asia that are lower than in their home regions and less well enforced, both companies today publish the manufacturing location of their suppliers and licensees. This allows us to gain an insight into the international network these firms control and how they might be able to influence economic conditions in other countries. In 2011, Nike procured products from 903 unaffiliated factories in 48 countries across 6 continents. About half of the contractors were located in emerging markets, mainly in China: 339. Across these factories, 1.1 million workers were employed (Nike 2011). Adidas, on the other hand, has direct business relationships with 1,232 suppliers in 63 countries as of early 2012 (Adidas 2012). A large share of these is again located in China (349). In addition, Adidas holds relationships with 269 licensee factories in 45 countries. These suppliers and licensees are spread across 6 continents. Assuming similar staffing numbers per factory as in the case of Nike, Adidas' partners employ more than 1.8 million workers. These numbers illustrate an impressive business network these two MNEs alone manage and control. Through the imposing of product quality requirements, regular but infrequent monitoring visits to check labor and environmental standards and other measures Adidas and Nike have in their power to change the operations of the related businesses which can stimulate economic developments (Buckley 2009; 2011). Adidas and Nike through their supplier network alone are businesses that have a global reach and therefore can be regarded as global companies.

International production networks often include the licensing out of technologies and innovation for manufacturing abroad. The best available data on this topic are provided by the U.S. Bureau of Economic Affairs (BEA) which surveys the international business activities of American firms. US firms received royalty and licensing fee payments of US$105 billion in 2010 (BEA various years). Of these, nearly US$40 billion were collected from unaffiliated businesses overseas. This is slightly higher than the average collection of one-third over the previous five years. Payments are received from all continents with the majority received from Asia, Pacific and the European Union which account for two-thirds of all payments.

The operations of Nestlé are an example of contract farming. The way Nestlé operates its contract farming involves significant input on behalf of Nestlé to its independent milk farmers. The non-equity based contractual relationship with some 600,000 milk farmers globally is supplemented with extensive training across all farming operations in order to increase quality and efficiency of the farms (Nestlé 2008; 2012). This supports the general development of the farmers and reduces any supply-chain risks for Nestlé.

Another form of non-equity internationalization is the engagement in trade relationships. Hereby a firm can internationalize its business through either exporting (outward internationalization) or importing (inward internationalization) (Welch and Luostarinen 1993). The opening remarks referred to a significant increase in international trade activities. In particular, small and medium-sized firms engage in this form of internationalization. These firms often possess the skills and resources to occupy niche markets in which they then flourish. They engage not at all or only very little in FDI because of resource and capacity constraints. Baader, the German food processing machinery company, or Galanz, the Chinese microwave manufacturing company, are examples of such firms.

The Global Company

Against the backdrop of the different kind of international business activities firms engage in and develop their international footprint, we can now discuss a typology of a global company. We have seen that firms internationalize by exporting goods and services. Within niche markets this can lead to global market leadership and dominance to the degree that industry sectors are dependent on the exporter. On the other hand, we have companies that invest long-term in economic entities overseas. Through their presence in overseas markets in production, research and development, or sales activities, they are seeking to penetrate the markets and take advantage of the local conditions. The physical presence in the host economy also provides them with a direct means to influence the business environment to their own advantage. Situated somewhere in between these two dimensions of international business, and related to them, are these different kinds of non-equity business relationships that firms conclude for contract research, manufacturing, or design purposes, among others. Common to all these kinds of business activities is that they establish or are part of international business networks. Through these networks, the contracting firm can have control over a large number of businesses in a wide range of countries. In order to do so, the firm does not actually have to have internationalized its own business.

Against the kind of international business activity we have to set the firm's performance and power. Performance relates here then to the standard measures of international activities which are international sales, employees, and assets. These proxies are normally used in ranking of 'global businesses'. Although a performance indicator, the extent to which a firm's brand name is globally recognized is often not explicitly included in such rankings. It is a good indicator of how well a firm's name has penetrated global markets with or without any physical presence. Lastly, firms exert influence on their business environment through dialogue with economic, political and social actors they identify as key stakeholders. At the political level, the focus rests with the industry policies of the country and its execution at the local level. The dialogue with social actors is sought to gain and sustain the legitimacy of the business. The economic interactions outside the equity and non-equity relationships discussed above include the setting of international standards and new trends. Examples of the latter are the hybrid and, subsequently, electric cars first developed by Toyota or the development of touchscreen smartphones by Apple. In both cases the industry had to react to and follow the trends established by these firms.

Bringing these different dimensions of activities and power together requires a complex data collection and analysis process. This more holistic picture will inform a fairer assessment of the existence and influence of global companies.

New Global Challengers

A new dimension in the economic and political discourse of the global company is the development of MNEs from emerging economies. Companies from Brazil, China, India, South Africa, or Taiwan have increased their international presence in the 2000s. Former contract manufacturers have developed into companies that sell products under their own brand globally (e.g. the electronic equipment producers Acer, Asus, or HTC), firms in the extractive industries secure their share of raw material resources, while others tap into the consumer markets in developed and developing markets alike. Governments from emerging markets have justified the push to establish multinational enterprises by arguing that the time is ripe for emerging market MNEs and their countries would need them in order to have a voice in the international economic order (Buckley *et al.* 2011). Firms from these countries have argued that internationalization is part of the natural growth of any firm (Voss, Buckley, and Cross 2010). As the above data has shown, and a number of rankings confirm, emerging market businesses have been fairly successful since the early 2000s in growing and internationalizing their businesses. Indeed, the Fortune Global 500 ranking lists 8 Brazilian, 73 Chinese, 8 Indian, and 13 South Korean companies – making Chinese firms the second largest group behind the US-based companies (Fortune 2012b).

These positive connotations are not shared by everyone. International investments and acquisitions by, in particular, mainland Chinese firms are viewed sceptically in some host and unaffected third countries. The partial acquisition of UK-based Weetabix by the Chinese state-owned company Bright Foods from private equity firm Lion Capital in spring 2012 was greeted by comments suggesting a Chinese global shopping spree, a buyout of industrialized countries' assets by Chinese firms, and a Chinese nationalization. The acquisition attempts of Unocal by CNOOC, 3com, and Marconi by Huawei, or Rio Tinto by Chinalco were all considered as increasing the influence of Chinese companies unduly and threatening the stability or security in the host economy if not the entire sector globally. All four businesses were subsequently acquired by established industrialized country businesses.[1] As a consequence of the rise of emerging markets MNEs, there has been renewed interest in the operations of inward investment approval agencies. Australia, Canada, and the United States have such an agency in place and it has been suggested the European Union should have one in response to the growth of Chinese investments (Okano-Heijmans and van der Putten 2009). Related to this discussion is the notion of the negative impacts Chinese firms will have in Africa (Ali and Jafrani 2012). While the discussion above remained at the general firm level, this one focuses on the contribution of businesses from particular countries. Although international investments by emerging markets are here to stay and likely to increase in the future (Rosen and Hahnemann 2011), they still account for a relatively small amount of global investments; thus barely representing a global force. They are encroaching onto economic fields that have once been the domain of industrialized country firms or, actually, that have not yet been developed by them. Exaggerated notions of global companies are in these cases used as a defense mechanism against growing competition.

Conclusion

Businesses are operating on a global scale, but identifying a global company is nevertheless difficult. The range of modes a firm can use to engage in international business operations leads to an international footprint that ranges from no physical international presence to affiliations in all markets. While either of these footprints can make it a firm with a global presence, neither makes it necessarily a global company.

The term 'global company' is often used as shorthand when very large businesses that have business operations in a number of countries are discussed. Businesses like Goldman Sachs, Shell, Vitol, or Wal-Mart fall into this category. These firms are not necessarily present in all countries or on all continents. Their direct business relationship with economies is only one side of the coin. Equally important are their indirect relationships that enable them to reach into the economies where they have no physical presence. The kind of indirect relationship depends on the industry sector. For a retailer like Wal-Mart this includes the expansive supplier network, for a resource extraction company like Shell it is the downstream operations network they deliver and fuel. Common to both is that they can influence businesses in a large number of countries because of the extensive direct and indirect network.

The possibility of influencing other businesses is not restricted to large corporations. Small and medium-sized businesses can also have a global influence and shape industry sectors. In these cases it is not the sheer size through which they exert the influence, but the product and service expertise. They are operating in niche markets and have acquired over time a degree of specialism that sets very high market entry barriers (Simon 2007). Global market shares significantly above 50% are not seldom.

From a policy and a social activism perspective, the SMEs play a negligible role when it comes to discussions of global companies and economic influence. The focus rests with businesses that are very visible and therefore more accessible. This is true for the positive as well as the negative expectations and perceptions of these businesses. A comprehensive analysis should not equate pure firm size with global economic influence. It should rather detail forensically the nature and extent of internationalization the firm is pursuing and the range of indirect measures through which it could exert influence. Doing so would bring us closer to a comprehension of a global company and devise appropriate policies.

Definitions of global companies can therefore focus on the physical globalization of the firm, on the importance of overseas markets for sales, on the extent to which an industry sector is dependent on one firm because of its specialized products or controlling stake in international trade, on the extent to which a firm's brand is globally appreciated, or on the extent to which the firms are able to influence the economic, political, and social environment in a number of markets. All of these definitions are appropriate for their purposes. They are trying to answer different sets of research questions and require different research strategies.

Note

1 Unocal by Chevron, 3com by HP, Marconi by Ericsson (Chevron, n.d.; Ericsson 2012; HP 2010).

References

Adidas. 2012. 2011 Performance Data, http://www.adidas-group.com/en/sustainability/Reporting_and_performance_data/Performance_data/default.aspx. Accessed December 1, 2012.

Ali, Shimelse and Jafran, Nidan. 2012. China's Growing Role in Africa: Myths and Facts, *International Economic Bulletin*, February 9, http://carnegieendowment.org/ieb/2012/02/09/china-s-growing-role-in-africa-myths-and-facts. Accessed December 1, 2012.

BEA (Bureau of Economic Analysis). Various years. Royalties and License Fees Receipts and Payments, http://www.bea.gov/international/international_services.htm. Accessed December 1, 2012.

Bernard, Andrew B., Jensen, J. Bradford, and Schott, Peter K. 2005. "Importers, Exporters, and Multinationals: A Portrait of Firms in the U.S. that Trade Goods." In *Producer Dynamics: New Evidence from Micro Data*, ed. Timothy Dunne, J. Bradford Jensen, and Mark J. Roberts, 513–552. Chicago: University of Chicago Press.

Buckley, Peter J. 2009. "The Impact of the Global Factory on Economic Development." *Journal of World Business*, 44 (2): 131–143.

Buckley, Peter J. 2011. "International Integration and Coordination in the Global Factory." *Management International Review*, 51 (2): 269–283.

Buckley, Peter J. and Casson, Mark. 1976. *The Future of the Multinational Enterprise*. London: Macmillan.

Buckley, Peter J., Voss, Hinrich, Cross, A.R., and Clegg, Jeremy L. 2011. "The Emergence of Chinese Firms as Multinationals: The Influence of Home Institutions." In *China and the Multinationals: International Business and the Entry of China into the Global Economy*, ed. RobertPearce, 125–157. Cheltenham: Edward Elgar.

Chevron. n.d. Chevron–Unocal Merger Fact Sheet, www.chevron.com/documents/pdf/merger_fact_sheet.pdf. Accessed December 1, 2012.

Clay, Jay. 2005. *Exploring the Links between International Business and Poverty Reduction: A Case Study of Unilever in Indonesia*. Oxford: Oxfam and Unilever.

Ericsson. 2005. Ericsson Acquisition of Marconi Key Assets Approved by Marconi Shareholders. Ericsson Press Release, December 21, http://www.ericsson.com/news/1027067. Accessed December 1, 2012.

Fortune. 2011. Global 500, http://money.cnn.com/magazines/fortune/global500/2010/full_list/. Accessed December 1, 2012.

Fortune. 2012a. If the Fortune 500 Were a Country, http://money.cnn.com/magazines/fortune/fortune500/world-economies-interactive/index.html. Accessed December 1, 2012.

Fortune. 2012b. Global 500 2012, http://money.cnn.com/magazines/fortune/global500/. Accessed December 1, 2012.

Ghemawat, Pankaj. 2007. *Redefining Global Strategy: Crossing Borders in a World Where Differences Still Matter*. Cambridge, MA: Harvard Business School Press.

Gupta, Anil K. and Govindarajan, Vijay. 2004. *Global Strategy and the Organization*. Hoboken: Wiley.

Gupta, Anil K., Govindarajan, Vijat, and Wang, Haiyan Wang. 2008. *The Quest for Global Dominance: Transforming Global Presence into Global Competitive Advantage*, 2nd edn. San Francisco: Jossey-Bass.

Hassel, A., Höpner, M., Kurdelbusch, A., Rehder, B., and Zugehör, R. 2003. Two Dimensions of the Internationalization of Firms. *Journal of Management Studies*, 40 (3): 705–723.

HP. 2010. HP Completes Acquisition of 3Com Corporation, Accelerates Converged Infrastructure Strategy, HP press release, April 12, http://www.hp.com/hpinfo/newsroom/press/2010/100412xa.html. Accessed December 1, 2012.

Moore, Karl, and Lewis, David. 1999. *Birth of the Multinational: 2000 Years of Ancient Business History – from Ashur to Augustus*. Copenhagen: Copenhagen Business School.

Nestlé. 2008. Nestlé's Management of Dairy Supply Chain in China, http://www.nestle.com/Media/PressReleases/Pages/AllPressRelease.aspx?PageId=142&PageName=2008.aspx. Accessed December 1, 2012.

Nestlé. 2012. Working with Dairy Farmers, http://www.nestle.com/Brands/Dairy/Pages/DairyCSV.aspx. Accessed December 1, 2012.

Nike. 2011. Manufacturing, http://www.nikeinc.com/pages/manufacturing. Accessed December 12, 2012.

Okano-Heijmans, Maaike and van der Putten, Frans-Paul. 2009. Europe Needs to Screen Chinese Investment. *East Asia Forum*, August 18, http://www.eastasiaforum.org/2009/08/18/europe-needs-to-screen-chinese-investment/. Accessed December 1, 2012.

Rosen, Daniel H. and Hanemann, Thilo. 2011. *An American Open Door? Maximizing the Benefits of Chinese Foreign Direct Investment*. New York: Asian Society.

Rugman, Alan M. 2005. *Regional Multinationals*. Cambridge: Cambridge University Press.

Rugman, Alan M. and Girod, Stephane. 2003. "Retail Multinationals and Globalization: The Evidence is regional." *European Management Journal*, 21 (1): 24–37.

Rugman, Alan M. and Collinson, Simon. 2004. "The Regional Nature of the World's Automotive Sector." *European Management Journal*, 22 (5): 471–482.

Rugman, Alan M. and Li, Jing. 2007. "Will China's Multinationals Succeed Globally or Regionally?" *European Management Journal*, 25 (5): 333–343.

Rugman, Alan M., Kudina, Alina, and Yip, George S. 2007. "The Regional Dimension of UK Multinationals." In *Regional Aspects of Multinationality and Performance*, ed. Alan M. Rugman, 297–315. Bingley: Emerald.

Simon, Hermann. 2007. *Hidden Champions des 21. Jahrhunderts: Die Erfolgsstrategien unbekannter Weltmarktführer*. Frankfurt: Campus.

Sullivan, Daniel. 1994. "Measuring the Degree of Internationalization of a Firm." *Journal of International Business Studies*, 25 (2): 325–342.

UNCTAD. 1997. *World Investment Report 1997: Transnational Corporations, Market Structure and Competition Policy*. Geneva and New York: UN.

UNCTAD. 2007. *World Investment Report 2007: Transnational Corporations, Extractive Industries and Development*. Geneva and New York: UN.

UNCTAD. 2011a. *UNCTADStat*. http://unctadstat.unctad.org. Accessed December 1, 2012.

UNCTAD. 2011b. *World Investment Report 2011: Non-Equity Modes of International Production and Development*. Geneva and New York: UN.

Vitol. 2012. About Vitol: Goup Performance, http://www.vitol.com/group-performance.html. Accessed December 1, 2012.

Voss, Hinrich, Buckley, Peter J., and Cross, Adam R. 2010. "The Impact of Home Country Institutional Effects on the Internationalisation Strategy of Chinese Firms." *Multinational Business Review*, 18 (3): 25–48.

Welch, Lawrence S. and Luostarinen, Reijo, K. 1993. "Inward–Outward Connections in Internationalization." *Journal of International Marketing*, 1 (1): 44–56.

World Bank. 2011. Gross Domestic Product 2010, http://siteresources.worldbank.org/DATASTATISTICS/Resources/GDP.pdf. Accessed December 1, 2012.

World Trade Organisation (WTO). 2012. Time Series on International Trade, www.wto.org. Accessed December 1, 2012.

Yip, George S. 2002. *Total Global Strategy II*. Saddle River, NJ: Prentice Hall.

Zeng, Ming and Williamson, Peter J. 2003. "The Hidden Dragons." *Harvard Business Review*, 81 (10): 92–103.

Chapter 3

The National Identity of Global Companies

Stephen Wilks

Introduction

The idea of a global company embraces a wide range of possible legal, economic, and political forms with multiple possible identities for the multinational corporations (MNCs) which are the subject of this chapter. We are concerned with a sub-set made up of the larger multinationals, but it is also necessary to recognize that "multinational" is a wasting and contested concept. The term "multinational corporation" was first coined in 1960 (Jones 2005: 4) and multinationals attracted substantial and often critical attention during the 1960s. Much of the writing at that time treated "the" multinational as a clear concept dealing with a coherent category of powerful corporations. In part this was because the concept was clearer then than it is now. Most multinationals were American or, like the British corporations, shared US characteristics. Thus Vernon's book, *Sovereignty at Bay*, was based on a study limited to 187 large US corporations, controlled primarily by US nationals (Vernon 1971: 146). Since then things have become much more complicated. Although many studies still revert to the discourse of "multinationals" as if they were a discrete category of political actors (for instance Roach 2005), there is increasing recognition that the diversity of corporations requires that study of individual corporations, or groups of corporations, should be contextualized according to what Morgan refers to as their "transnational social space" (Morgan 2011: 419).

This chapter seeks to explore that process of contextualization and the approach used is sociological and institutional. Corporations, it is suggested, are embedded in particular national, industrial, and historical contexts which shape their identities and mold behavior. The behavior with which we are primarily concerned is political. The chapter is concerned with corporations as political actors and with their abilities to lobby governments, to structure markets, to engage in governance partnerships,

The Handbook of Global Companies, First Edition. Edited by John Mikler.

and at the extreme to engage in private global governance. In these various forms of political engagement corporations influence public policy, and participate in the design and implementation of regulation (Büthe and Mattli 2011). The overarching argument, to which we return in the conclusion, is that the large multinational has become a governing institution within global governance, imbued with institutional authority and engaged in partnership with governments as part of a global managerial elite (Wilks 2013). In examining the varying institutional contexts in which the identities of such corporations are nested we can gain insight into the priorities, the processes, and the values that they bring to global governance.

Accordingly, the chapter begins with a section on the diverse home-country contexts which help shape corporate identities. It goes on to reflect on the comparative understanding of national contexts through a review of the "varieties of capitalism" literature which emphasizes national bases for corporate behavior. The fourth section engages with a disciplinary gap between the comparative politics literature and research on international political economy. There is a challenge in conceptualizing the interaction between political influence at the national level and how that translates into global influence and, in turn, how the global system disciplines national governments. This challenge has become more pointed by the increased salience of emergent country multinationals (EMNCs), especially those from China, whose identity is influenced by high levels of state ownership. The fifth section turns from the macro-political role of companies as actors, to consider the internal or micro-politics by presenting the company as a political system in its own right with alternative forms of corporate governance, with tensions between internal units and management strategies, and as an organization exposed to several modes of institutional authority. The sixth section explores the tensions between national and global sources of identity whilst the conclusion rehearses possible ways in which different nationally based companies might resolve those tensions.

The Diversity and National Context of Multinationals

The multinationals that constitute the global economy are bewilderingly diverse and the great majority, like smaller domestic corporations, will have very little individual influence. The usual working definition of a multinational is a corporation that has operations in at least two other countries in addition to its home state. Defined in this way UNCTAD (2008: 9–10) identified 79,000 transnational corporations and, up to 2007, it noted continued record growth in FDI which was growing three times faster than world trade. Increasingly MNCs are growing through cross-border mergers and acquisitions which is far easier in the Anglo-Saxon countries which encourage a market for corporate control that is not tolerated in countries such as Germany and Japan. The term "transnational corporation" is often used synonymously with "multinational" but, strictly speaking, a "transnational" is a corporation with no pre-eminent links to a single nation-state in terms of ownership or management. The prevailing view is that genuine transnationals are very rare. Most companies have a strong identification with a "home" country reflected in the location of production, the make-up of the board of directors, a nationally derived corporate culture or an expectation of support from the home government (Doremus et al. 1998). Prominent analysts of the corporation, notably Richard Whitley (1999; 2001; 2005a) have repeatedly emphasized the embeddedness of firms and their competitive strategies in national business systems. He has speculated on the development of "new cross national business systems" (Whitley 1999: 131) but doubted that they were yet emerging. Similarly Jones (2005: 40) notes that "Rugman and D'Cruz (2000) could only find nine 'global firms'" (see also Rugman 2005).

While the continued influence of national origins does need to be emphasized it is striking how genuinely global many large corporations have become. UNCTAD identifies the top 100 transnationals and applies a transnationality index based on the foreign percentage of assets, sales, and employees. Some 82% of the top 100 have a transnationality index of over 50% which indicates a high level of independence from home-country operations. An increase in the proportion of such highly multinationalized corporations does raise the prospect of a globally "denationalized" corporate sector, especially since the UNCTAD transnationality index only measures the internalized transactions within the hierarchy of the corporate organization. Corporations also operate through networks and alliances which increase their influence. The largest hosts and home countries for multinationals are the market-orientated developed OECD countries. Among these dominant players some countries are far more internationalized than others. UNCTAD also provides an index of country "transnationality." On this index Table 3.1 indicates the most internationalized economies. The high internationalization of Belgium or Singapore is not surprising but the table also emphasizes the high level of internationalization of the Netherlands, the United Kingdom, and France. Perhaps more surprising is that the large economies of Brazil, China, and Germany are only modestly

Table 3.1 Transnationality index for countries, 2005.

Countries	TNI
Belgium	66
Singapore	65
Chile	33
Netherlands	32
New Zealand	28
South Africa	25
UK	22
France	19
Switzerland	18
Egypt	17
Australia	16
Brazil	14
China	12
Germany	11
USA	7
India	4
Japan	2

Note: The index is based on the four indicators of: FDI flows; FDI stock; foreign affiliate value-added; and employment by foreign affiliates.
Source: UNCTAD (2008: 12).

internationalized and the United States, despite its huge role as home and host to MNCs, has a far smaller exposure to international pressures than the United Kingdom. The United Kingdom has an exceptionally "denationalized" industrial economy due partly to a very permissive (or neoliberal) stance by post-1979 governments which has allowed the market for corporate control to transfer a sequence of quintessentially "British" companies to foreign control. Examples include P&O (now the Dubai owned Dubai World); Pilkington (now Nippon Glass); and Cadbury (now part of the US Kraft Group).

These indices of country economic transnationality are potentially also indicators of national influence within global governance. The modes of behavior, styles of regulation, and form of political activism with which companies are familiar at the national level could be expected to be reproduced at the international level. Thus the more British companies operate overseas, and the more overseas companies operate in Britain, so the norms typical of the United Kingdom may be reproduced at the global level. This argument about the United Kingdom would also apply to the other transnationalized large OECD economies, especially France, Germany, and now China. In contrast familiarity with the United States might be less important than usually expected and the influence of Japan, as only a modestly transnationalized economy, might be regarded as less significant. The influence of the United Kingdom does indeed seem to be substantial in areas like privatization, negotiated regulation, and corporate governance. The UK shareholder value approach to corporate strategy and corporate governance model has had an extraordinary international influence. Similarly, the UK-style "partnership" between government and business has been taken to the global level by UK-based corporations acting as vigorous "norm entrepreneurs." As Flohr et al. (2010: 244–245) argue:

> UK business is used to a cooperative approach to policy-making with government as an individual partner – which above all stands in contrast to the US style of business–government relations. Therefore, British corporations are more likely to adopt the same expectations and style when interacting on the international level.

We come back to this point in the Conclusion, but here we can note that global companies have many characteristics in common but also bring identities to global political activity that reflect their national origins and continued national affiliations. To secure a better insight into these sometimes radical differences in national models of capitalism and of corporate political engagement we can turn to comparative political economy.

Comparison of National Context: Varieties of Capitalism

In the study of political economy there has been a rather weird gulf between scholars rooted in international relations who write in the well developed field of international political economy (IPE); and those who are rooted in comparative politics. The IPE literature is preoccupied with relations between nation-states and corporations and with the loss of state sovereignty. It barely mentions the national variations in the types of corporations and the way in which they are integrated into national economies. In contrast, the literature on comparative capitalism, or varieties of capitalism, is still firmly nested in national settings. The now substantial canon of literature on comparative political economy rejects assumptions of convergence, reaffirms national institutional differences, and downplays the independent power of multinationals (see Hall and Soskice 2001: 56). This body of work emphasizes national identities and is reviewed in more depth in this section.

The recognition and evaluation of different models of capitalism became a central concern of comparative politics and political economy after the fall of the Berlin Wall. Attention turned to the now striking contrasts between different types of capitalism and those types also proliferated as formerly socialist or communist states, from India to China, Brazil to Russia, began to develop their own distinctive variants on the capitalist theme. The new focus on the empirical and the normative differences between types of corporation and types of corporate governance was emphasized in an early influential and passionate polemic by a French businessman, Michel Albert, whose *Capitalisme contre Capitalisme* published in French in 1991 contrasted the cut-throat Anglo-American capitalism with the more caring continental Rhine model "which sees the company as a social institution and an enduring community deserving of the loyalty and affection of its members, who can expect a measure of company care and protection in return" (Albert 1993: 146). The confrontation between the two (or in reality several) variants of European capitalism has been a constant source of tension as corporate regulation has evolved and as the European Commission has moved to support a more Anglo-American system as an end-product of its attempts to harmonize corporate governance across Europe (Horn 2012).

These contrasting capitalist systems within which corporations are embedded have been categorized in a variety of frameworks. Something of a breakthrough in model building came from the work of Richard Whitley on "national business systems." He conceptualized business systems as modes of authoritative coordination and related distinctive national forms of economic organization to their national institutional contexts (Whitley 1999: 54). His emphasis on national embeddedness led him to affirm the continued influence of national origins on the behavior of firms arguing that "this is not to say that firms never alter when they internationalize... but to emphasise that they are unlikely to change central characteristics radically such that they become different kinds of economic actors" (Whitley 1999: 134). This approach was developed by Hall and Soskice who emphasized the central importance of corporations as defining features of these capitalist models in a hugely influential chapter which has fathered a "Varieties of Capitalism" (VoC) school of research which has become virtually an academic industry (Hall and Soskice 2001). They proposed a dichotomy of models, the Anglo-Saxon model becomes Liberal Market Economies (LMEs) and the Rhineland model becomes the Coordinated Market Economies (CMEs). Their argument has been so important in understanding the influence and role of the corporation that it deserves a brief summary.

The Hall and Soskice approach to comparative political economy is actor based with the assumption that actors (including corporations) seek to maximize goals in a rational way. They emphasize the role of the corporation, "this is a firm-centred political economy that regards corporations as the crucial actors in a capitalist economy" (Hall and Soskice 2001: 6). They concentrate their attention on the relationships that corporations develop with other actors and argue that the success of a corporation rests on its ability "to coordinate effectively with a wide range of actors" (Hall and Soskice 2001: 6). They emphasize the key importance of five sets of relation-ships: industrial relations; corporate governance; vocational training and education; inter-firm relations; and management of employees. LMEs manage this coordination primarily through markets, whilst CMEs manage coordination through networks and negotiation, structured by distinctive institutions (such as banks) and processes (such as interlocking directorships). They suggest that each capitalist model has assembled a portfolio of mutually supportive institutions, rules, and processes that facilitate coordination and are "complementary." Thus UK corporate governance rests on a liquid stock market (to permit shareholder sanctions), a flexible labor market (to allow cost cutting) and generalized education (to permit labor mobil-ity) whilst German corporate governance depends on "patient" long-term capital provided by banks, a restricted labor market (to avoid poaching of workers) and specialized education (to allow the development of firm-specific skills). This diag-nosis of complementarity has important implications for convergence of systems (Jackson and Deeg 2008).

The VoC framework suggests that both models can be successful and each embody distinctive sources of comparative advantage. The framework seeks to explain eco-nomic success measured in growth, although it can be productively employed to address many related questions including more political issues such as equality (CMEs could be expected to display greater income equality) and security (again, CMEs are likely to offer more job security and welfare benefits). This can also trans-late into policy leadership so that Mikler finds that German, and especially Japanese, motor companies are led by their home CME experience to regard social concerns as more strategically important (Mikler 2009: 230), whilst companies from LME coun-tries are more materialistic. More generally the VoC framework proved so creative that it has "revolutionised the study of contemporary political economy" (Hancke *et al.* 2007: 36) but it has also generated extensive criticism and adaptation (see Hancke *et al.* 2007: 5–8; Jackson and Deeg 2008: 686). Critics point out that the two models appear to be stylized accounts of the United States and Germany, never-theless, they can be used to emphasize and explain the way in which multinationals owe their success to supportive national systems and further, to speculate on how those national systems are projected onto the global level.

From National to Global Partnerships?

The focus on national sources of corporate identity within the comparative politics literature is invaluable but it needs to be extended to recognize the realities of global markets and global governance. This section therefore opens with a discussion of the enhanced power that corporations enjoy by virtue of international operations, it then reviews the range of national identities that are competing within the global arena, and turns to one peculiarly important emergent corporate identity in the shape of Chinese corporations.

The varieties of capitalism approach visualizes systematic processes of coordi-nation at the national level which involves varieties of "power sharing" involving cooperation between diverse units of government, organizations within civil society, and economic institutions. But, whilst government may share power, it is the ulti-mate sovereign authority and effectively the senior partner, able to change the terms of engagement and to disenfranchise other actors. This basic constitutional principle of ultimate sovereignty collapses when governance extends beyond the boundaries of the nation-state. Corporations operating internationally transcend dependency on national governments, there is no source of international (electoral) legitimacy and corporations themselves become agents of governance with a degree of absolute autonomy. Moreover, their enhanced international authority comes full circle to reinforce their domestic power so that governments dealing with international corporations become more dependent.

Susan Strange was particularly evangelical in stressing the influence of markets and firms in the international economy (Strange 1994). Her analysis of the declining power of the state was controversial but she was one of the first to advance the hypothesis that:

> the shift from state to market has actually made political players of the TNCs... They themselves are political institutions, having political relations with civil society. These political relations are even more important than their political involvement with other firms or with specific governments. (Strange 1996: 44)

In charting the growing political role of MNCs Strange was therefore inviting a more sophisticated analysis of the reconfiguration of state authority and a consideration of the political power of MNCs independent from the state. It is hard to see that Strange's invitation was widely accepted. Writing more recently, scholars of IPE have regretted the continued baleful influence of the zero-sum sovereignty debate. Goldman and Palan (2006: 182) bemoan the preoccupation with two types of corporate entities, "states" and "nonstate actors." "Within such a dichotomised conception of the world," they write, "IPE scholars have also tended to regard MNCs as constituting a direct challenge to state authority... the debates that focus on the interaction between states and MNCs are really a distraction from the real importance of these corporations." One exception is Sklair who accepted Strange's exhortation to concentrate on the corporation rather than the state and attempted "to replace the state-centric paradigm... with a paradigm of transnational practices." But he, like Strange, is too dismissive of the great variety of government-corporate relationships captured by comparativists (Sklair 2001: 10, 72). It is necessary to retain a focus on the various modes by which corporations engage with national governments while avoiding an obsession with loss of state authority. The state's power has not been reduced, it has been redistributed.

In the international arena, the idea that the corporation shares in governance as an institution has become widely accepted. The corporation should be regarded as a constituent institution of global governance so that Fuchs observes that "business has become a pivotal participant in global governance and an important source of global rules and regulation" (Fuchs 2007: 164). Independence from nation-states need not take on a confrontational character, it may be more about sharing the power of the nation-state than evading it. The adversarial attitudes of the 1970s and 1980s have been replaced by a far more positive and tolerant attitude since the early 1990s. Thus, at the turn of the century, one of the leading American scholars of international political economy could write that "as an institution the MNC is beneficial to peoples everywhere" (Gilpin 2000: 171). This viewpoint, reflective of the deepening neoliberal consensus, made it both instrumentally and ideologically respectable for governments to work with corporations in patterns of cooperation that involve partnership at the international level (Stern and Seligmann 2004). Thus Dunning (1997: 15) identified a move from an adversarial relationship to "a more cooperative relationship between *firms and governments*," a theme echoed with a more critical coloration by van Apeldoorn (2000: 159). The steady proliferation of "transnational public-private partnerships" has become a distinct area of research in international relations. These public-private partnerships (PPPs) tend to operate over more technical niche areas relating to industrial sectors or public policies and for Schäferhof *et al.* (2009: 452):

> PPPs are … an expression of the ongoing reconfiguration of authority in world politics, and reflect the fact that non-state actors, such as non-governments organisations (NGOs) … and transnational corporations (TNCs) … are increasingly engaged in authoritative decision-making. Indeed, some authors go further to maintain that private governance is replacing the public governance resting on international cooperation between nation-states. (Pattberg 2007; see also Ougaard 2008; and Hale and Held 2011)

We see in these debates an implication that all MNCs are similar. They engage in partnerships but there is little analysis of whether different corporations embedded in the institutional configurations of different states will participate differently in global governance. Could we, in other words, expect Japanese or Russian originated MNCs to behave differently from those originating in the United States or China? The commonsense assumption is that there will be differences and, given the increase in the diversity of the home countries of MNCs, this expectation of varying relationships is important. Corporate diversity has increased rapidly since 2000, as can be illustrated by the makeup of the *Fortune Global 500*. Corporations are ranked by global revenue and the results for 2011 show Wal-Mart as the largest corporation in the world with revenues of $422 billion and employing an astonishing 2,100,000 people. The biggest companies are in the biggest global industries including oil, motor vehicles, and financial services. The league table is relatively stable year by year but in the 15 years between 1996 and 2011 some clear trends have emerged. There are fewer large Japanese companies, the US predominance is decaying with more large companies now headquartered in Europe, and there has been a remarkable diversification of the global corporation with the rise of the BRICS, and especially China, as shown in Table 3.2.

The dominance of "the Triad" (the United States, Europe, and Japan) is thus breaking down and there are increasing numbers of government owned global corporations. The traditional assumption that most MNCs therefore shared the identities of American corporations, and that in the global arena European and even Japanese companies were converging on an American corporate form, begins to look dubious. In particular the rise of Chinese companies provokes the expectation that they will project Chinese identities as well as pursuing Chinese national interests.

In relation to national identity, the big questions about non-Western multinationals are first, whether they are emulating the Western corporate form of institution; and second, the degree to which they are becoming relatively autonomous from their

Table 3.2   National distribution of large corporations.

	1996	2007	2011
Europe (EU)	153	167	145
USA	153	153	133
Japan	141	64	68
China	2	29	61
Russia, Brazil, India	5	17	22
Others (in 2011, 12 countries)	46	70	71
Total Fortune 500	500	500	500

Source: Fortune Global 500, http://money.cnn.com, accessed December 19, 2012.

home states and governments to become part of a global business civilization. On the first point, the business corporation has become the standard mode of organizing economic activity in market economies. The model has spread to emergent economies and has eclipsed various alternatives such as state-managed industries, cooperatives, individual traders, partnerships, and so on. Moreover, the corporate form typically shares many of the characteristics of the limited liability joint stock corporation with larger corporations quoted on the rapidly developing stock markets of emergent economies. Within this general pattern of convergence there are a variety of alternative legal forms and governance structures which include such striking models as the huge Korean chaebols which are similar in organization to the pre-war Japanese zaibatsu; the rambling Indian conglomerate groupings and the Russian industrial empires headed by the so-called oligarchs such as the Sibneft oil group (now part of Gazprom) which formed the basis of the fortune of Roman Abramovich.

Perhaps the most interesting embrace of the corporate form is provided by China which began to encourage private enterprise after 1993. By 2000 the CCP officially moved to encourage development of privately owned businesses and "gave the private sector the same status as the public sector" (Dickson 2008: 39), a move followed by granting permission in 2001 for private entrepreneurs to become members of the Party (a measure so profoundly antagonistic to Maoist doctrine that it still seems bizarre) and by membership of the WTO in 2001. The corporatization of state owned enterprises proceeded from the late 1990s by converting them into shareholder owned corporations quoted on the new domestic Shanghai and Shenzhen stock exchanges. At the same time China began actively to promote inward investment thus accepting the presence and legal rights of foreign corporations. Indeed, Story (2010: 348) notes that China began "to make global corporations key allies for the regime in the global polity. China's adaptation is a magnificent achievement."

This striking convergence on the corporate form is one of the most important examples of "isomorphism" in the global economy. Isomorphism is the term used by organizational sociologists to explain convergence towards a particular organizational form. A standard explanation would be in terms of economic efficiency so that the corporate form is adopted simply because it generates greater added value but theories of isomorphism go beyond the efficiency perspective to try to explain convergence in non-economic settings. In one of the most influential treatments DiMaggio and Powell (1991) identify coercive, mimetic, and normative sources of isomorphism and this analytical approach is helpful in identifying the mix of factors that have led emergent countries towards endorsing the model of the corporation. The Chinese case is both fascinating and important, and so we can use it as an example of a more general syndrome.

From a coercive perspective the corporate model provided an entry ticket to participation in the global market by making Chinese economic organizations respectable in foreign markets and by gaining the endorsement and legitimacy provided by membership of the WTO in 2001. This was not coercion by blunt threats or ultimatums, the Chinese leadership has been spectacularly resistant to overseas pressure. Instead it was soft coercion through the acceptance of the rules, standards and expectation that characterize corporate trading practices so that Chinese corporations could be understood and trusted as trading partners. The Chinese leadership has proceeded gradually in its market reforms which has made "mimetic isomorphism" another significant factor. Mimetic pressures take the form of copying or contagion, of borrowing models that appear effective and offer convenient solutions. The American corporate model has been disseminated successfully across the globe (Djelic 1998) and, as the dominant economic unit in the most successful global economy, it was similarly attractive to a Chinese leadership who became determined to beat the Americans at their own game (see Story 2010: 348).

These coercive and mimetic influences are relatively straightforward but the Chinese leadership arguably had a far more powerful, pragmatic, and self-interested motive for building up Chinese corporations under the influence of a normative isomorphism. The corporate form preserved the key normative imperatives of stability and control. State-owned industries could be corporatized and privatized, thus protecting vested interests whilst opening up new possibilities for enrichment of elites in the CCP. At the same time the Party could retain control by becoming a major shareholder, by taking seats on the boards of corporations, and in many cases by appointing senior party members as chief executives. We have thus seen an extraordinary interpenetration of political and economic elites. Dickson (2008: 238) observes that "the CCP's strategy of integrating itself with the private sector, both by encouraging party members to go into business and co-opting entrepreneurs into the party, continues to provide dividends." Forecasts for the future development of the Chinese economy and polity tend to emphasize the apparent tensions arising from massive economic change confronting autocratic political continuity. But the Party has played the wealth card. Multinational corporations are now welcome in China and Chinese corporations have become the dominant domestic economic organizations and have established power in global markets. Thus, barely thirty years after the death of Mao Zedong in 1976, political power is no longer exerted through class struggle, but through the operations and strategies of business corporations whose boardrooms are the new battleground for control over corporate decision-making between the Party, business managers, and shareholders (see McGregor 2010: ch. 2). Indeed a revolutionary change, but not quite the one that Marxist-Leninist-Maoist theory anticipated.

In China, therefore, there has been substantial convergence on the Western corporate model, and the same is true of the bulk of emergent economies. In terms of their national identity a key question is whether these EMNCs will remain subject to family or state control, or whether they will become managerially controlled with a separation of ownership and control. Managers could be expected to share a more cosmopolitan, calculative mindset and be less tolerant of national cultural expectations. Again China provides an important example of growing managerial influence. The large Chinese state influenced corporations have managerial structures and corporate governance arrangements based largely on the regulations and practices of the West (Chen, Liu, and Lee 2010: 110). Thus, in a short space of time they have reproduced some of the least attractive features of the Western corporate model including over-powerful chief executives, poor protection for minority shareholders, excessive executive compensation and gross exploitation of workers. This has allowed CEOs to indulge their hubris in ways familiar to Western patterns (Haigh 2004) to engage in ambitious and risky ventures (Li and Tang 2010) and has permitted them to benchmark executive pay against foreign firms so that one by-product of foreign multinational investment in China has been for Chinese companies to emulate high executive pay (Chen, Liu, and Lee 2010: 112). Dickson has charted the deliberate way in which the CCP has co-opted entrepreneurs into the Party. He paints a picture of the Party brilliantly embracing entrepreneurs so that "the integration of political and economic elites in China may serve to sustain the existing authoritarian political system rather than pose a direct challenge to it" (Dickson 2008: 238) but this does not rule out the possibility of a corporate elite steadily gaining additional influence within the Party to produce a "crony communism" in which policy is tilted towards corporate interests and the state is operated in favor of the "red capitalists" and the corporations they control. Gourevitch and Shinn (2005: 192) rather provocatively term this "a unique form of insider kleptocracy, a sort of managerism with Chinese characteristics." But this remains a partnership between corporations and the state. Thus Chinese corporations, like those from other BRICs, are charged with pursuing strategic objectives and particularly access to vital inputs such as raw materials. UNCTAD has observed that "in the case of Chinese TNCs, the quest for raw materials is complemented by parallel and sustained Chinese diplomatic efforts" (UNCTAD 2006: xxvii). The proposition is therefore that in China state ownership has conceded a substantial element of control to corporate managers and that their discretion could be expected to be enhanced in those cases of Chinese MNCs operating outside the framework of domestic constraints. Although the emphasis here has been on China it seems to be a more general phenomenon in which many EMNCs have developed substantial managerial autonomy.

Our second big question was whether EMNCs are becoming part of a self-regulating global governance and whether they are joining what can be described as a global business civilization. EMNCs have become full participants in global business representative bodies such as the ICC (International Chambers of Commerce) and UNCTAD (2006, xxxii) notes that "more than half of the participating companies in the United Nations Global Compact are based in developing countries." Similarly, they are involved in global standard setting through private sector bodies and especially the ISO (International Organization for Standards) and, with their governments, they are involved in the international dispute resolution processes in the WTO thus engaging with international trade law. A more interesting question is whether their senior managers are becoming integrated into an international corporate elite through entry into the international executive labor market. This could happen through recruitment from business schools or through executives moving freely between Western and non-Western MNCs. While there are some hints that emergent country executives are becoming integrated into a global business elite, in the main they retain their home country identification although that does not prevent them from engaging fully in policy formulation for global business. The Davos meetings, for instance, encompass Indian and Chinese corporations and their chief executives. One of the beguiling and civilized aspects of multinational business is, of course, precisely its devotion to commerce and the rejection of the xenophobia that drives nations to pointless wars (Hirschman 1986: 107).

The Multinational Corporation as a Political System

The discussion so far has emphasized the national origins of MNCs and suggested that they will continue to operate internationally under the influence of behaviors learned at the national level. Further, the previous section has pointed out that the range of national origins has increased dramatically in recent years, so how do these contrasting cultures, expectations, and institutional alliances affect the operation of multinationals at the global level? This question is not addressed in the literature on comparative political economy and is barely considered in the IPE literature where the assumption seems to be that MNCs generate a global strategy with relative ease. Instead, the challenge of reconciling national and global constraints is considered by researchers working in international business and organizational sociology who have recently begun also to consider what the organizational complexity of multinationals implies for their role in global governance (Dorrenbacher and Geppert 2011). We can address this, firstly, in relation to the internal hierarchy of the corporation and its degree of centralization and, secondly, by reaching out beyond the corporation to consider what it implies for corporate networks.

The hierarchy within a large multinational can also be considered as a political system in which a range of actors debate and negotiate in an internal process of decision-making within a constitution structured by the national system of corporate governance. Despite the hierarchy, the corporate HQ often has difficulty in imposing policies on subsidiaries and functional specialists located overseas. Those subsidiaries may well be deeply integrated into the particular institutional framework of the host country, especially if they result from an acquisition of a domestic company and, indeed, local knowledge and legitimacy may be a valued competitive advantage. A rational response to a clash of home and host cultures may be to adopt a "multi-domestic strategy" (Fenton-O'Creevy et al. 2011: 101) and such MNCs might be regarded as federations. Alternatively the corporation may opt for a common global strategy and seek to impose it from the center. Corporations from liberal market economies (i.e. Anglo-Saxon corporations) are more likely to follow this approach and to impose standard organizational "best practices" since they are under pressure from shareholders and are less committed to sharing decisions with other stakeholders (Geppart and Dorrenbacher 2011: 23). The approach may be one of centralization or localization, or some synthesis along the lines of HSBC's "glocalization" strategy which illustrated local autonomy when "the world's local bank" conceded to a US Senate hearing that its Mexican subsidiary had been deeply implicated in money laundering for drug cartels (Guardian, July 17, 2012). Whichever is employed, the likelihood is of multinationals which display a range of national identities rather than enjoying one global identity. Morgan puts this well when he remarks that "the study of multinationals is... about how organizations are impacted on by the process of managing in multiple institutional contexts" (Morgan 2011: 417). One route out of this world of multiple identities is to turn to the identities of individuals and recruit from national managerial elites to a global management elite which can take directive positions in all the key units within the multinational and provide coherence around a global strategy (see Morgan 2011: 430; Whitley 2005b: 252).

These issues of defining and enforcing a corporate strategy within an organization divided by several nationally based institutional loyalties applies also when the MNC operates through outsourcing, contracts, networks, and supply chains. The "new economy" thesis argues that the key features of globalization, such as access to information, rapid communication and ease of transportation are changing the way in which corporations compete and organize themselves. Corporations have to be nimble, flexible, responsive, engage in rapid innovation and be prepared for continuous adaptation. Cairncross (2002: 152) anticipated that "companies will resemble constellations more than pyramids... corporate structure grows diffuse and fluid, more kaleidoscope in design." It is argued that the traditional corporate hierarchy will become a competitive disadvantage and will be replaced by franchises, joint ventures, networks, alliances, and outsourcing. In turn, this will militate against vertical integration, it will increase competition and lead to deconcentration of the global economy with more but smaller and less powerful MNCs. This implies that the economic power deployed by MNCs should be analyzed more widely as spheres of control rather than strictly defined by ownership. Those spheres of control are less likely to be embedded in national identities and more likely to support a globalizing strategy.

National and Global Identities

The discussion in the preceding sections emphasizes the range of national capitalist models which are in competition with one another. Clearly that competition is economic as states battle for competitive advantage in the global economy. But the competition is also political in that competitive advantage is affected by the way in which corporations engage with governments and with societal priorities. In both respects processes of convergence could allow one national model to become dominant either through emulation by other states or through reproduction at the global level as a globally dominant model. Prior to the 2007 financial crash the dominant model was widely regarded as the neoliberal or Anglo-American model of a market state based on stock market capitalism, shareholder value, and liberalized markets. After the crash and the ensuing recession the assumption was that the shareholder value model was discredited and that alternative models would find favor (Kaletsky 2010: 302). But the Anglo-American model appeared more resilient than critics had expected and appears still to offer a magnet upon which other systems are converging. An alternative possibility would be that no single national model has dominant influence in the global economy and instead there is developing a "global identity" or type of capitalism which has its own relationships, dynamics, and locations of authority. In other words, the possibility that the role of the corporation in global governance transcends its national origins to become a constituent of a new model of capitalist order. We consider this proposition before drawing final conclusions.

The treatment of national identity employed in this chapter has been concerned mainly with three aspects of corporate behavior which reflect national origins and are consistent with the VoC approach. First is the relationship of the corporation with its stakeholders and in particular whether it is responsive to its shareholders or to other stakeholders, especially workers but also suppliers and communities. A second, related, aspect is what sort of goals the corporation is likely to emphasize. Will it be concerned primarily with its short-term success in the market (which in LMEs is also assumed to generate a collective benefit) or will it be concerned with a longer-term focus on stability, growth, and meeting societal priorities. Third is the question of relationships to governments. Will the corporation anticipate relationships of cooperation or confrontation? In particular, will the corporation seek to develop or influence public policies in partnership with government bodies or will it seek to dictate policies by more confrontational tactics such as assertive lobbying, oppositional coalitions, threats, or even bribery. On this crucial third element, work by Flohr *et al.* (2010: 243) is suggestive. They examine the extent to which corporations engage with arrangements of global governance and, in particular, which corporations seek to innovate and mold global policies. Those corporations that are proactive are seen as "norm-entrepreneurs" and help to generate policies in areas like standards, reporting, human rights, and corporate social responsibility which become constitutive of the global system. Working within a VoC framework they find that corporations from the United Kingdom and Germany are far more active and effective norm entrepreneurs than those from the United States or France. This they explain by reference to domestic socialization in patterns of engagement with government. They suggest that some countries are marked by cooperative relations between business and government (in this case the United Kingdom and Germany) whilst others are typified by adversarial relations (including the United States and France). Corporations "learn" these patterns at home and reproduce them on the national stage. These conclusions are sympathetic to the VoC methodology but inconsistent with its predictions. We might have expected UK-based corporations to adopt market driven approaches and to operate at arm's length from government. But the UK state has changed. The state has become so business-friendly that it has become a "new corporate state" and the characteristic mode of policy-making is now based on partnership between government and corporations (Wilks 2013). The implication of the Flohr *et al.* approach is, of course, to suggest that evolving modes of global governance will be influenced in particular by national partnership models. National partnerships are parents to global partnerships.

If corporations did not operate at the global level in conformity to a national identity what sort of global identity could be expected? As regards stakeholders a genuinely global corporation would have a far broader potential range of stakeholders but a more superficial relationship with them. There would be no national set of stakeholders and no imperative to pursue national interests. Turning to the goals of the corporation again there would be a much vaguer set of societal goals which would be diffuse and globalized. It might be expected that corporations would pursue introverted, self-interested goals around profit maximization and rewards to senior employees. A less sinister alternative has been identified by Sklair who sees a possibility of more progressive goals arising from corporate concern with their own viability and survival. He speculates that corporations might find it in their own interests to alleviate poverty (thus creating long-term markets) and mitigate environmental harm (thus avoiding damaging environmental threats to their businesses) (Sklair 2001). In other words we might visualize either complete corporate cynicism or enlightened corporate citizenship. As to relations with government and input into political processes, corporations would be dealing with national government bodies and global regulatory agencies from a position of equality. They could be expected to be more confident and to displace elected governments entirely with regard to various areas of global governance. This theme of private governance undertaken within global civil society is attracting increasing attention (Büthe and Mattli 2011; Hale and Held 2011).

Conclusion

Global corporations do have a national identity, Toyota is quintessentially Japanese, just as General Electric (GE) is quintessentially American. But such corporations also have a global identity. Unilever operates in 137 countries and of necessity must transcend its Anglo-Dutch origins. Such major global corporations develop global strategies and engage in global governance. We see therefore a tension between the national and the global sources of identity: how is this tension likely to affect the political engagement of global companies? Looking first at the various national models, the tensions are likely to be less acute for companies from the anglophone countries who broadly follow the LME model. They operate in the international economy in a very similar fashion to their operations at home. They coordinate through the market and pursue profit maximization and shareholder value. For British companies in particular global political engagement is business as usual, based on cooperative partnerships with government. For companies based in CME economies adjusting to a global identity may be more difficult. It may involve conscious adaptation or a policy of overlaying national patterns of political engagement with a global strategy. Similar difficulties might also be expected for the new multinationals from the BRICs, but here perhaps corporate forms are more malleable. As explored above, Chinese companies appear to have adopted many features of the US corporate form and their global political engagement might not be so unlike that of US companies, substituting Chinese national interests for the traditional pursuit by American multinationals of US national interests. Their adoption of LME-style corporate reporting and even corporate governance may be an OECD inspired simulacrum, but it may equally be a genuine willingness to endorse an economic institution of extraordinary effectiveness.

This chapter has also considered the internal politics of the corporation as it seeks to balance identity choices. One method by which to align national and global identities is for the company to cohere around corporate loyalty and a corporate, rather than a national, identity expressed in a brand. For prominent brands this is a clear source of coherence and for McDonalds, Honda, or Apple the brand defines societal engagement as well as a product. More interesting for a political analysis is the possibility that the identity will be defined, communicated, and enforced by a managerial elite within the company. As senior executives are selected, promoted, and appointed to positions of leadership across the global corporation they are socialized and incentivized to exploit national identities but within a global corporate strategy. The managerial elite are the carriers of identity within the company but they themselves are mobile and may be regarded as the standard bearers of a global corporate identity (or ideology). They are the people identified by Sklair (2001) as the transnational capitalist class but it is not necessary to adopt a Marxist approach to accept both the existence of a global managerial elite or their role in carrying national identities and acting as the representative of business interests in global governance. Finally, these attempts at generalization about identity influences across types of company may be misleading. For Morgan (2011) each global corporation represents a "contested terrain" in which national elites migrate into global management and as actors "play crucial roles in the transnational social space of the MNC, setting standards and frameworks and engaging with actors in national contexts in ways that impact on micro-political struggles" (Morgan, 2011: 434). In other words identities are contingent and are continually being renegotiated within the company.

References

Albert, Michel. 1993. *Capitalism Against Capitalism*. London: Whurr.

Büthe, Tim and Mattli, Walter. 2011. *The New Global Rulers: The Privatization of Regulation in the World Economy*. Princeton: Princeton University Press.

Cairncross, Frances. 2002. *The Company of the Future: Meeting the Management Challenges of the Communications Revolution*. London: Profile.

Chen, Jean, Liu, Xuguang, and Li, Weian. 2010. "The Effect of Insider Control and Global Benchmarks on Chinese Executive Compensation." *Corporate Governance*, 18 (2): 107–123.

Dickson, Bruce. 2008. *Wealth into Power: The Communist Party's Embrace of China's Private Sector*. Cambridge: Cambridge University Press.

DiMaggio, Paul and Powell, Walter. 1991. "The Iron Cage Revisited: Institutional Isomorphism and Collective Rationality." In *The New Institutionalism in Organizational Analysis*, ed. Walter Powell and Paul DiMaggio, 63–82. Chicago: University of Chicago Press.

Djelic, Marie-Laure. 1998. *Exporting the American Model: The Postwar Transformation of European Business*. Oxford: Oxford University Press.

Doremus, Paul, Keller, William, Pauly, Louis, and Reich, Simon. 1998. *The Myth of the Global Corporation*. Princeton: Princeton University Press.

Dörrenbächer, Christoph and Geppert, Mike, eds. 2011. *Politics and Power in the Multinational Corporation: The Role of Institutions, Interests and Identities*. Cambridge: Cambridge University Press.

Dunning, John. 1997. *Alliance Capitalism and Global Business*. London: Routledge.

Fenton O'Creevy, Mark, Gooderham, Paul, Cerdin, Jean-Luc, and Ronning, Rune. 2011. "Bridging Roles, Social Skills and Embedded Knowledge in Multinational Organizations." In *Politics and Power in the Multinational Corporation: The Role of Institutions, Interests and Identities*, ed. Dörrenbächer Christoph and Mike Geppert, 101–136. Cambridge: Cambridge University Press.

Flohr, Annegret, Rieth, Lother, Schwindenhammer, Sandra, and Wolf, Klaus Dieter. 2010. "Variations in Corporate Norm-Entrepreneurship: Why the Home State Matters." In *Business and Global Governance*, ed. Morten Ougaard and Anna Leander, 235–256. London: Routledge.

Fuchs, Doris. 2007. *Business Power in Global Governance*. London: Lynne Rienner.

Geppert, Mike and Dörrenbächer, Christoph. 2011. "Politics and Power in the Multinational Corporation: An Introduction." In *Politics and Power in the Multinational Corporation: The Role of Institutions, Interests and Identities*, ed. Christoph Dörrenbächer and Mike Geppert, 1–38. Cambridge: Cambridge University Press.

Gilpin, Robert. 2000. *The Challenge of Global Capitalism*. Princeton: Princeton University Press.

Goldman, Ian and Palan, Ronen. 2006. "Corporate Citizenship." In *Global Corporate Power*, ed. Christopher May, 181–197. London: Lynne Rienner.

Gourevitch, Peter and Shinn, James. 2005. *Political Power and Corporate Control: The New Global Politics of Corporate Governance*. Princeton: Princeton University Press.

Haigh, Gideon. 2004. *Bad Company: The Strange Cult of the CEO*. London: Aurum.

Hale, Thomas and Held, David, eds. 2011. *Handbook of Transnational Governance: Institutions and Innovations*. Cambridge: Polity.

Hall, Peter and Soskice, David. 2001. "An Introduction to Varieties of Capitalism." In *Varieties of Capitalism: The Institutional Foundations of Comparative Advantage*, ed. Peter Hall and David Soskice, 1–68. Oxford: Oxford University Press.

Hancké, Bob, Rhodes, Martin, and Thatcher, Mark, eds. 2007. *Beyond Varieties of Capitalism: Conflict, Contradictions and Complementarities in the European Economy*. Oxford: Oxford University Press.

Hirschman, Albert. 1986. *Rival Views of Market Society: And Other Recent Essays*. New York: Viking.

Horn, Laura. 2012. *Regulating Corporate Governance in the EU: Towards a Marketization of Corporate Control*. Basingstoke: Palgrave Macmillan.

Jackson, Gregory and Deeg, Richard. 2008. "From Comparing Capitalisms to the Politics of Institutional Change." *Review of International Political Economy*, 15 (4): 680–709.

Jones, Geoffrey. 2005. *Multinationals and Global Capitalism: From the Nineteenth to the Twenty-First Century*. Oxford: Oxford University Press.

Kaletsky, Anatole. 2010. *Capitalism 4.0*. London: Bloomsbury.

Li Jiato and Yi Tang. 2010. "CEO Hubris and Firm Risk-Taking in China: The Moderating Role of Managerial Discretion." *Academy of Management Journal*, 53 (1): 45–68.

McGregor, Richard. 2010. *The Party: The Secret World of China's Communist Rulers*. London: Penguin.

Mikler, John. 2009. *Greening the Car Industry: Varieties of Capitalism and Climate Change*. Cheltenham: Edward Elgar.

Morgan, Glenn. 2011. "Reflections on the Macro-Politics of Micro-Politics." In *Politics and Power in the Multinational Corporation: The Role of Institutions, Interests and Identities*, ed. Christoph Dörrenbächer and Mike Geppert, 415–436. Cambridge: Cambridge University Press.

Ougaard, Morten. 2008. "Private Institutions and Business Power in Global Governance." *Global Governance*, 14: 387–403.

Pattberg, Philipp. 2007. *Private Institutions and Global Governance: The New Politics of Environmental Sustainability*. Northhampton, MA: Edward Elgar.

Roach, Brian. 2005. "A Primer on Multinational Corporations." In *Leviathans: Multinational Corporations and the New Global History*, ed. Alfred Chandler and Bruce Mazlish, 19–44. Cambridge: Cambridge University Press.

Rugman, Alan. 2005. *The Regional Multinationals: MNEs and "Global" Strategic Management*. Cambridge: Cambridge University Press.

Rugman, Alan and D'Cruz, John. 2000. *Multinationals as Flagship Firms*. Oxford: Oxford University Press.

Sklair, Leslie. 2001. *The Transnational Capitalist Class*. Oxford: Blackwell.

Stern, Susan and Seligmann, Elisabeth. 2004. *The Partnership Principle: New Forms of Governance in the 21st Century*. London: Archetype.

Story, Jonathan. 2010. "China and the Multinational Experience." In *The Oxford Handbook of Business and Government*, ed. David Coen, Wyn Grant, and Graham Wilson, 346–380. Oxford: Oxford University Press.

Strange, Susan. 1994. "Wake Up Krasner! The World *Has* Changed." *Review of International Political Economy*, 1 (2): 209–219.

Strange, Susan. 1996. *The Retreat of the State: The Diffusion of Power in the World Economy*. Cambridge: Cambridge University Press.

UNCTAD. 2006. *World Investment Report: FDI from Developing and Transition Economies: Implications for Development*. New York: United Nations Conference on Trade and Development.

UNCTAD. 2008. *World Investment Report: Transnational Corporations and the Infrastructure Challenge*. New York: United Nations Conference on Trade and Development.

Van Apeldoorn, Bastiaan. 2000. "Transnational Class Agency and European Governance: The Case of the European Round Table of Industrialists." *New Political Economy*, 5 (2): 157–181.

Vernon, Raymond. 1971. *Sovereignty at Bay: The Multinational Spread of US Enterprises*. Harmondsworth: Pelican.

Whitley, Richard. 1999. *Divergent Capitalisms: The Social Structuring and Change of Business Systems*. Oxford: Oxford University Press.

Whitley, Richard. 2001. "How and Why Are International Firms Different? The Consequences of Cross-Border Managerial Coordination for Firm Characteristics and Behaviour." In *The Multinational Firm: Organizing Across Institutional and National Divides*, ed. Glenn Morgan, Peer Hull Kristensen, and Richard Whitley. Oxford: Oxford University Press.

Whitley, Richard. 2005a. "How National Are Business Systems? The Role of States and Complementary Institutions in Standardizing Systems of Economic Coordination and Control at the National Level." In *Changing Capitalisms? Internationalization, Institutional Change, and Systems of Economic Organization*, ed. Glenn Morgan, Richard Whitley, and Eli Moen, 190–231. Oxford: Oxford University Press.

Whitley, Richard. 2005b. "Developing Transnational Organizational Capabilities in Multinational Companies: Institutional Constraints on Authority Sharing and Careers in Six Types of MNC." In *Changing Capitalisms? Internationalization, Institutional Change, and Systems of Economic Organization*, ed. Glenn Morgan, Richard Whitley, and Eli Moen, 235–276. Oxford: Oxford University Press.

Wilks, Stephen. 2013. *The Political Power of the Business Corporation*. Cheltenham: Edward Elgar.

Chapter 4

Big Business in the BRICs[1]

Andrea Goldstein

Introduction

The world has changed in the first decade of the twenty-first century and it would be far beyond the modest ambitions of this chapter to explore why the single largest change in the contemporary world has been the rise of post-WTO China and other emerging economies, and not the clash of civilizations that some pundits were predicting after 9/11. One particular domain in which great changes have occurred is in the composition of the universe of large global companies (Table 4.1 and Figure 4.1). From 27 in 2005 (the first year for which the Global *Fortune* 500 listing is available online), the number of BRIC (Brazil, Russia, India and China) entries skyrocketed to 83 in 2011. While the increase is much more spectacular for China – that by 2010 had more entries than any other country except the United States and Japan – it has been steady for each BRIC (with the exception of Russia which lost two firms in 2009–2010). In addition, the largest firm in each BRIC – always the same and invariably an oil company – has constantly climbed the global rankings, with the exception of 2009–2010 for Gazprom, Indian Oil, and Petrobras. As far as headquarters are concerned, only Tokyo and Paris host more Global 500 companies than Beijing.

This development challenges the convergence expectation that dominated much Western thinking only two decades ago. With the victorious end of the cold war, the world economy seemed such a pleasant place, with heterogeneity and differences on the way out, homogeneity and convergence toward the Washington Consensus, and *laissez faire* capitalism on the way in. Yoshihiro Francis Fukuyama wrote that "the century . . . seems at its close to be returning full circle to where it started . . . an unabashed victory of economic and political liberalism"; privatization and the demise of the state figured highly in John Williamson's Washington Consensus catalogue.

The Handbook of Global Companies, First Edition. Edited by John Mikler.

Table 4.1   BRIC companies in Fortune Global 500 (number of companies and global ranking of the largest company).

	Brazil		*Russia*		*India*		*China*	
2005	3	125	3	139	5	170	16	31
2006	4	86	5	102	6	153	20	23
2007	5	65	4	52	6	135	24	17
2008	5	63	5	47	7	116	29	16
2009	6	34	8	22	7	105	37	9
2010	7	54	6	50	8	125	46	7
2011	7	34	7	35	8	98	61	5
2012	8	23	7	15	8	83	73	5

Source: Author's elaboration on the Fortune Global 500, http://money.cnn.com, accessed December 19, 2012.

The view that there is only one way to organize economic activity at the nation's level extended in fact also to the internal organization of private business – ownership, governance, strategic orientation, etc. It was Paul Krugman who reminisced: "I am (just) old enough to remember the conglomerate-building era of the 1960's, an era that ended so badly that many thought the word 'synergy' would be permanently banned from the business lexicon." The 1997–1998 East Asian financial crisis provided additional ammunitions to convergence-towards-America supporters: corporate governance failures were blamed for the crisis and major international institutions requested "countries accepting financial assistance ... to commit to fundamental reform of their corporate governance system, in the direction of the American model" (Gilson 2001: 331).

Did all this talk convince decision-makers in emerging economies that it was time to shelve their pragmatic dreams and stop policy experimentation? The big

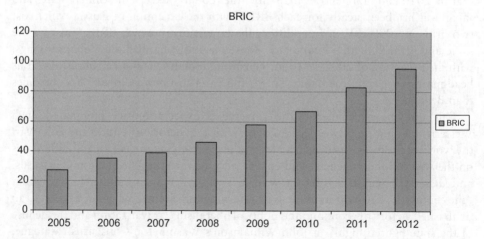

Figure 4.1   BRIC companies in Fortune Global 500 (number of companies and global ranking of the largest company).
Source: The Fortune Global 500, http://money.cnn.com, accessed December 19, 2012. Derived from Table 4.1.

success stories of business in the BRICs suggest that multiple socio-cultural and politico-economic forces accompanied the transition from post-WWII regulation of business to increasingly free – although not necessarily private – enterprise. This paper examines overall changes in the business environment and assesses the role of government and politics in shaping the structures and strategies of big business. It shows that government intervention remains pervasive in the BRICs and that this sometimes constrained and sometimes propeled the rise of modern business practices. In addition, it explores the longevity of diversified family controlled business groups as the main form of corporate organization in emerging economies, including the BRICs.

A Framework

As the late Alfred Chandler, for four decades the influential professor of business history at Harvard Business School, forcefully advanced in his writing, the large corporation is the productive engine of the modern industrial world. In fact, we still live in a world of large firms (Chandler 2005). From Google, Microsoft, and Apple to Wal-Mart and Ikea, from Boeing and Airbus to the majors that dominate the global oil industries, and almost any manufacturing or service sector, large corporations make a myriad of business, economic, social, and political decisions that influence the world we live in.

Bigness, primarily in undiversified firms, has many benefits in terms of economic growth (Chandler, Amatori, and Hikino 1997). They range from exploiting economies of scale and being the "locus of learning for the initial development and continued enhancement of their product-specific intangible organizational assets," to being the core of a "network of suppliers, equipment makers, retailers, advertisers, designers . . . " and the "primary driver of technological advancement through their heavy investment in research and development activities" (p. 26). For Dosi, "there are size thresholds for the ability of firms to internalize the capabilities of mastering the activities of innovation, production, and marketing in complex products, so that, other things being equal, 'bigness' confers a differential advantage" (p. 466).

Of course, that bigness is important does not mean that smallness is not, nor that bigness cannot have negative implications. Although it is very hard to measure the role played by big business in promoting economic growth, in a rigorous attempt big firms are found to have a significant positive effect on economic growth, both in terms of the number of big businesses and their sales volume in each country (Lee et al. 2012). Mahmood and Mitchell (2004) argue that there is an inverted-U relationship between group concentration and innovation. In practice the most productive form of capitalism involves a synergistic combination between large and small firms and allows for "creative destruction" (Baumol et al. 2007).

Against this background, gaining greater knowledge of the characteristics of large firms that dominate the global economy is inherently an important endeavor and should be a priority for economists. Unfortunately, the tendency in standard models is to abstract these powerful firms into general economic models, or absorb them as single anonymous data-points into large statistical samples, rather than to treat them as concrete actors (Teece and Winter 1984). Hence the importance of identifying large firms clearly, so that both their aggregate and their individual behaviors can be easily traced and their strategy, structure, ownership, and performance (SSOP) understood (Whittington 2011).

The main axes of this literature are the following:

- in terms of ownership, (a) private versus public, (b) domestic versus foreign, and (c) dispersion versus concentration;
- in terms of strategy, (d) related diversification versus single-business specialization and (e) internationalization versus domestic market focus;
- in terms of organizational structure, (f) Chandlerian multidivisionalization versus variants of the traditional and unsystematic holding company organizational structure and (g) internal versus market-based processes for executive jobs.

The SSOP tradition does not give a specific drift to the development dimension, i.e. to the possible peculiarities of business in lower-income, non-OECD countries. From another perspective, Amsden's list of common traits of successful late industrializ- ers ("the rest") is relevant: ownership is characterized by government intervention and domestic firms, strategy by large-scale diversification, organization by the group structure. In addition, the varieties of capitalism approach has shown how "hierar- chical market economies" have a distinctive way of organizing supply arrangements, structuring corporate governance and securing financial resources (Schneider 2007). Compared to industrial countries, in emerging economies, orders and directives from government, as well as other non-economic factors such as ethnic and religious ties, bear greater influence over relations between large firms and other actors than market incentives.

Big Business in the BRICs . . . before They Knew They Were the BRICs

The BRIC economies are different from each other and this is also true when exam- ining the heights of their respective business worlds nowadays. The situation aound 1990 was similar and could be summarized as follows:

In Terms of Ownership

- The government exercised wide-ranging control over the industrial sector through a mix of legislation and ownership (including of banks and financial institutions that invest in commercial organizations); in fact state ownership (although in most cases they were legally ministerial departments) was the only form of production in China and Russia, and accounted for 44% of the total turnover of the largest firms in Brazil (Siffert and Souza e Silva 1999).
- With the exception of Brazil – where there were 27 foreign firms among the top 100 – subsidiaries of foreign multinationals played almost no role in the heights of corporate power.
- In the universe of big business, private, listed or unlisted, companies were in practice a residual category. The main shareholders in both Brazil and India were families, representing 27% of the 100 largest companies in Brazil.

In Dimensional Terms

- BRIC corporations were, on average, relatively big. In particular, Chinese and Soviet corporations employed thousands of people and their plants "were deliberately designed as the largest in the world" (Yudanov 1997: 403).
- Still, very few of them had a turnover comparable with those listed in the Fortune 500. Only one (from India) was among the global 500 in 1962 (Chandler and Hikino 1997: 53), although by the early 1970s "Petrobras had become one of the hundred largest corporations in the world" (Evans 1979: 217). In 1990 Tata Steel had a turnover of US$1.3 billion, versus US$17.6 for Usinor-Sacilor, then the world's most global steelmaker. Even in 2003, the first year for which the *Fortune China 100* is available, the combined turnovers of the 25 largest companies was barely equal to that of Wal-Mart and the largest (CNPC) would have ranked 20th in the United States.
- Managerial structures were relatively unsophisticated. In SOEs, top management mostly had a engineering background and normally in-house career path; private business in Brazil and India was still mostly run by first-generation, self-made moguls such as Emirio de Moraes or Dhirubhai Ambani.[2] In India at least, religion and ethnicity played an important role: as late as 1997, 15 of the 20 largest industrial houses were of *vaishya* or *bania* trading caste, and 8 were Marwari.

In Terms of Strategy and Structure

- The prevalent strategies were based upon related diversification (for private firms) or prevailing activity (for SOEs) in Brazil and India, while in the socialist economies the most common behavior was the single business strategy, supplemented by the responsibility of providing a plethora of non-core activities such as education and health.
- The consequence was, as can be expected, a slow diffusion of multi-divisional structures in Brazil (Rago 2008) and India (Kudaisya 2003).
- Another structural characteristic of BRIC large firms was the low degree of internationalization – even if some early episodes of outward FDI had taken place in the previous decades (Wells 1982), in 1990 none appeared in the UNCTAD ranking of the largest 100 non-financial transnational corporations by foreign assets.

Ownership, Structure, Strategy, and Governance in the Twenty-First Century

In theory, the landscape of big business in the BRIC at the end of the 2010s should bear little resemblance to the 1990s. Globalization, structural reform (especially privatization), re-regulation, continuing government promotion, and "financiarization" have all shaped decisively the emerging corporate giants. In practice, however, path dependence and deliberate policy action have combined to maintain most of the ownership and structure (and at least some of the strategy and governance) that prevailed in the previous period.

Table 4.2 Data on big business in the BRIC.

	Brazil	Russia	India	China
Year	2010	2007	2010	2009
Industry coverage	Non-finance	All	All	All
Ownership coverage	All	All	All	Domestic
Source	*Exame*	RA Expert	*Fortune India*	China.org.cn

Analyzing responses of large business to global change therefore amounts to an ambitious program of research at any latitude, in the face of uneven access to data and information. When it comes to the analysis of large emerging economies, and the BRICs in particular, limitations are even greater. To the extent that this chapter is based on four different rankings of large companies and that there is great variance in data coverage (Table 4.2), the findings are indicative only. Nonetheless, the general contours are clear.

Ownership

With the exception of Brazil, big business in the BRIC remains dominated by domestic firms (Table 4.3). Obviously this finding must be interpreted with a lot of caution, in view of the exclusion of foreign companies from the Chinese ranking, but it also reflects the fact that most inward FDI since the late 1990s or so has been export-directed.[3] The private sector accounts for almost three-quarters of the top 100 firms' sales in Brazil and for slightly more than half in India; it is marginally smaller than the government in Russia and almost non-existent in China.

In Russia there are 6 oil companies (including state-owned Gazprom, Rosneft, and Surgutneftegaz) among the top 19 companies by turnover. The Kremlin has turned scattered companies into national champions. Rosneft took over most of Yukos from Mikhail Khodorkovsky, once Russia's richest man, and Gazprom bought Sibneft from Roman Abramovich. There is an equivalent number of mining and minerals companies risen from the ashes of Soviet *kombinat* (controlled by oligarchs such as Mikhaïl Prokhorov, Alexeï Mordachov, and Roman Abramovich), together with seven services companies. It is only in the 20th position that one can find a manufacturing firm, TAIF, and in 32nd a foreign-owned entity, Ford.

Industry-led financial-industrial groups (FIGs) emerged early in the privatization process. Bank-led FIGs emerged later, in relation to auctions initiated by President

Table 4.3 Top 100 companies' sales in the BRICs, by ownership.

	Brazil	Russia	India	China
Domestic	57.32	91.53	96.83	100.00
Government	28.02	51.74	47.96	95.25
Private groups	29.30	39.79	41.02	4.75
Independent			7.85	
Foreign	38.83	3.67	3.17	..
Joint ventures	3.85	4.81	..	..

Yeltsin favoring (some) buyers. The reach of the state has further expanded since 2008: VTB Bank, for instance, acquired 50% plus one share of the DON-Stroy Group in 2009. Russian Technologies rolled up hundreds of state companies, many of which had little to do with technology, into a vast conglomerate. As a result the Russian state once again controls the commanding heights of the economy – only this time through share ownership and cajoling, when not outright persecution (the Khodorkovsky saga), rather than directly.

India is *prima facie* similar – for 2010, among the top 11, there were seven state-controlled enterprises (four in petroleum, one each in banking, mining, and power) and, ranked 2nd, Reliance Industries, the energy and petrochemical private group. The two largest manufacturing companies among the top 11 are Tata Motors (5th) and Tata Steel. Maruti Suzuki was the largest foreign-owned company and ranked 19th only. Among the world's largest multinationals, only in the case of Unilever India has always been a very important location (Jones 2005: 169–174).

Nonetheless, it would be imprecise to consider each Indian firm among the top 100 as a stand-alone corporate entity. In most cases, they belong to diversified family controlled business groups and operate according to a different logic than traditional Western companies. Such business affiliates account for more than 70% of corporate sector assets. The most famous case is Tata, which groups dozens of firms in almost every sector, each of them applying a series of group-wide principles established in more than a century of existence (Goldstein 2008). Managers often rotate across different firms and other functions are performed centrally. The combined revenues of the six Tata firms (6th ranked Tata Motors, 8th Tata Steel, 20th TCS in ICT, 40th Tata Power, 68th Tata Comm, and 71st Tata Chemicals) equal 10% of the top 100 sales.

Brazil is yet another reality, more heterogeneous. In 2010 the two largest firms were in the petroleum industry, Petrobras (upstream) and BR Distribuidora (downstream), both controlled by the state albeit listed on the stock exchange and with sizeable stakes in the hands of private investors. Volkswagen in 5th place was the largest multinational and four more, all European (Fiat, Ambev, Shell, and Vivo), were in the top 10, together with three private, Brazilian firms, including Vale in third place. These seven multinationals, plus the four next largest (General Motors, Wal-Mart, Arcelor Mittal, and Ford), make more than 9% of their global sales in Brazil. There are four other local corporations ranked between 11th and 20th. While business groups exist, they are far less important and widespread than in India.

In China, all entries bar five (Huawei, Ping An Insurance, Haier, Suning Appliance, and Gome) correspond to state-owned enterprises. Petrochina and China Mobile alone recorded aggregate 2009 profits that were higher than for the 500 largest private companies in China! In fact not a surprising result when considering that China Mobile and two other state-owned companies, China Unicom and China Telecom, carve out the huge and very lucrative telecom market (in India, which is comparable in size, there are more than a dozen national operators), or that Petrochina values land at €20 cents per square meter, well below the market value. Control by the government is never far away. This model provides the government with continuing control of enterprises critical to the functioning of the economy. In particular, it facilitates the execution of big capital projects such as high-speed railways, steel plants, telecommunications networks, and ports.

Table 4.4 Varieties of state capitalism in China.

Typology	Sector	Ownership	Examples
Large SOEs	Capital-intensive, protected	Parent company fully owned by the state; operating company listed abroad, with minority shareholders	Banks (ICBC, China Construction Bank), utilities (China Mobile, Unicom), oil (CNPC, Sinopec)
Joint ventures	Capital-intensive, competitive	Public investor (central or province government) and foreign MNEs in need of market access	Car making (Shanghai Volkswagen, Iveco Hongyan), logistics (DHL Sinotrans)
Private companies with some state influence	Competitive, sometimes innovative	Private, although sometimes unclear	Huawei, BYD, Geely, Chery
Companies backed by publicly owned investment funds	Competitive, innovative	Foreign private equity and venture capital funds, jointly with city and province governments	Shanghai Environment, Nanhai Development, Digital China

Source: Adapted from "Capitalism Confined," *The Economist*, September 3, 2011.

In China state influence takes a variety of forms (Table 4.4). In a way the large SOEs that attract most interest are rather uncontroversial: they operate in sectors that are frequently state-dominated and the government (and the Party) are adamant that they intend to maintain control for the foreseeable future. Similarly for joint ventures and start-ups, despite contact negotiation between the parties there is clarity that these are not private entities. The "strange new beast . . . both commercial and communist at the same time" (McGregor 2010: 53) are the global champions like Haier, Huawei, and Lenovo, "in which managers and workers own the company's shares under the supervision of the local government" (p. 202). In addition, the People's Liberation Army has historically been involved in several business ventures, many of which are organized as business groups (Cheung 2004).

Corporate ownership remains highly concentrated in all BRICs, although with variance that reflects different ownership typologies. Under the impulse of SASAC (State-owned Assets Supervision and Administration Commission), property right management of Chinese SOEs changed significantly in recent years. More than 1,000 large SOEs, controlling high-quality assets, have listed either locally or internationally. SASAC typically owns 100% of the shares in the holding company. The holding company in turn owns a smaller proportion of shares in the listed subsidiary. For instance PetroChina, with a listing on the New York Stock Exchange, is the international division of China National Petroleum Corporation. In the overwhelming majority of cases, the public sector has remained the largest shareholder: among the 100 largest listed companies, when the state is the largest shareholder its stake is on average almost 50% (Bianco 2010). In fact, out of 1,453 A-share companies listed on the Chinese stock market in 2007, as few as six were widely held, with contestable control (Amit *et al.* 2010).

While the degree of separation between ownership and control is somewhat higher in the other BRICs, it remains much lower than in most OECD countries. In Brazil, the largest shareholder had a 50.3% stake in 2004, marginally declining to 49.2% in 2008 (Aguilera *et al.* 2012); for Russia, the largest direct shareholder owns 46.2% and the percentage of voting shares tied up in blocks over 5% is, on average, 70.7% (Chernykh 2008); in India, irrespective of the type of ownership affiliation, holdings by promoters constitute the single largest block – 50.2% for group affiliates, around 46% for stand-alones and the highest, 62.4%, for foreign firms (Sarkar 2010).

Structure

As already noted in the case of India, business groups – large, often family controlled organizations consisting of legally independent listed and unlisted firms operating across diverse industries and controlled through pyramidal ownership structures – are ubiquitous in emerging economies (Colpan *et al.* 2010). Business groups have been criticized as premodern forms of economic organization, at best a second-best substitute for weak institutions (the legal system, public capital and legal markets) and for weak governments in coordinating Big Push growth programs to establish numerous interdependent industries simultaneously (Khanna and Yafeh 2007). These groups, so the argument goes, place the governance of large swathes of many countries' big business sectors in the hands of a few of their wealthiest families. These have too cosy a relationship with the government and opaque corporate governance arrangements, being in fact synonyms of corruption and crony capitalism; in short a drag on national development.[4]

The pervasiveness of such structures – despite a decade of reforms to promote convergence towards dispersed share ownership, contestable markets for corporate control and Anglo-American management and governance practices – suggest that agency problems and political rent-seeking, while they exist, are not the only features of these groups. Missing or underdeveloped economic institutions still provide a rationale behind their remarkable resilience and ability to adjust to economic and political turbulence, international competition, and technological change. Despite profound changes in the operating environment, indigenous business groups have shown both resilience and continuous adaptability at the margin with respect to strategy and structure and remained the dominant players. Policies and state actions – especially regulatory policies and overall development strategies – promote and sustain business groups (Schneider 2009).

The Tata and Birla groups in India, created by indigenous entrepreneurs during the time of the British Empire, confirm the value of interested owners whose overriding aim is to ensure the long-term health of the company. Tata, possibly the quintessential family owned business group, reduced the number and range of sectors in which it is active, but has also continued to explore new possibilities and promote interesting business (Goldstein 2008). As a matter of fact the success of TCS in the globally competitive software industry is a vivid testimony that business groups can coexist with specialist firms (e.g. Wipro and Infosys) focused on a particular industry (Khanna and Palepu 2005). On the other hand, the Reliance soap opera also shows that a feud between heirs may jeopardize the stability and credibility of a nation's corporate sector (McDonald 2010). Clusters of business groups in India formed around ethnic, religious, and social communities, for example, the Marwaris of Rajasthan formed businesses in Bengal and elsewhere; the Gujeratis in the west, the Chettiars in the south, etc.

In China, "business groups are vertically integrated firms focused on a particular industry or sector, not diversified groups involved in a wide range of industries" (Lin and Milhaupt 2011: 13). Lee and Jin (2009) show the market forces, state-activism, and the firm's voluntary responses have driven the growth of "vertical" business groups. The Party state initially encouraged companies to band together into industry clusters by giving them preferential access to contracts and stock market listings. In recent years there is evidence that groups are becoming more "horizontal."[5] Under Beijing's 2009 stimulus, the government moved to support the economy by increasing bank loans. State-owned enterprises were the biggest beneficiaries, considered by banks to be more attractive borrowers than were private companies. When competition in their core business intensified, industrial groups started taking loans and branching out in other higher-return sectors. Baosteel Group, the world's third-largest steelmaker, has extensive subsidiaries that span a range of industries from real estate to telecommunications to manufacturing. Half of its net profit in 2011 came from non-steel businesses – up from 20% the previous year. Wuhan Iron & Steel, China's fourth-largest steelmaker by production, is investing $4.7 billion over the next five years in non-steel sectors, including pig, fish, and organic vegetable farming, as well as logistics and chemicals. Grains trader Cofco has channeled its access to funds into building luxury hotels in Beijing; copper producer Tongling is expanding into other base metals and timber; Ansteel has moved into coal, while Maanshan, a large mill in central China, has invested in wheel and axle manufacturing.

Large, privately owned conglomerates owned by wealthy individuals ("oligarchs") formed in the institutional void of the mid-1990s continued to dominate the Russian economy in the 2010s, despite regime change and the slow transition to a more stable business environment. Brazilian capitalism is similarly described as a "small world," where different actors "use relationships to explore market opportunities or to influence certain important decisions" (Lazzarini 2011: own translation).

Internationalization

In the broader context of the explosion of outward FDI from emerging economies (Goldstein 2007), the degree of internationalization of BRIC big business has substantially increased. Some of them, ranked by foreign assets, are CITIC and COSCO in China, Gazprom and Lukoil in Russia, Petrobras and Vale in Brazil, ONGC Videsh and various Tata companies in India.

The BRIC multinationals have developed various ownership-specific advantages – global brand names, management skills, and competitive business models – that allow them to be competitive in foreign markets as well as in their own markets. In China, Huawei, a telecoms-equipment firm, is the world's largest holder of international patents, while Haier, an appliance manufacturer, boasts 9,258 patents and 2,532 certified inventions; thanks to its prowess in ultra-deep exploration, Petrobras has twice won the Offshore Technology Distinguished Award.

In organizing their expansion abroad, BRIC MNEs have sought to establish port-folios of locational assets as increasingly important sources of their international competitiveness. Initially, firms from BRIC expanded mainly into their own region, often into countries with which they had close cultural links. Over time they have become much more daring in their international forays, targeting technology, engi-neering knowhow, and established brands. Europe has become a natural hunting-ground for industrial companies looking to move up the engineering value chain, for instance in clean technology. Suzlon, an Indian wind-turbine manufacturer, bought a Belgian designer called Hansen Transmission in 2006 so that it could develop bigger turbines for its domestic market; in 2011 China National Chemical Corpo-ration clinched the $2.2 billion purchase of Elkem, a Norwegian manufacturer of polysilicon, which is a key component of solar panels. Following the acquisition of Tetley, a beverages company, of Corus, a steelmaker, and of Jaguar Land Rover (JLR), a carmaker, the Tata Group is considered to be the largest foreign investor in the United Kingdom.

Nonetheless, the importance of developed Western economies in this process should not be exaggerated. China has largely concentrated its investments to date on developing regions that secure energy supplies and natural resources. Some of the largest Brazilian MNEs have focused on Latin America, either to increase size and consolidate specific global markets (e.g. JBS for meat packing), or to apply successful business models in similar markets. Bharti Airtel purchased the African assets of Zain to replicate its successful pre-paid mobile-telecom model.

Especially in China, and elsewhere to a lesser extent, state capitalism and sup-portive government policies have been at the heart of the rise of BRIC's outward FDI. Domestic enterprises have received financial support from state banks. Through the so-called Angola mode, China's Eximbank offers poor countries soft loans for infrastructure projects (usually built by China's contractors) in return for a guaran-teed supply of oil or some other raw material (Aguilar and Goldstein 2008). BNDES, the Brazilian development bank, has assisted companies in Latin America and Africa, especially Lusophone countries such as Angola and Mozambique. Even nominally private companies such as Huawei that have chosen to expand organically by export-ing and building operations on the ground have been supported by the Chinese state. The globalization of Indian firms owes more to changing domestic conditions such as the deregulation of finance and to leveraged takeovers. These firms used money borrowed largely from Western banks and money markets, in some cases secured only against their targets' cash flows. As the global crash began, their refinancing options dried up and the target firms' profits slumped in most cases.[6]

The Chinese model of state support for outward FDI is partly explained by scepti-cism regarding Western ideas about relying on the market, which prompts authorities to see the world in terms of brutal competition for limited resources and therefore to seek ownership rather than long-term, arm's length contracts. In the West, in turn, many consider Chinese corporate strategies as part of a wider plot to control the world's economy. These diverging views are bound to collide, as many failed attemps by Chinese companies to finalize overseas deals – from 2005 CNOOC's unsolicited bid for Unocal, one of America's largest oil companies, to the Australian refusal to buy broadband equipment from Huawei in 2012 – amply testify. The culture clash is causing major delays in some of the most visible Chinese deals abroad, such as iron ore mining in Australia.[7]

Management

In the United States and increasingly in other industrial countries, today's executives are younger, more likely to be to be hired from the outside and to be female, and less likely to have elite educations than their pre-globalization counterparts (Cappelli and Hamori 2005). Based on data collected for the 21 largest domestically owned firms, Brazil and India in 2012 resemble the United States in 1980, with relatively experienced and mostly male CEOs (Table 4.5). The percentage of "lifers" (i.e. executives who spent nearly their entire careers at the company they now lead) is high but this seems to mostly reflect family ownership: in the few companies with widespread ownership, it is not unusual to look for external talent.[8] The percentage of CEOs who studied at top Brazilian universities (in particular FGV in Rio) or overseas is also higher than for Ivy League education in the United States. Interestingly, few of the Indian CEOs for which this information was available studied in the country's top schools, the Indian Institutes of Management (IIM) and Technologies (IIT).

The way to the top differs. In China, as might be expected, many Chairmen or CEOs – 43% in listed SOEs according to Hung *et al.* (2012) – are current or former government bureaucrats. The state and the Communist Party's Organization Department appoint senior managers – including a Party committee headed by a party secretary (McGregor 2010). Compared with the three elite groups (provincial chiefs, cabinet ministers, and military leaders) that have long constituted the principal components of the CCP Central Committee and its Politburo, the proportion of CEOs of China's large enterprises in the national leadership is still relatively small (Li 2011). But it is evident that younger, business-savvy, politically connected, and globally minded Chinese CEOs have recently become a new source of the CCP leadership.

Obviously this is also a convenient career path for top managers in SOEs in other countries: for instance four out of five Brazilian SOEs' CEOs for which this information is available have spent at least a few years in government. As in Germany

Table 4.5   CEOs in the United States, Brazil, India, and China.

	USA 1980	USA 2001	Brazil 2012	India 2012	China 2011
Number of companies	100	100	21	21	130
Average age (years)	56	52	56	55	54
Female (number)	0	11	10	10	1
Years of education	17	17	18	17	16
Top universities' alumni (%)	14	10	75	n.a.	n.a.
"Lifers" (%)	53	45	48	69	55

Sources: Cappelli and Hamori (2005), Li (2011), and author's calculations based on Brazilian and Indian company websites.

and the United Kingdom, time in government is not a prerequisite to becoming a CEO in the private sector – unlike France where 26% of top managers have worked in the public sector (Heidrick and Struggles 2011).

The situation is different in Russia. State-sector "bureaugarchs," most of them former KGB officials who have close ties with Vladimir Putin, occupy the heart of the economy. The Chairman of the Russian Government himself is chairman of the supervisory board of Vnesheconombank, the state development bank; Igor Sechin, the deputy prime minister, was chairman of Rosneft until 2010, when President Dmitry Medvedev (who chaired Gazprom before entering politics) ordered government ministers to step down as chairmen of state companies' boards of directors to tidy things up. Sechin returned to Rosneft as company president in 2012, at the beginning of Putin's new term at the Kremlin.

Similarly obvious is the finding that in family held firms most CEO positions are occupied by family members: after many seasoned executives – including PepsiCo's Indra Nooyi or Citigroup's Vikram Pandit – were rumored as Ratan Tata's potential successors, Cyrus Mistry, the little-known son of a reclusive billionaire who is Tata Group's largest individual shareholder with an 18% stake was selected for the job. Familism itself is not necessarily bad, since the family may provide useful workplace experience. But family can also be the source of favoritism and nepotism and the next generation may prove less able than the founding entrepreneur.

The jury is definitely still out regarding the quality of management. Some scholars – such as Cappelli *et al.* (2010) for India – take a very sanguine view, considering that "far more than their Western counterparts, these leaders and their organizations take a long-term, internally focused view. They work to create a sense of social mission that is served when the business succeeds. They make aggressive investments in employee development, despite tight labor markets and widespread job-hopping. And they strive for a high level of employee engagement and openness." BRIC bosses are sometimes said to have other advantages, in handling diverse workforces and making money in complex business environments, that prepare them to make it anywhere.

On the other hand, Bloom *et al.* (2012) use double-blind survey techniques and randomized sampling to construct management quality data on over 10,000 organizations across 20 countries. They find that on average BRIC manufacturing firms tend to be poorly managed, with a long tail of badly managed firms and very few world-class examples (Table 4.6).

Table 4.6 The quality of management in Brazil, India, and China.[a]

	Overall	Monitoring	Targeting	Incentives	Firm interviews
Brazil	2.71	3.06	2.69	2.55	568
India	2.67	2.91	2.66	2.63	715
China	2.71	2.90	2.62	2.69	742
Maximum	3.35[b]	3.63[c]	3.34[d]	3.25[b]	n.a.
All-countries average	2.99	3.28	2.94	2.82	9079

Notes: (a) scale is 1-to-5; (b) United States; (c) Sweden; (d) Japan.
Source: Bloom *et al.* (2012).

Governance

On the whole, corporate and securities laws in the BRICs have been thoroughly reformed in recent years and appear by and large similar to OECD norms. Nonetheless, *de jure* reforms have not always translated in *de facto* application and better protection of the rights of shareholders to influence significantly the company. As Balasubramanian *et al.* (2008) observe in the case of India, compliance with legal norms is reasonably high in most areas, but not complete. As a recent episode featuring Reliance clearly showed, related party transactions is an area of particular concern and the source of permanent risks of tunneling and expropriation of minority shareholders.[9] This may also explain why, despite (at least partial) formal convergence in corporate law, it is impossible to identify the same or expected convergence in ownership or corporate structure. Ownership concentration is directly related to levels of uncertainty in emerging markets, where both agency and institutional problems persist (Aguilera *et al.* 2011, 2012). An additional problem is the poor quality, when not outright fraud, of accounting data, as shown in 2011 by dozens of scandals at Chinese companies listed in North America. In China, in fact, "the standard corporate mechanism for the appointment and evaluation of senior executives – the board of directors – is missing entirely from this process" (Lin and Milhaupt 2011: 39).

To the extent that a good governance framework should ensure that the board plays a central role in the strategic guidance of the company and the effective monitoring of management, while remaining accountable to all shareholders, its composition constitutes a dimension of corporate structure. In evaluating a board's role in governance, researchers and policy makers have typically focused on board independence, size, director characteristics in terms of education, age and multiple directorships (Kogut 2012).

Diversity is another dimension (Table 4.7). Focusing on nationality, there is a stark contrast between Brazil and India, where foreigner directors are very rare, China, and – even more so – Russia. In practice the situation in the latter is more complicated. Six of the 13 foreigners in Chinese boards are Hong Kong citizens and one of the Europeans is a Hong Kong resident with British nationality. In the case of Russia, two of the companies (TNK-BP and Vimpelcom) are effectively joint-ventures and eight non-Russian directors represent foreign directors; in addition, Evraz and Severstal, with their nine foreign directors, are listed on the London Stock

Table 4.7 Boards of directors in the BRICs.

	Brazil	Russia	India	China
Companies	9	9	11	10
Directors	96	100	127	124
Foreigners	3	27	8	13
Europe	2	24	6	4
Japan	1	0	0	8
United States	0	3	2	1
Women	7	5	5	8

Source: Author's calculations based on publicly available company reports.

Exchange. With these caveats the overall BRIC average compares unfavorably with OECD countries: in France, for instance, foreigners occupy 10% of board positions, and 30% in the case of the largest companies included in the CAC 40 index.[10] Foreign independent directors can be classified according to their profile function: retired industry executives (such as James Campbell at Evraz), top managers of a major company (such as Franco Bernabé at Petrochina), academics (such as Martin Gilman at Rosbank), and former civil servants (such as Andrew Wood at Kopeyka).

Most of the time foreignness and independence coincide. This is the case for China Mobile, where the three independent directors are from Hong Kong and Singapore[11] and these three are in turn the only foreigners on the board. China Construction Bank and Evraz both have five independents, of which four are foreigners (and no other non-nationals). At Severstal all four independents are foreigners, and so is the chairman. A contrasting example is Tata Motors (TMC) and its two (German) directors, who are respectively CEO at Jaguar Land Rover (Ralf Speth) and former TMC Managing Director.

While the board presence of foreigners may be surprisingly modest when compared to other indices of internationalization, three further issues must be noted. First, some Indian nationals belong to the academic diaspora – for instance Emory University's Jagdish N. Sheth who sits on Wipro board, or Dean of INSEAD Dipak C. Jain at Reliance Industries. Second, returnee entrepreneurs play a leading role in many Chinese companies, especially in the "going out" strategy (Wang *et al.* 2011). Third, and obviously not unlike in OECD countries, many BRIC executives have spent time studying and working abroad. The Gerdau example, where all six non-independent directors belong to the founding family, is revealing. The four first-generation brothers all went to the same state university in Southern Brazil (UFRGS) and only one, 1942-born Frederico, studied abroad, in Germany. Both second-generation cousins – who are now CEO and COO – studied in Canada and the United States.

The Challenges Ahead

The BRIC economies have recorded impressive growth rates since the early 2000s and the role of big business has been crucial in this regard. The process of economic development, however, is inherently dynamic and unstable and new challenges continuously emerge. With no pretense of exhaustion, nor of ranking them in importance, some such challenges are discussed in the following paragraphs.

First, the role of the state in the economy – in both quantitative and qualitative terms – remains a source of contention. This is especially true in the case of China, where many reformers have asserted that "the state [sector] is advancing and the private retreating." Weakening the grip of state-owned enterprises is needed in order to prevent the country from eventually falling into a "middle-income trap" of much slower growth (World Bank and DRC 2012). Control of SOEs should be taken over by new independent bodies that would hand over dividends to the state budget and gradually reduce the level of state ownership. Of course tackling economic reforms would affect powerful vested interests, such as SASAC.[12] But it is made all the more necessary by the expansion by China's SOEs into international markets and higher-profit areas, where they benefit from privileged conditions, jeopardize the principle of "competitive neutrality," and generate recurring friction.

Brazil's "Leviathan as a minority shareholder" model (Lazzarini and Musacchio 2011) is arguably subtler.[13] BNDES' loans and equity (through its investment subsidiary, BNDESPar[14]) do not seem to affect firm-level investment decisions and operational performance, although they do reduce firm-level cost of capital due to the governmental subsidies accompanying the loans. Next, examining the selection process through which BNDES' capital is allocated to firms, they find that BNDES apparently selects firms with good operational performance but also provides more capital to firms with political connections (measured as campaign donations to elected politicians). Yet, they do not find evidence that BNDES is systematically bailing out firms. In general, BNDES appears to be generally selecting firms with capacity to repay their loans, as regular commercial banks would do. The critical issue is whether this good judgment, in itself, is enough to justify the subsidies that the Brazilian Treasury grants to BNDES so that it can raise cheap capital to fund big business, especially to those firms which happen to have the greatest political clout. The logic of the BNDES model was clear when capital markets were thin, which is not the case in the BRICs these days, and should probably be limited to unaffiliated (non-group) firms with real capital needs.

More broadly, in systems where lines between Party, state, and business are blurred, a second and related challenge has to do with opacity in private-public interactions, bad corporate governance, and lack of competition. A few recent Brazilian cases are illustrative. In 2009 president Lula accused the management of Vale of laying off workers during the global crisis and purchasing large vessels to ship iron ore to Asia, instead of investing in integrated steel mills in Brazil. The government eventually removed Roger Agnelli from his post as CEO of Vale despite his outstanding record and is trying to force Petrobras to use expensive local equipment suppliers despite doubts about their competence. In China and Russia there have been numerous episodes where prominent businesspeople have accused political leaders of trampling on the law of property and human rights, attacking their competitors, and taking whatever they want in order to enhance their power.[15]

Third, the strategy of making huge strategic investments, even to the point of losing money for the sake of creating national champions and entire new industries, may be necessary to solve a market failure and substitute for financial intermediaries that are not doing their job properly, but it puts private companies at a severe disadvantage. The big question is whether this structure is less useful, and even counterproductive, when the country becomes more integrated into the world economy. If all countries were to implement state capitalism to accumulate a foreign currency surplus, this would result in a "fallacy of composition"; another danger is that the big groups will rig the market in their favor and inhibit the emergence of specialized players.[16] To prevent such an outcome, a financial system that gives start-ups easy access to capital is essential, as well as a vigorous competition policy. In fact it is not sufficient to uphold competition, it is necessary to understand the implications of business groups, cross-shareholdings and interlocked directors in this regard (Lazzarini 2011).

Fourth, even with substantial concentrated (state or family) ownership, corporate governance has been improving (especially in terms of disclosure and investor protection) in all BRICs. Reforms were initially mostly a formal-legalistic process, that with time have become more substantial as institutions (stock exchanges and government regulators) showed stronger commitment. Allocation of control, however, remains less dynamic than in more advanced market economies and the enforcement of rights is not always sufficient to protect minority shareholders and indeed other stakeholders. Diversification may also be motivated by expropriation – in Indian groups affiliates are found to engage in activities away from their core business to serve as destination points for funds tunneled from a group's core activity (Kali and Sarkar 2011). This should be a cause of concern insofar as dispersed shareholder firms are typically better managed (Bloom *et al.* 2012).

A note of cautious realism is needed here. There is a great deal of path dependence of corporate structure – the kind that an economy has at any point in time depends in part on those that it had at earlier times (Bebchuck and Roe 1999). In the case of China and Russia, their corporate ownership structures after 50 (pre-WTO era) and 75 years of socialism gave some stakeholders both incentives and power to impede changes in them, i.e. *de facto* privatization. In Brazil and India, corporate rules that favored the formation of business groups also reinforced the latter's power to resist pressures to converge. The paradox is that in the past the corporate model in emerging economies appeared adequate in protecting outside investors, as proven by the early experience of Brazil where financial markets flourished (Musacchio 2009). Politics is what counts: that experience came to an end once the most powerful interest groups of industrialists and labor reached consensus around preserving employment and consolidating domestic industry, to the detriment of the promotion of shareholders' rights.

Fifth, the rapid globalization of BRIC firms through takeovers may well have thrilled cheerleaders and corporate patriots, but the rate of success has not been equally spectacular. *The Economist* has examined the four largest Indian deals for which enough information is available.[17] Gross operating profits (EBITDA) have risen in one case only, while in the others earnings have failed to generate an adequate return on capital. Most Indian dominant shareholders dislike issuing equity and firms have fiddly holding chains, thus raising the risk of being too convoluted and puny to handle large foreign deals.

The learning curve in overcoming the liability of foreignness has always been very steep (Wilkins 2009) and the growing importance of M&A as entry mode adds post-merger integrations issues to the equation. Psychic distance between Russia, India, and China, on one hand, and OECD economies, on the other, is rather high and generates reciprocal bafflement at practices such as taking long holidays or making "facilitation" payments. In fact the greater success of Brazilian MNEs is explained by the much greater role of foreign MNEs in the domestic economy and managers' greater experience with cross-cultural deals.

The situation will gradually evolve as BRIC service companies start offering what MNEs need as they expand internationally – for instance knowledge of foreign-exchange trading and derivatives, especially important as the yuan internationalizes. But to the extent that state capitalism remains prevalent, suspicion and resentment at business practices and privileges will persist. Traditional beyond-the-border issues such as accounting, competition, anti-corruption, public procurement, and intellectual property are now discussed in fora such as the G20 and inter-governmental organizations. BRIC business will have to learn how to play the game of lobbying and advocacy effectively and transparently.

Conclusion

The early twenty-first century is witnessing an increasing internationalization of markets and regulatory institutions, the application of scientific knowledge to the commercialization of products in contexts where financial markets are becoming more uncertain and crisis-prone, and the vitality of new actors making different demands for more effective forms of corporate governance and corporate social responsibility. Drawing on a variety of interdisciplinary perspectives from economics and management, this chapter analyzes how national capitalisms are changing in this context, focusing on the ownership, structure, and strategy of the largest companies in each BRIC. Highlighting some critical themes, processes, events, and personalities that have shaped major corporations, it engages with debates that are central to global policy.

While corporate structures across the BRICs differ in this new environment, we found a common reinforcement of the key role of government in managing large corporations and driving economic development. Certainly there was a lot of privatization, which in Brazil and India included relinquishing control of hitherto strategic network industries and in all countries the sale of minority stakes in energy and natural resource SOEs. But various institutions extended or kept their influence in the governance of the commanding heights of the economy, such as policy and development banks, semi-public pension funds, and the ruling party. All these iterations of state engagement reflect how BRIC governments have adapted their economic policies and processes not only by holding on to economic control, but also finding subtle ways to extend it.

Private capitalists, for their part, have continued to organize their activity around business groups, deciding which industries to enter or leave and recruiting talented non-family associates. This partial transformation has shown that family control and diversification are far from incompatible with competitive success, even in the most demanding markets. Business groups, from a welfare standpoint, "can sometimes be 'paragons' and, at other times, 'parasites'" (Khanna and Yafeh 2007). Although they might be rent-seekers, the rents tend to remain within national boundaries: in practice, the alternative is not flourishing national SMEs, but, rather, a dissipation of rents abroad by MNCs.

Taken collectively, these phenomena constitute an important series of large-scale economic experiments and seem destined to create a plurality of new forms and new logics, with implications for the world's economy. At a minimum one can say that managers have proven that Fukuyama was wrong when he said that the "People's Republic of China can no longer act as a beacon for illiberal forces around the world," if liberalism means the American model of diffuse private ownership and coherent diversification as an inevitable outcome of economic development. On the contrary, the Fords, Morgans, and Sloans of the BRIC have proven that old structures can adapt somewhat successfully to new circumstances. An earlier generation of researchers studied strategy and structure in Japan and influenced management practice in the West. Today it is time to extend the research into emerging economies, to go beyond the clichés, devise appropriate policies to compete in international markets, and avoid the protectionism and even xenophobia that are often stirred by ignorance about the outer world.

Notes

1 The author thanks Jackie Evans, Sérgio Lazzarini, Keun Lee, John Mikler, Jayati Sarkar, and seminar participants at Manchester and Parma universities for most useful comments and suggestions on an earlier draft. The standard disclaimer applies.

2 Second-generation groups included Tata and Birla in India.

3 With a lower degree of precision, in all likelihood no foreign firm other than the car makers (for which such data are not available) generates sufficient China sales to qualify for the top 100 listing. Sales of five of the world's largest companies with large operations in China range from US$7.5 billion for Wal-Mart to US$3.1 billion for Nestlé, with Siemens, General Electric, and Procter & Gamble falling in between; 100th-ranked Beijing Railway had sales of US$8.3 billion. In a similar vein, Fosun International, China's largest private conglomerate, is not included in the ranking, but with sales of Rmb56.8 billion it would not be included in the top 100.

4 If sufficiently large, they may also add to economy volatility by rendering the risk of misgovernance systematic, rather than firm-specific.

5 "Chinese Steel Groups Forced to Diversify to Grow Profits," *Financial Times*, March 21, 2012.

6 "Running with the Bulls," *The Economist*, March 3, 2012.

7 "Dug in Too Deep," *Financial Times*, June 25, 2012.

8 By 2011, the percentage of "lifers" among the top 500 CEOs in the United States had fallen to roughly 30%.

9 According to the Financial Services Authority in the United Kingdom, the founder of Reliance, Anil Ambani, used a foreign vehicle to invest $250 million in a related company.

10 Communiqué: bilan de l'IFA sur la composition des CA après les AG 2011. Accessed December 19, 2012.

11 Frank Wong Kwong Shing, who also sits on the ICBC board.

12 "According to a Chinese newspaper, *21st Century Business Herald*, SASAC wrote to the finance ministry arguing that the proposal to scale back state ownership was unconstitutional" ("The Bees Get Busy," *The Economist*, March 3, 2012).

13 Since the early 1990s the Indian government has enacted gradual divestment in many public-sector enterprises, including State Bank of India, ONGC, and SAIL. Although they are now subjected to stock market discipline, control still rests firmly in the hands of the state.

14 By 2009 BNDESPar's holdings were worth $53 billion, or 4% of the stock market.

15 Recent examples include the Khodorkovsky–Yukos saga and the death of Sergei Magnitsky, the lawyer working for Hermitage Capital, in Russia and the incarceration of Huang Guangyu, founder and former CEO of retail appliance and electronics dealer Gome Electronics, and the Bo Xilai scandal in China.

16 I owe this point to Jorge Arbache.

17 "Running with the Bulls."

References

Aguilar, Renato and Goldstein, Andrea. 2009. "The Chinisation of Africa: The Case of Angola." *World Economy*, 32 (11): 1543–1562.

Aguilera, Ruth, deCastro, Kabbach, Ricardo, Luiz, and Crespí, Rafel. 2011. Corporate Ownership and Uncertainty: Evidence from Emerging Markets, http://demo.uib.es/IBEW/Papers2011/latam9may11.pdf. Accessed December 10, 2012.

Aguilera, Ruth, deCastro, Kabbach, Ricardo, Luiz, Ho Lee, Jun, and You, Jihae. 2012. "Corporate Governance in Emerging Markets." In *Capitalisms and Capitalism in the Twenty-First Century*, ed. Glenn Morgan and Richard Whitley. Oxford: Oxford University Press.

Aldrighi, Dante Mendes and Postali, Fernando A.S. 2010. "Business Groups in Brazil." In *Oxford Handbook of Business Groups*, ed. Asli M. Colpan, Takashi Hikino, and James R. Lincoln, 353–386. Oxford: Oxford University Press.

Amatori, Franco and Colli, Andrea. 2008. "European Corporations: Ownership, Governance, Strategies and Structures. A Review of Five Countries: United Kingdom, Germany, France, Italy and Spain." In *The European Enterprise: Historical Investigation into a Future Species*, ed. Harm Gustav Schroeter, 23–36. Berlin: Springer.

Amit, Raphael, Ding, Yuan, Villalonga, Belén, and Zhang, Hua. 2010. "The Role of Institutional Development in the Prevalence and Value of Family Firms." *HBS Working Papers*, 10–103.

Amsden, Alice. 2009. "Firm Ownership, FOEs, and POEs." *WIDER Research Paper*, 2009/46.

Balasubramanian, Bala N., Black, Bernard S., and Khanna, Vikramaditya. 2008. "Firm-Level Corporate Governance in Emerging Markets: A Case Study of India." *ECGI Law Working Paper*, 119/2009.

Baumol, William J., Litan, Robert E., and Schramm, Carl J. 2007. *Good Capitalism, Bad Capitalism, and the Economics of Growth and Prosperity*. New Haven and London: Yale University Press.

Bebchuk, Lucian A. and Roe, Mark J. 1999. "A Theory of Path Dependence in Corporate Ownership and Governance." *Stanford Law Review*, 52: 127–170.

Bianco, Magda. 2010. "Corporate Governance in China: A Changing Model?" Presented at the Banca d'Italia Workshop on "The Chinese Economy." Venice, November 25–27.

Bloom, Nicholas, Genakos, Christos, Sadun, Raffaella, and Van Reenen, John. 2012. "Management Practices across Firms and Countries." *NBER Working Paper*, 12–052.

Cappelli, Peter and Hamori, Monika. 2005. "The New Road to the Top." *Harvard Business Review*, 83 (1): 25–32.

Cappelli, Peter, Singh, Harbir, Singh, Jitendra V., and Useem, Michael. 2010. "How the Best Indian Companies Drive Performance by Investing in People." *Harvard Business Review*, March.

Chandler, Alfred D. Jr. 2005. *Inventing the Electronic Century: The Epic Story of the Consumer Electronics and Computer Industries*. Cambridge, MA: Harvard University Press.

Chandler, Alfred D. Jr., Amatori, Franco, and Hikino, Takashi, eds. 1997. *Big Business and the Wealth of Nations*. Cambridge: Cambridge University Press.

Chernykh, Lucy. 2008. "Ultimate Ownership and Control in Russia." *Journal of Financial Economics*, 88: 169–192.

Cheung, Tai Ming. 2004. "The Rise and Fall of the Chinese Military Business Complex." In *The Military as an Economic Actor: Soldiers in Business*, ed. Jörn Brömmelhörster and Wolf-Christian Paes, 52–73. Basingstoke and New York: Palgrave Macmillan.

Colpan, Asli M., Hikino, Takashi, and Lincoln, James R., eds. 2010. *Oxford Handbook of Business Groups*. Oxford: Oxford University Press.

Dosi, Giovanni. 1997. "Organizational Competences, Firm Size, and the Wealth of Nations." In *Big Business and the Wealth of Nations*, ed. Alfred D. Chandler, Jr., Franco Amatori, and Takashi Hikino. Cambridge: Cambridge University Press.

Evans, Peter. 1979. *Dependent Development*. Princeton: Princeton University Press.

Fukuyama, Francis. 1989. "The End of History?" *The National Interest*, Summer.

Gilson, Ronald. 2001. "Globalizing Corporate Governance: Convergence of Form or Function." *American Journal of Comparative Law*, 49 (2): 329–357.

Goldstein, Andrea. 1997. "Brazilian Privatization in International Perspective: The Rocky Path from State Capitalism to Regulatory Capitalism." *Industrial and Corporate Change*, 8 (4): 637–711.

Goldstein, Andrea. 2007. *Multinational Companies from Emerging Economies: Composition, Conceptualization and Direction in the Global Economy*. Basingstoke and New York: Palgrave.

Goldstein, Andrea. 2008. "Emerging Economies' Multinationals: Explaining the Case of Tata." *Transnational Corporations*, 17 (3): 85–108.

Guriev, Sergei. 2010. "Business Groups in Russia." In *Oxford Handbook of Business Groups*, ed. Asli M. Colpan, Takashi Hikino, and James R. Lincoln. Oxford: Oxford University Press.

Heidrick and Struggles. 2011. *La route vers le sommet: une comparaison des profils des PDG français, allemands, anglais et américains*. Paris: Heidrick & Struggles.

Hung, Mingyi, Wong, T.J., and Zhang, Tianyu. 2012. "Political Considerations in the Decision of Chinese SOEs to List in Hong Kong." *Journal of Accounting and Economics*, 53 (1): 435–449.

Jones, Geoffrey. 2005. *Reinventing Unilever*. Oxford: Oxford University Press.

Kali, Raja and Sarkar, Jayati. 2011. "Diversification and Tunneling: Evidence from Indian Business Groups." *Journal of Comparative Economics*, 39 (3): 349–367.

Kaur, Parmjit and Gill, Suveera. 2009. "The Effects of Ownership Structure on Corporate Governance and Performance: An Empirical Assessment in India." Panjab University Business School.

Khanna, Tarun and Palepu, Krishna. 2005. "The Evolution of Concentrated Ownership in India: Broad Patterns and a History of the Indian Software Industry." In *A History of Corporate Governance around the World*, ed. Randall K. Morck. Chicago: University of Chicago Press.

Khanna, Tarun and Yafeh, Yishay. 2007. "Business Groups in Emerging Markets: Paragons or Parasites?," *Journal of Economic Literature*, 45 (2): 331–372.

Kogut, Bruce, ed. 2012. *The Small Worlds of Corporate Governance*. Cambridge, MA: MIT Press.

Krugman, Paul. 2000. "Media Mania." *The New York Times*, January 12.

Kudaisya, Medha. 2003. *The Life and Times of G.D. Birla*. Oxford: Oxford University Press.

Lazzarini, Sérgio. 2011. *Capitalismo de laços*. Sao Paulo: Campus.

Lazzarini, Sérgio and Musacchio, Aldo. 2011. "Leviathan in Business: Varieties of State Capitalism and Their Implications for Economic Performance." Harvard Business School, *Working Paper*, 12–108.

Lee, Keun and Jin, Xuehua Jin. 2009. "The Origins of the Business Groups in China: An Empirical Testing of the Three Paths and the Three Theories." *Business History*, 51 (1): 77–99.

Lee, Keun, Kim, Byung-Yeon, Park, Young-Yoon, and Sanidas, Elias. 2012. "Big Business and National Economic Growth: Finding a Binding Constraint for Growth by a Country Panel Analysis." Mimeo. Seoul National University.

Li, Cheng. 2011. "China's Midterm Jockeying: Gearing Up for 2012 (Part 4: Top Leaders of Major State-Owned Enterprises)." *China Leadership Monitor*, 34.

Lin, Li-Wen and Milhaupt, Curtis J. 2011. "We Are the (National) Champions: Understanding the Mechanisms of State Capitalism in China." *Columbia Law and Economics Working Paper*, 409.

Liuhto, Kari and Vahtra, Peeter. 2009. "Who Governs the Russian Economy? A Cross-Section of Russia's Largest Corporations." *Electronic Publications of Pan-European Institute*, 12/2009. Turku School of Economics.

Mahmood, Ishtiaq P. and Mitchell, Will. 2004. "Two Faces: Effects of Business Groups on Innovation in Emerging Economies." *Management Science*, 50: 1348–1365.

McDonald, Hamish. 2010. *Ambani and Sons*. Delhi: Roli Books.

McGregor, Richard. 2010. *The Party: The Secret World of China's Communist Rulers*. London: Penguin.

Musacchio, Aldo. 2009. *Experiments in Financial Democracy: Corporate Governance and Financial Development in Brazil, 1882–1950*. Cambridge: Cambridge University Press.

Rago, Maria Aparacida dePaula. 2008. *José Ermírio de Moraes. A trajetória de um empresário nacional.* Rio de Janeiro: Paz e Terra.

Sarkar, Jayati. 2010. "Business Groups in India." In *Oxford Handbook of Business Groups*, ed. Asli M. Colpan, Takashi Hikino, and James R. Lincoln. Oxford: Oxford University Press.

Schneider, Ben Ross. 2009. "A Comparative Political Economy of Diversified Business Groups: Or How States Organize Big Business." *Review of International Political Economy*, 16 (2): 178–201.

Siffert, Nelson Filho and Souza e Silva, Carla. 1999. *Large Companies in the 1990s: Strategic Responses to a Scenario of Change.* Rio de Janeiro: BNDES (Banco Nacional de Desenvolvimento Econômico e Social).

Szamosszegi, Andrew and Kyle, Cole. 2011. *An Analysis of State-Owned Enterprises and State Capitalism in China.* Prepared by Capital Trade for the U.S.–China Economic and Security Review Commission. Washington, DC.

Teece, David J. and Winter, Sidney G. 1984. "The Limits of Neoclassical Theory in Management Education." *American Economic Review*, 74 (2): 116–121.

Wang, Huiyao, Zweig, David, and Lin, Xiaohua. 2011. "Returnee Entrepreneurs: Impact on China's Globalization Process." *Journal of Contemporary China*, 70 (20): 413–431.

Wells, Lou. 1982. *Third World Multinationals.* Cambridge, MA: MIT Press.

Whittington, Richard. 2011. "More SSOP: Commentary on the Special Issue." *Business History*, 53 (1): 169–173.

Wilkins, Mira. 2009. "The History of the Multinational Enterprise." In *The Oxford Handbook of International Business*, ed. Alan Rugman. Oxford: Oxford University Press.

World Bank and Development Research Center of the State Council. 2012. *China 2030: Building a Modern, Harmonious, and Creative High-Income Society.* Geneva: World Bank.

Yudanov, Andrei. 1997. "Large Enterprises in the USSR: The Functional Disorder." In *Big Business and the Wealth of Nations*, ed. Alfred D. Chandler, Jr., Franco Amatori, and Hikino, Takashi Hikino. Cambridge: Cambridge University Press.

Part II   Global Companies and Power

The Handbook of Global Companies, First Edition. Edited by John Mikler.
© 2013 John Wiley & Sons, Ltd. Published 2013 by John Wiley & Sons, Ltd.

Chapter 5

Theorizing the Power of Global Companies

Doris Fuchs

Introduction

The power of business actors and its implications for democracy have been a concern since the advent of large enterprises in the nineteenth century. While never completely disappearing again, such concerns have been voiced particularly loudly, again in specific periods and on specific occasions, such as the increasingly visible reach of corporations across the globe in the context of globalization in the 1970s and 1980s, or the recent financial crisis. However, it is difficult to move from the vague feeling that huge corporations may be a problem for democratic politics to a more systematic and differentiated understanding of why and how that may be the case. Some observers have argued, for instance, that numbers such as the turnover, workforce, or market share of a company say little about whether and how economic power may be turned into political power.

One approach to an analysis of business's political power that provides answers to this question is to differentiate between various dimensions of business power, specifically business's instrumental, structural, and discursive power. These dimensions differ regarding the sources of power on which they draw, as well as the channels through which power is exercised. An additional advantage of such a differentiated approach is that it allows targeting measures aimed at guaranteeing a democratic balance of interests strategically at trouble spots. Therefore, the aim of this chapter is to introduce a three-dimensional perspective on business power, to delineate some general developments in business power revealed by this perspective, and to point out implications for political reforms in the interest of democratic legitimacy.

The chapter proceeds as follows. The next section offers a brief theoretical overview of discussions on business power in political science, in general. The following section lays out instrumental, structural, and discursive perspectives on business

The Handbook of Global Companies, First Edition. Edited by John Mikler.
© 2013 John Wiley & Sons, Ltd. Published 2013 by John Wiley & Sons, Ltd.

power in more detail, pointing out their theoretical foundations, and the different sources and channels for the exercise of power identified by them. The subsequent section surveys perceivable developments in the extent of the various facets of business power over the last decades. Finally, the concluding section places these insights in a broader context, discussing normative preconditions for the observed developments and their political and societal handling.

Analyzing and Debating the Power of (Global) Companies

There is a long tradition in political science and neighboring disciplines of inquiries into the political influence exerted by economic actors, with increasingly critical voices being raised along the line. In the 1950s, pluralists still argued for the desirability of interest group participation in the political process as a precondition of the creation of a "market place of ideas" (Dahl 1961). Likewise, scholars of corporatism have emphasized the ability of non-state actors, especially associations, to aggregate societal interests, provide expertise, and assist the state in the implementation of regulations (Scharpf 1991).

However, these more optimistic evaluations have received harsh criticism over the years. Scholars have argued that pluralists merely rationalize asymmetric privileges due to their neglect of differences in organizing capacities and resources among societal sectors, as well as a lack of attention to structural sources of power (Schattschneider 1960; Lowi 1979). Moreover, they pointed out the failure of corporatism to discipline capital as a political actor and the need for active state support for the organization of weaker interests (Cohen and Rogers 1994; Streeck 1994). While tending to refrain from explicit normative evaluations, the conceptualization and analyses of rent seeking activities by business, conducted by public choice scholars, further has documented why an uneven distribution of resources may be a source of concern in the political "market" existing in democracies (Buchanan, Tollison, and Tullock 1980; Mitnick 1993).

Of course, corporate actors have received particular attention due to their size, resources, and reach. Critics of pluralism, in particular, depicted the increasing difficulty of assuming a comparably level playing field between interests (Miliband 1969; Lindblom 1977). Even traditional pluralist "advocates" eventually became increasingly pessimistic about the democratic implications of big business's influence on politics (Dahl 1994). In the 1970s and 1980s, moreover, scholars started to inquire into the socio-economic, environmental, and political implications of the increasingly global activities of corporations pointing to potential influences, ranging from downward pressures on social and environmental standards, to the support of Coup d'Etats (Barnet and Müller 1974; Caves 1982; Vernon 1971; 1991). Naturally, such concerns grew as globalization sparked mergers and acquisitions between corporations, creating economic actors of a size, reach, and (increasingly mobile) wealth previously unknown (Lawton, Rosenau, and Verdun 2000; Strange 1996; 1998). Critical observers argued that "corporations rule the world" and that they are simultaneously the "principal agent and architect," as well as major "villain" and "beneficiary" of globalization and global governance (Drache 2001: 6; Korten 1995). At the same time, scholars identified growing engagement by business actors in a range of "new"[1] political activities, such as self-regulation, quasi-regulation, and PPPs, as well as the broadening of the societal reach of business interests due to the increasing privatization of the public domain (Cutler, Haufler, and Porter 1999; Brühl *et al.* 2001).

But how does one gauge the actual political power of global companies? After all, economic resources do not necessarily and not always translate into political resources. To gain a first impression, one may juxtapose comparisons of resources between global companies and other actors, in particular countries with small economies. There, one may see that today's largest global companies each have annual sales revenues greater than the GNP of a substantial number of countries (Ferguson and Mansbach 1999). Alternatively, one can look at market shares controlled by one or a few global companies in important global supply chains. In a considerable number of market segments, three to seven global companies control market shares of 50–90% (Bagdikian 1997; Clapp 2012; Finger and Allouche 2002; Friends of the Earth International 1999; Thomas 2000).

However, such indicators can only serve as rough and indirect measures of political power. They need to be integrated into analyses of the political process, examining, for example, how such numbers translate into political influence. In consequence, systematic approaches, allowing the identification of channels and instruments of the political influence of global companies, are required to gain an understanding of their power and its implications for democracy and societies.

Yet, analyzing the power of business or the ways in which it is exercised is not easy. Power is not only one of the core concepts in political science, it is also one of the most controversial ones. There is little agreement on the definition of power or its operationalization for empirical assessments across different theoretical frameworks. Most political scientists would agree on very broad definitions of power, such as the ability of A to somehow affect the behavior of B. Likewise, Weber's definition of power as "the probability that one actor within a social relationship will be in a position to carry out his own will despite resistance, regardless of the basis on which this probability rests" (1947: 153) is generally cited as one of the authoritative definitions. Yet, these broad definitions allow a range of views on sources, exercise, and influence of power. Weber himself pointed out the complexity of power relationships, since "All conceivable qualities of a person and all conceivable combinations of circumstances may put him in a position to impose his will in a given situation" (p. 153). Moreover, analyses of the power of global companies are particularly challenging for the subdiscipline of International Relations. For a long time, analyses of power in the international system tended to focus almost exclusively on the power of states, due to the preponderance of the (neo-)realist perspective in IR (Baldwin 2002; Schimmelfennig 1998).

Dimensions of the Power of Global Companies

Approaches to the analysis of power differentiate between actor-specific and structural, as well as between material and ideational sources of power (Fuchs 2007; Fuchs and Glaab 2011).[2] Instrumentalist approaches analyze direct, observable relationships of power deriving from actor-specific material resources, while structural material and discursive approaches situate power and its use in material and ideational institutions and structures.[3] A theoretically grounded analysis of the power of business in global governance should draw insights from all of these perspectives.

Instrumentalist approaches to power employ an actor-centered, relational concept of power based on notions of individual voluntary action and linear causality. They focus on the direct influence of one actor on another. Such perspectives are often related to Machiavelli and his interest in the strategic acquisition, maintenance, and use of power. In political science, instrumentalist perspectives have tended to explore how actors influence decisions by formal political decision-makers, for example via lobbying and campaign finance.[4] Moreover, they have been employed by realist approaches in IR to analyze the use of power by states in pursuit of national interests, as well as by liberal institutionalists arguing that states decide on the exertion of power in the international system, if it allows them to realize absolute gains (Keohane and Nye 1977; Morgenthau 1948; Waltz 1979).[5]

Instrumentalist approaches provide a good framework for conceptualizing the exercise of direct influence by special interests on political decision-makers. However, the underlying assumptions of a mechanistic kind of causality and of the autonomy of actors' choices lead to a neglect of structural and systemic sources of power (Lukes 1974; 2004). As a consequence, instrumentalist approaches only provide partial insights into power in the political process.

Structuralist perspectives on power focus on the material and ideational structures shaping actors' choice sets and allocating indirect and direct political influence. In addition, they concentrate their analyses on the input side of the political process. They identify factors that make alternatives more or less acceptable before the actual and observable political bargaining starts and help explain why some issues never appear on the political agenda. Thereby, structuralist approaches reveal the second and third "faces of power" (Bachrach and Baratz 1970; Lukes 1974; 2004).

From a material structuralist perspective, which has been at the core of studies analyzing structural power in the past, actors derive power from their position in institutional processes and from the dependence of politicians on private-sector profitability, investments, and jobs (Shepsle 1979; Cox 1987).[6] Moreover, material structural conditions may place global companies in the position to not just influence political decision-makers, but to adopt, implement, and enforce rules and standards themselves, i.e. replace those holding formal decision-making power. Thus, economic and organizational structures, processes, and interdependencies of today's globalized world mean that actors in control of financial and technological networks and resources have acquired rule-setting power.[7]

In sum, material structuralist approaches to power capture important aspects of power relationships in so far as material structures predetermine actors' behavioral options. Thereby, they allow a broader understanding of decision-making and nondecision-making, thus widening the scope of power politics to be analyzed. However, such approaches only focus on observable conflicts of interest, as well as the influence of material structures on the distribution of power.

Ideational structuralist approaches, also called discursive approaches, are necessary to reveal ideational and normative conditions of power located before decisions and non-decisions by actors (Fuchs 2005; 2007; Fuchs and Glaab 2011). Ideational power is reflected in discourses, practices, and cultural institutions, shaping perceptions, values, and identities (Koller 1991). Via ideas, political contests take place in discourse, as frames are attributed to policy problems and solutions, actors, politics, and the political as such (Hajer 1997; Holzscheiter 2005). Both agency and structure play an important role with respect to discursive power. Actors strategically shape norms and ideas for instance through the use of selected symbols and story-lines, and via the linking of issues and actors to certain connoted norms and ideas. At the same time, the discursive power of actors depends on existing structures in the form of norms and values.

A core insight derived from a perspective on this "third face of power" is that power does not pursue interests but creates them, thereby allowing an explanation of why some potential political demands never arise (Lukes 1974; 2004). It highlights the role of accepted "truths" about desirable policies and political developments, thereby revealing the close link between discursive power and legitimacy and authority (Arendt 1970; Nye 2002). Authority, in turn, can derive from a range of sources. Public actors tend to have authority on the basis of electoral processes and political offices. Non-state actors can have authority on the basis of the trust the public places in their ability to obtain desired results as well as in their intentions (Cashore 2002).

The different dimensions of power offer alternative as well as complementary means to exercise political influence. They can employ material and ideational, actor-specific and structural resources at the same time or use them as substitutes, relying on "voice" in the absence of "exit" power, for example, i.e., intensifying lobbying if their structural power is weak. Likewise, global companies can attempt to foster the diffusion of selected ideas and norms, supporting their cause, thereby reducing the need for lobbying. In other words, global companies can draw simultaneously on their various sources of power and employ different activities in contingent strategies. Likewise, lobbying can be used to foster the development of structural material and ideational power in terms of lobbying against capital controls, for self-regulatory arrangements (rather than governmental regulation), and for the privatization of infrastructure and other service sectors, for example.

Such interaction can be delineated particularly well between ideational and material sources of power through a focus on access and reproduction (Fuchs and Glaab 2011). The extent to which actors gain access to political decision-makers, for instance, depends on their financial resources as well as their perceived political legitimacy. Moreover, access to political decision-makers is also a function of the ability to provide information, considered necessary and trustworthy, and the ability to generate such information, in turn, is at least partly a function of material resources. At the same time, material and ideational power interact with respect to the promotion and repetition of messages. In the era of mediatized politics, financial resources allow actors to strengthen their preferred ideas and norms through repetition and reproduction.

Importantly, even a differentiated framework focusing on different dimensions of business power will only allow us to plausibilize the extent of business power in today's politics, however. This is partly the case, because of a lack of data. Lobbying, for instance, is notorious for the lack of transparency of activities involved, even in countries in which regulation exists and lobbyists are supposed to register. It is also the case, however, because some forms of this power work subtly and comprehensively. Agenda-setting and discursive forms of power may not "leave a trace" to begin with, for example. Threats to move investments and jobs, in the case that governments make unfavorable policy choices, generally need not even be voiced.[8] In turn, due to its reliance on persuasion and voluntary "compliance," the exercise of discursive power frequently will not even be perceived as an exercise of power.

Developments in the Power of Global Companies

Given the difficulties with respect to the empirical analysis of business power just described, the following section can only spotlight some of the most interesting developments in the instrumental, material structural and discursive power of global companies in the past decades.

Developments in Instrumental Power

The instrumental power of global companies has gone through both quantitative and qualitative changes, especially compared to their competitors in the political game. On the quantitative side, the political mobilization of business since the 1970s and the rising need of policy-makers for technical and economic information, as well as financial contributions, have fostered a notable growth in lobbying activity. The direct pursuit of political interests via the establishment of (long-term) relationships with political decision-makers and top-level bureaucrats has become a core part of business's strategy in today's world. It is carried out by high-level executives, including CEOs, and coordinated by corporate offices in the capitals of the world, which draw on financial and personnel resources from headquarters as needed (Berry 1997; Kroszner and Stratmann 2000; Shaiko 1998).

At the same time, the access granted to global companies by political decision-makers has increased considerably as well, due to policy-makers' need for technical and economic information and financial support (Clapp 2001; Hall and Deardorff 2006; Herrnson, Shaiko, and Wilcox 1998; Schuler and Rehbein 2011).[9] The former is a function of increasing constraints on public finances and the complexity and speed of economic and societal developments in the era of globalization. The latter is a function of dramatic increases in the cost of election campaigns in times of mediatized politics, the professionalization of political PR, as well as growing shares of swing voters (Dalton and Wattenberg 2000; Kepplinger 1999; von Alemann and Marshall 2002). The result is a situation allowing top level executives to regularly and directly converse with political decision-makers (Kaiser 2000; Verba and Orren 1985). This leads to long-term "semi-contractual" relationships between representatives of global companies and members and staff of legislatures and bureaucracies (Lord 2000), and provides global companies with an increasing share of seats on governmental advisory committees and delegations (Farnsworth 2004; UNDP 2002). It is a situation, in which "private interests are simultaneously the object of regulation/supervision and the chief counsellors in the formulation of official policy" (Underhill 2001: 290) – if they do not directly write the legislative drafts themselves, as repeated scandals in Germany have shown, for instance.

The combination of increasing business interest in and political dependence on business involvement in politics has strongly tilted the representation of interests in the political game in favor of the interests of global companies. Already around the turn of the millennium, corporations outspent labor by 14 times and other interest groups by 16 times in US election campaigns (UNDP 2002). Moreover, scholars have reported that conservative governments seek contact with business and provide little access for labor and environmental interests, while leftist governments are forced to provide access for both (Herrnson, Shaiko, and Wilcox 1998; Hirscher and Sturm 2001). In turn, regulatory efforts to limit the asymmetry in influence[10] have frequently proven to be too weak, if not completely failed in their purpose, having been interspersed with reforms fostering the opposite (Berry 1997; Greenwood and Thomas 1998; Kropp 2000; Shaffer 2001). For example, many individuals representing business's interests in the political game in Brussels/Strasbourg or Washington, for instance, are not registered as lobbyists despite requirements to do so.

Interestingly, there is a growing asymmetry of political influence even within the business community. This is due to a qualitative change in the political activities of global companies, which keep developing their political toolbox. Increasingly, such companies pursue their interests not via general business associations but do so either individually or in small informal clubs, roundtables, or temporary issue-based coalitions, due to the greater homogeneity in interests, flexibility, and lower organizational costs and inertia (Braithwaite and Drahos 2000; Brand *et al.* 2000; Coen 2005; Eising and Kohler-Koch 1994; Grande 2003; Kaiser 2000; Kohler-Koch 2000; Mazey and Richardson 1997; Smith 2000; van Apeldoorn 2002). Moreover, global companies are simultaneously pursuing their interests at various levels of governance.

Lobbying activities by global companies are particularly notorious at EU institutions, such as the Commission and the Parliament in particular (Greenwood 2002; Tenbücken 2002). The dynamics above, in terms of the combination of business interest in political activity and the dependence of policy-makers and bureaucrats on information, apply at the EU level at least as much. Critical observers have deplored the development of "clientilist relationships" between the two groups there (Nollert 1997).

However and most importantly, the asymmetry in interest representation is even larger at the EU level due to the higher costs of representation beyond the national level, the larger spatial reach of the interests of global companies, the greater removedness of activities from public view, the specific characteristics of the institutional set-up, and business's superior ability to organize transnationally compared to most competing interests (especially labor) (Cadot and Webber 2002; Eising and Kohler-Koch 1994; Fischer 1997; Knill 2001; Nollert 1997; Paul 2001; Streeck 1994; Traxler and Schmitter 1994). Some 75% of all associations represented in Brussels are business associations (to which one has to add all of the representatives of individual corporations as well as the informal clubs mentioned above), while unions make up less than 5% (Ronit and Schneider 1997). At the same time, regulation of lobbying activities has been limited, with the Commission favoring self-regulation due to its traditional dependence on input from practitioners (Greenwood and Thomas 1998). Moreover, efforts to improve civil society participation as an attempt to reduce the asymmetry have proven half-hearted in their implementation (Geiger 2005). The Commission itself has shown a tendency to draw on individual companies with a record proving their ability to invest the necessary financial and human means and the potential for political leaderships over the course of protracted regulative processes, criteria advantaging global companies (Kohler-Koch 1996). Furthermore, the divergence in available resources plays such an important role, because lobbying strategies tend to target different levels of governance simultaneously, thus proving costly (Neuman, Bitton, and Glantz 2002; Streeck and Schmitter 1991; Walter 2001).

The same picture develops in global governance arenas. Here too, political activities by global companies have increased, creating major lobbies on international regulation, as well as at international organizations (Clapp 2001; Farnsworth 2004; Higgott, Underhill, and Bieler 2000; Ledgerwood and Broadhurst 2000; Susskind 1992). In particular, global companies have shown a strong presence at the Bretton Woods triad, lobbying for trade liberalization, private property rights, deregulation, and privatization (Finger and Allouche 2002; Levy and Egan 2000; Sell 2000). However, business lobbies also have pursued profitable public private partnerships at the UN (Hummel 2001; Paul 2001) as well as effectively prevented regulation (Chatterjee and Finger 1994; Mintzer and Leonard 1994; Parto 1999). Moreover, business interests benefit from the fact that decision-making processes at global institutions tend to be more removed from public view, too, as well as from a lack of institutionalized processes of participation, which could define procedures for the creation of a level playing field.

Developments in Structural (Material) Power

The structural material power of global companies has expanded as well, both in its passive, agenda-setting and in its active, rule-setting form. Regarding the passive form, it is obvious that capital mobility has increased over the last decades, as has the share of highly flexible finance capital compared to productive capital (Brand *et al.* 2000). More importantly, developments on the side of business as well as states have increased the power of companies vis-à-vis political decision-makers. On the side of business, we have companies flexibly shifting short-term production contracts between local subcontractors, thus with little risk of losing capital investments. On the political side, the fall of the Iron Curtain as well as the active search for private investment at all levels of governance have meant that more political units than ever before are competing for capital (Altvater 1996; Gill 1995; Strange 1998; Walter 1998). As a result, we have seen an increasing orientation of "the competition state" towards global capital (Hewson and Sinclair 1999), a decrease in corporate tax rates across OECD countries (Ganghof 2005), an extension of arenas for competition for capital to education, transport, and communication policies as well as ethical standards (Gill and Law 1993; Kobrin 1997), political arguments against the increase of environmental and social standards above an established minimum level (Braithwaite and Drahos 2000; Farnsworth 2004), and the indirect influence of global companies in international negotiations via the exercise of structural power in national arenas (Newell and Paterson 1998). Importantly, the structural power of certain global companies has grown in particular. Coordination service firms, such as rating agencies, global accounting firms, or international law firms set standards for policies and practices of states and economic actors worldwide – a phenomenon which was evaluated critically by scholars long before it moved into public view in the context of recent financial crises (Boyer and Drache 1996; Hillebrand 2001; Kerwer 2002; Nölke and Perry 2007; Sinclair 1999). Today, this development is contextualized in the financialization literature, which depicts its broader sources, facets, and most importantly, far reaching implications (Epstein 2005).

In terms of the active side of structural material power, global companies have greatly expanded their rule-setting activities in the last decades (Brühl *et al.* 2004; Cutler, Haufler, and Porter 1999; Hodess 2001; Weiser and Zadek 2000). Via private governance initiatives, today global companies set rules and standards influencing the sustainability of production and consumption activities across the world (Clapp 1998; Dauvergne and Lister 2010; Fuchs, Kalfagianni, and Arentsen 2009; Gulbrandsen 2010). Importantly, most of these private rules and standards are developed without input from and control by public authorities, an important difference to the self-regulatory arrangements or public private partnerships known under corporatism, for instance (Lütz 1995). At the same time, governments have increasingly taken self-regulation into account in the design and implementation of national policies and global regulations (Clapp 2001; Nadvi and Wältring 2002; Ungericht and Hirt 2010).

Why would one consider private standards a form of exercise of power? After all, aren't private actors imposing constraints on their own behavior? While they may be doing so, they are also imposing constraints on everybody else (Buthe 2010; Fuchs and Kalfagianni 2010; Nölke and Perry 2007). Moreover, by setting certain rules, business influences political agendas, policies, and enforcement. This is particularly important, as numerous studies have argued that some of the business-led private standards represent marketing ploys, attempts to pre-empt public regulation or to marginalize more stringent civil society-led private standards, or show very weak results (Clapp 2001; Gibson 1999; Haufler 2001; King and Lenox 2000; von Mirbach 1999).[11]

Developments in Discursive Power

The discursive power of global companies has only recently moved into the focus of research. It draws substantial attention due to perceptions of the increasing relevance of discursive contests in politics (Cigler and Loomis 1995; Hojnacki and Kimball 1998; Kooiman 2002), as well as visible efforts by global companies to exercise discursive power. Some observers claim that the ability to send repeated messages in the public debate is a crucial determinant of political influence today (West and Loomis 1999).

In efforts to exercise discursive power, scholars have documented public opinion campaigns on specific political issues, the use of surveys testing the public reception of different arguments, the hiring of PR firms as agents in political communication, as well as the sponsoring of research and creation of think tanks to generate evidence on policy issues in their interest (Bowman 1996; Levy and Egan 2000; Scherrer 1999; West and Loomis 1999). The increasing ability of global companies to exercise discursive power is a function of their acquisition of political authority, i.e. "decision-making power over an issue area that is generally regarded as legitimate by participations," which endows their influence in their relationships with other actors with an "obligatory quality" (Cutler, Haufler, and Porter 1999: 362).

This increasing authority results from a rise in trust in the ability of economic actors to deliver desired results, placed in global companies by civil society and political decision-makers (Cashore 2002). In turn, this trust derives from dominant norms suggesting that economic growth, efficiency, and competitiveness have to be the core strategies for improving societal well-being, which turns business into the expert for the pursuit of public objectives.

Challenges to this acquisition of political authority by global companies have arisen with respect to questions of the divergence between private and public interests and intentions, especially in political contests with NGOs, who tend to be associated with moral authority in the public view. Business has answered these challenges with efforts to improve its own moral legitimacy via image campaigns ranging from "green economy" to "corporate citizenship" discourses. Also coalition-building with NGOs and even the creation of NGOs, if no NGOs with corresponding views and interests could be found, as well as campaigns attempting to undermine the legitimacy of civil society and governmental actors are part of the tool set (Bennis 2001; Bowman 1996; Clapp 2001; Fuchs and Kalfagianni 2009; Levy and Newell 2005; Ong and Glantz 2000; Ougaard 2006; Smith 2000; Yergin and Stanislaw 1998).

Importantly, however, the discursive power of global companies reaches much farther than specific political campaigns. This discursive power is also exercised via sponsoring and advertisement activities as well as so-called "report" formats on TV, which can often be particularly found in branches with restrictions on advertising, such as cosmetic surgery. The values, lifestyles, and identities communicated through these channels relate to the shaping of politics and society, currently fostering individualistic and materialistic values and depoliticized lifestyles, for instance (Reljić 2001; Schmidt 1998; Solomon 2003).[12] In addition, media dependence on advertising has allowed business to indirectly influence news reporting as well. Importantly, while one cannot assume a direct impact of the media on what people think, according to research, one can identify a strong impact on what people think about, i.e. an agenda-setting, priming, and gate-keeping effect (Brettschneider 2005; Cohen 1963; Iyengar and Simon 1993; McCombs and Shaw 1972).

Similar to the special role of coordination service firms such as rating agencies in terms of the structural power of global companies, the media have a special role in terms of their discursive power (Mast 1996). After all, many media actors are global companies. Moreover, within media corporations, marketing departments have acquired increasing power, while news reporting has been streamlined according to what attracts viewers (Bergsdorf 1980; Kepplinger 1998).

In sum, developments in the discursive power of global companies deserve attention and, most importantly, require a more systematic analysis. The discursive power of business is particularly challenging for democracies, because in a discursive polity, as Hajer (1997) argues, it allows the redefinition of political order. Or to put it in the words of Beck (2002), business's new authority provides it with the revolutionary privilege to rewrite the rules of the game. Empirical analyses of the discursive power of global companies are difficult, due to the subtle and diffuse nature of this power, as pointed out above. But it is all the more relevant, because discursive power entails "a presence at multiple levels in society and a place in multiple conversations, which allows a set of voices to be heard and a set of interests to be taken seriously almost everywhere" (Himmelstein 1997: 143).

Conclusion: Normative Foundations of the Power of Global Companies

As the previous section has shown, there is a lot of evidence that the political power of global companies has increased in all of its dimensions. In addition, there is evidence of an increasing asymmetry of resources and influence between global companies and their competitors in the political game. Labor organizations, in particular, have lost cohesion and resources in times of global competition (Sklair 1998; Wilson 1990). In a six-month period, the largest NGOs may be able to invest considerable resources in a couple of highly controversial policy contests. Large global companies, however, tend to lobby on more than 100 distinct issues in the same time period (Baumgartner et al. 2001). According to critical observers, today the scales are tilted so strongly that the only remaining threat to business influence is business influence (Berry 1997). In other words, the political investments by global companies may cancel each other out, in cases of competition and disagreement on policy objectives. Given that most political activities either concern very specific aspects, such as tax reductions for individual corporations, or broad normative issues, such the necessity and determinants of economic growth, in many cases such competition will not exist (Clawson, Neustadt, and Scott 1992; Smith 2000). Especially considering the values transmitted via advertising, lifestyle magazines, and a majority of films and other entertainments, we can notice the huge amount of resources pushing society in one particular direction.

While resources do not automatically translate into political influence, as pointed out above, they do matter for the various dimensions of power from lobbying and campaign finance activities, to media campaigns and research funding. Financial resources, in particular, can be utilized for a multitude of objectives and in a large variety of forms due to their fungibility.

Accordingly, one would expect a huge asymmetry in resources between global companies and civil society as well as small and medium-sized businesses to represent a challenge for democracy. Similarly, one should expect more stringent regulation of political activities of actors with such predominance in resources. However, such regulation exists only in certain areas and has been rather weak in the past, interspersed by reforms pointing in the opposite direction, as indicated above. How is that possible? Why do we allow actors with such predominance in financial resources in the supposedly democratic political game?

The answer to this question points to the normative embedding of the depicted developments in power. The dominance of neoliberal norms in the past decades, with the associated focus on growth and efficiency, has meant that business has come to be seen as the primary expert, able to deliver in "the public interest" (Bowman 1996; Fuchs and Kalfagianni 2010; Tooze 2000).[13] Beck (2002) speaks of a melting of the identities of capital and the state in this respect, to which one could add the notion of a melting of identities of capital and civil society.

While thus provided with a form of political authority and legitimacy as a political actor in the wider sense, the neoliberal frame has also meant that global companies have not come to be seen as political actors in the narrow sense, their money not as a political resource. In contrast to Marxist, neo-Gramscian or critical approaches, who see an unavoidable intertwining of politics and economics, neoliberal ideas rather strictly differentiate between the economic and political spheres. Only on this premise, i.e. the view that business's resources are economic and not political resources, can actors of the size of corporations be allowed political voice. Indeed, when the institution of "incorporation" was first developed, such rights were granted by governments only for a given period of time, due to concerns about undue influence (Bowman 1996). In this context, it took the constructed notion of "corporate individualism" to provide corporations with "natural rights," including the right of speech.

In other words, the surprising acceptance of asymmetries in political power between today's huge global companies and other non-governmental (and governmental) actors is a function of the attribution of individual rights and freedoms to corporate actors and the attribution of these actors to the economic sphere. The contradictions arising from such constructions with the trust placed in private governance by some practitioners and academics may seem equally surprising, but have been veiled by the creation of an assumption of wide-ranging cohesion between public and corporate interests.

It would take challenges to these normative frames, then, to allow fundamental challenges to the power of global companies to develop. Clearly, restrictions on political donations, as well as on both lobbying activities and improvements in the independence of political decision-makers and bureaucrats from business's resources may go some way in improving the balance between different interests in the political game. In addition, restrictions on advertising and a detangling of business and media interests may help to reduce the societal influence of global companies in the broader sense. However, it will require a public debate on underlying normative frames to have a chance at restoring a level playing field in democratic contests.

Notes

1 While the actual newness of these activities can be debated, their nature, extent, and influence have changed dramatically over the last decades (see below).

2 See also Arts 2003; Barnett and Duvall 2005; Holzscheiter 2005; Levy and Egan 2000; Levy and Newell 2002; Murphy 2011; Okereke, Bulkeley, and Schroeder 2009.

3 Recent theoretic approaches to political power in international relations have added a focus on "power with" to the traditional emphasis on "power over" concepts (Fuchs, Partzsch, and Glaab 2010). While such perspectives are starting to provide interesting insights with respect to "social entrepreneurs" (Partzsch 2011), they have yet to be systematically employed in the study of the power of global companies.

4 Critical state theorists, however, use the term "instrumental power" to refer to a range of more structural mechanisms of business influence on politics such as "revolving doors" and social networks, which in turn support lobbying and campaign finance activities (Miliband 1969; Poulantzas 1978).

5 The focus on the relative power of states, which Waltz relates back to the distribution of power in the global system, also shows the influence of structural aspects, however.

6 Please note that Strange (1996; 1998) takes a different approach in her concept of structural power, as she combines aspects of the second and third faces of power.

7 Simultaneously, the existence of these technical and financial networks is limiting the scope for rule-setting by states (McDowell 2006).

8 Likewise, unvoiced threats of being sued by investors may cause governments to refrain from certain policy choices, including attempts by highly indebted governments to obtain a debt cut.

9   In this respect, reports on the dramatic expansion in "sponsoring" of politicians and parties by private actors indicate that systematic research on new developments in this area is urgently needed (Rose 2011).

10 For instance through registration requirements of lobbyists, limits on the size of contributions, disclosure requirements, and constraints on the use of private media.

11 Such weak or rhetorical private governance initiatives are leading to increasing skepticism towards self-regulation even among certain sectors of the economic community, a development that is likely to increase with the continuing rise of Southern TNCs (which tend to be less in the focus of a critical public) (Gjolberg 2011; Nölke 2011).

12 Research on developments in advertising strategies, which include especially activities that are no longer recognizable as advertising, indicates that more research into similarly veiled strategies of political advertising is needed (Walker 2008).

13 This normative embedding relates to the design and implementation of antitrust regulation, which allowed the development of companies of such size and market power to begin with (Buch-Hansen and Wigger 2010; Page 2008).

References

Alemann, Ulrich von, and Marshall, Stefan, eds. 2002. *Parteien in der Mediendemokratie.* Wiesbaden: Westdeutscher Verlag.

Altvater, Elmar. 1996. *Grenzen der Globalisierung.* Münster: Westfälisches Dampfboot.

Arendt, Hannah. 1970. *On Violence.* London: Penguin.

Arts, Bas. 2003. "Non-State Actors in Global Governance." Max-Planck-Projektgruppe Recht der Gemeinschaftsgüter, http://www.coll.mpg.de/pdf_dat/2003_04online.pdf. Accessed December 1, 2012.

Bachrach, Peter and Baratz, Morton. 1970. *Power and Poverty.* New York: Oxford University Press.

Bagdikian, Ben. 1997. *The Media Monopoly.* Boston: Beacon.

Baldwin, David. 2002. "Power and International Relations." In *Handbook of International Relations,* ed. Carlsnaes, Risse-Kappen, and Simmons, 177–192. London: Sage.

Barnet, Richard and Müller, Ronald. 1974. *Global Reach.* New York: Simon & Schuster.

Barnett, Michael, and Duvall, Raymond. 2005. *Power in Global Governance.* Cambridge: Cambridge University Press.

Baumgartner, Frank, Berry, Jeffrey, Hojnacki, Marie, Kimball, David, and Leech, Beth. 2001. "Issue Advocacy and Interest Group Influence." Paper presented at the ECPR, Canterbury, September 6–10.

Beck, Ulrich. 2002. *Macht und Gegenmacht im globalen Zeitalter.* Frankfurt: Suhrkamp.

Bennis, Phyllis. 2001. "Mit der Wirtschaft aus der Finanzkrise?" In *Die Privatisierung der Weltpolitik,* ed. Brühl, Debiel, Hamm, Hummel, and Martens, 130–150. Bonn: Dietz.

Bergsdorf, Wolfgang. 1980. *Die vierte Gewalt.* Mainz: Von Hase & Koehler.

Berry, Jeffrey. 1997. *The Interest Group Society.* New York: Longman.

Bowman, Scott. 1996. *The Modern Corporation and American Political Thought.* University Park: Pennsylvania State University.

Boyer, Robert and Drache, Daniel, eds. 1996. *States Against Markets.* New York: Routledge.

Braithwaite, John, and Drahos, Peter. 2000. *Global Business Regulation.* Cambridge: Cambridge University Press.

Brand, Ulrich, Brunnengräber, Achim, Schrader, Lutz, Stock, Christian, and Wahl, Peter. 2000. *Global Governance: Alternative zur neoliberalen Globalisierung?* Münster: Westfälisches Dampfboot.

Brettschneider, Frank. 2005. "Massenmedien und politische Kommunikation." In *Handbuch Politisches System der Bundesrepublik Deutschland*, ed. Gabriel and Holtmann. Munich: Oldenbourg.

Brühl, Tanja, Debiel, Tobias, Hamm, Brigitte, Hummel, Hartwig, and Martens, Jens, eds. 2001. *Die Privatisierung der Weltpolitik*. Bonn: Dietz.

Brühl, Tanja, Feldt, Heidi, Hamm, Brigitte, Hummel, Hartwig, and Martens, Jens, eds. 2004. *Unternehmen in der Weltpolitik*. Bonn: Dietz.

Buchanan, James, Tollison, Robert, and Tullock, Gordon, eds. 1980. *Toward a Theory of the Rent-Seeking Society*. College Station: Texas A&M.

Buch-Hansen, Hubert and Wigger, Angela. 2010. "Revisiting 50 Years of Market-Making in the Neoliberal Transformation of European Competition Policy." *Review of International Political Economy*, 17 (1): 20–44.

Buthe, Tim. 2010. "Private Regulation in the Global Economy." *Business and Politics*, 12 (3): 1–12.

Cadot, Olivier and Webber, Douglas. 2002. "Banana Splits." *Business and Politics*, 4 (1): 5–39.

Cashore, Benjamin. 2002. "Legitimacy and the Privatization of Environmental Governance." *Governance*, 8 (4): 503–529.

Caves, Richard. 1982. *The Multinational Enterprise and Economic Analysis*. Cambridge: Cambridge University Press.

Chatterjee, Pratap and Finger, Matthias. 1994. *The Earth Brokers*. New York: Routledge.

Cigler, Alan and Loomis, Burdett, eds. 1995. *Interest Group Politics*. Washington, DC: CQ Press.

Clapp, Jennifer. 1998. "The Privatization of Global Environmental Governance." *Global Governance*, 4: 295–316.

Clapp, Jennifer. 2001. *Toxic Exports*. Ithaca: Cornell University.

Clapp, Jennifer. 2012. *Food*. Cambridge: Polity Press.

Clawson, Dan, Neustadtl, Alan, and Scott, Denise. 1992. *Money Talks*. New York: Basic Books.

Coen, David. 2005. "Environmental and Business Lobbying Alliances in Europe." In *The Business of Global Environmental Governance*, ed. Levy and Newell, 197–223. Cambridge, MA: MIT Press.

Cohen, Bernhard. 1963. *The Press and Foreign Policy*. Princeton: Princeton University Press.

Cohen, Joshua and Rogers, Joel. 1994. "Solidarity, Democracy, Association." In *Staat und Verbände*, ed. Streeck, 236–267. Opladen: Westdeutscher Verlag.

Cox, Robert. 1987. *Production, Power, and World Order*. New York: Columbia University Press.

Cutler, Claire, Haufler, Virginia, and Porter, Tony, eds. 1999. *Private Authority and International Affairs*. Albany: SUNY.

Dahl, Robert. 1961. *Who Governs?* New Haven: Yale University Press.

Dahl, Robert. 1994. *The New American Political (Dis)order*. Berkeley: Institute of Governmental Studies.

Dalton, Russell and Wattenberg, Martin, eds. 2000. *Parties without Partisans*. Oxford: Oxford University Press.

Dauvergne, Peter and Lister, Jane. 2010. "The Power of Big Box Retail in Global Environmental Governance." *Millennium*, 39: 145–160.

Drache, Daniel, ed. 2001. *The Market or the Public Domain?* New York: Routledge.

Eising, Rainer and Kohler-Koch, Beate. 1994. "Inflation und Zerfaserung." In *Staat und Verbände*, ed. Streeck, 175–206. Opladen: Westdeutscher Verlag.

Epstein, Gerald, ed. 2005. *Financialization and the World Economy*. Cheltenham: Elgar.

Farnsworth, Kevin. 2004. *Corporate Power and Social Policy in a Global Economy*. Bristol: Policy Press.

Ferguson, Yale and Mansbach, Richard. 1999. "Global Politics at the Turn of the Millennium." *International Studies Review*, 1: 77–107.

Finger, Matthias and Allouche, Jeremy. 2002. *Water Privatization*. New York: Spon Press.

Fischer, Klemens. 1997. *Lobbying und Kommunikation in der Europäischen Union*. Berlin: Spitz.

Friends of the Earth International. 1999. Food and Food Security. Seattle Series of Briefings 4, http://www.foei.org/publications/gmo/food.html.

Fuchs, Doris. 2005. "Commanding Heights?" *Millennium*, 33 (3): 771–803.

Fuchs, Doris. 2007. *Business Power in Global Governance*. Boulder: Rienner.

Fuchs, Doris and Kalfagianni, Agni. 2009. "Discursive Power as a Source of Legitimation in Food Governance." *International Review of Retail, Distribution and Consumer Research*, 19 (5): 553–570.

Fuchs, Doris and Kalfagianni, Agni. 2010. "The Causes and Consequences of Private Food Governance." *Business and Politics*, 12 (3). DOI: 10.2202/1469-3569.1319.

Fuchs, Doris and Glaab, Katharina. 2011. "Material Power and Normative Conflict in Global and Local Agrifood Governance." *Food Policy*, 36 (6): 729–735.

Fuchs, Doris, Kalfagianni, Agni, and Arentsen, Maarten. 2009. "Retail Power, Private Standards, and Sustainability in the Global Food System." In *Corporate Power in Global Agrifood Governance*, ed. Clapp and Fuchs, 29–60. Cambridge, MA: MIT Press.

Fuchs, Doris, Partzsch, Lena, and Glaab, Katharina. 2010. "Assessing Non-State Power in Global Governance." Getidos Workshop, October 19–20, 2010. Greifswald.

Ganghof, Steffen. 2005. "Konditionale Konvergenz." *ZIB*, 12 (1): 7–40.

Geiger, Stephanie. 2005. *Europäische Governance*. Marburg: Tectum.

Gibson, Robert, ed. 1999. *Voluntary Initiatives and the New Politics of Corporate Greening*. Peterborough: Broadview Press.

Gill, Stephen. 1995. "Globalisation, Market Civilisation, and Disciplinary Neoliberalism." *Millennium*, 24 (3): 399–423.

Gill, Stephen and Law, David. 1993. "Global Hegemony and the Structural Power of Capital." In *Gramsci, Historical Materialism and International Relations*, ed. Gill, 93–124. Cambridge: Cambridge University Press.

Gjolberg, Maria. 2011. "Explaining Regulatory Preferences." *Business and Politics*, 13 (2): 1–31.

Grande, Edgar. 2003. "How the Architecture of the EU Political System Influences Business Associations." In *The Challenge of Change in EU Business Associations*, ed. Justin Greenwood, 213–225. Basingstoke: Palgrave.

Greenwood, Justin, ed. 2002. *The Effectiveness of EU Business Associations*. Basingstoke: Palgrave.

Greenwood, Justin and Thomas, Clive. 1998. "Introduction: Regulating Lobbying in the Western World." *Parliamentary Affairs*, 51 (4): 487–499.

Gulbrandsen, Lars H. 2010. *Transnational Environmental Governance*. Cheltenham: Elgar.

Hajer, Maarten. 1997. *The Politics of Environmental Discourse*. Oxford: Clarendon.

Hall, Richard and Deardorff, Alan. 2006. "Lobbying as Legislative Subsidy." *American Political Science Review*, 100 (1): 69–84.

Haufler, Virginia. 2001. *A Public Role for the Private Sector*. Washington: Carnegie Endowment for International Peace.

Herrnson, Paul, Shaiko, Ronald, and Wilcox, Clyde, eds. 1998. *The Interest Group Connection*. Chatham: Chatham House.

Hewson, Martin and Sinclair, Timothy, eds. 1999. *Approaches to Global Governance Theory*. Albany: SUNY.

Higgott, Richard, Underhill, Geoffrey, and Bieler, Andreas, eds. 2000. *Non-State Actors and Authority in the Global System*. London: Routledge.

Hillebrand, Ernst. 2001. "Schlüsselstellung im globalisierten Kapitalismus." In *Die Privatisierung der Weltpolitik*, ed. Brühl *et al.*, 150–174. Bonn: Dietz.

Himmelstein, Jerome. 1997. *Looking Good and Doing Good*. Bloomington: Indiana University Press.

Hirscher, Gerhard, and Sturm, Roland, eds. 2001. *Die Strategie des "Dritten Weges."* Munich: Olzog.

Hodess, Robin. 2001. "The Contested Competence of NGOs and Business in Public Life." In *The Market or the Public Domain?*, ed. Drache, 129–148. New York: Routledge.

Hojnacki, Marie, and Kimball, David. 1998. "Organizational Interests and the Decision of Whom to Lobby in Congress." *American Political Science Review*, 92 (4): 775–790.

Holzscheiter, Anna. 2005. "Discourse as Capability." *Millennium*, 33 (3): 723–746.

Hummel, Hartwig. 2001. "Die Privatisisierung der Weltpolitik." In *Die Privatisierung der Weltpolitik*, ed. Brühl *et al.*, 22–58. Bonn: Dietz.

Iyengar, Shanto and Simon, Adam. 1993. "News Coverage of the Gulf Crisis and Public Opinion." *Communication Research*, 20 (3): 365–383.

Kaiser, Wolfram. 2000. "Europäisch und pragmatisch." In *Unternehmerverbände und Staat in Deutschland*, ed. Bührer and Grande, 119–131. Baden-Baden: Nomos.

Keohane, Robert and Nye, Joseph. 1977. *Power and Interdependence*. Boston: Longman.

Kepplinger, Hans. 1998. *Die Demontage der Politik in der Informationsgesellschaft*. Freiburg: Alber.

Kepplinger, Hans. 1999. "Die Mediatisierung der Politik." In *Massenmedien und Zeitgeschichte*, ed.Wilke. Konstanz: UvK Medien.

Kerwer, Dieter. 2002. "Standardizing as Governance." In *Common Goods*, ed. Heritier, 293–315. Lanham: Rowman & Littlefield.

King, Andrew and Lenox, Michael. 2000. "Industry Self-Regulation without Sanctions." *Academy of Management Journal*, 43 (3): 698–716.

Knill, Christoph. 2001. "Private Governance across Multiple Arenas." *Journal of European Public Policy*, 8 (2): 227–246.

Kobrin, Stephan. 1997. "The Architecture of Globalization." In *Governments, Globilization, and International Business*, ed. John Dunning, 146–171. Oxford: Oxford University Press.

Kohler-Koch, Beate. 1996. "Die Gestaltungsmacht organisierter Interessen." In *Europäische Integration*, ed. Jachtenfuchs and Kohler-Koch, 193–222. Opladen: Leske & Budrich.

Kohler-Koch, Beate. 2000. "Unternehmensverbände im Spannungsfeld von Europäisierung und Globalisierung." In *Unternehmerverbände und Staat in Deutschland*, ed. Bührer and Grande, 132–148. Baden-Baden: Nomos.

Koller, Peter. 1991. "Facetten der Macht." *Analyse und Kritik*, 13: 107–133.

Kooiman, Jan. 2002. "Governance: A Socio-Political Perspective." In *Participatory Governance*, ed. Grote and Gbikpi, 71–96. Opladen: Leske & Budrich.

Korten, David C. 1995. *When Corporations Rule the World*. West Hartford: Kumarian Press.

Kropp, Sabine. 2000. "Parteienfinanzierung im 'Parteienstaat'." *Gegenwartskunde*, 49 (4): 435–446.

Kroszner, Randall and Stratmann, Thomas. 2000. "Congressional Committees as a Reputation-Building Mechanism." *Business and Politics*, 2 (1): 35–52.

Lawton, Thomas, Rosenau, James, and Verdun, Amy, eds. 2000. *Strange Power*. Aldershot: Ashgate.

Ledgerwood, Grant and Broadhurst, Arlene. 2000. *Environment, Ethics and the Corporation*. New York: St Martin's Press.

Levy, Daniel and Egan, Daniel. 2000. "Corporate Political Action in the Global Polity." In *Non-State Actors and Authority in the Global System*, ed. Higgott, Underhill, and Bieler, 138–153. London: Routledge.

Levy, David and Newell, Peter. 2002. "Business Strategy and International Environmental Governance." *Global Environmental Politics*, 2 (4): 84–101.

Levy, David and Newell, Peter, eds. 2005. *The Business of Global Environmental Governance*. Cambridge, MA: MIT Press.

Lindblom, Charles. 1977. *Politics and Market*. New York: Basic Books.

Lord, Michael. 2000. "Constituency-Based Lobbying as Corporate Political Strategy." *Business and Politics*, 2 (3): 289–308.

Lowi, Theodore. 1979. *The End of Liberalism*. New York: Norton.

Lukes, Steven. 1974. *Power: A Radical View*. London: Macmillan.

Lukes, Steven. 2004. *Power: A Radical View*, 2nd edn. Basingstoke: Palgrave Macmillan.

Lütz, Susanne. 1995. "Politische Steuerung und die Selbstregulierung korporativer Akteure." In *Gesellschaftliche Selbstregelung und politische Steuerung*, ed. Mayntz and Scharpf, 169–197. Frankfurt: Campus.

Mast, Claudia, ed. 1996. *Markt, Macht, Medien*. Konstanz: UvK Medien.

Mazey, Sonja and Richardson, Jeremy. 1997. "Policy Framing." *West European Politics*, 20 (3): 111–133.

McCombs, Maxwell and Shaw, D.L. 1972. "The Agenda-Setting Function of the Mass Media." *Public Opinion Quarterly*, 36: 176–187.

McDowell, Stephen. 2006. "Commercial Control of Global Electronic Networks." In *Global Corporate Power*, ed. May, 127–157. Boulder: Rienner.

Miliband, Ralph. 1969. *The State in Capitalist Society*. New York: Basic Books.

Mintzer, Irving and Leonard, J.A., eds. 1994. *Negotiating Climate Change*. Cambridge: Cambridge University Press.

Mirbach, Martin von. 1999. "Demanding Good Wood." In *Voluntary Initiatives and the New Politics of Corporate Greening*, ed. Gibson, 211–225. Peterborough: Broadview.

Mitnick, Barry. 1993. *Corporate Political Agency*. Newbury Park: Sage.

Morgenthau, Hans. 1948. *Politics Among Nations*. New York: Knopf.

Murphy, James. 2011. "Perspectives on Power." *Journal of Political Power*, 4 (1): 87–103.

Nadvi, Khalid and Wältring, Frank. 2002. "Making Sense of Global Standards." INEF Report 58. Institute for Development and Peace, Duisburg.

Neuman, Mark, Bitton, Asaf, and Glantz, Stanton. 2002. "Tobacco Industry Strategies for Influencing European Community Tobacco Advertising Legislation." *Lancet*, 359: 1323–1330.

Newell, Peter and Paterson, Matthew. 1998. "A Climate for Business." *Review of International Political Economy*, 54 (4): 679–703.

Nölke, Andreas. 2011. "Non-Triad Multinational Enterprises and Global Economic Institutions." In *Governing the Global Economy*, ed. Claes and Knutsen. New York: Routledge.

Nölke, Andreas and Perry, James. 2007. "The Power of Transnational Private Governance: Financialization and the IASB." *Business and Politics*, 9 (3). DOI: 10.2202/1469-3569.1185.

Nollert, Michael. 1997. "Verbändelobbying in der Europäischen Union." In *Verbände in vergleichender Perspektive*, ed. von Alemann, 107–137. Berlin: Sigma.

Nye, Joseph. 2002. *The Paradox of American Power*. Oxford: Oxford University Press.

Okereke, Chukwumerije, Bulkeley, Harriet, and Schroeder, Heike. 2009. "Conceptualizing Climate Governance beyond International Regime." *Global Environmental Politics*, 9 (1): 56–76.

Ong, Elisa, and Glantz, Stanton. 2000. "Tobacco Industry Efforts Subverting International Agency for Research on Cancer's Second-hand Smoke Study." *Lancet*, 355: 1253–1259.

Ougaard, Morten. 2006. "Instituting the Power to Do Good?" In *Global Corporate Power*, ed. May, 227–249. Boulder: Rienner.

Page, William. 2008. "The Ideological Origins and Evolution of U.S. Antitrust Law." In *Issues in Competition Law and Policy*, ed. Collins and Angland. Chicago: ABA Section of Antitrust Law.

Parto, Saeed. 1999. "Aiming Low." In *Voluntary Initiatives and the New Politics of Corporate Greening*, ed. Gibson, 182–199. Peterborough: Broadview.

Partzsch, Lena. 2011. "Power Over and Power With." Presented at the Meeting on International Relations of the DVPW, Munich, October 6–7.

Paul, James. 2001. "Der Weg zum Global Compact." In *Die Privatisierung der Weltpolitik*, ed. Brühl *et al.*, 104–130. Bonn: Dietz.

Poulantzas, Nicos. 1978. *Political Power and Social Classes*. London: Verso.

Reljić, Dušan. 2001. "Der Vormarsch der Megamedien und die Kommerzialisierung der Weltöffentlichkeit." In *Die Privatisierung der Weltpolitik*, ed. Brühl *et al.*, 58–82. Bonn: Dietz.

Ronit, Karsten and Schneider, Volker. 1997. "Organisierte Interessen in nationalen und supranationalen Politökologien." In *Verbände in vergleichender Perspektive*, ed. von Alemann, 29–63. Berlin: Sigma.

Rose, Mathew. 2011. *Korrupt? Wie unsere Politiker und Parteien sich bereichern – und uns verkaufen*. Munich: Heyne.

Scharpf, Fritz. 1991. "Die Handlungsfähigkeit des Staates am Ende des zwanzigsten Jahrhunderts." *Politische Vierteljahresschrift*, 32 (4): 621–634.

Schattschneider, Elmer. 1960. *The Semi-Sovereign People*. NY: Holt, Rinehart, Winston.

Scherrer, Christoph. 1999. *Globalisierung wider Willen?* Berlin: Sigma.

Schimmelfennig, Frank. 1998. "Macht und Herrschaft in Theorien der Internationalen Beziehungen." In *Macht und Herrschaft*, ed. Imbusch, 317–333. Leverkusen: Leske & Budrich.

Schmidt, Rudi. 1998. "Zur politischen Semantik von 'Globalisierung'." In *Arbeit, Gesellschaft, Kritik*, ed. Hirsch-Kreinsen and Wolf, 135–149. Berlin: Sigma.

Schuler, Douglas and Rehbein, Kathleen. 2011. "Determinants of Access to Legislative and Executive Branch Officials." *Business and Politics*, 13 (2): 1–30.

Sell, Susan. 2000. "Structures, Agents and Institutions." In *Non-State Actors and Authority in the Global System*, ed. Higgott, Underhill, and Bieler, 91–107. London: Routledge.

Shaffer, Gregory. 2001. "The Blurring of the Intergovernmental." In *Transatlantic Governance in the Global Economy*, ed. Pollack and Shaffer, 97–123. Lanham: Rowman & Littlefield.

Shaiko, Ronald. 1998. "Lobbying in Washington." In *The Interest Group Connection*, ed. Herrnson, Shaiko, and Wilcox, 1–24. Chatham: Chatham House.

Shepsle, Kenneth. 1979. "Institutional Arrangements and Equilibrium in Multidimensional Voting Models." *American Journal of Political Science*, 23 (1): 27–59.

Sinclair, Timothy. 1999. "Bond-Rating Agencies and Coordination in the Global Political Economy." In *Private Authority and International Affairs*, ed. Cutler, Haufler, and Porter, 153–169. Albany: SUNY.

Sklair, Leslie. 1998. "As Political Actors." *New Political Economy*, 3 (2): 284–287.

Smith, Mark. 2000. *American Business and Political Power*. Chicago: University of Chicago.

Solomon, Michael. 2003. *Conquering Consumerspace*. New York: Amacom.

Strange, Susan. 1996. *The Retreat of the State*. Cambridge: Cambridge University Press.

Strange, Susan. 1998. *Mad Money*. Ann Arbor: University of Michigan Press.

Streeck, Wolfgang, ed. 1994. *Staat und Verbände*. Opladen: Westdeutscher Verlag.

Streeck, Wolfgang and Schmitter, Philippe. 1991. "From National Corporatism to Transnational Pluralism." *Politics and Society*, 19 (2): 133–161.

Susskind, Lawrence. 1992. "New Corporate Roles in Global Environmental Treaty-Making." *Columbia Journal of World Business*, 27: 62–73.

Tenbücken, Marc. 2002. *Corporate Lobbying in the European Union*. Frankfurt: Peter Lang.

Thomas, Caroline. 2000. *Global Governance, Development and Human Security*. London: Pluto.

Tooze, Roger. 2000. "Ideology, Knowledge and Power in International Relations and International Political Economy." In *Strange Power*, ed. Lawton, Rosenau, and Verdun, 175–194. Aldershot: Ashgate.

Traxler, Franz and Schmitter, Philippe. 1994. "Perspektiven europäischer Integration, verbandlicher Interessenvermittlung und Politikformulierung." In *Europäische Integration und verbandliche Interessenvermittlung*, ed. Eichener and Voelzkow, 45–70. Marburg: Metropolis.

Underhill, Geoffrey. 2001. "The Public Good versus Private Interests and the Global Financial and Monetary System." In *The Market or the Public Domain?*, ed. Drache, 274–296. New York: Routledge.

UNDP. 2002. *Human Development Report 2002*. Oxford: Oxford University Press.

Ungericht, Bernd, and Hirt, Christian. 2010. "CSR as a Political Arena." *Business and Politics*, 12 (4): 1–22.

Van Apeldoorn, Bastian. 2002. "The European Round Table of Industrialists." In *The Effectiveness of EU Business Associations*, ed. Greenwood, 194–205. Basingstoke: Palgrave.

Verba, Sidney and Orren, Gary. 1985. *Equality in America*. Cambridge: Harvard University.

Vernon, R. 1971. *Sovereignty at Bay:* New York: Basic Books.

Vernon, R. 1991. "Sovereignty at Bay: Twenty Years After." *Millennium*, 20 (2): 191–196.

Walker, Rob. 2008. *Buying In*. New York: Random House.

Walter, Andrew. 1998. "Do They Really Rule the World?" *New Political Economy*, 3 (2): 288–292.

Walter, Andrew. 2001. "NGOs, Business, and International Investment." *Global Governance*, 7: 51–73.

Waltz, Kenneth. 1979. *Theory of International Politics*. Reading: Addison-Wesley.

Weber, Max. 1947. *The Theory of Social and Economic Organization*. Oxford: Oxford University Press.

Weiser, John and Zadek, Simon. 2000. Conversations with Disbelievers, http://www.zadek.net/wp-content/uploads/2011/02/Conversations-with-Disbelievers_November2000.pdf. Accessed December 7, 2012.

West, Darrell and Loomis, Burdett. 1999. *The Sound of Money*. New York: Norton.

Wilson, Graham. 1990. *Interest Groups*. Oxford: Blackwell.

Yergin, Daniel and Stanislaw, Joseph. 1998. *The Commanding Heights*. New York: Simon & Schuster.

Chapter 6

Why, When, and How Global Companies Get Organized

Tony Porter and Sherri Brown

Introduction

While chapters in the first part of this volume analyzed global transformations in the geographic and material spatiality and scope of corporations, this chapter explores how corporate power, both in its organizational and legal forms and operating more broadly within systemic processes, is organized within global policy processes and outcomes. The central question guiding this chapter asks how corporations, which have grown in size and scope and are increasingly regarded as powerful and authoritative actors in global policy processes, organize themselves to wield power and authority? To address this question demands mapping, conceptual, and theoretical exercises to locate and explore modalities of corporate power in policy processes.

There is the growing perception that corporate power is "everywhere" and that it intersects and shapes policy and governance processes in increasingly complex ways. The literature on private business authority confirms widespread interfaces of corporate power across multiple policy issues and levels. Corporate power shapes policy processes and outcomes in environment and the biosphere (Green 2010; Pattberg and Stripple 2008), finance (Büthe 2004; Kobrin 2002), communication and information technologies (Salter 1999; Spar 1999), and other policy areas, at local, national, regional, and international levels.

In this chapter we map the ubiquity of corporate power in various spheres, to understand its organizational and legal forms, interfaces, and articulations, as well as its larger systemic implications. This involves an examination of power as a construct and a typology, which includes Dahl's (1957) conventional definition of compelling compliance to a direct command, known as direct or instrumental power (Fuchs and Lederer 2007) to comprehensive typologies, differentiating between direct,

The Handbook of Global Companies, First Edition. Edited by John Mikler.
© 2013 John Wiley & Sons, Ltd. Published 2013 by John Wiley & Sons, Ltd.

structural, and discursive power (2007). Drawing upon Gramscian, post-structural, and other theoretical frameworks, we explore themes of organization, transformation, consolidation, and disaggregation in corporate power and its interfaces and effects on global public policy processes and outcomes.

In so doing, we explore disaggregation as the most distinctive mode by which corporate power is organized today. A disaggregated authority structure resembles a web of networks in which sources of authority are discrete, but boundaries intersect in shaping policy processes and outcomes. The original authority source may retain an important role in this structure, but disaggregation implies decentralizing transformations in the sites and sources of power and authority (Hansen 2008; Porter 2008; Slaughter 2004). Our analysis suggests that the growth, ubiquity, and complexity of corporate power is increasingly organized through a disaggregated authority structure that supplies new entry points for corporate power and corporate actors in global policy processes and outcomes.

Coherence and Disaggregation, and the Notion of Spheres

How then can we best understand the multiple ways that corporate power extends beyond the organizational boundaries of the MNC itself, producing effects that can seem quite distant from more centralized locations of power, such as corporate board rooms or elite networks of owners of capital? A first task is to acknowledge the complexity of power itself. A second task is to identify the various locations where corporate power operates beyond the organizational boundaries of the MNC. We do this by identifying five locations, or *spheres*: public authority; civil society; consumption; production relations; and the biosphere. In this section we carry out these two tasks. The following section examines disaggregated corporate power in each of the five spheres in turn.

To understand the disaggregated operations of corporate power it is important to recognize the complexity of power itself. Many typologies of the dimensions of power have been created (for example Barnett and Duvall 2005; Fuchs 2007; Lukes 1974; Strange 1990).[1] A key message from these typologies is that power involves much more than the issuing of a command. The type of *direct* power associated with such commands is important, but limitations on the choices of those subject to power can also come more indirectly from the conditions of life that they experience. For instance, elites may create rules or operational systems that contribute to the reproduction of social inequality over time, and thereby produce power relations, even without an elite actor directly commanding a subordinate to do something. This is often labeled *structural* power. A second message from these typologies is that power operates through both ideas and material objects. For instance ideas may produce dominant or subordinate identities, or they may inspire compliance or resistance. However objects such as weapons, biometric identity systems, assembly lines, concrete walls, or written contracts can also be important in the production or reproduction of power (Law and Hetherington 2000).

How can we organize our analysis of the different locations outside the MNC's organizational boundaries to which corporate power extends? The ability of the MNC to exercise power over other actors has long been recognized, such as when the "seven sisters," the oil oligopoly, were seen as controlling oil markets, or the United

Fruit Company was implicated in the 1954 coup in Guatemala. More recently the organizational form of the MNC has become more complex, shifting from reliance on a more hierarchical, wholly owned, internally financed corporate structure to one in which the MNC is one node in an extended set of networks, including suppliers on contract, marketing, and retailing networks, third party standards-setters, public-private partnerships, and global financial markets. This has complicated the exercise of power by MNCs, creating both new opportunities for their power to be extended, but also uncertainties and obstacles. It is helpful to distinguish the different locations in which MNC power is exercised by constructing a typology. This typology should be varied enough to capture the wide range of MNC influences, but concise enough to be manageable. As noted above, we have such a typology, with five spheres.

These spheres are not self-contained mutually exclusive categories, but rather overlapping spaces. The first sphere is public authority, which includes governments and states, but also international organizations and laws that were established by states, and less formal public networks or spaces in which public authority is generated. *Authority* here refers to a recognition that it is right to comply with an actor or institution. The second sphere is civil society, which includes non-governmental actors and institutions that are concerned with social or political matters rather than commercial transactions. The third sphere is consumption, which includes all activities related to the purchase and use of products sold in markets. The fourth sphere is production relations, which includes all the social relations that make it possible for MNCs to produce goods or services. The fifth sphere is the biosphere, which includes our planet's biological and physical environments. In the next sections we shall see that in each of these spheres the disaggregated power of the MNC is experienced, but in distinctive ways.

Public Authority

Seeking to directly influence public authority is one of the most recognized ways in which corporate power is exercised. This includes lobbying, funding electoral campaigns, directly positioning corporate executives or representatives in policy networks, the initiation of private litigation to alter a public policy, or carrying out the implementation of public policy, for instance when formerly public prisons or schools are privatized. The undue influence of corporate money in politics has been a particularly prominent issue in the US (Lessig 2011; Reich 2007). Sometimes corporations directly wield authority in a way that closely resembles the public functions of states, such as when private military companies secure a contested territory, or when business associations create and manage sets of rules.

Disaggregation can occur when the power of corporations is exercised in or targeted at locations that are some distance from such traditionally central organs of the state as the cabinet or legislature. The more distant locations have become more important due to the disaggregation of public authority, and can include, for example, quasi-independent regulatory agencies or central banks, international organizations, transnational policy networks, public–private partnerships, or self-regulatory arrangements. A literature on "regulatory capture" has usefully analyzed the way that companies can manipulate such processes (Baker 2010).

The structural power of corporations over public institutions is also well recognized. In capitalist societies growth is dependent on corporations, elections are often dependent on growth, and thus politicians have an incentive to respond to their concerns to make the economy grow. With globalization and the cross-border liberalization of capital flows, governments increasingly adopt corporation-friendly policies in an effort to make their economy competitive (Cerny 1997). A corporation can play one government off against another, threatening to move to a different jurisdiction if its interests are not served (Gill and Law 1989). An increasing number of domestic policies are constrained by business-friendly international laws, such as the thousands of bilateral investment treaties that protect the rights of investors against interference from domestic legislatures. Gill (2003) has called this the "new constitutionalism." International organizations such as the International Monetary Fund may dictate market-friendly policies to states that are dependent on IMF funding, a phenomenon that Gill (1995; 2003) has called "disciplinary neoliberalism." In general, all the ways that corporations exercise power in the remaining spheres that this chapter discusses are forms of structural power relative to public authority, since they indirectly constrain or influence the actions of states and other public actors. The increasing omnipresence of corporations in all spheres of life, and their increased mobility and connectedness across borders, contributes to the growth of disaggregated and structural forms of corporate power.

Both direct and structural corporate power can be produced and transmitted in various mixes of ideas and material objects. The role of ideas in corporate power has been labeled "discursive power" by Fuchs (2007). Corporations can seek to directly influence the thinking of public authorities by threatening or convincing them that not acceding to their demands will be immoral, destructive of the economy, or have some other negative consequence. Ideas may also work more indirectly, for instance when corporate ways of operating influence academic literatures such as the new public management, regulatory policy, or law and economics, which then work to reshape the contours of the state. Ideas may be highly technical but consequential for public policy, such as the role played by accounting companies in promoting accounting standards compatible with Anglo-American styles of capitalism (Nölke 2010). In general the exercise of indirect ideational power is a form of disaggregation that is increasingly important as states find it difficult to manage a complex fast-moving world and turn to the knowledge that is produced by corporations.

Material power can take well recognized forms such as the cash in an envelope that a lobbyist hands secretly to a politician. Material power can take a less visible form when material objects produced by corporations influence or constrain public authorities. The role of mobile phones and internet connections in destabilizing authoritarian regimes is a positive example. More negatively, the proliferation of shopping malls, privately owned parks, and corporate media can reduce the public spaces needed for citizens to constitute a public. To police their borders or airports, states rely upon security systems that are often dependent on material objects produced and managed by corporations, such as biometric scanners or databases of personal information. Firms can have tremendous discretion over how these are configured. The military has become increasingly dependent on technology produced by corporations, including the use of modified Xbox game controllers to control drone aircraft (Economist 2009).

Civil Society and Corporate Power

Frequently depicted as a third and separate sphere of social relations (Macdonald 1994), mediating between public and private sector spheres, civil society brings together individuals and social groupings, playing a key role in the construction of a public sphere. The next section addresses individuals' consumer identities, and this section focuses on the role of civil society in constituting communities, including political communities at the state and transnational levels. Civil society's relations with the private sector and corporate power range from latent interactions where corporations shape social preferences or behaviors through ownership and production of media, cultural and sports outlets, natural, built, and virtual spaces, and other goods and services, to relations of contestation where civil society and corporate power encounter one another as opponents. Contestation has taken the form of struggles over ideas and ideologies and the exercise and boundaries of corporate power in social and political life. Corporate power thus shapes social preferences and behavior with respect to transmission and reproduction of ideas and material resources and capabilities.

Corporations and corporate power leverage these capacities directly by influencing civil society preferences and behavior with respect to information and culture through media, philanthropy, and financial and other supports for civil society organizations (particularly think tanks and research institutes, but also "astroturf" groups that present themselves misleadingly as spontaneous grassroots organizations). Corporations also exercise direct power through ownership and governance of natural and virtual public spaces, including parks and the Internet. The civil society "Occupy Wall Street" movement in New York City, for example, was subject to the effects of direct corporate power when the private owners of Zuccotti Park, a key assembly site of the movement, evicted protesters from their park (Bell and Flock 2011), a strategy that was quickly adopted by other Occupy movement sites across North America. Corporate power is also exercised through private governance forums and modalities in virtual spaces that influence and impact civil society, including the growing influence of corporate power in shaping the rules of the internet and online activity (Bislev and Flyverbom 2007; Spar 1999). The ability of Visa, MasterCard, and Paypal to disable Wikileak's capacity to fund itself is an example.

Corporate structural power manifests itself through structures of world order, which provide support for existing systems of production and accumulation. Corporate structural power thus implies the privileging of corporate imperatives in social relations. This not only extends to the public sphere, as discussed above, but also to patterns of hierarchical social relations. The TRIPs Agreement, for example, secured broad property rights for corporations, including 20-year patent protections for innovations. The effects of TRIPs on access to medicines are widely recognized as contributing to monopolistic pricing, undersupply, and therefore, reduced access (Atik and Lidgard 2006; Heywood 2002; t'Hoen 2009), validating commercial principles while undermining alternative community-enhancing tendencies in civil society. Global civil society movements and activism helped to secure discretionary pricing reductions from pharmaceutical companies. These concessions, while critical to enhancing access to medicines, particularly in developing countries, transpire within the structural constraints of disciplinary neoliberalism and new constitutionalism

(Gill 1995; 1998; 2003) which entrenches and extends the prerogative of capital to behave in ways that resist, sublimate, or violate the interests of working, marginalized, and/or excluded populations. Concessions are not substitutes for structural reform, and offer poor protection from future abuses of structural power. Indeed, the proliferation of new constitutionalist arrangements, including trade and investment treaties, represent the disaggregation of corporate power and increasingly, sites where corporate power encounters both civil society engagement and resistance.

Corporate power in civil society is also exercised in part through ideas. Corporations, for example, employ discursive strategies, such as branding and public relations campaigns, and responsibility and sustainability discourses, to appeal to and defend their role in the world order, as with BP branding itself as "Beyond Petroleum" while continuing to extract oil in environmentally damaging ways. Corporations may also transmit normative and policy ideas through media ownership and production and thus shape the content of popular discussion and the public sphere. Corporations also develop and advance technical ideas and rules of practice in areas of social life such as health, family, education, and so forth. For example, corporations configure and promote technical ideas and solutions to health problems, notably pharmacological or technological interventions, either on their own or by funding others, such as think tanks or universities. They also develop standards and rules around private insurance for family, education, death benefits, and so forth, and, accordingly, influence civil society behaviors, preferences, and experiences.

Although typically corporate material power has most often been understood as synonymous with financial resources, corporations wield material power through a variety of other products, including technologies, patents, production materials, and consumer goods. Civil society often makes extensive use of these products as both tools and targets in their resistance. The use of "smart phones" to support communication and dissemination efforts during the Arab Spring and Occupy Wall Street movements underscores the importance of these objects for rapid social feedback and interaction, but other commercial internet technologies have been complicit in government efforts to track dissidents. Other objects, such as those encoded with Digital Rights Management controls, or that administer password access to networks can severely restrict the flow of information. Branded commercial products, such as toys, apparel, or electronic gadgetry can often encode in material form the celebration of corporate culture at the expense of alternative civil society orientations (Klein 2000).

Consumption

Corporate power has become increasingly integrated into our daily lives in our roles as consumers. In liberal economic theory, the idea that a corporation could exercise power over consumers in competitive markets would seem impossible since consumers could always choose to buy from a different corporation. The notion of consumer sovereignty implies that consumers are even more powerful, shaping structures of production more broadly as firms respond to their preferences. However there are many reasons that this is misleading. Corporations exercise control over consumers in increasingly complex and disaggregated ways.

Corporations often seek to control consumers through mixes of direct and indirect structural power. This is especially evident in attempts to prevent competition, which alters the structure of markets and thereby allows the firm to exercise direct power over consumers. The possibility of anti-competitive conduct is well recognized in economic literatures, even if they tend to understate its prevalence. A firm may seek to prevent competition on its own, or working together with a few firms that constitute an oligopoly. Explicit collusion in cartels, such as dividing up markets, price-fixing, or control of technology, which was widespread internationally before World War II, has generally been outlawed (Porter 1999) but more informal means of controlling competition are common. This may occur through predatory pricing, where products are temporarily priced below the level that would allow strong competitors to emerge.[2] It may occur through control of a key technology, as Microsoft was accused of doing in promoting Explorer against competitors like Netscape. "Pre-competitive" collaboration is often encouraged, as with government endorsement of the Sematech and EUCAR consortia which have sought to coordinate the development of microchip and automotive technologies respectively.[3] VISA and MasterCard, which are owned collectively by banks, were charged by US anti-trust authorities with unfairly dominating retail payment systems, settling for a record $3 billion (Levitin 2007). Firms also try to entangle consumers in complex products or technologies that initially seem cheap but that lock consumers into longer-range profitable relations, as with the deceptively low initial interest rates that contributed to the 2007 subprime mortgage crisis, the provision of cheap computer printers that require expensive supplies and replacement parts, or the aggressive promotion of banks by online payments to make it difficult for consumers to switch banks (Schwartz 2011). Firms may use abusive "terms of service agreements" on websites, where "users never get a chance to negotiate their contents and can often be entirely unaware of their existence" (EFF 2011).

Both direct and structural power may operate through ideas. The manipulation of knowledge is a tool in the direct exercise of power, such as when the tobacco industry conceals the harmful effects of smoking, or when realtors try to prevent the online dissemination of information about housing that would help consumers control their own affairs (CBC 2011). All of the anti-competitive practices discussed above rely on ideas to some extent, but there are more subtle and insidious ways that corporations may manipulate the desires and identities of consumers. An increasing proportion of the value in products is symbolic rather than material, as evident in massive expenditures on advertising and the heavy emphasis on aesthetics and design in objects (Lash and Urry 1994). Marketing is becoming embedded in new social contexts such "viral marketing" that uses new social media (Brown 2006). Anxieties, affections, and other feelings are elicited with increasing sophistication. Scholars have differed greatly in their analysis of the degree to which individuals are controlled by or control the meanings of products. For instance Giddens (1991) stresses the new opportunities for self-fulfilment that they provide, Bourdieu argues that powerful individuals use them to reinforce their dominance through "symbolic capital" (1986), Baudrillard linked the growth of sign-value to the development of capitalism (1973) while Deleuze has linked advertising and marketing to psychoanalytical processes that strongly challenge the notion that individuals have control over their own identities (1995).

Direct and structural power both operate through material objects. All the above examples of corporate power over consumers involve objects that reinforce that power, including the technical artifacts that empowered VISA and MasterCard at the point of sale; fostered Explorer's dominance; are the focal point of "pre-competitive" consortia; make it difficult for a customer to switch banks; automatically administer terms of service agreements, or embody consumer desires. Indeed a shift can be identified from earlier simple forms of domination, such as the pre-World War II cartel agreements, or the manipulations of traveling snake oil salesmen, to increasingly complex and extended forms of power which, as with other aspects of our "post-social" world, work through objects, such as the corporate logo that presents itself as a gamer works a game controller (Knorr Cetina 1977; Roustan 2009).

Production

One of the most well recognized expressions of corporate power is in the realm of production, particularly the globalization of production and transformations in global production structures and relations. For the latter, the drive to decrease production costs and transform production processes directly impacts labor and suppliers through automation, flexibilization, routinization, declining employment and social protections, and lay-offs. Corporations exercise control over labor and suppliers by increasingly moving towards automation and routinization; circumscribing the scope and scale of production processes. The use of automated voice technology in telephone transactions, self-checkout mechanisms at grocery stores, and robots in assembly lines and factories, is a reflection of not only the current technological age, but also corporate interests in controlling production processes and costs. In July 2011, Foxconn, a Taiwanese electronics company, for example, announced that they intended to replace 1 million workers with robots within three years (Knapp 2011). These trends extend to suppliers and farmers who are increasingly expected to automate production to achieve economies of scale and competitiveness in a globalized economy. Both automated and non-automated production often involves a growing degree of routinization, in which workers and suppliers universalize production processes through adherence to standardized principles and procedures. The use of standardized production procedures, scripts, and uniforms in service work in fast-food restaurants exercise a high degree of control over labor and restaurant suppliers. This can include efforts to control gestures and emotions, generating negative physical and psychological effects for workers who lack autonomy and self-expression in their work environment (Leidner 1991).

Corporations are also achieving greater control and reduced costs through trends in flexible labor arrangements, including growing rates of part-time, temporary, and insecure employment (Kalleberg 2009). These trends are consistent with corporate interests in achieving flexible workforces through sectoral collective bargaining, union-busting, and factory closings or mass lay-offs. Sectoral bargaining, or "two-tiered bargaining" (Aarvaag Stokke 2008), is an illustration of the disaggregation of corporate power in production, whereby corporations may achieve better outcomes through decentralized sector-specific bargaining. There are also familiar examples of direct circumvention of bargaining processes such as Wal-Mart's union-busting tactics or decisions to close down whole or parts of stores, including stores in Quebec and Texas, that had become unionized (Hays 2003; MacNeil 2010). Corporations also conduct mass and/or cyclical lay-offs to exercise their power over labor during periods of economic uncertainty or downturn, such as when Home Depot eliminated 500 jobs and froze or reduced wages in the wake of the 2008 financial crisis (Barbaro 2008). These trends directly reduce the power of workers relative to corporations. They impact workers' job and income security as well as access to employment and social protections, including union, employment insurance, and other health and social insurance protections.

The globalization of production reinforces these trends through corporate productive outsourcing, offshoring, and fragmentation in global international production and distribution networks. A key feature of these networks is that they involve more indirect and disaggregated forms of control over production. Corporate outsourcing refers to the transfer of in-house goods and service production to other firms. Corporations may elect to transfer production to domestic firms, or may outsource production to other countries, for example, transferring call center services to India, and goods manufacturing to China, to obtain greater productive cost savings and/or comparative advantage (Plank, Staritz, and Lukas 2009). Corporations are also fragmenting production, which entails parceling out the production process into modules to be performed by different firms (Arndt and Kierzkowski 2001). Computers are commonly produced in a fragmented fashion, with individual components produced by different firms in various locales (Ernst 2004). These processes offer corporations significant flexibility in controlling labor and production costs, while also strengthening their structural power to extract favorable business conditions in domestic and international locales.

Corporate power in production also operates through ideas. Business codes of conduct and private standard setting establishes rules, principles, and procedures governing production methods and procedures. Codes of conduct or standards may be generated at the level of the firm; Nike, Coca-Cola, and Barrick Gold all have business codes of conduct, within sectors, such as accounting, communications, and tourism (see Harrison 1994; Neill, Stovall, and Jinkerson 2005; Payne and Dimanche 1996) or in networks, such as the International Organization for Standardization (ISO) which develops commercial and industrial standards for its network of 162 national member organizations (see www.iso.org). Corporations are also adopting benchmarking practices; the identification and sharing of ideas and practices in production methods and processes (Holger Kohl 2004). Codes and standards allow corporations to enforce uniform expectations for employees and production processes, while benchmarking establishes a centralized clearinghouse of best practices which can be used to control disaggregated global production networks. As production has becomes increasingly disaggregated, corporations seek uniformity and access to excellence in production procedures and flexibility in production networks and mobility.

Corporate power over production is also exercised through material objects. The use of robots and other forms of automation has transformed production processes. The procedures and standards mentioned above are inscribed in material objects, such as checklists or procedure manuals. Building architectures and transportation infrastructures are configured to maximize power and efficiency. Transnational value chains are increasingly connected electronically, facilitated by objects such as bar codes, scanners, or radio frequency identity (RFID) tags (Ferguson 2002). RFID allows objects to transmit recorded information through radio waves, and can be linked electronically to databases, sensors, thermostats, or other controls. While controversial on privacy grounds, retailers have begun to add unique RFID tags to individual products. The proliferation of objects that can communicate directly to one another has been labeled the "internet of things." Such connections facilitate far greater corporate control of extended value chains, mediated through objects.

Biosphere

The exercise of corporate power in the biosphere has long been associated with manipulation and transformation of water, land, and the atmosphere. As in the other spheres we have examined, corporate power over the biosphere today is exercised in increasingly extensive and disaggregated ways. The negative effects of corporate power in the biosphere have become more complex, uncertain, and dangerous. Individually and collectively corporations have also become much more actively engaged in the governance of environmental problems.

Direct corporate interaction with the biosphere has resulted in increasingly complex environmental disasters, including the April 2010 leakage of over 4.9 million barrels of oil from the British Petroleum (BP) "Macondo" well into the Gulf of Mexico (Bryant 2011). The disaster caused extensive loss of bird, marine, and animal life, and contamination of seawater and beaches. The deepwater drilling involved added to the complexity of the disaster since humans could not access the spill directly, but instead needed to rely on deepwater devices. Regulators relied too heavily on the management by the firms (BP, Halliburton, and Transocean) of those devices and the risks involved, despite the ultimately catastrophic extensive exposure of the public and the biosphere to those risks. "Fracking" – high-pressure pumping of water, sand, and chemicals to break open shale thousands of feet below the surface to release natural gas – is another recent technology that intervenes in the biosphere far more deeply and hazardously than before. In other cases the complexity of the risk is due to the sheer size of the disaster. For instance the Texaco Corporation (now Chevron) has been held responsible, following a class-action lawsuit, for environmental damage associated with an estimated 18 billion gallons of waste in the Amazon rainforest in northern Ecuador dating back to the 1970s and 1980s (Feige 2008; Reuters 2011).

More indirect negative structural effects of corporate power occur when the ongoing expansion of production, without regard for its negative externalities, leads to deforestation, soil degradation, climate change, loss of biodiversity, and other problems. The poorly regulated purchase of massively large tracts of land in Africa by multinational corporations and sovereign wealth funds ("land grabbing"), at times for speculation, and stimulated by the promise of biofuels, integrates financial markets, energy markets, agriculture, and the biosphere in new and hazardous ways (Zoomers 2010). Genetic engineering similarly represents an unprecedented modification of life forms, in both the instrumental sense of producing a new organism, and in the potentially longer term transformative sense of disrupting ecosystems or agricultural processes (for example Monsanto's terminator seeds which are engineered to be sterile), introducing unknown environmental and human health hazards.

Climate change is emblematic of the complex and disaggregated character of the negative effects of corporate power. Unlike more localized problems, any consumption of fossil fuels – which involves almost all aspects of contemporary life – contributes to truly global risks of catastrophic climate change, including inter alia depletion of snow, ice, and frozen ground, transformations and disappearances in plant, animal, and marine species, changes to growing seasons, and increases in forest fires, droughts, and floods (Rosenzweig *et al.* 2007). Not just the corporation's inadequately constrained search for growth and profitability, but also the increasing complexity of its production processes and products, add to the difficulty of addressing the climate change problem. For instance, road vehicles contribute to between 15 and 20% of worldwide CO_2 emissions (IEA 2009: 3, 29), but most of these come from the vehicles themselves rather than the manufacturing process, creating mobile sources of emissions that require complex coordination between vehicle engineers, fuel, and transportation infrastructures, and consumer preferences and identities if they are to be addressed.

Corporate power over the environment is also facilitated through structural power that constrains the ability of governments to regulate. This structural power includes global production networks, trade liberalization, and pressures on policy-makers for favorable regulatory standards. The pollution haven thesis, for example, posits that corporations may opt to relocate polluting production to developing countries with more favorable regulatory standards (Daly and Goodland 1994), together with more general concerns about regulatory "races to the bottom" whereby jurisdictions seeking to attract or retain corporate investment implement minimum environmental obligations or constraints on corporate behavior. Although there is evidence to substantiate both theses (cf. Konisky 2007; Spatareanu 2007), studies show evidence of "regulatory chill" (Neumayer 2001) or stagnation, as well as "races to the top" and ratcheting up of environmental standards. Prakash and Potoski's (2006) study finds, for example, that contrary to the race to the bottom thesis which emphasizes the role of structural power and capital flight risk, trade and global production networks may help to ratchet up environmental standards from importing countries to exporting countries.

Corporations have become far more directly and extensively involved in the governance of environmental issues. This can operate through ideational processes to shape governance action and inaction for the biosphere. The "Global Climate Coalition" was a coalition of various firms, engaged in discursive strategies and framings to generate public and political skepticism around the causes of climate change (Levy and Egan 2000). Similarly, several industry associations funded studies prior to the adoption of the Kyoto Protocol, highlighting profound economic effects of the protocol (Levy and Egan 1998). These efforts are an attempt to cast doubt on scientific data, and failing that, propound economic consequences of stronger regulatory obligations.

Corporations also are increasingly engaging in voluntary environmental codes of conduct, management, and production practices. These include environmental sustainability discourses and performance reporting, management practices to reduce and/or offset pollution, conformance with ISO 14001 environmental standards, and "green" (reduction of carbon footprint, retrofitting plants to environmental standards, etc.) processes and products. These can be individual programs, such as Dell Computer, which offers consumers the option of offsetting their carbon footprint when purchasing a Dell Computer by investing in their "Plant a Tree Program" (see: http://content.dell.com/us/en/corp/dell-environment.aspx). They can also involve more complex collaborations with other corporations or civil society actors, such as the Forest Stewardship Council. Voluntary initiatives are numerous and varied enough that many have collaborated through the ISEAL Alliance on a set of standards to govern their own standard-setting (see www.isealalliance.org).

While reputational factors may under some conditions provide the basis for effective voluntary standards (Prakash and Potoski 2007) they have often been seen as mere "greenwashing" ideational strategies used to deflect from more stringent regulatory obligations (Levy and Prakash 2003). The "greening" of products and processes may also, borrowing from Baudrillard's (1977) concepts of hyperreality and seduction, elicit new consumption behaviors, as consumers become drawn to environmentally "chic" products and corporations.

Corporate power also operates through objects to both generate and mitigate environmental risks and impacts. Previously mentioned objects, including industrial waste, genetically modified products, consumer goods, and production tools and technologies create risks to the biosphere. Genetic engineering can provide corporations exclusive access to the physical mechanisms that alter life-forms because of the material complexity of the science, even without intellectual property protection. Corporations, however, also create and invest in objects designed to mitigate environmental risk, such as green productive equipment and technologies (Boiral 2006; Dunn 2002; Schultz and Williamson 2005), buildings and plants (such as the Toyota and Bank of America buildings which are certified by the Green Building Council) (see: http://www.usgbc.org/) or enact changes to product specifications for renewable and/or recyclable materials and final products (Jeswani, Wehrmeyer, and Mulugetta 2008).

Conclusion

This chapter has focused on the disaggregated ways that corporations exercise power. In order to examine these we started by discussing the complexity of power, which can be more direct or structural, and which may be exercised through ideas and material objects. We then identified and analyzed five spheres in which disaggregated corporate power can be exercised. This analysis showed that the exercise of power by companies goes far beyond any narrow category of activities, such as lobbying or direct control over employees. The disaggregated exercise of corporate power can shape public policy through its influence on states, but it can also create effects that are quite independent of states, but comparable to public policies in their significance, such as when control of technologies or marketing campaigns produce major changes in a population's health that work with or against public health policy.

This power can be generated and operate at considerable distances from locations, such as a CEO's suite or an exclusive club of bankers and industrialists, from which centralized corporate power is often seen to emanate. This disaggregated corporate power is enabled by forms of power that go beyond direct commands to operate more independently through structures. However an insight from our analysis is that a sharp distinction between direct and structural power is inadequate for capturing the process of disaggregation. A direct exercise of power can shift into an embedded or automated form of power, such as when lobbying for intellectual property rules is followed by alterations of rules in a workplace or computer program. The direct exercise of power in one sphere can appear as a structural constraint in a second sphere, such as when direct efforts to control production processes creates a monopoly that constrains consumer choices.

The disaggregated operation of corporate power is also enabled by complex mixtures of ideas and objects that connect command centers with distant operations. Free-floating ideas that celebrate the superiority of business over other forms of activity may be inscribed and disseminated in documents or television scripts, but less inspiring ideas that also empower business are often also embedded in material artifacts, such as when biometrics or barcodes allow precise automated control of commercial activities with minimal human managerial presence. These mechanisms of control extend into more and more aspects of life in the five spheres we identified, such as when managerial systems go beyond the control of workers' bodies to regulate their emotions when engaging with customers.

Disaggregation poses challenges for the theorization and practical exercise of corporate power. Disaggregation extends corporate power, but complicates the relationship between its presence in any particular instance, such as the particular legal, organizational, social, cultural, and material things that together make the firm we know as Wal-Mart, and the more generalized properties of business that give it a degree of coherence, including an ability to produce and reproduce modes of thinking and behavior that sustain and reinforce the dominance of business transnationally. Today this coherence is accomplished through the types of disaggregated activities we have discussed, such as the dissemination of business-friendly ideas or the way that business associations, value chains, or other forms of networking bring business actors together. At the same time the disaggregated character of this control creates new challenges, risks, and failures in the exercise of corporate power. Failures can appear in control systems, lost court cases, ineffective lobbying, unexpected resistance from civil society, and in many other forms. The autonomy of the subsystems can lead them to go in unexpected directions, such as when digital rights management controls embedded on CDs damage customers' audio systems and damage corporate reputations, when a formerly submissive subcontractor becomes a competitor, when a malfunctioning risk model leads to bankruptcy, or when critics of business like Adbusters make use of business systems to subvert them. In studying the role of corporations in public policy, it is crucial to consider not only conventional forms of corporate power, such as lobbying, but the complex and disaggregated mechanisms that are present in the five spheres outlined in this chapter.

Notes

1 Barnett and Duvall's definition of power is useful: "power is the production, in and through social relations, of effects that shape the capacities of actors to determine their circumstances and fate" (Barnett and Duvall 2005: 8).

2 Predatory pricing is difficult to detect and its prevalence is hotly contested on theoretical and empirical grounds. Nevertheless, public authorities consider it a serious threat possibility and have developed many legal mechanisms to deter it. See for instance Organization for Economic Cooperation and Development (1989) Predatory Pricing, at http://www.oecd.org/dataoecd/7/54/2375661.pdf, accessed November 24, 2011, and Phlips and Moras (1993: 315).

3 www.sematech.org, www.eucar.be, both accessed December 19, 2012.

References

Aarvaag Stokke, T. 2008. "The Anatomy of Two-Tier Bargaining Models." *European Journal of Industrial Relations*, 14 (1): 7–24.

Arndt, S. and Kierzkowski, H. 2001. "Introduction." In *Fragmentation: New Production Patterns in the World Economy*, ed. S. Arndt and H. Kierzkowski, 1–16. Oxford: Oxford University Press

Atik, J. and Lidgard, H.H. 2006. "Embracing Price Discrimination: TRIPs and the Suppression of Parallel Trade in Pharmaceuticals." *University of Pennsylvania Journal of International Economic Law*, 27 (4): 1043–1076.

Baker, A. 2010. "Restraining Regulatory Capture? Anglo-America, Crisis Politics, and Trajectories of Change in Global Financial Governance." *International Affairs*, 86 (3): 647–663.

Barbaro, M. 2008. Home Depot Will Lay Off 500 Workers, *New York Times*, http://www.nytimes.com/2008/02/01/business/01depot.html. Accessed December 19, 2012.

Barnett, M. and Duvall, R. 2005. "Power in Global Governance." In *Power in Global Governance*, ed. M. Barnett and R. Duvall, 1–32. Cambridge: Cambridge University Press.

Baudrillard, J. 1973. *For a Critique of the Political Economy of the Sign*. St Louis: Telos Press.

Baudrillard, J. 1977. *Forget Foucault*. Paris: Éditions Galilée.

Bell, M. and Flock, E. 2011. "Zuccotti Park Evicted: Protesters Lose Right to Stay in Park with Tents." *Washington Post*, November 15.

Bislev, S. and Flyverbom, M. 2007. "Global Internet Governance: Joined-Up Powers and Perspectives." In *Critical Perspectives on Private Authority in Global Politics*, ed. H. Krause Hansen and D. Salskov-Iversen, 72–92. Basingstoke: Palgrave Macmillan.

Boiral, O. 2006. "Global Warming: Should Companies Adopt a Proactive Strategy?" *Long Range Planning*, 39 (3): 315–330.

Bourdieu, P. 1986. "The Forms of Capital." In *Handbook of Theory and Research for the Sociology of Education*, ed. J.R. Richardson, 241–258. New York: Greenwood.

Brown, E. 2006. Product Placement on the Rise in Video Games, *Forbes*, http://www.msnbc.msn.com/id/13960083/ns/technology_and_science-tech_and_gadgets/t/product-placement-rise-video-games/. Accessed December 19, 2012.

Bryant, B. 2011. Deepwater Horizon and the Gulf Oil Spill: The Key Questions Answered, *The Guardian*, http://www.guardian.co.uk/environment/2011/apr/20/deepwater-horizon-key-questions-answered. Accessed December 19, 2012.

Büthe, T. 2004. "Governance through Private Authority: Non-State Actors in World Politics [Book Review]." *Journal of International Affairs*, 58 (1): 281–290.

CBC. 2011. Competition Board Sues Real Estate Board, http://www.cbc.ca/news/business/story/2011/05/27/competition-bureau-treb.html. Accessed December 19, 2012.

Cerny, P. 1997. "Paradoxes of the Competition State: The Dynamics of Political Globalization." *Government and Opposition*, 32 (2): 251–274.

Dahl, R.A. 1957. "The Concept of Power." *Systems Research and Behavioral Science*, 2 (3): 201–215.

Daly, H. and Goodland, R. 1994. "An Ecological-Economic Assessment of Deregulation of International Commerce under GATT." *Ecological Economics*, 9: 73–92.

Deleuze, G. 1995. *Negotiations, 1972–1990*, trans. Martin Joughin. New York: Columbia University Press.

Dunn, S. 2002. "Down to Business on Climate Change: An Overview of Corporate Strategies." *Greener Management International*, 39: 27–41.

Economist. 2009. The Military-Consumer Complex: Military Technology Used to Filter Down to Consumers: Now It's Going the Other Way, *Economist*, http://www.economist.com/node/15065709. Accessed December 19, 2012.

EFF. 2011. Terms of (Ab)use, http://www.eff.org/issues/terms-of-abuse. Accessed December 19, 2012.

Ernst, D. 2004. "Global Production Networks in East Asia's Electronics Industry and Upgrading Perspectives in Malaysia. In *Global Production Networking and Technological Change in East Asia*, ed. S. Yusuf, M. Altaf, and K. Nabeshima, 89–157. Washington, DC; Oxford: World Bank, Oxford University Press.

Feige, D. 2008. Pursuing the Polluters: An Environmental Lawsuit May Open the Door for Small Countries to Take on the Multinationals. *Los Angeles Times*, April 20, http://articles.latimes.com/2008/apr/20/opinion/op-feige20. Accessed December 19, 2012.

Ferguson, G.T. 2002. "Have Your Objects Call My Objects." *Harvard Business Review*, June: 138–144.

Fuchs, D. 2007. *Business Power in Global Governance*. Boulder: Lynne Rienner.

Fuchs, D. and Lederer, M.M. 2007. "The Power of Business." *Business and Politics*, 9 (3): 1–17.

Giddens, A. 1991. *Modernity and Self-Identity: Self and Society in the Late Modern Age*. Stanford: Stanford University Press.

Gill, S. 1995. "Globalisation, Market Civilisation, and Disciplinary Neoliberalism." *Millennium*, 24: 399–423.

Gill, S. 1998. "New Constitutionalism, Democratisation and Global Political Economy." *Global Change, Peace and Security*, 10 (1): 23–38.

Gill, S. 2003. *Power and Resistance in the New World Order*. Basingstoke; New York: Palgrave Macmillan.

Gill, S. and Law, D. 1989. "Global Hegemony and the Structural Power of Capital." *International Studies Quarterly*, 33: 475–499.

Green, J. 2010. "Private Standards in the Climate Regime: The Greenhouse Gas Protocol." *Business and Politics*, 12 (3): 1–37.

Hansen, H.K. 2008. "Investigating the Disaggregation, Innovation and Mediation of Authority in Global Politics." In *Critical Perspectives on Private Authority in Global Politics*, ed. H.K. Hansen and D. Salskov-Iversen, 1–23. Basingstoke; New York: Palgrave Macmillan.

Harrison, S. 1994. "Codes of Practice and Ethics in the UK Communications Industry." *Business Ethics: A European Review*, 3: 109–116.

Hays, C.L. 2003. "Here's the Beef: So Where's the Butcher?," *New York Times* (C1), http://www.nytimes.com/2003/02/15/business/here-s-the-beef-so-where-s-the-butcher.html?pagewanted=allandsrc=pm. Accessed December 19, 2012.

Heywood, M. 2002. "Drug Access: Patents and Global Health: 'Chaffed and Waxed Sufficient.'" *Third World Quarterly*, 23 (2): 217–231.

Holger Kohl, I. 2004. "Process Benchmarking at the German Fraunhofer Information Center Benchmarking (ICB)." *Best Practice Digest*, 1–27, http://www.globalbenchmarking.org/images/stories/PDF/members/01_Best_practices/npc_icb_process_benchmarking.pdf. Accessed December 19, 2012.

IEA. 2009. *Transport, Energy and CO2: Moving Toward Sustainability*. Paris: International Energy Agency/Organization for Economic Cooperation and Development.

Jeswani, H.K., Wehrmeyer, W., and Mulugetta, Y. 2008. "How Warm Is the Corporate Response to Climate Change? Evidence from Pakistan and the UK." *Business Strategy and the Environment*, 17 (1): 46–60.

Kalleberg, A.L. 2009. "Precarious Work, Insecure Workers: Employment Relations in Transition." *American Sociological Review*, 74 (1): 1–22.

Klein, N. 2000. *No Logo: Taking Aim and the Brand Bullies*. Toronto: Vintage Canada.

Knapp, A. 2011. FoxConn to Replace Workers with Robots: Aim for One Million Robots in Three Years. *Forbes*, http://www.forbes.com/sites/alexknapp/2011/07/31/foxconn-to-replace-workers-with-robots-aim-for-one-million-robots-in-three-years/. Accessed December 19, 2012.

Knorr Cetina, K.D. 1977. "Sociality with Objects: Social Relations in Postsocial Knowledge Societies." *Theory, Culture and Society*, 14 (4): 1–30.

Kobrin, S.J. 2002. "Economic Governance in an Electronically Networked Global Economy." In *The Emergence of Private Authority and Global Governance*, ed. R.B. Hall and T.J. Biersteker, 43–75. Cambridge; New York: Cambridge University Press.

Konisky, D.M. 2007. "Regulatory Competition and Environmental Enforcement: Is There a Race to the Bottom?," *American Journal of Political Science*, 51 (4): 853–872.

Lash, S. and Urry, J. 1994. *Economies of Signs and Space*. London: Sage.

Law, J. and Hetherington, K. 2000. "Materialities, Spatialities, Globalities." In *Knowledge, Space, Economy*, ed. J. Bryson, P. Daniels, N. Henry, and J. Pollard, 34–49. London: Routledge.

Leidner, R. (1991). "Serving Hamburgers and Selling Insurance: Gender, Work, and Identity in Interactive Service Jobs." *Gender and Society*, 5 (2): 154–177.

Lessig, L. 2011. *Republic, Lost: How Money Corrupts Congress – and a Plan to Stop It*. New York: Twelve.

Levitin, A.J. 2007. "Payment Wars: The Merchant-Bank Struggle for Control of Payment Systems." *Stanford Journal of Law, Business and Finance*, 12: 425–485.

Levy, D.L. and Egan, D. 1998. "Capital Contests: National and Transnational Channels of Corporate Influence on the Climate Change Negotiations." *Politics and Society*, 26: 337–361.

Levy, D.L. and Egan, D. 2000. "Corporate Political Action in the Global Polity." In *Non-State Actors and Authority in the Global System*, ed. R. Higgott, G.R.D. Underhill, and A. Bieler. London: Routledge.

Levy, D.L. and Prakash, A. 2003. "Bargains Old and New: Multinational Corporations in Global Governance." *Business and Politics*, 5 (5): 131–150.

Lukes, S. 1974. *Power: A Radical View*. London: Macmillan Press.

Macdonald, L. 1994. "Globalising Civil Society: Interpreting International NGOs in Central America." *Millennium*, 23 (2): 267–285.

MacNeil, M. 2010. "Freedom of Association in a Free Enterprise System: Wal-Mart in Jonquière." *Canadian Labour and Employment Law Journal*, 15: 495–540.

Neill, J.D., Stovall, O.S., and Jinkerson, D.L. 2005. "A Critical Analysis of the Accounting Industry's Voluntary Code of Conduct." *Journal of Business Ethics*, 59 (1–2): 101–108.

Neumayer, E. 2001. "Do Countries Fail to Raise Environmental Standards? An Evaluation of Policy Options Addressing 'Regulatory Chill.'" *International Journal of Sustainable Development*, 4 (3): 231.

Nölke, A. 2010. "The Politics of Accounting Regulation: Responses to the Subprime Crisis." In *Global Finance in Crisis: The Politics of International Regulatory Change*, ed. E. Helleiner, 37–55. New York: Routledge.

Pattberg, P.H. and Stripple, J. 2008. "Beyond the Public and Private Divide: Remapping Transnational Climate Governance in the 21st Century." *International Environmental Agreements: Politics, Law and Economics*, 8 (4): 367–388.

Payne, D. and Dimanche, F. 1996. "Towards a Code of Conduct for the Tourism Industry: An Ethics Model." *Journal of Business Ethics*, 15 (9): 997–1007.

Phlips, Louis and Moras, Ireneo Miguel. (1993) "The Akzo Decision: A Case of Predatory Pricing?" *Journal of Industrial Economics*, 41 (3): 315.

Plank, L., Staritz, C., and Lukas, K. 2009. Labour Rights in Global Production Networks: An Analysis of the Apparel and Electronics Sector in Romania, http://www.arbeiterkammer.at/bilder/d103/LabourRights.pdf. Accessed December 19, 2012.

Porter, T. 1999. "Hegemony and the Private Governance of International Industries." In *Private Authority and International Affairs*, ed. A.C. Cutler, V. Haufler, and T. Porter, 257–281. Albany: SUNY.

Porter, T. 2008. "Disaggregating Authority in Global Governance." In *Critical Perspectives on Private Authority in Global Politics*, ed. H.K. Hansen and D. Salskov-Iversen, 27–50. Basingstoke; New York: Palgrave Macmillan.

Prakash, A. and Potoski, M. 2006. "Racing to the Bottom? Trade, Environmental Governance, and ISO 14001." *American Journal of Political Science*, 50 (2): 350–364.

Prakash, A. and Potoski, M. 2007. "Collective Action through Voluntary Environmental Programs: A Club Theory Perspective." *Policy Studies Journal*, 35 (4): 773–792.

Reich, R. 2007. *Supercapitalism: The Transformation of Business, Democracy, and Everyday Life*. New York: Knopf.

Reuters. 2011. Chevron Ordered to Pay $8 Billion by Ecuador Court, *Los Angeles Times*, February 14, http://articles.latimes.com/2011/feb/14/business/la-fi-chevron-20110214. Accessed December 19, 2012.

Rosenzweig, C., Casassa, G., Karoly, D.G., Imeson, A., Liu, C., Menzel, A., *et al.* 2007. "Assessment of Observed Changes and Responses in Natural and Managed Systems." In *Climate Change 2007: Impacts, Adaptation and Vulnerability. Contribution of Working Group II to the Fourth Assessment Report of the Intergovernmental Panel on Climate Change*, ed. M.L. Parry *et al.*, 79–131. Cambridge: Cambridge University Press.

Roustan, M. 2009. "From Embodied Ethnography to the Anthropology of Material Culture: Gaming in the Field." In *Material Culture and Technology in Everyday Life: Ethnographic Approaches*, ed. P. Vannini, 89–100. New York: Peter Lang.

Salter, L. 1999. "The Standards Regime for Communication and Information Technologies." In *Private Authority and International Affairs*, ed. A.C. Cutler, V. Haufler, and T. Porter, 97–127. Albany: SUNY.

Schultz, K. and Williamson, P. 2005. "Gaining Competitive Advantage in a Carbon-Constrained World: Strategies for European Business." *European Management Journal*, 23 (4): 383–391.

Schwartz, N.D. 2011. Online Banking Keeps Customers on Hook for Fees, *New York Times*, http://www.nytimes.com/2011/10/16/business/online-banking-keeps-customers-on-hook-for-fees.html?pagewanted=all. Accessed December 19, 2012.

Slaughter, A.M. 2004. "Disaggregated Sovereignty: Towards the Public Accountability of Global Government Networks." *Government and Opposition*, 39 (2): 122–155.

Spar, D.L. 1999. "Lost in (Cyber)Space: The Private Rules of Online Commerce." In *Private Authority and International Affairs*, ed. A.C. Cutler, V. Haufler, and T. Porter, 31–51. Albany: SUNY.

Spatareanu, M. 2007. "Searching for Pollution Havens." *The Journal of Environment and Development*, 16 (2): 161–182.

Strange, S. 1990. "Finance, Information and Power." *Review of International Studies*, 16: 259–274.

t'Hoen, E. 2009. *The Global Politics of Pharmaceutical Monopoly Power: Drug Patents, Access, Innovation and the Application of the WTO Doha Declaration on TRIPS and Public Health*. Diemen: AMB.

Zoomers, A. 2010. "Globalisation and the Foreignisation of Space: Seven Processes Driving the Current Global Land Grab." *Journal of Peasant Studies*, 37 (2): 429–447.

Chapter 7

How Governments Mediate the Structural Power of International Business

Stephen Bell

Introduction

The last few decades have witnessed an unprecedented spread of international business in an age of "globalization," marked by the hyper-mobility of multinational corporations and footloose business investment, the astonishing growth and spread of international financial markets, and the rapid emergence and integration of emerging market economies, including those from former communist regimes. All this suggests the rising power and influence of business interests. Ironically, however, serious examination of key questions about the clout of business investors and about business power has been all too limited in recent decades. As Hacker and Pierson (2002: 277) suggest, "with the growing interest in 'the state' and institutions, the debate over business power essentially ended." Indeed, Culpepper (2011: 185) has noted that "the study of business power is currently more neglected than it has been for the last half century" (see also Fuchs 2005).

True, a debate developed during the 1990s about the impacts of "globalization," with many analysts arguing that governments have been forced to offer "business friendly" policies in order to attract or hold business or financial market investment (Gill and Law 1989; Gill 2003). The implication here is that capital mobility had increased the power of business and financial interests and markedly reduced the policy discretion of national governments (Ohmae 1995; Strange 1996). A counter response has since argued that states in fact still have considerable policy discretion and that the alleged dominance of mobile business interests had been exaggerated (Weiss 1998; Mosley 2003; Garrett 1998; Bell 2005). This detour into the realm of globalization, however, tended to focus on the structure of the world economy and the policy capacities of national states, with less attention to the precise dynamics of business power.

The Handbook of Global Companies, First Edition. Edited by John Mikler.
© 2013 John Wiley & Sons, Ltd. Published 2013 by John Wiley & Sons, Ltd.

A re-examination of the power of business interests in national and international settings is thus overdue. Such power is usually understood in at least three ways. First, business interests attempt to exert influence through lobbying, public relations campaigns, supporting political parties or candidates, and other forms of overt political activism (Lindblom 1977). Second, and relatedly, business interests can wield ideas and shape public discourse to further their interests. Indeed, in liberal systems, prevailing ideas and discourses, about, for example, the virtues of private property or markets typically support business interests (Fuchs and Lederer 2007). This chapter however focuses on a third dimension of business power – the "structural" power of business. This is a form of power that derives from business's structural position and distinctive role in a capitalist economy. Business interests own and control most of the economy in a liberal capitalist system. Important decisions about innovation, the allocation of resources, investment, and employment are thus largely in the hands of business leaders. In the classic argument, business interests have structural power because governments and the wider society depend on the investment decisions and other activities by business to sustain a healthy economy, jobs growth, government tax revenues, etc. In an early statement Lindblom (1977; 1982) argued that business interests have a "privileged position" in politics and that the market system was akin to a "prison" radically limiting the policy options available to governments. The strength of such arguments is that they highlight the state's broad dependence on the aggregate results of capitalist economic activity. The clear implication of such a division of responsibilities between government and business is that governments will face strong incentives to adopt business friendly policies and/or to keep policies distasteful to business off the political agenda (Crenson 1971). A generalized loss of "business confidence" is something that governments typically seek to avoid. Disinvestment, capital flight, and a faltering economy are a high price to pay for policies which undermine business confidence. This effect is increased by capital mobility and competition between states for mobile investment in an increasingly globalized world. Moreover, the structural power instrument is distinctive in that it does not necessarily require overt political activism on the part of business to be effective. As Hacker and Pierson (2002: 281) point out: "This power is structural because the pressure to protect business interests is generated automatically and apolitically." It results from private, individual investment decisions taken by thousands of enterprises, rather than from any organized effort to influence policy-makers. As Hall (1986: 274) explains:

> The conjunction of a liberal democratic polity and a capitalist economy confers an unusual degree of systemic power on capital. Their power is systemic in the sense that capitalists need not take concerted action to actualize it. Timely reminders from the spokesman for business are never amiss, but structural incentives, already apparent to politicians, tend to discourage them from pursuing policies that might endanger investment, even in the absence of collective action on the part of capital.

It is not hard to find evidence of the structural power of business interests. Governments routinely worry about financial market reactions to macroeconomic policy settings. They are also faced with actual or potential threats of disinvestment or capital flight if their policies do not satisfy business policy demands (Crenson 1971).

In extreme cases, whole economies can be decimated by capital flight, as occurred in a number of countries during the Asian financial crisis of the late 1990s.

Notwithstanding the obvious importance of these arguments, a well-known criticism of the structural power thesis is that they are too "structuralist," implying a world of limited options for governments and overweening notions of business supremacy. Such a theory cannot explain cases where governments stand up to business pressures. More generally, a critical deficiency in such structuralist accounts is their limited focus on *agency*, especially on the part of governments. After all, it is governments and state leaders who must confront, interpret, and react to business pressures.

A key argument of this chapter is that the agency of governments and state leaders can matter a great deal in such structural power contexts. The chapter shows how by exploring sophisticated contemporary understandings of agent–structure interaction in this context, arguing that the exercise of structural power is not about the imposition of power from above but is instead best seen as the outcome of a *relationship* between actors with differing attributes and capacities. In unpacking agency in this manner we focus on how state actors operate with a degree of discretion in such settings, being shaped by but also potentially shaping wider structural environments. In particular, it is useful to explore the way in which state leaders use ideas and inter-subjective understandings to appraise and navigate the environments they confront. Here contemporary constructivist approaches are helpful. Structural power arguments say very little about how target governments and state leaders perceive and interpret business power challenges. This is a big gap because perceptions about power on the part of target agents and the changing ideas and contexts that inform such perceptions actually matter in shaping such power.

Most accounts of the relationship between power and ideas argue that power shapes ideas and helps constitute forms of domination. Arguments such as Lukes's (1974) "third face" of power point to the way in which power is exercised through preference shaping. Gramscian arguments about ideological hegemony are somewhat similar (Cox 1987). According to these approaches ideas have a causal force in the service of power. For example, in recent strands of constructivist political economy, scholars have explored how government leaders confronting either real or perceived threats from globalization, such as capital flight, are potentially capable of constructing their own policy straitjackets, reflecting prevailing discourses about the impacts of globalization (see, for example, Rosamond 1999; Watson and Hay 2003; Hay and Rosamond 2002; Hay 2006a; 2006b; Hay and Smith 2005). Hence, if policy-makers believe their tax rates or labor standards are internationally "uncompetitive" they may act to effect pre-emptive change, irrespective of any real or immediate impacts from globalization. In this sense, ideas can have real effects and the impacts of globalization become almost a self-fulfilling reflex. If policy-makers believe a "golden straitjacket" exists, then, in effect, it exists. The argument from these constructivists is that ideas mediate and can indeed magnify the power of capital, a view that is consistent with wider constructivist arguments about the ideational shaping of agents and the ideational construction of reality (Onuf 1989; Adler 1997; Ruggie 1998; Abdelal *et al.* 2010).

This chapter is consistent with such an approach and agrees with the constructivist globalization scholars above in suggesting that ideas can mediate power. However, instead of amplifying power, this chapter uses two case studies to show how the structural power of international business was *reduced* through the ideational constructions adopted by government leaders in particular contexts. Hence, instead of power shaping ideas, it is ideas that shaped power. This ideational shaping is quite consistent with constructivist thinking, but it has been underexplored in the literature, especially in relation to questions regarding the power of business interests. The chapter also goes further than at least some strands of constructivist thinking in arguing that agents and their ideas and constructions of reality are heavily mediated by institutional and material contexts.

All this suggests that the structural power of business in liberal capitalist settings is not automatic. Instead it can be shaped and mediated by the ideas and conceptions held by key agents, such as state leaders, depending on how they assess the relative costs and benefits of particular relations with business and how such relations are interpreted and assessed. This explanatory logic implies greater attention to agency. It can help us explain the ideational mediation of the structural power of business and how and why such power varies (Vogel 1983; Hacker and Pierson 2002).

The chapter first briefly reviews relevant debates about the structural power of business and shows how these lack a detailed account of agency. Then, it is shown how insights from contemporary constructivist research and agency/structure debates can help deepen our understanding of how state leaders respond to the structural power of business. This approach is then illustrated using empirical evidence from Australia and United Kingdom. The Australian case illustrates how the ideas of policy-makers reduced the structural power of international currency markets in the late 1990s amidst pressure on the Australian dollar and impacts from the Asian financial crisis. The second case illustrates how ideation revision on the part of the UK policy-makers allowed government to defy the demands of major international banks and City financial interests and press ahead with significant and much resisted banking reform in the wake of the recent financial meltdown.

Structural Power Arguments and the Question of Agency

Arguments about the structural power of business have typically been pitched at a high level of abstraction and have often had little to say about the details of interactions between structures and relevant agents. This is an important lacuna because, as argued more fully below and illustrated empirically, structural power relations are always mediated and actualized by agents. This is why Lindblom's generalized claim that the capitalist market amounts to a policy prison (Lindblom 1982) cannot fully explain the comparative diversity of business–government relations under different types of capitalist systems: a research agenda now embodied in the Varieties of Capitalism approach (Hall and Soskice 2001). Nor can Lindblom's approach explain how governments periodically triumph over business opposition. This question has occasioned responses mainly from Weberian "statist" scholars who have been keen to show that the state's authority and institutional capacities can potentially counter or mediate the power of business interests. Skocpol's (1980) analysis of the bold policy-making in the American New Deal in the face of widespread business opposition is a good case in point. Arguments about the historical variability of business power have also been explored in the work of David Vogel (1983; 1987; 1989). In a research program explicitly designed to challenge "static" conceptions of business power (such as Lindblom's), Vogel sets out to explain the political ascendency of American social reformism in the late 1960s and early 1970s in the face of widespread business opposition. A key explanation, Vogel argues, involved the organizational weakness of business during this period, as well as the way in which prosperous national economic conditions reduced the public and policy-makers' concerns about levels of business investment. As Vogel (1983: 42) states in a key passage:

> Seen from this perspective, Lindblom is partially correct; business is in a uniquely privileged position to persuade the public that the satisfaction of its demands is essential if high growth rates are to be restored. But there is nothing automatic about this business confidence weapon... it is apt to have limited political significance in a relatively prosperous period.

A further refinement is to connect detailed institutionalist analysis to arguments about structural power. For example, Hacker and Pierson (2002) argue that the structural shifts wrought by the Depression of the 1930s helped the consolidation of the state at the national level in the United States. The shift from a decentralized state to a more centralized one reduced the structural power of business interests that had hitherto exploited a key resource, capital mobility, or the ability to play off state governments against each other in their efforts to attract footloose business investment. As these scholars show, the "structural power of business will increase in decentralized federal systems" (2002: 282). Smith's (1999; 2000) evidence from the United States also suggests that institutional incentives, such as electoral pressures on governments in high stakes contests, can override the need to secure business investment, even during economic downturns. The business world can also remain opaque to government decision-makers, and, in such a situation, as Crouch (1979: 43) argues; uncertainty and ambiguity can increase the discretionary power of government:

> The state in a capitalist society will always be responsive to the interests of capital, but it may do so with varying degrees of precision and vary in its responsiveness to capital's interpretation of its own needs. For example, it may always be the case that governments must acknowledge capital's concern about the impact of taxation levels on the incentive to invest, but given the difficulties of acquiring firm knowledge of the precise relationships involved, there is always an area for *discretion* in the extent to which governments *take seriously* industry's complaints (emphasis added).

Similar points about agency, the role of perceptions and the potential discretion of government policy-makers have also been made by Hacker and Pierson (2002: 282) when they argue that government fears about potential disinvestment "will depend on how credible policy-makers believe the threat to be" (see also Smith 1999: 861; Barry 2002: 179).

These revisionist studies all hint that agency matters and that the ideas and attitudes of government policy-makers are a potentially important factor in mediating the structural power of business. Thus far, however, such agency-based dynamics have not been explored in sufficient depth. Relatively crude or aggregated notions of the structural power of business tend to black box the state, as well as details about the agency of state leaders. Clearly, it would be useful to understand more about how state policy-makers actually appraise and interpret the structural power of business in particular contexts. As Blyth (2003) puts it, "structures do not come with an instruction sheet"; implying that the meaning and ramifications of structural dynamics need to be worked out "on the ground" by relevant agents. Indeed, as Hacker and Pierson (2002: 282) suggest, "structural power is a signaling device: by itself it does not indicate policy choices" (p. 282). Hence, what government policy-makers actually think and the inter-subjective contexts in which they operate is a crucial part of the equation.

Based on such reasoning we can define the structural power of business as working through the real or potential benefits or costs of real or threatened business activities in relation to state actors who must *perceive* such benefits, costs, or threats as significant and meaningful. To understand their interests and the meaning of things, agents rely on ideas, interpretation, and inter-subjective understandings. Hence, power is not just an objective condition but is also shaped subjectively and inter-subjectively; it is a relational artifact, produced and mediated through social and ideational realms. All this points to the importance of constructivist theory.

Constructivism and Institutionalism

According to constructivists, *ideas shape or constitute the situation or context of action*. Constructivists also argue that *ideas also shape or constitute agents themselves*, especially their interests, preferences, and identities. Constructivism varies. There are post-modern approaches, which argue that ideas *fully constitute* the situation or context of action and also *fully constitute* agents themselves. Alternatively, there is a "modern" constructivist approach in which ideas are not fully primitive and where the external material world is assumed to exist in some "real" manner. Adler (1997) calls this the "middle ground" between rationalism and the fully interpretivist position of post-modernism. It is an approach in which ideas mediate the relationship between agents and material reality and where the latter is accepted as "real" or efficacious. Here ideas or "collective understandings, such as norms, endow physical objects with meaning or purpose and therefore *help* constitute reality" (Adler 1997: 324) (my emphasis). In other words, there is "a real world out there" that matters (Adler 1997: 324), albeit one that is interpreted using ideas. This approach recognizes that ideas, language, and discourse provide crucial building-blocks for establishing meaning and understanding and thus of purposeful action in politics and institutional life. This is essentially the type of "modern" constructivist stance adopted here.

Constructivists also typically wish to engage with the structure–agency debate, often endorsing a dialectical approach, arguing that "agents and structures are mutually constituted" (Price and Rues-Smit 1998: 267; Finnemore and Sikkink 2001: 393). Agents are thus embedded within an ideational realm, but importantly, agents are also shaped by wider institutional and structural environments. As Price and Reus-Smit (1998: 266) argue, "systems of meaning define how actors interpret their material environment." Ideas and inter-subjective understandings play a central role in mediating reality (social or material) and as mediating between agents and the world "out there"; a world which has ramifications for human action and, importantly, which can change in ways which help re-shape ideas and interpretations.

In order to better understand how institutionally-situated agents operate, we need the resources of institutional theory, and here an agency-based form of historical institutionalism is used (Bell 2011). Institutions and structures matter because of the ways they reflect, refract, restrain, and enable human behavior, whilst in turn, it is the behavior of agents that reproduces or transforms institutions and structures over time. Institutions are ontologically prior to the individuals who populate them at any given time. The temporal dimension is important here. Institutions have properties that help structure thought and behavior at one remove from the immediacy of thought or action by agents at any given point in time. Institutions can thus shape or even impose behavior. This is what gives institutions causal properties and why at bottom we pursue institutional analysis. Hence, at one level, institutional or structural environments are analytically distinguishable from agents and are "out there" to the extent that they are not just constituted by real time subjective ideational construction. Institutional or structural environments can exert real (though always interpreted) effects by imposing costs or benefits on agents, by shaping actor interpretations and preferences, the scope of "bounded discretion" of agents in institutional life, and the resources and opportunities that are available to actors.

Institutions and structures are often conflated by analysts. However, it is useful to distinguish between agents, institutions, and structures. Institutions can be defined as rules, norms, or operating procedures that shape agents' behavior whilst structures can be defined as wider economic, social, or political forces that shape both agents and institutions. For example, Australia's changing terms of trade can be thought of in such structural terms and below it is shown how this shaped the behavior of agents within institutions, such as the Reserve Bank of Australia (RBA). Structures operate in a "strategically selective" manner, establishing incentives or disincentives or other rationales that may lead agents to favor certain developments or choices over others (Hay 1996; Jessop 1990). Because structural factors are typically the result of embedded historical processes they arguably form a broader background context in which specific institutions operate.

In dealing with the dialectical interactions between agents, institutions, and structures, the approach here follows the work of Archer (1995: 2003) and (a) models agents, institutions, and structures as being analytically distinct in the sense that each has properties that are not simply reducible to the other at any given point in time; (b) models agents as operating in institutional and structural contexts that are pre-given at any given point in time; (c) models agents, institutions, and structures as operating in a dialectical, mutually constitutive relationship over time; and (d) sees institutional and structural effects as ultimately mediated and actualized by agency (for a fuller discussion see Bell 2011). The account being developed here thus has situated agents as a key component of the analysis, albeit agents who are dialectically engaged in shaping and being shaped by their relevant contexts over time.

Australian Economic Policy and the Power of Financial Markets

The case study in this section empirically illustrates the theoretical claims above, particularly the way in which structures and agents mutually interact, with agents mediating and actualizing structures and with structures helping to shape the ideas and the scope of bounded discretion available to actors. The intervening role of institutions in mediating such dialectics between agents and structures is also illustrated. Such an empirical illustration of the role of ideas in shaping and being shaped by structural elements is central to a dialectical understanding of the relations between agents and structures. The arguments presented also question the widespread interpretation of power as something which simply shapes or conditions ideas and behavior as part of wider processes of domination or hegemony. Instead it shows how changing ideas and perceptions can also shape or constitute forms of power, in this case the structural power of financial markets. The account shows how changing structural conditions in the Australian economy during the 1980s and 1990s, especially improving terms of trade, encouraging policy-makers to revise their perceptions of vulnerability regarding Australia's current account deficit. This in turn saw a revision of threat perceptions regarding the possibility of a currency sell-off, a major weapon wielded by financial markets. The net effect was that changing institutional and structural conditions in the economy helped change policy-makers' perceptions about the structural power of financial markets, culminating in a showdown during the Asian financial crisis in 1998 when the Reserve Bank and wider authorities weathered a currency sell-off and stood up to the financial markets.

The Australian government had floated the dollar in 1983. Despite the fact that the institutional and policy regime had been altered fundamentally by the float, the mindset of the policy authorities remained locked in a prior era of fixation on activist management of the current account and the value of the currency. This fixation was primarily driven by the fear of a falling dollar if financial markets lost confidence in domestic policy settings and the management of Australia's relatively high current account deficit (CAD). By 1985–1986 amidst falling terms of trade and a rising CAD this scenario began to unfold as market reactions produced a substantial depreciation of the dollar. This culminated in the current account crisis of July 1986; one that prompted the then Treasurer, Paul Keating, to proclaim that Australia could become a "banana republic" if solutions were not found. As one leading journalist recalls:

> The currency crisis hit Australia on Monday 28 July when ministers were finalizing the budget. [Treasurer] Keating had his little Reuters screen on the Cabinet table and kept pointing to the falling $A rate. An exchange rate of US 60 cents was seen as a psychological barrier but on this day the dollar fell from around 63 to 57.2 cents. The slide was only arrested by Reserve Bank intervention. The Cabinet was infiltrated with a distinct mood of panic. Keating's banana republic warning never seemed so real . . . It is doubtful if any budget meeting in the last twenty-five years has ever been subjected to such pressure. (Kelly 1992: 220)

To appease the markets, both fiscal and monetary policies had been targeting the CAD (Bell 2004: 54). The current account crisis of 1986 saw a tough restrictionist policy stance with official interest rates jacked up to 19%. After a fortuitous soft landing in 1987, interest rates were raised again to similar levels in 1989 amidst a surging post-financial deregulation asset price boom and further pressure on the CAD. In August 1990, Reserve Bank Governor Bernie Fraser devoted an entire speech to affirming the commitment to tackle the CAD, arguing that worsening current accounts and growing external debt made Australia excessively vulnerable to adverse market reaction. "Confidence, as we all know, is a fragile thing," he warned: "Even countries without large foreign debts can be subject to adverse re-assessments by international markets" (1990: 13). As it eventuated, the high interest rates of 1989 led to a deep policy-induced recession in the early 1990s.

In the intense policy debates that had led up to the float of the Australian dollar in the early 1980s, the then head of the federal Treasury had argued that relinquishing control over the exchange rate would be an excessive gift of power to the markets. And in the 1980s, as just outlined, the policy authorities thought and acted in a way which fully recognized and underlined such market power. This is an object lesson in the way in which ideas and wider structures interacted; shaping a policy mindset that was focused on the value of the dollar and fixated on market reactions, even amidst the newly created floating rate regime. Hence, the ideas and mindsets of policy-makers placed them in a situation where they were highly vulnerable to the sentiments of financial markets and their structural power.

Crucially however, this mindset changed substantially during the 1990s. First, the experience of the policy-induced recession of the early 1990s proved that using official interest rates to fight the CAD was an uncertain and risky business with huge downside risks. This had a sobering effect on policy-makers and helped shape a policy rethink. Second, a senior economist, John Pitchford (1989) suggested that the authorities should simply stop worrying about the CAD. Pitchford argued the CAD was driven primarily by *private* external debt obligations that were largely servicing productive domestic investment and that the authorities should not be trying to second-guess such market outcomes or potential market reactions to them. Pitchford's sanguine "consenting adults" view about external private debt and the CAD also reflected the increasing salience of neoliberal views about markets and economic policy; views that were becoming increasingly influential in the top policy circle in Canberra and at the RBA in Sydney (Pusey 1991; Bell 1997). In fact, the RBA led the push to revise official thinking. As the Bank's then Deputy-Governor put it, the "mindset" within the Bank began to change (Bell 2004: 67). The RBA finally convinced Keating, who became Prime Minister in late 1991, to stop fixating on the CAD.

Third, by the mid-1990s, important structural and institutional shifts were also occurring in the Australian economy, which further helped entrench this new mind-set. Most importantly, there was a shift towards far stronger terms of trade for Australia as commodity exports (especially to a booming China) strengthened. This was enough to reverse a process of declining terms of trade that had been underway for decades in Australia. It was a profound structural shift that further emboldened policy-makers regarding the CAD and was a further strong facilitator in helping to alter mindsets and the stance of economic policy. Indeed, even during episodes when the CAD rose to historically high levels during the 1990s, the policy authorities remained sanguine, pointing out that mounting debt servicing obligations could be handled by rising export incomes and the new strength of Australia's terms of trade. There were also a series of major institutional and associated structural changes in the economy that were also important. Institutionally, there were major reforms in tariff protection, the labor market, and other areas of microeconomic reform that led to structural economic changes, including increased productivity growth and greater flexibility in the economy which also reduced the "pass through" effects of exchange rate changes on domestic prices and inflation. Together with the lower levels of inflation after the early 1990s recession, these changes meant that the economy was in a far stronger position to flexibly absorb changes (even large changes) in the exchange rate. These institutional and structural changes in turn helped reshape mindsets about policy and emboldened policy-makers. Crucially, the lowering of concerns about the CAD during the 1990s placed the government and the authorities in a new and more authoritative position in relation to the financial markets. Finally, after many years, the full ramifications of the floating rate regime and new perceptions about the CAD were filtering through, helping to alter the power landscape in which policy-makers and the markets operated.

This new relationship was illustrated graphically during the Asian financial crisis of 1997–1998, which in effect proved to be a contest between the authorities (especially at the RBA, though supported by the government) and global currency markets. In the context of the Asian crisis, the RBA's leaders developed novel interpretations and exercised policy discretion. Market concerns about the potential fallout of the crisis in Australia, particularly on the export front, were reflected in a rapidly depreciating currency. The Bank's leaders could have attempted to defend the currency, ward off potential imported inflation, and attempt to appease the markets by adopting higher interest rates, but they chose not to (Bell 2005). In contrast to the more orthodox approach of defending the currency through higher interest rates, as adopted in New Zealand (and which led to a domestic recession), the RBA held its nerve and essentially defied the markets. In fact the Bank was well aware that a good deal of the market making was the result of aggressive, speculative action by hedge funds that had already wreaked havoc in East Asia. The RBA's leaders were anxious not to see this happen in Australia and were keen to stand up to the hedge funds and their efforts at short-selling the dollar. As it eventuated the RBA's views about the economy's strong fundamentals prevailed and the hedge funds lost their bets. Crucially, interest rates were not raised during the crisis and domestic growth and employment were protected. John Edwards, a wellknown Sydney-based economist comments that the RBA's Governor Macfarlane did well: "A more easily rattled Governor, someone with less monetary experience, someone with more reliance on models and theories and less on accumulated wisdom, would quite easily have cost Australia billions of dollars in lost output and a hundred thousand jobs" (quoted in Burrell 1999). Hence the Bank's responses cushioned the impact on the domestic economy and absorbed the short-term shock on the exchange rate. This is exactly the flexible response that a floating rate regime is supposed to facilitate, but it had taken fifteen years since the dollar float for this mindset to be fully worked through and expressed in policy behavior.

Overall, then, changing institutional and structural conditions in the economy, the institutional capacities of the RBA, and new policy mindsets amongst key agents were important in mediating the relations between agents and structures, in helping to empower the bank, and in helping to moderate the power of the financial markets at key moments. This case shows how the ideas and perceptions of policy-makers were heavily shaped not just by particular ideational innovations but also by changing institutional and structural contexts. By the late 1990s the mindsets of the policy authorities, in contrast to the 1980s, had arrived at a point where their changing conceptions and attitudes to the CAD and the dollar had effectively reshaped power relationships with financial markets, allowing a greater degree of "relative autonomy" from market pressures. To be sure, Governor Macfarlane (1992: 16) had recognized that "the financial markets set a corridor in which monetary policy can act," but it is still the case that policy-makers were actively engaged in consciously pushing the discretionary policy envelope; further illustrating the role of ideas and agency in appraising and in navigating a path through complex structural environments (Bell 2005).

How the UK Government Withstood the Structural Power of the City

In this second case example, we again use the theoretical approach outlined, but this time we use it to analyze and explain how the UK government was able to withstand the structural power of the banks and London's financial interests – the City – amidst the politics of banking sector reform in the wake of the 2008 banking and financial meltdown. In the wake of the crisis that had decimated the UK banking system and seen massive government bailouts, the government pursued a substantial reform agenda and, in particular, endorsed the far-reaching reforms set out by the Independent Commission on Banking in its final September 2011 report. The government has thus far withstood a concerted campaign by the banks to water down the reform measures. It has not been cowed by classic structural power threats from the banks about credit impairment or threats to move offshore, and has moved ahead and formulated its own response to banking reform. Crucially, its approach has been shaped and mediated by beliefs that the threats of the banks are not credible and that, contrary to calls from the banks, far reaching reform will actually strengthen rather than weaken the banking and financial sector. Amidst this battle and amidst the material shifts wrought by the crisis, the hand of the government has also been strengthened because the institutional context of the bank-government relationship has also changed. Banking regulation has been dragged from the informal and cloistered world of "quiet" politics analyzed by Culpepper (2011) into the glare of a highly politicized arena involving aggressive new actors in government and the regulatory sphere armed with new ideas that are far more skeptical and critical of the City than was the case prior to the crisis.

In the immediate wake of the banking crisis, banks and financial sector lobby groups had warned about "excessive" or "draconian" additional regulations on banking and finance. The Labour government under Gordon Brown seemed overwhelmed by the crisis and took only minimal reform steps. Indeed, Labour's Chancellor, Alistair Darling (2009), expressed his "determination" to work with the banking sector to "maintain the United Kingdom's position as the world centre for financial services." Frustrated, the Governor of the Bank of England, Mervyn King, criticized the UK banking sector as being "too big" (2009a), and in October (2009b) he gave a speech containing some entirely un-coded attacks on elected politicians, publicly expressing mounting frustration with the banks and the government by telling his audience that: "never in the field of financial endeavor has so much money been owed by so few to so many. *And, one might add, so far with little real reform*" (emphasis added). Johal, Moran, and Williams (2012) argue the government's timid responses reflected the power of the "traditional narrative" about the central role of finance in the UK economy and the "reassertion of City power."

Nevertheless, the reform debate continued, fueled by what the *Economist* (2011a) called "the still seething public anger" over the crisis and the bailouts. This eventually proved crucial in changing the political and institutional terrain of banking politics in the United Kingdom. In a recent comparative study, Culpepper (2011) found that changes in such terrains, particularly the level of political salience and the degree of institutional formality or informality, can have a marked effect on business power. Culpepper distinguishes between open and highly politicized policy arenas which actively engage politicians and voters and compares these to more cloistered and informal arenas of "quiet" politics. The latter are marked by low visibility, technical complexity, and informality; arenas where the business resources of focused lobbying, networking, and expertise have often paid off. This of course is a perfect description of the long-standing traditions of "quiet" politics surrounding bank regulation in the United Kingdom, where regulatory relations were constructed in a cloistered world well beyond the public gaze, where the supposedly expert judgments, technical acumen, and market efficiency of bankers were largely accepted by the authorities and where the latter trusted the former to be prudent. Such an environment of institutional informality, expertise, and trust gave bankers and financiers a great deal of discretion, facilitated the tradition of "light touch" regulation, and provided ample room for byzantine forms of financial innovation.

As we now know, the latter proved to be very costly. Amidst the ensuing financial and economic crisis, the political and institutional context rapidly shifted, catapulting bankers and regulators into the full glare of a highly politicized and hostile environment. Smith's research on business politics in the United States suggests that business power can decline substantially in such highly politicized contexts where government leaders often face strong electoral pressures that may not align with business preferences (Smith 2000). This scenario did not initially unfold in the United Kingdom, because the Labour government continued to support the City. However, as the scale of the economic fallout from the crisis became more obvious and in the face of growing public anger over the bank bailouts, the Labour government was defeated in the 2010 general election. The incoming Coalition government, partly for electoral advantage and partly because of pressure from its coalition partners, adopted a more aggressive reform stance, championed not least by Liberal Democrat Vince Cable, the new Business Secretary, who was highly critical of the banks. This was a new form of electoral contingency that punctured the cloistered world of British finance. The City was now confronted by a more critical and assertive government and Bank of England and by hostile voters.

In this new political and institutional context, banking policy has shifted substantially. Shortly after taking office, the new government moved to abolish the largely discredited regulator, the Financial Services Authority (FSA) and repudiate the previous tradition of "light touch" regulation. Regulatory power was shifted to the Bank of England. But the changing dynamics of the relationship between government and the banks is most clearly revealed in the Coalition government's reaction to the recommendations made by the Independent Commission on Banking (ICB), headed by Sir John Vickers. The ICB was established at the insistence of the Liberal Democrats during their negotiations to join a governing coalition with the Conservatives and was established in June 2010 to "consider the structure of the UK banking sector, and look at structural and non-structural measures to reform the banking system and promote competition" (ICB 2011a). In its interim report published in April 2011 and in its final report published in September 2011 the ICB proposed institutionally separating, that is "ring fencing," normal high street or retail banking from riskier investment banking activities (ICB 2011b). Ring fencing aims to isolate risky investment banking activities from implied government bailouts, reduce risk-taking within investment banks, and help to deal with the "too big to fail" problem. Ring-fenced high-street banks could be self-standing, or subsidiary companies in wider banking groups. They would have their own capital, a separate board of directors and be constituted as a distinct legal entity. The retail entity will thus be required to be operationally separable from the other entities within its banking group to ensure that it would be able to continue providing services irrespective of the financial health of the rest of the group. The *Financial Times* has argued that the ICB was proposing the "biggest shake-up of British banking in a generation" (Goff 2011). Chancellor George Osborne described the final ICB report as an "impressive piece of work" and crucially the government has committed to implement its recommendations (quoted in Parker 2011).

Prior to the release of the ICB's final report, amidst frenzied lobbying, the banks argued that ring-fencing would threaten UK banking and the City's role as a global financial center. They also argued that new regulation would raise the costs of credit, reduce the supply of credit available to UK businesses, and threaten economic recovery. Because of its high level of investment banking activities, Barclays, squarely in the firing line of the reforms, argued in a submission to the ICB that "a major and unilateral change to the structure of UK banks would simply lead to a reduction in the competitiveness of the UK banking industry." Lloyds (2010) similarly argued that the proposed changes "would lead to a much-reduced availability of credit to households and small businesses." There were also warnings that the Euro-crisis made it unwise to pursue bank reform, with John Cridland, the head of the Confederation of British Industry (CBI), arguing that "taking action at this moment – this moment of growth peril, which weakens the ability of banks in Britain to provide the finance that businesses need to grow – is just, to me, barking mad" (quoted in Wachman and Curtis 2011). The lobbying was also fueled by analysts' reports that ring-fencing would jeopardize the profitability of the banks and lead to job losses. There were also ongoing rumors that HSBC and Standard Charter were considering moving their headquarters and stock market listing from the United Kingdom to, respectively, Hong Kong and Singapore, and that Barclays was also planning to move parts of its operations offshore (Jenkins, Goff, and Parker 2011; Griffiths 2011).

To be sure, the proposed reforms fall short of requiring a formal separation of ownership, reflect a degree of compromise within the Coalition, and have a substantial lead-in. On the other hand, the reforms do impose direct costs upon the industry which the banks themselves have denounced. This is significant because the ICB's recommendations have been accepted by the government *despite* having been strongly opposed by the banks and their political supporters. Reforms of this nature would have been unthinkable prior to the crisis. Indeed, the new reforms mark a substantial political shift in government–bank relations in the United Kingdom. Of course, there will be ample opportunity for the banks to lobby over implementation. And as one banker told the *Economist* (2011b), the "banks don't think the war is over yet." Nevertheless the conclusion remains that the reforms represent a crucial moment when the government stood up to the City and defied its structural power.

New ideas and new conceptions were a key part of the armory of the government and the Bank of England in the bid for reform. The earlier prevailing discourse about banking and the economic value of the City has been revised and, even more importantly, has provided policy-makers with ways of countering structural power threats from banks and the City. Indeed, the recent push on bank reform offers a classic illustration of the dialectical interaction between changing contexts and ideas and of the way changes in the latter have rebounded on the structural power of the banks. In particular, in the changed post-crisis context, threats made by the banks have been *reinterpreted* by government leaders to produce far less challenging or even perhaps welcome outcomes, thus modifying threat perceptions normally associated with structural power or investment threats.

For example, arguments about the costs of reform to the banks came to be viewed as a positive development given the earlier scale of bank profits and the size of banking in the UK economy; not to mention exorbitant bank bonuses. In a similar fashion, calls to delay banking reforms because of the Eurocrisis were rejected. Vince Cable responded by saying that "the uncertainty and instability in the markets makes it all the more necessary that we press ahead and make our banks safe and reform them" (quoted in Wachman and Curtis 2011). The argument that reform was inevitable gained considerable traction, not least because of increasingly clear perceptions about the full scale of the banking crisis and the huge collateral damage in its aftermath. Clearly, the crisis had weakened the structural bargaining position of the banks, casting them in part as an economic liability. As Deputy Prime Minister Nick Clegg, put it, "we cannot ever again allow the banking system to blow up in our face in the way that it did before." In this context, critiques by the banks of the costs of reform tended to pale by comparison with memories of the costs of the bank bailouts amidst the crisis and of subsequent huge costs to the economy. The credibility of the banks' threats to exit the United Kingdom was also questioned. Critics of the banks' position have argued that they benefit from being in London because of its time zone, social cosmopolitanism, and high-quality legal and information technology support services (King 2011). For example, in his memoirs, Alistair Darling recounts how, when he introduced a new tax on bankers' bonuses:

> The outcry was predictable. The right-wing press . . . ran lurid stories of bankers planning to flee the country and decamp to Switzerland. I did not believe it. As one banker said: "have you ever been to Geneva?" And he was Swiss. (Darling 2011)

Critics have also pointed out that if major UK banks were to move to Asia they would be just as heavily regulated, if not more regulated, and that if HSBC moved to Hong Kong it would be required to undertake delicate regulatory negotiations with the Chinese Government. As the *Financial Times* (2011) put it amidst the showdown with the UK banks, "threats [to exit] should be faced down, not just because they are unreasonable but because they are of questionable credibility." As the paper went on:

> It is not clear what "moving abroad" actually means. Were a bank such as Barclays to shift its headquarters, the impact on the United Kingdom would surely be minimal as it would still do much of its business and pay taxes in the country. What is more likely anyway is rather than upping sticks altogether, some banks may reduce their new investments in Britain. This might make the City slightly less of a hot spot, but it would not be a disaster. And were it to be the price of financial stability, this would be a price worth paying. It is hardly as if Britain has an under-developed banking sector.

The views and ideas of government leaders are thus crucial in this context. The credibility of any threat cannot be reduced to an objective or determinate function of the structural environment. Judgements about the credibility of any threat and views about the value of a sector's real contribution to the overall economy are shaped by ideas. Moreover, there is always uncertainty about the potential impacts of capital flight and whether business is serious about carrying through its threats.

Clearly, banks in the United Kingdom are now operating from a structurally weaker position, especially compared to their pre-crisis position. Yet the shift in power has also occurred because the mindsets of key policy-makers have shifted to a position that is critical of the banks, highly aware of their actual and potential costs, and increasingly dismissive of their threats. Revised and more critical views about the economic value of riskier forms of banking have also conditioned policy-makers' views on regulatory reform. These changing mindsets are important. It may even be true that the Coalition government's reform responses have effectively tackled Chancellor George Osborne's "British dilemma," insisting that the United Kingdom will remain a key financial center, but of a more stable and durable kind. In this view, reform is *good* for the banks, and potentially for taxpayers too. As the *Financial Times* notes (2011), "While it is fine to be concerned about the competitiveness of the entrepot City, there is no value in an unstable financial system."

Conclusion

This chapter reviewed debates about the structural power of business and criticized the limited attention to agency in such accounts, especially in relation to the views and reactions of government or state leaders. The chapter attempted to fill this gap using insights from contemporary constructivist research and agency/structure debates to help deepen our understanding of how government or state leaders respond to the structural power of business. This approach was illustrated first using evidence from Australia that showed how the ideas of policy-makers *reduced* the structural power of international currency markets in the late 1990s amidst pressure on the Australian dollar and impacts from the Asian financial crisis. A second case study illustrated how ideation revision on the part of the UK policy-makers allowed government to defy the demands of major international banks and City financial interests and press ahead with significant and much resisted banking reform in the wake of the 2008 financial meltdown.

Overall, the chapter attempted to show how arguments about the structural power of business in relation to government policy-makers need to focus on the dynamics of a particular type of constitutive *relationship* between agents. Structural power works by inflicting real or perceived constraints on governments or state leaders, yet ultimately it is up to these agents to appraise such situations using ideational resources and assessments of structural pressures to establish their preferences and policy agendas. This involves complex ideational processes whereby policy-makers assemble and assess information, make risk assessments, and construct pictures of reality which shape their behavior and ultimately help mediate and shape the power of business.

References

Abelelal, Rawi, Blyth, Mark, and Parsons, Craig. 2010. *Constructing the International Political Economy*. Ithaca: Cornell University Press.

Adler, Emanuel. 1997. "Seizing the Middle Ground: Constructivism in World Politics." *European Journal of International Relations*, 3: 319–363.

Adler, Emanuel. 2002. "Constructivism and International Relations." In *Handbook of International Relations*, ed. Walter Carlsnaes, Thomas Risse-Kappen, and Beth A. Simmons. London: Sage.

Archer, Margaret. 1995. *Realist Social Theory: The Morphogenetic Approach*. New York: Cambridge University Press.

Archer, Margaret. 2000. "For Structure: Its Reality, Properties and Powers: A Reply to Antony King." *Sociological Review*, 48: 464–472.

Archer, Margaret. 2003. *Structure, Agency and the Internal Conversation*. Cambridge: Cambridge University Press.

Barnett, Michael and Duvall, Raymond. 2005. "Power in International Politics." *International Organization*, 59: 39–75.

Barry, Brian. 2002. "Capitalists Rules OK? Some Puzzles about Power." *Politics, Philosophy and Economics*, 1: 155–184.

Bell, Stephen. 1989. "State Strength and Capitalist Weakness: Manufacturing Capital and the Tariff Board's Attack on McEwenism, 1967–1974." *Politics*, 24: 23–38.

Bell, Stephen. 1997. *Ungoverning the Economy*. Oxford: Oxford University Press.

Bell, Stephen. 2004. *Australia's Money Mandarins: The Reserve Bank and the Politics of Money*. Cambridge: Cambridge University Press.

Bell, Stephen. 2005. "How Tight Are the Policy Constraints? The Policy Convergence Thesis, Institutionally Situated Actors and Expansionary Monetary Policy in Australia." *New Political Economy*, 10: 67–92.

Bell, Stephen. 2011. "Do We Really Need a New 'Constructivist Institutionalism' to Explain Institutional Change?" *British Journal of Political Science*, 41: 883–906.

Bell, Stephen and Feng, Hui. 2011. "The Rise of the People's Bank of China: The Structural Foundations of Institutional Change." Unpublished.

Berger, Peter L. and Luckman, Thomas. 1966. *The Social Construction of Reality*. New York: Anchor.

Bevir, Mark and Rhodes, Rod A.W. 2010. *The State as Cultural Practice*. Oxford: Oxford University Press.

Block, Fred. 1977. "The Ruling Class Does Not Rule." *Socialist Revolution*, 7: 6–28.

Block, Fred. 1980. "Beyond Relative Autonomy: State Managers as Historical Subjects." In *The Socialist Register*, ed. Ralph Miliband and John Saville. London: Merlin Press.

Blyth, Mark. 2002. *Great Transformations: Economic Ideas and Institutional Change in the Twentieth Century*. Cambridge: Cambridge University Press.

Blyth, Mark. 2003. "Structures Do Not Come with an Instruction Sheet: Interests, Ideas and Progress in Political Science." *Perspectives in Politics*, 1: 695–706.

Burrell, Steve. 1999. "Yes, He's the Gov." *Sydney Morning Herald*. November 27.

Campbell, John L. 2004. *Institutional Change and Globalization*. Princeton: Princeton University Press.

Capling, Ann and Galligan, Brian. 1992. *Beyond the Protective State*. Melbourne: Cambridge University Press.

Cerny, Phillip. 2005. "Globalisation and the Logic of Collective Action." *International Organisation*, 49: 595–625.

Checkel, Jeffrey T. 1998. "The Constructivist Turn in International Relations Theory." *World Politics*, 50: 324–348.

Cortell, Andrew and Peterson, Susan. 1999. "Altered States: Explaining Domestic Institutional Change." *British Journal of Political Science*, 29: 177–203.

Cox, Robert. 1987. *Production, Power and World Order*. New York: Columbia University Press.

Crenson, Matthew. 1971 *The Un-Politics of Air Pollution: A Study of Non-Decision-Making in the Cities*. Baltimore: Johns Hopkins University Press.

Crouch, Colin. 1979. *State and Economy in Contemporary Capitalism*. London: Croom Helm.

Crouch, Colin. 2005. *Capitalist Diversity and Change*. Oxford: Oxford University Press.

Culpepper, Pepper D. 2005. "Institutional Change in Contemporary Capitalism: Coordinated Financial Systems since 1990." *World Politics*, 57: 173–199.

Culpepper, Pepper, D. 2011. *Quiet Politics and Business Power: Corporate Control in Europe and Japan*. Cambridge: Cambridge University Press.

Darling, Alistair. 2009. Speech by the Chancellor of the Exchequer, the Rt Hon Alistair Darling MP, at Mansion House, London, 17 June, http://www.hm-treasury.gov.uk/press_57_09.htm. Accessed August 23, 2011.

Darling, Alistair. 2011. *Back from the Brink*. London: Atlantic Books.

Dessler, David, and Owen, John. 2005. "Constructivism and the Problem of Explanation." *Perspectives on Politics*, 3: 597–610.

Dowding, Keith. 2008. "Agency and Structure: Interpreting Power Relationships." *Journal of Power*, 1: 21–36.

Economist. 2011a. "Commission Accomplished." *Economist*, April 16.

Economist. 2011b. "To Rip Asunder." *Economist*, September 17.

Eichengreen, Barry. *International Monetary Arrangements for the 21st Century*. Washington: Brookings Institution.

Fearon, James and Wendt, Alexander. 2002. "Rationalism vs. Constructivism: A Skeptical View." In *Handbook of International Relations*, ed. Walter Carlsnaes, Thomas Risse-Kappen, and Beth A. Simmons. London: Sage.

Financial Times. 2011. "King Helps the Case for Banking Reform." *Financial Times*, March 9.

Finnemore, Martha. (1966) *National Interests in International Society*. Ithaca: Cornell University Press.

Finnemore, Martha and Sikkink, Kathryn. 2001. "Taking Stock: The Constructivist Research Program in International Relations and Comparative Politics." *Annual Review of Political Science*, 4: 391–416.

Fligstein, Neil. 2001. "Social Skill and the Theory of Fields." *Sociological Theory*, 19: 105–125.

Foucault, Michel. 1979. *Discipline and Punish: The Birth of the Prison*. Harmondsworth: Penguin.

Fraser, Bernie W. 1990. "Understanding Australia's Foreign Debt and the Solutions." *Reserve Bank of Australia Bulletin*, August.

Fuchs, Doris. 1992. *The Professional Quest for Knowledge: A Social Theory of Science and Knowledge*. Albany: SUNY.

Fuchs, Doris. 2005. "Commanding Heights? The Strength and Fragility of Business Power in Global Politics." *Millennium*, 33: 771–801.

Fuchs, Doris and Lederer, Markus. 2007. "The Power of Business." *Business and Politics*, 9: 1–19.

Garrett, Geoffrey. 1998. *Partisan Politics in the Global Economy*. Cambridge: Cambridge University Press.

Gaventa, John. 1980. *Power and Powerless: Quiescence and Rebellion in an Appalachian Valley*. Oxford: Clarendon Press.

Gill, Stephen. 2003. *Power and Resistance in the New World Order*. London: Palgrave Macmillan.

Gill, Stephen and Law, David. 1989. "Global Hegemony and the Structural Power of Capital." *International Studies Quarterly*, 33: 475–499.

Goff, Sharlene. 2011. "The Future of Banking." *Financial Times*, September 12.

Griffiths, Katherine. 2011. "Ringfence Will Cost Britain's Banks Dear, Wall Street Says." *The Times*, September 1.

Griffiths, Katherine, and Watson, Roland. 2011. "Ringfence Will Cost Britain's Banks Dear, Wall Street Says." *The Times*, September 1.

Guzzini, Stefano. 2000. "A Reconstruction of Constructivism in International Relations." *European Journal of International Relations*, 6: 147–182.

Hacker, Jacob S. and Pierson, Paul. 2002. "Business Power and Social Policy: Employers and the Formation of the American Welfare State." *Politics and Society*, 30: 277–325.

Hall, Peter A. 1986. *Governing the Economy: The Politics of State Intervention in Britain and France*. New York: Oxford University Press.

Hall, Peter A. and Soskice, David. 2001. "An Introduction to Varieties of Capitalism." In *Varieties of Capitalism: The Institutional Foundations of Comparative Advantage*, ed. Peter A. Hall and David Soskice. Oxford: Oxford University Press.

Hardie, Iain. 2006. "The Power of the Markets? The International Bond Markets and the 2002 Election in Brazil." *Review of International Political Economy*, 13: 53–77.

Hay, Colin. 1996. *Re-Stating Social and Political Change*. Buckingham: Open University Press.

Hay, Colin. 2002. *Political Analysis*. Basingstoke: Palgrave.

Hay, Colin. 2006a. "Globalisation and Public Policy." In *Oxford Handbook of Public Policy*, ed. Martin Rein, Michael Moran, and Robert Goodin. Oxford: Oxford University Press.

Hay, Colin. 2006b. "What's Globalisation Got to Do with It? Economic Interdependence and the Future of Welfare States." *Government and Opposition*, 41: 1–23.

Hay, Colin. 2007. "Constructivist Institutionalism." In *The Oxford Handbook of Political Institutions*, ed. Rod A.W. Rhodes, Sarah Binder, and Bert A. Rockman. Oxford: Oxford University Press.

Hay, Colin and Wincott, Daniel. 1998. "Structure, Agency and Historical Institutionalism." *Political Studies*, 46: 951–957.

Hay, Colin and Rosamond, Ben. 2002. "Globalisation, European Integration and the Discursive Construction of Economic Imperatives." *Journal of European Public Policy*, 9: 147–167.

Independent Commission on Banking (ICB). 2011a. Terms of Reference, http://bankingcommission.independent.gov.uk/terms-of-reference. Accessed May 30, 2012.

Independent Commission on Banking (ICB). 2011b. *Final Report: Recommendations*. London: ICB.

Jenkins, Patrick, Goff, Sharlene, and Parker, George. 2011. "Banks Hope Their Lobbying Pays Off." *Financial Times*, April 10.

Jessop, Bob. 1990. *State Theory: Putting Capitalist States in their Place*. Cambridge: Polity Press.

Johal, Sukhdev, Moran, Michael, and Williams, Karel. 2012. "Post-Crisis Financial Regulation in Britain." In *Crisis and Control: Institutional Change in Financial Market Regulation*, ed. Renate Mayntz. Cologne: Campus Verlag/Max Planck Institut für Geselschaftsforschung.

Kelly, Paul. 1992. *The End of Certainty: The Story of the 1980s*. Sydney: Allen & Unwin.

King, Mervyn. 2009a. Speech by Mervyn King, Governor of the Bank of England, at the Lord Mayor's Banquet for Bankers and Merchants of the City of London at the Mansion House, London, June 17, http://www.bankofengland.co.uk/publications/Documents/speeches/2009/speech394.pdf. Accessed May 30, 2012.

King, Mervyn. 2009b. Speech by Mervyn King, Governor of the Bank of England, to Scottish Business Organisations, Edinburgh, October 20, http://www.bankofengland.co.uk/publications/Documents/speeches/2009/speech406.pdf. Accessed May 30, 2012.

King, Mervyn. 2011. Speech Given by Sir Mervyn King, Governor of the Bank of England, at the Lord Mayor's Banquet for Bankers and Merchants of the City of London at the Mansion House, London, 15 June, http://www.bankofengland.co.uk/publications/Documents/speeches/2011/speech504.pdf. Accessed May 30, 2012.

Konings, Martijn. 2009. "The Construction of US Financial Power." *Review of International Studies*, 35: 69–94.

Krasner, Stephen D. 1984. "Approaches to the State: Alternative Conceptions and Historical Dynamics." *Comparative Politics*, 16: 223–246.

Lindblom, C.E. 1977. *Politics and Markets: The World's Political-Economic Systems*. New York: Basic Books.

Lindblom, C.E. (1982) "The Market as Prison." *Journal of Politics*, 44: 324–336.

Lloyds Banking Group. 2010. Lloyds Banking Group Response to the Independent Commission on Banking: Issues Paper Response. http://bankingcommission.s3.amazonaws.com/wp-content/uploads/2011/02/Lloyds-Issues-Paper-Response-1.pdf. Accessed 30 May, 2012.

Lukes, Steven. 1974. *Power: A Radical View*. London: Macmillan.

Macfarlane, Ian J. 1992. "Making Monetary Policy in an Uncertain World." *Reserve Bank of Australia Bulletin*, September 9–16.

Mahoney, James. 2000. "Path Dependence in Historical Sociology." *Theory and Society*, 29: 507–548.

Mann, Michael. 1984. "The Autonomous Power of the State: Its Origins, Mechanisms and Results." *European Journal of Sociology*, 25: 185–213.

Marsh, David. 2009. "Keeping Ideas in Their Place: in Praise of Thin Constructivism." *Australian Journal of Political Science*, 44: 679–696.

McAnulla, Stuart. 2005. "Making Hay with Actualism? The Need for a Realist Concept of Structure." *Politics*, 25: 31–38.

McAnulla, Stuart. 2006. "Challenging the New Interpretivist Approach: Towards a Critical Realist Alternative." *British Politics*, 1: 113–138.

Meyer, John W. 2010. "World Society, Institutional Theories, and the Actor." *Annual Review of Sociology*, 36: 1–20.

Miliband, Ralph. 1973. *The State in Capitalist Society*. London: Quartet.

Mosley, Layna. 2000. "Room to Move: International Financial Markets and National Welfare States." *International Organisation*, 54: 737–773.

Mosley, Layna. 2003. *Global Capital and National Governments*. Cambridge: Cambridge University Press.

Mulholland, Helene and Quinn, Ben. 2011. Cable Claims Coalition Unity over Banking Reforms *The Guardian*, August 31, http://www.guardian.co.uk/politics/2011/aug/31/vince-cable-bankers-derail-reforms. Accessed 30 May, 2012.

Nye, Joseph. 1990. *Soft Power: The Means to Succeeed in World Politics*. New York: Public Affairs Press.

Offe, Claus and Wiesenthal, Helmut. 1980. "Two Logics of Collective Action: Theoretical Notes on Social Class and Organisational Form." *Political Power and Social Theory*, 1: 76–115.

Ohmae, Kenichi. 1995. *The End of the Nation State*. New York: Harper Collins.

Olson, Johan P. 2009. "Change and Continuity: An Institutional Approach to Institutions and Democratic Government." *European Political Science Review*, 1: 3–32.

Onuf, Nicholas. 1989. *World of Our Making: Rules and Rule in Social Theory and International Relations*. Columbia: University of South Carolina Press.

Parker, George. 2011. "Osborne Praises 'Impressive' Proposals." *Financial Times*, September 12.

Peters, B. Guy. 1999. *Institutional Analysis in Political Science: The New Institutionalism*. London: Pinter.

Pierson, Paul. 2000a. "The Limits of Design: Explaining Institutional Origins and Change." *Governance*, 13: 475–499.

Pierson, Paul. 2000b. "Increasing Returns, Path Dependence, and the Study of Politics." *American Political Science Review*, 94: 251–267.

Pitchford, John. 1989. "A Sceptical View of Australia's Current Account and Debt Problem." *Australian Economic Review*, 22: 5–14.

Pontusson, Jonas. 2005. "From Comparative Public Policy to Political Economy: Putting Institutions in Their Place and Taking Interests Seriously." *Comparative Political Studies*, 28: 117–147.

Price, Richard and Reus-Smit, Christian. 1998. "Dangerous Liaisons? Critical International Theory and Constructivism." *European Journal of International Relations*, 4: 259–294.

Pusey, Michael. 1991. *Economic Rationalism in Canberra*. Melbourne: Cambridge University Press.

Risse, Thomas. 2007. "Social Constructivism Meets Globalisation." In *Globalisation Theory*, ed. David Held and Anthony McGrew. Cambridge: Polity Press.

Rosamond, Ben. 1999. "Discourses of Globalisation and the Social Construction of European Identities." *Journal of European Public Policy*, 6: 652–668.

Ruggie, John G. 1998. *Constructing the World Polity*. London: Routledge.

Schmidt, Vivien. 2008. "Discursive Institutionalism: The Explanatory Power of Ideas and Discourse." *Annual Review of Political Science*, 11: 303–326.

Searle, John. 1995. *The Social Construction of Reality*. New York: Free Press.

Skocpol, Theda. 1980. "Political Responses to Capitalist Crisis: Neo-Marxist Theories of the State and the Case of the New Deal." *Politics and Society*, 10: 155–201.

Smith, Mark A. 1999. "Public Opinion, Elections and Representation within a Market Economy: Does the Structural Power of Business Undermine Popular Sovereignty?" *American Journal of Political Science*, 43: 842–863.

Smith, Mark, A. 2000. *American Business and Political Power: Public Opinion, Elections and Democracy*. Chicago: Chicago University Press.

Steinmo, Sven and Thelen, Kathleen. 1992. "Historical Institutionalism in Comparative Perspective." In *Structuring Politics: Historical Institutionalism in Comparative Analysis*, ed. Kathleen Thelen, Sven Steinmo, and Frank Longstreth. Cambridge: Cambridge University Press.

Strange, Susan. 1996. *The Retreat of the State: The Diffusion of Power in the World Economy*. Cambridge: Cambridge University Press.

Vogel, David. 1983. "The Power of Business in America: A Reappraisal." *British Journal of Political Science*, 13: 19–43.

Vogel, David. 1987. "Political Science and the Study of Corporate Power: A Dissent from the New Conventional Wisdom." *British Journal of Political Science*, 17: 385–408.

Vogel, David. 1989. *Fluctuating Fortunes: The Political Power of Business in America*. New York: Basic Books.

Wachman, Richard and Curtis, Polly. 2011. City Hits Back at Vince Cable over Banking Reform Comments, *The Guardian*, August 31, http://www.guardian.co.uk/business/2011/aug/31/city-vince-cable-banking-reform. Accessed 30 May, 2012.

Watson, Matthew and Hay, Colin. 2003. "The Discourse of Globalisation and the Logic of No Alternative: Rendering the Contingent Necessary in the Political Economy of New Labour." *Policy and Politics*, 3: 289–305.

Weiss, Linda. 1998. *The Myth of the Powerless State: Governing the Economy in a Global Era*. Cambridge: Polity Press.

Wendt, Alexander. 1987. "The Agent-Structure Problem in International Relations Theory." *International Organization*, 41: 335–370.

Wendt, Alexander. 1992. "Anarchy Is What States Make of It." *International Organization*, 46: 391–425.

Wendt, Alexander. 1999. *Social Theory of International Politics*. Cambridge: Cambridge University Press.

Wrong, Dennis. 1961. "The Over-socialized Conception of Man in Modern Sociology." *American Sociological Review*, 26: 183–193.

Chapter 8

How Global Companies Wield Their Power

The Discursive Shaping of Sustainable Development

Nina Kolleck

Introduction[1]

Recently, business representatives have begun to create networks that help shape public understanding of political concepts by influencing the establishment of norms, institutions, and discourses. At the same time, there is wide consensus that the power of transnational private actors in global (environmental) governance has been neglected thus far by social science scholars, particularly those in political science and economics (e.g. Levy and Newell 2005; Sklair 2002). In the past few years, new theoretical frameworks have been developed in order to identify different dimensions of business power in global governance (e.g. Falkner 2010; Fuchs 2007; Levy and Egan 1998; Levy and Newell 2005; Newell 2004). These approaches highlight the growing importance of the discursive power of business representatives and the lack of studies in this field.

This chapter addresses this research gap by exploring how global companies wield discursive power in order to shape the discourse on sustainable development. It does not consider whether companies should integrate sustainable development strategies into their activities nor the extent of diffusion of global firms' discursive use of sustainable development in social and political processes. Instead, the purpose of this chapter is to focus on how global companies use the concept of sustainable development in order to wield discursive power. It introduces a research design that draws on constructivist ideas and uses a discourse analytical approach.

The demand for corporate responsibility is not new, but has "a long and wide-ranging history" (Carroll 2008: 19). Evidence can be seen as early as the eighteenth century, for example, in Adam Smith's *The Theory of Moral Sentiments*. According to Smith, the economic prosperity granted by the "invisible hand" does not come with self-interest and profit-seeking but from "sympathy" for others. Thus, the act

The Handbook of Global Companies, First Edition. Edited by John Mikler.
© 2013 John Wiley & Sons, Ltd. Published 2013 by John Wiley & Sons, Ltd.

of observing others makes people aware of the morality of their own behavior and provides the basis for general social order (Smith 1761). While in the past companies' responsibility to society was realized at the local level, the phenomenon of Corporate Social Responsibility (CSR) can be seen as the development of responsibility on a global scale. Since the mid-1990s, the number and scope of civil regulations have increased significantly (Vogel 2006) and sustainable development has become an important subject in business strategy. Changing attitudes, investor expectations, and public pressures have urged businesses to integrate emerging ecological and social norms into their practices and to take part in the debate on sustainable development. Today, global companies "are not only under pressure to respond to these new sources of authority, they are also increasingly engaged in their development" (Levy and Kaplan 2008: 433). Several initiatives have already been developed that deal with topics surrounding "sustainability and business." Environmental and social standards have become strategically significant components of global corporate policy.[2] While globalization has reconfigured power relations between governmental and private actors, transnational companies are confronted with political expectations (Zadek 2007) and are increasingly held responsible for problems like pollution or human rights violations. Reframing these private actors from pure profit-seeking entities to "corporate citizens" has raised expectations and encouraged companies to ascertain their role in society (Wright and Rwabizambuga 2006). Business representatives have started to create networks that help shape public understanding of the concept of sustainable development.

At the same time, there is broad consensus that both the power of "non-state actors and movements" (Ruggie 2003: 13) and transnational processes of legitimization, which grant companies the right to wield power, have been neglected by social scientists. In the past, research on the power of global companies was primarily conducted in rationalist terms and limited to questions of legitimacy and how effectively sustainable development was integrated into business strategies (Conzelmann and Wolf 2007). From this point of view, businesses are treated as interest groups, wielding their power within the state (Falkner 2010). Hence, there is an apparent need to analyze business's discursive use of development concepts as both their definition and operationalization have consequences on the identification of policy needs and outcomes. Equally, they are of crucial importance in terms of global and national problem solving, which also has political implications. The use of development concepts influences how policies are formulated and how actors understand their concerns with respect to development and growth. Additionally, the discursive shaping of sustainable development has the ability to draw on new sources of legitimacy because it gives new meaning to existing norms.

This chapter avoids implementing an exclusively rationalist perspective in order to focus on the shaping of norms and ideas. Consequently, companies are treated here not only as economic but also as social and political actors. They are not only embedded in social and political systems, but are also part of the political process, which they try to shape. While the global business networks examined here describe business as solution providers that "cannot succeed in societies that fail" (WBCSD 2006: 1), they are considered as an integral part of global politics.

The chapter is divided into six sections. This introduction presents the research focus and background information. The second section briefly defines crucial concepts of discourse analysis, argues the value of a discourse analytical approach that draws on Michel Foucault in analyzing the discursive shaping of sustainable development, and provides the methodological approach. The third section introduces the cases – the World Business Council of Sustainable Development (WBCSD) and the business network econsense – and presents data collected through empirical analysis of their corporate members' published documents. The fourth section shows how companies wield discursive power in order to shape norms, values, and perceptions and analyzes businesses' use of elements of discursive power in the context of sustainable development. Here it is demonstrated that companies seek to shape the discourse on sustainable development in order to strengthen their global position and gain legitimacy as political and social actors. Fifthly, it is argued that the specific social constructions of "sustainable development" stem from the concept's inherent vagueness and ambivalence.

With this in mind, the strengths and limits of business discursive power are discussed. This section also identifies a discrete type of influence that can be traced back to rules inherent in the discourse that companies have to deal with. The last section summarizes major arguments.

Analyzing Discursive Power

The social science literature is rich with various understandings of the notion of "discourse." This lack of definitional clarity can even be noted with respect to the different methodologies of discourse analysis. However, scholars primarily distinguish between approaches that draw on either Foucault (e.g. 1971) or Habermas (e.g. 1981). Habermas focuses his attention on analyzing communication structures and assumes that even in the face of social inequality discourses may be free of domination. In contrast, Foucault concentrates on analyzing power (re)production and links discourses to the struggle for power and dominance.

According to a general definition of Foucault, "discourse" has to be distinguished from "discussion" and can be understood as an entity of sequences of signs and enouncements (or statements) that belong to a single system of formation (e.g. Foucault 1969). Discourses are produced by the regularities of discursive formations. Discursive formations, in turn, can be seen as fields of knowledge (Foucault 1966), such as medical history, political economy, or sustainable development. The Foucauldian conception of discourse is closely connected with power, truth, and knowledge. The conditions of truth related to a specific historical period constitute what can be expressed as discourses. As such, discourses define what can be said, what is not possible to say, and who can say what with what effect. They shape perceptions, identities, and interpretations and they (re)produce and structure reality. Hence, discourses have an important impact on political processes.

This chapter employs a specific approach to discourse and discourse analysis that draws on Foucault and integrates further theoretical and methodological elaborations of his discourse analysis (e.g. Hajer 1995; Lukes 2005). A "strict" application of a research program according to Foucault is not executed. Thus, the discourse of global companies within the business networks WBCSD and econsense is conceptualized as a typical example of a *discourse coalition*. This concept assumes that in the struggle for hegemony actors become connected on the basis of common story lines. This does not mean that actors of the same discourse coalition do not utter different arguments. Even so, they represent the same story lines and realize collective activities in which story lines become manifest (Hajer 1995). On this note, discourse coalitions themselves can be regarded as certain types of social networks. Analysis of discourse coalitions can determine what holds networks together and what ideas and norms they are based on. Discursive material produced by these companies introduces relevant discourse-analytical categories such as story lines, image cultivations, ambiguities, and stylistic devices.

The term *story line* refers to the dramaturgical shaping of events in literature, film, and lyrics. Since Aristotle, the analysis of story lines has been a significant part of the theatre. This chapter considers story lines as instruments of discursive power on the world stage (Shakespeare 2002). Thus, story lines characterize discourses, link discursive elements, and give meaning to social and physical phenomena (Hajer 1995). Identifying story lines can clarify how discursive complexities are reduced within a given discourse and how issues can be constructed as "impossible."

Another salient element of discourse analysis is the notion of *discourse connections*, which emerge if at least two different discourses are interlinked. In other words, different discursive approaches are combined in a given discourse. The discourse on CSR, for example, often refers to the discourses on climate change, biodiversity, or social justice.

Discursive power emphasizes the exercise of power in discursive processes. It refers to the shaping of identities, perceptions, interpretations, and the creation of trust and confidence (e.g. Fuchs and Lederer 2007; Levy and Egan 1998; Levy and Egan 2000; Lukes 2005). In the scientific literature, discursive power is often understood as the third dimension of power. In contrast to the instrumental and structural facets, this third face of power is related to norms, ideas, and social interactions. It is reflected in discourses, cultural values, and communicative practices (Koller 1991). The "three faces of business power" perspective can be traced back to Levy and Egan (1998), who have argued that the influence of business within a capitalist system derives from three sources of power: instrumental power, structural power, and discursive power. They further note that the power of business in global governance should be examined from three theoretical perspectives: power elite or instrumentalist, structural dependence, and cultural or discursive perspectives (Levy and Egan 2000).

While "power is at its most effective when least observable" (Lukes 2005: 64), discursive power provides particularly strong instruments of influence. Therefore, the discursive dimension of business power is often regarded as the "most nuanced, and the hardest to observe" (Mikler 2011b: 157). Drawing on discursive techniques such as story lines, discourse connections, and metaphors, discursive power can be extended. Analyses of these elements lead to a better understanding of how discursive power is wielded by global companies.

It is important to note that discourse analysis should not be confused with discourse theories (e.g. Laclau and Mouffe 2001: 1987). However, scholars often conflate these concepts. In general, discourse theories can be understood as theoretical perspectives on the linguistic construction of meaning. In contrast, discourse analytical approaches refer to empirical investigations of discourses. Of course, discourse theoretical approaches contain statements about discursive effects. Nevertheless, they act on structuralist assumptions and cannot sufficiently explain actor-centered elements of the exercise of discursive power. The theoretical starting point of this chapter conceptualizes "discourse as the power-suffused result on many people speaking to each other" (Onuf 2007: xv). The notion of business and sustainable development is regarded as "a set of discursive texts and practices that construct corporate subjectivity and the fields within which corporate operations take place as domains of socially responsible actions" (Levy and Kaplan 2008: 438).[3]

At the same time, the notion of "sustainable development" seems to be a very important field in which to wield power. Civil society, governments, media, international organizations, and companies all use the term, giving the impression that they are addressing the same phenomenon. The increased use of the catchphrase creates a conceptual vagueness. Mostly, scholars use the Brundtland report definition: "Sustainable development is development that meets the needs of the present without compromising the ability of future generations to meet their own needs" (WCED 1987).

After the late 1980s, the concept became an integral part of the political vocabulary in western democracies (Schreurs and Papadakis 2007). While the struggle since has been for a holistic conception of what sustainable development means – with many actors emphasizing a balance between economic, social, and environmental aims – business representatives often argue for the primacy of economic success (Schmidheiny 1998), sometimes as a prerequisite for social and environmental sustainability. As will be shown in the following sections, companies try to shape the concept in more economic terms by relating it not to social and environmental aims but to the company's economic growth.

However, sustainability is not the only vague concept companies use to deal with these issues; a lack of definitional clarity can also be seen with the term "CSR" (Mikler 2007). There is still no common understanding "about what it means to be socially responsible, or even whether firms should have social responsibilities in the first place" (Crane 2008: 4). Global business networks that deal exclusively with issues surrounding businesses' sustainability strategies, such as the WBCSD or econsense, use a broad definition of CSR and criticize the "call for no growth" for being "at worst cruel and inhumane" (WBCSD 1998: 7). In the literature, CSR is often referred to as the integration of the principles of sustainable development into all aspects of economic behavior. Furthermore, CSR is understood as "a set of discourses and practices that reflects the particular balance of forces in a contested issue arena" (Levy and Kaplan 2008: 445).

Global Business Networks on Sustainable Development

In order to show how discursive power as wielded by global companies can be understood, this chapter draws on an analysis of the discourse of global companies that are members of the WBCSD or econsense, two business networks devoted to sustainability. An analysis was conducted of all documents dealing with business and sustainable development that were published by WBCSD, econsense, and any of their members and were available online by 2010. Relevant documents include statements issued by the business networks, their members' sustainability reports, and published interviews with relevant business representatives related to the businesses' sustainable

Table 8.1 WBCSD and econsense.

	WBCSD	econsense
Founded in	1995	2000
Members	About 200	33
Headquarters	Geneva, Switzerland	Berlin, Germany
President	Björn Stigson	Hans-Peter Keitel
Selected members	adidas, BP, Coca-Cola, DuPont, General Motors, IBM, Sony, Royal Dutch Shell	Telekom, Danone, DuPont, Ernst & Young, KPMG, Linde, ThyssenKrupp
Members in both networks	Allianz, BASF, Bayer, BMW, Deutsche Bank, Deloitte & Touche, E.ON, Evonik Industries, HeidelbergCement, KPMG, PricewaterhouseCoopers, Siemens, Unilever, Vodafone, Volkswagen	
Sectors	Utilities & power, oil & gas, chemicals, engineering, consumer goods, cement, mining & metals, tires, forest & paper products, auto, IT & telecoms, services, bank & insurance, construction, food & beverages, logistics, maritime, healthcare, media, retail, water services, aviation, trading	

development strategies. These documents were analyzed as representative material of what each business network or company "believes to be its key message" (Mikler 2007: 76). The analysis was supported by the computer program ATLAS.ti. The process of coding followed the rules of qualitative content analysis (Kolleck 2011). Codes were related to the way companies intend to wield discursive power and shape the discourse on sustainable development.

The WBCSD and econsense were chosen because they include the world's largest and most powerful transnational companies. Furthermore, both are global business networks whose members are exclusively global companies. Their membership base is pan-sectoral, including among others the pharmaceutical, automobile, and energy industries (see Table 8.1). The networks deal exclusively with issues related to members' sustainable development strategies and seek to present global companies in a favorable light on sustainable development issues. They are embedded in the global discourse on business and sustainability and try to shape the discourse on sustainable development by promoting dialogues and encouraging discussion between business representatives, politicians, and other stakeholders.

Emphasizing that businesses' technological knowhow, innovation, and investments have an important role in the success of sustainable development, these global business networks argue that their members "participate in policy development to create the right framework conditions for business to make an effective contribution to sustainable human progress" (WBCSD 2011a). Furthermore, networks highlight that their members "have pledged to move forward the implementation of these approaches through an open discussion process" (econsense 2011).

The networks could be regarded as promoting change in corporate behavior in favor of sustainable development. Yet they could also be seen as organizations that engage in *greenwashing* efforts and allow businesses to artificially bolster their image as promoters of sustainability. However, these business networks attempt to position themselves as leading pro-sustainable development organizations. They promote

global companies as providing solutions in the debate on long-term policy and regulations and have sought to showcase their members as stewards of environmental
and social objectives.

WBCSD consists of around 200 global companies with registered head offices
around the world, making it the largest network of global companies that deals with
sustainability. econsense's 33 members are some of the world's largest global firms,
each of which has at least one office in Germany. Along with the United States and
Japan, Germany is one of the three largest economies within the OECD and includes
the highest number of global companies (Kolleck 2011: 36).[4]

Nevertheless, national policy and culture continue to play an important role in
international politics (e.g. Mikler 2011b; Schreurs, Selin, and VanDeveer 2009).
Differences between corporations' sustainability strategies can be related to the location of their home country (Mikler 2007; 2011a) and states still employ differing
approaches to regulating industry (Beem and Mikler 2011). The WBCSD itself refers
to the influence of national institutional variations (WBCSD 2004b), but also highlights the need for global solutions and international commitment (WBCSD 2004b).
Of course, companies that are members in one of these business networks are very
diverse. However, although membership is different between these two networks,
empirical analysis of their discourse clearly identifies a common global business
voice on sustainable development. In recent years, topics around "business and sustainability" have become increasingly internationalized (Crane *et al.* 2008), mainly
pushed by global companies operating in OECD countries. The current debate on
these issues is particularly characterized by the emergence of global networks – such
as the WBCSD and econsense – and the lack of coherent international regulatory
policy or a global welfare state. With the catchphrase "sustainable development"
companies now refer to facts that can no longer be solely related to their home
country or headquarters because they affect many countries (Mühle 2010). Involved
in transnational discourses, global companies' sustainability policy has become a
global corporate strategy. Being "commonly recognized worldwide as an accepted
business model" (Mühle 2010: 21), companies' sustainability programs "currently
do not reach out to the headquarters of a firm but also try to include organizations along the supply chain" (Mühle 2010: 19). Transnational business networks
initiate international dialogue in order to find common global definitions and strategies related to CSR (e.g. WBCSD 2000). CSR resembles the transnational spread
of other normative ideas (such as democracy) and "companies have increasingly
become the diffusion agents of social ideas" (Mühle 2010: 21). Thus, instead of
analyzing the national differences between documents, the focus here is on how
global companies use their discursive power to influence the discourse on sustainable
development.

The Discursive Shaping of Sustainable Development

This section analyzes companies' use of elements of discursive power in the context
of sustainable development. It examines how global companies seek to shape the discourse on sustainable development in order to gain legitimacy as political and social
actors. It first shows how business networks are getting involved in the discourse

in order to gain *legitimacy* as a discursive actor. Secondly, it demonstrates how companies *underestimate conflicts of interest* and what this means with respect to their discursive shaping. Thirdly, this section explores the way businesses try to become legitimized as *political actors* and concludes by referring to their use of *religious allusions* and the trend towards *individualization*.

Legitimacy

Published documents of the discourse coalition demonstrate that companies are taking part in the debate on sustainable development in order to wield discursive power. In other words, global companies pursue the aim to "move from being 'observer and victim' to being 'shaper and advocate'" (WBCSD 2000: 7). CSR is, for example, implicitly seen as a chance to influence public beliefs:

> concerns often center on the belief that social and environmental standards are being compromised, or that investment decisions are insensitive to local needs and circumstances. CSR provides business with an opportunity to demonstrate that this does not have to be the case. (WBCSD 2000: 6)

The WBCSD regards companies that participate in the discursive shaping of sustainable development as better positioned to become the world's most powerful private actors. Put another way, the WBCSD argues that only companies that engage in the field of sustainable development will get the chance to gain power in the discourse.

> The companies that will be able to take advantage of those opportunities are the ones that anticipate trends and respond with smart solutions. They are the ones whose leaders not only lead their companies, but also help guide society toward major investments in sustainability. (WBCSD 2010: 23)

In general, the business discourse on sustainable development is highly complex and emotionally charged. It is characterized by imagery, euphemisms, exaggerations, and inconsistencies. Corporate sustainability reports often highlight managerial processes rather than assessing outcomes (Levy and Kaplan 2008). Terms and phrases are chosen to evoke positive or negative connotations. As such, the term "genetic engineering" is replaced with "life sciences" (Bayer 2008), "biotechnology" (e.g. BASF 2009; Bayer 2008), or with "green biotechnology" (DuPont 2005) in order to avoid negative associations. Stories related to company history are often used to generate confidence by creating the impression that the company has a tradition of reliability: consequently, social and environmental concerns are part of a traditional self-conception (Bosch 2006; Siemens 2009). "Protecting the environment has a long tradition at Siemens. Over the years, we've invested heavily in waste water treatment, air pollution control, and environmental management systems" (Siemens 2009: 125). Traditionalism conveys the impression of being reliable, conservative, and convincing. Thus, this description may counter the perception that CSR is just a fad. On the one hand, global companies present themselves as enlightened, energetic, reform-minded, and progressive actors in international politics (WBCSD 2006). On the other hand, outdated social attitudes are criticized:

> the crucial factors are often social and corporate structures, as well as outdated social attitudes and opinions. . . . It still continues to be difficult for women to achieve a reasonable work-life balance. (econsense 2006: 14)

After all, many different concepts and topics can be considered in the sustainability discourse. The conceptual openness of sustainable development invites connections with further discourses. Hence, the business discourse on sustainable development shows several connections with other important social discourses (such as the discourses on war, globalization, and demographic change). These connections can be regarded as attempts to extend discursive power on additional areas, probably in order to increase the overall weight of the arguments and the general dominance of global companies. Put another way, the concept of sustainable development is used in order to wield discursive power and to extend the general influence of global companies.

Downplaying Conflicts

A strategy of increasing discursive power may also be seen in how corporations underestimate conflicts of interest. By taking part in the debate on sustainable development, global companies address civil society, states, and other actors. Yet conflicts between these different actors are regarded as a thing of the past:

> groupings that were previously in opposition (e.g. the old adversarial relationships between NGOs and business) are realizing that they are often likely to achieve their objectives through constructive dialogue and working in partnership. (WBCSD 2010: 21)

Furthermore, civil society criticism of business behavior is carried through the media. In this respect, global companies have an equivalent: a growing number of companies and business networks have begun to award prizes recognizing the best professional journalism in the field of business and sustainable development. Part of the selection criteria is that journalists can persuasively describe how companies succeed in tackling the "alleged area of conflict" between competing sustainability goals. This entails the conflict-free pursuit of all three pillars of sustainability. A further goal of these awards is to influence public perception related to the performance of global companies with respect to sustainable development: "[We] strongly support journalists who, through their engagement, help to anchor the idea of sustainable development in people's minds"[5] (econsense 2009). By following this strategy companies pursue the aim "that the ideas of 'sustainable development' and 'corporate responsibility' gain power"[6] (Fickel 2009: 2). Syntactic links between sustainable development and profit, good deeds and corporate responsibility, idea and power are generated through juxtapositions. Business's role as problem solver is stressed by highlighting the resolution of the seemingly conflicting imperatives of economic growth and environmental protection. Stability and strength are reflected in wordings such as "anchor" or "strongly support." Companies implicitly argue that economic and definitional power belong together.

The ways that companies downplay areas of conflict in realizing sustainable development are not marginal or accidental, but systematic, as shown in several passages. For companies this is necessary. Other actors could argue that companies should not have the chance to talk and act like a *Praeceptor Mundi* (global teacher). At the same time, global companies see the need to respond to obvious discursive power of civil society actors in framing these issues. If other players are viewed as legitimate world teachers, it is appropriate to use their language in order to themselves take part in the discussion on social values.

Other passages show that businesses try directly to prevent regulations or intend to influence the design of public policy. However, the quotations above show that business networks attempt to establish a connection between sustainable development and economic activities and, as a result, to wield discursive power. While this inevitably involves a certain degree of self-regulation, definite general proposals for binding regulations are not suggested. At the same time, these arguments strengthen the legitimacy of individual companies and business networks, establish them as necessary and sophisticated players in the definition of societal goals, and foster their influence in the free-market system.

Businesses as Political Actors

Sustainable development and CSR are not only discursive struggles "over practices" but also over the "locus of governance authority," offering potential paths "toward the transformation of stakeholders from external observers and petitioners into legitimate and organized participants in decision-making" (Levy and Kaplan 2008: 446). The analysis of story lines in this chapter shows that global companies are conceptualized as the most competent, indispensable, and strongest player in the field of sustainable development. According to this framing strategy, global companies do not only make a "substantial contribution," but they form a *necessary* basis for sustainable development because they have "surpassed government in the pursuit of sustainable development" (WBCSD 2007: 5). It is highlighted that "it is in the interest of business to support governments in establishing effective and accountable institutions and developing sound policy and regulatory frameworks" (WBCSD 2010: 19). Furthermore, the description of the economy as a vital player for cooperation in the field of sustainable development is linked to political demands that call for more political influence and business-friendly frameworks.

> The role of business on this issue [sustainability] is clear: these challenges cannot be solved without the innovative power of the business world. But the force of innovation requires room to prosper and flourish. (econsense 2007a: 6)

Under no circumstances, however, should these stable and predictable frameworks get the chance to impede the free development of global corporations:

> econsense actively supports the federal government in avoiding a rigid regulatory framework at the national and particularly at the international level. Furthermore, it supports the promotion and institutionalization of policies based on the successful principle of voluntary and flexible approaches. Proactive, creative global corporations should not be hampered by bureaucratic rules. (econsense 2007b: 4)[7]

By asserting its active support for the government, the business network implicitly tries to persuade national governments to use its approach and to gain authority and legitimacy as a political actor. In this way, global companies try to legitimize their dominance in the area of sustainable development. They accuse governments of having failed to provide adequate solutions and highlight that governments need the support of business:

> Governments find it increasingly difficult to deliver societal infrastructure and services ... In searching for solutions, governments are more and more turning to business for support via partnerships and privatization. (WBCSD 2004a: 6)

Thus, cooperative and proactive approaches are regarded as effective means to increase influence by falling back on discursive power.

Religious Allusions and Individualization

Religious allusions and metaphors are also used to gain discursive power. ThyssenKrupp Steel's sustainability report, for example, argues that sustainability lies in the nature of human creation (ThyssenKrupp Steel 2005a: 11) which is "geared, if not [for] eternity, then at least long-term survival" (ThyssenKrupp Steel 2005b: 11). econsense (2005) refers indirectly to the social responsibility of companies that arises solely from the existence of the companies themselves:

> In the beginning was the product – and because people need products in their everyday lives, there are companies. Day in, day out, they invent, design, and modify products and product-oriented services for people. This lies at the heart of Economic Value Added. Today, this means striving to produce the best product ideas in a tough competitive environment. (econsense 2005: 2)[8]

The reference to Genesis is apparently used to promote faith in the intentions of businesses. Only upon second glance does this seem flat or at best ironic ("In the beginning was the product"). The allusion to the myth of God's creation in combination with industrially manufactured goods is just as absurd as the philosophical-sounding statements about sustainability in the nature of human creation. By not telling the story of God's creation, the originally religious content is obscured (Kolleck 2012). However, on the evidence of the manifold dangers and risks it cannot be seriously asserted that sustainability inherently belongs to "human creation." Therefore, the statement's meaning comes not from its content but from the allusion to the myth itself. Companies try to highlight their capacity to give meaning and transcendence ("eternity") and, ultimately, to take over the norm-creating role of the church. In this way, they take up the discourse on the loss of meaning of modernity and respond to some extent to the argumentation of many environmental organizations.

This notion is also reflected elsewhere. As such, global companies react to the "trend to greater individualization" (Evonik 2009: 13) by pursuing a "family-conscious human resources policy" (Evonik 2009: 53) and when they are keen to "harmonize the demands of careers and family" (Bosch 2009: 53). The idea of social-market radicalism is opposed by "corporate culture" (WBCSD 2011c) and the promotion of "regional commitment" (Bosch 2009: 56ff) can be seen as a response to perceived negative impacts of globalization. On the one hand, such argumentation may be in answer to public perceptions of corporate behavior as driven by unconditional profit-seeking and destroying values. On the other hand, this may reflect companies' desire to participate in social life beyond narrow economic objectives. In the long term, however, the quality of the arguments matters as well: Discursive elements that are created by outsiders can be accused of being pure advertising.

Discourse-Inherent Rules and the Limits of Business's Discursive Power

Discourse-inherent rules are to be understood as forms and content that define a social boundary on what can be communicated and what cannot be communicated about a specific topic at a certain point in time. Thus, rules inherent in the discourse contain paradigms that are related to historical circumstances. They also describe the currently accepted ways to pursue a specific discourse.

A basic rule of the business discourse on sustainability can be seen in the demand for a conflict-free pursuit of economic, ecological, and social benefits. This central rule results not only from countless repetition but also from an agreement between the different actors which serves as the basis for further negotiations. Furthermore, it reflects the discourse status quo and social and political consensus. In contrast, other passages within the documents (implicitly) argue that economic growth should have priority within the concept of sustainable development. Some companies even consider lay-offs an activity that promotes sustainable development (see also Telekom 2006):

> Our commitment to ensuring customer satisfaction involves offering the best possible value, and this has meant unavoidable reductions in staff numbers ... we do so in the knowledge that making these difficult changes will help ensure a sustainable and competitive future. (Allianz Group 2007: 2)

This understanding implies that sustainable development is not related to social and environmental aims but to the company's economic vitality or well-being. In addition, the reduction of jobs is labeled as "unavoidable." In this way, it is constructed as necessary; any alternatives are ignored.

It becomes apparent that the concept of sustainable development is used to pursue traditional economic goals. Thus, the debate on the balance of the three dimensions of sustainability is pursued on the back of the highlighted consensus. This may also be considered a "rule." As long as economic success remains the most important objective, it cannot be expected that ecological and social dimensions be considered equal. Other actors such as environmental organizations may face similar problems with regard to ecological or social dimensions. The three pillars of sustainable development, however, are not automatically in equilibrium with each other. Although various actors and global initiatives struggle for mandatory regulations, standards are still missing. Considering the legitimization of the free-market economy and the promotion of "market-based solutions" (WBCSD 2011b: 32), sustainable development and CSR are extremely important issues on which global companies can wield power.

Discourse-inherent rules and argumentative guidelines such as the primacy of economic aims often become evident in such obvious contradictions. Ambivalences are left, allowing one to emphasize that which is closest to one's own interests. Inconsistencies can be interpreted based on the reader's judgement. On the one hand, the business discourse on sustainable development principally requires proceeding on the balance of the three pillars. On the other hand, however, global companies seek ways to interpret purely economic interests in terms of sustainable development.

Further rules inherent in the discourse (here without quotations) highlight ambivalences between conservation and development, global and national orientations, as well as external and internal expectations. Global companies try to deal with underlying tensions between these values by ignoring contradictions or interpreting discursive elements according to their own preferences. As such, the business networks try to avoid the ambiguity between preservation ("sustainable") and development – the demands of the present and more or less probable demands of future generations – by linking the term "sustainable" to the well-being of the private sector and the term development to the increase of corporate productivity (e.g. econsense 2006; WBCSD 2002). However, predictions about what will be are uncertain; the companies themselves do not seem to understand the objectives to be achieved. There is no fixed status quo for an ever-changing nature and restless world. Development is the only alternative and development consumes resources. While some technical applications have known negative impacts, the full range of consequences is unknown. Ambivalences inherent in the discourse and uncertainties along with the diverse aims of different agents form the platform for ongoing political negotiations and create a forum for political debate.

Other actors in the sustainability discourse may also face the difficulties described above. A balance between ecological, social, and economic interests does not seem likely, at least not over a longer time period. As yet, there are no conventions or optimal parameters but only conflicting goals that must be resolved. Ambivalences are indicators for these conflicting goals. They offer opportunities to force opportunistic interests and they demonstrate the need to combat undesired developments. In the struggle for discursive power, global companies benefit from monetary advantages, free-market systems, structural connections between mass media and politics and the dominant influence of neo-liberal norms. Furthermore, some discourses are more successful sources of power than others and may imply a particular stabilization of business's discursive power. Sustainable development can be regarded as a particularly strong source of discursive power, characterized by its high social legitimacy and its open, malleable character. It can be used strategically to influence global norms, avert regulatory pressure, shape media attention, shift societal expectations, and generate social legitimacy.

Nevertheless, the discursive power of global companies requires more than just the use of material resources. It is based on legitimacy and the acceptance of business-friendly norms and ideas. Thus, discursive power also faces limits. Business representatives themselves indirectly point out that their powerful position is challenged today (Stigson 2000: 5). Scholars often distinguish between two types of challenges to business's discursive power. First, global companies are particularly vulnerable to economic crises and scandals. Second, a change with respect to dominant norms and socially accepted ideas may limit business's discursive power (e.g. Fuchs 2007). The social acceptance of sustainable development can also challenge business's discursive power. Complex normative concepts such as sustainable development need to be considered legitimate in order to provide a source for discursive power.

However, the empirical analysis for this chapter identifies a third way to challenging business's discursive power, which is related to the discourse-inherent rules that companies have to deal with. Participation in the discourse requires following these rules. Companies that don't follow the rules of the larger sustainability discourse can be sidelined. If the rules are violated, for example due to inability to deal with ambivalences, negligence in the development of discursive scripts and story lines, or even the breaking of taboos, credibility and influence may be diminished. Conversely, convincing concepts, innovative ideas, helpful coalitions, or simply argumentative skills may increase the power of corporations.

As such, former WBCSD member Wal-Mart has not been very successful in using sustainable development as a source of discursive power. While the company has implemented a sustainability strategy since 2005 and continues to pour into its sustainability strategy (e.g. WBCSD 2009a), its lobbying expenses have increased enormously since the early 2000s (Wal-Mart Watch 2011: 10). However, the company is still subject to criticism. Several groups and media reports have emerged alerting the public to the company's policies and business practices on issues such as working conditions, environmental practices, and child labor violations. Although Wal-Mart has launched initiatives to counter criticisms, it loses credibility and discursive power.

Conclusion

Ambivalences, uncertainties, and contradictory values within contested concepts form a platform for ongoing political discussion. They open a fascinating stage for discourses that involve actors with different positions. This chapter has examined how global companies wield discursive power in order to gain legitimacy as political and social actors. Hence, global companies were treated as an integral part of global political processes, which they try to shape. It was shown how business networks use elements of discursive power; for example, by underestimating conflicts of interest or using story lines, metaphors, religious allusions, and euphemisms. Furthermore, this chapter has argued that companies combine important social discourses to extend discursive power in additional areas, probably to increase the overall weight of their arguments. The analysis of story lines has illustrated that global companies see themselves as the most competent and indispensable players in defining societal goals. At the same time, global companies benefit from the dominance of neoliberal norms, financial benefits, free-market systems, and structural connections between mass media and politics.

Nevertheless, the discursive power of global companies is also based on legitimacy and the acceptance of business-friendly norms and ideas. Corporations' discursive power faces limits: Discourse-inherent rules, which describe currently accepted ways to interact within a specific discourse, may present a way to challenge business's discursive power. Participation in discourses requires following these rules. If they are violated, companies can be sidelined and their credibility and influence may be diminished.

In order to better understand the way businesses wield discursive power, this chapter has explored how the business networks WBCSD and econsense intend to shape the discourse on sustainable development. It gave evidence that business networks are using the inherent ambivalences of sustainability to reframe the discourse to their own benefit. Furthermore, it argued that the various social constructions of "sustainable development" stem from the concept's inherent vagueness.

However, the "new business paradigm" (Stigson 2002) of sustainability has so far consisted of the "old" one of economic growth. Even with respect to the recent economic crisis, global companies refer to sustainable development and highlight the economic dimension (WBCSD 2009b: 3). It is unlikely that the economic crisis will cause significant changes in the business discourse on sustainable development. In the end, global companies have the chance to shape how the concept of sustainable development is realized in the global governance system. The "reality" of sustainable development is negotiated and constructed through social discourse. At the same time, the possibilities of "governance without government" (Rosenau and Czempiel 1992) are especially high due to the "Retreat of the State" (Strange 1996) and the absence of a global regulatory state. In the future, the story lines of actors engaged in the discourse may emphasize social and ecological realities. After all, "whoever sets the terms of discourse will almost always determine the outcome. Naming the game is the name of the game, and admission to this contest is controlled by gatekeepers" (Lowi 2001: 131–132). Nevertheless, the real risks that take place outside of the discourse must be recognized. Beyond the discursive shaping of the concept, actors involved in the discourse have a real responsibility to represent factual reality in their statements. Actors should keep in mind that there are real consequences beyond the short-term bottom line at the company.

Notes

1 I am grateful for useful comments of John Mikler, Miranda Schreurs, and Lisa Pettibone.
2 Social and environmental business standards are not to be confused with a so-called "business ethics" that implies a moral evaluation of business conduct (Haufler 1999: 201).
3 It is a moot point whether Foucault's notion of discourse can be treated as a discourse theory since the term itself is more of a concept than a full theory. Thus, discourse analyses implement Foucault's definition of discourse without referring to discourse theory.
4 Of course, it is not just the number of multinational corporations (MNCs) but also their degree of concentration and "control over the world's key industrial sectors" (Mikler 2012: 56) that indicates dominance.
5 Author's translation.
6 Author's translation.
7 Author's translation.
8 Author's translation.

References

Allianz Group. 2007. In Pursuit of a Sustainable World. Sustainable Development Summary Report 2007, http://www.allianz.com/static-resources/en/responsibility/media/documents/v_1303069088000/allianz_sd_report_2007.pdf. Accessed November 26, 2009.

BASF. 2009. We Shape the Future. Corporate Report 2008, http://basf.com/group/corporate/
    en/function/conversions:/publish/content/about-basf/facts-reports/reports/2008/ZOAC090
    6E_BASF_SE_Financial_Statements_2008.pdf. Accessed November 26, 2009.
Bayer. 2008. Science for a Better Life. Sustainable Development Report 2007, http://www
    .bayer.com/en/sustainable-development-report-2007.pdfx. Accessed November 26, 2009.
Beem, Betsi and Mikler, John. 2011. "National Regulations for a Borderless Industry:
    US versus UK Approaches to Online Gambling." *Policy and Society*, 30 (3): 161–176,
    DOI:10.1016/j.polsoc.2011.07.001.
Bosch. 2006. Corporate Social Responsibility Report 2005/2006, http://www.unglobalco
    mpact.org/system/attachments/2138/original/COP.pdf?1262614311. Accessed November
    26, 2009.
Bosch. 2009. Corporate Social Responsibility Report 2007/2008, http://www.econsense.de/_
    CSR_MITGLIEDER/_CSR_NACHHALTIGKEITSBERICHTE/images/Bosch/Bosch_CSR_
    Report_2007_2008.pdf. Accessed November 26, 2009.
Carroll, Archie B. 2008. *A History of Corporate Social Responsibility: Concepts and Practices.*
    Oxford: Oxford University Press.
Conzelmann, Thomas and Wolf, Klaus D. 2007. "Doing Good While Doing Well?
    Potenzial und Grenzen grenzüberschreitender privatwirtschaftlicher Selbstregulierung."
    In *Macht und Ohnmacht internationaler Institutionen: Festschrift für Volker Rit-
    tberger*, ed. Andreas Hasenclever and Volker Rittberger, 145–175. Frankfurt am Main:
    Campus.
Crane, Andrew. 2008. *Corporate Social Responsibility in Global Context*, 2nd edn. Los
    Angeles: Sage.
Crane, Andrew, Matten, Dirk, McWilliams, Abigail, Moon, Jeremy, and Siegel, Donald S.,
    eds. 2008. *The Oxford Handbook of Corporate Social Responsibility*. Oxford: Oxford
    University Press.
DuPont. 2005. A DuPont Perspective on Biotechnology: Speech by Chad Holliday, Chairman
    and CEO, http://www.wbcsd.org/DocRoot/3WQKubr7aOuQN1rZAeup/ITBiotech.pdf.
    Accessed November 26, 2009.
econsense. 2005. Produkte des 21. Jahrhunderts. Innovativ, Effizient, Nachhaltig. Ein Beitrag
    zur Politischen IPP Diskussion, http://www.econsense.de. Accessed November 26, 2009.
econsense. 2006. Successfully Tackling Demographic Challenges, http://www.econsense.de/_
    ENGLISH/_publications/images/WorkingDoc_Demography.pdf. Accessed November 26,
    2009.
econsense. 2007a. Climate Protection: On Successful Paths? Econsense Discussion Paper
    on Climate Protection, http://www.econsense.de/_PUBLIKATIONEN/_ECONSENSE_
    PUBLIK/images/Climate_Protection_Paper.pdf. Accessed November 26, 2009.
econsense. 2007b. Stellungnahme zum Indikatorenbericht 2006 des Statistischen Bunde-
    samtes zur Nachhaltigen Entwicklung in Deutschland, http://www.econsense.de/_PUBL
    IKATIONEN/_ECONSENSE_PUBLIK/images/Stellungnahme%20Indikatorenbericht.pdf.
    Accessed November 26, 2009.
econsense. 2009. econsense-Journalistenpreis, http://www.econsense.de/_presse/_journalistenp
    reis/. Accessed November 26, 2009.
econsense. 2011. Profile and Objectives, http://econsense.org/_ENGLISH/. Accessed Novem-
    ber 26, 2009.
Evonik. 2009. Living Up to Our Responsibility: Corporate Responsibility Report 2008, http://
    corporate.evonik.com/_layouts/Websites/Internet/NewsAttachmentHandlerSec.ashx?fileid
    =3288&newsid=7390&NewsSecToken=wtQuV4YnNvn5oArzh0H2nPa0%2ftczROQis
    FfwgBiLzg%2bT1KZxvbu6pPc%2f45joycIu&AllowNews=True. Accessed November
    26, 2009.
Falkner, Robert. 2010. "Business and Global Climate Governance: A Neo-Pluralist Perspec-
    tive." In *Business and Global Governance*, ed. Morten Ougaard and Anna Leander, 99–117.
    London: Routledge.

Fickel, Brigitte. 2009. Laudatio. econsense-Journalistenpreis 2009, http://www.econsense.de/_
PRESSE/_JOURNALISTENPREIS/images/Laudatio_2009.pdf. Accessed December 1, 2010.

Foucault, Michel. 1966. *Les mots et les choses: une archéologie des sciences humaines.* Paris:
Gallimard.

Foucault, Michel. 1969. *L'archéologie du savoir.* Paris: Gallimard.

Foucault, Michel. 1971. *L'ordre du discours.* Paris: Gallimard.

Fuchs, Doris A. 2007. *Business Power in Global Governance.* Boulder: Rienner.

Fuchs, Doris A. and Lederer, Markus. 2007. "The Power of Business." *Business and Politics,*
9 (3): 1–17. DOI:10.2202/1469-3569.1214.

Habermas, Jürgen. 1981. *Theorie des kommunikativen Handelns.* Frankfurt am Main:
Suhrkamp.

Hajer, Maarten A. 1995. *The Politics of Environmental Discourse: Ecological Modernization
and the Policy Process.* Oxford: Clarendon Press.

Haufler, Virginia. 1999. "Self-Regulation and Business Norms: Political Risk, Political
Activism." In *Private Authority and International Affairs,* ed. Claire Cutler, Virginia Haufler, and Tony Porter, 199–222. New York: State University of New York Press.

Kolleck, Nina. 2011. *Global Governance, Corporate Responsibility und die diskursive Macht
multinationaler Unternehmen: freiwillige Initiativen der Wirtschaft für eine nachhaltige
Entwicklung?* Baden Baden: Nomos.

Kolleck, Nina. 2012. "Shaping Sustainability. Zu den Chancen und Grenzen der diskursiven
Macht multinationaler Unternehmen." *Zeitschrift für Wirtschafts- und Unternehmensethik
(zfwu),* 13 (2): 154–168.

Koller, Peter. 1991. "Facetten der Macht." *Analyse und Kritik,* 13 (2): 107–133.

Laclau, Ernesto, and Mouffe, Chantal. 1987. "Post-Marxism without Apologies." *New Left
Review* 166 (1): 79–106.

Laclau, Ernesto and Mouffe, Chantal. 2001. *Hegemony and Socialist Strategy: Towards a
Radical Democratic Politics.* London: Verso.

Levy, David and Egan, Daniel. 1998. "Capital Contests: National and Transnational Channels
of Corporate Influence in the Climate Change Negotiations." *Politics and Society,* 26 (3):
337–361. DOI:10.1177/0032329298026003003.

Levy, David L. and Egan, Daniel. 2000. "Corporate Political Action in the Global Polity:
National and Transnational Strategies in the Climate Change Negotiations." In *Non-State
Actors and Authority in the Global System,* ed. Richard A. Higgott, Geoffrey R.D. Under-
hill, and Andreas Bieler, 138–154. London: Routledge.

Levy, David L. and Kaplan, Rami. 2008. "Corporate Social Responsibility and Theories of
Global Governance: Strategic Contestation in Global Issue Arenas." In *The Oxford Hand-
book of Corporate Social Responsibility,* ed. Andrew Crane, 433–451. Oxford: Oxford
University Press.

Levy, David L. and Newell, Peter J., eds. 2005. *The Business of Global Environmental Governance.* Cambridge: MIT.

Lowi, Theodore J. 2001. "Our Millennium: Political Science Confronts the Global Corporate Economy." *International Political Science Review,* 22 (2): 131–150. DOI: 10.1177/
0192512101222001.

Lukes, Steven. 2005. *Power: A Radical View,* 2nd edn. Basingstoke: Palgrave Macmillan.

Mikler, John. 2007. "Framing Responsibility: National Variations in Corporations' Motivations." *Policy and Society,* 26 (4): 67–104. DOI: 10.1016/S1449-4035(07)70121-2.

Mikler, John. 2011a. "Plus ca Change? A Varieties of Capitalism Approach to Concern for
the Environment." *Global Society,* 5 (3): 331–352. DOI:10.1080/13600826.2011.577033.

Mikler, John. 2011b. "Sharing Sovereignty for Policy Outcomes." *Policy and Society,* 30 (3):
151–160. DOI:10.1016/j.polsoc.2011.07.007.

Mikler John. 2012. "The Illusion of the Power of Markets." *Journal of Australian Political
Economy,* 68: 41–61.

Mühle, Ursula. 2010. *The Politics of Corporate Social Responsibility: The Rise of a Global Business Norm.* Frankfurt am Main: Campus.

Newell, Peter J. 2004. "Business and International Environmental Governance. The State of the Art." In *The Business of Global Environmental Governance*, ed. David L. Levy and Peter J. Newell, 21–45. Cambridge, MA; London: MIT.

Onuf, Nicholas G. 2007. "Foreword." In *The Social Construction of Climate Change. Power, Knowledge, Norms, Discourses*, ed. Mary E. Pettenger, 10–15. Aldershot: Ashgate.

Rosenau, James N. and Czempiel, Ernst-Otto. 1992. *Governance without Government: Order and Change in World Politics.* Cambridge: Cambridge University Press.

Ruggie, John G. 2003. "Taking Embedded Liberalism Global: The Corporate Connection." In *Taming Globalization: Frontiers of Governance*, ed. Matthias Koenig-Archibugi and David Held, 1–37. Aldershot: Ashgate.

Schmidheiny, Stephan. 1998. *Changing Course: A Global Business Perspective on Development and the Environment.* Cambridge, MA: MIT.

Schreurs, Miranda A. and Papadakis, Elim. 2007. *Historical Dictionary of the Green Movements*, 2nd edn. Lanham: Scarecrow Press.

Schreurs, Miranda A., Selin, Henrik, and VanDeveer, Stacy D. 2009. "Expanding Transatlantic Relations: Implications for Environment and Energy Politics." In *Transatlantic Environment and Energy Politics: Comparative and International Perspectives*, ed. Miranda A. Schreurs, Henrik Selin, and Stacy D. VanDeveer, 1–20. Farnham: Ashgate.

Shakespeare, William. 2002. *As You Like It.* New York: Sparknotes.

Siemens. 2009. Sustainability Report 2008, http://www.siemens.com/responsibility/report/08/pool/en/sustainability_report_2008.pdf. Accessed October 26, 2011.

Sklair, Leslie. 2002. "The Transnational Capitalist Class and Global Politics: Deconstructing the Corporate-State Connection." *International Political Science Review*, 23 (2): 159–174. DOI:10.1177/0192512102023002003.

Smith, Adam. 1761. *The Theory of Moral Sentiments*, 2nd edn. London: Millar.

Stigson, Björn. 2000. Globalization and Corporate Responsibility for Environment and Social Development: The WBCSD Perspective, http://www.wbcsd.org/DocRoot/Qdwgf00L7VtIshuPK2Oc/Goteborg.pdf. Accessed October 26, 2011.

Stigson, Björn. 2002. Corporate Social Responsibility: A New Business Paradigm, http://www.docstoc.com/docs/69006950/Corporate-social-responsibility–a-new-business-paradigm. Accessed October 26, 2011.

Strange, Susan. 1996. *The Retreat of the State: The Diffusion of Power in the World Economy.* Cambridge: Cambridge University Press.

Telekom. 2006. Leading Change, http://www.download-telekom.de/dt/StaticPage/47/28/72/PuN_06_engl.pdf_472872.pdf. Accessed October 26, 2011.

ThyssenKrupp Steel. 2005a. Das Richtige tun. Richtig? Nachhaltigkeitsbericht 2004/2005, http://www.econsense.de/_CSR_MITGLIEDER/_CSR_NACHHALTIGKEITSBERICHTE/images/ThyssenKrupp_AG/TKS_NH-Bericht_2004_2005.pdf. Accessed October 26, 2011.

ThyssenKrupp Steel. 2005b. Doing the Right Thing. Right? Sustainability Report 2004–2005, http://www.thyssenkrupp-steel-europe.com/en/publikationen/unternehmensinformationen.jsp. Accessed October 26, 2011.

Vogel, David. 2006. The Private Regulation of Global Corporate Conduct, Paper Prepared for the Annual Meeting of the American Political Science Association, http://escholarship.org/uc/item/8g66g3hf#page-2. Accessed October 26, 2011.

Wal-Mart Watch. 2011. What's Right? Wal-Mart's Words vs. Wal-Mart's Political Priorities, http://walmartwatch.org/files/2011/06/WW-Political-Giving_0602.pdf. Accessed October 26, 2011.

WBCSD. 1998. Signals of Change. Business Progress towards Sustainable Development, http://www.wbcsd.org/DocRoot/hkaopUSqok425SLACneQ/signals.pdf. Accessed October 26, 2011.

WBCSD. 2000. Corporate Social Responsibility: Making Good Business Sense, http://www.wbcsd.org/templates/TemplateWBCSD5/layout.asp?type=p&MenuId=MTE0OQ. Accessed October 26, 2011.

WBCSD. 2002. Sustainable Development: A Learning Tool, http://www.wbcsd.org/DocRoot/omMth9T0juWwQ2XDHa7O/20021118_sdmap.pdf. Accessed October 26, 2011.

WBCSD. 2004a. Annual Review 2004: A Decade of Action and Learning, http://www.wbcsd.org/DocRoot/4fLbdTRkS0gfTk7cq2Ov/ar2004.pdf. Accessed October 26, 2011.

WBCSD. 2004b. Mobility 2030: Meeting the Challenges to Sustainability, http://www.wbcsd.org/web/publications/mobility/mobility-full.pdf. Accessed October 26, 2011.

WBCSD. 2006. Catalyzing Change: A Short History of the WBCSD, http://www.wbcsd.org/DocRoot/acZUEFxTAKIvTs0KOtii/catalyzing-change.pdf. Accessed October 26, 2011.

WBCSD. 2007. Annual Review 2006. Then & Now: Celebrating the 20th Anniversary of the "Brundtland Report," http://www.sustentabilidad.uai.edu.ar/pdf/info/annual-review2006.pdf. Accessed 26 October 2011.

WBCSD. 2009a. Wal-Mart's Fertile Partnership with Small Farmers in Central America, http://www.inclusivebusiness.org/2009/03/walmart-tierra-fertil.html. Accessed September 9, 2011.

WBCSD. 2009b. WBCSD Annual Review 2008 – What a Way to Run the World, http://www.wbcsd.org/DocRoot/KsdOfKvIONwQuWjPmZl8/rapport_annuel_08.pdf. Accessed November 1, 2011.

WBCSD. 2010. Business and Development: Challenges and Opportunities in a Rapidly Changing World, http://www.wbcsd.org/web/development/business_and_development.pdf. Accessed October 26, 2011.

WBCSD. 2011a. About the WBCSD, http://www.wbcsd.org/templates/TemplateWBCSD5/layout.asp?type=p&MenuId=NjA&doOpen=1&ClickMenu=LeftMenu. Accessed October 26, 2011.

WBCSD. 2011b. Annual Review 2010/2011. Transformation in the Turbulent Teens, http://www.wbcsd.org/DocRoot/9hSGwxf2cX5DULniplTL/wbcsd_annualReview2010-11.pdf. Accessed October 26, 2011.

WBCSD. 2011c. People Matter Reward. Linking Sustainability to Pay, http://www.wbcsd.org/DocRoot/fXxvKXV3CbppJvboQgG3/WBCSD_People%20Matter%20Reward.pdf. Accessed October 26, 2011.

WCED. 1987. Our Common Future: Report of the World Commission on Environment and Development, Chapter 2: Towards Sustainable Development, http://www.un-documents.net/ocf-02.htm. Accessed October 26, 2011.

Wright, Christopher and Rwabizambuga, Alexis. 2006. "Institutional Pressures, Corporate Reputation, and Voluntary Codes of Conduct: An Examination of the Equator Principles." *Business and Society Review*, 111 (1): 89–117. DOI:10.1111/j.1467-8594.2006.00263.x.

Zadek, Simon. 2007. *The Civil Corporation: The New Economy of Corporate Citizenship*, 2nd edn. London: Earthscan.

Part III   Global Companies and the State

Chapter 9

How Global Companies Make National Regulations

Terry O'Callaghan and Vlado Vivoda

Introduction

Regulation is essential if chaos and disorder are to be prevented. Individuals need to regulate their behavior, not only to keep the body functioning efficiently, but also to ensure it performs optimally. An impaired capacity for self-regulation generally leads to a breakdown. It is the same with the social order. If communities are to function, they need to have regulations to govern the conduct of their members. Consequently, regulation can be thought of as the parameters that are required to benefit the whole of society. This is why states are essential for a healthy society.

States make regulation across a wide spectrum. These include regulations governing the economy, law and order, health, taxation, and customs, as well as the regulation governing the political system itself. Yet they do not make these rules in a vacuum. Various individuals and actors also have input, as each seeks to shape the rules in various ways. The role of the state is as much about charting a course through these competing interests, as it is about developing and implementing regulation itself.

This chapter looks at how one group of actors – global companies – make national regulation. Or, perhaps more correctly, how global companies influence decision-making and ultimately the regulatory agenda of the state itself. In order to understand this influence, it is necessary first to understand the nature of regulation and its various forms. Following that, we examine a range of specific "tools" used by global companies to shape the regulation agenda in such a way as to benefit them. We support our discussion with two cases – the petroleum and pharmaceutical industries. We frame the discussion in this chapter by mainly focusing on the United States, as it exemplifies the liberal case where the state regulates the market, and therefore global companies.

The Handbook of Global Companies, First Edition. Edited by John Mikler.
© 2013 John Wiley & Sons, Ltd. Published 2013 by John Wiley & Sons, Ltd.

Regulation

The concept of "regulation" is defined in at least three ways in the academic literature. The first definition refers to all the mechanisms of social control that the state has at its disposal. This includes not only the state's capacity to regulate the market, but also its capacity to set policy prescriptions in areas such as law enforcement, health, and labor. The second definition refers to the aggregate efforts by government to steer the economy. This is a narrower rendering of "regulation" and focuses primarily on the rules which help to stop or reduce market failure (Jordana and Levi-Faur 2005: 3). The third definition, and the one primarily employed in this chapter, is "the promulgation of an authoritative set of rules, accompanied by some mechanism, typically a public agency, for monitoring and promoting compliance with these rules" (Baldwin and Scott 1998: 3). This definition locates the idea of regulation within an institutional framework in order for the regulation to function effectively and achieve its purpose. We might call this a regulatory architecture or a regulatory regime. The latter term is useful because the word "regime" highlights the importance of a monitoring and compliance capability. Without it, a regulatory regime is a pointless artifact of a toothless government.

A regulatory regime serves multiple functions. At its most basic, it prevents anarchy and provides a legal basis upon which societies are able to flourish. In Hobbes's notion of the state of nature, there were no rules upon which to found a social order. Consequently, life was "solitary, poor, nasty, brutish, and short" (Hobbes 1986: 186). It was only when, through the use of force, the Leviathan was able to put an end to the state of nature, that individuals could begin to act socially and pursue higher order pursuits such as science and culture. In other words, the Leviathan brought regulation to people's lives and allowed them to think about other things besides survival.

In a more modern sense, however, a regulatory regime can serve a twofold purpose. First, it seeks to promote certain activities. In the context of foreign investment, for example, the state establishes incentive schemes to attract investment. These may include tax holidays, profit repatriation, 100% ownership of assets, and exemptions from land tax. These are enabling forms of regulation (Baldwin and Cave 1999: 2), which allow the state to take advantage of the benefits that MNCs bring: capital, technology, and knowhow. Providing such incentives to investors potentially leads to improvements in the economic performance of the state, including better employment outcomes, education and training, and wealth creation. In contrast, there are restrictive regulations. These seek to curtail or manage certain kinds of behavior. They set limits on what MNCs may do in the course of their commercial activities. Regulations to ensure that they do not pollute the environment or ones that set out working conditions for employees are good examples of these kinds of rules. Enabling and restrictive regulations provide a set of guidelines which, in theory, enable MNCs to operate in ways that satisfy their commercial ambitions, but also serve a government's long-term economic and social interests.

Effective administration of an industry sector, then, is determined by how effectively a state is able to put into practice these two policy trajectories and achieve an appropriate balance between the two. Investment rules that are too restrictive tend to deter foreign investors, while too much emphasis on enabling rules may undermine a state's economic interests by reducing its income stream. Getting the balance right is, essentially, the art of government.

Regulatory regimes form and develop within unique social and political contexts. They are influenced by such factors as language and culture, history, norms, taboos, conventions, forms of government, and institutional structures. This is sometimes referred to as a country's "institutional endowment" (Levy and Spiller 1994: 205). The key point is that institutions and regulatory frameworks evolve according to the particular institutional endowment of a country, and this ultimately determines the efficacy of its regulatory regimes, its capacity for reform, and its ability to attract foreign investment. As Levy and Spiller (1994: 202) note, "the credibility and effectiveness of a regulatory framework – and hence its ability to facilitate private investment – varies with a country's political and social institutions." For example, mining regulation in a number of countries in the Asia-Pacific region suffers from poor institutional capacity. This generally means that foreign direct investment levels in the sector are lower than in those countries with well-developed regulatory environments (O'Callaghan 2009; 2010; Vivoda 2008; 2011a). Yet, regulatory regimes in developed economies such as the United States are not immune from these sorts of problems. The global financial crisis (GFC) was caused, in part, by poor regulation of the financial services sector (Omarova and Feibelman 2009). Similarly, part of the blame for BP's recent oil spill in the Gulf of Mexico (2010) has been leveled at the US Department of Interior's Minerals Management Service (MMS), the regulatory body which was responsible for regulatory compliance of drilling operations in the Gulf (Urbina 2010). The official verdict of the inquiry into the spill suggested that regulatory capture by the oil and gas industry may have occurred. Regulatory capture can be defined as "de facto control of the state and its regulatory agencies by the 'regulated' interests, enabling these interests to transfer wealth to themselves at the expense of society" (Mattli and Woods 2009: 10). It occurs when an industry gains enough political power to undermine the neutrality of regulatory agencies or is able to reduce their effectiveness. Bribes and gifts to politicians and regulators are key ways in which capture takes place. In the case of the Gulf oil companies, the co-chairman of the inquiry into the spill has suggested that "there has been a cozy relationship between the regulator and the industry, largely driven by the fact that the same regulator responsible for setting and enforcing industry safety is also the agency that collects almost $20 billion a year in royalties" (O'Brien 2011).

The most common form of restrictive regulation is "command and control" (Ogus 1994). The state makes laws which are then policed by a government agency to ensure compliance. Command and control is generally seen in areas where the government wants to ensure certain standards of behavior are met. Issue areas such as food hygiene, weights and measures, pollution control, construction, and consumer protection are all examples where governments seek to limit certain activities and set appropriate standards. In other words, the main role of command and control forms of regulation is to correct for market failure. Until the 1980s, this form of regulation predominated. However, a number of scholars and policy makers began to question the efficiency of such techniques and leveled a number of criticisms against this sort of regulation (Parker 2002: 7–14). While command and control forms of regulation are not without their difficulties, effective regulation of societies and economies will always rely on them and other regulatory techniques, in order to achieve good governance outcomes. But problems with command and control led to a shift in thinking by governments and the employment of new methods of regulation. This occurred in the United States and Great Britain in the 1980s, but became a feature of most advanced economies from the 1990s onward (Vogel 1996; Hodgson 2006). The centerpiece of this shift has been the trend toward deregulation and privatization. It is within this context that the emergence of self-regulation needs to be understood. As Levi-Faur (2005: 13) notes, "a new division of labor between state and society (e.g. privatization) is accompanied by an increase in delegation, proliferation of new technologies of regulation, formalization of inter-institutional and intra-institutional relations, and the proliferation of self-regulation in the shadow of the state."

Regulation is not simply a top down process imposed by governments. As part of attempts to self-regulate, companies also have a significant role to play in the regulatory process. In some cases, this is seen as controversial, with a number of commentators concerned about the capacity of companies to lobby governments, but in other cases it may be a genuine attempt to improve the image of industry or to reduce red-tape in order to stream-line an industry. In the next section of this paper, we examine some of the more important ways in which firms influence regulation.

Mechanisms of Influence

Government actions affect global companies' economic value more than any other group of stakeholders, with the exception of customers (Dua, Heil, and Wilkins 2010). The effects of government on competitive position of firms are an important determinant of profitability as acts of government create individual winners and losers in the marketplace (Boddewyn and Brewer 1994: 121). Global companies may support regulation that benefits their positions vis-à-vis rivals, entrants, substitute products, buyers, and suppliers. This may be termed the strategic use of public policy for the purpose of gaining competitive advantage. When government uses its authority to implement public policies through the regulatory process, the main response of firms is adaptation. Given such importance of government actions on their operations, global companies use various strategies to influence national regulations and public policy in order to improve their business environment (Hillman and Hitt 1999: 825). Business interests are selective about exerting their influence and when they do get involved it is on issues that have high stakes for their operations (Kamieniecki 2006). In general, corporations influence government regulation through lobbying, campaign contributions and captured regulatory agencies (Lux, Crook, and Woehr 2011: 223–224; Shaffer 1995: 495). They also do so via industry and corporate self-regulation. The choice of strategy is contingent on the nature of the issue (Getz 1997). Global companies engage in these activities to enhance their revenues and reduce costs, but also to influence the use of government resources and coercive powers that influence their profits (Hillman, Keim, and Schuler 2004: 838). Research has shown that corporate political activity is positively related to firm performance (Lux, Crook, and Woehr 2011: 243) and that corporations are significant contributors to the shape and content of national regulation, with their contributions having significant effect on social welfare (Danielsen 2005: 411). One dimension of corporate political activity is not necessarily a good proxy for all forms as the different dimensions have differences in their properties (Hansen and Mitchell 2000: 899).

Lobbying

Lobbying is the act of attempting to influence decisions made by government officials, most often legislators or members of regulatory agencies. Various individuals or groups of people can be lobbyists, including private-sector individuals or corporations, legislators or government officials and advocacy or interest groups. More specifically, lobbying can be defined as the expenditure of resources by a firm or group of firms in order to secure a favorable political or legal environment for their activities (Polk and Schmutzler 2005: 915). Although lobbying actions are most frequently geared toward achieving preferable domestic policies, larger governments with regional or international influence can be petitioned for favorable foreign policies. Domestic interest groups attempt to gain, often indirectly, economic benefits through a government's exclusive diplomatic channels. Governments often hold a great deal of information unknown to the private sector, as well as direct contacts with officials and lawmakers of foreign countries. As monopolists of force, states also reserve the threat of war as a means to their ends. Economic interest groups can, instead of expending resources on adjusting their business to market conditions, expend those resources on adjusting market conditions to their business or, in other words, to enhance their "rent-seeking" (Murphy, Shleifer, and Vishny 1993: 409).

The United States is the prime example of a powerful nation whose foreign dealings and economic policies are highly responsive to special interests. Both the structures of the electoral system and the government's coercive powers grant a significant level of policymaking access to private organizations. A thorough examination of the government's scope of powers, the structure of policymaking institutions, and the long-term trend of increasing reported lobbying expenditure reveals considerable evidence that political proficiency is part of an essential set of skills for the modern US multinational corporation.

American institutions have a long history of lobbying, beginning in essence with the first amendment of the Constitution: "[Congress shall make no law abridging] the right of the people peaceably to assemble, and to petition the government for a redress of grievances." Increasing demand for lobbyists in the late 1980s led to a growth in popularity of the practice, and the "Washington Game" began to perpetuate itself. The high demand also changed the traditional viewpoint that it was inappropriate for former elected officials to become lobbyists. Since 1998, 43% of the 198 members of Congress who are no longer in any elected office have registered as lobbyists at least once (Congress Watch 2005). The overall result of this evolution is the ever-increasing presence of private money circulating in public affairs. The bottom line is that to the American politician, money matters greatly.

In 2011, US interest groups spent $3.32 billion on reported lobbying expenses – over $6 million per Congressman (OpenSecrets.org 2012a). A large portion of that expenditure came from global companies that generate and control large amounts of money. Important lobbying strategy lies in promoting favorable ideas to support firm or industry-specific goals. The aim is to achieve ideological or empirical consensus in policymakers and in, more importantly, the public. While some expenditure for this objective is through private organizations, the end result when it is successful is a favorable alteration of the law.

Besides the standard range of direct government benefits which global companies seek for their domestic markets (direct subsidies, tax breaks, etc.), MNCs often pursue policies that positively affect their standing as global companies (or negatively affect their competitors). This could mean, for example, arguing for a tariff that may not be necessary to inhibit a rival's trade, but to make its production inputs more expensive if it depends heavily on outsourced components. MNCs can lobby for direct negotiations or even the use of force between its home country and a potential host country in order to increase its stock of investment abroad. These are but two examples of the many ways in which global companies can attain indirect subsidies, whose legislative elements frequently obscure their ultimate beneficiaries who, in public discussion, are supplanted by symbolic language.

Campaign Contributions

Another mechanism which global companies use to influence regulation is through campaign funding. In the United States, although the Federal Corrupt Practice Act of 1925 had contained very strong provisions on campaign funding, they were never enforced. The Federal Elections Commission (FEC) was established in 1974 to enforce the Federal Elections Campaign Act. This was very important because it was the first time an enforcement mechanism had been established in connection with a campaign finance law. The 1974 Act was thus a very significant step toward campaign finance reform when it was first passed as it put limits on both campaign contributions and campaign spending. However after the Act was passed, there was a very important Supreme Court case in 1976 (*Buckley v. Valeo*). The decision in that case was that campaign spending could not be limited. The Court felt that to limit spending was a violation of freedom of speech. Moreover, the Court ruled that individuals could contribute as much of their own money as they wanted to their own campaigns (Schultz 1998).

What the decision allowing individuals to spend an unlimited amount of their own personal money on their own campaigns did was to increase the tendency of the Senate to be a "millionaires' club." It also affected the House in a similar way. Since the Democrats do not have as many corporate and wealthy connections as the Republicans, and therefore have trouble raising money, the Democrats tend to nominate candidates for the Senate who have a lot of their own money to spend on their election campaigns. A glance at the roster of Democrats in the Senate reveals numerous millionaires.

The 1974 Act also allowed for political action committees (PACs) to be established in the United States. A political action committee is a separate fund or organizations to which members of a group – such as a corporation, labor union, or trade association – can donate money. These funds, in turn, are used to contribute to political campaigns in the name of the group. All employees of a corporation can make voluntary contributions to the corporation's PAC, which gives a lot of strength to corporate PACs. Even if a corporation has a PAC, in addition it can also contribute to the PAC of a trade association that represents its industry. In the period since 1974, corporate and trade association PACs have come to dominate PAC contributions and gain far more influence on the government than other PACs. Thus instead of limiting corporate influence, the 1974 Act set up a mechanism – the PAC – for legitimizing that influence (Milyo, Primo, and Groseclose 2000). Consequently, global companies have benefited greatly from the provision allowing for PACs.

Since the mid-1970s, other ways have emerged to get around the campaign financing law in the United States, and one is referred to as soft money. As PACs became major sources of funding, political parties began to lose some of their influence with their own candidates. Consequently, Congress amended the Act in 1979 in such a way as to try to strengthen political parties. These amendments allowed political parties to collect money for party building activities and for voter registration drives as long as their efforts did not support any particular candidate. These contributions, commonly referred to as soft money, do not have to be reported. In addition, the amount that can be contributed this way is unlimited. The political party can use it to advertise for candidates in general, without focus on a particular candidate (Ansolabehere and Snyder 2000). The soft money provision is an additional contribution method which has made contribution limitations ineffective.

Independent expenditures are another important mechanism often used to manipulate campaign limitations in the United States. An independent expenditure is made by an individual or organization that is not connected with a candidate's campaign, but favors that particular candidate. Recently, some of these independent expenditures have become very suspicious. Many obviously support a particular candidate and they are made during election time. The difficulty here is that the issue involves freedom of speech. People or organizations must be allowed to express their views freely. Yet, independent expenditures can be used in ways to get around the election laws. Issue advertisements by political parties are a fourth mechanism which has been used recently to get around election laws. Political parties, labor unions or corporations can run ads that do not mention a particular candidate by name, but support issues that the candidate is known to stress. Given that issue advertisements are not coordinated with the individual candidate's campaign they are completely unregulated. Thus, if the Republican or Democratic candidate's campaign is unable to collect sufficient funds because it has reached its limit, there are other mechanisms at its disposal through which the campaign can be supported (Malbin and Gais 1998).

Thus far we have discussed PACs, soft money, independent expenditures, and issue advertisements in the US context. These mechanisms allow global companies to indirectly or directly support political campaigns. In return, corporations get access to potential policy makers. A corporation will usually donate money to those representatives or senators who are on the specific committees or subcommittees responsible for decision-making which affects their industry. It is very difficult to determine the effect of access or campaign contributions. One of the reasons is that corporations often do not want a new law to be passed or new regulations adopted, and their aim is to maintain the status quo. Often, corporations desire a minor change in regulations which gets very little media attention. However, a small modification can result in massive additional profits for that company, while costing consumers or taxpayers a great deal more. Without doubt, on key issues senators or representatives are likely to vote in the public interest as they conceive of it; but on minor regulatory issues they may vote with the special economic interests that support their campaigns.

Captured Regulatory Agencies

As people work together, they begin to form similar opinions about particular issues. Many regulatory agencies work very closely with the industry they regulate. Consequently, after some time, the regulators adopt similar views to those of the industry. This does not imply that the regulators or corporations engage in corrupt activity per se; this is simply an example of natural human behavior: regulators develop close relationship with the industry and they want to protect their interests.

In fact, the regulatory agencies are always the targets of corporate influence. In the United States, in each area of policy, a triangular relationship exists. The players are the lobbyists and corporations and other private organizations in that area, the congressional committees and subcommittees who make decisions about that subject area, and the executive agencies and regulatory commissions that operate in that field. The connections between these players are as follows: corporations, for whom the lobbyists work, give campaign contributions to members of the congressional committees that make decisions about that field. These committees and subcommittees in turn determine the jurisdictions, and sometimes the budgets, of the executive agencies and regulatory commissions that work in the field. Finally, the executive agencies give out government contracts, which can be very lucrative to the industry; while the regulatory commissions adopt regulations, which can be beneficial or restrictive to the industry at hand. If everyone in the triangle cooperates everyone benefits. These triangles are sometimes referred to as Iron Triangles or Washington Triangles (Jordan 1981; Gais, Peterson, and Walker 1984). These symbiotic relationships, which exist in every policy area, are also known as sub-governments.

Self-Regulation

Global companies use the public policy process as a means of enhancing their legitimacy in the eyes of external constituents. Efficiency in markets as attained through competitive advantage must be balanced with social legitimacy in order for the firm to be allowed to function as part of the broader social system. Legitimacy is a political resource which must be secured prior to the attainment of economic goals, and often global companies gain legitimacy through self-regulation. In the context of global companies, two forms of self-regulation are of relevance: industry self-regulation and corporate self-regulation.

Industry self-regulation is a sector specific form of regulation set up by industry to advance the collective interests of MNCs in that sector (Lad and Caldwell 2009). It is a body charged by its members with a degree of rule-making capacity. Its purpose is to govern the behavior of its members by setting standards and ensuring compliance. The motivation for industry self-regulation varies. Industries may perceive benefits from banding together. First, there may be an enhancement of their reputation over non-members (Lenox 2006: 677). Second, it may be a way for an MNC to reduce its overall risk. Imposing certain limits on its own commercial practices may lead to efficiencies and, ultimately, increased profitability. Third, it may be a mechanism to control the exploitation of a particular natural resource and the collective action problems inherent in common property resources. Ostrom's (1990) seminal work on how collective action can be achieved in order to deal with "tragedy on the commons" problems is perhaps the most notable exploration of this issue. Finally, MNCs may benefit from submitting to industry self-regulation in order to forestall stricter regulation by governments. In each of these cases, it is a sense of enlightened self-interest that drives MNCs to submit to such a regulatory arrangement.

In recent years the number of these associations has grown dramatically in industry sectors such as chemical production, nuclear power, electronic retailing, advertising, and even tourism. Omarova (2011: 413) has argued that self-regulation of the financial services sector may be the best solution for avoiding future systemic risks to the global economy. Such a suggestion is likely to prove controversial, given recent events, but it highlights the growing interest in industry self-regulation and the growing value that it represents to MNCs.

Perhaps the earliest and most striking example of industry self-regulation is the "Responsible Care" program developed by the Chemical Manufacturers Association (CMA) in the United States in 1988. In response to a large number of incidents, in particular, the devastating Bhopal tragedy in India, the industry decided that it needed to reform the sector, not only to restore confidence in the industry's capacity to keep the public safe, but also to limit the possibility of regulation being imposed on the whole industry (Delmas and Montiel 2009). Responsible Care is a voluntary code of conduct which revolves around three major themes: health, safety, and the environment (HSE). According to the International Council of Chemical Associations website, the program also encourages open and transparent dialogue with stakeholders. It was first introduced in Canada in 1985 and then in the United States in 1988. Currently, 50 national chemical associations participate in the program. Moreover, 159 companies have signed agreements to participate in it (ICCA 2012a). In the early 1990s, the program produced a set of guiding principles. These were regarded as the basis for entry into Responsible Care and were used to orient the industry along a more responsible path. Since then, as the program has become better established, and as more chemical MNCs have become signatories, a new global charter has been developed to deal with a changing business environment and stakeholder expectations. The charter now includes, for example, a commitment to sustainable development (ICCA 2012b).

The key characteristic of industry self-regulation is that it is based on a principle of voluntarism. MNCs voluntarily decide whether to sign up to the regime or not. Some critics argue that voluntary regimes have no real capacity to enforce the rules and so are procedurally weak. Others have suggested that such regimes produce free riding behavior because, as noted earlier, an MNC may sign on to gain the benefits of membership, yet not actually change the way it behaves in the marketplace. However, the most serious criticism of industry self-regulation is that an industry in charge of itself is akin, in Etzioni's (2009: 42) words, to "the fox that is supposed to guard the chicken coop." He argues that there is an information deficit which arises from the market. First, it is difficult to get the kind of information that consumers need to make informed choices. Second, corporations routinely skew relevant information to deliberately deceive consumers (Etzioni 2009: 42). For him, the key solution to this problem lies in "filters," that is, government regulation with "teeth" (Etzioni 2009: 43). In his view, these filters are necessary to ensure consumers are not duped by industries keen to improve their bottom line.

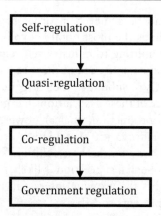

Figure 9.1   A simplified spectrum of regulation.
Source: Office of Regulation Review (1998: 64).

Etzioni's (2009) views are an interesting case of a problem that bedevils much of the discussion about self-regulation. It dichotomizes regulation and self-regulation, or, to put it slightly differently, regulation and the free market, as if these are the only two possibilities at hand. The difficulty with this framing is that it fails to recognize that regulation is located on a continuum of regulatory possibilities. Australia's Office of Regulation Review, for example, employs the following flowchart to highlight this continuum (see Figure 9.1).

Moreover, as Omarova (2011: 426) points out, as "a matter of principle, the concept of industry self-regulation is not inherently incompatible with some form of direct government regulation." Indeed, she suggests that the best governance model may be some combination of both government regulation and industry self-regulation. Part of the reason for this is that industry has a much better overview of the health of its sector than the government and, consequently, is able to respond in a more timely fashion. Some years ago, Ayres and Braithwaite (1992: 3) made a similar point:

> Good policy analysis is not about choosing between the free market and government regulation. Nor is it simply deciding what the law should proscribe. If we accept that sound policy analysis is about understanding private regulation – by industry associations, by firms, by peers, and by individual consciences – and how it is interdependent with state regulation, then interesting possibilities open up to steer the mix of private and public regulation.

Moreover, arguments which dismiss forms of industry self-regulation as simply regulatory deception, as Etzioni (2009: 42) does, fail to understand the nature and modes of regulation and are reductionist. Finally, there is a growing body of literature which suggests that industry self-regulation can work and alter the behavior of industry participants. King and Lenox (2000: 701) highlight three ways that this occurs. The first is through informal, coercive means such as naming and shaming free riders and those who fail to live up to the standards of the association. The second is through codifying new sets of norms and values. The third way is through providing industry participants with information about best practice. These points are equally valid in the context of individual corporations as well.

Corporate self-regulation is defined as a form of regulation where the company regulates itself. It does this in various ways. Invariably, it sets up codes of practice and appoints internal compliance officers to monitor and police them. These practices can be developed from a mixture of sources. First, they are sometimes developed in conjunction with NGOs. Second, they can be derived from industry self-regulation. The World Business Council for Sustainable Development (WBCSD), for example, has recently developed an online Guide to Corporate Ecosystem Valuation (WBCSD 2011). The purpose of the guide is to provide businesses with strategies to better value the ecosystem that their industry depends on. Third, corporate self-regulatory practices may be derived from international organizations and international norms. The UN Extractive Industries Transparency Initiative (EITI) has been adopted by a large number of oil and mining MNCs. Finally, a company may tailor its own principles to guide its behavior.

A self-regulating corporation exhibits a number of characteristics. The first is a strong commitment to meaningful self-regulation. A corporation that appears to use green-washing techniques to boost its image, supports charitable organizations only for their public relations potential, or engages in shallow cause-related marketing is not making a real commitment to self-regulation. A pivotal part of this first characteristic is a willingness on the part of management to develop a self-regulating philosophy within the organization. In this sense, sound leadership within an organization is crucial if self-regulation is to be more than merely tokenistic. At its most basic, this means adherence to corporate codes of conduct. But while leadership is essential, it cannot be a top down approach only. It also needs to be bottom up. Parker (2002: 168–196) employs the notion of self-regulating professionals as delegated by the state or regulators to highlight the need to make self-regulation everybody's business. In this, it must be treated the same way risk management professionals understand their craft. Just as risk management is a whole-of-organization task, so is self-regulation. The second characteristic is possession of adequate internal compliance, audit and monitoring systems that are capable of ensuring that self-regulation is effective. The growth in the number of corporate social responsibility (CSR) officers within MNCs in recent years demonstrates that they are taking self-regulation seriously. The third characteristic is that it makes an effort to take seriously and respond adequately to the concerns of various stakeholder groups. This includes not only those with a direct stake in the company's operations, but also those with an unfavorable view of the company. This is potentially the hardest aspect of being a self-regulating corporation. There are some in society who regard themselves as stakeholders and who simply deny the right of MNCs to exist. The extractive industries have probably been the worst affected by this attitude. The final characteristic is that the company demonstrates leadership in self-regulation. By this is meant that it is not just leadership internally in the organization, but leadership in the industry sector and in the broader community.

It is important to note that there are degrees of self-regulation. Some global companies may be described as underdeveloped self-regulators. While they understand the importance of acting according to certain community standards and have adopted CSR, they may do no more than this. Jaffe and Weiss (2006) make an interesting observation in this respect. Royal Dutch/Shell's General Business Principles commit it to upholding applicable laws and regulations. According to Jaffe and Weiss (2006: 882), "This statement is vague. It only commits the company to not violating the law, but by using the term 'applicable' they may, for example, employ child labor, where doing so is legal." Of course, Royal Dutch/Shell also has a statement of principle which commits it to upholding human rights. Presumably, this means that the company would not employ child labor as it would violate that commitment. Jaffe and Weiss's point is valid. An underdeveloped self-regulating company would not necessarily feel the need to move beyond this position. In this instance, a company may equate self-regulation with a commitment to abiding by the laws of the land and can still potentially be seen to a significant extent as a state regulated corporation (Friedman 1970).

Pharmaceutical and Petroleum Industry Examples

Given the general claims stated up to this point, the next inquiry must be into their actual historical relevance: what contemporary examples are there of global companies demonstrating a palpable influence on US regulation? The difficulty of finding information on the topic is testament to the lack of transparency that MNCs often enjoy in their corporate political activities, at least in regard to the general public. To discover the appropriate connections, one must integrate diffuse pieces of information from diverse sources in order to draw the connection between a particular firm's action and how a government policy was determined. In addition, there are numerous methods of influencing government regulation that have no legal disclosure requirements. These include "revolving door" offers, personal favors, insider information, and other transactions that frequently have no official paper trail. Discovering these obscure relationships beyond mere speculation is a matter of intensive research, including investigative reporting across many sources that only provide small amounts of information individually. We will briefly explore two major and well-known contemporary examples of multinational industries that engage in, and profit from, abundant political activity: pharmaceuticals and petroleum.

In terms of campaign contributions, the pharmaceuticals and health products industry contributed a record $166.8 million to federal candidates during the 2008 election cycle and close to $1.1 billion since 1990 (OpenSource.org 2012b). Their critical policy objectives focus on international recognition of "intellectual property" rights to their drugs, in order to undermine cheaper competitive drugs which cut into their market shares, and the elimination of price controls caused by growing desires for healthcare guarantees. The pharmaceutical industry deals primarily with products that prolong or improve the well-being of humans. In most societies the act of "saving lives" is a moral priority, or at least a noble deed. It is no surprise, then, that all related regulations are couched in strongly symbolic terms. Their public claims are broadly reflected by statements in which they claim that without assistance from government, expensive research on important drugs will stop and many life-saving implements will not be available.

The industry's influence on international trade is very palpable and significant. With regard to lobbying, its trade association in the United States, Pharmaceutical Research and Manufacturers of America (PhRMA) includes Pfizer Inc.,

Glaxo-SmithKline Plc, Merck & Co. Inc. primarily functioning as a means to increase transparency of individual companies' political influence. PhRMA has filed 59 lobbying reports concerning the Office of the US Trade Representative, more than any other organization historically. Drafts of the Dominican Republic–Central American Free Trade Agreement (DR-CAFTA) echo the pharmaceutical industry's sentiments about price controls and intellectual property. Under its provisions, member nations will be required to comply with deregulated pricing and international patent laws. An examination of the voting record for implementing DR-CAFTA demonstrates almost unanimous votes along party lines: only 15 Democrats voted for the measure, and only 27 Republicans voted against it (*The Washington Post* 2005). Furthermore, in light of DR-CAFTA in 2005, Guatemala was pressured to repeal a law that would allow for increased marketing of generic drugs as long as the drugs were demonstrated to behave like approved drugs. The US ambassador to Guatemala issued an ultimatum: Guatemala had to change its law to provide the clinical study data exclusivity mandated by DR-CAFTA, or the US Congress would not allow them membership (Shaffer and Brenner 2009).

Individuals and political action committees affiliated with oil and gas companies have donated $615 million to candidates and parties since the 1990 US election cycle, 70% of which has gone to Republicans (OpenSource.org 2012c). The oil and gas industry is a major source of greenhouse gas emissions and a particularly powerful actor in the US domestic arena (Levy and Egan 1998: 344). The oil industry, especially in extraction and transportation, is the beneficiary of a large amount of both direct and indirect subsidies. Two of the most significant (relating to their international position) are in the use of government resources in protecting their assets abroad as well as expanding their potential asset base, and in their lack of responsibility for environmental externalities caused by the consumption of fossil fuels. The physical security of oil drills, pipelines, and shipping lanes constitutes billions of dollars of US government services. Friendly diplomatic relations must be maintained with major exporter countries, especially those with US-owned holdings. Likewise, military force must be readily available to combat any attempt to seize or otherwise disrupt oil supplies by foreign aggressors (Engdahl 2004). Besides maintaining existing American assets and relationships, the government has also engaged in policies in seeking out new sources of oil. It is misleading, of course, to characterize the US government's heavy interest in maintaining and expanding oil supplies as only a resource transfer to large oil companies, as much income in America is authentically dependent on the energy generated by oil. Nonetheless, it is still a subsidy that discourages substitutes and conservation.

Given a large share of campaign contributions going to their party, it is no surprise that Republicans under former President George W. Bush advocated the very symbolic policy goal of an aggressive outward foreign policy. While oil interests may not have been the sole explanation of their foreign policy goals, they stand as part of a wider variety of interests that share common goals, such as defense contractors and other service companies such as Halliburton (Briody 2004). In addition, during George W. Bush's presidency, evidence of a "revolving door"-style administration was abundant with respect to the petroleum industry. In 2001, ExxonMobil lobbyist Randy Randol sent a memo to the White House requesting that Intergovernmental Panel on Climate Change (IPCC) chairman Robert Watson resign (Lawler 2002:

232). Although he did not resign, his re-election was blocked one year later. In 2003, the Bush administration officially denounced the Kyoto protocols. Three out of every four lobbyists who represent oil and gas companies previously worked in the federal government, a proportion that far exceeds the usual revolving-door standards on Capitol Hill (Eggen and Kindy 2010).

The issue of global climate change has led to political gamesmanship from major corporate interests in the oil industry. The Kyoto protocols, negotiated and signed by the Clinton administration in 1997, were drafted with the objective of stabilization of greenhouse gas concentrations in the atmosphere at a level that would prevent dangerous anthropogenic interference with the climate system. This would entail the reduction of emissions, either via increased automobile efficiency among other conservation measures, or even possibly the development of permanent alternative fuel sources – a clear threat to the oil industry's many sunken capital costs. Exxon-Mobil, the largest oil company in the world and contributor of the greatest amount of US lobbying dollars in its industry, has undertaken a strong anti-global-warming campaign, funding private think tanks to promote uncertainty over global warming and the economic danger of environmental regulations (Levy and Egan 1998: 350; Kolk and Levy 2001: 501; Skjærseth and Skodvin 2003).

Global oil companies such as ExxonMobil had quickly realized that they needed to win the war against the Kyoto protocols and all other climate control policies, and doing so would require the scientific agreement of the public, and in turn Congress (van den Hove, Le Menestrel, and de Bettignies 2002). In 1998, the *New York Times* revealed a leaked American Petroleum Institute (an organization whose membership includes ExxonMobil) memo aimed at addressing the ubiquitous presence of global climate concerns. Its proposed organization, the Global Climate Science Data Center, would serve several useful functions, among them, "identifying and establishing cooperative relationships with all major scientists whose research in this field supports our position," and "developing opportunities to maximize the impact of scientific views consistent with ours with Congress, the media and other key audiences" (American Petroleum Institute 1998). It is quite clear that no matter where the evidence lies for global warming phenomena, money is pushed into politics in a manner concurrent with partisanship over science. The major international oil companies, such as ExxonMobil, BP, Chevron, Royal Dutch/Shell, ConocoPhillips and Total, are some of the world's largest and most powerful corporations. In 2010, their combined profits amounted to over $80 billion and their sales revenues to over $1.6 trillion (Vivoda 2011b: 6). These global oil companies have stymied the public debate over climate change despite strong scientific evidence that human activity is generating greenhouse gases that are accelerating global warming (Kamieniecki 2006). From a business standpoint, climate change strategies employed by these companies have been supportive of profit for corporations that favor them (van den Hove, Le Menestrel, and de Bettignies 2002: 17).

Conclusion

One of the major challenges facing democratic societies is the incorporation of the conflicting goals and views of its citizens into legislative action and public policy. A free society allows its members to interact with political bodies and political figures and thereby attempt to influence or shape regulation. Given a complex society of many actors and coalitions, the variety of political influence strategies becomes immense. Moreover, in this political environment it is likely that certain influence strategies would be more effective than other strategies. The goal of this chapter has been both to illuminate the strategies that are used by companies to gain influence in a pluralist society, but also to highlight the emerging trend towards self-regulation. Firms are beginning to realize that they can no longer simply act as profit maximizers. Instead, they are becoming cognizant of the need to take other actors and stakeholders into account. They are using CSR strategies as one way to achieve this. In this sense, the influence is largely positive, as firms push governments for greater clarity around the "rules of the game." Put differently, effective CSR requires effective regulation. However, in other cases, the influence is less positive as the interpersonal nature of relationships can undermine good governance.

Given the unavoidable interdependence of business and government in modern society, the public policy process comprises a central aspect of the competitive environment for many firms and one that can be managed. Due to society's dependence on global companies for attaining macroeconomic goals such as growth in employment and national income, firms play a legitimate role in the public policy process by advocating regulations deemed desirable with regard to their business operations and competitive position. Global companies have demonstrated that they can effectively manage the political environment through politically oriented strategies and tactics, such as lobbying, campaign contributions, regulatory capture, and self-regulation. The omnipresence of private interests bearing significant influence on government regulation is not unknown or surprising to most people. However, an understanding of the process of how these interests come to affect government policies is important for the MNC strategy theorist, for the foundations that underlie it must be considered as new developments in global governance begin to surface.

References

American Petroleum Institute. 1998. "Global Climate Science Communications: Action Plan." Memo published in the *New York Times*, April 26.

Ansolabehere, Stephen and Snyder, James M., Jr. 2000. "Soft Money, Hard Money, Strong Parties." *Columbia Law Review*, 100 (3): 598–619.

Ayres, Ian and Braithwaite, John. 1992. *Responsive Regulation: Transcending the Deregulation Debate*. Oxford: Oxford University Press.

Baldwin, Robert and Scott, Christopher. 1998. *A Reader on Regulation*. Oxford: Oxford University Press.

Baldwin, Robert and Cave, Martin. 1999. *Understanding Regulation: Theory, Strategy, Practice*. Oxford: Oxford University Press.

Boddewyn, Jean J. and Brewer, Thomas L. 1994. "International-Business Political Behavior: New Theoretical Directions." *Academy of Management Review*, 19 (1): 119–143.

Briody, Dan. 2004. *The Halliburton Agenda: The Politics of Oil and Money*. Hoboken: John Wiley & Sons.

Congress Watch. 2005. "Congressional Revolving Doors: The Journey from Congress to K Street." *Public Citizen's Congress Watch*, July, Washington, DC.

Danielsen, Dan. 2005. "How Corporations Govern: Taking Corporate Power Seriously in Transnational Regulation and Governance." *Harvard International Law Journal*, 46 (2): 411–425.

Delmas, Magali and Montiel, Ivan. 2009. "Greening the Supply Chain: When Is Customer Pressure Effective?" *Financial Economics*, 18 (1): 171–201.

Dua, Andrea, Heil, Kerrin, and Wilkins, Jon. 2010. "How Business Interacts with Government: McKinsey Global Survey Results." January. McKinsey.

Eggen, Dan and Kindy, Kimberly. 2010. "Three of Every Four Oil and Gas Lobbyists Worked for Federal Government." *Washington Post*, July 22.

Engdahl, William. 2004. *A Century of War: Anglo-American Oil Politics and the New World Order*. London: Pluto Press.

Etzioni, Amitai. 2009. "The Free Market versus a Regulating Government." *Challenge*, 52 (1): 40–46.

Friedman, Milton. 1970. "The Social Responsibility of Business is to Increase Its Profits." *The New York Times Magazine*, September 13.

Gais, Thomas L., Paterson, Mark A., and Walker, Jack L. 1984. "Interest Groups, Iron Triangles and Representative Institutions in American National Government." *British Journal of Political Science*, 14 (2): 161–185.

Getz, Kathleen A. 1997. "Research in Corporate Political Action Integration and Assessment." *Business Society*, 36 (1): 32–72.

Hansen, Wendy L. and Mitchell, Neil J. 2000. "Disaggregating and Explaining Corporate Political Activity: Domestic and Foreign Corporations in National Politics." *American Political Science Review*, 94 (4): 891–903.

Hillman, Amy J. and Hitt, Michael A. 1999. "Corporate Political Strategy Formulation: A Model of Approach, Participation and Strategy Decisions." *Academy of Management Review*, 24 (4): 825–842.

Hillman, Amy J., Keim, Gerald D., and Schuler, Douglas. 2004. "Corporate Political Activity: A Review and Research Agenda." *Journal of Management*, 30 (6): 837–857.

Hobbes, Thomas. 1986. *The Leviathan*. Harmondsworth: Pelican.

Hodgson, Geoffrey. 2006. *Economics in the Shadows of Darwin and Marx*. Cheltenham: Edward Elgar.

International Council of Chemical Associations. 2012a. Responsible Care Members, http://www.icca-chem.org/en/Home/About-us/Members-of-the-ICCA/. Accessed December 19, 2012.

International Council of Chemical Associations. 2012b. 'Vision and Mission.' http://www.icca-chem.org/en/Home/About-us/Our-vision-mission-and-goals/. Accessed December 19, 2012.

Jaffe, Natasha Rossell and Weiss, Jordan D. 2006. "Self-Regulating Corporation: How Corporate Codes Can Save Our Children." *Fordham Journal of Corporate & Financial Law*, 11 (4): 851–893.

Jordan, A. Grant. 1981. "Iron Triangles, Woolly Corporatism and Elastic Nets: Images of the Policy Process." *Journal of Public Policy*, 1 (1): 95–123.

Jordana, Jacint and Levi-Faur, David. 2005. *The Politics of Regulation: Institutions and Regulatory Reforms for the Age of Governance*. London: Edward Elgar.

Kamieniecki, Sheldon. 2006. *Corporate America and Environmental Policy: How Often Does Business Get Its Way?* Palo Alto: Stanford University Press.

King, Andrew A. and Lenox, Michael J. 2000. "Industry Self-Regulation without Sanctions: The Chemical Industry's Responsible Care Program." *Academy of Management Journal*, 43 (4): 698–716.

Kolk, Ans and Levy, David L. 2001. "Winds of Change: Corporate Strategy, Climate Change and Oil Multinationals." *European Management Journal*, 19 (5): 501–509.

Lad, Lawrence J. and Caldwell, Craig B. 2009. "Collaborative Standards, Voluntary Codes and Industry Self-regulation." Butler University, Scholarship and Professional Work – Business, *Paper*, 75.

Lawler, Andrew. 2002. "Battle Over IPCC Chair Renews Debate on U.S. Climate Policy." *Science*, 296 (5566): 232–233.

Lenox, Michael J. 2006. "The Role of Private Decentralized Institutions in Sustaining Industry Self-Regulation." *Organization Science*, 17 (6): 677–690.

Levi-Faur, David. 2005. "The Global Diffusion of Regulatory Capitalism." *Annals of the American Academy of Political and Social Science*, 598 (1): 12–32.

Levy, Brian and Spiller, Pablo. 1994. "The Institutional Foundations of Regulatory Commitment: A Comparative Analysis of Telecommunications Regulation." *Journal of Law, Economics and Organization*, 10 (2): 201–246.

Levy, David L. and Egan, Daniel. 1998. "Capital Contests: National and Transnational Channels of Corporate Influence on the Climate Change Negotiations." *Politics & Society*, 26 (3): 337–361.

Lux, Sean, Crook, T. Russell, and Woehr, David J. 2011. "Mixing Business with Politics: A Meta-Analysis of the Antecedents and Outcomes of Corporate Political Activity." *Journal of Management*, 37 (1): 223–247.

Malbin, Michael J. and Gais, Thomas. 1998. *The Day after Reform: Sobering Campaign Finance Lessons from the American States*. Albany: Rockefeller Institute Press.

Mattli, Walter and Woods, Ngaire. 2009. *The Politics of Global Regulation*. Princeton: Princeton University Press.

Milyo, Jeffrey, Primo, David, and Groseclose, Timothy. 2000. "Corporate PAC Campaign Contributions in Perspective." *Business and Politics*, 2 (1): 75–88.

Murphy, Kevin M., Shleifer, Andrei, and Vishny, Robert W. 1993. "Why Is Rent-Seeking So Costly to Growth?" *American Economic Review*, 83 (2): 409–414.

New York Times. 1989. "Move to Ban Offshore Oil Drilling Debated," August 20.

O'Brien, Kerry. 2011. "Interview: Bob Graham." Australian Broadcasting Corporation. *Four Corners*, March.

O'Callaghan, Terry. 2009. "Regulation and Governance in the Philippines Mining Sector." *Asia Pacific Journal of Public Administration*, 31 (1): 91–114.

O'Callaghan, Terry. 2010. "Patience Is a Virtue: Regulation and Governance in the Indonesian Mining Sector." *Resources Policy*, 35 (3): 218–225.

Office of Regulation Review (Australia). 1998. *A Guide to Regulation*, 2nd edn. Belconnen: Productivity Commission.

Ogus, Anthony. 1994. *Regulation: Legal Form and Economic Theory*. London: Oxford University Press.

Omarova, Saule T. 2011. "Wall Street as Community of Fate: Toward Financial Industry Self-Regulation." *University of Pennsylvania Law Review*, 159: 411–492.

Omarova, Saule T. and Feibelman, Adam. 2009. "Risks, Rules, and Institutions: A Process for Reforming Financial Regulation." *University of Memphis Law Review*, 39 (4): 881–930.

OpenSecrets.org. 2012a. "Lobbying Database." Center for Responsive Politics, April 30.

OpenSecrets.org. 2012b. "Health." Center for Responsive Politics, April 30.

OpenSecrets.org. 2012c. "Energy/Natural Resources." Center for Responsive Politics, April 30.

Ostrom, Elinor. 1990. *Governing the Commons: The Evolution of Institutions for Collective Action*. Cambridge: Cambridge University Press.

Parker, Christine. 2002. *The Open Corporation: Effective Self-Regulation and Democracy*. Cambridge: Cambridge University Press.

Polk, Andreas and Schmutzler, Armin. 2005. "Lobbying against Environmental Regulation vs. Lobbying for Loopholes." *European Journal of Political Economy*, 21 (4): 915–931.

Schultz, David. 1998. "Revisiting Buckley v. Valeo: Eviscerating the Line between Candidate Contributions and Independent Expenditures." *Journal of Law and Politics*, 14: 33–108.

Shaffer, Brian. 1995. "Firm-level Responses to Government Regulation: Theoretical and Research Approaches." *Journal of Management*, 21 (3): 495–514.

Shaffer, Ellen R. and Brenner, Joseph E. 2009. "A Trade Agreement's Impact on Access to Generic Drugs." *Health Affairs*, 28 (5): 957–968.

Skjærseth, Jon Birger and Skodvin, Tora. 2003. *Climate Change and the Oil Industry: Common Problem, Varying Strategies*. Manchester: Manchester University Press.

Stern, Jon and Holder, Stuart. 1999. "Regulatory Governance: Criteria for Assessing the Performance of Regulatory Systems." *Utilities Policy*, 8 (1): 33–50.

Urbina, Ian. 2010. "U.S. Said to Allow Drilling Without Needed Permits." *The New York Times*, May 13.

Van den Hove, Sybille, Le Menestrel, Marc, and de Bettingnies, Henri-Claude. 2002. "The Oil Industry and Climate Change: Strategies and Ethical Dilemmas." *Climate Policy*, 2: 3–18.

Vivoda, Vlado. 2008. "Assessment of the Governance Performance of the Regulatory Regime Governing Foreign Mining Investment in the Philippines." *Minerals & Energy: Raw Materials Report*, 23 (3): 123–145.

Vivoda, Vlado. 2011a. "Determinants of Foreign Direct Investment in the Mining Sector in Asia: A Comparison between China and India." *Resources Policy*, 36 (1): 49–59.

Vivoda, Vlado. 2011b. "Bargaining Model for the International Oil Industry." *Business and Politics*, 13 (4): 1–34.

Vogel, Stephen K. 1996. *Freer Markets, More Rules: Regulatory Reform in Advanced Industrial Countries*. Ithaca: Cornell University Press.

Washington Post. 2005. "The U.S. Congress Votes Database." Vote 443, July 28.

World Business Council for Sustainable Development (WBCSD). 2011. Corporate Ecosystem Valuation, April, http://www.wbcsd.org/work-program/ecosystems/cev.aspx. Accessed December 19, 2012.

Chapter 10

Making Government More "Business-Like"

Management Consultants as Agents of Isomorphism in Modern Political Economies

Denis Saint-Martin

Introduction

Management consultancy is a US$300 billion global business that provides expert advice intended to improve the organizational performance of the world's largest companies and large government bodies, such as the National Health Service in the United Kingdom, and various defense ministries in Europe and North America (IBIS*World* 2012). Government is a booming sector and accounts for almost a third of the global management consulting market (*Economist* 2005). If management consultants from the private sector were once described as being part of a "shadow government" (Guttman and Willner 1976), this is no longer the case today. With the rise of the New Public Management since the past 1980s, consultants have become increasingly visible actors in the process of government restructuring. Some have written about the "new cult of the management consultant" in government (Smith 1994: 130), and described consultants as "intellectual mercenaries" (Leys 1999) or "hired guns" that "politicians use to bypass reluctant civil servants" (Bakvis 1997: 106). Others have coined the term "consultocracy" (Hood and Jackson 1991: 224) to underline the growing influence of consultants in public policy. In Australia, a study goes as far as suggesting that consultants "reoriented" the nation's social policy framework (Martin 1998), while in France, a former minister of industry once claimed that a minister arriving at a cabinet meeting with a report from McKinsey or the Boston Consulting Group is like "Moses coming down from the mountain with the Tables of the Law" (*Le Monde* 1999).

Global consulting firms are non-state actors that assume an important political role in today's world. Over time, as they developed more intimate links with governments, large consulting firms mutated into somewhat less "private" and more "public" entities by creating arm's length, not-for-profit, research institutes that

The Handbook of Global Companies, First Edition. Edited by John Mikler.
© 2013 John Wiley & Sons, Ltd. Published 2013 by John Wiley & Sons, Ltd.

produce analyses on key public policy issues. For instance, the Government of the Future Center is a think tank established in 2009 by Accenture in partnership with the Lisbon Council and the College of Europe. The Center is similar to the KPMG Public Governance and Government Institute and the McKinsey Global Institute, the research arm of McKinsey, created in 1990 to "provide leaders in the commercial, public and social sectors with the facts and insights on which to base management and policy decisions."

I have described elsewhere the growing inclination of consulting firms to take a more active policy advocacy role as the *"think tank-ization"* of management consultancy (Saint-Martin 2005). This transformation is an indication of the discursive power that global management consulting corporations increasingly exercise in public debates on the definition of political problems and solutions. How they have acquired that power and the political legitimacy to become co-pilots in the steering of government organizations are among the key questions addressed in this chapter. The first section below introduces the concept of institutional isomorphism to highlight the role of consultants as experts active in defining the norms and disseminating models of appropriate action in the management of large organizations. The second section provides an overview of the origins and evolution of management consultancy cross-nationally. The third section looks at the role of consultants in government since the 1960s and the subsequent growth of the public sector market for management consulting services. Using the "varieties of capitalism" approach (Hall and Soskice 2001) to compare national trajectories reveals that governments and businesses use more consulting services in liberal than in coordinated market economies, and that managerial reforms seeking to make government more "business-like" have had more impact in countries associated with the former than the latter model of capitalism (Pollitt and Bouckaert 2000; Saint-Martin 1998). This link is not a coincidence. As argued in conclusion, it is an indication of the institutional complementarities or "tight coupling" between managerial practices in business and government organizations in modern political economies.

Managerial Expertise and Institutional Isomorphism

Management consulting has not been the object of much attention in either international relations or comparative politics. Management consultants are nowhere to be seen in studies of global "private regulation" regimes (Vogel 2008), and the same absence prevails in much of the research on business and government in political economy (Coen, Grant, and Wilson 2010). In this literature, the focus is not on consultants *per se* but on managerial elites building political coalitions with other groups to oppose pro-shareholder reforms in corporate governance (Gourevitch and Shinn 2005). In a recent book on business power, Pepper Culpepper argues that "managerial expertise" and the "deference of legislators and reporters" toward it is the "weapon of choice" in the arsenal that business uses to wield influence in politics and policy-making (2011: 4). Managerial expertise in these studies is a crucial power resource and yet it is largely taken as a given. How it is constructed, how it acquires social and political recognition, are questions outside the theoretical radar screen. Managerial expertise is merely a tool of business power, as if it had no autonomous existence of its own (Culpepper 2010). But as the study of the management consulting industry suggests, managerial expertise is also a thriving business with distinctive economic interests. Whereas big business in general might want freer markets and lower taxes, management consultants prefer "smarter," and not necessarily smaller, governments (Deloitte 2009). Consultants think of themselves as technocrats. They do not portray themselves as a business, but rather as experts and trusted professional advisors (Kipping 2011).

Expertise and professionalism, as "new institutionalists" in sociology have argued, play a central role in defining the norms of legitimate behavior in highly rationalized social contexts (DiMaggio and Powell 1983; Dobbin 1994). Defined as "organizational fields," these contexts are populated by experts and groups of professionals who are densely networked and have considerable resources and incentives to disseminate models of appropriate action (Lodge and Wegrich 2005; Simmons, Dobbin, and Garrett 2008). Management consultants constitute one such group of experts, acting as agents of institutional isomorphism between large organizations in business and government. The concept of institutional isomorphism focuses on processes of homogenization leading organizations to become more similar to one another. According to DiMaggio and Powell, organizations tend to model themselves after organizations in similar fields that they perceive to be more legitimate or successful (1983: 152). Copying organizational structures is a process not driven by efficiency considerations alone; it is also a way of securing legitimacy in political life (Radaelli 2002: 28).

Consultancies disseminate and advocate management "fashions" and benchmarks that lead to isomorphism (Abrahamson 1996). They play a knowledge-brokering role between businesses and other large organizations in the public and the not-for-profit sectors (Lapsley 2001). Consultants have acquired norms-setting power in public management by taking on a more active role in governance processes through contracting-out and public-private partnerships (Saint-Martin 2000).

Consultants are typically brought in by government to make it more "business-like." As one can read on the website of McKinsey's Public Sector Practice, "By drawing on our private sector experience, we work to enhance the effectiveness and efficiency of government institutions, enabling them to better fulfill their mission to the public."[1] Consultants are brought in by government to model public organizations after what is perceived to be the more legitimate or superior management model in the business sector. They provide the language and styles of the corporate world that government organizations imitate to appear more efficient.

Management consultants' claims to expertise are based on their knowledge of business management approaches and practices. Consultants use this knowledge to build and market their reputation as knowledge brokers able to move knowledge among client groups (Semadeni 2001). As a glossy document describing the KPMG Government and Public Sector Services explains, the firm "is uniquely positioned to deliver highly-tailored local solutions, based on key insights gained from our work with similar public and private sector organizations around the world" (KPMG 2011: 1).

Reputation matters crucially for a sector that is unregulated in most countries. Any individual or firm can label their services as "consulting." The lack of formal institutional standards such as professionalization and porous industry boundaries create substantial uncertainty when client organizations buy consulting services

(Corcoran and McLean 1998). Reputation, as a result, becomes most important in reducing uncertainty and controlling opportunistic behavior (Glückler and Armbrüster 2003: 270).

As agents of isomorphism, management consultants facilitate coordination between organizations in the corporate and government sectors. In the words of Powell and DiMaggio, "similarity can make it easier for organizations to transact with other organizations" (1991: 73). Consultants help define what Hall and Soskice describe as the "set of shared understandings" that lead actors to a specific equilibrium. These "shared understandings," they argue, "are important elements of the 'common knowledge' that lead participants to coordinate on one outcome, rather than another" (2001: 13). According to the "varieties of capitalism" (VOC) approach there are two broad types of equilibrium in modern political economies defined as "liberal market" and "coordinated market" institutional arrangements, respectively. In each case, characteristic institutional structures and power relations are replicated at multiple levels of the state, market, and corporate firm. The institutional framework governing the political economy in "liberal market" (LMEs) and "coordinated market" (CMEs) economies are highly path dependent. They consist of interlocking pieces that are, in broad terms, complementary and self-reinforcing over time. As we shall see next, differences between LMEs and CMEs generate systematic differences in the development of the management consulting industry and in the share of public management functions assumed by consultants.

The Historical Development of Management Consultancy

Management consultancy is an industry largely dominated by US-based firms (McKenna 2006). In 2011, the size of the global market for consulting services was estimated to be around US$313 billion (IBIS*World* 2012). The United States represents half of this market, compared to a third for Europe. The European market developed later than in the US. As one study concluded, "culturally and politically, the United States was a more fertile ground than Europe for embracing consultancy, either as a practical pursuit or as a professional service – or both" (Gross and Poor 2008: 70).

Management consulting first emerged in the US in the early 1900s with Frederick Taylor and his "scientific management" approach to the work process (Rassam and Oates 1991). Consulting has both an engineering and accounting background. The industry is diverse and generally divided between the large accountancy-based firms and the so-called "elite strategy consultancies" such as McKinsey, the Boston Consulting Group, Bain, A.T. Kearney and Booz & Company. Unlike the accounting firms, which specialize in financial management and information technology, these consultancies focus more on strategic advice, brand management, and organizational development, especially business-process re-engineering (Rassam 1998: 13). It is estimated that large strategy consultancies such as McKinsey spend about US$100 million annually on research.

McKinsey also publishes a review (the *McKinsey Quarterly*), and has published 54 books on management since 1980 (*Economist* 1995: 57). The most famous book produced by two McKinsey consultants is the best-selling *In Search of Excellence* by Peters and Waterman (1982). This book, which has sold more than five million copies, has been described as one of the "most influential" sources of ideas in the development of the New Public Management (Aucoin 1990: 117). For large consultancies such as McKinsey, Booz, Gemini, and Arthur D. Little, one of the key instruments for disseminating ideas is the publication of articles or books, which has become a favored marketing tactic in the firms' attempts to increase their market share (Dwyer and Harding 1996). Consultancies arrange for such books to be serialized in magazines, advertised in newspapers, and endorsed by well-known business persons. For instance, since its publication in 1993, *Re-Engineering the Corporation* by Champy and Hammer has sold nearly two million copies worldwide. The consulting firm that employed the two authors subsequently increased its annual revenues from US$70 million the year preceding publication to more than US$160 million the year after (*Economist* 1995: 57).

Consultancies in the "strategy" category are keen to be seen at the forefront of management thinking. Some firms have formed alliances with business schools by sponsoring research on issues such as the future shape of companies or the changing role of the chief executive (Wooldridge 1997: 17). Consultants are often seen as the conduit between business schools and the business world. It is largely management consultants who transfer new ideas from the academic world to the commercial one. This is especially true of the American-owned consultancies (McKinsey, Boston Consulting Group, etc.), which have always had strong links with the leading US business schools (Rassam and Oates 1991: 23). In their search for new groundbreaking ideas, consultancies offer their brightest consultants time to write books, and then the firms throw the full weight of their marketing divisions behind the final products.

The Institutional Link to Accountancy

Management consulting emerged in the early twentieth century, but only started to establish itself as a multi-billion dollar industry in the 1960s when the large international accounting firms moved into consultancy (Stevens 1991). These firms, then known as the "Big Eight" included: Arthur Andersen, Coopers & Lybrand, Ernst & Whinney, Arthur Young, KPMG Peat Marwick, Deloitte Haskins & Sells, Touche Ross, and Price Waterhouse. In moving into management consulting, accountants brought with them a reputation for seriousness and professionalism. Contrary to the industrial engineers, the involvement of accountants in management consulting was not seen as that of an "intruder or snoop" in company operations, since accountants had already developed an organized relationship with their audit clients (Mellett 1988: 5). As auditors for blue chip North American and European businesses and industries, many of the Big Eight firms had earned a reputation for being the world's premiere accountants. The prestige they garnered helped them become the world leaders in management consulting services (Hanlon 1994). Following a series of mergers, the "Big Eight" became the "Big Four" and shared at the turn of the millennium global revenues of US$25 billion, representing 35% of the world market (Industry Week 2000).

The Big Four trace their origins to London-based accountants who first came to the United States in the nineteenth century to oversee the interests of British industrialists and entrepreneurs. The first international accounting firms began to emerge, as London accountants, following the trail of UK investment, set up offices in North America. Deloitte was created in 1845; Price Waterhouse in 1849; KPMG in 1870, and Ernst & Young in 1849. Together, the Big Four have offices in more than 130 countries and employ a total of about 400,000 professionals worldwide.

These firms have long acted as the reputational agents of large international corporations (Poullaos and Sian 2010). They first emerged in the United Kingdom and the US as a result of the separation of ownership and management that came with the corporate form of governance in the nineteenth century (Stevens 1991). In political economies where firms finance themselves largely through the capital markets, investors stay at arms' length from the companies. They rely heavily on accountants to provide calculable measures on profitability and performance (Vitols 2001). This is typically the case of LMEs, where investors do not have – unlike their counterparts in CMEs – access to private or inside information about the operation of the company (Hall and Soskice 2001: 23). The accounting profession is, accordingly, much older and larger in size in the United Kingdom and the US than in more "coordinated" European markets (Chatfield and Vangermeersch 1996).

In moving into management consulting, accountants had a head start, since they already knew their audit clients and were party to their business secrets. At the same time, however, they faced potential conflicts of interests between their roles as certified public accountants and management consultants. This is exactly what happened in 2002, when it was found that Arthur Andersen had broken the law by shredding Enron Corp. documents while Enron, a client of Andersen, was under investigation by the US government for hiding debts and concealing its imminent collapse from creditors and investors (Glater 2002). The fact that over half of the US$52 million Andersen earned from Enron in 2000 came from consulting fees, led observers in the US and politicians in Congress to argue that this might have played a role in Andersen's "decision not to expose Enron's ongoing lies" (Hastings 2002). Fearing that the US Securities and Exchange Commission might weaken the self-regulatory practices of the accounting profession and intervene to make it illegal for accountants to provide consulting work to their audit clients, the big accounting firms cut their ties with their consulting arms. Arthur Andersen became Accenture, KPMG Consulting became BearingPoint, while Ernst & Young sold its consulting business to Cap Gemini in 2000 and IBM bought PricewaterhouseCoopers' consulting arm in 2002 for US$3.5 billion.

The European Consulting Market

In several European countries (especially those where the Napoleonic code formed the basis of the private law system), government regulation restricts accountants from providing consulting and auditing services to the same client (Ridyard and De Bolle 1992: 67). This is one reason why management consulting has been slower to develop in continental Europe than in the US and the United Kingdom. Another is that large corporations have more resources than small and medium-sized enterprises (SMEs) to afford expensive management consulting services from top elite firms. SMEs in Europe are more numerous than in the US and they account for a larger share of GDP (European Capital Markets 2001: 2). Governments in Europe have long nurtured the development of the management consulting profession and industry by providing SMEs with resources and incentives to buy management consulting services to improve their efficiency and competitiveness (Saint-Martin 2001).

In 2010, the European market for management consulting services was estimated at around €90 billion. Germany (32%) and the United Kingdom (22%) alone constitute 54% of the European market, followed by Spain (11%), France (10%), Italy, and The Netherlands (3% each). US consultancies dominate the European consulting market. They benefited from the growing presence of American multinationals throughout Europe during the postwar period. The Marshall Plan, in particular, facilitated the expansion of US consulting firms to Europe and the spread of American management ideas and models (Djelic 1998).

Table 10.1 lists some of the top consulting markets in Europe in 2010 and the percentage of income by client sector. Differences between the United Kingdom and German "varieties of capitalism" and corporate governance are most visible when looking at revenues by sector. If the category "industry" represents the most important source of income for the German consulting market, in the United Kingdom that category is the public sector. The public sector as a whole forms 1% of the European consulting market.

At 46%, Greece – in deep financial and political crisis at the moment of writing (2012) – is an exceptional case. In second place is the United Kingdom. The public sector in the United Kingdom consumes three times more management consulting services than its German counterpart, and twice as much as Spain and France. Ireland closely follows the United Kingdom with 27%, suggesting that smaller public sectors consume more management consulting services than in countries where the state plays a larger role in the economy and society. Similar patterns have been in found in Canada and the US (Saint-Martin 2006). The overall trend reflects the *laissez-faire* attitude of the state towards the market typical of LMEs and "liberal" welfare states (Esping-Andersen 1990).

Management Consultants and Public-Sector Reform

LMEs have also been leading the way in the dissemination and adoption of New Public Management ideas and practices. The central idea behind the NPM program is that the efficiency and effectiveness of public services can be improved by lessening or removing differences between the public and private sectors. In their use of market-oriented mechanisms and private sector management techniques, the United Kingdom, New Zealand, the US, Canada, and Australia have been described as "first mover countries" (Bach and Bordogna 2011: 2282). As Lynn argued, "there are really only two groups of great interest in the context of [public sector] reform: the core, Anglo-American NPM marketizers and the continental European modernizers" (2008: 1). The first group of NPM enthusiasts is represented by "the Anglophone countries characterized by majoritarian political systems and an individualist pro-market culture . . . By contrast, the continental European countries embody a strong state tradition reflected in a larger and more active state role" (Bach and Bordogna 2011: 2290). As discussed below, in countries of the first group politicians have, over time and regardless of party affiliation, made policy-making institutions more open to outside consultants and framed their use in government in three different ways: (a): consultants as rational planners in the 1960s; (b) as "cost-cutters" and

Table 10.1 European consulting market, 2010.

	Germany	UK	Spain	France	Finland	Switzerland	Ireland	Slovenia	Hungary	Greece
Total turnover (million €)	27,900	19,009	9903	8814	1142	1056	438	271.1	215	208
Industry (%)	32.4	6	6	14.5	38.7	27	9.8	29.5	11	11.9
Banking & insurance (%)	23.7	24.4	25	30	5.1	26	21.6	14.5	25	5.6
Public sector (%)	10.1	29.9	16	15	11.8	9	27.3	13	28	46.6
Aerospace & defense (%)	0	1.7	8	3	0	n.a.	0.1	n.a.	0	0
Telecoms & media (%)	8.2	3.6	17	5	8.3	5	13.3	7.5	9	12.7
Wholesale & retail (%)	4.3	n.a.	3	5	9.4	5	3.8	7.5	8	6
Energy & utilities (%)	7.6	9.7	11	11	7.3	6	7	13.5	14	3
Transport & travel (%)	5.3	3.1	9	4	2.8	5	4.7	2	1	1.9
Healthcare (pharmaceuticals & biotech included) (%)	3.5	3.3	2	3	7.7	15	7.1	5.5	3	2.8
Other (%)	4.9	3	3	8.6	0	2	5.3	7.5	1	9.5
Total (%)	100	100	100	100	100	100	100	100	100	100

Source: Saint-Martin (2005).

apostles of the NPM in the 1980s, and (c) as partners in the new governance in the twenty-first century.

Rational Planning and Technocratic Politics in the 1960s

In the 1960s, at a time when Keynesianism was still influential and faith in the capacity of the social sciences to help solve public problems was high, decision-makers in government were looking for new ways to strengthen and rationalize the interventions of the state in society and the economy. This was the era of "rational management" (Aucoin 1986), of the Planning, Programming and Budgeting System (PPBS) and the beginning of the so-called "policy analysis industry" (Pal 1992: 66). The goal was to make management of the modern welfare state more "scientific" and professional (Fischer 1990). For instance, in Britain the 1966 Fulton Committee on the Civil Service complained that, "too few civil servants are skilled managers" (Fulton 1968: 12). It sought to open up the civil service and argued that it was too closed: "there is not enough awareness of how the world outside Whitehall works" (p. 12). Fulton encouraged the "free flow of men, ideas and knowledge" between the civil service and the world of industry and research (p. 13).

In Canada, the 1962 Royal Commission on Government Organization argued in favor of "letting the managers manage" (Canada 1962). To professionalize government management, Glassco saw the need to learn from the private sector. In becoming more open to the use of consultants from the private sector, Glassco and Fulton followed a path similar to that taken earlier by the Hoover Commission on the reorganization of the US government in 1947. The Commission sought to make the presidency more "managerial" and use business management practices to transform the president into a chief executive officer with centralized authority for decision-making (Arnold 1996). The Commission contracted 15 of its 34 studies to consulting firms. According to McKenna:

> The Hoover Commission represented the first high-profile use of management consulting firms by the Federal Government, and the potential for favorable publicity from the assignment was not lost on the management consulting firms. Each of the firms, in varying degrees, gained prestige and future clients from its work for the Hoover Commission (Arnold 1996: 104).

In 1968, the UK Treasury, with the support of the British Institute of Management Consultants (IMC), established a register of management consultants that departments were required to consult before using external consulting services (Archer 1968). In 1970, the Civil Service Department began to develop a secondment program between Whitehall and large consulting firms. In a speech to the IMC in 1971, Prime Minister Heath noted that, "the practice has grown of seconding management consultants to work alongside civil servants" (Civil Service Department 1972: 5). He added that, "consultants [were] playing a valuable role in improving the quality of central government management." In Canada, some have argued that, "the practice of using external consultants was given a significant boost by the Royal Commission on Government Organization" (Mellett 1988: 22).

The requirement to evaluate policy more systematically imposed by PPBS, opened a lucrative market for management consulting firms (Pattenaude 1979). PPBS is based on systems theory, which itself became a booming business in the 1960s. As one American critic noted: "Taught in universities, bought by private business and government agencies, and sold by a cadre of experts, systems analysis is a commodity commanding high prices and ready acceptance at home and abroad" (Hoos 1972: 1–2). In the early 1970s, it was estimated that the American government was spending "billions of dollars" in subcontracting to consulting firms work "concerned with policy formation, organizational models and even the recruitment of Federal executives" (Nader 1976: x). The title of a book published in 1976 by two American lawyers is evocative: *The Shadow Government: The Government's Multi-Billion Dollar Giveaway of Its Decision-Making Powers to Private Management Consultants, "Experts," and Think Tanks.*

The New Public Management in the 1980s

In the 1970s, as governments were consolidating their internal policy-making capacities, and as the fiscal crisis led to cutbacks in public expenditures, the use of consultants in the public sector became less prevalent than it had been in previous years (Wilding 1976: 69). However, that changed in the 1980s when, as a result of the influence of public choice theory and the rise of the New Right, governments, seeking to improve efficiency, increased their reliance on outside consultants as a way to transfer business management ideas and practices into the public sector (Saint-Martin 2000).

When Mrs. Thatcher was elected in 1979 the UK government was spending about £6 million on consulting services. By the end of her tenure as prime minister in 1990, this amount had grown to £246 million. In Canada, when the Conservative Mulroney government was in power, spending on consultancy went from CAD$56 million in 1984 to almost CAD$190 million in 1993. In Australia, during the Hawke–Keating Labor government, spending on consultancies rose from AUD$91 million in 1987 to AUD$342 million in 1993 (Howard 1996: 70). This increase was so significant that it led to a parliamentary committee inquiry on the engagement of consultants by government departments (Parliament of the Commonwealth of Australia 1990). In New Zealand, growth in expenditures on consultants also led to an investigation by the Comptroller and Auditor General in 1994 (Audit Office 1994). That same year, the Efficiency Unit in the United Kingdom issued a study on the use of external consultants. It noted that, "Over the past 10 years the Government has substantially increased its use of external consultants" (Efficiency Unit 1994: 19).

The release of that study, which showed that government spending on external consultancy increased "nearly fourfold" between 1985 and 1990 (Efficiency Unit 1994: 46), created a political backlash as civil service unions, the media, and Labour MPs denounced what they saw as a too cozy relationship between consultants and the Tories (Willman 1994). It has thus been argued that "the era of Conservative government since 1979 has certainly been the age of management consultancy" (Beale 1994: 13); and that "the rise of management consultants was one of the distinctive features of the Thatcher years" (Smith and Young 1996: 137). Nevertheless, government spending on management consultants continued to grow even after the election of center-left governments. Under New Labour, the UK government was spending £3 billion on consultants in 2006. In Canada, expenditures on consulting contracts grew from CAD$534 million in 2004 under a Liberal government, to almost CAD$1 billion in 2008 under a Conservative government (Donovan 2008).

The New Governance in the Twenty-First Century

Starting in the mid-1990s, after almost two decades of focusing on reforming the *management* of government, decision-makers began to worry more about the *policy* side of the governing process (Peters 1996). To use Osborne and Gaebler's distinction (1992), the focus of reform shifted from *rowing* to *steering*. After coming to power, the Blair government issued a White Paper on *Modernising Government* (1999). The document argued that whereas earlier management reforms brought improved productivity and better value for money, they paid little attention to the policy process. It underlined in particular the problem of ensuring that policies are devised and delivered in a consistent and effective way across institutional boundaries to address issues that cannot be tackled on a departmental basis – the need for what came to be called "joined-up" policies – against a background of increasing separation between policy and delivery, and more diverse and decentralized delivery arrangements (Williams 1999: 452). Similarly, in Canada, once the government had solved its deficit problem, the focus of reform in the mid-1990s shifted to building policy capacity and horizontal management (Bakvis 2000).

Largely inspired by the new politics of the "Third Way" developed by Clinton and Blair, these reforms were designed to make government more "intelligent" and better able to meet the needs of the people (Giddens 1998). Whereas the political right of the 1980s was anti-statist or anti-bureaucratic, the politics of the Third Way in the late 1990s was more pragmatic and less inclined to denigrate the role of the public sector (Newman 2001). The new focus was on "partnerships" with either the private or voluntary sectors. As Neil Williams observed in the case of Britain, modernizing the policy process has meant a "greater role for outsiders" (1999: 456) as a way to ensure that a wider range of viewpoints, knowledge, and experience is brought to bear on policy. It is in this context that management consultants redefined themselves in the late 1990s as "partners in governance." As one can read on Accenture's website, "Citizens now expect government to be more like the 24/7 world of the private sector – more efficient, and always aligned with the people it serves. And government needs a partner who will help improve the way it serves citizens . . . Accenture is that partner."

Being a partner means that consultancy is no longer simply about providing advice to a client organization that is then solely responsible for subsequently deciding whether to implement the consultants' recommendations. In 1986, the International Labour Office defined a consultant as an expert detached from the employing organization (Kubr 1986). But now, with the growth of "outsourcing consultancy," consultants are more involved in service delivery and less detached from their clients than in the past. "Outsourcing consultancy" – which in the past few years has become the fastest growth sector for consultants – is when an organization assigns whole business or administrative functions to a consulting firm (Tewksbury 1999). In Britain, a survey of consulting services users found in 2001 that 96% of clients said that they wanted "some form of relationship with their consultancy firm rather than keeping them at arms length. There is no doubt that consultants are increasingly seen as partners rather than suppliers" (MCA 2001: 4). Quick intervention is less the norm today, and the new trend is for large firms to have long-term contracts, such as the six-year contract between PwC and the UK Ministry of Defence and the ten-year contract with the Home Office covering immigration programs and services (Huntington 2001). Consultants are keen to take up large contracts because this is a way of protecting their business from the ups and downs of the economy.

"Outsourcing consultancy" is especially strong in the field of information technology (IT). Consulting firms have become increasingly active in the development of eGovernment, promoting the use of IT as a tool to transcend organizational boundaries and make government more "joined up." Some have described eGovernment as the "new paradigm" of public sector reform (Accenture) and according to Patrick Dunleavy and his colleague, it has "overtaken and superseded" the NPM whose time, they argue, is now "over" (Dunleavy and Margetts 2000: 1). Whether eGovernment is different from the NPM is still an open question. But like the NPM whose emergence in the 1980s increased public spending on consulting services, eGovernment is also becoming a fast growing market for management consultancies. In Europe, the eEurope Action Plan first adopted by the European Union in 2000 is driving the demand for information technologies in the public sector. Research indicates that eGovernment spending by governments in Western Europe was around US$2.3 billion in 2002 (IDC 2002).

In the United States, it is estimated that federal, state, and local spending on eGovernment was about US$6 billion in 2003 (CIBER 2003). Moreover, in the US, the use of IT in government has taken a new, more security-oriented direction following 9/11 and the creation of the Homeland Security Department. Consulting firms in Washington are now involved in providing the technology that could help, in the words of the Head of the Public Sector Branch of BearingPoint (formerly KPMG Consulting), "mitigate the risk of exposing valuable information to our enemies" (BearingPoint 2002). Consultants see the global war against terrorism as a growing market where governments worldwide are expected to spend an estimated US$550 billion on homeland security (Reuters 2003).

Lobbying Strategies

As the demand for consultancy in government became more pronounced in countries like Britain, Canada, or Australia, most consulting firms, as well as the associations that represent their interests, began in the 1980s to develop various institutions and practices designed to build networks of contacts with government officials.

In Britain, following the introduction of Mrs. Thatcher's "Efficiency Strategy" in 1980, it was noted that, "the Management Consultancies Association (MCA) moved swiftly to consolidate its position by developing its network of contacts within the civil service" (Smith and Young 1996: 142). In the early 1980s, the MCA created within its organization a "Public Sector Working Party" (PSWP) in order to develop a more coordinated strategy for promoting management consulting to government. According to the MCA, "the Group dealing with the public sector has established close links with departments employing management consultancy services with the intention not only of establishing a better understanding within Whitehall of the services that we can offer, but of equal importance, ensuring that our membership is aware of the needs and constraints faced by Ministries" (MCA 1989: 4). The PSWP is made up of various "sub-groups" one of which is directly linked to the Cabinet Office and whose role is to ensure, in the words of the MCA director, that there is "a regular dialogue between the MCA and members of Cabinet and with senior officials" (MCA 1995: 3).

Following its creation, the PSWP began to organize a number of events to facilitate the exchange of ideas between Whitehall officials and consultants. Each year, the MCA runs half-day seminars for civil servants on management reform and on the use of consultants in the public sector. In the past, such seminars were sometimes attended by no less than 200 civil servants (MCA 1995: 3). The PSWP also holds a series of meetings (four or five a year) attended by member firms and Permanent Secretaries, the purpose of which is to receive an authoritative update on activities within a particular sector of government. As explained in the letters sent by the MCA to the senior officials invited to speak at PSWP meetings, the goal is to see "how consultants can act as advisers and partners in helping the Civil Service to face future management challenges." These meetings are supplemented by a series of small monthly business lunches involving the participation of senior staff from member firms and policy-makers. For the MCA, these luncheons "provided an ideal 'off the record' opportunity for wide ranging discussions on subjects of particular interest to both guests and hosts" (MCA 1996: 5). In the past, MCA guests included the head of the Policy Unit, senior Treasury officials, and members of the Efficiency Unit and of the Cabinet Office. Following the example of their business association, MCA member-firms began in the 1980s to organize various lobbying activities targeted at Whitehall officials and created "Government Services Divisions" within their organizational structures. These divisions are often made up of "former bureaucrats and others with public sector expertise [who] have been hired to develop a rapport with civil servants and to sell the firms' many and varied services" (Bakvis 1997: 109).

As the government became a more important client, management consultants increasingly sought to obtain inside knowledge of Whitehall's current and future plans for management reform. In this search for information, MPs became an important asset in helping to secure valuable Whitehall contacts. In 1988 Tim Smith, a British Conservative MP and consultant to Price Waterhouse, asked no less than eighteen parliamentary questions for detailed information on management consulting. The answers disclosed the nature of the contracts, the successful companies, their assignments, and the government expenditures involved (Halloran and Hollingworth 1994: 198).

In Britain, some have also noted the "revolving door" between government and management consulting firms. For instance, before becoming minister in Tony Blair's government in 2003, Margaret Hodge worked at PricewaterhouseCoopers and the Secretary of State for Trade, Patricia Hewitt, was research director at Andersen (Simms 2002: 34). Large consultancies also offer some of their staff for free on secondment to various government departments. An investigation by *The Observer* in 2000, which led to the "staff-for-favours row" (Barnett 2000), found that firms like PricewaterhouseCoopers and Ernst & Young, which had donated staff free to departments, had subsequently won lucrative government contracts. One consultant to the Treasury quoted in the *Observer* article said: "I did work on policy issues and got amazing access . . . It is now much easier for me to ring up Treasury officials and get the information I need" (reported in Barnett 2000).

In the United States, financial contributions to parties and candidates for Congress are a common practice among large consulting firms. For instance, in the 2000 election cycle, the "Big Five" donated US$8 million to the two major political parties: 61% to the Republicans and 38% to the Democrats. In the aftermath of the Enron scandal, observers of the American political scene uncovered the fact that "very few politicians in Washington haven't been on the receiving end of Arthur Andersen" (Centre for Responsive Politics 2002). Andersen was the fifth-biggest donor to Bush's White House run, contributing nearly US$146,000 via its employees and political action committee (PAC). Since 1989, Andersen has contributed more than US$5 million in soft money, PAC and individual contributions to federal candidates and parties, more than two-thirds to Republicans. It is also reported that more than half of the current members of the House of Representatives were recipients of Andersen cash since the early 2000s. In the Senate, 94 of the chamber's 100 members reported Andersen contributions since 1989 (Centre for Responsive Politics 2002).

Finally, at the European level, management consulting firms' national associations are grouped together in a Brussels-based organization called the FEACO: the European Federation of Management Consulting Associations. The FEACO presents itself as the "united voice" of consultants, promoting "the interests of management consultants with various international organizations by maintaining close contacts with European institutions, such as the European Commission" (FEACO 2001: 3). The FEACO is organized into various committees such as the European Community Institutions Committee (ECIC). Following publication of the White Paper on Reforming the Commission in 2000, members of the ECIC met to develop their "action plan." In that document, one can read that:

> The main objective of the ECIC should be to monitor, influence and provide input into the modernization of the European Commission . . . The ECIC should maintain close contacts with key persons in the European Commission . . . and maintain close contacts with the European Parliament by inviting MEPS to lunches and organize meetings with them, to help them better understand the role of consultants and their contribution to the improvement of the efficient management of all EU activities. (FEACO 2000a)

Conclusion

This broad comparative historical overview has focused on the relationships between management consultants and governments and suggested that this link has been closer in some countries than others because of differences in the institutional framework governing the political economy. The management consulting industry has historically been more developed in LMEs than in CMEs, and the available evidence suggests that governments in LMEs have delegated a greater portion of public management functions to outside consultants than governments in CMEs.

One type of reform that consultants helped design and implement in LMEs is "agencification," i.e. the breaking up of large public-sector bodies into semi-autonomous agencies that operate at arms' length and under more business-like conditions than the government bureaucracy (Pollitt *et al.* 2004). This so-called "agency model" is heavily influenced by corporate governance arrangements characteristic of LMEs. Corporate structures in LMEs concentrate authority in top management. A hands-off approach to regulation prevails, as companies are regarded as a domain of private transaction, regulated by contract rather than by statute. Investors generally stay at arm's length from the companies in which they invest and intervene only in periods of crisis. In government, the application of these practices led to reforms that sought to "let the managers manage" (James 2001). Civil servants were turned into managerial executives accountable for performance to legislators and the public, re-defined as "shareholders" and "stakeholders" respectively.

As agents of isomorphism, management consultants make organizations more similar to one another. However, making government more "business-like" in LMEs and CMEs involves different organizational forms and practices. These differences seem to be reinforced rather than weakened by consultants' work in government. The "agency model" is an illustrative case of isomorphic modeling. It is no coincidence that it was first emulated by governments in LMEs. There is a greater "fit" with this form of corporate arrangement than in CMEs, reflecting the "institutional complementarities" between managerial practices in business and government in modern political economies.

Note

1   http://www.mckinsey.com/Client_Service/Public_Sector.aspx#Defense_and_Security, accessed June 27, 2012.

References

Abrahamson, E. 1996. "Management Fashion." *Academy of Management Review*, 21 (1): 254–285.

Archer, J.N. 1968. "Management Consultants in Government." *O&M Bulletin*, 23 (1): 23–33.

Arnold, Peri E. 1996. *Making the Managerial Presidency: Comprehensive Reorganization Planning, 1905–1996*. Kansas: University Press of Kansas.

Aucoin, Peter. 1986. "Organizational Change in the Machinery of Canadian Government: From Rational Management to Brokerage Politics." *Canadian Journal of Political Science*, 19 (2): 3–27.

Aucoin, Peter. 1990. "Administrative Reform in Public Management: Paradigms, Principles, Paradoxes and Pendulums." *Governance*, 3 (2): 115–137.

Audit Office. 1994. "Employment of Consultants by Government Departments." In *Report of the Comptroller and Auditor General: Third Report for 1994*. Wellington: Auditor General.

Bach, Stephan and Bordogna, Lorenzo. 2011. "Varieties of New Public Management or Alternative Models?" *International Journal of Human Resource Management*, 22 (11): 2281–2294.

Bakvis, Herman. 1997. "Advising the Executive: Think Tanks, Consultants, Political Staff and Kitchen Cabinet." In *The Hollow Crown: Countervailing Trends in Core Executives*, ed. Patrick Weller, Herman Bakvis, and R.A.W. Rhodes, 84–125. London: Macmillan.

Bakvis, Herman. 2000. "Rebuilding Policy Capacity in the Era of the Fiscal Dividend." *Governance*, 13 (1): 71–104.

Barnett, Anthony. 2000. Staff for Favours Row Hits Treasury, *The Observer*, June 25, http://www.guardian.co.uk/Archive/Article/0,4273,4033309,00.html. Accessed June 27, 2012.

Beale, Dave. 1994. *Driven by Nissan? A Critical Guide of New Management Techniques*. London: Lawrence & Wishart.

BearingPoint. 2002. Homeland Security Testimonials. Statement of S. Daniel Johnson, Executive Vice-President, Public Services, Committee on House Government Reform, http://www.bearingpoint.com/about_us/features/home_sec_testimony.html. Accessed June 27, 2012.

Canada. 1962. *The Royal Commission on Government Organization, Volume 1: Management of the Public Service*. Ottawa: The Queen's Printer.

Centre for Responsive Politics. 2002. Enron and Andersen, http://www.opensecrets.org/news/enron/index.asp. Accessed June 27, 2012.

Chatfield, Michael and Vangermeersch, Richard, eds. 1996. *The History of Accounting: An International Encyclopedia*. New York: Garland.

CIBER. 2003. Overview of State Government Solutions Provided by CIBER, http://ciber.com/services_solutions/other_services/egovt/images/CIBER-SGS-Overview.pdf. Accessed June 27, 2012.

Civil Service Department. 1972. *CSD News*, 3 (2): February.

Coen, David, Grant, Wyn, and Wilson, Graham, eds. 2010. *The Oxford Handbook of Business and Government*. New York: Oxford University Press.

Corcoran, Jan and McLean, Fiona. 1998. "The Selection of Management Consultants: How Are Governments Dealing with this Difficult Decision? An Exploratory Study." *International Journal of Public Sector Management*, 11 (1): 37–54.

Culpepper, Pepper D. 2010. "Corporate Control and Managerial Expertise." In *The Oxford Handbook of Business and Government*, ed. David Coen, Wyn Grant, and Graham Wilson, 497–511. New York: Oxford University Press.

Culpepper, Pepper D. 2011. *Quiet Politics and Business Power*. New York: Cambridge University Press.

Deloitte. 2009. *Government Reform's Next Wave: Redesigning Government to Meet the Challenges of the 21st Century*. Washington, DC: Deloitte Research.

DiMaggio, Paul J. and Powell, Walter W. 1983. "The Iron Cage Revisited: Institutional Isomorphism and Collective Rationality in Organizational Fields." *American Sociological Review*, 48 (2): 147–160.

Djelic, Marie-Laure. 1998. *Exporting the American Model: The Postwar Transformation of American Business*. Oxford: Oxford University Press.

Dobbin, Frank. 1994. *Forging Industrial Policy: United States, Britain and France in the Railway Age*. New York: Cambridge University Press.

Donovan, Kevin. 2008. "Tories Outspent Liberals on Consultants." *The Toronto Star*, December 8.

Dunleavy, Patrick and Margetts, Helen. 2000. "The Advent of Digital Government: Public Bureaucracies and the State in the Internet Age." Paper prepared for delivery at the 2000 Annual Meeting of the American Political Science Association. Washington, September 4.

Dwyer, A. and Harding, F. 1996. "Using Ideas to Increase the Marketability of Your Firm." *Journal of Management Consulting*, 9 (2): 56–61.

Economist. 1995. "Manufacturing Best-Sellers: A Scam Over a 'Best-Selling' Business Book Shows How Obsessed Management Consultancies Have Become with Producing the Next Big Idea," August 5, 57.

Economist. 2005. "From Big Business to Big Government: How Public Sector Work Is Re-Shaping Management Consultancy," September 8, 61.

Efficiency Unit. 1994. *The Government's Use of External Consultants: An Efficiency Unit Scrutiny.* London: HMSO.

Esping-Andersen, Gosta. 1990. *The Three Worlds of Welfare Capitalism.* Princeton: Princeton University Press.

European Capital Markets Institute. 2001. A Comparison of Small and Medium Sized Enterprises in Europe and in the USA. Manuscript, http://www.eurocapitalmarkets.org/system/files/SMEE_book.pdf. Accessed June 27, 2012.

FEACO. 2000. *Newsletter,* 1: Winter.

FEACO. 2000a. *ECIC Action Plan 2000.*

FEACO. 2001. *Survey of the European Management Consultancy Market.*

Fischer, Frank. 1990. *Technocracy and the Politics of Expertise.* Newbury Park: Sage.

Fulton, Lord. 1968. *The Civil Service, Volume 1: Report of the Committee 1966–1968.* Cmnd. 3638. London: HMSO.

Giddens, Anthony. 1998. *The Third Way: The Renewal of Social Democracy.* Cambridge: Polity Press.

Glater, Jonathan D. 2002. "Longtime Clients Leave Arthur Andersen." *New York Times,* March 16, 1.

Glückler, Johannes and Armbrüster, Thomas. 2003. "Bridging Uncertainty in Management Consulting: The Mechanism of Trust and Networked Reputation." *Organization Studies,* 24 (2): 269–297.

Gourevitch, Peter A. and Shinn, James. 2005. *Political Power and Corporate Control: The New Global Politics of Corporate Governance.* Princeton: Princeton University Press.

Gross, Andrew C. and Poor, Jozsef. 2008. "The Global Management Consulting Sector." Focus on Industries. *Business Economics,* October, 69–79.

Guttman, Daniel and Willner, Barry. 1976. *The Shadow Government: The Government's Multi-Billion Dollar Giveaway of its Decision-Making Powers to Private Management Consultants, "Experts," and Think Tanks.* New York: Pantheon Books.

Hall, Peter A. and Soskice, David, eds. 2001. *Varieties of Capitalism. The Institutional Foundations of Comparative Advantage.* New York: Oxford University Press.

Halloran, P. and Hollingworth, M. 1994. *A Bit on the Side: Politicians and Who Pays Them? An Insider's Guide.* London: Simon & Schuster.

Hanlon, G. 1994. *The Commercialization of Accountancy.* London: Macmillan.

Hastings, Alcee. L. 2002. *The Need for Auditor Independence.* U.S. House of Representatives, http://www.house.gov/alceehastings/op_eds/oped_auditor_indep.html. Accessed June 27, 2012.

Hood, Christopher and Jackson, Michael. 1991. *Administrative Argument.* Aldershot: Dartmouth.

Hoos, Ida. 1972. *Systems Analysis in Public Policy: A Critique.* Berkeley: University of California Press.

Howard, Michael. 1996. "A Growth Industry? Use of Consultants Reported by Commonwealth Departments, 1974–1994." *Canberra Bulletin of Public Administration,* 80 (September): 62–74.

Huntington, Mary. 2001. "Careers: Public Sector: Working in the Public Eye." *Management Consultancy,* March 12.

IBIS*World.* 2012. Global Management Consultants: Market Research Report, March, Santa Monica, http://www.ibisworld.com/industry/global/global-management-consultants.html. Accessed June 27, 2012.

IDC. 2002. Survey: IT Purchasing Patterns in Western European Public Sector: IDC # PP08J, http://www.idcresearch.com/getdoc.jhtml?containerId=PP08J. Accessed June 27, 2012.

Industry Week. 2000. *Global Manufacturers' Resource Guide: Top Consulting Firms.* http://www.industryweek.com/iwinprint/data/chart6-2.html. Accessed June 27, 2012.

James, Oliver. 2001. "Business Models and the Transfer of Businesslike Central Government Agencies." *Governance*, 14 (2): 233–252.

Kipping, Matthias. 2011. "Hollow From the Start? Image Professionalism in Management Consulting." *Current Sociology*, 59 (4): 530–550.

KPMG. 2011. *Cutting Through Complexity: KPMG Government and Public Sector Services.* Washington, DC: KPMG International.

Kubr, Milos. 1986. *Management Consulting: A Guide to the Profession.* Geneva: International Labour Office.

Lapsley, Irvine. 2001. "Transforming the Public Sector: Management Consultants as Agents of Change." *European Accounting Review*, 10 (3): 523–543.

Le Monde. 1999. "Les cabinets de conseil, les géo-maîtres du monde." Economic Section, January 19.

Leys, Colin. 1999. "Intellectual Mercenaries and the Public Interest: Management Consultants and the NHS." *Policy & Politics*, 27 (4): 447–465.

Lodge, Martin and Wegrich, Kai. 2005. "Control over Government: Institutional Isomorphism and Governance Dynamics in German Public Administration." *Policy Studies Journal*, 33 (2): 213–233.

Lynn, Laurence E. Jr. 2008. "What Is A Neo-Weberian State? Reflections on a Concept and Its Implications." Manuscript, January 24.

Martin, John F. 1998. *Reorienting a Nation: Consultants and Australian Public Policy.* Aldershot: Ashgate.

MCA: Management Consultancies Association. 1989. *President's Statement and Annual Report.* London.

MCA: Management Consultancies Association. 1995. *President's Statement and Annual Report.* London.

MCA: Management Consultancies Association. 1996. *President's Statement and Annual Report.* London.

MCA: Management Consultancies Association. 2001. *President's Statement and Annual Report.* London.

McKenna, Christopher D. 1996. "Agents of Adhocracy: Management Consultants and the Reorganization of the Executive Branch, 1947–1949." *Business and Economic History*, 25 (1): 101–111.

McKenna, Christopher D. 2006. *The World's Newest Profession: Management Consulting in the Twentieth Century.* Cambridge: Cambridge University Press.

Mellett, Edward Bruce. 1988. *From Stopwatch to Strategy: A History of the First Twenty-Five Years of the Canadian Association of Management Consultants.* Toronto: CAMC.

Nader, Ralph. 1976. "Introduction." In *The Shadow Government: The Government's Multi-Billion Dollar Giveaway of its Decision-Making Powers to Private Management Consultants, "Experts," and Think Tanks*, ed. Daniel Guttman and Barry Willner. New York: Pantheon Books.

Newman, Janet. 2001. *Modernising Governance: New Labour, Policy and Society.* London: Sage.

Pal, Leslie A. 1992. *Public Policy Analysis: An Introduction*, 2nd edn. Scarborough: Nelson Canada.

Parliament of the Commonwealth of Australia. 1990. *Engagement of External Consultants by Commonwealth Departments.* Report 302, Joint Committee of Public Accounts. Canberra: Australian Government Publishing Service.

Pattenaude, Richard L. 1979. "Consultants in the Public Sector." *Public Administration Review*, May/June: 203–205.

Peters, B. Guy. 1996. *The Policy Capacity of Government.* Ottawa: Canadian Centre for Management Development. Research Paper 18.

Peters, Thomas J. and Waterman, Robert H. 1982. *In Search of Excellence*. New York: Harper & Row.

Pollitt, Chritopher and Bouckaert, Geert. 2000. *Public Management Reform: A Comparative Analysis*. Oxford: Oxford University Press.

Pollitt, Christopher, Talbot, Colin, Caulfield, Janice, and Smullen, Amanda. 2004. *Agencies: How Governments Do Things Through Semi-Autonomous Organizations*. London: Palgrave.

Poullaos, Chris and Sian, Suki. 2010. *Accountancy and Empire: The British Legacy of Professional Organization*. London: Routledge.

Powell, W.W. and DiMaggio, P.J. 1991. *The New Institutionalism in Organizational Analysis*. Chicago: Chicago University Press.

Radaelli, Claudio. M. 2002. "Policy Transfer in the European Union: Institutional Isomorphism as a Source of Legitimacy." *Governance*, 13 (1): 25–43.

Rassam, C. 1998. "The Management Consulting Industry." In *Management Consultancy: A Handbook for Best Practice*, ed. Philip Sadler, 3–29. London: Kogan Page.

Rassam, C. and Oates, D. 1991. *Management Consultancy: The Inside Story*. London: Mercury.

Reuters. 2003. Governments around the World Will Spend an Estimated $550 Billion on Homeland Security in 2003," Washington, July 7, http://www.world-am.com/body_03-04-2.html. Accessed June 27, 2012.

Ridyard, D. and De Bolle, J. 1992. *Competition in European Accounting: A Study of the EC Audit and Consulting Sectors*. Dublin: Lafferty Publications.

Saint-Martin, Denis. 1998. "The New Managerialism and the Policy Influence of Consultants in Government: An Historical Institutionalist Analysis of Britain, Canada and France." *Governance: An International Journal of Public Policy and Administration*, 11 (3): 319–356.

Saint-Martin, Denis. 2000. *Building the New Managerialist State: Consultants and the Politics of Public Sector Reform in Comparative Perspective*. Oxford: Oxford University Press.

Saint-Martin, Denis. 2001. "When Industrial Policy Shapes Public Sector Reform: The Case of TQM in Britain and France." *West European Politics*, 24 (4): 105–124.

Saint-Martin, Denis. 2005. "Management Consultancy." In *The Oxford Handbook of Public Management*, ed. Ewan Ferlie, Laurence E. Lynn, Jr., and Christopher Pollitt, 671–694. New York: Oxford University Press.

Saint-Martin, Denis. 2006. "Le consulting et l'État." *Revue française d'Administration publique*, 120: 743–756.

Semadeni, Matthew. 2001. "Toward a Theory of Knowledge Arbitrage: Examining Management Consultants as Knowledge Arbiters." In *Current Trends in Management Consulting*, ed. Anthony F. Buono, 43–63. Greenwich, CT: Information Age Publishers.

Simmons, Beth, Dobbin, Frank, and Garrett, Geoffrey, eds. 2008. *The Global Diffusion of Markets and Democracy*. New York: Cambridge University Press.

Simms, Andrew. 2002. *Five Brothers: The Rise and Nemesis of the Big Bean Counters*. London: New Economics Foundation.

Smith, T. 1994. "Post-Modern Politics and the Case for Constitutional Renewal." *Political Quarterly*, 65 (2): 128–138.

Smith, T. and Young, A. 1996. *The Fixers: Crisis Management in British Politics*. Aldershot: Dartmouth.

Stevens, M. 1991. *The Big Six: The Selling Out of America's Top Accounting Firms*. New York: Simon & Schuster.

Tewksbury. 1999. "Survey: Public Sector Go Slow." *Management Consultancy*, February 11.

Vitols, Sigurt. 2001. "Varieties of Corporate Governance: Comparing Germany and the UK." In *Varieties of Capitalism*, ed. Peter A. Hall and and David Soskice, 337–360. New York: Oxford University Press.

Vogel, David. 2008. "Private Global Business Regulation." *Annual Review of Political Science*, 11 (4): 261–282.

Wilding, R.W.L. 1976. "The Use of Management Consultants in Government Departments." *Management Services in Government*, 31 (2): 60–70.

Williams, Neil. 1999. "Modernising Government: Policy-Making within Whitehall." *Political Quarterly*, 70 (4): 452–459.

Willman, John. 1994. "Con Artists or Cost-Cutters? Do Whitehall's Outside Consultants Provide Value for Money?" *Financial Times Week-End*, April 30, 7.

Wooldridge, Adrian. 1997. "Trimming the Fat: A Survey of Management Consultancy." *The Economist*, March 22, 1–22.

Chapter 11

East Asian Development States and Global Companies as Partners of Techno-Industrial Competitiveness

Sung-Young Kim

Introduction

It has long been recognized that large corporations (as opposed to small firms) are endowed with a structurally privileged position in the public domain based on their contribution to the economic well-being of a country, to resist changes which are perceived to threaten their interests (Block 1992; Lindblom 1977). The "global companies" label has been used to describe the development of large corporations which have become more numerous, grown in size, entrenched their domestic and international sales positions, extended their production networks internationally, and maintain monopolistic control over virtually every market sector (Harrod 2006: 24–28). To this, we may add the important role that knowledge accumulation, specifically technological capabilities, plays in strengthening the market positions of global companies. A radical view of the impact of global companies argues that transnational corporations have become "denationalized" through abandoning their ties to the country of origin while simultaneously converging into a single organizational form (Ohmae 1990: 94). There are, however, strong doubts over how "global" global companies really are. An abundance of studies have empirically demonstrated the fact that the world's leading transnational corporations operate in a manner heavily influenced by the institutions of their home countries.[1] In light of the findings produced in such works, global companies should be viewed as "national corporations with international operations" (Dicken 2007: 126). Any serious analysis of global companies and their relationship to the state must therefore take as its starting point the domestic institutional context from which global companies maintain their headquarters.

East Asia is home to many of the world's most formidable players in automobile manufacturing such as Toyota, the world's largest shipbuilding firms

The Handbook of Global Companies, First Edition. Edited by John Mikler.
© 2013 John Wiley & Sons, Ltd. Published 2013 by John Wiley & Sons, Ltd.

including Hyundai Heavy Industries and Mitsubishi Heavy Industries, and semiconductor manufacturers such as the Taiwan Semiconductor Manufacturing Company.
Arguably the most visible illustration of this point, South Korea is home to some
of the world's most powerful corporations such as Samsung and Hyundai who represent two companies in a handful of family-owned mammoth conglomerates or
chaebol modeled after the Japanese *zaibatsu* of the colonial period (Woo 1991).
The Samsung *chaebol* may be best known internationally as the manufacturer of
electronics products yet Samsung Electronics is only one, although a major, part of
a conglomerate which includes the Shinsegae (department store chain), Cheil Jedang
or CJ (retail, distribution, and entertainment) and Bokwang (finance, public relations, convenience store chain, and high-tech parts and components). In the case of
Hyundai, the conglomerate includes not only Hyundai Motors, but also Hyundai
Department Store, Hyundai Heavy Industries, Sungwoo, and Halla. In turn, each
of these affiliates also spawned multiple subsidiaries. The owner families of the
chaebol control the management of their respective conglomerates through cross-
shareholding arrangements. Overall, the activities of the *chaebol* have dominated
almost every aspect of economic life imaginable in Korea.

The growth of the *chaebol* did not come about by the vicissitudes of the free
market; they were a creation and reflection of the Korean state's development strategy over the postwar era. From the 1960s onwards, the Korean state privileged the
chaebol as the main partners in the drive towards catching-up with the industrially
advanced economies to the detriment of nurturing other entrepreneurs such as small
and medium-sized enterprises (SMEs) (Park, H-J 2007). The state provided *support*
in the form of low-interest policy loans and protection from foreign competition but
in a *disciplined* manner which typically involved their ability to meet monitorable
performance standards such as pre-negotiated export targets (Amsden 1989) and
investments in ever more technology-intensive sectors (Mathews and Cho 2000).
From the late 1980s onwards, however, the state found it increasingly difficult to
work constructively with the *chaebol* as they began to engage in business activities
such as real estate speculation, which were at odds with the state's strategic goals of
encouraging them to streamline their activities and concentrate on core competencies
(Weiss 1998: 60–62). Not only did the ability of the *chaebol* to spread their tentacles
into non-related business sectors reflect a level of financial and technological independence previously unseen, but as Thurbon (2003) argues it was also a reflection of
the ideological inconsistency within the state itself which ultimately played a critical
role in the extent to which Korea was impacted by the Asian Financial Crisis of
1997. It was not until the aftermath of the 1997 crisis, which provided the Korean
state with the opportunity to pursue long-held goals of industrial restructuring and
streamlining through a series of state-orchestrated industrial mergers and sell-offs
("the Big Deals") and part of wider restructuring measures (Hundt 2009: 97–108;
Thurbon and Weiss 2006: 7–11).

The state's role in streamlining the activities of the *chaebol* has undoubtedly
played a major role in "saving flagship firms from their own worst selves" (Woo-
Cumings 2003: 214) and in bringing about leaner firms that are now more focused on
building on their core strengths (Weiss 2003: 251–252). In fact, the *chaebol* are now
more powerful than ever. One report notes that in 2011 the annual sales of Korea's
thirty largest *chaebol* of 1.134 quadrillion won (approximately USD$1 quadrillion)

accounted for 96.7% of Gross Domestic Product (GDP) (Kim 2012). Another report mentioned by the same author notes that from 2001 to 2010, the sales of the five largest *chaebol* alone which includes Samsung, Hyundai Motors, SK, LG, and Lotte increased from 59% to 70.4% of GDP. This figure includes the core company and the affiliate companies of the conglomerates. Each market sector has traditionally been monopolized by two to three companies related to the *chaebol*, which dominate sales and production. The key point is that the concentration of economic activities by the *chaebol* in Korea has increased, which suggests an enhancement of their structural power.

A more recent although understudied sector in which Korean firms have now become significant international players is in telecommunications. In the Korean domestic market alone, over 70% of sales is dominated by just two firms, Samsung Electronics and LG Electronics, who held 53% and 23.8% of the domestic handset market in 2010 respectively (*Telecoms Korea* 2010). Their market leadership is also reflected in their sales internationally; Samsung and LG were the second- and fourth-largest manufacturers of mobile phones by the end of 2011 (Arthur 2012). As will be discussed at greater length in the sections which follow, the creation of the Korean telecommunications sector and wireless communications sector more specifically, began in the late 1980s with the cooperation of Korea's conglomerates or the *chaebol* such as Samsung Electronics who at that time had almost no knowledge of how to manufacture such high-tech products. Driven by a strategic commitment to creating a national presence in an infant technological growth sector, the state played a role akin to what Evans (1995) describes as "midwifery" in his study of the beginnings of the broader Korean electronics industry. The state facilitated the technological learning of the *chaebol* and within the space of just over a decade many of the firms which participated in this project became the world's leading manufacturers of mobile communications products. In more recent years, Korean firms have set out to challenge the technological standards created by rivals from Europe and the United States such as Nokia and Qualcomm by utilizing their market positions and most importantly through increasingly utilizing their own technological innovations to create alternative technological standards. What this suggests is that Korea's *chaebol* have "grown up"; they now possess the capacity to finance and undertake technological innovation more independently of the state than ever before.

In light of the above, a key question arises: how have the developmentally oriented states of East Asia coped with the unprecedented levels of structural power that global companies now possess? The core argument presented in this chapter is that under conditions of intensifying knowledge-based competition, states with strategic industry objectives seek new ways of managing collaborative ties between public and private actors. As will be shown through the case of the Korean telecommunications sector, the state's role has changed from that of a midwife for the growth of conglomerate enterprises to one since the early 2000s which increasingly expects the *chaebol* themselves to accept greater responsibilities in the formulation and implementation of policies for promoting national techno-industrial competitiveness.

Before analyzing the Korean telecommunications sector in greater depth, I begin by discussing various conceptualizations of the relationship between government and business in the developmental state literature, which may provide clues to how we should expect the developmentally oriented states to cope with the increasing structural power of global companies. After examining the evolution of the relation-ship between the state and the *chaebol*, I conclude this chapter by considering the implications of the findings for the broader concerns of this book over the rise of global companies and outline a number of areas for future research.

The Structural Power of Global Companies and the Transformative Power of States

In order to understand how states might cope with the growing power of corporate actors in East Asia, we first need to understand the nature of the relationship between government and business in developmental states over the postwar era. The seminal works on the developmental state idea provide propositions about how we can expect developmentally oriented states to cope with the increased structural power of global companies. Before doing so, however, I will discuss a popular although limited understanding of the government-business relationship in East Asia, which I call the "end-of-the-developmental state" or endist thesis. In doing so, my aim is to contrast this narrow view of the nature of government and business relations with the key point of the seminal works on this subject, which was to show that the basis of successful industrial transformation in East Asia's developmental states over the postwar period was due to the existence of a cooperative relationship in which both the state and the private sector were strong in the pursuit of pre-negotiated transformative goals set and monitored by the state.

The Limitations of the Endist Thesis

A popular line of argument in the end of the developmental state thesis (the "endist thesis") which has been repeated since the mid-1990s to recent years is that the state's capacity to play a developmental role is dependent on the existence of a highly autonomous state and a weak business sector (Callon 1995; Minns 2001). When applied to explain developments in the Korean context since the early 2000s, some writers such as Kalinowski (2009) have argued that market-oriented reforms undertaken by successive Korean governments led by Roh Moo-Hyun and conse-quently by the current President, Lee Myung-Bak, have strengthened the structural power of the *chaebol* which in effect has undermined the state's capacity to play a developmental role. Kalinowski (2009: 288) makes two key propositions: first, the Korean state's developmental role was based on its ability to remain insulated from the *chaebol* which enabled government officials to implement a transformation of the economy and second, that the growth in the power of the *chaebol* has undermined the state's autonomy and therefore forced a retreat of the Korean state's develop-mental role.[2] These propositions are problematic. While there is no doubt that the *chaebol* have grown in power over the postwar era and unsurprisingly since the early 2000s, there is little reason to assume that this should come at the *expense* of the state's power to guide economic activities. This zero-sum logic appears to arise from a misunderstanding of the cooperative, but not conflict-free, nature of government and business relations in the developmental idea as originally developed by Chalmers Johnson (1982), which I discuss below.

Public and Private Cooperation as the Basis of Successful National Development

As originally conceived by Johnson (1982: 19) in his study of the role of the Ministry of International Trade and Industry in Japan's postwar economic growth, the "developmental state" concept was reserved for a state that was committed to strategically oriented long-term goals to transform the economy. Subsequent studies applied the framework to explain the rapid postwar industrialization of Korea and Taiwan amongst other countries in East Asia and elsewhere.[3] For Johnson (1982: 315–320), the effectiveness of the Japanese state in the economic realm was based on its priorities, which reflected a commitment to strategic long-term focused goals, the existence of an insulated pilot agency responsible for industrial transformation, a supportive political environment, and the final element of greatest relevance for my purposes in this chapter is the existence of institutionalized mechanisms for public and private cooperation. Throughout *MITI and the Japanese Miracle*, as Johnson (1999: 56–60) himself explains, he went to some lengths to recognize the structural power of business through explaining the patterns of interactions between the Japanese bureaucracy and the managers of privately owned companies. From 1931 to 1940 evolution of the relationship between government and business was one of "private-control" where the governance of manufacturing was left almost completely at the behest of the Japanese *zaibatsu*. The result was protest from workers and other groups within Japanese society such as the military over the oligopolistic holding of economic power by the *zaibatsu*. From 1940 to 1952 the relationship evolved to one of "state-control" where the state took almost full control of the means of production with disastrous consequences for the economy. It was only with the failure of such forms of governance that a more mature relationship between government and business based on *genuine public and private cooperation* came into evolution in the early 1950s. It was the existence of such a relationship which explained the phenomenal Japanese economic transformation over the following four decades.

These insights into the Japanese political economy were influential in the development of conceptualizations of the government–business relationship in other developmental states throughout East Asia and elsewhere, which accepted the idea that national development not only rested on the state's capacity but also on the structural power of business but to varying degrees as will be explained below.

Conceptualizing Strong State Power and Strong Business Power

In the case of Korea, Peter Evans (1995: 12) argues that the Korean state's capacity to play a developmental role from the 1960s to the early 1990s was dependent on the existence of a coherent and well-qualified bureaucracy, which formed the basis of its *autonomy*. Bureaucratic autonomy, however, was no guarantee for the successful execution of a developmental project. The Korean state also *embedded* itself in society and used business networks in order to pursue developmental goals. While Evans's work did much to advance our understanding of the institutional basis of Korea's successful development in contrast to so many cases of development failure of states in the Third World, the idea of embedded autonomy still fell somewhat short in conceptualizing a situation where the state is strong and business is strong

(Weiss 1998: 36–37), which is precisely the situation that Johnson describes in his 1982 publication. For Evans, the Korean state's capacity seems to rest on its ability to use its embedded autonomy to achieve its goals through the business class. The implications of this are that when the structural power of business grows stronger, the state's capacity must get weaker. In this regard, the idea of "governed interdependence" (Weiss 1998) has gone the furthest in taking state power and business power seriously.

For Weiss (1998: 38–39), the strategies for successful industrial transformation are dependent on the level of maturity of an institutionalized relationship of negotiation between government and business. In a relationship of governed interdependence, the power of the state and the power of business are strong by virtue of the fact that each side maintains their autonomy but negotiate to work towards broader goals, which are ultimately set and monitored by the state. The state does not act alone in isolation; unilaterally "imposing" its will *over* the private sector. The state's capacity to effect industrial development and technological upgrading is derived from its ability to induce cooperation from business into a negotiating relationship, not from its ability to impose its will over the private sector which as the case of Japan during the wartime years of 1940–1952 had negative impacts in the economic arena. The concept can not only be contrasted with *statist* notions of state strength but also of *interest-based* notions of captured governments where interdependence is "ungoverned" (Weiss 2006: 167–169). Several features in the organization of the state and in its relationship with business are conducive to this type of negotiated relationship, which could readily be identified in the East Asian states of Japan, Korea, and Taiwan during their periods of catch-up (Weiss 1998: 49–64). This includes insulated pilot agencies, institutionalized linkages between public and private actors, and the organization of business actors in industrial representation associations which sufficiently encompass firms in a given sector and are capable of achieving consensus amongst its members. The key point is that the success of national development strategies in East Asia involved the participation of state actors and corporate actors in a mutually beneficial relationship of coordination.

Various forms of governed interdependence such as "disciplined support" as mentioned earlier were recognizable during Korea's drive to establish heavy industries in the 1960s and 1970s. One could readily identify each of the three features discussed above which facilitated governed interdependence in the postwar Korean model with one exception, namely, the fact that the state increasingly relied on the *chaebol* as functional alternatives to industrial associations due to the fact that so much economic activity was concentrated within the conglomerates (Weiss 1998: 60-62). As the state negotiated with the *chaebol* directly, industry associations simply became less relevant. This situation proved to be highly successful in mobilizing rapid economic development until the Korean state began phasing out the use of policy loans and encouraged the *chaebol* to source capital from international sources in the mid-1980s. At the same time, the state sought to encourage greater private self-governance although as Weiss notes, this has proved to be difficult due to the weakness of industrial associations in the Korean political economy and the over-diversification of the *chaebol* into unrelated areas. As mentioned earlier, it was not until Korea edged towards the brink of bankruptcy during the 1997 crisis that state efforts to streamline their operations were achieved. The difficulties in the state-*chaebol* relationship in Korea, however, should come as no surprise when we cast our eyes back to the cooperative, but not conflict-free, nature of public and private relations in the archetypical developmental state, Japan. Even during the heyday of the Japanese developmental state (1950s to 1960s) – the country which is often typified to having gone the furthest in perfecting the art of managing public and private cooperation – experienced frequent conflict between the managers of corporations and economic bureaucrats.[4] As Johnson (1982) remarks:

> the cooperative government–business relationship in the capitalist developmental state is very difficult to achieve and maintain [p. 312]... the state inevitably will go too far, and private enterprise inevitably will resent state interference in its decisions [p. 312]... One clear lesson from the Japanese case is that the state needs the market and private enterprise needs the state; once both sides recognized this, cooperation was possible and high-speed growth occurred. (p. 318)

The main point of this section is that instead of adopting the zero-sum logic evident in the works of those in the endist camp, the nature of the government and business relationship in East Asia's developmental states over the postwar era were essentially based on cooperative ties between strong states and strong business. The lesson for the present study is that the growing structural power of business does not necessitate a diminution of the state's transformative power. Rather, we should be focused on how states seek ways to *govern* newer forms of *interdependence* between public and private actors.

With these points in mind, let us now examine how East Asia's developmentally oriented states have coped with the growth in the structural power of global companies. As explained in the introductory section, the Korean telecommunications sector provides an ideal case study to examine how the state has coped with the rise of global companies aided by their technological knowledge capabilities in this sector. In order to fully appreciate what the Korean state has done since the early 2000s, however, we first need to understand precisely what types of public and private cooperation were deployed as part of the state's midwifery role from the late 1980s to the 1990s.

The State as Midwife in the Creation of the National Telecommunications Sector

By the early 1980s, the *chaebol* had emerged as serious players in the international heavy and chemical industries – an outcome of the state's successful role as "midwife" to the birth of Korea's national champions (Evans 1995: 124–126). The Korean state, however, had even greater ambitions based on nurturing the entry of the conglomerates into technologically more intensive sectors beyond labor-intensive industries such as shipbuilding. The creation of the wireless communications sector in the 1990s provides a clear demonstration of state's role as midwife and later into a more equal partnership to promote knowledge-intensive development.

Korea's entry into the mobile communications system began in earnest with the knowledge accumulated by the participation of the private sector in collaborative projects to create a digital landline communication system known as the

TDX Project.[5] The technological learning of firms and the state's management of research and development (R&D) projects was brought to bear on promotional efforts during the late 1980s to create second-generation (2G) wireless communications technologies, namely, CDMA. Korean firms, however, simply did not possess the capabilities to create 2G technologies themselves and required the coordinative role of the Korean state. Despite efforts to establish technology licensing agreements with European and American firms such as Nokia and Motorola, these companies were unsurprisingly guarded about licensing their technologies and thereby aiding Korean firms in establishing a foothold in a lucrative new industry (Jho 2007a: 639).

Even if European firms like Nokia and Ericsson were to become more willing to share their knowledge of the 2G GSM standard mandated throughout Europe, Korean firms would have been relegated to a position of catching-up in another industry. For these reasons, the Korean Ministry of Information and Communication (MIC) coordinated the creation, commercialization and domestic standardization of CDMA technology as the national mandatory standard for the delivery of 2G services. Firms including Samsung Electronics, LG Information and Communication, Hyundai Electronics, and Maxon Electronics collaborated with the Electronics and Telecommunications Research Institute (ETRI) which was an R&D institute established under the MIC, in R&D activities to create CDMA network infrastructure (Mani 2005: 43). The key source of knowledge was an American-based start-up known as Qualcomm who was willing to share its untested and as yet, prototype proprietary CDMA technology with Korean firms and ETRI in return for the purchase of its Qualcomm chipsets in Korean-manufactured mobile handsets and the payment of royalties by Korean manufacturers to Qualcomm. The MIC also used its ownership of Korea Mobile Telecom to guarantee an initial market for products developed by participants in the R&D project. Perhaps most importantly, however, the state's financial support for the CDMA project was not given freely. Not only did firms have to repay the MIC's contributions through licensing fees to the state itself (through ETRI), but as Jho (2007a: 640–642) shows in her study, state support was dependent on the ability of firms to develop internationally competitive products and services. The MIC used its authority over licensing as part of its arsenal of carrots and sticks to carefully manage liberalization and privatization of telecommunications services in the mid-1990s. These developments helped to provide a large domestic market for manufacturers which could be used as a test-bed before an export offensive and to build internationally competitive service providers.

After the development of 2G telecommunications products and services, in the mid-1990s, the MIC promoted the further technological upgrading of firms by initiating development of third-generation (3G) technologies (Wang and Kim 2007: 124–128). In the development of 3G technologies, the MIC expected firms to accept a greater share of the burden in developing new technologies since firms could utilize and build upon the technological learning they had accumulated through the development of the 2G CDMA system. Firms followed through with this expectation by launching two separate R&D consortiums and standardization bodies to develop technologies based on specifications in the American-based CDMA2000 3G standard and the European-based W-CDMA standard. While the MIC provided support for the former, the latter was left to the responsibility of the private sector.[6]

The State and Chaebol as Equal Partners in the Promotion of New Technological Growth Sectors

By the early 2000s, Korean firms had demonstrated the ability to produce 3G chipsets utilizing their own innovations (Pringle and Tam 2003; *Telecoms Korea* 2003). This meant that Korean firms were capable of substituting the importation of Qualcomm's chipsets with those created by domestic manufacturers, which fulfilled a long-held goal by the MIC of closing the technology gap between Korea and industrially more advanced countries in the telecommunications sector (Larson 1995: 125). In order to facilitate the transition from catching-up to staying ahead, since 2003 the Korean state and the *chaebol* have collaborated in various ways which I detail below.[7]

Setting New Technological Standards

One of the most striking features of the Korean state's support for a transition to innovation-led development has been its focus on the international standardization of Korean-developed technologies. This includes the development of new technologies for mobile broadcasting such as Digital Multimedia Broadcasting, software such as the Wireless Internet Platform for Interoperability, and fourth-generation (4G) communication systems such as Mobile Wimax amongst many others that have been promoted as competing standards to those developed by foreign firms such as Qualcomm and Nokia. To this end, the MIC established "technology-centred forums" which coordinate all aspects of the promotion of new technologies. This includes defining and agreeing upon the specifications of new technologies, formulating and implementing R&D projects, setting commercialization schedules, and participating in international standardization strategies in regional and international standards development bodies such as the International Telecommunications Union. These forums, which I have discussed at greater length elsewhere (Kim 2012a: 157–158) are composed of representatives from the full spectrum of companies involved in the technological value chain: typically high-tech start-ups involved in the development of core components, software, and solutions, and also conglomerates which dominate the manufacture of end products such as handsets and the provision of services. Representatives of the *chaebol* typically act as Chairpersons in collaboration with government officials from public agencies affiliated with the MIC in the complex network of working groups established in these technology-centered forums.

The state's ability to induce the participation and leadership of the *chaebol* in such forums is not based on the provision of financial support for activities such as R&D, which is increasingly less relevant. Indeed, in the words of the President of ETRI, Yim Chu-Hwan (Han 2004: 54–55):

> We currently have 1,800 ETRI researchers . . . The era when ETRI developed *everything* has passed. There are numerous firms that far surpass ETRI in the number of researchers and research expenses. ETRI must now concentrate its efforts on strengthening the competitiveness of domestic companies by acting as a source of R&D and having Korean technology reflected in international standards.

Instead, the participation of the *chaebol* in technology-centered forums is based on the potential benefits that they can reap from having their technologies recognized as part of an international standard such as the likelihood of royalty payments derived from the adoption of the standard by other countries and perhaps more importantly, to be able to have greater influence over the pace and direction of innovation in the international telecommunications sector. The MIC has induced the cooperation of the *chaebol* in other ways as discussed below.

Commercializing Innovations Developed by High-Tech Start-Ups

It is widely recognized that high-tech start-ups are a major source of new innovations. The fact that so many governments in the advanced industrial economies such as Germany and the United States have established venture capital funds for sponsoring promising new small firms provides support for this idea (cf. Weiss 2005; Block 2008). It is therefore hardly surprising that since the early 2000s, the Korean state in collaboration with the *chaebol* have pursued various ways to nurture small high-tech firms in the country as part of its innovation-led strategy.

This new approach is evident in the MIC's provision of R&D subsidies for the development of prototypes of core components and handheld devices of a new mobile broadcasting technology known as Terrestrial-Digital Mobile Broadcasting (T-DMB), which was assumed as part of a broader national R&D fund of $100 million established by the MIC to develop next generation digital television technologies (Lee *et al.* 2005; Ministry of Information and Communication 2003). Terrestrial-DMB was promoted as an alternative technological standard to compete against technologies delivering similar services such as Nokia's DVB-H and Qualcomm's MediaFLO. The project involved participation from ETRI, start-ups spun off by ETRI such as "Net&TV" and "Perstel" and those founded by senior researchers that formerly worked in the laboratories of the leading *chaebol* such as "Pixtree" and "OnTimetek" (*Korea IT Times* 2005a, 2005b). While the Ministry absorbed the financial and technological risks faced by small firms in developing this new technology, the *chaebol* were expected to extend their support to the project through investing their own financial and technological resources into creating new commercially ready products which utilized the innovations developed by high-tech start-ups (Cho and Kim 2004: 12). To this end, LG Electronics invested $20 million and 130 researchers to create a mobile phone with integrated DMB functions in 2004.[8] Samsung Electronics also displayed its willingness to support high-tech start-ups by utilizing the multimedia solutions developed by Pixtree.[9]

When the risks faced by firms in the development of new technologies were low, the MIC delegated the promotion of new products to R&D projects financed purely by the private sector itself. This was evident in the MIC's support for the development of a related mobile broadcasting technology called Satellite-Digital Multimedia Broadcasting. Since the technology on which the Satellite-DMB system was based was similar technology to CDMA, the MIC expected Korean participants in the project to hold a technological advantage since participating firms could utilize their existing knowledge of CDMA technology (Kim 2004). Korea's largest provider of telecommunications services, SK Telecom, and Japan's "Mobile Broadcasting Corporation" jointly undertook the R&D for the satellite. To develop broadcasting

contents, chipsets, and handsets, SK Telecom launched a research consortium consisting of 200 companies in 2003 with the participation of a significant number
of high-tech start-ups (Shim, 2004: 62–63). Initially, handset manufacturers developed products with the Satellite-DMB chipsets purchased from Toshiba. However,
LG Electronics and a number of domestic start-up firms including "Integrant" and
"Tel Ace" developed a chipset, which integrated signals with CDMA networks (Kim
2005: 23–24; Kim 2004). In 2005, handset manufacturers including Pantech &
Curitel and Sky Teletech began to substitute Toshiba's chips for chipsets produced
by LG and Tel Ace respectively, which was in keeping with the MIC's goals of
reducing Korea's dependence on imports as mentioned earlier and securing an initial
market for high-tech start-ups (iPark Silicon Valley, 2005).

The key point of the discussion presented in this section is that since the early
2000s, the MIC has supported a national transition from a strategy based on
catching-up to one based increasingly on innovation-led development by inducing the
cooperation of the *chaebol* in the international standardization of Korean-developed
technologies and to secure an initial market for the innovations created by high-tech
start-ups.[10]

Discussion: The Evolution of Cooperation between the State and the *Chaebol*

What does the Korean state's promotion of the telecommunications sector since the
early 2000s tell us about what the state has done to cope with the rise of global
companies in this sector? How does this compare with the state's governance of
interdependence between public and private actors to create the telecommunications
sector in the late 1980s to 1990s? In short, to support companies in their attempts
to transition from catching-up to a position of staying ahead, the Korean state instituted newer forms of governed interdependence to undertake a coordinated approach
to international standardization and to support the commercialization of innovations developed by high-tech start-ups. Two types of governed interdependence can
be identified.

First, the state has instituted *elements* of what Weiss (1998: 76–78) and others (cf.
Schaede and Grimes 2003: 247–248) refer to as "private-sector governance" in which
the state delegates the formulation and implementation of public policies for specific
industries to the private sector itself. This type of governance has been apparent in the
MIC's willingness to delegate promotional functions to technology-centered forums
with the expectation that the *chaebol* play leadership roles in the organization of
such forums in collaboration with public officials from agencies affiliated with the
MIC. The *chaebol* have played their part in these forums by participating in domestic
and international standards-setting activities while also becoming major purchasers
of domestically manufactured core components, software, and solutions. The MIC's
encouragement for the *chaebol* to accept a greater share of the burden in promoting
techno-industrial competitiveness represents a shift away from a situation where the
state, particularly in the earlier stages of the telecommunications sector, absorbed
most of the risks involved in creating a completely new national presence in this
sector. This shift is a reflection of the changing needs of the *chaebol* and provides
evidence of the state's ability to adapt to the current needs of the *chaebol* and

the needs of new industrial actors such as high-tech start-ups who may be highly innovative but face barriers in accessing markets dominated by conglomerates such as Samsung Electronics and LG Electronics.

Second, the state continued to utilize "disciplined support" in state-sponsored R&D projects involving high-tech start-ups which need financial support but also in the state's collaboration with the conglomerates. The state's support for the representation of the interests of the *chaebol* in inter-governmental regional and international standards development bodies was implicitly tied to the participation of the *chaebol* in the state-sponsored technology-centered forums. A major function of these forums was to coordinate the commercialization of innovations developed in high-tech start-ups and in this respect, conglomerates which dominate the final assembly of telecommunications products cooperated by providing initial markets for these small firms. The *chaebol* may be less reliant on the state as a source of financial support and technology transfer as made clear in the words of the President of ETRI, Yim Chu-Hwan, mentioned earlier. However, the *chaebol* like any other firm in advanced industrial countries who have ambitions to get their technologies reflected in international standards, require the state to play a coordinative role in reducing the uncertainties faced by firms in investing into the development of new technologies, which may not become recognized as part of future international standards. The continuing use of disciplined support reflects a continuation of a form of public and private cooperation seen in the formative stages of the Korean telecommunications sector, in completely new ways.

Conclusion

The changing forms of governed interdependence between the Korean state and the *chaebol* from the 1980s to the 2000s in the telecommunications sector provides an ideal case to examine how states with strategic industry objectives in East Asia have coped with the growth in the structural power of global companies. Rather than revealing any signs of diminishing the state's coordinative role, developmental states such as Korea have sought new ways of managing collaborative ties between public and private actors. From a relationship based initially on midwifery where the state absorbed most of the risks faced by the *chaebol* in creating a completely new technological growth sector, in more recent years, the Korean state has increasingly encouraged the *chaebol* to collaborate as equal partners with the state and accept greater responsibilities over the promotion of national techno-industrial competitiveness. The *chaebol* have cooperated in two main ways. First, the state has induced their collaboration in state-sponsored efforts to promote the international standardization of Korean-developed technologies. The second is more a precondition for the state's continued support of international standardization activities with the *chaebol* which involves their provision of initial markets for the innovations created by fledgling high-tech start-ups who provide crucial sources of innovation in the pursuit of the Korean state's emphasis on transitioning towards innovation-led development.

What can these findings in the East Asian region tell us about broader questions over the relationship between the structural power of global companies and the transformative power of states? The state's transformative capacity has been critical to the transformation of global companies from their typically humble origins to the formidable players in their respective domestic markets and international markets that they now are. The structural power of global companies depends in large part on the transformative power of states and this relationship is likely to continue in light of external pressures brought about by ever increasing levels of economic openness and intensifying knowledge-based competition.

Are governmental responses to the growing structural power of business uniform across all states? The findings presented in this chapter show that states which embody the ideological commitment to strategic goals and possess specific institutional features which enables a relationship of governed interdependence are the most capable of instituting mutually beneficial relations with global companies. I have merely touched on such features throughout this chapter. In arguments presented elsewhere, I have provided fuller accounts of how erstwhile developmental states such as Korea have recombined core institutional features (Kim 2012a) and rearticulated strategic goals as part of renewing their domestic legitimacy (Kim 2012b). States which are absent of the ideational and institutional features which contribute to a relationship of governed interdependence would appear ill-equipped as effective partners for global companies. Testing such a claim in setting outside of the state-guided economies such as the more corporatist and liberal types may a useful task for future studies of comparative capitalism.

While I have pursued a line of inquiry from the perspective of a political scientist, the extent to which the state's transformative capacity is dependent on the structural power of global companies begs a different question and may provide a fruitful area for further investigation. A research agenda of this type may help us to understand the *conditions* which obstruct or facilitate cooperation. In this regard, David Hundt's (2009: 108–112) fine work on governmental, industrial, and societal factors which enable or constrain a "developmental alliance" has gone the furthest. There is still, however, much more work that needs to be done in understanding the conditions underlying public and private cooperation particularly with regards to how the characteristics of specific sectors may influence outcomes. This will require a multidisciplinary approach incorporating existing insights from public policy, strategic management, comparative capitalism, and international political economy.

Notes

1 Amongst the many studies on this subject see for example, Dicken (2007: 124–135), Lansbury, Suh, and Kwon (2007), and Mikler (2009).

2 It is important to note that such interpretations of recent events differs with the most radical exponents of the endist thesis such as those who argue that the Korean developmental state has transformed into something that approximates a neoliberal model (cf. Pirie 2008). Such views have already been subject to challenge both empirically and conceptually (Kim 2012a; 2012b; Thurbon 2011).

3 See the seminal works of Amsden (1989), Johnson (1982), Fields (1995), Wade (1990/2004), Onis (1991), Woo (1991). For countries outside of East Asia who applied the developmental state idea, see Loriaux (1999) on France and Levi-Faur (1999) on Israel.

4 See Johnson (1982: ch. 7).

5 See Larson (1995), Evans (1995), and Mani (2005) for more information on the TDX and other projects.

6 For a deeper analysis of the politics involved in the launch of two separate R&D consortiums and the problems involved in the standardization process, see Wang and Kim (2007) and Jho (2007b).

7 For an empirical examination of the politics underlying the efforts by bureaucratic actors and industrial actors in establishing political support for embarking on innovation-led development, see Kim (2012b).

8 See: http://americas.kgin.or.kr/eng/overview/world.asp#09, accessed August 27, 2007.

9 See: http://www.pixtree.com/, accessed July 5, 2009.

10 This is not to deny the challenges the MIC faced in the launch of Terrestrial and Satellite-DMB services, which resulted in significant delays (cf. Lee and Kwak 2005; Shin 2006).

References

Amsden, Alice H. 1989. *Asia's Next Giant: South Korea and Late Industrialization*. Oxford and New York: Oxford University Press.

Arthur, Charles. 2012. "Nokia and Samsung Lead Mobile Phone Sales as Apple Leaps into Third Place." *The Guardian*, February 2.

Block, Fred. 1992. "Capitalism without Class Power." *Politics and Society*, 20 (3): 277–303.

Block, Fred. 2008. "Swimming Against the Current: The Rise of a Hidden Developmental State in the United States." *Politics and Society*, 36 (2): 169–206.

Callon, Scott. 1995. *Divided Sun: MITI and the Breakdown of Japanese High-tech Industrial Policy, 1975–1993*. Stanford: Stanford University Press.

Cho, Sammo and Kim, Songmin. 2004. "T-DMB Approach in Korea: Technical and Economic Aspects of T-DMB." Presentation at Bayerische Medien Technik GmbH, Germany. October 20–22.

Dicken, Peter. 2007. *Global Shift: Mapping the Changing Contours of the World Economy*, 5th edn. London: Sage.

Evans, Peter. 1995. *Embedded Autonomy: States and Industrial Transformation*. Princeton: Princeton University Press.

Fields, Karl J. 1995. *Enterprise and the State in Korea and Taiwan*. Ithaca: Cornell University Press.

Han, Ji-young. 2004. "Interview: ETRI President Yim Chu-hwan." *IT Korea Journal*, 5 (January): 54–55.

Harrod, Jeffrey. 2006. "The Century of the Corporation." In *Global Corporate Power*, ed. Christopher May, 23–34. Boulder: Lynne Rienner.

Hundt, David. 2009. *Korea's Developmental Alliance: State Capital and the Politics of Rapid Development*. London and New York: Routledge.

iPark Silicon Valley. 2005. Satellite DMB Phone Makers Move to Adopt Domestically Developed Chips, *iPark Silicon Valley News*, September 9, http://www.kiica-sv.com/homepage_main.php?menu=it_korea&sub=news&id=340&action=view. Accessed February 21, 2005.

Johnson, Chalmers. 1982. *MITI and the Japanese Miracle: The Growth of Industrial Policy, 1925–1975*. Stanford: Stanford University Press.

Johnson, Chalmers. 1999. "The Developmental State: Odyssey of a Concept." In *The Developmental State*, ed. Meredith Woo-Cumings, 32–60. New York: Cornell University Press.

Jho, Whasun. 2007a. "Liberalization as a Development Strategy: Network Governance in the Korean Mobile Telecom Market." *Governance*, 20 (4): 633–654.

Jho, Whasun. 2007b. "Global Political Economy of Technology Standardization: A Case of the Korean Mobile Telecommunications Market." *Telecommunications Policy*, 31: 124–138.

Kalinowski, Thomas. 2009. "The Politics of Market Reforms: Korea's Path from Chaebol Republic to Market Democracy and Back." *Contemporary Politics*, 15 (3): 287–304.

Kim, Jin-cheol. 2012. "Chaebol Control Pervades Life in Korea." *Hankyoreh*, February 13.

Kim, Jong-ryul. 2005. "Many Non-Memory Venture Firms Enter Market." *IT Korea Journal* 11 (January/February): 22–24.

Kim, Kyu-tae. 2004. "Semiconductor Makers Develop 3 Core Chips for Satellite DMB Receiver." *The Electronic Times Internet*, August 17.

Kim, Sung-Young. 2012a. "Transitioning from Fast-Follower to Innovator: The Institutional Foundations of the Korean Telecommunications Sector." *Review of International Political Economy*, 19 (1): 140–168, http://dx.doi.org/10.1080/09692290.2010.503125.

Kim, Sung-Young. 2012b. "The Politics of Technological Upgrading in South Korea: How Government and Business Challenged the Might of Qualcomm." *New Political Economy*, 17 (3): 293–312.

Kim, Tae-gyu. 2004. "Korea Loses in Global Digital Mobile Broadcast Race." *The Korea Times*, October 5.

Korea IT Times. 2005a. "Maximizing the Punch of DMB by Facilitating Interactive Services." *Korea IT Times*, February, volume 8.

Korea IT Times. 2005b. "Making DMB a Reality." *Korea IT Times*, February, volume 8.

Lansbury, Russell, Suh, Chung-Sok, and Kwon, Seung-Ho. 2007. *The Global Korean Motor Industry: The Hyundai Motor Company's Global Strategy*. London and New York: Routledge.

Larson, James F. 1995. *The Telecommunications Revolution in Korea*. Hong Kong: Oxford University Press.

Lee, Gwangsoon, Cho, Sammo, Yang, Kyu-Tae, Hahm, Young Kwon, and Lee, Soo In. 2005. "Development of Terrestrial DMB Transmission System Based On Eureka-147 DAB System." *IEEE Transactions on Consumer Electronics*, 51 (1): 63–68.

Lee, Seungwhan and Kwak, Dong Kyun. 2005. "TV in Your Cell Phone: The Introduction of Digital Multimedia Broadcasting (DMB) in Korea." Paper presented at the annual Telecommunications Policy Research Conference, Arlington, September 23–25.

Levi-Faur, David. 1999. "Warfare, Polity-Formation, and the Israeli National Policy Patterns." In *Israel: The Dynamics of Change and Continuity*, ed. David Levi-Faur, Gabriel Sheffer, and David Vogel, 156–168. London: Frank Cass.

Lindblom, Charles E. 1977. *Politics and Markets: The World's Political-Economic Systems*. New York: Basic Books.

Loriaux, Michael. 1999. "The French Developmental State as Myth and Moral Ambition." In *The Developmental State*, ed. Meredith Woo-Cumings, 235–275. New York: Cornell University Press.

Mani, Sunil. 2005. "Keeping Pace with Globalisation Innovation Capability in Korea's Telecommunications Equipment Industry." *Center for Development Studies, Working Paper*, 370, March.

Mathews, John A. and Cho, Dong-Sung Cho. 2000. *Tiger Technology: The Creation of a Semiconductor Industry in East Asia*. Cambridge: Cambridge University Press.

Mikler, John. 2009. *Greening the Car Industry: Varieties of Capitalism and Climate Change*. Cheltenham; Northampton, MA: Edward Elgar.

Ministry of Information and Communication. 2003. "Digital Broadcasting in Korea." *MIC Policy News*, February 28, http://eng.mic.go.kr/eng/user.tdf. Accessed July 7.

Minns, John. 2001. "Of Miracles and Models: The Rise and Decline of the Developmental State in South Korea." *Third World Quarterly*, 22 (6): 1025–1043.

Ohmae, Kenichi. 1990. *The Borderless World: Power and Strategy in the Interlinked Economy*. London: Fontana.

Onis, Ziya. 1991. "The Logic of the Developmental State." *Comparative Politics*, 24 (1): 109–126.

Park, Hun-Joo. 2007. "Small Business' Place in the South Korean State–Society Relations." *Asian Journal of Political Science*, 15 (2): 195–218.

Pirie, Iain. 2008. *The Korean Developmental State: From Dirigisme to Neo-Liberalism*. London and New York: Routledge.

Pringle, David and Tam, Pui-Wing. 2003. "Samsung to Use Its Own CDMA Chip." *The Wall Street Journal*, April 14.

Schaede, Ulrike and Grimes, William. 2003. "Permeable Insulation and Japan's Managed Globalization." In *Japan's Managed Globalization: Adapting to the Twenty-First Century*, ed. Ulrike Schaede and William Grimes, 243–254. Armonk, New York: M.E. Sharpe.

Shim, Woo-sung. 2004. "Special Interview: Developers of Multi Mobile Telephone Contents." *IT Korea Journal*, 7 (May): 59–75.

Shin, Dong Hee. 2006. "Prospectus of Mobile TV: Another Bubble or Killer Application?" *Telematics and Informatics*, 23: 253–270.

Telecoms Korea. 2003. "Korea's Struggle for Independence from Qualcomm: Defiance and Compromise." *Telecoms Korea*, June 11.

Telecoms Korea. 2010. "Samsung, LG Report Fall in March Handset Sales in Korea." *Telecoms Korea*, April 2.

Thurbon, Elizabeth. 2003. "Ideational Inconsistency and Institutional Incapacity: Why Financial Liberalisation in South Korea Went Horribly Wrong." *New Political Economy*, 8 (3): 341–361.

Thurbon, Elizabeth. 2011. "Why the Declinists are Wrong: (Mis)-Constructing the 1970s Authoritarian Korean State as *the* Developmental State Model." Paper Prepared for the International Studies Association Asia-Pacific Regional Section Inaugural Conference, University of Queensland, September 29–30.

Thurbon, Elizabeth and Weiss, Linda. 2006. "Investing in Openness: The Evolution of FDI Strategy in South Korea and Taiwan." *New Political Economy*, 11 (1): 1–22.

Wade, Robert H. 1990. *Governing the Market: Economic Theory and the Role of Government in East Asian Industrialization*. Princeton: Princeton University Press; reprinted (2004) with a new introduction by the author.

Wang, Jaesun and Kim, Seoyong. 2007. "Time To Get In: The Contrasting Stories About Government Interventions In Information technology Standards (The Case of CDMA and IMT-2000 in Korea)." *Government Information Quarterly*, 24: 115–134.

Weiss, Linda. 1998. *The Myth of the Powerless State: Governing the Economy in a Global Era*. Ithaca: Cornell University Press.

Weiss, Linda. 2003. "Guiding Globalisation in East Asia: New Roles for Old Developmental States." In *States in the Global Economy: Bringing Domestic Institutions Back*, ed. Linda Weiss, 245–270. Cambridge: Cambridge University Press.

Weiss, Linda. 2005. "Global Governance, National Strategies: How Industrialized States Make Room to Move Under the WTO." *Review of International Political Economy*, 12 (5): 723–749.

Weiss, Linda. 2006. "Infrastructural Power, Economic Transformation, and Globalization." In *The Social Theory of Michael Mann*, ed. John A. Hall and Ralph Schroeder, 167–186. Cambridge: Cambridge University Press.

Woo, Jung-en. 1991. *Race to the Swift: State and Finance in Korean Industrialization*. New York: Columbia University Press.

Woo-Cumings, Meredith. 2003. "Diverse Paths Towards 'The Right Institutions': Law, the State, and Economic Reform in East Asia." In *States in the Global Economy: Bringing Domestic Institutions Back In*, ed. Linda Weiss, 200–222. Cambridge: Cambridge University Press.

Chapter 12

Varieties of the Regulatory State and Global Companies

The Case of China

Shiufai Wong

Introduction

Since China's recent emergence as the world's second largest economy after the United States, global companies have not only accelerated their presence in the country, but stretched out their economic hands to become involved in social and political affairs. Such involvement, to a certain extent, has significantly altered the stance and strategy of the Chinese government in managing national development. Sometimes global companies gain the upper hand, while at other times the government predominates. After gradually replacing arbitrary administrative guidance with statutory regulation, regulators and regulations in China are now more important and powerful than ever. Today, China can be considered a regulatory state (e.g. Pearson 2003/05; Bach, Newman, and Weber 2006).

Yet, understanding what kind of regulatory state/capitalism China is can be a grim task. In addition to the "*laissez-faire* regulatory capitalism" (under both weak state and civil regulation) in Western market-oriented economies, there are also "command-and-control regulatory capitalism" (under strong state regulation and weak civil regulation), "pluralist regulatory capitalism" (under weak state regulation and strong civil regulation) and "corporatist regulatory capitalism" (under both strong state and civil regulation) in the rest of the world (Levi-Faur 2006b). No single variety of regulatory capitalism can explain why and how China has inconsistently behaved in its relationship with global companies. It is noted that the regulatory game plan in China has continually changed to integrate itself into the world capitalism, especially after China was admitted to WTO membership in December 2001. The government is running more than one kind of regulatory capitalism in parallel. Why do these variants of regulatory capitalism co-exist after the massive entry

The Handbook of Global Companies, First Edition. Edited by John Mikler.
© 2013 John Wiley & Sons, Ltd. Published 2013 by John Wiley & Sons, Ltd.

Table 12.1 Conflicting features of Chinese regulations.

Strong regulation (toward developmental orientation)	Weak regulation (toward regulatory orientation)
(A) Discourage heavily polluting industries	(a) Provide a business-friendly market
(B) Change the economic structure	(b) Reduce business barriers
(C) Improve the safety, quality, and standard of products and services	(c) Clamp down on preferential policies
(D) Prevent activities harmful to China's sovereignty	(d) Ensure more corporate/transactional transparency/integrity

Source: Table constructed with reference to the developmental and regulatory orientations conceptualized by Johnson (1982; 1995).

of global companies (which formulate civil regulations) into China (which enacts state regulations)?

The literature has found that the usual (*laissez-faire*) regulatory approach to governance without a sense of purpose or a clear national target inside it has large loopholes that invite abuse by market players (Mathews 2001). China's regulatory policies have thus become more sophisticated to realize both their regulatory and developmental functions. This proposition shares the view of some scholars that China's developmental aspiration remains unchanged (e.g. Bramall 2000; Xu and Yeh 2005). Therefore, in addition to regulatory orientation of reform initiatives through which Chinese rulemakers promote/maintain fair competition and market transparency, developmental orientation may also have been employed. While China has increasingly become the factory of the world under the WTO to provide a fair and transparent legal system for the protection of foreign companies, its regulatory requirements for foreign companies have inevitably had to adapt to certain needs of the country and this developmental function has to be achieved through regulation. It could mean embedding state power in regulation so that the state's tasks become much less "visible" than before but may manage to meet its development goals or to effect industrial transformation. However, the regulatory orientation is supposedly contradictory to the developmental orientation (Table 12.1). How can the Chinese government manage to smooth out the contradiction? Due to the need that new regulatory mechanisms in China have been harnessing the behavior of global companies with an intention of retaining developmental power intact, this prompts the leadership in Beijing of trying to balance the two conflicting orientations by alternative or more innovative means.

After all, why and how has China managed to regulate toward the two conflicting orientations after mingling with global companies? To reveal the "black box" process of China's integration into global capitalist markets, very few empirical studies on China from a dynamic regulatory capitalism perspective have been conducted. The next section uses historical analysis to present four rationales of why Chinese regulatory capitalism becomes dynamic and partly developmental, and then uses statistics across the 100 largest global companies to illustrate actually how the Chinese government regulates global companies.

China in Need of Going beyond *Laissez-Faire* Regulatory Capitalism

Governments in Anglo-Saxon countries usually govern through regulatory agencies to enforce a variety of behavior standards, e.g. an effective and fair market mechanism as well as a sufficient and stable provision of public goods and services undersupplied by the market (e.g. Moran 2001; Jordana and Levi-Faur 2004; Cook *et al.* 2004). The emergence of China's regulatory state like this as a means to integrate itself into the world economy has become an irreversible process (Pearson 2003; 2005). Since the rise of economic neoliberalism and the new public management policies adopted across governments in the early 1980s to restructure their bureaucracies, regulation has increasingly become a legally acceptable policy tool for public administrators to replace unpopular direct state involvement or interventionist administrative guidance.

Moran (2001) describes this increasing replacement of discretionary state intervention with institutional regulation as "the rise of the regulatory state" asserting that neoliberal economic outcomes are not so much the result of deregulation but, rather, a diversified form of regulation including (a) the regulation of newly privatized industries, (b) self-regulation in enterprises, (c) social regulation to respond to the subversion of justice, and (d) internal regulation of the public sector. By employing them, the state may achieve the following: First, the state can fix any market or systemic failure by so-called "pro-competition regulation" which is actually designed to remove market entry barriers (e.g. access regulation in telecommunications sectors), to provide rules of the game (e.g. settlement procedures of stock markets), to improve information asymmetry (e.g. disclosure regulation in financial markets) and to permit a sufficient number of market players competing with one another (e.g. antitrust regulation of mergers and acquisitions) (Loughlin and Scott 1997; Stirton and Lodge 2001).

Second, the state may stop excessive government spending in Keynesian welfare capitalism by transferring ownership of public utilities such as water and electricity to the private sector through "small government regulation" (e.g. licensing requirements or privatization rules in Cook *et al.* 2004).

Third, the state may improve the utilitarian problems of *laissez-faire* capitalism by establishing more "social regulation" (e.g. minimum wages and social security) rather than steering the economy solely by profit-oriented business (e.g. Jordana and Levi-Faur 2004; Levi-Faur and Jordana 2005).

Fourth, the state may reduce the heavy administrative burden and the costs of information necessary for public sector decision-making by allowing "professional regulation" in professional associations or technical organizations (e.g. the Association of American Medical Colleges in Ogus 2004).

All these regulatory approaches resemble Levi-Faur's (2006b) "*laissez-faire* regulatory capitalism" which lacks a noticeable function of building national developmental and/or transformative capability. The early emergence of Chinese rulemakers in this style has implied the demise of a developmental China (e.g. Pang 2000; Keeley 2003; Pekkanen 2004). However, to avoid jeopardizing national development and autonomy, China has had to seek a different rationale behind its regulatory approach, and therefore regulatory agencies empowered by statutory laws will need to implement a wide range of different types of governance as circumstances of regulated industries require.

The second rationale for China steering a different regulatory mechanism may have regarded the fundamental role of the Communist Party of China (CPC) in its Party Constitution that "the realization of communism is the highest ideal and ultimate goal of the Party." This is an ideal supposed to continuously transform the country, along with the famous dictum of Deng Xiaoping that "development is the only cardinal principle." This dictum has long been the guiding developmental tenet of the CPC both during and after his rule (Yang 2005). The Chinese state may thus not be satisfied with being only a market-oriented or non-interventionist mechanism toward regulatory orientation, but may be aspiring to a more aggressive development model. According to China's 12th Five-Year Plan (2011–2015), its recent national development goals include a short-term target of 7% national economic growth annually on average, and medium-term goals of removing massive labor-intensive enterprises away from cities to outer suburbs. They seek to upgrade locally made products from low-end to advanced technologies with larger expenditure on R&D, shifting overheated investment growth to underdeveloped internal demand growth, and improving environment including energy consumption and carbon dioxide emission per unit of GDP to be cut by 16% and 17% respectively through developing non-fossil fuel energy-related techniques. Since most of the policy areas are located away from the WTO territory, these developmental goals seem not to contradict the current perception of a predominantly market-oriented or non-interventionist regulatory orientation, and seem to share the views of "command-and-control regulatory capitalism" (under strong state regulation but weak civil regulation).

The third and fourth rationales for China respectively being "corporatist regulatory capitalism" and "civil regulatory capitalism" may also be good descriptors of current policy. Despite the dilemma that Chinese state regulation has had to become even less strategic and political especially within the jurisdiction of the WTO, the Chinese leadership is reluctance to abandon its heretofore interventionist and dirigiste developmental policies and thus may have been forced to carefully and selectively choose amongst civil regulators and regulations from professional/technical civil society to achieve its national development objectives. To enable Chinese enterprises to meet its national development interests and goals, the state has not retreated but has, instead, introduced some alternative policy measures through regulatory decentralization of renowned or credible professional/technical civil society so as to encourage Chinese enterprises to take up the challenge from foreign competitors. This has been aimed at orienting civil regulation toward national goals and interests, leading to the rise of either "corporatist regulatory capitalism" (under both strong state and civil regulation) and/or "pluralist regulatory capitalism" (under weak state regulation but strong civil regulation).

To statistically and empirically illustrate these four rationales, this chapter observes the 100 largest global companies chosen from Fortune's Global 500 in 2011 to examine the latest Chinese regulatory reforms and answers the following questions: (a) whilst China has entered the global market and has been transforming itself into a competition and market-based regulatory regime, does this signal an end to China's former strategic development policies? (b) Is the Chinese state still directly intervening in the economy in order to govern and orient the targeted market players towards its national goals, albeit that its nomenclature system and shareholding ownership appear less effective than before, with a variety of regulatory means dominated by the government and global companies? (c) Which or what type(s) of regulatory governance has China chosen to deal with global companies? (d) How has (dynamic) regulatory governance helped China pursue market liberalization without its further growth and long-term development interests necessarily being compromised? To find answers to these questions, we should have a historical discussion on the four rationales.

Rationale 1: To Bring Prices Down and/or to Ensure Availability of Products/Services

Such a governance mode refers to the predominance of regulatory orientation over developmental orientation during regulation-making by both the state and the civil society. It is generally suitable for markets where prices and/or availability of products/services have a higher concern than the quality or technological development of products or services, e.g. clothing, groceries, food, housing, transport, energy, or fuel. The state is inclined to let a large number of market players compete in price, and to regulate independently to ensure sufficient availability of products/services in the market.

Since China's WTO accession required the country to open markets to foreigners, reliable and transparent regulatory instruments and mechanisms have more commonly and increasingly replaced administrative order and personal trust methods (Tan, Yang, and Veliyath 2008). The above-mentioned type of global companies may enjoy a few regulatory advantages. First, China's policy instruments to provide a business-friendly market include regulations such as relaxation of foreign investment rules, simplified trade procedures, protection of foreign equity investors, stronger antidumping rules, and so on. Profits earned by foreign direct investors, and their other legal rights and interests in the country, are protected by the new law "Circular on Amending the Law of the PRC on Foreign Capital Enterprises" amended and promulgated at the National People's Congress (NPC) on October 31, 2000 (A in Table 12.1).

Second, the government introduced regulations to reduce business barriers. For example, an amendment to the 1993 "Company Law" made on October 27, 2005 to lower minimum registered capital and the draft "Measures for the Administration of Procurement Transactions between Retailer and Supplier" to lower entry fees levied by retailers. In addition, any promulgation of local regulations and measures that would lead to sectoral monopoly or regional barrier without approval from the State Council has had to be amended to fit into WTO rules or otherwise revoked[1] (B in Table 12.1).

Third, under the WTO rules, China has also had to clamp down on preferential policies in order to allow foreign investors to compete more fairly in its markets (except for areas outside the WTO-contingent economic center). Accordingly, dramatic changes from the subsidizing of industry policy to the reduction of tariffs and a level-playing-field competition policy have come about. For example, first, import and export tariff rates of some 5000 items have been gradually reduced since 2002; the average tariff rate of industrial products was reduced from 14.7% in 2001 to 11.6% in 2002; and the average tariff rate of agricultural goods dropped from 18.9% in 2001 to 15.6% in 2002[2] (C in Table 12.1).

Fourth, there are new regulations to ensure more corporate/transactional transparency/integrity (e.g. the Direct Sales Management Rules which took effect on December 1, 2005) in line with the announcement of the State Council on June 2, 2000, at the opening of the 3rd Session of the 9th NPC. During this time the then premier Zhu Rongji revised his strategy and regulatory targets and declared "war" through a new form of regulatory governance on all corporate misbehavior and malpractice. Both Chinese and foreign companies are the targets (D in Table 12.1).

The retail and consumer goods industries out of the sampled largest 100 global companies are fitting cases to show the characteristics and policy trends of this type of regulatory governance. It is discovered that eight of them belong to these industries and of which six have structural co-operation with Chinese companies. [3] Of these 8 companies, 6 of them have extensive cooperation with or substantial investment in Chinese companies.

Amongst these sampled global companies, latest examples to bring prices down and/or to ensure availability of products/services are as follows: in 2011 China fined Wal-Mart for misleading prices and fake organic pork;[4] in the same year China fined Carrefour for misleading prices.[5]

Rationale 2: To Relocate Industries to Central/Western China and/or to Upgrade Technological Level

Despite allowing new or foreign investors to break into de facto monopolies of state-owned enterprises, barriers resulting from negative externalities (e.g. pollution, dangerous production, supply–demand bottleneck, and even detriment to national sovereignty) remain to be redressed.

For this reason, first, since the mid-2000s new state regulations have discouraged heavily polluting industries including metallurgy, smelting, paper-making, breweries, heavy and chemical production, and oil refining in, for example, Guangdong Province. Meanwhile, manufacturing of shoes, furniture, textiles and garments, plastics, and luggage and bags in many urban areas of the country is conditionally restricted.[6] Under the restricted category, producers have to pay a customs duty deposit to compensate for the externality (A in Table 12.1).[7]

Second, preferential regulations are also reemployed to change the economic structure in areas outside the WTO-contingent economic center. For example, the "Priority Industrial Catalogue of Foreign Investment in the Central and Western Region" offers preferential treatment to encourage foreign investors to explore the central and western regions of China. A milestone in this process was reached when on July 1, 2004 the Standing Committee of the NPC promulgated the "Foreign Trade Law of the People's Republic of China." It stipulates that although some others should remain restricted from import or export, some goods and technologies promoted by the national department of development planning are no longer subject to quota or licensing control. In certain important industries (e.g. automotive, healthcare and pharmacy), technology transfer is promoted through related laws and regulations on Sino-foreign contractual joint ventures in 2000 and on Sino-foreign contractual equity joint ventures in 2001. Both of them were first enacted in the 1980s, and then revised to exempt foreign direct investors from submitting production and operational plans, along with the proportion of sales of products between the domestic and foreign markets, to governmental departments (B in Table 12.1).

Third, state regulations to improve the safety, quality, and standard of products and services have been formulated. For example, Regulations of the PRC on Production Licences of Industrial Products took effect on September 1, 2005; the Measures for the Administration of Second Hand Car Distribution of Taxation took effect on October 1, 2005; and the new Rules for Registration and Management of Freight Forwarders took effect on February 1, 2005 (C in Table 12.1).

Fourth, state regulations to prevent activities harmful to China's sovereignty have been enacted. For example, Article 4 of Regulations for the Implementation of the Law on Sino-foreign Equity Joint Ventures (2001) stipulates that applications to establish joint ventures shall not be granted approval if the project involves detriment to China's sovereignty[8] (D in Table 12.1).

All these examples illustrate that the increasing employment of regulations in China does not necessarily refer to the predominance of regulatory orientation over developmental orientation, but the other way round. A total of 46 of the sampled 100 largest global companies cooperate closely with Chinese/foreign companies. [9] Of these 46 companies, 40 of them have between 9–60% of a stake in (or sold to) Chinese counterparts.

Amongst these sampled global companies, latest examples of "command-and-control regulatory capitalism" to drive economic transformation and/or technological upgrade include the following: Toyota was required to reveal the electric vehicle technology before being allowed to sell their wares in China;[10] in 2007 Chinese regulators coerced Nanjing Automobile Corp (NAC) to merge with SAIC Motor and let NAC build the MG in Oklahoma, leading to the termination of an 8-year-long JV between Fiat with NAC;[11] in 2010 since new laws to require technology transfers in return for market access, Peugeot had to rethink its gasoline-electric hybrid technology plans in its second JV with China Changan Automobile Group;[12] in 2011 ArcelorMittal was accused by the Chinese regulator CSRC of failing to provide hot-rolling technologies and to allow Valin Steel to realize its global iron ore purchasing scheme.[13]

Rationale 3: To Improve Chinese Companies' Quality Control and/or to Build Investor Confidence

Regulatory failure in China, nonetheless, has often arisen from the unproven status of regulatory enforcement, for example, in the banking sector (e.g. Barth, Trimbath, and Yago 2004), or in stock markets (e.g. Pistor and Xu 2005). This implies that, despite using the state's strategic regulation as a basis to create competition and to relocate and/or transform industries, a positive outcome is not guaranteed, particularly when decentralized regulatory power is being abused by state and local government officials (Pei 2006; O'Brien and Li 2006). This problem has led to the reaffirmation by the State Council of its commitment to the improvement of regulatory implementation. In China's legal system, laws are primarily enacted by its legislature. But provisions, measures, or regulations promulgated by the State Council or executive branch agencies were not necessarily pursuant to delegation by a rule-making authority from the legislature. This supremacy of bureaucratic power had the advantage of flexible and quick governance but it also resulted in abused regulatory power remaining unchecked and distinct interpretations of law through state regulation proving untrustworthy in terms of regulatory enforcement.

To solve this problem, the 2000 "Legislative Law" to clarify under what conditions the State Council, ministries, and NPC at local levels could make administrative regulations or local laws was enacted.[14] In addition, one would further recommend state regulations to be made and implemented under the approval and supervision of the legislature. Also, the need to offer a reliable, easy-to-operate competitive business environment had prompted the state to consider simplifying its "complicated" regulatory system. A revolutionary review had thus emerged since the 15th National Congress of the Communist Party of China (CPC) in September 1997, which reaffirmed that the legal principle of legislature should take precedence over the government. More significantly, since the first draft of the "Supervision Law" in the 1990s attempting to supervise the performance of governments (and courts and other prosecuting bodies) by the legislature, there had also been a heated debate in the mainland about whether the CPC or the legislature should rule over the country. Finally, at the 23rd Meeting of the Standing Committee of the 10th NPC on August 27, 2006, the legislators passed the "Supervision Law" which took effect on January 1, 2007, stipulating that administrative and judicial officials must serve statutes.

Despite being able to improve the legitimacy of state regulation, the above legislative review may, however, jeopardize the flexibility and efficiency of the regulatory capacity of the state. Hence, delegation to civil society regulation (hereinafter abbreviated as civil regulation) could be one of the solutions. On one hand, a narrow understanding of civil regulation (or semi-state regulation) may refer to those provisions and rules formulated by independent regulators. In recent years, such regulators and regulatory violation investigation mechanisms are being increasingly established. More such kinds of new regulatory packages and/or exclusive regulators can be found from the most disordered sectors such as insurance (e.g. the 2001 China Insurance Regulatory Commission), banking (e.g. the 2004 China Banking Regulatory Commission), securities (e.g. the 2005 China Securities Regulatory Commission), postal services (e.g. the 2007 restructured State Post Bureau) and the like.

On the other hand, a broad understanding of civil regulation generally refers to demands and expectations of non-state actors or civil societies including consumers, investors, NGOs, media, and local communities to regulate business behavior (Vogel 2005), and the scope of civil regulation here in the field of national development has a focus on regulation formulated by the professional/technical civil society. Over the past few years, the Chinese government has been working hard to employ more reliable, systematic, and accumulated regulation (such as best-practice codes, industrial data sharing, technical standardization and operating procedures) produced by trustworthy people who are not necessarily government technocrats. They are politically neutral professional/technical civil societies that are responsible for producing, certifying and/or licensing industrial/product standards, ratings, values and/or ethics for a profession, product line, or industrial sector, in order that businesses can gain public trust and accreditation status by complying with required civil regulations and standards. However, these regulatory agencies or non-state regulators are actually governed by central planning to exert a variety of state intervention. This euphemistical or fake regulatory decentralization would thus improve the aforesaid bureaucratic problems of regulatory making and implementation and also circumvent legislative restraint.

Such civil regulations, however, do not necessarily refer only to those produced by the Chinese professional/technical civil society (e.g. in the accounting and auditing sectors) of which some are presently not sufficiently sophisticated or credible to industries and investors. But even though the deadline to fulfil WTO liberalization commitments was drawing near, improving domestic civil regulations would still take a very long time. A quick solution would be simply to adopt regulations and standards of foreign civil societies. For example, dominant global professional/technical systems and rules such as the International Electrotechnical Commission (IEC), the Occupational Health and Safety Management System (OHSAS), the International Organization for Standardization (ISO), the International Accounting Standards Board (IASB), and the International Auditing and Assurance Standards Board (IAASB) have increasingly become complementary or transitional working standards in industries, financial institutions, and many other businesses operating in China (e.g. ISO9001/OHSAS18001 in the Chinese banking and financial sector, Wang 2006; ISO/TS16949 for internal auditors on quality, safety, and environmental management systems, Yin and Zhang 2006).

A total of 29 of the sampled 100 largest global companies have integrated into China, mainly engaging in insurance, banking, and other financial services.[15] Of these 29 companies, 25 of them have between 2.8–60% of a stake in (or sold to) Chinese counterparts. They could be included in "corporatist regulatory capitalism." In contrast to the previous first type of regulatory governance, a stronger preference for quality over price, and/or a need to build investor confidence, especially when corporate governance is in crisis, has prompted the Chinese government and business communities to pursue foreign quality assurance standards in tandem with local ones.

The double-auditing system for listed companies and banks is one of the latest examples amongst the sampled global companies to build investor confidence. The first so-called independent auditing system in China was written into the constitution after the 5th Plenary Session of the 5th NPC in December 1982. Accordingly, the National Audit Office (NAO), as a ministry and state institution to supervise audits at different (provincial, municipal, and county) levels, has been affiliated to the State Council. Four Auditor Generals, who are also members of the State Council, are supervising some 80,000 government auditors all over the country. The 1995 "Audit Law of the PRC" and the 1997 "Implementation Rules for the Audit Law of the PRC" have empowered government auditors to refer to judicial or administrative inspection agencies, and to sanction or penalize enterprises which have breached the relevant laws and regulations. With the help of "Professional Codes of Ethics for Government Auditors" issued on December 16, 1996 and under the "Golden Audit Project," many other auditing standards, guidelines, and procedures have been computerized. As a result, on January 1, 1997, the NAO issued 38 auditing standards and guidelines. In principle, while the primary function of audits in the West is to scrutinize financial statements in an objective manner for ensuring their truthfulness and fairness, the main objective of audits in China is to protect the legal interests of both the company and the state. In the West, independent external auditors are responsible for auditing companies, but in China government auditors at various levels directly carry out the audit work. For this very reason, Chinese auditing standards set by the state institution have substantially differed from their American or British counterparts or the International Standards on Auditing (ISA) set by the International Auditing and Assurance Standards Board (IAASB).[16]

Another remarkable difference between them is their professionalism and reputation. The growing number of scandals involving government (and local private) auditors has prompted the state to rethink the statutory role of government auditors (Bertin and Jaussaud 2003; Wang, Wong, and Xia 2006). This has led to a revision of Chinese national accounting standards making it compatible with the ISA so as to reduce the costs of raising foreign capital by enterprises. Meanwhile, the government has begun to realize that foreign independent auditors might help Chinese companies engage in a more reliable, internationally compatible accounting practice which is highly important to investors in the country.

Hence, at this point, the state critically came up with the idea of a double auditing requirement. To facilitate this, the "Accounting System for Business Enterprises" (ASBE, applicable to joint equity limited companies taking effect from January 1, 2001 and to foreign-invested companies taking effect from January 1, 2002) was enacted to replace the 1992 "Accounting System for Joint Stock Limited Enterprises," the "Accounting System for Foreign Investment Enterprises," and the "Charter of Accounts and Accounting Statements for Foreign Investment Industrial Enterprises." These revisions of the accounting systems, regulations, and standards have enabled the China Securities Regulatory Commission (CSRC) to pursue double auditing standards, which require listed Chinese companies (classified as B shares in Chinese stock exchanges and H shares in foreign stock exchanges) to be audited by both Chinese and foreign auditors. This requirement was then extended to all listed companies in banking, securities, and insurance industries through "Measures for Adopting the System of Temporary Licenses to Foreign Accounting Firms for Engaging in the Business of Auditing for Financial Listed Companies" jointly promulgated by the CSRC and the Ministry of Finance on January 12, 2001. To facilitate this special requirement, temporary licenses were granted to the internationally renowned "Big Five" (today only the "Big Four") foreign auditors to carry out the additional audit work.[17] Later, from January 1, 2002 onwards, such a double-auditing system was further extended to all newly listed companies classified as A shares (in Chinese stock exchanges) and to all existing A-share companies that raise new funds on the stock exchanges. There had been a huge controversy in the business sector over the double-auditing arrangement; but as soon as the state made some concession by moving to confine its requirement to large companies who issue more than 300 million shares of stock, the resistance was pacified. The idea of double audits may sound ridiculous to the West; even so, it aims to help the Chinese auditing standards incorporate the international ones quickly.

Finally the CSRC announced the abolition of the double audit of all PRC listed companies (i.e. B-Share companies in 2007 and of A- and H-share companies in 2010) due to China's accounting and auditing standards increasingly matching up to international practice. After the latest collaboration between the Chinese Auditing Standards Board (CASB) and the International Accounting Standards Board (IAASB), new Chinese auditing standards for auditors (and new accounting standards for listed companies) in the mainland have just been released, taking effect on January 1, 2007. These new auditing standards are the result of 17 drafts and revisions over the past few years. Whilst modifying some of the existing Chinese standards to meet the need for international convergence bringing ASBE substantially in line with the International Financial Reporting Standards (IFRS), the CASB has managed to strike a balance by maintaining some original standards, such as the verification of capital contributions, and communication between predecessor and successor auditors, to reflect China's unique business practices and developmental needs.[18] This arrangement of dual state-civil regulator exemplifies another example of China's developmental orientation in its regulatory regimes to improve the Chinese auditing system and also to eliminate possible domestic resistance.

Rationale 4: To Let Chinese Companies Participate in the Making of Dominant Technical Standards for the World Market

However, if foreign professional/technical civil regulations dominate over domestic ones, it might be detrimental to Chinese development goals, due to the fact that under-developed Chinese professional/technical civil societies with much poorer capacity in civil regulation-making and standard-setting would be heavily suppressed by their well-developed and reputable foreign counterparts. This would then create intellectual hegemony by foreign professional/technical civil societies which would in turn control the direction of China's product/industrial development without considering the technical levels of (and/or without considering a need to cooperate with) local producers. Concern over this issue has triggered the Chinese government to reconsider its regulatory approach. Lacking many choices, Chinese authorities have been obliged to strategically allow a tandem combination of weak foreign civil regulation and strong Chinese civil regulation to exist.

Due to the need for national security and political stability, at some stage and place, the government is inclined to encourage organized Chinese industrial civil society. In doing so, an industry alliance model has been adopted. The transition to an open economy recently has brought a paradigmatic change to the product standardization of China: for example, Intelligent Grouping and Resource Sharing (IGRS) industry, which is shaped by a well-connected industrial civil society. This paradigmatic change has sparked off a new China-made universal standard, which is a home grown interoperable standard to facilitate network interactions among all kinds of electronic and digital devices. The IGRS is designed to link up PCs, TVs, digitally controlled air conditioners, intelligent refrigerators, or any other digital products, and the design work was initially a collaboration between a handful of Chinese brand names affiliated directly or indirectly to the central government like the three largest computer manufacturers, Lenovo, Great Wall, and TCL, and two mega-sized consumer electronics and communications manufacturers, Konka and Hisense. These first five Chinese producers were then extended to some 40 local manufacturers, research institutes, and universities with strong transnational linkages from, for example, Taiwan, South Korea, and Japan, who are highly supported by the Ministry of Information and Industry (MII). This cooperation by giant Chinese companies is obviously a self-defense "crusade" against the foreign standards developed by the US Digital Home Working Group (DHWG), in which 134 foreign manufacturers including Microsoft, Sony, and Philips collaborate to penetrate the Chinese digital-home market.

The IGRS includes a common protocol and an IGRS-1.0 version meeting Chinese standards, using a TCP/IP-based application and taking the HTTP protocol as its framework, supporting wired LAN, and many other network media. The Chinese government seeks to solicit its foreign counterpart, DHWG, to adapt to the Chinese standard, not the other way around. In January 2004, notably Lenovo Computers ceased its cooperation with Time Warner and turned to working with China Telecom through its service arm Sunny Information Technology Service and preinstalled an Asymmetric Digital Subscriber Line (ADSL) broadband to allow consumers to access China Telecom's China Vnet. Actually there has been a tug-of-war between foreign and Chinese standardizations in the information technology industry since the early 2000s. In mid-2003, having seen several Chinese manufacturers such as TCL, Konka, Huawei, UTStarcom, and ZTE join with the American DHWG, quite a few Chinese IT manufacturers have faced strong pressures from foreign standardization forcefully pushing Chinese companies away from the dominance of core technologies, and foreign standards have become technical barriers to Chinese technological upgrading.

Having experienced this, Chinese industrial civil society with the support of the Chinese government decisively submitted a proposal on April 5, 2006 to the Secretariat of the Subcommittee of the ISO/IEC Joint Technical Committee in Germany to request permission for the Chinese IGRS to become an international standard.[19] This is a joined-up liberalist Chinese industrial civil society dissimilar to the case of the protectionist or mandatory Wireless LAN Authentication and Privacy Infrastructure (WAPI), another Chinese unified standard which failed to become accepted as an international standard, driving many foreign makers out of the Chinese markets for the reason that they did not meet the required Chinese technical standards, unless they modified their products to adopt Chinese standards. Tremendous negative responses from foreign countries to these Chinese confrontational attitudes have taught the Chinese government how to offset the risk by giving up the protectionist approach and focusing on liberalist standardization.

As a result, Chinese industries have drafted some two dozen Chinese liberalist product standards, for example Chaoji VCD and TD-SCDMA, to become approved international standards, though far from making any success in collecting royalty fees from the participants. While Chaoji VCD is made compatible with the foreign standard HQ-VCD and the other two Chinese standards CVD and SVCD, the four Chinese TD-SCDMA vendors, namely ZTE, Huawei, Datang, and Potevio, are working closely with foreign producers Siemens, Erricson, Alcatel, and Nortel respectively.[20] Except for the earlier on protectionist WAPI, the promotion of transnational business linkages between the Chinese and foreign industry would expect China's industry alliances to continue to employ liberalist strategies; and the state will continue to play a high profile and supportive role in industry alliances as long as the resulting product standards and the national goals do not conflict.

There are also many other such Chinese enterprise technology alliances such as 3D Video Industry Alliance of China, ITopHome Alliance, China Software Alliance, or alliances in the drugs and medicines industry, under which industrial civil societies are responsible for at least 50% of the cost of establishing research, development, and demonstration facilities, providing human resources, and setting up their own industry standards. This episode illustrates not only China's new civil regulatory capacity to become a rule maker (Bach, Newman, and Weber 2006), but the Chinese state's delicate balancing act between regulatory and developmental orientation to reposition the standardization approach in an appropriate marketplace. For example, owing to the increasingly dominant role of DisplayPort (supported by Apple, Dell, HP, Lenovo, Fujitsu, Toshiba, and Acer) and HDMI (developed by Hitachi, Panasonic/National/Quasar, Philips, Silicon Image, Sony, Thomson, and Toshiba) to replace LVDS (fadeout from 2013), and DVI and VGA (fadeout from 2015), many Chinese computer vendors and display makers have chosen to enter joint ventures or partnerships with these dominant standardization makers.

A total of 17 out of the sampled 100 largest global companies can be categorized into this type of regulatory governance.[21] Of these 17 companies, all of them have partnerships or joint-ventures with Chinese counterparts. Latest examples amongst the sampled global companies to bring a paradigmatic change to the product standardization of China's global companies include the co-development of HDMI, the de facto standard for HDTV with Sony, Panasonic, and Toshiba respectively; the co-development of ADSL2 or VDSL on telephone lines and ITU's G.hn standard for home networking with AT&T; the co-establishment of the LTE as a global radio access technology; the co-establishment of cloud computing services to cities worldwide with Verizon; the co-development of WCDMA, dual-mode dual-standby mobile communications system to bridge the gap between CDMA and GSM with Telefónica; the co-deployment of TD-LTE networks as a standard 4G mobile technology with Vodafone.

Conclusion

Much of the regulatory state/capitalism literature fails to satisfy readers who want a more widesweeping view of the process of transforming China itself into a significant market player in the global economy. In view of conflicting evidence showing that market liberalization and competition-oriented regulatory measures in China have gradually taken shape and that the country has managed to move ahead towards both its regulatory and developmental goals, observers today need a combination of different rationales to understand why and how these most recent Chinese apparently conflicting economic systems have evolved in such a way and functionally worked.

In response to the research questions, the usual strategic development policies in China's regulatory reform process are not really over. Despite the presence of market-oriented regulation ("*laissez-faire* regulatory capitalism"), China has replaced its usual interventionist administrative guidance with strategic regulation as well ("command-and-control regulatory capitalism"). Despite a certain degree of regulatory decentralization to professional/technical civil society ("pluralist regulatory capitalism") or the co-production of technical standardization between the Chinese and foreign industry ("corporatist regulatory capitalism"), developmental orientation in addition to regulatory orientation is also seen in the case studies. In any case, the purposes of intervention in terms of introducing state and/or civil regulations are just to protect China's interests. It can be observed that they are to bring prices down and/or to ensure availability of products/services, relocate industries to central/western China and/or upgrade technological level, improve quality control, and/or build public confidence in Chinese companies, and join forces of producers to participate in the making of dominant technical standards.

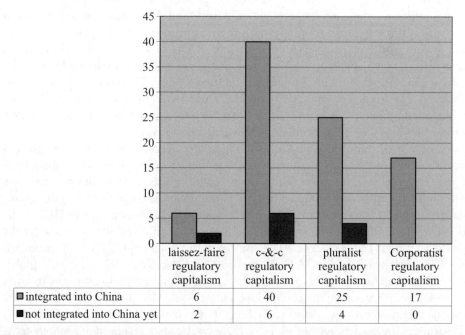

	laissez-faire regulatory capitalism	c-&-c regulatory capitalism	pluralist regulatory capitalism	Corporatist regulatory capitalism
◨ integrated into China	6	40	25	17
◼ not integrated into China yet	2	6	4	0

Figure 12.1   Varieties of Chinese regulatory capitalism across the 100 largest global companies. Source: Fortune Global 500 (2011).

Overall, the cases of the 100 largest global companies show at least three characteristics of the Chinese regulatory governance. First, China is flexible enough to mingle with foreign global companies with different forms of regulatory governance to achieve its national goals and interests. While command-and-control is the most popular type of regulatory capitalism in China, *laissez-faire* is the least (see Figure 12.1). Second, despite close connection between Chinese local firms and foreign global companies under the pluralist and corporatist regulatory capitalisms, China's strategic regulations have restrained the latter to a minority in joint ventures or partnerships to maintain the Chinese leadership. Third, exchanges of interests are commonly seen. Under this practice, China not only uses Sino-foreign structural collaboration to help local development, but treats it as a bridge to enter foreign markets. In any case, the effort in this chapter is just a take-off. As the evidence tends to suggest, in no respect can China's regulatory choices be looked upon as the regulatory state/capitalism in the literature. Further critical examination of such dynamically and strategically regulated, and interest swapping Sino-foreign relationships should be directed towards new models different from the other, especially Western, forms of the regulatory state/capitalism.

Notes

1   Sourced from the website of Hong Kong Trade Development Council, *New Enterprise Accounting System Implemented*, 1, January 15, 2002, http://www.tdctrade.com/alert/cba-e0201a.htm, accessed

November 16, 2006; MOF Bans Unauthorized Tax Incentives, *Business Alert – China*, 4, April 1, 2004, http://www.tdctrade.com/alert/cba-e0404a-2.htm, accessed November 16, 2006.

2   Sourced from the website of Hong Kong Trade Development Council, *New Enterprise Accounting System Implemented*, 1, January 15, 2002, http://www.tdctrade.com/alert/cba-e0201a.htm, accessed November 16, 2006; MOF Bans Unauthorized Tax Incentives, *Business Alert – China*, 4, April 1, 2004, http://www.tdctrade.com/alert/cba-e0404a-2.htm, accessed November 16, 2006.

3   They are, except for Kroger and Costco which have not entered into the Chinese market yet, Wal-Mart's 2004 agreement with the government to set up a trade union, Carrefour's 2007 and Tesco's 2009 compliance with new labor laws to set up a trade union, Metro's 2011 agreement with Shuanghui Logistics who would provide storage, processing, transfer, and distribution services for Metro, Procter & Gamble's 2010 construction of its second-largest distribution center in the world jointly funded by Procter & Gamble and local government, and Glencore's 2009 agreement with the China Investment Corp to invest $200 billion sovereign wealth fund in Glencore.

4   *Sing Tao Daily*, October 18, 2011.

5   *China Daily*, July 19, 2007.

6   *Ming Pao*, September 16, 2006.

7   *Ming Pao*, August 23, 2008.

8   Invest in China, http://www.fdi.gov.cn, accessed October 1, 2011.

9   Except for Toyota, McKesson, CVS Caremark, AmerisourceBergen, Pemex, and Indian Oil which have not structurally cooperated with China yet, they are Volkswagen which has 14 subsidiaries in China including major partnerships with SAIC in Shanghai and FAW in Changchun since 1984, GM's 1998 partnership with Shanghai Automotive Industry Corporation, Daimler's 2011 partnership to form Shenzhen BYD Daimler New Technology Co Ltd, Ford's 2010 memorandum with Chongqing Municipal Government to build its second engine plant in China, Honda which has four car assembly factories in China including three joint ventures, Nissan's 2003 partnership with Dongfeng Motor, Hyundai which has three car plants in China, BMW's 2003 joint venture with Brilliance China, EXOR (Fiat)'s joint ventures in Zhanjiang City (2001), Pudong (2001), Zhongqing (2008), and Changsha (2011), Peugeot's 1992 partnership with Dongfeng Motor, ArcelorMittal's 2008 joint venture with Valin Steel, Hon Hai's first processing plant in Shenzhen in 1988 with expansion to 13 factories in nine cities to produce consumer electronics for famous brandnames, Cardinal Health's 2010 acquisition of China's biggest pharmaceuticals importer Zuellig Pharma, Nestlé's 2011 agreement to take a 60% stake in family-owned Yinlu Foods Group, State Grid Corp's 2007 award of a tender for a 25-year license to run the Philippines power grid, Transco, GDF Suez's 2010 agreement with CNOOC to supply 2.6 million tons of LNG from 2013 to 2017, E.ON's 2009 partnership with Dongjiang to engage in Clean Development Mechanism projects in China, Enel's 2009 agreement with China to share the carbon capture and storage technology, Électricité de France's 2006 agreement with China Guangdong Nuclear Power to extend nuclear power project cooperation, Royal Dutch Shell's 2010 partnership with PetroChina to jointly work on a coalbed methane block in North China, ExxonMobil's 2009 long-term LNG sales and purchase agreements with PetroChina and Sinopec, BP's 2010 partnership with CNOOC for an exploration project in the South China Sea, Sinopec's 2010 acquisition of a 9% stake in the Canadian oil firms, Syncrude, PetroChina's 2009 investment in Iraq to develop oil fields and 2011 in Iran to develop oil fields, Chevron's 2010 partnership with CNOOC for an exploration project in the South China Sea, Total's 2008 agreement with CNOOC for up to one million tons annual sales of LNG, ConocoPhillips' 2002 partnership with CNOOC to develop the Peng Lai 19-3 Field, ENI's 2011 memorandum with CNPC to jointly expand operations in shale gas in Africa, Petrobras' 2009 $10 billion loan from the China Development Bank to sell 100,000 barrels of oil to Sinopec, Gazprom's 2011 agreement with a 20-year loan from China Development Bank to supply gas to China, JX Holdings' 2010 agreement with a unit of PetroChina to jointly run JX Energy's Osaka refinery in Japan, PDVSA's 2010/2011 agreement with PetroChina to pump crude and extract natural gas from Venezuela and to build a refinery in China, Statoil's 2011 team-up with PetroChina to tap shale gas in China, Lukoil's 2010 partnership with PetroChina

on projects at Kumkol & Severnye Buzachi in Kazakhstan and is ready to supply gas to China, Valero Energy's 2011 in talk with PetroChina to sell a refinery in Aruba, SK Group's 2005 establishment of two wholly foreign-owned gas stations in Shenyang, Petronas' 2006 25-year contract to sell LNG to Shanghai LNG Company, Repsol YPF's 2010 agreement with Sinopec to sell 40% of Repsol-YPF Brazil operations, Marathon Oil's 2010 agreement with CNOOC and Sinopec to sell 20% stake in Angola Block 32, and BASF's 2009 second phase of joint venture with Sinopec to invest $1.4 billion in a petrochemical project.

10 *Paul Tan's Automotive News*, September 22, 2010.

11 *China Daily*, August 31, 2009.

12 *Bloomberg*, October 1, 2010.

13 *SteelHome*, July 27, 2011.

14 The Legislative Law of the PRC (Order No. 31 of the President of the PRC) was passed at the Third Session of the Standing Committee of the Ninth NPC on March 15, 2000 and took effect on July 1, 2000.

15 Except for United Health Group, Lloyds Banking Group, Groupe BPCE and Dexia group which have not structurally cooperated with China yet, they are AXA's 2010 agreement to sell a 60% stake in AXA's China insurance operation to ICBC, AIG's 2009 selling all shares of AIG Finance (HK) to China Construction Bank Asia, Aviva's 2009 joint-venture with Henan-based Central China Securities, Nippon Life Insurance's 2009 joint-venture with China Great Wall Asset Management Corp, Prudential's 2011 joint-venture with a unit of Fosun Group, Fannie Mae's bond largely sold to the Chinese Government, Freddie Mac's bond largely sold to the Chinese Government, Berkshire Hathaway's 2008 acquisition of a 10% stake in Chinese electric car company BYD, ING Group's 2007 strategic collaboration with China Construction Bank (Asia), Bank of America Corp's selling its BoA (Asia) to China Construction Bank in 2006, BNP Paribas's acquisition of a 19.2% stake in Nanjing City Commercial Bank in 2005, Allianz's acquisition of a 2.8% stake in China Pacific Insurance in 2011, Assicurazioni Generali's 2002 joint venture with PetroChina to form Generali China Life Insurance, JP Morgan Chase's 2010 joint venture with First Capital Securities, Citigroup's 2011 joint venture with Oriental Securities, Crédit Agricole's 2011 selling its 19.9% stake to Citic Securities, HSBC's 2004 acquisition of a 19.9% stake in Bank of Communications, Banco Santander's 2011 joint venture with China Construction Bank, Wells Fargo's 2011 agreement with Baoding Tianwei Group to build a polysilicon production plant in Pocatello, United States, Société Générale's 2011 ended car financing joint venture with BYD, Industrial & Commercial Bank of China's 2005 acquisition of the Hong Kong subsidiary of Fortis Bank, Munich Re Group's 2011 agreement with Ping An Property and Casualty Insurance to provide insurance for the domestic renewable energy industry, Royal Bank of Scotland's 2011 33% stake joint venture with Guolian Securities, Japan Post Holdings' 2010 agreement with China Post to deliver goods ordered online by Chinese consumers, Deutsche Post DHL's selling its domestic express operations to Shenzhen-based Uni-top Industry in 2011.

16 IAASB is one of the boards of the International Federations of Accounts, which is a global organization founded in 1977 with members from the accountancy and auditing professional sector of 118 countries.

17 They are PricewaterhouseCoopers, Deloitte Touche Tohmatsu, Ernst & Young, and KPMG.

18 Sourced from Department of Accounting of Ministry of Finance, *Joint Statement by the Chairman of the Chinese Auditing Standards Board and the Chairman of the International Auditing and Assurance Standards Board* (Economic Science Press, 2006).

19 In August 2006, IGRS became first China-initiated ISO standard.

20 The 3G mobile phone standards also include the American CDMA 2000 and the European WCDMA but the Chinese government has chosen its home-made standard TD-SCDMA for its own 3G market.

21 They are General Electric's 2009 joint venture agreement with Aviation Industry Corporation of China, Samsung's 2010 partnership with TCL Group to build factories in Suzhou, Siemens' 2004 partnership with Huawei Technologies Company Ltd, Sony's 2004 joint venture with Hua Long Film

Digital Production Co., Panasonic's 1995 joint venture with Shandong Taishan Electric Group & State Capital Management Co. Ltd, Hewlett-Packard's 2006 partnership with Beijing Hejia Software Technology Ltd, IBM's 2004 selling PC business to Lenovo, Hitachi's 2006 joint venture with Bao Steel to produce cast rolls for hot strip mills, Toshiba's 2009 joint venture with Greentech Group Ltd and a Hong Kong LCD panel distributor, AT&T's 2002 joint venture with China Telecom Corp and Shanghai Information Investment Inc., NTT's sixth-largest shareholder in 2011 being OD05 Omnibus supported by China Sovereignty Fund, Verizon's 2009 partnership with China Mobile, Verizon Wireless and Vodafone to develop the next-generation technology LTE, Deutsche Telekom's 2011 partnership with Chinese telecom equipment maker Huawei, Telefónica's 2009 tie-up with China Unicom by investing $1 billion in each other, China Mobile's 2007 fully acquired Paktel to launch the ZoNG brand in Pakistan, Vodafone's 2011 agreement with China in Barcelona Mobile, China Railway's 2009 award of a tender to build a highway in Europe inclusive of the 50 km A2 highway in Poland.

References

Bach, D., Newman, Abraham L., and Weber, Steven. 2006. "The International Implications of China's Fledgling Regulatory State: From Product Maker to Rule Maker." *New Political Economy*, 11 (4): 499–518.

Barth, James R., Trimbath, Susanne, and Yago, Glenn. 2004. *The Savings and Loan Crisis: Lessons from a Regulatory Failure*. Dordrecht: Kluwer.

Bertin, E. and Jaussaud, J. 2003. "Regulation of Statutory Audit in China." *Asian Business & Management*, 2 (2): 267–280.

Bramall, C. 2000. *Sources of Chinese Economic Growth*, 1978–1996. Oxford: Oxford University Press.

Cook, Paul, Kirkpatrick, Colin, Minogue, Martin, and Parker, David, eds. 2004. *Leading Issues in Competition, Regulation and Development*. Cheltenham: Edward Elgar.

Johnson, Chalmers A. 1982. *MITI and the Japanese Miracle: The Growth of Industrial Policy 1925–1975*. Stanford: Stanford University Press.

Johnson, Chalmers A. 1995. *Japan, Who Governs? The Rise of the Developmental State*, New York: Norton.

Jordana, Jacint and Levi-Faur, David, eds. 2004. *The Politics of Regulation: Institutions and Regulatory Reforms for the Age of Governance*. Cheltenham: Edward Elgar.

Keeley, James. 2003. "The Biotech Developmental State? Investigating the Chinese Gene Revolution." *IDS Working Paper*, 2007, Institute of Development Studies, Brighton, Sussex BN1 9RE, England.

Levi-Faur, David. 2006a. "Varieties of Regulatory Capitalism: Sectors and Nations in the Making of a New Global Order." *Governance*, 19 (3): 363–366.

Levi-Faur, David. 2006b. "Regulation in the Age of Governance: Beyond the Zero-Sum Narratives." Conference Paper for "Frontiers of Regulation. Assessing Scholarly Debates and Policy Challenges," University of Bath, September 7–8.

Levi-Faur, David and Jordana, Jacint. 2005. "The Rise of Regulatory Capitalism: The Global Diffusion of a New Order." *Annals of the American Academy of Political and Social Science*, 598 (March): 200–217.

Loughlin, M. and Scott, C. 1997. "The Regulatory State." In *Developments in British Politics: P. Dunleavy*, ed. A. Gamble, I. Holliday, and G. Peele, 205–219. London: Macmillan.

Mathews, John A. 2001. "Fashioning a New Korean Model out of the Crisis: The Rebuilding of Institutional Capabilities." In *Financial Liberalization and the Asian Crisis*, ed. Ha-JoonChang, Gabriel Palma, and D. Hugh Whittaker, 156–174. Hampshire; New York: Palgrave.

Moran, M. 2001. "The Rise of the Regulatory State in Britain." *Parliamentary Affairs*, 54 (1).

O'Brien, Kevin J., and Li, Lianjiang Li. 2006. *Rightful Resistance in Rural China*. New York: Cambridge University Press.

Ogus, Anthony. 2004. "Comparing Regulatory Systems: Institutions, Processes, and Legal Forms in Industrialized Countries." In *Leading Issues in Competition, Regulation and Development*, ed. Paul Cook, Colin Kirkpatrick, Martin Minogue, and David Parker, 146–164. Cheltenham: Edward Elgar.

Pang, Eulsoo. 2000. "The Financial Crisis of 1997–98 and the End of the Asian Developmental State." *Contemporary Southeast Asia*, 22 (3): 570.

Pearson, M. 2003. "Mapping the Rise of China's Regulatory State: Economic Regulation and Network and Insurance Industries." Paper Prepared for the Annual Meeting of the Association of Asian Studies.

Pearson, M. 2005. "The Business of Governing Business in China: Institutions and Norms of the Emerging Regulatory State." *World Politics*, 57: 296–322.

Pei, Minxin. 2006. *China's Trapped Transition: The Limits of Developmental Autocracy*. Cambridge, MA: Harvard University Press.

Pekkanen, Robert. 2004. "After the Developmental State: Civil Society in Japan." *Journal of East Asian Studies*, 4: 363–388.

Pistor, Katharina and Xu, Chenggang. 2005. "Governing Stock Markets in Transition Economies: Lessons from China." *American Law and Economics Review*, 7 (1): 184–210.

Stirton, L. and Lodge, M. 2001. "Transparency Mechanisms: Building Publicness into Public Services." *Journal of Law and Society*, 28 (4): 471–489.

Vogel, David. 2005. *The Market for Virtue: The Potential and Limits of Corporate Social Responsibility*. Washington, DC: Brookings Institution Press.

Wang, Guibing, ed. 2006. *ISO9001/OHSAS18001and the Internal Regulatory System of the Banking Sector* (in Chinese). Beijing: China Economic Publishing House.

Wang, Qian, Wong, T. J., and Xia, Lijun. 2006. "State Ownership, the Institutional Environment and Auditor Choice: Evidence from China." Paper presented at the China Research Conference at the CUHK.

Xu, Jiang and Yeh, Anthony G.O. 2005. "City Repositioning and Competitiveness Building in Regional Development: New Development Strategies in Guangzhou, China." *International Journal of Urban and Regional Research*, 29 (2): 283–308.

Yang, Baoguo. 2005. "From 'Development is the Cardinal Principle' to 'the Development View of Science': On the Innovation and Development of the Thoughts of the Party's Leaders." *Journal of Lianning University*, Philosophy and Social Sciences Edition, 1: 105–112.

Yin, Zhewu and Zhang, Zhiyong. 2006. *Internal Controller and Management Representative: ISO9001(ISO/TS16949), ISO14001, GB/T28001* (in Chinese). Beijing: China Machine Press.

Chapter 13

Global Companies and Emerging Market Countries

Caner Bakir and Cantay Caliskan

Introduction

The age of globalization has transformed the nation-state-dominated Westphalian system in a significant manner: the twentieth century has witnessed the rise of the power of multinational corporations (MNCs), which increasingly share the authority for governance with nation-states and even undermine their sovereignty. Since the 1980s this is due to the processes of market liberalization and economic globalization. States in emerging countries face intense competition with each other in a world of global capital mobility in order to attract inward Foreign Direct Investment (FDI), which is seen as a significant means of achieving national economic growth and development objectives. Not surprisingly, host state (HS) and multinational corporation (MNC) bargaining increasingly takes place in domestic political economies. This chapter has two aims. First, it analyzes the multi-actored and multi-level entry bargaining processes where state capacity plays a pivotal role in the outcome which has dual meaning as an investment and a non-investment decision that merits explanation. Second, in the light of this analysis, the chapter focuses on a crucial aspect of the vast literature on MNC–state relations: the impact of the MNC on sovereignty, state capacity, and governance with particular emphasis on bargaining between HS and MNCs.

States, MNCs, Bargaining, and Public Goods

A discussion of state and MNC relations can be broadly located in the globalization literature based on a typology of theories of globalization proposed by Held *et al.* (1999: 10) consisting of "hyper-globalist," "sceptic," and "transformationalist" categories.

The Handbook of Global Companies, First Edition. Edited by John Mikler.
© 2013 John Wiley & Sons, Ltd. Published 2013 by John Wiley & Sons, Ltd.

Hyper-globalists argue that "the nation state has become an unnatural, even dysfunctional, unit for organizing human activity and managing economic endeavor in a borderless world" (Ohmae 1993: 78). If the state is not dysfunctional, at the very least it is in retreat so that "the impersonal forces of world market ... are now more powerful than the state's to whom ultimate political authority over society is supposed to belong" (Strange 1996: 4).

For sceptics, states are still relevant actors. They are "'pivotal' institutions, especially in terms of creating the conditions for effective international governance" (Hirst and Thompson 1996: 170). Further, "[in]ternational businesses are still largely confined to their home territory in terms of their overall business activity; they remain heavily 'nationally embedded' and continue to be multinational, rather than transnational, corporations" (p. 98).

For transformationalists such as Rosenau (1997) or Giddens (1990), globalization occurs as "states and societies across the globe are experiencing a process of profound change as they try to adapt to a more interconnected but highly uncertain world" (Held et al. 1999: 2). In this view, the globalization process has transformed state power where immobile nation-states are constrained by mobile developed country MNCs and their powerful host states.

There are several views on bargaining between nation-states and MNCs that may be considered in the context of these debates (e.g. see Yeung 1995; Salehizadeh 2007; Haslam 2007). However, the first point to make is that there has been only limited study in the politics literature of how competition among states to host the investment of MNCs takes place with special reference to an entry bargaining process. In contrast, the bargaining between HSs and MNCs has been subject to extensive research in the International Business (IB) literature. The traditional model of entry bargaining employed in this literature is the "obsolescing bargain model" (OBM), and it is a conflict model of firm/state interaction. It reflects *conflictual* bargaining between developing country governments and developed country MNCs in natural resource industries in the 1960s and 1970s. Sector-specific investments, as the argument goes, make the relatively immobile MNC vulnerable to opportunistic decisions of HS, making the original bargain obsolete. The primary focus is on HSs' and MNCs' *economic* sources of relative bargaining power as an ability or capacity to achieve their respective ends in the outcome, the investment deal (Vachani 1995: 159–180). It is assumed that an MNC's bargaining power resources include ownership advantages such as capital and technology, while a HS's bargaining power resources include its location-specific advantages such as access to the home market, natural resources, and cheap and skilled labor (Poynter 1985; Boddewyn 1988). This view focuses on the bargaining powers of HSs and MNCs in the 1960s and 1970s: power of an MNC is highest at the time of entry but the balance of power shifts in favor of the state once an initial investment is made. The bargain is expected to obsolesce over time as an HS is likely to have new demands from the relatively immobile MNC following its sector-specific investments. The key vulnerabilities of MNCs include expropriations, adverse regulatory changes, renegotiation of contracts, and performance requirements imposed by HSs. However, Bennett and Sharpe argue that the balance of bargaining power, especially in high-technology manufacturing, shifts in favor of MNCs (Bennett and Sharpe 1979). Once car manufacturers, for example, have access to a market, they are integrated into the local economy and establish relationships within the host country, strengthening their bargaining power *vis-à-vis* the HS.

Following a FDI liberalization trend across national economies since the 1980s, restrictions on inward FDI such as screening or performance requirements, ownership restrictions, and licensing agreements featuring technology transfer have been gradually removed by HSs (UNCTAD 2000). Not surprisingly, from the 1990s onwards, interaction between HSs and MNCs has changed from being "predominantly adversarial and confrontational to being non-adversarial and cooperative" (Dunning 1998; Vernon 1998). More recently, it is accepted that bargaining does not define HS and MNC relations. As a result, "the widely held view among [IB] scholars is that the OB model has outlived its usefulness" (Eden and Molot 2002: 362). In response to these views, there have been efforts among IB scholars to show the utility of the OBM for understanding bargaining outcomes (Eden and Molot 2002; Eden, Lenway, and Schuler 2005).

Following this cooperative view on bargaining, the model of "triangular diplomacy" is an earlier work focusing on the competition of states and firms for world market share (Stopford and Strange 1991). This model moved beyond the traditional bargaining model and described the triangle of bargaining among states (in terms of trade policy, bi- and multi-lateral treaties, and domestic policies), between states and firms (in terms of attracting inward FDI), and among firms (in terms of enhancing their global success). More recently, the "two-tier bargaining model" offered a novel insight to the OBM and the triangular diplomacy model by incorporating Tier-1 bargaining between the developing country host governments and developed country home governments (Ramamurti 2001). It has been noted that Tier-1 bargaining that occurs bilaterally or through multilateral institutions produces macro rules on FDI that affect micro negotiations in Tier-2 (per the traditional bargaining model). It is argued that the bargaining between developing-country host governments and home governments of developed country MNCs provide additional leverage to their MNCs over developing country HSs through bilateral or multilateral agreements and/or organizations. These models discussed above focus on how the bargain changes over time to the benefit of HS or MNC rather than the dynamic entry bargaining process itself.

Moreover, the competition between states gives the MNCs a fertile basis for bargaining. As states are not the producers, "it is the firm that is adding value to the labor, materials and knowhow going into the product. States are therefore competing with other states to get the value-added done in their territory and not elsewhere, [which is the basis of the bargain]" (Strange 1992: 7). However, it is important to note that the bargaining positions of the MNCs are more effective before the investment. After the FDI goes into a particular country, then the MNCs are reluctant to leave the country because of the local operations developed and the job training provided by the MNCs. In the case of bargaining, John Stopford notes that both states and the MNCs have a strong incentive to work on building partnerships that create wealth in the first place (Vernon 1971; Vernon 1977; Moran 1974; Moran 1978; Mytelka 2000). Thus, territory constitutes the main advantage that nation-states possess facing the corporations in the bargaining process, which proves to be a relatively weak position compared to the potential of economic growth and technological spillover effects caused by the MNCs. Hence, the market competition aspect of the relationship between MNCs and states also has a symbiotic nature; however, states may need MNCs more than MNCs need states. States welcome FDI, as they need to be globally competitive for their survival, in which MNCs receive the majority of the relative gains.

For example, such competition did take place in 2005 when the world's 95th largest South Korean MNC, Hyundai Motors Corporation (HMC), considered establishing an approximately USD1.5 billion car manufacturing plant in one of the two countries, the Czech Republic and Turkey, in order to host HMC investment. The Czech Republic used its sovereignty at the expense of its citizens when landowners were required either to sell their land to the government or face forced land expropriation as a legitimate action (Bakir 2011). The threat of expropriation enabled the regional authorities to obtain the consent of owners for the sale of all necessary land at the desired site by the HMC. This led to the conclusion of the investment deal among the parties.

Job training, labor quality, and the ways of doing business constitute a major aspect of bargaining. For developing economies, job training is especially important, as many of these countries do not have the means to provide enough technical education to their labor force. In this aspect, MNCs largely use cross-border comparisons of costs and performance in local negotiations in manufacturing (European Foundation for the Improvement of Living and Working Conditions 2009).

The economic power of the MNCs is strong (Kaplan 1997), and therefore can be translated into political power by forming interest groups and using lobbyists. Some scholars suggest that MNCs can aim to maximize their profits by seeking corrupt governments and destroying domestic economies, as seen with Wal-Mart's deplorable labor practices like underpaying their employees and overcharging for produce. Thus, MNCs are self-optimizers that invest in countries where they can receive the highest profit. This puts the countries in a disadvantageous position, as they continuously need to fight for providing the best conditions in a situation where there are only few winners.

Generalizations are problematic though. In a comparative perspective, MNCs' role in collective bargaining varies between different countries. In many countries, MNCs have been a major source of pressure for decentralization of bargaining arrangements by introducing greater scope for company negotiation within sector and inter-sector arrangements. For example, in Portugal, sectors in which MNCs are concentrated are expected to be prominent in taking advantage of new provisions by the state which enable either party to terminate agreements that have technically expired, but until now remained in force, and replace them with agreements that provide greater scope for company negotiation (XX SASE Annual Meeting 2009: 1–20). This role, however, can be played by domestic MNCs with centers in the home country or foreign-owned MNCs. For instance, in northern Europe, mainly home-based MNCs play this role, whereas in the Mediterranean countries it is the foreign-owned MNCs (European Foundation for the Improvement of Living and Working Conditions 2009). Thus, the cross-country differences in national jurisdictions and labor costs emerge as the important factors for the MNCs to further develop or reduce their investments in that country.

Similarly, previous research indicates that the most important benefit of FDI is that it provides, along with financial resources, access to the whole range of technological, organizational, and skill assets, as well as the markets of the parent company. With few exceptions, the vast majority of the fast-growing economies relied heavily on FDI to jump-start and sustain their rapid economic transformation (Sun 2002). As such, the countries that are more restrictive in terms of their FDI policies are usually those that are economically less developed, as in the cases of Botswana, Chile, and Mauritius. Thus, nations can retain their sovereignty only if they are less connected with the global market.

Finally, a major aspect of the MNCs is the public goods that they provide in the countries in which they invest (Rondinelli 2003: 14). For example, Rondinelli (2003) focuses on the privatization of public goods and services in developing countries. For the analysis, the concept of "corporate citizenship" is used to define "activities that ensure compliance with laws and regulations, maintain ethical behavior, contribute to social and economic welfare, and generate profits that provide a fair return to investors" (p. 14). The author focuses on three distinct types of TNCs' activities that have impact on policies: private foreign aid, international standard-setting and policymaking. However these activities pose serious challenges: "corporate citizen-ship movements allows TNCs to shift liability and risk by focusing on voluntary codes of conduct, plea agreements, and civil and administrative actions in place of criminal indictments, thereby undermining criminal law and – when pursued internationally – national sovereignty" (p. 19).

However, there are very few past experiences with MNCs bringing a substantial amount of public goods and thus adding a new dimension to the relationship between MNCs and states.[1] Thus, John Kline (2006) suggests that MNCs appear to operate as a surrogate sovereign by taking over traditional government functions and making efforts to construct schools, health centers, new roads, etc. However, MNCs can only act in this way when the governments are greatly absent. MNCs generally prefer to avoid the role of surrogate sovereign (Kline 2006: 132). The literature on the reaction of states against the public goods provided by the MNCs suggests that these goods are mainly provided to help the corporations benefit economically and to receive state incentives. Similarly, MNCs are hesitant to play the role of the government, when it comes to public goods, as this might receive criticism.

This section provides support for the transformationalist view of globalization in the context of state-MNC interactions. The globalization process transforms power, authority, and functions of nation-states which are increasingly adjusted to cope with the challenges posed by this process. The next section focuses on state sovereignty and MNCs.

MNCs and State Sovereignty

Market competition in a globalizing economy emerges as an additional important factor that puts into question the sovereignty and authority of the state versus the MNCs. Following Krasner, sovereignty refers to "an institutional arrangement for organizing political life that is based on two principles: territoriality and the exclusion of external actors from domestic authority structures" (Krasner 1999: 20). FDI by definition refers to ownership and control of domestic assets by foreigners. Not surprisingly, HSs are sensitive to loss of sovereignty and "resist giving up their freedom to impose performance requirements" (Graham 2000: 189, cited in Crystal

2009: 229). Especially before the liberalization era of the 1980s and 1990s, "many less developed countries sought to preserve their sovereignty as much as possible vis-à-vis MNCs, even if that meant sacrificing material gains from economic exchange" (Crystal 2009: 225). This view is in line with a conflictual bargaining perspective. Following the economic and financial liberalization, developing countries were still sensitive to preserving their sovereignty with respect to MNCs, as in the case of China, which acknowledges the economic importance of MNCs, but also views them as a form of external interference in their internal matters.

Nevertheless, what is to be produced, by whom, under what conditions, where, when, and at what price (or economic costs and benefits) are increasingly decided by MNCs in a world of capital mobility (Stopford and Strange 1991). Thus, developing countries have increasingly adopted FDI friendly policies and regulations. As Crystal (2009: 130) notes: "Among the explanations for this shift that analysts have put forward are: a renewed appreciation by governments for FDI as a source of long-term investment in the wake of recent debt and financial crises, pressure from developed countries or international financial institutions to liberalize, an increased reliance on the technology, managerial skills, and exporting channels that foreign firms bring with them, and the increasing power of liberal ideas in the wake of past economic failures."

It should also be noted that FDI policies of developing nations are increasingly shaped by the home governments of MNCs via state to state "bargaining through bilateral or multilateral negotiations" (Ramamurti 2001: 37). For example, the US protects and advances the interests of its MNCs via bilateral trade agreements (e.g., MNCs enjoy most favored nation status with strong limits on expropriation). Similarly, FDI liberalization and privatization of national entities attached to structural adjustment loans by the IMF and World Bank (p. 31). Thus, developing nations are increasingly sharing their sovereignty with extraterritorial actors.

Market competition in a globalizing world raises concerns especially in developing countries, some of which desperately need the knowhow and education brought into countries through FDI. Thus, to be competitive in trade, some developing countries allow FDI at the expense of negative effects on domestic corporations. Theodore Moran indicates that FDI often has a negative short-run effect on domestic competitors with a possible positive long-run impact in the domestic market (Moran, Gramham, and Blomstrom 2005: 375–393). As such, FDI hurts the current account balance initially, but spillover effects such as managerial and technological advancements in an economy through FDI may compensate for this in excess of any initial damage. In a similar vein, following the success stories of emerging country multinationals such as Motorola – which grew through spillover effects of MNCs – many developing countries welcome FDI. However, as the extent of the spillover is also controlled by the MNCs, it may be hard for particular sectors in some countries to receive technological knowhow. For example, the automotive sector in Turkey has long benefited from foreign investment and knowhow for around two decades without being able to develop the local technology necessary to produce cars.[2]

Nevertheless, states share their sovereignty particularly because of the economic implications of FDI: economic growth, market competition, and the training of the local labor together with the business operations of the MNCs. Who gets what from FDI is determined by the bargaining between MNCs and HSs. Hence, with

the advent of economic globalization and the adoption of neoliberal economic policies across market economies from the 1980s onward, there has been a gradual
shift from conflictual to cooperative relations which face greatly intensified competition for world market shares (Stopford and Strange 1991; Dunning 1991; Luo
2001). States increasingly began considering inward FDI as complementary to their
own development objectives. Thus, it is widely believed that economic benefits from
inward FDI outweigh the erosion of sovereignty. For example, development aid is
not used as effectively as FDI and that states need long-established governments and
transparency to benefit from development aid (Pritchett, Murgaj, and Wes 2006). As
a great portion of the development aid goes directly under control of the recipient
government, the society might welcome the FDI hoping that it would have positive
spillover effects on the society. This is because MNCs create expectations about
reducing unemployment and raising income levels. In this case, states have to share
their sovereignty with the MNCs by providing them with an attractive ground for
investment, as MNCs can move the production to another country or invest in other
states in the future, when they are faced with unfavorable conditions. This characteristic of MNCs however is both an advantage and a disadvantage for territorially
immobile states: states need MNCs, as MNCs are operationally flexible and can relocate resources easily, whilst states have become vulnerable to exit options exercised
by MNCs (Reich 1992).

In fact, the economic needs of the countries can be so high that their sovereignty
is "for sale" to MNCs. To illustrate, many micro-states, which are vulnerable to
natural disasters and global economic shocks, and have limited resources, are selling
their country-code top-level domain names (CCTLDN) of the worldwide web to
MNCs (Campbell, Thacker-Kumar, and Slagle 2010). In so doing, they are willingly
relinquishing much of the control that they would otherwise exercise over internet
functions within their borders. This helps governments to raise money; however, it
also gives the MNCs the ability to essentially influence the reputation of a particular
state – an investment too risky for the state. In this vein, academics from the glob-
alist school believe that states do not share their sovereignty, but their sovereignty
is directly attacked by the MNCs. For example, Walters (1972: 127–138) notes
that "MNCs are sometimes seen as instruments of a predator state through which
the predator can achieve its self-interested ambitions by penetrating and securing
effective economic and political dominance over the less developed state."

Comparably, MNCs may choose to exert political influence on a state by manip-
ulating government officials, corrupting them thus to achieve lucrative investment
goals. As a result, this allows those governments to raise money, but at the same
time it undermines state sovereignty. Non-market knowhow is useful to MNCs in a
variety of ways including "economic ones (such as monetary contributions to political agents), but also true political (power), social (solidarity) and cultural (status
or respect) ones." The evidence for MNCs' non-market knowledge is evidenced by
the number of "risk assessors, advisors, door-openers, '5-percent men,' negotiators,
public relations specialists, and the like" that MNCs hire in order to pursue foreign
investment. Additionally, MNCs can target social groups in order to eliminate any
opposition to investment. For many MNCs "political means must be chosen because
they are superior or complementary to traditional economic ones" (Boddewyn
1988: 341–363).

In fact, there are many examples of MNCs undermining state sovereignty, especially through economic power. Of course, in wealthy industrialized states MNCs are very effective in policy making, as well. In the case of the United States, they hire lobbyists to put pressure on the government, so that they can have laws which allow them to lay off US workers more easily and outsource work to foreign lands. To achieve their goals, MNCs frequently donate money to presidential campaigns (Biazoto 2011). However, the results are more dramatic in developing countries. For example, under the disguise of "agricultural development," many American firms are buying large pieces of land in Africa. In 2010, New York-based Jarch Capital bought an area equal to the size of Dubai from a warlord in South Sudan, whereas Dominion Farms Ltd bought a swampland in Kenya in 2003 and flooded local farms to force the relocation of farmers (Nichols 2012). However, American firms are not the only examples of this phenomenon: oil-rich Arab countries such as Qatar and Saudi Arabia have also attempted to secure large pieces of land in Africa most importantly to increase their potential food supply. Similarly, Suez, a multinational corporation, bought the water rights in certain parts of Bolivia in 1999. Thus, citizens lost control of the cost of water and were occasionally locked out from the use of it, which resulted in riots and severe changes in governmental policy (Segers 2010: 26). These examples show that the territoriality and the law-making aspects of state sovereignty were undermined.

In addition, the economic power of the MNCs can also be used by foreign states – the owners of those particular MNCs – as an instrument of their governments' foreign policy. As nation-states exercise less control under conditions of globalization, MNCs can complicate the regulatory execution of a national government's policy. John Kline provides the example of oil companies that are among the largest and most financially powerful MNCs. He shows that single firms, even when allied with their home governments, cannot successfully challenge another government's sovereign power, when alternative MNC investors are increasingly available (Kline 2006: 126), noting that MNCs are "more likely to be used by governments or civil society groups seeking to influence foreign government policies than to initiate or direct such efforts themselves" (2006: 132). For example, many MNCs brought more pressure to bear on the apartheid regime of South Africa in comparison to states, and an alliance between the MNCs and their respective state of origin can dilute the sovereignty of the target country for FDI. Furthermore, the economic aspect of the relationship between states and MNCs is often a vicious circle for the states: they can join international organizations to effectively regulate and mitigate MNCs; however, joining such organizations also results in the relinquishment of some state authority.

A significant aspect of the problems regarding MNCs arises from the jurisdictional characteristics of the states and the extraterritorial dimensions of FDI. As MNCs are potentially global in their operations, it is always a question as to which laws and regulations apply to their business practices. MNCs can benefit from the jurisdictional conflict. If international declarations, such as the Human Rights Declaration, reduce the profits of the MNCs, they can overcome this barrier by relying on the legitimacy provided by the local laws, as seen with the sweatshops in East Asia.[3] Secondly, if local laws are not strong enough to defend the interests of MNCs, then the MNCs can take initiatives on their own to make sure that the business runs more efficiently. For instance, MNCs can hire "private armies" to stabilize situations in countries where the governments have failed to provide stability in ethnic and tribal wars (European Foundation for the Improvement of Living and Working Conditions 2009); if they face opposition from governments, MNCs always have the option to leave. The economic aspect of the relationship between MNCs and states shows that MNCs have caused a noteworthy amount of fragmentation in sovereignty and authority possessed by actors, such as states and international organizations. They are the winners in such a relationship with states and can act flexibly due to the bottom-up and top-down pressures of economic prosperity among societies and also of the economic knock-on effect induced by globalization: if one country hosts a MNC, then it is almost economically irresistible for others not to do so as well.

Conclusion

This chapter reviewed state and MNC bargaining interactions and state sovereignty in the context of the broader globalization debate. It has shown that states and MNCs and their bargaining interactions are seen as one of the key elements in the globalization process. MNCs have significant economic and political power in a world of mobile capital, whilst immobile states still play a very crucial role in domestic economic governance with the significant political and institutional resources at their disposal such as tax instruments and regulation.

An area into which this study can be extended is state capacity in governance literature. We need to learn much more about how states effectively achieve their chosen policy outcomes in their bargaining interactions with MNCs where the exercise of power and deployment of resources are key; and how they build administrative capacity and institutions to attract and maintain inward FDI over their sovereign territory that contributes to their national economic goals such as sustainable development, growth, welfare, and employment.

Notes

1   One of the few examples found out is an Italian construction company operating in Africa that automatically sends out a small field hospital, properly staffed and supplied, with every construction job it undertakes. To this are welcomed not only its own local workers, but anyone in need. Presumably it has found this practice a good investment in government–firm diplomacy (Strange 1992).

2   In the Turkish press, many scholars indicate that it is too costly for Turkey to develop its own cars (e.g. see Cumhuriyet Science Review, http://bilimteknik.cumhuriyet.com.tr/?kn=18/, accessed December 19, 2012).

3   The following quotation is highly illustrative: "Before opening up its economy in 1978, China had stringent controls on the movement of people between rural and urban areas, preventing migration to cities. These controls were part of the permit (*hukou*) system, in which welfare entitlements such as pensions, housing, health, and education were tied to a person's place of birth. As China moved towards a market economy, cheap rural labor helped fuel the country's growth and constraints on migration were reduced, however the restrictions on household registration of the *hukou* have remained in place, so migrant workers become outcasts without access to any state benefits or protection, despite Chinese laws enshrining 'equal rights' for all." See http://www.waronwant.org/overseas-work/sweatshops-and-plantations/china-sweatshops, accessed December 19, 2012.

References

Bakir, C. 2011. "A Southern Multinational and an Emerging European State in an Entry Bargaining Process." In *The Emergence of Southern Multinationals and Their Impact on Europe*, ed. Louis Brennan, 342–364. London: Palgrave Macmillan.

Bennett, D.C. and Sharpe, K.E. 1979. "Agenda Setting and Bargaining Power: The Mexican State versus Transnational Automobile Corporations." *World Politics*, 32: 57–89.

Biazoto, J. 2011. U.S.-based Multinational Corporations Are Buying Up Massive Chunks of Africa, Ethiopia.org, http://www.ethiopia.org/index.php/component/content/article/6-world/365-usbased-multinational-corporations-are-buying-up-massive-chunks-of-africa. Accessed March 13, 2012.

Big Players, Different Rules?: Multinationals and Collective Bargaining in Europe. 2009. XX SASE Annual Meeting.

Boddewyn, J. 1988. "Political Aspects of MNC Theory." *Journal of International Business Studies*, 19: 341–363.

Campbell, J.R., Thacker-Kumar, L., and Slagle, S. 2010. "International Sovereignty: State Power and Networked Governance in a Globalizing World." *International Social Science Review*, 85 (3): 107–123.

Crystal, J. 2009. "Sovereignty, Bargaining, and the International Regulation of Foreign Direct Investment." *Global Society*, 23 (3): 225–243.

Dunning, J.H. 1991. "Governments and Multinational Enterprises: From Confrontation to Co-operation?" *Millennium*, 20 (2): 225–244.

Dunning, J.H. 1998. "An Overview of Relations with National Governments." *New Political Economy*, 3 (2): 280–284.

Eden, L. and Molot, M.A. 2002. "Insiders, Outsiders and Host Country Bargains." *Journal of International Management*, 8: 359–388.

Eden, L., Lenway, S., and Schuler, D.A. 2005. "From the Obsolescing to the Political Bargaining Model." In *International Business and Government Relations in the 21st Century*, ed. R. Grosse, 251–272. Cambridge: Cambridge University Press.

Giddens, A. 1990. *The Consequences of Modernity*. Cambridge: Polity Press.

Graham, E.M. 2000. *Fighting the Wrong Enemy: Antiglobal Activists and Multinational Enterprises*. Washington, DC: Institute for International Economics.

Haslam, P.A. 2007. "The firm rules: Multinational corporations, policy space and neoliberalism." *Third World Quarterly*, 28 (6): 1167–1183.

Held, D., McGrew, A., Goldblatt, D., and Perraton, J. 1999. *Global Transformations: Politics, Economics and Culture*. Cambridge; Stanford: Polity and Stanford University Press.

Hirst, P. and Thompson, G. 1996. *Globalization in Question: The International Economy and the Possibilities of Governance*. Cambridge: Polity Press.

Kaplan, R.D. 1997. "Was Democracy Just a Moment?" *Atlantic Monthly*, December: 55–80.

Kline, J.M. 2006. "MNCs and Surrogate Sovereignty." *Brown Journal of World Affairs*, 13 (1): 123–133.

Krasner, S.D. 1999. *Sovereignty: Organized Hypocrisy*. Princeton: Princeton University Press.

Luo, Y. 2001. "Toward a Cooperative View of MNC–Host Government Relations: Building Blocks and Performance Implications." *Journal of International Business Studies*, 32 (3): 401–419.

Moran, T.H. 1974. *Multinational Corporations and the Politics of Dependence: Copper in Chile*. Princeton: Princeton University Press.

Moran, T.H. 1978. "Multinational Corporations and Dependency." *International Organization*, 32 (1): 79–100.

Moran, T.H., Graham, E.M., and Blomstrom, M. 2005. "Conclusions and Implications for FDI Policy in Developing Countries, New Methods of Research, and a Future Research Agenda." In *Does Foreign Direct Investment Promote Development?*, 375–395. Washington, DC: Institute for International Economics.

Multinational Companies and Collective Bargaining. 2009. Dublin: European Foundation for the Improvement of Living and Working Conditions.

Mytelka, L. 2000. "We the People: The Transformation of State–TNC Relations at the Turn of the Millennium." *Journal of International Management*, 6 (4): 313–325.

Nichols, J. 2012. "Multinational Corporations Try to Buy an Election," The Nation, October 12, http://www.thenation.com/blog/155269/multinational-corporations-try-buy-election. Accessed December 1, 2012.

Ohmae, K. 1993. "The Rise of the Region State." *Foreign Affairs*, 72: 78–87.

Poynter, T.A. 1985. *Multinational Enterprises and Government Intervention*. New York: St Martin's Press.

Pritchett, L., Murgai, R., and Wes, M. 2006. *Building on Success: Service Delivery and Inclusive Growth*. New Delhi: Macmillan Press.

Ramamurti, R. 2001. "The Obsolescing Bargaining Model: MNC–Host Developing Country Relations Revisited." *Journal of International Business Studies*, 32 (1): 23–39.

Reich, R.B. 1992. *The Work of Nations: Preparing Ourselves for 21st Century Capitalism*. New York: Vintage.

Rondinelli, D.A. 2003. "Transnational Corporations: International Citizens or New Sovereigns?" *Business and Society Review*, 107: 391–413.

Rosenau, J. 1997. *Along the Domestic–Foreign Frontier*. Cambridge: Cambridge University Press.

Salehizadeh, M. 2007. "Emerging Economies' Multinationals: Current Status and Future Prospects." *Third World Quarterly*, 28 (6): 1151–1166.

Segers, J. 2010. "Privatization of Water in Latin America: A Case Study in Bolivia." Master's thesis. California Polytechnic State University.

Stopford, J.M. and Strange, S. 1991. *Rival States, Rival Firms*. Cambridge: Cambridge University Press.

Strange, S. 1992. "States, Firms and Diplomacy." *International Affairs*, 68 (1): 1–15.

Strange, S. 1996. *The Retreat of the State: The Diffusion of Power in the World Economy*. Cambridge: Cambridge University Press.

Sun, X. 2002. *Foreign Direct Investment and Economic Development: What Do the States Need to Do?* Marrakech: United Nations.

UNCTAD. 2000. *World Investment Report 2000: Cross-Border Mergers and Acquisitions and Development*. Geneva; New York: United Nations.

Vachani, S. 1995. "Enhancing the Obsolescing Bargain Theory: A Longitudinal Study of Foreign Ownership of US and European Multinationals." *Journal of International Business Studies*, 26 (1): 159–180.

Vernon, R. 1971. *Sovereignty at Bay: The Multinational Spread of US Enterprises*. New York: Basic Books.

Vernon, R. 1977. *Storm over Multinationals: The Real Issues*. Cambridge, MA: Harvard University Press.

Vernon, R. 1998. *In the Hurricane's Eye: The Troubled Prospects of Multinational Enterprises*. Cambridge, MA: Harvard University Press.

Walters, R.S. 1972. "International Organizations and the MNC: An Overview and Observations." *Annals of the American Academy of Political and Social Science*, 403 (September): 127–138.

Yeung, H.W. 1995. "Third World Multinationals Revisited: A Research Critique and Future Agenda." *Third World Quarterly*, 15 (2): 297–317.

Part IV Global Companies and International Organizations

The Handbook of Global Companies, First Edition. Edited by John Mikler.
© 2013 John Wiley & Sons, Ltd. Published 2013 by John Wiley & Sons, Ltd.

Chapter 14

Regulating Global Corporate Capitalism

Sarianna M. Lundan

Introduction

The relationship between the corporation and the state has undergone a major transformation since the 1980s, with corporations becoming more global and state regulation becoming more international in nature. As part of this dynamic process, new forms of global governance are beginning to emerge, that combine the participation of international organizations, states, corporations, and civil society. In particular, multinational enterprises (MNEs) have become important contributors to the creation of new hybrid institutions involving public and private participation. The focus of this chapter is on examining the role of MNEs in transnational or global governance in light of the changing relationship between corporations and the nation-state.

The modern welfare state that came into being in the aftermath of World War II, and reached its peak in the 1970s, began to gradually retreat from the economic sphere as a result of deregulation and privatization that started in the United Kingdom during the Thatcher years. Alongside the diminished participation of the state in the economy, its regulatory role also changed, providing increasing opportunity for corporate self-regulation to complement, and sometimes replace, the regulatory functions of the state.

Underpinning this state transformation was the second wave of globalization. This was the outcome of the progressive trade and investment liberalization that was pursued with the advent of the GATT, and accelerated by advances in both communication and transportation technologies. Just as the railroads, steamships, and the telegraph had acted as enabling technologies during the first wave of globalization that reached its peak on the eve of World War I, the personal computer, the internet, and advances in civil aviation and containerization fueled the second wave (Jones

The Handbook of Global Companies, First Edition. Edited by John Mikler.
© 2013 John Wiley & Sons, Ltd. Published 2013 by John Wiley & Sons, Ltd.

2004). Deepening globalization induced further changes to the regulatory role of the state, by shifting some of its regulatory functions to the supranational (regional or global) level (Held *et al.* 1999).

In the aftermath of the still ongoing financial and economic crisis, governments have reasserted their role in the financial markets, and various plans have been put forward to re-regulate different aspects of the financial sector. These developments, as well as the continuing efforts to formulate an effective response to the challenges posed by climate change, are likely to accelerate the development of new governance institutions for the global economy. Characteristic of these issues is that they not only touch on several traditional policy domains (what might be called the horizontal policy challenge), but they typically also range across multiple levels of governance, from the local to regional and national to supranational levels, imposing the challenge of vertical policy coordination.

In addition to taking place at multiple levels, the processes that result in the creation of new governance institutions involve a variety of different actors, from governments to firms and civil society organizations. This melding together of public and private forms of governance, where hard regulation is complemented by soft or voluntary elements, and where sometimes voluntary private initiatives become accepted as de facto forms of regulation, results in hybrids of public and private governance that are a characteristic component of the emerging institutional infrastructure of the global economy.

This chapter will examine corporate self-regulation and supranational regulation as responses (and complements) to the retreat of the regulatory state. The chapter begins with a short historical overview, after which various forms of corporate self-regulation existing in the contemporary global economy are outlined. This is followed by a short review of the development of supranational corporate regulation, and some reflections on possible future directions concerning new forms of transnational governance involving multinational enterprises.

This chapter suggests that there is an emerging global governance paradigm that reflects three essential elements: A rebalancing of the rights and obligations of firms and governments, new institutional forms that meld together public and private governance, and MNEs as actors in both the economic and institutional transformation of host countries. In this emerging paradigm, different kinds of change processes are converging, including changes in the role of the state in relation to the market, and changes in the strategies and structures of MNEs in response to a changing marketplace with new competitors, and new sources of growth, particularly in the emerging economies.

A Short Historical Overview

The balance between public and private, or the respective roles and responsibilities of governments and markets, have undergone many changes over time. In the 1960s and 1970s, governments were generally seen as powerful actors, both in developed and in developing countries (Lundan and Mirza 2010). However, in historical terms, this golden era of the comprehensive welfare state was an anomaly, as for many decades, life in towns and smaller cities had often been dominated not by the state, but by a large mill or a factory, which provided many of the public services now associated with the state, such as infrastructure, subsidized housing, education, and healthcare.

By the 1980s and 1990s, political discussion began to be increasingly dominated by liberal market ideologies that sought to limit the role of the state, and to enhance the role of the market.[1] Beginning with the Thatcher and Reagan administrations, the privatization of formerly state-owned enterprises began to take place. Privatization and deregulation were also increasingly being regarded as means of containing costs and providing more efficiency in the provision of public services. The drivers and many manifestations of the subsequent process of transformation of the modern welfare state have been the subject of extensive study since the early 2000s, particularly by political scientists (Castles *et al.* 2010; Obinger *et al.* 2010).

The different responsibilities assumed by governments can be divided into three basic types (Zürn and Leibfried 2005). The state bears outcome responsibility if it is the ultimate guarantor over the provision of normative goods such as security, legal certainty, democratic self-determination, economic growth, and social welfare. The state has regulatory responsibility if it decides the processes through which such normative goods are to be provided, and it has operational responsibility if state institutions actually perform the necessary tasks. Thus the changes in the role of the state can be conceptualized in terms of the level of responsibility for the provision of normative goods, the type of institution to which responsibilities are transferred, and the extent to which responsibilities are de-monopolized (Hurrelmann *et al.* 2007). The main shift has been in the direction of shifting responsibility from public to private actors, and from national to supranational institutions (Zürn and Leibfried 2005).

Thus while in the 1960s and 1970s, Western governments assumed full responsibility for the provision of all the normative goods, this is much less often the case in the contemporary global economy. For example, the role of the state may have been curtailed because international law may restrict the legislative competence of the state in a particular issue area, or its operational responsibility may have been reduced through the process of privatization.

The market-driven policies that gained popularity in the 1980s began to gradually alter the contours of the modern welfare state in areas ranging from education and healthcare to increasing economic integration and the privatization of former state monopolies in sectors such as telecommunications and transportation (Zürn and Leibfried 2005). These changes reduced the relative importance and influence of the state, while giving more opportunities for private firms to deliver either contractually or through some form of co-production the services that were previously supplied as public goods by the government.[2]

This shifting of service provision from the public to the private sector[3] not only opened up new markets for firms, but with increasing economic integration, it also opened up new cross-border markets for MNEs in areas that were previously closed to them. The increasing involvement of MNEs in the provision of public services has in part also legitimated and broadened their role in the host countries in both political and social terms.

At the same time, the relationship of MNEs with regulatory institutions also underwent substantial changes, as regulatory authorities became less inclined to adopt an adversarial stance, and more likely to engage in negotiation with firms and industry associations (Harrison 1999; Willman *et al.* 2003). Among other reasons, this is because in many industries, MNEs possess significant knowledge related to both technologies and markets, that is an essential input to the regulatory process. Indeed, the quality of the regulatory institutions directly affects MNEs' compliance cost, and a credible governance environment in the home and host countries is a precondition for investment that employs advanced technologies and managerial processes (Lundan 2004).

Due to the complexity of the changes confronting governments, firms, and civil society alike, the importance of appropriate governance institutions has become paramount to achieving economically and socially sustainable societies. Such institutions consist both of formal rules (e.g. constitutions, laws, and regulations) as well as informal constraints (norms of behavior, conventions, and self-imposed codes of conduct). Institutions (and their enforcement mechanisms) set the "rules of the game," which firms and other organizations need to follow to maintain or gain legitimacy (North 1990; 2005). The design and functioning of formal institutions reflect the underlying informal institutions, and as a consequence, the transfer of "best-practice" institutions across borders is subject to adaptation and incomplete transfer (Kipping and Bjarnar 1998; Zeitlin and Herrigel 2000).

Following this definition, the government is the primary source of formal institutions in the form of laws, regulations, and their enforcement mechanisms. This includes the rules that underpin markets, such as enforcement of property rights and contract law (Fligstein 2002; Hall and Soskice 2001). However, the market economy also generates its own contingent of rules, including private law relating to the enforcement of contracts, codes of conduct, as well as systems of technical standards (Morgan 2005). There is an increasingly diffused boundary between the private and public rules, and some private rules have become pseudo-public rules. For example, this is the case with international accounting standards, which are developed by the International Accounting Standards Board, whose membership comprises individuals with corporate and regulatory experience (Zimmermann, Werner, and Volmer 2008).

In terms of informal institutions, civil society comprising both community and cultural organizations generates both civic norms and values reflecting religious and cultural identity. The business sector also generates its own set of informal norms and values, which can be either firm or industry-specific. These are implicit and shared among participants, but not formalized into an explicit code.

There is considerable evidence that good governance in terms of the institutions that support market exchange, such as property rights protection, reliable contract enforcement, and a predictable and transparent regulatory structure, is conducive to investment and economic growth (Rodrik, Subramanian, and Trebbi 2002). Similarly, an environment of good public governance with low levels of corruption and a high degree of policy consistency are generally necessary to achieve economic development (Keefer 2004).[4] Indeed, most scholars attribute a causal relationship between good governance and higher economic growth, although one must also acknowledge that there are likely to be feedback loops with economic growth providing the resources necessary to improve the institutional infrastructure (Glaeser *et al.* 2004). At the same time, all countries are likely to suffer from some types of market and nonmarket failures, and such institutional voids or deficits are particularly evident in emerging economies (Khanna, Palepu, and Sinha 2005; Palazzo and Scherer 2008).

The increasing intermingling of public and private forms of governance in connection with issues that cut across regulatory borders can be described in terms of the balance between public and private orderings (Backer 2008; Zumbansen 2006). *Public ordering* rests on laws and regulations backed by a legal system of civil enforcement and criminal penalties. While public ordering is a "top-down" process which ultimately rests on the threat of the use of sovereign force, *private ordering* is a consensual "bottom-up" practice that derives its efficacy and legitimacy from the participants involved. A private ordering system allows exchanges to take place even when pricing is difficult, property rights are unclear or insecure, and consequently transaction costs are high.[5]

The basis of private ordering is contractual (Backer 2007), and contract management and dispute settlement are often dealt with directly by the parties involved, or through mutually agreed-upon arbitration schemes. In lieu of relying on well-defined property rights and contract laws, exchanges are embedded in a continuing relationship with the same party, so that non-performance in one exchange can be penalized in later ones. Private ordering by groups or networks based on personal or kinship ties is often used in emerging markets to compensate for the failures in public ordering (Khanna and Yafeh 2007; Meyer and Peng 2005).

However, private ordering may also be employed in markets where public ordering is of high quality, because it is more flexible and faster in adjusting to changing circumstances. Examples of this are found in connection with the regulation of transactions in emerging electronic cross-border markets (Calliess 2008), and this practice is also illustrated by the increasing popularity of private-arbitration agreements among firms (Calliess *et al.* 2007). In such cases, private ordering works in the shadow of a well-functioning public-ordering system, which lends it additional legitimacy.

Corporate Self-Regulation

Within the complex governance structures that characterize the global economy, new combinations of public and private governance have emerged that involve MNEs in either complementing or substituting for public rulemaking and the provision of public goods. In the latter case, firms are involved in partnerships to provide some public goods, which extends their involvement from private rulemaking to assuming operational responsibility.

The first example of private regulation that is complementary to public regulation involves the codes of conduct and environmental and labor standards adopted by MNEs. Since the various non-financial factors constituting corporate social responsibility (CSR) are very difficult to measure, social responsibility reporting generally provides a selective and incommensurate range of measures (Fortanier, Kolk, and Pinkse 2011). While some countries provide regulatory guidelines on social reporting, in most cases, firms are free to choose what to report and how. The adoption of ISO 14000 standards in MNE supply chains, the publication of codes of conduct, the publication of social performance reports, and a variety of labeling initiatives have been some of the tools by which MNEs have sought to self-regulate their activities.

Some of the best-known cases involve firms that initially became targets of NGOs and suffered loss of reputation due to the exposure of their labor, environmental, or human rights practices such as Nike (Backer 2008) and Shell (Frynas 2005). However, self-regulation is also becoming quite common among other large MNEs such as Wal-Mart (Backer 2007), and an increasing number of them are beginning to report on their activities in separate social or corporate responsibility reports (Kolk 2010).

Another type of self-regulation involves collaboration between firms in an industry sector to arrive at the common rules to undo the need for public regulation. Examples of such codes include the chemical industry's Responsible Care initiative (Hoffman 1997; Holm and Pedersen 2000), and the codes developed in sporting goods (van Tulder and Kolk 2001) and coffee (Kolk 2005). These are sometimes complemented by standards and codes of conduct developed by governments and NGOs, such as Publish What You Pay, which was developed by a coalition of NGOs and promotes the idea that MNEs engaged in natural resource extraction should disclose all the revenue they pay to host governments. On the other side, there is the Extractive Industries Transparency Initiative promoted by the UK government, which encourages disclosure by host governments of their natural resource revenues.

The second group of governance forms include bilateral and multi-stakeholder initiatives. Many modern NGOs, like modern MNEs, are global in reach, and different kinds of partnerships with NGOs can form an integral part of the value-creating process of MNEs (Fransen and Kolk 2007; Rondinelli and London 2003; Teegen, Doh, and Vachani 2004). One of the most well known of these is the Chiquita-Rainforest Alliance partnership. In all of these cases, the rulemaking that results from the shifting of responsibility from the state to private actors is soft, as it relies on mutually agreed-upon methods of enforcement, but does not have the backing of the coercive power of the state.

The third group involves public-private partnerships. Partnerships involving the state are often aimed at providing public services at higher quality or lower cost than was possible with state provision (UNCTAD 2008). Other kinds of public-private partnerships are geared towards e.g. the distribution of HIV/AIDS medications, and involve cooperation with international organizations as well as private donors and national governments (Bexell and Mörth 2010).

Supranational Regulation

As a result of the ongoing process of globalization, the role of the territorially bound nation-state has changed. In addition to states having devolved more of the operational responsibility for economic activity to the market, some of the locus of regulation has also shifted to the regional or global level. The supranational regulation that covers the activities of MNEs does not consist of a uniform set of rules, but, rather, a patchwork consisting of contractual and treaty obligations, both on a multilateral and a bilateral level.[6]

While the rules governing world trade are quite comprehensive, the hard rules governing foreign investment only cover some areas of activity, and have mainly sought to ensure non-discrimination in the access to resources and markets, and to protect investors from host governments' opportunistic behavior.[7] The most important agreement for investment remains the WTO agreement which came into force in 1995 as a result of the Uruguay round of negotiations. This set of agreements includes the General Agreement on Trade in Services (GATS), which contains several areas relevant to foreign investment, the Agreement on Trade-Related Investment Measures (TRIMs) that outlawed many types of post-entry performance requirements, and the Agreement on Trade-Related Aspects of Intellectual Property Rights (TRIPs), which has been particularly important for investment in knowledge-intensive activities, and which was actively promoted by MNEs, particularly from the pharmaceutical industry (Ramamurti 2005).[8]

Various international investment agreements (IIAs) complete the framework of investment rules, with 2807 bilateral investment treaties (BITs) in force by the end of 2010 (UNCTAD, 2011). In addition to the provisions contained in BITs concluded between states, agreements between individual investors and the host state may also include, e.g. concessions with respect to taxation and the extent of other social obligations pertaining to foreign investors, particularly in special enterprise zones.

A common concern with much of the earlier generation of investment treaties has been that they grant foreign investors privileges that are not available to domestic firms. This is particularly in terms of the right to be compensated for regulatory takings, for example in the case of tightening of environmental regulations (Sanders 2010; UNCTAD 2012).

In addition to the treaty obligations, there are multilateral agreements that provide general guidelines for the social responsibilities of MNEs. The most prominent among these are the OECD Guidelines for Multinational Enterprises (adopted in 1976, and revised most recently in 2011), which oblige the governments of the signatory countries to promote the observance of the guidelines by their MNEs. Specific guidelines against corrupt practices are provided by the OECD Anti-Bribery Convention (adopted in 1997), with governments being responsible for introducing and enforcing legislation at the national level.[9] The UN Global Compact (introduced in 1999) is a voluntary initiative, that derives its ten core principles from the Universal Declaration of Human Rights of the UN, the ILO Declaration on Fundamental Principles and Rights at Work, the Rio Declaration on Environment and Development, and the UN Convention Against Corruption. The Global Compact has gained more than 6000 corporate members, who are expected to set in motion changes in business practices pursuant to the principles, and to report on these in their annual reports or other corporate reporting.[10]

Although these guidelines articulate in general terms the responsibilities of MNEs, the enforcement of these responsibilities remains problematic due to the great diversity of operating contexts, and the inability to clearly define and delimit the boundaries of that responsibility. The mismatch between the economic interdependence that characterizes the integrated MNE, and the legal tradition that reinforces the independence and limited liability pertaining to the constituent parts of the corporation serve to further complicate the matter (Muchlinski 2010; Stephens 2002; Teubner 2009).

As already discussed, a partial solution to the question of how responsibilities should be defined has been the development of various instruments of (transnational) private law, which serve to fill in some of the voids in the existing institutional structure comprised of local law and treaty obligations (Calliess and Zumbansen

2010; Dunning and Lundan 2011). Such initiatives involve various types of voluntary standards that can be firm or industry specific, bilateral between governments and investors or governments and civil society organizations, or multilateral between governments, civil society organizations, and foreign investors. They are reinforced by standards developed by other organizations such as the International Organization for Standardization, whose voluntary social responsibility guidance standard ISO 26000 was introduced in 2010, as well as other social responsibility standards such as SA 8000 by Social Accountability International. The Global Reporting Initiative, which works in collaboration with the UNEP and the Dow Jones Sustainability Index, is dedicated to developing common standards of measurement in corporate CSR (Dingwerth 2007; Fortanier, Kolk, and Pinkse 2011).

A major new supranational initiative was started in 2005, when John Ruggie was appointed the United Nations Special Representative of the Secretary General on the Issue of Human Rights (SRSG). He was given the task of examining the interplay between the different actors in transnational regulation, and to define the respective responsibilities of states, firms, and civil society. This process resulted in the Protect-Respect-Remedy framework, and a continuation of his mandate enabled further examination of the issues related to the operationalization of these principles (Ruggie 2008; 2010).

The UN Framework places a great deal of emphasis on the responsibility of states to effectively protect human rights within their own jurisdiction, while also obliging multinational enterprises to respect the efforts of national governments to achieve these goals, and where rights violations have occurred, to provide timely and adequate access to judicial and non-judicial remedies to those affected. It also specifically urges firms to apply processes of due diligence with respect to their human rights obligations.

The concept of due diligence has more recently acquired a wider role in relation to the revised OECD Guidelines for Multinational Enterprises, where it is endorsed as a general principle of corporate action across a wide range of CSR related issues including but also going beyond human rights observance.[11] It is also included in the International Finance Corporation's (IFC) Human Rights Impact Assessment Guide for corporations launched in 2010, which provides guidance on all elements of human rights due diligence, as advanced in the UN Framework.[12]

In practice, this might mean for example, that having set its policy objectives, a government could oblige firms above a certain size, including but not limited to MNEs, to undertake a process of due diligence concerning the social and political risks they encounter in their operating environment. The firms should then put forward a plan that addresses at the very minimum how the firm intends to do no harm, i.e. not to further exacerbate existing vulnerabilities, but also to put forward a positive plan on how their activities might contribute to meeting the social objectives of the government in the long run.

There should also be a grievance procedure that would address the consequences of nonperformance. The state has the choice of both judicial and non-judicial mechanisms of enforcement, but in a partnership-based model, a natural choice would be to adopt some of the best practices of alliance management employed by firms in the market context. This includes the definition of some stop-gates where performance is assessed, as well as the identification of the corrective mechanisms that can be employed to align interests and to achieve the desired targets. Should this fail, the state should also be willing to employ judicial means, while not forgetting other methods such as the exclusion of nonperforming firms from government procurement, or making incentives conditional on performance.

The Emergence of New Governance Institutions

The challenges presented by the interdependent global economy have resulted in the evolution of new governance structures that involve public and private participation, and hard and soft rulemaking (Abbott and Snidal 2000). The attempts in the aftermath of the global financial crisis to rein in the global economy do not represent a return to an earlier era of direct regulation, but they should, rather, be seen as efforts to find a new balance in an evolving institutional context, where MNEs and civil society actors are seen as partners along with governments in shaping new governance institutions.

In the golden era of the modern welfare state, national governments held a monopoly of action, policy making was mainly conducted on the national level, and it was targeting MNEs whose activities were mainly contained within the ownership boundaries of the firm. Over time, both the regulatory space and the scope of MNE activities has widened considerably, with liberalization bringing in public-private partnerships and regional integration, as well as new agreements on the supranational level. At the same time, important economic players such as China have emerged, embracing an economic model that involves considerably more state participation, also in terms of direct or indirect state ownership.

One of the essential implications of the changing role of both firms and governments is that the wider policy space creates an unprecedented demand for new governance institutions. Contributing to the creation of these new institutions are firms, civil society, and governments at different levels (Crane, Matten, and Moon 2008). The emerging body of transnational private law is filling some of the space that is left vacant either because no institutions are in place to govern activities that cross borders, or because the national framework of rules and regulations is less flexible than the framework of rules that is introduced by MNEs. MNEs and civil society actors are increasingly involved in all stages of the policy process, from policy formulation to implementation, and this is likely to result in some political contestation in different policy areas (Dryzek 2012; Levy and Scully 2007).

Following Cantwell, Dunning, and Lundan (2010), three basic types of engagement between MNEs and the institutional environment can be identified. The first is *institutional avoidance*, in which MNEs take the external institutional environment as a given, but in which they are able to make choices between different institutional environments. Faced with a weak institutional environment, characterized by a lack of accountability and political instability, poor regulation, and deficient enforcement of the rule of law, the response of most MNEs is likely to be characterized by an "exit" rather than a "voice" strategy (Hirschman 1970). Exceptions to this are natural resource seeking investment and some forms of infrastructure investment, where the number of alternative investment locations is often limited. The prevalence of this type of behavior is evident in the results of many studies confirming that the more footloose forms of MNE activity are mostly concentrated in countries characterized by good governance (Dunning and Lundan 2008; Kaufmann, Kraay, and Mastruzzi 2007).

The second form of engagement is *institutional adaptation*. As in the previous case, the MNE treats the institutional environment as essentially exogenous, but in this case it seeks to adjust its own structure and policies to better fit the environment. The means to achieve this objective include the use of political influence and, in some cases, bribery, but it may also involve efforts by the MNE to intentionally emulate the behavior, commercial culture, and institutional artifacts that are most desirable in the host country context. Indeed, the MNE may wish to "go native," and to become an insider in the host country market, by acquiring the use of local brands for example.

In contrast to the first two cases, in the third one, the institutional environment is assumed to be partly endogenous, and the MNE is engaged in a process of co-evolution. In *institutional co-evolution*, while firms may employ some of the same tactics they used under the previous scenario, their objective is no longer simply to adjust, but to affect change in the local institutions – be they formal or informal. For example, a MNE might engage in political activities to advance specific kinds of regulation or market structure that give it an advantage over its competitors. In doing so, the MNE might also align itself with domestic firms in lobbying the government for economic protection or support.

The model of the global economy we have presented in this chapter is one that is based neither on command-and-control regulation nor voluntary bottom-up activity, but a combination of the enhanced ability and duty of states to set their objectives in operational policy terms, and the responsibility of firms to develop the means whereby these can be addressed, including processes of effective monitoring.

From a normative standpoint, the impact of firms clearly differs by sector, and by the size and type of the operations they undertake. Large firms have a more sub-stantive task in both mapping the impact and risks of their activities, and the ways in which these can be mitigated in any given market. Some activities are inherently more sensitive than others, owing to their environmental or employment impact. At the same time, the regulatory approach should be neutral in terms of the ownership of the firms in question (domestic/foreign, public/private), as well the modality (con-tractual or ownership-based) whereby activities are carried out. Achieving neutrality in the latter dimension is a challenge, since it would obligate both the seller and the buyer in an economic transaction equally, but this is not essentially different from the current practice of large MNEs, which extend their codes of conduct to contrac-tual suppliers. The parameters of responsible corporate citizenship should be set in consultation with civil society and firms, but in the last instance these need to be put in operational policy terms by governments. As suggested by Lundan and Mirza (2010) "National treatment is one of the cornerstones of the liberal trading system, but a guarantee of national treatment should be accompanied by a requirement for responsible corporate citizenship" (p. 41).

Of course, there are many instances where the activities of MNEs take place where the governments are unable or even unwilling to interfere with destructive practices in order to preserve the political status quo, and to maintain government revenue. In line with the UN framework, the goal should be to enhance the ability and desire of governments to uphold social regulation, and to provide a solid framework against which company and industry-specific voluntary initiatives can be built.[13] Equally important is the role of civil society organizations, which are vital in engaging the media by exposing abuses and bringing them to the consciousness of consumers.

For the MNE, this requires the application of due diligence analysis to identify its vulnerabilities, and to address these in a responsible manner. It calls on the firm to employ its capabilities in control and coordination to establish transparent and effective monitoring processes. Such processes are reliant on information from a range of relevant stakeholders, and managing such multi-stakeholder partnerships is a key step to achieving a process of due diligence that fulfils not only the formal reporting criteria, but that might allow the firm to develop new standards of corporate citizenship as participants in "deliberative democracy" (Palazzo and Scherer 2006; Scherer and Palazzo 2007).

Conclusion

This chapter has examined the role of multinational enterprises in shaping the emerging institutions of transnational governance. We began by briefly reviewing the changing relationship between corporations, whose value adding operations and sources of revenue are increasingly global, and the nation-state, that is adjusting its role in the context of the global economy. Multinational enterprises that not only sell goods and services abroad, but also engage in various types of value-adding activities in an increasing number of host countries are not only concerned with their relationship to the home country, but they are also subject to and involved in negotiations concerning the regulation of their operations in host countries. The tension that exists between the demands and desires of the home country, and those of the host country, force the MNE to develop new corporate policies, and to contribute to the emergence of governance institutions that populate a transnational regulatory space.

One specific solution to the problem of divergent expectations we examined has been the proactive engagement of MNEs in corporate self-regulation that is global in scope, particularly in the area of environmental and social issues. These efforts have generated codes of conduct and corporate procedures that have acted as benchmarks for other firms operating in the same sector. Alongside the corporate initiatives, we also examined the role of supranational institutions such as the UN and OECD in developing codes and guidelines for MNEs that could act as global meta-norms to govern the cross-border activities of MNEs. Finally, we examined the process of co-evolution that allows the firm to adjust to changing expectations by contributing to the creation of hybrid institutions that combine public and private participation.

The new framework of governance for the global economy raises a number of issues that are likely to occupy scholars of political science and international business in the foreseeable future. On one hand, there is a need to gain a better understanding of the co-evolutionary process of institutional development to understand how new institutions come about, and what are the respective roles of states, corporations, and civil society in this process. On the other hand, there is a pressing need to examine the evolving institutions as they appear, and to evaluate how they meet different normative standards such as legitimacy, transparency, and equity, as governance shifts from the national context to the global level.

For example, the fact that corporations increasingly participate in the creation of the rules they are subject to raises obvious concerns about legitimacy. At the same time, the knowledge that corporations accumulate concerning both the needs and wants of host countries, as well as the demands articulated by civil society organizations, make them valuable and quite possibly irreplaceable partners in the process of generating new transnational forms of governance for the global economy. Corporate self-interest and the public interest are not always easily reconciled, particularly in an era dominated by shareholder capitalism. The historical experience suggests that this is by no means impossible, but thus far the experience of corporate citizenship has been limited mainly to corporations acting in their home country. The new transnational forms of governance require a new definition of responsibility that is not easy to articulate. The UN framework on human rights is one of the first attempts to outline a process by which such definitions could be developed, and as such, it gives an indication of a possible way forward for transnational governance.

Notes

1 Since the start of the new millennium, however, there has again been something of a resurgence of the importance of the state, particularly in connection with issues of global importance, such as climate change, the economic and financial crisis, and sustainable development (UNCTAD 2010; 2012).

2 While the shift has occurred across the developed world and in many developing countries, it should also be noted that conceptions of public and private have not been the same in different parts of the world.

3 By public we mean service provision that is paid by taxpayers and delivered by state employees. By private provision of public services we mean services that may be entirely or in part funded by taxpayers, but where the services are actually rendered by private firms. In contrast to the purely private sector, the state still retains residual involvement by setting guidelines in terms of access and affordability, or by running parallel public services.

4 However, it is debatable whether developing countries should have intellectual property protection to the same extent as developed countries (Heath and Kamperman Sanders 2005). From an investor perspective this should clearly be the case, but the actions taken by some of the more powerful developing countries such as Brazil, India, and China either to explicitly challenge the intellectual property regime imposed on them, or only partially to enforce the intellectual property regulations illustrate that there may be room for renegotiation also in terms of some of the institutions that support market exchange.

5 One of the advantages of South–South investment seems to be the degree of familiarity of the investors with the institutional shortcomings they encounter in the host market (Cuervo-Cazurra and Genc 2008).

6 This section draws on Dunning and Lundan (2011).

7 The existing agreements refer to trade and investment only, although it is increasingly recognized that nonequity (contractual) modes of activity constitute an important part of the cross-border value adding activities of MNEs: see e.g. Dunning and Lundan (2008) and UNCTAD (2011).

8 See Brewer and Young (2000) for a history of the multilateral system from the inception of the GATT and the Bretton Woods institutions, and an analysis of their impact on MNE activity.

9 However, enforcement of these and other guidelines is a major issue, also in developed countries.

10 Relatively few US firms have joined the Global Compact due to concerns about legal liability. See e.g. Williams (2004); see also Rasche (2009).

11 OECD Guidelines for Multinational Enterprises (revision of May 25, 2011), http://www. oecd.org/dataoecd/43/29/48004323.pdf, accessed December 19, 2012.
12 IFC Guide to Human Rights Impact Assessment and Management, www.ifc.org/hriam, accessed December 19, 2012.
13 See e.g. the *Investment Policy Framework for Sustainable Development* (IPFSD) and UNCTAD (2012); see also Lundan and Mirza (2010).

References

Abbott, K.W. and Snidal, D. 2000. "Hard and Soft Law in International Governance." *International Organization*, 54 (3): 421–456.

Backer, L.C. 2007. "Economic Globalization and the Rise of Efficient Systems of Global Private Law Making: Wal-Mart as Global Legislator." *Connecticut Law Review*, 39 (4): 1739–1784.

Backer, L.C. 2008. "Multinational Corporations as Objects and Sources of Transnational Regulation." *ILSA Journal of International and Comparative Law*, 14 (2): 1–26.

Bexell, M. and Mörth, U., eds. 2010. *Democracy and Public-Private Partnerships in Global Governance*. Basingstoke: Palgrave.

Brewer, T.L. and Young, S. 2000. *The Multilateral Investment System and Multinational Enterprises*. Oxford: Oxford University Press.

Calliess, G.-P. 2008. "Transnational Consumer Law: Co-regulation of B2C E-Commerce." In *Responsible Business: Self-Governance and Law in Transnational Economic Transactions*, ed. Olaf Dilling, Martin Herberg, and Gerd Winter, 225–258. Oxford: Hart.

Calliess, G.-P. and Zumbansen, P. 2010. *Rough Consensus and Running Code: A Theory of Transnational Private Law*. Oxford: Hart.

Calliess, G.-P., Dietz, T., Konradi, W., Nieswandt, H., and Sosa, F. 2007. "Transformations of Commercial Law: New Forms of Legal Certainty for Globalized Exchange Processes?" In *Transforming the Golden-Age Nation State*, ed. A. Hurrelmann, S. Leibfried, K. Martens, and P. Mayer, 83–108. Basingstoke: Palgrave.

Cantwell, J.A., Dunning, J.H., and Lundan, S.M. 2010. "An Evolutionary Approach to Understanding International Business Activity: The Co-Evolution of MNEs and the Institutional Environment." *Journal of International Business Studies*, 41 (4): 567–586.

Castles, F.G., Leibfried, S., Lewis, J., Obinger, H., and Pierson, C., eds. 2010. *The Oxford Handbook of the Welfare State*. Oxford: Oxford University Press.

Crane, A., Matten, D., and Moon, J. 2008. *Corporations and Citizenship*. New York: Cambridge University Press.

Cuervo-Cazurra, A. and Genc, M. 2008. "Converting Disadvantages into Advantages: Developing Country MNEs in the Least Developed Countries." *Journal of International Business Studies*, 39 (6): 957–979.

Dingwerth, K. 2007. *The New Transnationalism: Transnational Governance and Democratic Legitimacy*. Basingstoke: Palgrave Macmillan.

Dryzek, J.S. 2012. "Global Civil Society: The Progress of Post-Westphalian Politics." *Annual Review of Political Science*, 15 (1): 101–119.

Dunning, J.H. and Lundan, S.M. 2008. *Multinational Enterprises and the Global Economy*, 2nd edn. Cheltenham: Edward Elgar.

Dunning, J.H. and Lundan, S.M. 2011. "The Changing Political Economy of Foreign Investment: Finding a Balance between Hard and Soft Forms of Regulation." In *The Evolving International Investment Regime: Expectations, Realities, Options*, ed. José E. Alvarez and Karl P. Sauvant, 125–152. New York: Oxford University Press.

Fligstein, N. 2002. *The Architecture of Markets: An Economic Sociology of Twenty-First Century Capitalist Societies*. Princeton: Princeton University Press.

Fortanier, F., Kolk, A., and Pinkse, J. 2011. "Harmonization in CSR Reporting." *Management International Review*, 51 (5): 665–696.

Fransen, L.W. and Kolk, A. 2007. "Global Rule-Setting for Business: A Critical Analysis of Multi-Stakeholder Standards." *Organization*, 14 (5): 667–684.

Frynas, J.G. 2005. "The False Developmental Promise of Corporate Social Responsibility: Evidence from Multinational Oil Companies." *International Affairs*, 81 (3): 581–598.

Glaeser, E.L., La Porta, R., Lopez-de-Silanes, F., and Shleifer, A. 2004. "Do Institutions Cause Growth?" *NBER Working Paper*, 10568.

Hall, P.A. and Soskice, D. 2001. "An Introduction to Varieties of Capitalism." In *Varieties of Capitalism: The Institutional Foundations of Comparative Advantage*, ed. Peter A. Hall and David Soskice, 1–68. Oxford: Oxford University Press.

Harrison, K. 1999. "Talking with the Donkey: Cooperative Approaches to Environmental Protection." *Journal of Industrial Ecology*, 2 (3): 51–72.

Heath, C. and Kamperman Sanders, A., eds. 2005. *New Frontiers of Intellectual Property Law*. Oxford: Hart.

Held, D., McGrew, A., Goldblatt, D., and Perraton, J. 1999. *Global Transformations: Politics, Economics and Culture*. Stanford: Stanford University Press.

Hirschman, A.O. 1970. *Exit, Voice and Loyalty*. Cambridge, MA: Harvard University Press.

Hoffman, A.J. 1997. *From Heresy to Dogma: An Institutional History of Corporate Environmentalism*. San Francisco: New Lexington Press.

Holm, U. and Pedersen, T., eds. 2000. *The Emergence and Impact of MNC Centers of Excellence*. Basingstoke: Macmillan.

Hurrelmann, A., Leibfried, S., Martens, K., and Mayer, P. 2007. "The Golden-Age Nation State and Its Transformation: A Framework for Analysis." In *Transforming the Golden-Age Nation State*, ed. A. Hurrelmann, S. Leibfried, K. Martens, and P. Mayer, 1–23. Basingstoke: Palgrave.

Jones, G. 2004. *Multinationals and Global Capitalism: From the Nineteenth to the Twenty First Century*. New York: Oxford University Press.

Kaufmann, D., Kraay, A., and Mastruzzi, M. 2007. "The Worldwide Governance Indicators Project: Answering the Critics." *Policy Research Working Paper, 4149*. Washington, DC: World Bank.

Keefer, P. 2004. "What Does Political Economy Tell Us about Economic Development – and Vice Versa?" *Policy Research Working Paper Series, 3250*. Washington, DC: World Bank.

Khanna, T. and Yafeh, Y. 2007. "Business Groups in Emerging Markets: Paragons or Parasites?" *Journal of Economic Literature*, 45 (2): 331–372.

Khanna, T., Palepu, K., and Sinha, J. 2005. "Strategies That Fit Emerging Markets." *Harvard Business Review*, June: 63–76.

Kipping, M. and Bjarnar, O., eds. 1998. *The Americanization of European Business: The Marshall Plan and the Transfer of US Management Models*. London: Routledge.

Kolk, A. 2005. "Corporate Social Responsibility in the Coffee Sector: The Dynamics of MNC Responses and Code Development." *European Management Journal*, 23 (2): 228–236.

Kolk, A. 2010. "Trajectories of Sustainability Reporting by MNCs." *Journal of World Business*, 45 (4): 367–374.

Levy, D. and Scully, M. 2007. "The Institutional Entrepreneur as Modern Prince: The Strategic Face of Power in Contested Fields." *Organization Studies*, 28 (7): 971–991.

Lundan, S.M., ed. 2004. *Multinationals, Environment and Global Competition*. Oxford: JAI (Elsevier).

Lundan, S.M. and Mirza, H. 2010. "TNC Evolution and the Emerging Investment-Development Paradigm." *Transnational Corporations*, 19 (2): 29–52.

Meyer, K.E. and Peng, M.W. 2005. "Probing Theoretically into Central and Eastern Europe: Transactions, Resources, and Institutions." *Journal of International Business Studies*, 36 (6): 600–621.

Morgan, G. 2005. "Introduction: Changing Capitalisms? Internationalization, Institutional Change, and Systems of Economic Organization." In *Changing Capitalisms? Internationalization, Institutional Change, and Systems of Economic Organization*, ed. Glenn Morgan, Richard Whitley, and Eli Moen, 1–18. Oxford; New York: Oxford University Press.

Muchlinski, P. 2010. "Limited Liability and Multinational Enterprises: A Case for Reform?" *Cambridge Journal of Economics*, 34 (5): 915–928.

North, D.C. 1990. *Institutions, Institutional Change and Economic Performance*. Cambridge: Cambridge University Press.

North, D.C. 2005. *Understanding the Process of Economic Change*. Princeton: Princeton University Press.

Obinger, H., Starke, P., Moser, J., Bogedan, C., Gindulis, E., and Leibfried, S. 2010. *Transformations of the Welfare State: Small States, Big Lessons*. Oxford: Oxford University Press.

Palazzo, G. and Scherer, A.G. 2006. "Corporate Legitimacy as Deliberation: A Communicative Framework." *Journal of Business Ethics*, 66 (1): 71–88.

Palazzo, G. and Scherer, A.G. 2008. "Corporate Social Responsibility, Democracy, and the Politicization of the Corporation." *Academy of Management Review*, 33 (3): 773–775.

Ramamurti, R. 2005. "Global Regulatory Convergence: The Case of Intellectual Property Rights." In *International Business and Government Relations in the 21st Century*, ed. Robert Grosse, 341–60. Cambridge: Cambridge University Press.

Rasche, A. 2009. "'A Necessary Supplement': What the United Nations Global Compact Is and Is Not." *Business and Society*, 48 (4): 511–537.

Rodrik, D., Subramanian, A., and Trebbi, F. 2002. "Institutions Rule: The Primacy of Institutions over Geography and Integration in Economic Development." *NBER Working Paper*, 9305.

Rondinelli, D.A. and London, T. 2003. "How Corporations and Environmental Groups Cooperate: Assessing Cross-Sector Alliances and Collaborations." *Academy of Management Executive*, 17 (1): 61–76.

Ruggie, J.G. 2008. *Protect, Respect and Remedy: A Framework for Business and Human Rights*. Report of the Special Representative of the Secretary-General on the issue of human rights and transnational corporations and other business enterprises. Geneva: United Nations.

Ruggie, J.G. 2010. *Business and Human Rights: Further Steps toward the Operationalization of the "Protect, Respect and Remedy" Framework*. Report of the Special Representative of the Secretary-General on the issue of human rights and transnational corporations and other business enterprises. Geneva: United Nations.

Sanders, A.B. 2010. "Of All Things Made in America Why Are We Exporting the Penn Central Test?" *Northwestern Journal of International Law and Business*, 30 (2): 339–381.

Scherer, A.G. and Palazzo, G. 2007. "Toward a Political Conception of Corporate Responsibility: Business and Society Seen From a Habermasian Perspective." *Academy of Management Review*, 32 (4): 1096–1120.

Stephens, B. 2002. "The Amorality of Profit: Transnational Corporations and Human Rights." *Berkeley Journal of International Law*, 20 (1): 45–90.

Teegen, H., Doh, J.P., and Vachani, S. 2004. "The Importance of Nongovernmental Organizations (NGOs) in Global Governance and Value Creation: An International Business Research Agenda." *Journal of International Business Studies*, 35 (6): 463–483.

Teubner, G. 2009. "Coincidentia Oppositorum: Hybrid Networks beyond Contract and Organization." Storrs Lecture Series, Yale Law School. In *Contractual Networks: Legal Issues of Multilateral Cooperation*, ed. Marc Amstutz and Gunther Teubner, 3–30. Oxford: Hart Publishing.

UNCTAD. 2008. *World Investment Report 2008: Transnational Corporations and the Infrastructure Challenge*. New York and Geneva: United Nations Conference on Trade and Development.

UNCTAD. 2010. *World Investment Report 2010: Investing in a Low-Carbon Economy.* New York and Geneva: United Nations Conference on Trade and Development.

UNCTAD. 2011. *World Investment Report 2011: Non-Equity Modes of International Production and Development.* New York; Geneva: United Nations Conference on Trade and Development.

UNCTAD. 2012. *World Investment Report 2012: Towards a New Generation of Investment Policies.* New York; Geneva: United Nations Conference on Trade and Development.

Van Tulder, R. and Kolk, A. 2001. "Multinationality and Corporate Ethics: Codes of Conduct in the Sporting Goods Industry." *Journal of International Business Studies,* 32 (2): 267–284.

Williams, O.F. 2004. "The UN Global Compact: The Challenge and the Promise." *Business Ethics Quarterly,* 14 (4): 755–774.

Willman, P., Coen, D., Currie, D., and Siner, M. 2003. "The Evolution of Regulatory Relationships: Regulatory Institutions and Firm Behaviour in Privatized Industries." *Industrial and Corporate Change,* 12 (1): 69–89.

Zeitlin, J. and Herrigel, G., eds. 2000. *Americanization and Its Limits.* Oxford: Oxford University Press.

Zimmermann, J., Werner, J.R., and Volmer, P.B. 2008. *Global Governance in Accounting: Rebalancing Public Power and Private Commitment.* Basingstoke: Palgrave Macmillan.

Zumbansen, P. 2006. "The Parallel Worlds of Corporate Governance and Labor Law." *Indiana Journal of Global Legal Studies,* 13 (Winter): 261–312.

Zürn, M. and Leibfried, S. 2005. "Reconfiguring the National Constellation." In *Transformations of the State?*, ed Michael Zürn, and S. Leibfried, 1–36. Cambridge: Cambridge University Press.

Chapter 15

Global Companies as Agenda Setters in the World Trade Organization

Cornelia Woll

Introduction

The World Trade Organization (WTO) strikes many as the international organization that caters most to the agenda of powerful global companies. With the explicit objective to facilitate trade across borders, a primary interest of multinational enterprises, the WTO had come under attack in the 1990s as a symbol of "corporate globalization" (e.g. Wallach and Sforza 1999; Klein 2000). The anti-globalization movement chose the ministerial meetings of the WTO, most notably in Seattle in December 1999, to demonstrate against the influence of big firms and economic actors on policy making (see Seoane and Taddei 2002).

What influence do global companies have in the WTO? This chapter examines their lobbying activities on trade-related issues. To be sure, economic activities across borders are central for global companies: they have closely followed the stakes dealt with by the WTO and actively sought to influence negotiations in their favor. However, the political activities of companies reflect the evolution of the WTO itself. Formally created in 1995, the WTO builds on the negotiation rounds of the General Agreement on Tariffs and Trade (GATT) of 1947. While initial rounds of the GATT were intergovernmental attempts to reduce tariff barriers, the scope of the organization widened during the Uruguay Round (1986–1994) to include service trade, intellectual property, investment, and a dispute settlement mechanism. In the late 1990s, the WTO came under growing criticism from participants, observers, and civil society groups and members agreed to focus the new negotiation round on economic development rather than market access. Since the start of the Doha round in 2001, the ambitious objectives have not been matched by any noteworthy outcomes. While the WTO's dispute settlement system is growing into a strong mechanism of economic integration, the negotiation side of the organization appears to be weak

The Handbook of Global Companies, First Edition. Edited by John Mikler.
© 2013 John Wiley & Sons, Ltd. Published 2013 by John Wiley & Sons, Ltd.

and ineffective (Cottier and Elsig 2011). Sidelined by the financial crisis in the late 2000s, trade negotiations are currently making few headlines.

Business lobbying at the WTO has parallels with these developments. Initially, companies concentrated on affecting their governments' negotiation position through domestic lobbying. During the early rounds, such lobbying can be most accurately described as the support for or opposition to trade barriers in their respective sectors. As the negotiation scope expanded, companies began to participate in the definition of objectives and operating procedures, most notably in the context of service trade negotiation, intellectual property, and health. During this period, global companies did indeed affect the agenda of trade negotiations, when they successfully worked with their respective governments during the Uruguay Round and after. By the time the WTO was formally created, some companies moved their lobbying activities to the supranational level in Geneva. Simultaneously, the WTO sought to increase its transparency and engage other stakeholders beyond economic actors. The most important advocacy skill companies developed in the following years was judicial lobbying to affect the rulings of the dispute settlement body. Presently, the organization struggles to move forward with the development agenda of the Doha round, which is mired with governance problems and tensions between industrialized and developing countries. For many observers, trade negotiations are stuck. It is therefore of little interest for companies to invest much effort into further lobbying. This institutional deadlock thus led to a disengagement of business lobbyists as well as civil society organizations (Young 2007; McGuire 2012).

This chapter discusses the different phases and approaches of business lobbying at the WTO. It begins by presenting the literature on trade policy lobbying focused on support or opposition to liberalization. A second section discusses under what circumstances companies were able to affect agenda setting during the Uruguay Round negotiations. Showing the changes brought about by the creation of the WTO, both with respect to negotiations and dispute settlement, a third section then lays out current trends in political representation. A final section evaluates the WTO's attempt to encourage a greater diversity of stakeholder participation and discusses what this means for the strategy of business lobbyists.

Because of its interest in the actual lobbying activities of companies on trade-related matters, the chapter will concentrate on studies in political economy, rather than international economics or international trade theory, which tends to rely on general equilibrium analysis with a somewhat abstract understanding of firm activities (see Markusen 2001 for discussion).

Classic Trade Policy Lobbying: Protectionism vs. Liberalization

The lobbying of firms has long been considered central for an understanding of trade policy. Following Schattschneider's (1935) seminal study of the protectionist lobbying that brought about the Smoot Hawley bill of 1930, scholars have studied for generations which pressure groups supported or opposed trade liberalization. Although an extensive empirical study by Bauer, Pool, and Dexter (1963) showed early on that businesses tended to support liberalization more than was previously expected, most scholarship focused initially on pressures for protection of local and national production. According to the school of economic regulation, lobbying over trade policy became equated with "rent-seeking," where deviation from the welfare maximizing policy of free trade was explained by the power of special interests (Buchanan, Tollison, and Tullock 1980; Magee, Brock, and Young 1989). During the 1980s, it became apparent that this approach failed to explain the general move towards more open trade arrangements (Peltzman 1989). Several authors therefore tried to explain why and when firms supported liberalization (Milner 1988; Gilligan 1997; Dür 2010).

Both perspectives share a demand-side conception of politics. Accordingly, politicians are confronted with a combination of pressures from special interest groups and the broad public demanding trade policy, they are not autonomously "supplying" policies. This conceptualization is rooted in economic theory or, alternatively, in analytical Marxism and continues to dominate the field of international political economy today (Alt et al. 1996; Frieden and Martin 2002). Understanding the making of trade policy implies understanding when firms would lobby for protectionism and when for liberalization, and sophisticated models have been developed to predict industry behavior according to factor distribution, sectors, or firm strategies (Alt and Gilligan 1994; Milner 1999; Hiscox 2002).

Moreover, it becomes important to understand the institutional conditions that allow industry demands to be more or less successful (O'Halloran 1994; Lohmann and O'Halloran 1994; Gilligan 1997). In these accounts, firm lobbying might not have an impact on trade policy, but only because politicians were sufficiently insulated from industry pressure or because firms were unable to act collectively. Similarly, Grossman and Helpman (1994; 2001) have postulated most prominently that government preferences for "political support" from firms can change, which affects the government's willingness to protect particular sectoral interests. In all of these studies, the basic assumption is shared: depending on their economic interests, firms lobby their governments for protection or liberalization. Trade policy then evolves depending on how these different demands are aggregated and how individual governments were able to defend their firms and industries in international negotiations.

A central concern in this literature is therefore to identify what shapes the economic interests of firms. This question has led to a burgeoning literature on trade preferences, which deduces trade preferences from the distributional effects of the policy in question. The basic logic links preferences to income: policies that will lead to a gain in income should be supported, while policies that lead to a loss will be opposed. Scholars have therefore turned to international trade theory to predict the distributional effect of market opening or protectionism (see Alt et al. 1996).

Two theories have received particular attention: factoral models that focus on the distribution of labor, land, and capital endowment and sectoral models that concentrate on different industries and the specificities of their assets. Based on the Stolper-Samuelson theorem, factor endowment models predict that owners of factors of production that are scarce in a country will benefit from trade protection, while owners of relatively abundant productive factors will form free-trading coalitions (e.g. Rogowski 1989). Specifically, labor in capital-rich countries and capital in labor-rich countries should be protectionist. The second model is based on the Ricardo-Viner or specific factors approach and emphasizes comparative costs of foreign trade. It asserts that factors of production specific to import-competing industries will be affected most by international trade (e.g. Milner 1988). Hiscox (2002) suggests that mobility of factors determines which one of the two perspectives is most relevant.

Unfortunately, the nature of corporate activities is highly stylized, and authors oftentimes speak about "industries" rather than individual firms. With an increasing attention to the organization of the individual companies, studies have pointed out the importance of scale economies for the trade preferences of large firms. Firms with increasing returns to scale will be supportive of access to new markets (Milner and Yoffie 1989), in particular if they have a small home market (Casella 1996), but also if their production chains depend on foreign markets (Chase 2003). Moreover, once one studies decision-making within firms and the evolution of preferences over time, it becomes clear that the construction of preferences is a rather political process, not just an equilibrium outcome (Woll 2008).

The move away from stylized understandings of individual firms has shown the limits of the dichotomy between liberalization and protectionism (Milner and Yoffie 1989: 239). This dichotomy is not only insufficient to account for the complexity of business stances, it is also based on a misunderstanding of the content of international trade negotiations. Cowhey and Aronson (1993) suggest that the stakes for firms in international trade negotiations are no longer simply the height and scope of tariff barriers. More central are regulations applying to both foreign and domestic firms that fundamentally shape market access. This perspective is mirrored and confirmed by research on corporate political activities in the field of business administration and international business, which has long moved away from a simple dichotomy between open or closed borders (e.g. Rugman and Verbeke 1990; Dunning 1997). According to business-centered studies, the stakes in international trade negotiations are foreign investment and market access relevant to the strategic positioning of firms.

The classic perspective on trade policy lobbying thus suffers from a unidirectional conception of business-government interactions, where firms demand policies that the government can decide to put into place or not. It also oversimplifies the policy options firms support. More recent qualitative studies have highlighted that the objectives of firms and governments in international trade negotiations co-evolve, in particular in a context where trade negotiations have grown increasingly complex. This becomes very visible when one considers the negotiations during the Uruguay Round, where global companies significantly influenced the global trade agenda.

Companies as Agenda-Setters: Service Trade and Intellectual Property

The first six negotiation rounds of the GATT had exclusively concentrated on the multilateral reduction of tariffs before the Tokyo Round raised the issue of non-tariff barriers to trade and voluntary export restrictions from 1973–1979. The Uruguay Round launched in 1986 was marked by an even more ambitious set of issues, in particular intellectual property or service trade (Sauvé and Stern 2000; Mattoo and Sauvé 2003), and the renegotiation of older regimes, most importantly the reduction of agricultural subsidies and the textile agreement.

The desire to move beyond tariff barriers opened up the opportunity for a more active participation of business groups. Since the stakes for government were no longer the simple reduction or maintenance of restrictions, the work of business lobbying changed from pressuring for protection or liberalization towards shaping the content of new regimes (Woll and Artigas 2007). Harmonizing regulatory standards and creating new regimes for market access necessitates detailed knowledge about the details of commercial exchange and competition, often even including very fundamental definitions of what is subject to exchange or not. As in regulatory decision-making, the search for such information implies a very close interaction of companies and public officials (Coglianese, Zeckhauser, and Parson 2004; Coen 2005). By offering expertise, firms become part of the epistemic communities that thus structure global business regulation (Braithwaite and Drahos 2000). Moreover, the new scope of negotiations created new dynamics in the governmental negotiation strategies, who could link issues to advance in areas where talks had stalled (Young and Peterson 2006).

In this new context, global companies emerged as important participants who shaped the agenda of trade negotiations during the Uruguay Round. This was particularly visible in the emergence of service trade and the protection of intellectual property rights, but also affected other issues. It is helpful to examine these two prominent cases, before turning to other areas, where business interests have been equally involved but less influential, most notably concerning investment protection and textiles.

Financial service companies from the United States and its Coalition for Service Industries played a key role in bringing the issue onto the international negotiating table (Drake and Nicolaïdis 1992; Sell 2000; Woll 2008). As a result, the emergence of a General Agreement on Trade in Services (GATS) is often cited as a proof that big financial companies can obtain exactly what they want in international trade negotiations (Arkell 1994; Wesselius 2002).

Previously, service exchanges were not considered as trade and categorized as part of the "tertiary sector," which regrouped everything that was neither manufacturing nor agriculture. National accounts referred to services as "invisibles." With shifts in the economic structures, the growth of service sectors, and the increased international activities of large multinational service companies, this conception began to change in the 1970s and early 1980s. Large companies encountered difficulties when they tried to penetrate into foreign markets and inquired whether there were instruments in trade policy to address these issues. Preparing for a new round of trade negotiations, the US government was enthusiastic about the idea of broadening the GATT framework to move the pressure away from the difficult agricultural negotiations (Drake and Nicolaïdis 1992; Feketekuty 1988). Companies such as American International Group (AIG), American Express, CitiCorp or the consulting group Arthur Andersen worked with the government to advance the issue and appeared in media and newspapers to make their case and convince opponents and trading partners. In 1982, they founded the Coalition of Service Industries to continue lobbying on the issue.

The coalition of multinational companies and US government officials benefited from early discussion in the OECD and among economists and contributed to redefining the stakes in terms of trade, which helped to make the demands more pressing both internally and externally. Even though the coalition of US firms was originally only from the financial sector and parts of the professional services sector, their ambition was from very early on to achieve a more global agreement on services.

Financial services, consulting, advertising, data processing, telecommunications, and transport were all relevant services to their international operations, so they lobbied both for the benefits of their own service expansion and as user companies of other services, in particular through the United States Council for International Business. In a variety of multinational business associations, American firms urged their foreign counterparts to take up the cause.

The lobbying contributed to the diffusion of ideas on service exchanges and helped to unify the position of American business on the issue. Large companies from all sectors of the economy started conceiving of themselves as user companies of services. This allowed for new alliances of "user groups," which continued to push for a general agreement once the Uruguay Round was launched in 1986. The final agreement, the GATS, one of the Marrakech agreements of the Uruguay Round in 1994, eventually brought service exchanges under the same trade regime as the exchange of goods under the GATT, and integrated it under the umbrella of the newly founded WTO. Without the contribution of large companies in the early phases of these discussions, service trade might have never taken the form of a separate agreement (Hoekman and Kostecki 2001: 250).

A similar story can be told about the Agreement on Trade-Related Aspects of Intellectual Property Rights (TRIPS) (Sell 1999; 2000; Drahos and Braithwaite 2002). Like GATS, the achievement of a separate regime protecting intellectual property rights was the result of very intensive lobbying by a small group of companies from pharmaceutical, entertainment, and software industries that pushed the US government to advance on an international framework to protect their investment through a generalized intellectual property regime.

Founded in the United States in 1986, the Intellectual Property Committee brought together Bristol Myers, CBS, DuPont, General Electric, General Motors, Hewlett-Packard, IBM, Johnson and Johnson, Merck, Monsanto, and Pfizer. The group of companies was later joined by European and Japanese counterparts. Intellectual property protection had initially been a matter of national legislation, governed internationally by the Paris Convention for the Protection of Industrial Property of 1883 for patents and industrial design and by the Berne Convention of 1886 for copyright. The traditional framework provided for non-discrimination and national treatment of foreign producers, but left the details of protection up to individual national legislation (Picciotto 2011: 385–389). With respect to this regime, the TRIPS agreement was a "revolution" (Deere 2011: 1). As part of the WTO agreements, it is binding to all members, covers patents, trademarks, copyrights, and trade secrets, including new technologies and media. The patent law minimum imposed by TRIPS is well above the previous standards and extends to virtually all subject matter for twenty years, requiring states to provide adequate and effective enforcement within their borders. Failure to do so can be pursued through the WTO's Dispute Settlement Body and lead to sanctions (see Sell 2003: 8–9).

The fundamental stake in the debate about intellectual property rights is the tension between creation and diffusion. By instituting a heavy-handed regime to protect the investment at the origin of the product, the TRIPS agreement increases the costs of diffusion, which weigh particularly hard on developing countries and consumers of such products that have only reduced financial means (Drahos and Braithwaite 2002). In the years following the agreement, these issues were heavily contested and NGOs fought very effectively to loosen the requirement to allow for easier access to essential medication, in particular in the context of the fight against AIDS (Sell and Prakash 2004). These evolutions not withstanding, intellectual property protection through the WTO is clearly one of the most noteworthy cases of business influence over the global negotiation agenda.

Failure to Influence Effectively: Investment and Textiles

Even though the new trade issues provided global companies with new opportunities to shape policy agendas, not all attempts to influence negotiations were equally successful. For agenda-setting success, it is crucial that demands are interesting and acceptable not only to the government the companies first lobby in order to convince it to push for a proposal, but also to the negotiating partners. This is not always the case, as investment negotiations and the reform of the textile agreement illustrate.

The WTO agreement on trade-related investment measures (TRIMS) was another agenda item that companies heavily lobbied for. As in the case of TRIPS and service trade, US private sector activists led efforts to achieve an ambitious investment agreement similar to the GATT, that would establish non-discrimination, national treatment, and rights of establishment for foreign companies, in particular through the elimination of requirements for investment (e.g. conditions mandating local content). The targets were above all Asian markets. US companies lobbied through the same associations used to push for GATS and TRIPS, in particular the US Council for International Business and the Coalition of Service Industries. Even though the US government integrated these demands into their negotiation agenda, the efforts ultimately failed to create an effective multilateral investment agreement. As Sell (2000; 2003: 168–171) highlights, the lobbying efforts of companies were stymied by the fact that none of the parties involved could agree on all aspects of the future agreement: the US government and business lobbyists grappled over security issues, OECD member states did not arrive at a common conception about an optimal agreement, and developing countries were opposed to many aspects of the proposal. In the end, the United States conceded on investment in order to keep TRIPS and service trade on the agenda (Low and Subramanian 1997). The success of lobbying during the agenda-setting phase thus depends on the compatibility of demands with the most central negotiating governments.

Not all lobbying during global trade talks aims at agenda setting, however. As traditional political economy suggests, a substantial amount of lobbying still aims at maintaining protection, for instance by being exempt from the standard multilateral regime. This has most notably been the case for textile industries. Protectionism in textiles and clothing was enshrined in four successive Multi Fibre Arrangements (MFA) from 1974 to 1994, which imposed quotas on the amounts developing countries could export to developed countries (Aggarwal 1985). The protection of textiles and clothing was suspended with the Agreement on Textiles and Clothing negotiated during the Uruguay Round, which stipulated the phasing out of quotas over a ten-year period until January 1, 2005.

The decision to end the protective regime did not happen because companies had reduced their lobbying for exception, on the contrary. After three agreements that corresponded to US calls and the interests of several European member states for strict protectionism, the shift toward gradual liberalization under MFA IV (1986-1994) was tied to the desire of developed countries to open up trade in services and other new issues (Woolcock 2000: 378). In particular the European Commission, which acts as the negotiator for the European member states, aimed to treat textiles as any other industry. Despite intense lobbying from the European industry association COMITEXTIL, trade unions, and other textile associations, member states decided to work towards liberalization in the Uruguay Round. Without the backing of the member states, protectionist lobbying in textiles and clothing at the EU level was a failure. In a last attempt to secure special treatment in EU trade policy, industry representatives formed a new coalition in the early 1990s, the European Textile and Clothing Coalition, to avert the dangers of the new policy orientation. Simultaneously, the European Trade Union Committee for Textiles began to organize meetings and demonstrations. All of these efforts were largely ignored and at the conclusion of the Uruguay Round, the EU had endorsed the WTO's Agreement on Textiles and Clothing. Faced with this new reality, the textile industry had to reinvent its lobbying effort, changed the name of its organization to EURATEX in 1995 and decided to work in a more cooperative manner with the European Commission, embracing a strategy centered on market access rather than protection (cf. Woll 2007).

When lobbying on multilateral trade issues does not fit the objectives of the lead negotiators, it is very difficult for companies to shape negotiations effectively. The example of investment protection shows that this holds true at the agenda-setting phase, but it is also valid in repeated negotiations, as the textile agreement illustrates. Generally speaking, one can note that the Uruguay Round has led to a shift in business lobbying. As the scope of trade talks expanded and interest moved to behind-the-border issues such as regulatory standards, companies were able to engage in close working relationships with governments to define the new stakes. Depending on the sectors, governments solicit firm input and even delegate tasks to business actors (see also Cutler, Haufler, and Porter 1999). Especially in areas where regulation is central, we should expect the continued influence of global companies, although some of this activity might happen outside of the direct purview of the WTO (Levi-Faur 2013: ch. 5). Still, subsidies, and lately safeguards remain an important issue (Hoekman and Kostecki 2001: 453), so we should expect traditional lobbying at the national level to continue as well.

Direct Lobbying at the WTO

With the creation of the WTO in 1995, companies have increasingly sought to establish a presence in Geneva directly and maintain ties with the WTO's secretariat. In many cases, however, associations are better equipped than companies to maintain stable relationships over time. For business interests, the International Chamber of Commerce (ICC) is very active and has close links to the WTO secretariat, in particular through networking and exchanges of personnel. For example, Arthur Dunkel, a former Director General of GATT during the Uruguay Round, has subsequently become a board member at Nestlé and chair of the ICC working group on international trade and investment (Balanyà *et al.* 2003: 137). Similarly Peter Sutherland, a former European Commissioner who succeeded Dunkel as Director General and presided over the conclusion of the Uruguay Round and creation of the WTO, had a long career in business afterwards, including the directorship of the Royal Bank of Scotland and non-executive chairmanships at Goldman Sachs and BP. He also served on the steering committee of the Bilderberg Group, which brings together corporate and political elites, and was vice chairman of the European Roundtable of Industrialists from 2006 to 2009, one of Europe's foremost corporate lobbying associations.

Although such revolving doors are common and strengthen the ties between companies, their associations, and the WTOs secretariat, the most important part of lobbying still targets the negotiating governments. The ICC, for instance, works closely with its national committees in over sixty countries to lobby governments in the periods leading up to intergovernmental negotiations (Balanyà *et al.* 2003: 137). Companies seeking to participate in WTO negotiations use associations such as the Transatlantic Business Dialogue (TABD), which brings together CEOs from American and European companies, to develop joint policy proposals and submit them to their respective governments (Cowles 2001). Despite the creation of the WTO, a substantial part of its work is still based on intergovernmental negotiations, so national lobbying strategies will continue to remain central for affecting their evolution.

Activities have become much more centralized with respect to dispute settlement. With the establishment of the Dispute Settlement Body in 1995, companies began to develop a new kind of judicial lobbying which depended both on public-private partnerships with their respective governments (Shaffer 2003) and the submission of opinion to the settlement panels directly. The Dispute Settlement Body, a session of representatives of the WTO member states, adjudicates trade disputes between member states on the basis of recommendations of a Dispute Settlement Panel and possibly its Appellate Body in case of appeal. If countries do not comply with the judgments, the WTO can authorize the withdrawal of trade concessions. This mechanism has been extremely effective and even powerful states have agreed to modify domestic practices in response to a ruling or, less frequently, accepted sanctions. Between 1995 to 2012, 427 formal complaints have been received by the WTO, upon which 161 panels were established (World Trade Organization 2011).

Global companies are central drivers in bringing their governments to file a complaint (Davis 2012). After all, they have the information about competitive practices and restrictions on their operations abroad that would fall under the purview of the WTO. Traditionally, the US government worked most effectively with private companies to identify and dismantle trade barriers abroad. In the 1980s, the European Commission sought to emulate US practices, but initial attempts to gather information from companies were highly bureaucratic and rather unsuccessful (Shaffer 2003: 84–94). With the launch of the WTO, the EU had put into place a new instrument, the Trade Barriers Regulation, which it again replaced in 1996 with a new Market Access Strategy. A close examination of these reforms show how actively the Commission was seeking to work with companies to identify and launch complaints, in order not to find itself overtaken by the United States (Shaffer 2006; Woll 2009). Indeed, dispute settlement through the WTO was most notably used for disputes between the United States and the EU and involved much less developing countries (Busch and Reinhardt 2003).

Once a panel is constituted, third parties have the possibility to participate directly by submitting arguments to the panel in the form of *amicus curiae* briefs. Under the GATT system, unsolicited statements from non-members were not accepted, and the introduction of such briefs in the dispute settlement system was much criticized by members that were not acquainted with the use of such procedures (Ala'i 2000). Filed in only highly visible and controversial cases, the submissions of arguments brought forward by third parties was nonetheless accepted as "information from relevant sources," which Article 13 of the Dispute Settlement Understanding authorizes. Both companies and other stakeholders have made use of this possibility, making judicial lobbying a new pillar of political representation at the WTO. To be sure, not all panels receive such briefs: until the end of 2011, only 35 out of 161 panels or Appellate Body reports have seen the submission of these unsolicited statements. However, private parties have the possibility to obtain access to information through hearings and consultations. Between 2006-2012, twenty such meetings with stakeholders have been held by the dispute settlement panelists (Johansen 2012).

Judicial lobbying can thus take several forms. Companies or NGOs can submit their arguments directly to the WTO or they can gather information and press their governments to defend their interests in a given case. In fact, Busch and Reinhardt (2006) show that direct lobbying might not be the most effective way to influence WTO cases. They underline that the most advantageous resolution of WTO disputes is early settlement, i.e. an agreement on a complaint before a panel is actually constituted (Busch and Reinhardt 2000). Direct participation by third parties, however, undermines pretrial negotiations. That said, once a panel is constituted third party support does seem to increase chances for a dispute settlement victory.

Business vs. Civil Society?

With the rise of direct participation, the WTO secretariat became increasingly vulnerable to accusations of favoring corporate interests. As a target of the anti-globalization movement in the late 1990s, the organization had to justify itself to those that pointed out that the increasing scope of its activities was not matched by consultation and inclusion of the affected stakeholders beyond the business community. Indeed, not only business lobbies, but also labor unions, environmentalists groups, civil rights organizations, development groups, consumer associations, and various other non-governmental organizations (NGOs) mobilized increasingly on trade-related matters and sought to influence both trade negotiations and the WTO secretariat from the 1990s onwards.

The participation of NGOs, i.e. non-commercial interest associations, has indeed been provided for in the constitution of the WTO through article V(2) which stipulates that "arrangements for consultation and cooperation with non-governmental organizations" should be made. Subsequently, Director General Renato Ruggiero and his successors have repeated the intention to improve contacts with a diverse set of stakeholders (Scholte, O'Brien, and Williams 1999).

Even if civil society groups often appear to be weak compared to corporate interests, their mobilization has significantly affected the atmosphere of negotiations. Environmental NGOs have been very persistent in pointing out the ecological effects of trade, which put multinational companies in a much more defensive position than they had previously been (Esty 1998; Levy and Kolk 2002). Labor unions have drawn considerable attention to issues of labor protection and groups in the health sector have been instrumental in bringing about modifications to the TRIPS agreement (Sell and Prakash 2004; He and Murphy 2007). Development NGOs insisted on the need to consider economic development rather than trade in and of itself. Together with the clout of member states from emerging economies, these activities have certainly contributed to put development at the heart of the current Doha Round. Finally, consumer protection groups have argued that global competition policy and codes of conduct are crucial to counter corporate power in foreign markets.

For the political activities of companies, the participation of these new stakeholders had important consequences. During the negotiations of investment protection through TRIMS but also the failed multilateral agreement on investment (MAI) negotiated between members of the OECD, companies learned that they would not obtain their interests in the face of stiff opposition from other societal stakeholders. During trade negotiations, as in other areas of global governance, companies therefore had to learn to accommodate NGOs, at least partially.

However, interest group mobilization, whether from business or from non-commercial interests is only as strong as an organization itself. When one studies the mobilization of companies and civil society groups over time, one can see that there is no linear increase of participation from either one. Both business and NGO flocked to ministerial conferences when public attention was high, most notably in Seattle in 1999 and Cancun in 2003. Since then, however, participation in steadily declining (De Bièvre and Hanegraaff 2011). As the Doha Round has slipped into deadlock, third party interest fades steadily, in particular in the context of other international negotiations such as financial reform or climate change, that seem to be much more pressing.

Conclusion

Companies have continuously invested time and effort into multilateral trade negotiations, since they fundamentally shape the context in which they can operate globally. Lobbying on trade-related matters nonetheless evolved over time, primarily as a function of the changes in the multilateral trading system itself. When GATT negotiations dealt largely with the reduction of tariff barriers, companies pressured their government for protection or access to foreign markets. Traditional theorizing in political economy reflects this dichotomy.

As the scope of trade negotiation expanded and the activities of companies abroad evolved, they became engaged with trying to shape the multilateral agenda. In particular during the Uruguay Round, we can see that companies have fundamentally affected the course of intergovernmental negotiations, most notably by contributing to the conclusion of a separate agreement on service trade and on intellectual property rights. However, the mere presence and activities of these global companies do not condition their success. In several instances, companies have pressed hard for agreements that did not end up in the way they had hoped. Investment protection and the phasing out of an exemption for textile and clothing are cases in point.

With the establishment of the WTO, companies have also invested in the supranational level directly, if only partially. On the one hand, they have sought to establish ties with the WTO secretariat, most notably through personal relationships and networks. On the other hand, they have developed judicial lobbying to affect dispute settlement at the WTO. Indeed, companies are crucial in helping government gather information and file complaints against other countries at the WTO. Moreover, companies can submit arguments as private parties in the form of *amicus curiae* briefs.

In the context of direct lobbying at the WTO, the secretariat has made a concerted effort to address a diverse set of stakeholders, and not just business interests. The increasing pluralism of non-governmental actors has had important consequences for the strategies of global companies both at home and during trade talks. However, the participation of business and civil society groups has fallen in recent years, when trade talks stalled and moved into the background of global issues.

This hints at the fact lobbying on trade-related issues is a bit of a gamble for companies, because the long-term timing involved is profoundly foreign to their decision-making horizons. Although companies can decide to become active on trade in order to construct "political capital" (Yoffie and Bergenstein 1985), they tend to be more interested in issues with more immediate pay-offs. Despite the fervor of companies lobbying for service trade in the 1980s and 1990s, business representatives and lobbyists acknowledged that they would have not engaged in these activities had they known it would take eight years to achieve the Uruguay Round. For business executives, who evaluate investment returns over the period of financial quarters, such efforts would have been difficult to justify. This speaks volumes about companies' involvement in the Doha Round, which started in 2001, so far with no end in sight.

References

Aggarwal, Vinod K. 1985. *Liberal Protectionism: The International Politics of Organized Textile Trade*. Berkeley: University of California Press.

Ala'i, Padideh. 2000. "Judicial Lobbying at the WTO: The Debate over the Use of Amicus Curiae Briefs and the U.S. Experience." *Fordham International Law Journal*, 24 (1): 62.

Alt, James E., Frieden, Jeffry, Gilligan, Michael J., Rodrik, Dani, and Rogowski, Ronald. 1996. "The Political Economy of International Trade: Enduring Puzzles and an Agenda for Inquiry." *Comparative Political Studies*, 29 (6): 689–717.

Alt, James E. and Gilligan, Michael J. 1994. "The Political Economy of Trading States: Factor Specificity, Collective Action Problems, and Domestic Political Institutions." *Journal of Political Philosophy*, 2 (2): 165–192.

Arkell, Julian. 1994. "Lobbying for Market Access for Professional Services." In *Marketing Strategies for Services*, ed. Michel M. Kostecki. Oxford: Pergamon Press.

Balanyà, Belén, Doherty, Ann, Hoedeman, Olivier, Ma'anit, Adam, and Wesselius, Erik. 2003. *Europe Inc.: Regional and Global Restructuring and the Rise of Corporate Power*. Brussels: Pluto Press.

Bauer, Raymond A., De Sola Pool, Ithiel, and Dexter, Lewis Anthony. 1963. *American Business and Public Policy: The Politics of Foreign Trade*. Chicago: Aldine.

Braithwaite, John and Drahos, Peter. 2000. *Global Business Regulation*. Cambridge: Cambridge University Press.

De Bièvre, Dirk and Hanegraaff, Marcel. 2011. "Non-State Actors in Multilateral Trade Governance." In *Ashgate Companion to Non-State Actors*, ed. Bob Reinalda. Aldershot: Ashgate.

Buchanan, James, Tollison, R.D., and Tullock, Gordon. eds. 1980. *Towards a Theory of the Rent-Seeking Society*. College Station: Texas A&M University Press.

Busch, Marc L. and Reinhardt, Eric. 2000. "Bargaining in the Shadow of the Law: Early Settlement in GATT/WTO Disputes." *Fordham International Law Journal*, 24 (1): 158.

Busch, Marc L. and Reinhardt, Eric. 2003. "Transatlantic Trade Conflicts and GATT/WTO Dispute Settlement." In *Dispute Prevention and Dispute Settlement in the Transatlantic Partnership*, ed. Ernst-Ulrich Petersmann and Mark Pollack, 465–485. Oxford: Oxford University Press.

Busch, Marc L. and Reinhardt, Eric. 2006. "Three's a Crowd: Third Parties and WTO Dispute Settlement." *World Politics*, 58 (3): 446–477. 10.1353/wp.2007.0000.

Casella, Alessandra. 1996. "Large Countries, Small Countries, and the Enlargement of Trading Blocs." *European Economic Review*, 40 (2): 389–415.

Chase, Kerry A. 2003. "Economic Interests and Regional Trading Arrangements: The Case of NAFTA." *International Organization*, 57 (1): 137–174.

Coen, David. 2005. "Business-Regulatory Relations: Learning to Play Regulatory Games in European Utility Markets." *Governance*, 18 (3): 375–398.

Coglianese, Cary, Zeckhauser, Richard, and Parson, Edward. 2004. "Seeking Truth for Power: Informational Strategy and Regulatory Policymaking." *Minnesota Law Review*, 89 (2): 277–341.

Cottier, Thomas and Elsig, Manfred. eds. 2011. *Governing the World Trade Organization: Past, Present and Beyond Doha*, 1st edn. Cambridge: Cambridge University Press.

Cowhey, Peter and Aronson, Jonathan David. 1993. *Managing the World Economy: The Consequences of Corporate Alliances*. New York: Council on Foreign Relations.

Cowles, Maria Green. 2001. "The Transatlantic Business Dialogue and Domestic Business-Government Relations." In *Transforming Europe: Europeanization and Domestic Change*, ed. James Caporaso, Maria Green Cowles, and Thomas Risse, 159–179. Ithaca: Cornell University Press.

Cutler, A. Claire, Haufler, Virginia, and Porter, Thomas, eds. 1999. *Private Authority and International Affairs*. Albany: SUNY.

Davis, Christina L. 2012. *Why Adjudicate? Enforcing Trade Rules in the WTO*. Princeton: Princeton University Press.

Deere, Carolyn. 2011. *The Implementation Game: The TRIPS Agreement and the Global Politics of Intellectual Property Reform in Developing Countries*. Reprint. New York: Oxford University Press.

Drahos, Peter and Braithwaite, John. 2002. "Intellectual Property, Corporate Strategy, Globalisation: TRIPS in Context." *Wisconsin International Law Journal*, 20: 451–480.

Drake, William J. and Nicolaïdis, Kalypso. 1992. "Ideas, Interests, and Institutionalization: Trade in Services and the Uruguay Round." *International Organization*, 46 (1): 37–100.

Dunning, John H., ed. 1997. *Governments, Globalization, and International Business*. Oxford: Oxford University Press.

Dür, Andreas. 2010. *Protection for Exporters: Discrimination and Liberalization in Transatlantic Trade Relations, 1930–2010*. Ithaca: Cornell University Press.

Esty, Daniel C. 1998. "Non-Governmental Organizations at the World Trade Organization: Cooperation, Competition, or Exclusion." *Journal of International Economic Law*, 1 (1): 123–148. doi:10.1093/jiel/1.1.123.

Feketekuty, Geza. 1988. *International Trade in Services: An Overview and Blueprint for Negotiations*. Cambridge, MA: Ballinger.

Frieden, Jeffry and Martin, Lisa L. 2002. "International Political Economy: Global and Domestic Interactions." In *Political Science: The State of the Discipline*, ed. Ira Katznelson and Helen Milner, 118–146. New York: W.W. Norton.

Gilligan, Michael J. 1997. *Empowering Exporters: Reciprocity, Delegation, and Collective Action in American Trade Policy*. Ann Harbor: Michigan University Press.

Grossman, Gene and Helpmann, Elhanan. 1994. "Protection for Sale." *American Economic Review*, 84 (4): 833–850.

Grossman, Gene M. and Helpman, Elhanan. 2001. *Special Interest Politics*. Cambridge, MA: MIT Press.

He, Baogang and Murphy, Hannah. 2007. "Global Social Justice at the WTO? The Role of NGOs in Constructing Global Social Contracts." *International Affairs*, 83 (4): 707–727. doi:10.1111/j.1468-2346.2007.00648.x.

Hiscox, Michael J. 2002. *International Trade and Political Conflict: Commerce, Coalitions, and Mobility*. Princeton: Princeton University Press.

Hoekman, Bernard M. and Kostecki, Michel M. 2001. *The Political Economy of the World Trading System*. Oxford: Oxford University Press.

Johansen, Elin Østebø. 2012. WTO Dispute Settlement Body Developments in 2011, http://www.wto.org/english/tratop_e/dispu_e/speech_johansen_13mar12_e.htm. Accessed December 19, 2012.

Klein, Naomi. 2000. *No Logo: Taking Aim at the Brand Bullies*. Toronto: Alfred Knopf.

Levi-Faur, David. 2013. "Regulation and Capitalism," unpublished book manuscript.

Levy, David L. and Kolk, Ans. 2002. "Strategic Responses to Global Climate Change: Conflicting Pressures on Multinationals in the Oil Industry." *Business and Politics*, 4 (3): 275–300.

Lohmann, Susanne and O'Halloran, Sharyn. 1994. "Divided Government and US Trade Policy: Theory and Evidence." *International Organization*, 48 (4): 595–632.

Low, Patrick and Subramanian, Arvind. 1997. "TRIMs in the Uruguay Round: Unfinished Business?" In *The Uruguay Round and the Developing Countries*, ed. Will Martin and L. Alan Winters, 380–408. Cambridge University Press.

Magee, Stephen P., Brock, William A., and Young, Leslie. 1989. *Black Hole Tariffs and Endogenous Policy Theory: Political Economy in General Equilibrium*. Cambridge: Cambridge University Press.

Markusen, James R. 2001. "International Trade Theory and International Business." In *Oxford Handbook of International Business*, ed. Alan M. Rugman and Thomas L. Brewer, 69–87. Oxford: Oxford University Press.

Mattoo, Aaditya and Sauvé, Pierre, eds. 2003. *Domestic Regulation and Service Trade Liberalization*. Washington, DC: World Bank and Oxford University Press.

McGuire, Steven M. 2012. "What Happened to the Influence of Business? Corporations and Organized Labor in the WTO." In *The Oxford Handbook on the World Trade Organization*, ed. Amrita Narlikar and Robert M. Stern, 320–339. Oxford: Oxford University Press.

Milner, Helen. 1988. *Resisting Protectionism: Global Industries and the Politics of International Trade*. Princeton: Princeton University Press.

Milner, Helen. 1999. "The Political Economy of International Trade." *Annual Review of Political Science*, 2: 91–114.

Milner, Helen and Yoffie, David B. 1989. "Between Free Trade and Protectionism: Strategic Trade Policy and a Theory of Corporate Trade Demands." *International Organization*, 43 (2): 239–272.

O'Halloran, Sharyn. 1994. *Politics, Process, and American Trade Policy*. Ann Arbor: University of Michigan Press.

Peltzman, Sam. 1989. "The Economic Theory of Regulation after a Decade of Deregulation." *Brookings Papers on Economic Activity, Microeconomics 1989*, 1–41. Washington, DC: Brookings Institution Press.

Picciotto, Sol. 2011. *Regulating Global Corporate Capitalism*, 1st edn. Cambridge: Cambridge University Press.

Rogowski, Ronald. 1989. *Commerce and Coalitions: How Trade Affects Domestic Political Alignments*. Princeton: Princeton University Press.

Rugman, Alan M. and Verbeke, Alain. 1990. *Global Corporate Strategy and International Trade Policy*. London: Routledge.

Sauvé, Pierre and Stern, Robert Mitchell. 2000. *GATS 2000: New Directions in Services Trade Liberalization*. Washington, DC: Brookings Institution Press.

Schattschneider, E.E. 1935. *Politics, Pressures and the Tariff: A Study of Free Private Enterprise in Pressure Politics, as Shown in the 1929–1930 Revision of the Tariff*. New York: Prentice-Hall.

Scholte, Jan Aart, O'Brien, Robert, and Williams, Marc. 1999. "The WTO and Civil Society." *Journal of World Trade*, 33 (1): 107–123.

Sell, Susan K. 1999. "Multinational Corportations as Agents of Change: The Globalization of Intellectual Property Rights." In *Private Authority and International Affairs*, ed. A. Claire Cutler, Virginia Haufler, and Tony Porter, 169–198. Albany: SUNY.

Sell, Susan K. 2000. "Big Business and the New Trade Agreements: The Future of the WTO." In *Political Economy and the Changing Global Order*, ed. Richard Stubbs and Geoffrey R.D. Underhill. Oxford: Oxford University Press.

Sell, Susan K. 2003. *Private Power, Public Law: The Globalization of Intellectual Property Rights*. Cambridge: Cambridge University Press.

Sell, Susan K. and Prakash, Aseem. 2004. "Using Ideas Strategically: The Contest Between Business and NGO Networks in Intellectual Property Rights." *International Studies Quarterly*, 48 (1): 143–175.

Seoane, José and Taddei, Emilio. 2002. "From Seattle to Porto Alegre: The Anti-Neoliberal Globalization Movement." *Current Sociology*, 50 (1): 99–122.

Shaffer, Gregory C. 2003. *Defending Interests: Public-Private Partnerships in WTO Litigation*. Washington, DC: Brookings Institution Press.

Shaffer, Gregory C. 2006. "What's New in EU Trade Dispute Settlement? Judicialization, Public–Private Networks and the WTO Legal Order." *Journal of European Public Policy*, 13 (6): 832–850. 10.1080/13501760600837153.

Wallach, Lori and Sforza, Michelle. 1999. *The WTO: Five Years of Reasons to Resist Corporate Globalization*. New York: Seven Stories Press.

Wesselius, Erik. 2002. *Behind GATS 2000: Corporate Power at Work*. Transnational Institute Briefing Series, 6.

Woll, Cornelia. 2007. "Leading the Dance? Power and Political Resources of Business Lobbyists." *Journal of Public Policy*, 27 (1): 57–78.

Woll, Cornelia. 2008. *Firm Interests: How Governments Shape Business Lobbying on Global Trade*. Ithaca: Cornell University Press.

Woll, Cornelia. 2009. "Who Captures Whom? Trade Policy Lobbying in the European Union." In *Lobbying in the European Union: Institutions, Actors and Issues*, ed. David Coen and Jeremy Richardson, 268–288. Oxford: Oxford University Press.

Woll, Cornelia and Artigas, Alvaro. 2007. "When Trade Liberalization Turns into Regulatory Reform: The Impact on Business–Government Relations in International Trade Politics." *Regulation and Governance*, 1 (2): 121–138.

Woolcock, Stephen. 2000. "European Trade Policy: Global Pressures and Domestic Constraints." In *Policy-making in the European Union*, ed. Helen Wallace and William Wallace, 373–399, 4th edn. New European Union Series. Oxford: Oxford University Press.

World Trade Organization. 2011. *Dispute Settlement Body Annual Report*. Geneva: World Trade Organization.

Yoffie, David B. and Bergenstein, Sigrid. 1985. "Creating Political Advantage: The Rise of the Corporate Political Entrepreneur." *California Management Review*, 28 (1): 124–139.

Young, Alasdair R. 2007. "Trade Politics Ain't What It Used to Be: The European Union in the Doha Round." *Journal of Common Market Studies*, 45 (4): 789–811.

Young, Alasdair R. and Peterson, John. 2006. "The EU and the New Trade Politics." *Journal of European Public Policy*, 13 (6): 795–814.

Chapter 16

Business Interests Shaping International Institutions

Negotiating the Trans-Pacific Partnership Agreement

Deborah Elms

Introduction

Companies have always tried to influence government policies. This chapter is an extended look at one international institution – the birth of the Trans-Pacific Partnership (TPP) – and the various approaches different member governments and business firms have used to try to influence the course of its institutional development. The TPP is a free trade agreement that will link together at least eleven countries in three continents. Negotiations began in 2010 and the first tranche of bargaining is projected to continue through at least the end of 2013.

   The TPP is both an institution and an organization, although it currently does not exist in the same form as an institution like the World Bank or the International Monetary Fund. To quote Nobel-prizewinning economist Douglass North (1990: 3), institutions "are the rules of the game in a society" while organizations are "groups of individuals bound by some common purpose to achieve objectives." In the TPP, it is possible to watch business attempt to influence policy outcomes from the very beginning of the institutional foundations. Given the diverse nature of membership, moreover, it is possible to observe behavior of firms and government from different countries and regions. This makes this an interesting case for observing the interactions between business and government as each jockey for influence over the resultant institution.

The Creation of the TPP

The Trans-Pacific Partnership (TPP) talks got underway in early 2010. The TPP is a free trade agreement (or preferential trade agreement) between countries from three continents of extremely different sizes and varying levels of economic development.

The Handbook of Global Companies, First Edition. Edited by John Mikler.
© 2013 John Wiley & Sons, Ltd. Published 2013 by John Wiley & Sons, Ltd.

As of early 2012, membership included nine states, including Australia, Brunei, Chile, Malaysia, New Zealand, Peru, Singapore, the United States, and Vietnam. Participants hope to create a "high-quality, 21st century" preferential trade agreement (PTA).[1] It aims to go beyond the normal areas of discussion like tariff cuts (imagine them as acting like taxes on imports) for goods and includes new measures and wholly original topics for possible inclusion in a PTA. Many of these new areas, like the harmonization of standards and regulations across member states, could be highly intrusive into domestic political and economic spheres. By early 2012, officials had met in 11 official "rounds" of negotiations, in addition to many smaller meetings held with subgroups on specific issues.

PTAs have proliferated tremendously. In 2007, the Asian Development Bank counted 204 agreements signed in and between Asian economies. Most are bilateral or regional agreements, largely focused on liberalizing trade in goods, especially through reductions in tariff levels. The TPP is supposed to be different. Not only does this agreement bring together countries in three continents, but it aims to produce a "high quality, 21st century" outcome. By this, officials mean it should have broader and deeper commitments than typical PTAs.

Another highly unusual feature of the TPP is that it has continued to expand its membership. It began with just four countries: Brunei, Chile, New Zealand, and Peru. It expanded to seven, and then added Vietnam and Malaysia. Finally, in the wake of the G20 meetings in June 2012, Canada and Mexico were officially welcomed as members of the TPP. Given the complex domestic requirements in the United States, the two countries were not able to participate in the talks until nearly the end of 2012. This chapter, therefore, concentrates on the negotiations that have taken place with nine countries involved.

Further expansion of the TPP is also possible. Japan also indicated a formal interest in joining in November 2011 and held all the necessary bilateral consultation meetings with the current nine member states in late 2011 and early 2012 to become a participant. Its membership has been on hold, pending confirmation of its intent to restructure its domestic economy to the level that will be required of all TPP members. Other countries, like South Korea and Costa Rica, had also expressed keen interest in the talks, albeit at a less formal level.

The original nine member states in the TPP were already connected by a dense web of existing bilateral and regional preferential or free trade agreements. Of the 36 bilateral preferential arrangements possible between the nine TPP members, only ten were not covered by existing agreements, most with Peru and the United States. In some instances, partners have multiple agreements. For instance, Singapore and New Zealand have three different PTA agreements in force: the New Zealand-Singapore Closer Economic Partnership (NZSCEP), the P4 (a forerunner to the TPP), and the Association of Southeast Asian Nations (ASEAN)–Australia–New Zealand agreement (AANZFTA), in addition to their commitments to one another under the World Trade Organization (WTO). Each of these agreements has different provisions and commitments.

As a result of all this activity, the TPP member states have ample prior experience negotiating preferential trade agreements. The TPP agreement is more comprehensive than many existing PTAs. But for some elements, like market access for the majority of goods trade, all of the countries have discussed these topics before. Officials have already dealt with their internal politics and have worked out the mechanisms for approaching their own conflicts with internal ministries and departments required to open trade to new countries.

They have also put into place some specific approaches for handling the concerns of business. After all, a preferential trade agreement is designed to be used by business. It grants businesses in partner markets preferential access to each others' markets at terms that are better than the access granted to non-partners. But this access only counts if businesses use the specific rules and benefits. If the rules are too complex or too cumbersome, business will not take advantage of the PTA provisions for trade. Business will instead trade using normal, non-PTA rules governing trade. This makes it imperative that government pay attention to the needs of business in drafting the rules that govern a PTA. Otherwise, all the effort that goes into creating the PTA will have been wasted on creating an institution that does not facilitate trade any more than the status quo.

It might seem obvious then that business should drive PTA negotiations forward, with government actors going to great lengths to gather information on what various businesses need and want from a preferential trade agreement. As this case study information on the TPP negotiations makes clear, however, this is actually not quite how it happens. In fact, what is particularly striking about the TPP is that the nine governments involved have gone to rather extraordinary lengths to solicit business feedback – especially during negotiations – and have still received relatively little input. Also striking is the range of government/business interaction between states with some TPP members having clear, formal channels for receiving feedback from business and other states having almost no connection between the groups at all.

Governments do create PTAs for the purpose of encouraging trade and fostering business. But they also sign these agreements for non-economic reasons as well. For example, some governments sign PTAs for strategic or political objectives to reward friends or strengthen allies. Officials could sign agreements for pragmatic domestic reasons to draw attention to themselves in election seasons or to keep bureaucrats busy.

This chapter examines the specific interactions between business and government in the TPP negotiations. Each has attempted to influence the scale and scope of the final agreement. Each has tried to bend the TPP in ways that fit their own interests. Because the TPP includes nine different member states, each with hundreds of business firms and industry associations actively involved in lobbying government actors, the negotiations have been extremely complex.

Obtaining Feedback through Comment Periods

The nine governments involved in the talks have different procedures in place to handle relations with business interests. For most of the countries, business consultations at the outset of negotiations were handled informally. For example, in the case of Singapore, officials from the lead agency, the Ministry of Trade and Industry, had already established close ties to major industry groups as a result of extensive past negotiations. By the commencement of talks in early 2010, Singapore had 17 PTAs in force.

As the start date approached for launching discussions on the TPP, Singaporean officials reached out to business officials for feedback on their key interests in this new agreement. Of particular interest was feedback from apex industry associations like the various chambers of commerce. Singapore has chambers of commerce not only for domestic firms but also a number of different chambers for multinational companies of various nationalities, such as AmCham, EuroCham, BritCham, and so forth. Firms are frequently members of more than one chamber. These groups are quite active and often provide the most meaningful feedback to government.

In general, Singaporean negotiators believed they were well prepared to start talks in areas like goods or services, since these topics had been covered in past agreements. But they were particularly eager to get input on new issues like supply chain connectivity from industry leaders such as the courier giants United Parcel Service (UPS) or DHL which have a large presence in Singapore. These companies, working together with their industry association, put together specific policy recommendations of what they wanted to see in any liberalization plans for the TPP.

Because UPS and DHL and other express logistics companies operate in multiple TPP members, the Singapore-based firms also worked with their counterparts in other countries to present the same materials to government officials elsewhere. This strategy of working through their subsidiaries has been highly effective in the TPP. In logistics, for example, the final TPP agreement is likely to contain a good deal of the language from that original document drafted by the businesses.[2]

Many other TPP countries have similar, more informal mechanisms for soliciting business feedback. Malaysia and Vietnam, for instance, also obtained comments from business at the outset of negotiations in a similar fashion to Singapore.

The situation is different for New Zealand, Australia, and the United States. These three countries followed specific procedures for obtaining comments, largely aimed at increasing the transparency of the process. These open procedures were accompanied by multiple meetings between business industry associations or representatives and government officials over the course of negotiations.

For example, New Zealand received 64 written comments from companies and individuals when the Ministry of Foreign Affairs and Trade asked for public comment on the proposed negotiations in the TPP. Most of the feedback was related to rules on intellectual property rights, which has become a particular hot topic for New Zealand in these negotiations.

In Australia, the government asked for public comments on Australia's proposed plans to enter the TPP in early 2009. The Department of Foreign Affairs and Trade received 42 submissions. These included many comments from industry associations ranging from the dairy, pork, and grain industries to mining, minerals, and movies. It also included comments from organizations with affiliations outside of Australia, including the American Chamber of Commerce in Australia and the Australian Chamber of Commerce in Singapore.

The United States has the most institutionalized mechanisms for soliciting business feedback on government action. Before the government can launch new negotiations, it must publish a notice of its intentions in the *Federal Register* and open a comment period. During the comment period through the end of 2011, 118 companies filed written comments with the United States Trade Representative's (USTR) Office. Nearly all were prepared by legal counsel or lobby groups on behalf of various industry associations, ranging from some of the largest organizations and firms in the US economy to some of the smallest such as the dehydrated garlic and onion association.

The open comment periods provide an especially useful feedback mechanism for government officials. It gives businesses across the spectrum the opportunity to weigh in with their concerns as a negotiation gets underway. These written letters highlight many issues that government officials already knew from past experience. For instance, in the TPP negotiations as the chapter discusses in further detail below, officials knew that talks over market access in dairy products would be difficult. This is because dairy has been a sensitive topic in previous PTA negotiations and because the dairy industry, especially in the United States, has been highly organized and politically well connected. As a result of this long history, dairy has received a high degree of protection from foreign competition. Any negotiations aimed at lower barriers to trade – and especially talks with a very competitive dairy producer like New Zealand – were going to be problematic for the dairy industry.

But these written comments also throw up some issues that were likely not well understood by trade officials. For instance, even the most knowledgeable agricultural expert may not have realized the specific problems likely to be faced by California dehydrated garlic farmers from market liberalization. Or officials in New Zealand may not have known that persimmons were prohibited from the American market outside of Guam or that exporters of blueberries have had problems with exporting to the US markets over incidents of immature mealybugs even though these should not have been an issue under American agricultural rules.

The Stakeholder Process

Such procedures for collecting comments, however, are not institutionalized through all TPP member states. Nor are the comments always made public. In part to help facilitate transparency in the links between government and business, officials opted to try something different in the TPP negotiations. They opened up something called "stakeholder meetings" on the sidelines of each official TPP round of negotiations. In the beginning, these were somewhat haphazard affairs, but by the Singapore round in June 2011, the stakeholders were brought together into an all-day forum held at the start of each round. These forums quickly grew in size. Officials from TPP negotiating teams were encouraged to attend the different stakeholder presentations to get a better understanding of the needs and concerns of business.

To get a sense of these meetings, the March 2012 meeting in Melbourne, Australia, featured 250 different individuals and 38 presentations. Presentation topics included investment, intellectual property rights, food, and public health. Although many of the presenters at this meeting were NGOs or academics, businesses included the Emergency Committee for American Trade, the Business Council of Australia, IBM, Ford, Dairy Australia, Gap, Distilled Spirits Industry Association of Australia, and the Australian Directors Guild.

In addition to the formal presentations made at the forum, stakeholders were also invited to attend a reception during the round. This gave business a direct opportunity to speak to the various trade officials from each of the TPP member countries. Some business officials have spent time hanging around the conference room venues waiting for the opportunity to catch an official or two for a short meeting.

Many of the savvier businesses also set up meetings with officials in their respective areas during the round whenever meetings were not being held. This, especially, gave them the opportunity to exchange views with government officials from different countries as often as every round or every two months. Such frequent meetings gave interested businesses the chance to weigh in with suggestions along the way as rules and procedures were being discussed at the negotiating table.

This institutionalized process of stakeholder meetings is highly unusual for PTA negotiations. Interested participants were encouraged to register their attendance in advance of each round. The host government of the round was responsible for scheduling specific presentations and sorting out which stakeholders would be granted a seat at the table. Some businesses, like Google or the Pharmaceutical Research and Manufacturers of America (PhRMA), were present at nearly every stakeholder function, while others attended only one or two.

The format of the stakeholder meetings changed over time as well. In an effort to see what might facilitate the best exchange of ideas between government and business, the American hosts in the Dallas round in 2012 shifted to make the stakeholder meetings a one-on-one event. Each registered stakeholder was given a space beside a table for a four-hour time period. Government delegates could circulate and talk directly with each participant about specific issues of concern. Because this format was criticized by some, it was later replaced with a hybrid system that allowed stakeholders to choose whether they wanted the one-on-one presentation slots or to make a formal presentation to a larger audience.

The stakeholder concept is entirely new in the TPP. No other PTA negotiation has attempted anything similar. If, at the end of the day, it proves to have been useful, other states may attempt to implement a similar feedback mechanism in future negotiations. The system appears most helpful in getting government officials to better understand the complex needs of business in negotiations that span multiple countries. It provides a mechanism for letting smaller firms and industries give feedback directly to government and allows smaller states an opportunity to receive input that is generally not available in their own countries.

Specific Issues of Concern to Business in the TPP

As the largest country – by far – in the TPP, the United States dominates the negotiations. The demands of US business also reign over the proceedings. American multinationals operate in nearly all the TPP member countries, so their influence is frequently felt far beyond Washington, DC. Given the open nature of the feedback loop between business and government in the United States, it is also easier to see how business has attempted to shape these negotiations by looking to Washington.

The Trade Policy Staff Committee in the US Congress held the first public hearings on the proposed TPP talks on March 4, 2009. This was the first opportunity for industry groups to weigh in on the planned talks.[3] At the time, Vietnam was not a full member in the TPP and Malaysia had not yet joined the negotiations.

These public statements of firms in Washington, however, were important to study, as they revealed the lines of argument that were used once the official talks got underway. They also pinpointed the sources of disagreement.

Many businesses highlighted the relatively modest size of the grouping from the very beginning and pointed out that new export opportunities for American business might be minimal. Of the three partners not already covered by a PTA with the United States, New Zealand was already substantially open for trade; Brunei represented almost no market of any kind (beyond limited trade in oil and oil-related equipment); and most of what the United States wanted from Vietnam had been incorporated into Vietnam's recent accession package for the World Trade Organization (WTO). Malaysia's 20 million person strong market joined later and did not substantially change the overall market picture for US exports.

However, any effort to expand to additional partners in the future could reach into economically significant markets that were previously closed through bilateral negotiations. In addition, there was some concern that if the United States failed to participate in the TPP negotiations, it risked being left out of key markets going forward. Particularly for businesses with supply chains in Asia, the downside to being caught on the outside of proliferating PTAs could be significant.

Firms also raised a host of specific issues, both large and small, for officials going forward with negotiations. For example, businesses pushed to have the service sectors opened as much as possible in TPP member states. They asked to have this done using a technique called a "negative list." Under this approach, government promises to liberalize or open up the markets in all sectors except for those that are explicitly listed as closed to foreign competition. This approach is broadly seen as more market opening than the alternative. Given that Vietnam and Malaysia had never worked in this style before, it was an important consideration for trade officials. Business specifically raised concerns about market barriers in financial services, telecommunications, audiovisual services, media, electronic payment systems, e-commerce, energy services, and express delivery services.

Firms also raised a host of issues related to protections of intellectual property rights (IPR) and enforcement of IPR. This was not an unexpected concern, as Brunei, Chile, Peru, and Vietnam had all been on the US government's Special 301 watch list for IPR protection problems in the past. Many companies urged USTR to use the most recent FTA templates as models for handling IPR issues in the TPP. These were seen as providing better, more advanced rules on IP protections than the older models.

Another early area of concern for firms related to the connections between labor and the environment. Although it was widely held that a US Congress, especially when controlled by Democrats, could not approve a final TPP agreement without robust labor and environmental provisions, few businesses began lobbying USTR for tough labor or environmental rules from the beginning. Most firms seemed to adopt a "wait and see" attitude towards these issues.

Another hot topic for some companies concerned the entry of New Zealand's competitive agricultural industry into the American market. Because there has never been a free trade agreement between the United States and New Zealand for historical reasons (mostly related to New Zealand's ban on refueling of American nuclear warships and then on the Kiwis' lack of support for the war in Iraq), the United

States had been able to maintain high barriers to trade in key agricultural products. In particular, US limits on dairy, beef, and lamb severely limited the supply of New Zealand products in the lucrative American market.[4]

Under the TPP, however, officials were already talking about market liberalization with "no exceptions." The primary bone of contention for American milk producers was that New Zealand's dairy industry was viewed as a monopoly, with one firm (Fonterra) in control of 90% of the market and substantial barriers to entry into the market.[5] If the American market was opened to competition through an FTA like the TPP, they feared that New Zealand dairy would receive unfair competitive advantages. Equally worrisome to some American firms like the US Cattleman's Association was the opening of the US beef market to highly competitive New Zealand beef. Firms and industry associations urged USTR to block the opening of the US market.

Many industry associations believed that the largest source of economic gains from a TPP could come from further liberalization and market access in Vietnam. But not everyone in the United States was enthusiastic about Vietnam's possible inclusion in the TPP talks. In particular, the US garment and textile industries expressed strong reservations about a free trade agreement with a non-market economy. The National Council of Textile Organizations noted that after the removal of quotas from Vietnam in 2007, textile and apparel imports increased by 60% or $2 billion in two years.[6]

The American Manufacturing Trade Action Coalition came out strongly against any FTA agreement with Vietnam, noting that Vietnam did not purchase finished goods from the United States, nor did it use substantial amounts of American-made products in its supply chains.[7] The coalition recommended excluding textiles, apparel, and other sensitive products from any agreement with Vietnam. The Rubber and Plastic Footwear Manufacturers Association urged officials to exclude core products of the domestic rubber footwear industry from any agreement with Vietnam.[8]

The National Association of Manufacturers (NAM) noted that the United States ran a large and growing manufactured goods trade deficit of $8.6 billion with Vietnam in 2008. NAM highlighted high Vietnamese tariffs (which would be lowered under Vietnam's WTO accession terms, although not to zero) and the potential benefits that could arise from Vietnamese participation in the TPP.[9] The National Confectioners Association made a similar point. Vietnamese tariffs on chewing gum and sugar confectionary products could be as high as 35%. Reduction of these tariffs to an MFN rate of 5% could generate $2 million in export sales in the first year.[10]

The National Association of Retailers highlighted the importance of Vietnam to the supply chains of many American firms, as well as growing opportunities for retail investment.[11] It argued strongly that liberalizing trade in textiles and clothing would benefit American consumers. Other benefits could accrue to the US dairy industry, as a result of further market opening in Vietnam.[12]

Australia

In an expansion of the TPP beyond the original four founding members, perhaps the second most important state to consider was Australia. Like the United States, the Australian government faced conflicting pressures from industry groups.

Understanding these interests was important, as they have shaped the direction of the final agreement.

Australia's trade minister, Simon Crean, announced Australia's planned participation in TPP talks on the margins of the APEC ministerial meeting in Lima, Peru, on November 20, 2008. This announcement followed nearly two months of intensive discussions within the government and industry over the priorities and objectives for the negotiations.

Australia had bilateral FTAs with New Zealand (1983), Singapore, and the United States (2003). It concluded an FTA with Chile in 2009. Brunei was included in the ASEAN/Australia/New Zealand agreement. Given this network of FTAs (and similar overall templates to the American FTA agreements) with TPP members, negotiating in the TPP should have been relatively straightforward.

Australia had strong trade ties to most of the TPP member states. The United States was Australia's third largest trading partner in 2008, with a two-way goods trade of AUD $38.8 billion and services trade of $15.9 billion. Singapore was the fourth largest partner with goods of $22.3 billion and services of $8.7 billion.[13] Peru and Chile are members of the Cairns group of agricultural exporting countries with a long history of working together in multilateral trade negotiations.

Like the United States, Australia viewed the TPP as a building block to further regional integration. With this perspective, policymakers preferred to be in "on the ground floor" to shape the overall direction of the agreement. The Australian government issued an important report reviewing export policies and programs (Mortimer 2008). The report warned of the potential for Australia to be caught out by the proliferation of trade deals in the region. As a hedge against this possibility, the report recommended developing multiple "clusters" of FTA deals that could ultimately be knit together into something like a Free Trade Area of the Asia Pacific (FTAAP) among the 21 member economies of the Asia Pacific Economic Cooperation (APEC).

The TPP negotiations fit within this cluster approach to trade. The report noted that among states with recently negotiated FTAs, there has not "yet been a strong export response, but the full benefits of the agreements are expected to emerge over time" (Mortimer 2008: 92).

In announcing Australia's intention to pursue membership, Trade Minister Simon Crean (2008) outlined the following priorities:

- Promote trade and investment flows with the partners of the Trans-Pacific Partnership negotiations;
- Ensure that the Trans-Pacific Partnership provides a platform for comprehensive liberalization across goods, services and investment;
- Substantially improve trade and economic integration with Peru, with which we do not currently have a free-trade agreement, given our growing commercial interests, particularly in services and commodities trade;
- To pursue commercial interests more broadly in the Asia-Pacific region as other countries start to take a closer interest in the Trans-Pacific Partnership process;
- To build on WTO rules covering goods, services, and investment; and
- To provide a model arrangement which might stimulate other initiatives to multilateralize bilateral FTAs.

Australian Industry Approaches to the TPP Negotiations

Again, like the Americans, the Australian Department of Foreign Affairs and Trade (DFAT) solicited public comment on the TPP negotiations on October 3, 2008.[14] The responses – in many ways – mirrored the reactions from American industry groups.

One striking difference between the two states, however, was the importance that Australian firms placed on widening the TPP process to include other states. Industry after industry recommended bringing Japan, China, and Korea into the negotiations.[15] Given the trade liberalization already flowing from Australia's bilateral FTAs with most of the presumptive TPP partners, the economic gains from negotiations could be best captured with the inclusion of some of the bigger Northeast Asian markets. Several industry officials questioned whether the seven markets in the TPP negotiations (plus Vietnam as an associate member) would be sufficient to attract the interest of these economies in joining. If not, they suggested that perhaps DFAT's focus should be on negotiating bilateral or regional agreements with the key markets of Japan, China, or South Korea.

Australian dairy asked for a high degree of trade liberalization in agriculture (and specifically dairy products) to include both tariff and non-tariff barriers to trade. The Australian sugar industry noted that the TPP might be a mechanism for bringing liberalization into the American sugar market that was not possible in the US–Australian FTA.[16] Sugar products were substantially liberalized under the P4 agreement, so, industry noted, it might prove difficult to exclude sugar from the TPP.[17]

Like American firms, several Australian companies also noted issues related to intellectual property rights. Several industry associations asked the government to ensure that the TPP include strong IP protections. They asked to have Australian FTA rules harmonized with the goal of building a broader agreement in the future.

Several coalitions requested labor standards to be incorporated into the TPP, while expressing concerns about the movement of persons and rights of indigenous peoples. One asked government to strengthen multilateral environmental agreements. Another submission highlighted problems of marine management in particular.

Industry officials also expressed a set of concerns at the domestic level. They called on DFAT to continue to negotiate in the context of an open and transparent process with sufficient access for public consultations.

Conclusion

After nearly two years of negotiations, it is remarkable how prescient business interests in the United States and Australia were in predicting the challenging points of the negotiations. The TPP talks have not yet concluded, but many of the pressure points highlighted by industry in their various submissions have become some of the most contested areas of negotiation.

On goods trade, for example, the most heated discussions have been around the areas of market access for dairy, beef, sugar, textiles, and footwear. Many of the member governments face difficult challenges at the domestic level managing their own business interests. The United States, for instance, faces demands to both liberalize the sugar market from users of sugar as well as strident objections to any attempts to open the market further in the TPP negotiations from producers. While US consumers would undoubtedly benefit from more open markets in sugar in the form of lower prices for everything made with sugar, consumers are not well represented in the lobbying efforts in Washington. Government negotiators have to manage these competing business interests at home as well as try to get an agreement among the nine TPP member governments that will satisfy everyone. For dairy liberalization or sugar, this has proven challenging.

In some areas, business suggestions from the beginning appear to have been taken on board by officials. For example, services negotiations have been conducted on the basis of a negative list – all service sectors will be opened to foreign competition unless explicitly listed as closed. Some aspects of the talks have been relatively smooth, including services overall or even discussions over standards and regulations that have proceeded with limited disagreements after two years of discussions.

But there remain a few areas that business did note from the earliest moments as a source of likely deep sensitivities. These areas include intellectual property rights, investment protections, and especially investor–state dispute mechanisms, government procurement particularly for state-owned enterprises, and labor and environmental provisions.

Getting an agreement with nine countries is difficult. Officials have to balance competing interests. Businesses need to provide their input to the process. After all, if they are not satisfied with the eventual result, they are unlikely to take advantage of the provisions of this preferential trade agreement. It will not open markets and it will not improve trade prospects among the member countries.

In the TPP negotiations, government officials have taken advantage of multiple methods of soliciting feedback from business. They have received comments informally and utilized the connections of business associations and industry groups. Some countries have clear methods in place for business groups to lobby government directly. This can involve written and oral feedback during open comment periods.

During the course of negotiations, business has been involved through a series of stakeholder meetings. These have included both formal and informal meetings with officials on the sidelines of each negotiating round.

These multiple approaches have been important, since the negotiations themselves are conducted in private. Businesses and other interested parties receive little news and information about the ongoing bargaining and will not have access to specific texts until the whole agreement has been completed and signed off by government actors. It is only at the end that business will find out how successful they have been in arguing their case.

Notes

1   To the extent that this is so, see Low *et al.* (2012).
2   Various interviews with company representatives in Singapore as well as government officials in Singapore, Malaysia, and Vietnam on express logistics services in 2011.

3 Groups testifying or supplying messages of support included: US Chamber of Commerce; National Foreign Trade Council; National Council of Textile Organizations (supportive, except for Vietnamese participation); Pharmaceutical Research and Manufacturers of America (PhRMA); International Intellectual Property Alliance; Coalition of Service Industries; National Association of Manufacturers; the United States–New Zealand Council; Emergency Committee for American Trade; New Zealand–United States Council; Biotechnology Industry Association; Grocery Manufacturers Association; National Pork Producers; Land O'Lakes Farmers Coop; Motion Picture Association of America; Croplife America; Northwest Horticulture Council; TechAmerica; National Retail Federation; Boeing; Novartis Corporation; Wal-Mart; Distilled Spirits Council of the United States; California Table Grape Commission; Advanced Medical Technology Association; National Electrical Manufacturers Association; National Confectioners Association; United States Association of Importers of Textiles and Apparel; and the American Chamber of Commerce in Japan.

Several commodity groups and agribusiness organizations including the National Association of Wheat Growers, the National Association of Barley Growers, and the American Soybean Association, sent a letter of support to President Obama in March 2009. See *Inside US Trade*, April 10, 2009, 23. Testimony or letters opposed include: American Manufacturing Trade Action Coalition; National Milk Producers Federation (NMPF); Rubber and Plastic Footwear Manufacturers Association; Public Citizen; American Sugar Alliance, and the US Dairy Export Council.

4 The World Trade Organization has had only limited rules – so far – governing trade in agricultural products.

5 The WTO's review of New Zealand (2003) found that dairy was no longer a monopoly, but the company had exclusive licenses to export to some markets from 2010 onwards. Fonterra (USA), Inc. submitted a letter to USTR during the open comment period (through the legal firm of Blank, Rowe, LLP, on March 11, 2009). It argued that the market in New Zealand was open for competition, with no government subsidies, import tariffs, or quota restrictions. It also argued that the entire New Zealand dairy industry was smaller than that of California and that it was no more globally competitive than American dairy in various export markets.

6 The NCTO argued that it was not a fair competition, as the government of Vietnam had "poured billions of dollars of government support into the sector over the last ten years." Testimony of Cass Johnson, National Council of Textile Organizations, February 24, 2009. In addition, this surge in imports did not merely harm domestic American producers, but also competitors in trade preference areas like Africa, Central America, and Mexico. The National Association of Manufacturers urged officials to take careful note of the apparel sector concerns, if Vietnam moved from being an observer to a full participant. Testimony of Franklin Vargo, National Association of Manufacturers, March 4, 2009.

7 Sara Ormand said, "A potential free trade agreement with Vietnam would be a disaster and would represent the worst aspects of the failed 'one-way' trade policy of the Bush Administration." Testimony, American Manufacturing Trade Action Coalition, March 4, 2009.

8 The industry did not take a position on trade talks with any of the other states in the TPP talks. Rubber footwear has some of the highest tariffs in the United States and has maintained these tariff levels through successive rounds of negotiations in the WTO and elsewhere. The high tariffs stem in part from a concern over defense needs. See Testimony, Mitchell Cooper, Rubber and Plastic Footwear Manufacturers Association, March 4, 2009.

9 Testimony of Franklin Vargo, National Association of Manufacturers, March 4, 2009.

10 See the submission of National Confectioners Association, March 10, 2009.

11 See submission of National Association of Retailers, March 11, 2009.

12 Vietnam's tariff levels have been generally low, and largely falling in areas of significant export promise as a result of WTO accession commitments. See US Dairy Export Council, March 10, 2009. Land O'Lakes Farmers Coop was specifically enthusiastic about the potential for market expansion in Vietnam. See submission, March 9, 2009.

13   *Trade at a Glance, 2009*, Australian Department of Foreign Affairs and Trade. Overall trade with APEC members accounted for AUD $560.8 billion in total two-way trade and a 68% share of Australian trade.

14   Weighing in support of the negotiations were: ABB Grain Ltd; American Chamber of Commerce in Australia; Australian Dairy Industry Council Inc.; Australian Industry Group; Australian Recording Industry Association; Australian Sugar Industry Alliance Limited; Australian Tourism Export Council; Investment & Financial Services Association Ltd; Minerals Council of Australia; Music Industry Piracy Investigations Pty Limited; and the Screen Producers Association of Australia.

Writing in opposition to negotiations were: Australian Fair Trade and Investment Network (AFTINET); and Australian Pork Limited.

15   For example, see the submissions of Australian Industry Group, or Australian Pork Limited.

16   The US–Australian FTA, the industry noted, was the only one that either country has concluded that completely excludes sugar. See Ian McMaster, Australian Sugar Industry Alliance Limited, submission on October 31, 2008. The US National Confectioners Association specifically asked USTR to relook at the exclusion of Australian sugar in the TPP negotiations. See their USTR submission, March 10, 2009. In the P4 agreement, Chile got a special agricultural safeguard mechanism, the "sugar treatment," based on a trade surplus mechanism. This was the only sector-specific provision in the P4 goods agreement. See WTO Factual Presentation, p. 38. Wal-Mart asked USTR to avoid such sector-specific exclusions in the TPP. See submission of Wal-Mart, March 11, 2009. This was opposed by the American Sugar Alliance, as noted in their submission of March 11, 2009.

17   New Zealand noted that it only agreed to liberalization of sugar products (in solid form, HS 1701) because it did not export such products to Chile. See "Trans-Pacific Strategic Economic Partnership Agreement: National Interest Analysis," New Zealand Ministry of Foreign Affairs and Trade, July 2005, 8.

References

Crean, Simon. 2008. November 26. Ministerial Statement. Australian Parliament, Canberra.

Low, C.L., Elms, Deborah, and Low, Patrick, eds. 2012. *Trans-Pacific Partnership: A Quest for a 21st Century Trade Agreement*. Cambridge: Cambridge University Press.

Mortimer, David. 2008. *Winning in World Markets: Review of Export Policies and Programs*. Canberra: Department of Foreign Affairs and Trade, September 1.

North, Douglass. 1990. *Institutions, Institutional Change and Economic Performance*. Cambridge: Cambridge University Press.

Chapter 17

Global Companies and the Environment

The Triumph of TNCs in Global Environmental Governance

Matthias Finger

Introduction

This chapter is about the evolving (strategic) relationship between transnational corporations (TNCs) and the environment. In it, I make a distinction between the discourse about the environment – i.e., what TNCs consider to be environmental problems and issues – and environmental behavior, i.e., what TNCs actually do in regard to these issues and problems. The discourse about the environment was mainly shaped during the 1990s in the context of several UN conferences and has led, recently, i.e., during the Rio+20 Summit, to the new concept of "green growth." This is a clear triumph of the transnational corporations over the international organizations, both in terms of discourse and in terms of how environmental problems are now addressed in practice. It may well be that, now that the discourse on "green growth" is well in place, the environmental behavior of the TNCs will be about gaining competitive advantage over other TNCs, rather than about promoting green growth.

The literature about the relationship between TNCs and the environment is broadly of two kinds. There is, on the one hand, the business literature which, especially after the United Nations Conference on Environment and Development (UNCED) in 1992, has started to apply the traditional concepts and tools of management to environmental issues inside and sometimes outside of the firm. There is notably literature on "how to green the firm" by way of optimizing processes, introducing environmental management systems, as well as by way of developing green products (e.g. see Prakash 2000; Stead and Stead 2009; Welford 1996). Other business literature talks about environmental strategies, environmental leadership, and entrepreneurship (e.g. see Bennett 1991; Bennis et al. 1994; Piasecki 1995). I will not discuss this literature any further in this chapter, as it is already very well

The Handbook of Global Companies, First Edition. Edited by John Mikler.
© 2013 John Wiley & Sons, Ltd. Published 2013 by John Wiley & Sons, Ltd.

developed, concerns mainly intra-firm matters and has not really contributed to any major management or management theory innovation. Rather, the opposite is the case: the "environment" has been molded into the already well-known management concepts and practices. Also, this literature does not particularly address the very reasons for such environmental management. There is indeed, at times, reference to compliance or regulation. Yet, most of the time this literature considers environmental management to be a good thing in its own right and focuses mainly on how such environmental management has to be put into practice, rather than why it is done to begin with. Also, it does not really address the question of the (strategic) relationship between firms and the environment either. Finally, this literature does not refer to the particular situation of the TNCs. Unfortunately, this still today constitutes the dominant business literature in environmental matters, and, as I will show below, comes now very handy when companies seek to attain competitive advantages over one another thanks to the "environment."

On the other hand, there is a significant amount of more recent literature about "governance" of the environment, also called (global) "environmental governance." Generally, this literature addresses also firms, especially TNCs, and discusses how these TNCs have to come under some sort of (global) "environmental governance regime" (e.g. see Delmas and Young 2009; Levy and Newell 2005). "Governance," in fact, becomes the appropriate concept in a situation where environmental problems are beyond the capabilities of national governments and where TNCs have become significant global economic actors (e.g. see Dunning 1993; Fuchs 2007; Stopford, Strange, and Henley 1991; UNCTAD 1996). Literature has focused here on soft and hard law, i.e., "governance instruments," by which TNCs are engaged in addressing environmental issues (e.g. see Cutler, Haufler, and Porter 1999; Uetting and Clapp 2008). Among the soft law instruments one may mention government-driven guidelines (for example by the OECD or the World Bank), business-initiated principles and guidelines (such as for example the Global Compact, or initiatives by the Business Council for Sustainable Development), industry standards (e.g., ISO standards) or other industry-specific instruments (e.g., certification systems, financing standards, lending standards, and other CSR standards). Among the hard law instruments one must mention multilateral agreements (e.g., the Basle convention on the transboundary movement of hazardous waste), as well as environmental conditionalities built into investment and trade agreements. While this governance literature does indeed talk about the strategic relationship between TNCs and the environment, it contains a strong pro-government bias, as it is dominated by (international) environmental lawyers or political scientists interested in designing policy instruments for "regulating" TNCs. Less legally- and less policy-oriented political scientists, along with scholars holding a more civil-society-oriented perspective, have recently tried to enlarge this approach somewhat by involving civil-society actors (especially non-governmental organizations) into such environmental governance schemes, thus making governance more accountable and more inclusive (e.g. see Adger and Jordan 2009). However, this does not constitute a fundamental change to the above approach, as it generally only ends up in an appeal to governments and intergovernmental actors to take on their responsibility and regulate TNCs, this time in the name of the peoples, i.e. with a stronger legitimacy.

This chapter is *not* about such governance of TNCs in matters of environment. Much has been written about it and probably not much new can be said, except to further complain that most of these governance instruments are ineffective, owing to the lack of political will, lack of corporate leadership, lack of social pressure, lack of legitimacy, and so on. More importantly though, the assumption underlying this approach is outdated, as it is grounded on the idea that TNCs *can* be controlled or "regulated" by nation-states and the international state system. Indeed, all these currently dominant governance approaches do not, in my mind, adequately reflect how the (strategic) relationships between TNCs, the nation-states and their governments, and the "environment" have changed since the 1990s. Such an inadequate understanding will only lead to ineffective (and naive) solutions. This chapter is not about the global ecological crisis either, nor will it discuss whether what TNCs do is good or bad for the environment. Rather, this chapter is about the evolving attitude of TNCs *vis-à-vis* the environment, both in terms of discourse and behavior, with the state and international organizations as the hidden, yet central, mediator. It is grounded in my personal observations of this very evolving attitude. The chapter is therefore structured into four sections: the first two sections describe the change in the very perception TNCs have of the "environment." The other two sections describe TNC behavior in regard to this perception. Overall, I will distinguish two phases in this evolving attitude of TNCs vis-à-vis the environment, namely a first phase (from the 1970s to the late 1990s) where TNCs have come to see (section 1) and to promote (section 3) the environment as a business opportunity and a second phase, where certain TNCs are now seeing (section 2) and possibly using (section 4) the environment as a strategic competitive advantage for themselves.

The "Environment": From Existential Threat to Business Opportunity

In order to understand and appreciate the evolution of the attitude of the TNCs vis-à-vis the environment one has to recall the very beginning of environmental concerns during the late 1960s and throughout the 1970s. At that time, the environment, or rather "ecology" as it was then called, was considered, both by firms and governments, to be a threat to industrial development and therefore to the corporations benefiting from such industrial development. Indeed, environmental problems, at that time, were generally considered to be only a symptom of the much broader problem of so-called "advanced industrial societies" caused by industrial development (e.g. see Commoner 1971; Marcuse 1964). Such industrial development was said to be "unsustainable" (in today's words), not only from an ecological (chemical and nuclear pollution, population growth, resources depletion, biodiversity loss[1]), but also from social (poverty, inequity), cultural (consumerism, loss of cultural diversity, Westernization), and political points of view (militarization, technocracy, exploitation of the Third World). This comprehensive critique of industrial development was mostly carried by social movements (the green movement, the anti-nuclear movement, the counter-cultural movement, the anti-war movement), emerging green parties, and selected academics from both the social and the natural sciences. But this comprehensive critique was rarely directly targeted at TNCs or industries, as it focused on the "industrial system" in general. Nevertheless, some

TNCs (Nestlé, Union Carbide, Exxon, and others), as well as some industries (the nuclear industry, the chemical industry, the oil industry, the arms industry, as well as others) had already then come under direct attack, often as a result of accidents (nuclear, chemical, oil spills), related scandals, or concrete industrial projects.

The 1972 Report to the Club of Rome on the "Limits to Growth" may best capture this broad and rather unspecific critique of industrial development from a scientific point of view, even though the Report does not really address its social, economic, political, and cultural dimensions (Meadows *et al.* 1972). To recall, the report developed 12 scenarios which "illustrate how growth in population and natural resource use interacts with a variety of limits. In reality limits to growth appear in many forms. In our analysis we focused principally on the planet's physical limits, in the form of depletable natural resources and the finite capacity of the earth to absorb emissions from industry and agriculture. In every realistic scenario we found that these limits force an end to physical growth ... sometime during the twenty-first century" (Meadows *et al.* 2004: x–xi). In this chapter, I will not discuss whether the Club of Rome or all the other critiques of industrial development at that time (and today) were (are) right or wrong. There is ample literature on this topic (e.g. Bardi 2011). My argument simply is that, at that time, the very foundations of industrial development, economic growth, capitalistic expansion and more generally postwar Western lifestyle were under attack. Even though this critique, at that time, was not directly targeted at nation-states and TNCs – it was rather addressed to the "industrial system" as such – it nevertheless constituted a serious challenge to the nation-states and their governments which, by their very nature, live off economic growth. It also was an existential threat to firms, and especially TNCs which were emerging precisely at that time, fueled by decolonization and the beginnings of globalization. Indeed, postwar economic growth and industrial development in the United States, Europe, and Japan had led to the gradual emergence of first international, then multinational, and finally transnational corporations, whose growth (and profits) depended (and still depend) precisely on ever more global and ever accelerated industrial development. And even though nation-states and national governments were (and still are) themselves equally dependent upon industrial development and economic growth as are TNCs, they were, at that time, much more responsive to their citizens and to the social movements than is the case today. Emerging TNCs were therefore rightfully worried, during the 1970s, that governments, pressured by their citizens, green parties, and critical scientists, would impose limits to *their* growth. Consequently, governments were seen, at that time, rather as enemies of TNCs and not, as is the case today, as "partners."

The challenge for the emerging TNCs of that time, i.e. mostly European and Western TNCs, was first of all to avert this "environmental" threat. Only approximately twenty years later – i.e. around the time of the UN Conference on Environment and Development in 1992 – the challenge evolved into turning the "environment" also into a business opportunity. In this first section, I will present the conceptual transformations that were operated so that this threat to industrial development, and thus to business and TNCs, could be successfully averted. It must also be said that, in retrospect, these conceptual transformations may well appear more rational than they were in reality at that time. In section 3 I will then describe *how* such conceptual transformations have been operated concretely.

Overall, it can be observed that the "environment as a threat" to industrial development, business, and TNCs has been transformed into an opportunity for further industrial development, for more economic growth, and especially for the continued expansion of TNCs. Instead of talking about "Limits to Growth," we now talk, some decades later, i.e. as of the United Nations Rio+20 Conference on Environment and Development (in short Rio+20), about "green growth." Even though the concept of "green growth" may not yet be the last word in this "conceptual turnaround," it is nevertheless already a significant one. Indeed, the last word may well be "growth *tout court*," as the word "growth" would automatically imply being green. In any case, the challenge is now "growth," not "green." The "environment" is no longer a Limit to Growth, but rather its backdrop to growth, the foil on which growth can now take place. For example, it is no longer the natural resources that are the limit; rather, today, the limits are investments, innovative capacity, efficiency gains, entrepreneurship, stimulus, and, more generally, additional financial resources for further development, as stated in the Rio+20 Final Declaration.

Two conceptual elements are essential to this turnaround: environmental globalization or the "global environment" on the one hand and the concept of "sustainable development" on the other. Parallel to economic globalization during the 1980s also emerged the concepts of "global ecology" and "global change" (e.g. see Malone and Roederer 1985). Global ecology and global change were mainly scientific concepts which drew attention to global bio-geo-chemical cycles – the carbon cycle, climate change more generally, ocean circulation, atmosphere–ocean interactions – which were increasingly affected by industrial activities. Global change became indeed very handy, as it removed the question of the environment from being a local problem and concern against which peoples could protest and for which governments could take action and transformed it into a global, i.e. somewhat remote, problem, by which everybody should be concerned but for which nobody was really responsible. Furthermore, in global ecology there was no longer any real connection between cause and consequence: not only were the consequences of environmental destruction no longer borne by those who caused them, but, moreover, environmental action would not necessarily benefit those who initiated them. It appears therefore only natural that global environmental problems should be addressed by global actors such as global conferences or global companies.

Even though the concept of "sustainable development" emerged independently of, yet after the concept of "global ecology," it nevertheless built on it: sustainability and sustainable development were meant to be globally and not locally defined. Sustainable development, which was to become the key concept of the UN Conference on Environment and Development in 1992 (UNCED or Rio-Conference or Earth Summit), was popularized by the so-called Brundlandt report in preparation of UNCED (World Commission on Environment and Development 1987) and basically allows for multiple trade-offs: trade-offs between the present and the future, trade-offs between the local and the global and, most importantly, trade-offs between economic, social, and environmental sustainability. Even though there remain some abstract limits to growth, these limits are basically removed by the very possibility of "trade-offs," a basically economic concept. For example, development may be unsustainable in the short run if this is to generate the necessary means to create sustainable development in the long run. Also, development may be locally unsustainable if this, instead, contributes to global sustainability, and most importantly social sustainability (i.e. social equity), economic sustainability (i.e. continued growth), and environmental sustainability must be balanced or at least considered together. This very idea of trade-offs implicit in the concept of sustainable development has allowed for the concept's evolution in recent years to the point that, after UNCED, economic growth (i.e. economic sustainability) has become a condition for social sustainability, and both together have now become a condition for environmental sustainability. The argument goes that social inequity, especially poverty, leads to environmental destruction, while the lack of economic growth will hamper scientific and technological innovation, which is a condition for managing the environment sustainably. The final outcome of this conceptual turnaround since the past 1970s is that growth is now good for the environment and that the real challenge is "green growth" and not the environment. In short, the "environment" has been turned from an existential threat to a (green) business opportunity. This is a remarkable change, for which at least certain TNCs can take credit, as will be shown below.

The "Environment" as Competitive Advantage

Since the early 1990s, roughly since UNCED, the environment has no longer been a threat to industrial development and growth, but a business opportunity, especially for TNCs. The environment is now also a global problem, to the solution of which all actors, especially the global actors have to contribute. Simultaneously, TNCs are no longer a threat to the environment, but engines of growth, or even *the* engines of growth, and are such an indispensable partner of governments in the "green economy," another concept actively promoted by the recent Rio+20 Earth Summit. In this section, I will argue that, in a global economy facing global environmental problems, TNCs are now able to present themselves as being *the* natural actors of the green economy. I will then highlight the types of challenges that the green economy faces and I will finally show how TNCs can credibly argue to have the best answers in store to these challenges.

Indeed, once environmental problems have been defined as being global problems of green growth, TNCs naturally acquire a prominent position. This evolution has of course substantially been aided by the fact that, in the meantime, i.e. since the 1970s, TNCs have also substantially grown in size and number, and this in a dialectical relationship with globalization: globalization has promoted TNCs and TNCs, in turn, have promoted globalization (e.g. see Mitriuc, Mitriuc, and Adrusca 2011). Furthermore, TNCs are now the dominant actors of the global economy, as illustrated, for example, by their sheer size and clout in comparison with governments (e.g. see Ietto-Gillies 2005; Korten 1995) or by their significant share in global trade (Lanz and Miroudot 2011). TNCs are also these firms that most have an interest in the liberalization of the global economy, at least in an initial phase when global and especially emerging markets are up for grabs. At the least, they have a vital interest in continued growth and expansion of geographical and product markets. In a global economy, characterized by an international division of labor, by global flows of goods and services, and by global financial flows, TNCs are therefore naturally better positioned than governments to do anything – from promoting growth to "protecting" the environment – as they simultaneously control the(ir) supply chains and have access to the final consumers. While the TNCs do not really control the natural resources they need for their production – there is indeed a certain evolution towards a re-nationalization of natural resources (but which is rather a sign of weakness of national governments than a sign of government power) – they can increasingly play governments (and their resources) against one another, owing to their competitive advantage of mobility over geographical boundedness. In this sense, national governments are now global stakeholders of TNCs, as nicely theorized by (business) stakeholder theory (e.g. see Freeman 2010). In other words, once the "environment" has been defined as a problem of "green growth" and once green growth problems are considered to be global problems, TNCs naturally can legitimately claim to hold the key to addressing these global green growth challenges in the following three key areas that are efficiency, externalities, and resources, in this order of importance, to which I will turn now.

The most important challenge of green growth is clearly efficiency, or resources efficiency: as growth is the overarching goal, being green now means to operate in the most efficient way possible, i.e., to use the environmental resources (energy, minerals, and materials more generally) most efficiently given a certain state of technology. And this is precisely what markets and (global) firms operating in these markets are or should be all about. Therefore, an efficient economy is automatically also a green economy, or the other way round. Green now equals efficiency, and efficiency can be actively promoted by neoliberal economic policies and practices, combined with the active use of the information and communication technologies (e.g. see Rifkin 2011). In short, resources efficiency is not a threat to TNCs, but a great opportunity, as the most efficient companies, i.e. the greenest companies, will also be the most global ones. TNCs can thus legitimately claim to hold the key to global resources efficiency, at least in theory (see below).

The second major challenge of green growth is externalities or more generally market failures. This is indeed the area where governments, international organizations, and corresponding agreements and governance instruments (see above) are normally brought in and could potentially threaten TNCs. Also, framing environmental problems as green growth problems does not necessarily do away with externalities or market failures. TNCs are thus challenged to present themselves as the most appropriate actors for the internalization of environmental externalities. This challenge is in fact twofold: the first challenge is to convince the political actors and the public that all environmental externalities can actually be properly calculated and priced and subsequently internalized into the market. This is done by way of the active promotion of a new discipline called "environmental economics" since the 1990s (e.g. see Hanley *et al.* 1997). While the internalization of the costs of particular pollutants has now been generally accepted by the consumers, the idea that even climate change is simply a market failure and that a proper internalization can remedy this failure was a more difficult challenge. But the recent "Stern review" has achieved precisely that (Stern 2009). From now on, all environmental problems can be defined as market failures, leading to the need to internalize their mitigation costs. The second challenge for TNCs therefore now is to demonstrate that they are the most appropriate actors in doing so, ideally by way of private or self-regulatory instruments. This appears to be a more difficult, but not entirely impossible task (e.g. see Hall and Biersteker 2002). Indeed, TNCs can claim that, by virtue of their global presence, they are ideally placed to define globally valid (private) rules. In addition, by virtue of their direct contact with the consumers, they can also claim that they are better placed to internalize the environmental costs. Ultimately, this will lead to governments and international organizations playing only a subsidiary role as competition regulator, i.e., as an actor that makes sure that the privately negotiated regulations are respected by all the parties so as not to create market distortions.

The third major challenge of green growth are the limited resources, especially the finite natural resources in the areas of energy and materials. The market-based instruments of efficiency and internalization of their growing scarcity cannot be a satisfactory answer, even though these two arguments are often used by both business and academics. TNCs are therefore challenged to present themselves as the most appropriate answer to the resources problem. This is done first by promoting the belief in unlimited scientific and technological progress, meaning that innovation will lead to the development of new technologies, which in turn increase resources efficiency (thus gaining time) or which will allow for the substitution of the scarce by less scarce resources (thus eliminating the problem). On the basis of this belief, the economic argument of the internalization of the costs of developing these new technologies, i.e., the costs of innovation, is then applied: either the citizens (and future consumers) should pay upfront for innovation (by way of subsidies to firms, startups, or research centers) or the consumers should pay ex post by way of intellectual property rights protection, or a combination of both (e.g. see Cullet 2005). In both cases, governments only have a subsidiary role and TNCs can legitimately claim to be in the driver's seat.

In summary, TNCs, by having managed to redefine the environment as being a problem of green growth, can now convincingly offer themselves as the most appropriate answers to the three main challenges that green growth faces, namely efficiency, internalization of externalities, and innovation. This, they can first do because environmental problems have been redefined as market problems, leading automatically to the acceptance of market actors as being more appropriate than non-market actors. But, in addition, TNCs can also claim to be the most appropriate actors by virtue of the fact that they are more global than governments (i.e. not as limited geographically as are nation-states), that they often control the entire value chain, and that they have direct access to the consumers. They can therefore claim to be in the best possible position to internalize the externalities, either by translating consumer demand into upstream supply or by passing internalized costs directly onto the consumers (without government interference). A similar argument goes for innovation: not only are TNCs best positioned to impose innovations along the value chain, but moreover they also have the financial clout to invest in innovations and, again, to internalize these costs and distribute them along the value chain. There remains one little problem, as the literature generally states, that big companies are less innovative than small and medium-sized companies, or start-ups for that matter. But this is rather an organizational issue, as TNCs can organize for innovation, for example by way of spin-offs, innovation eco-systems, open innovation, and others more.

To conclude, it is obvious that, once environmental issues have been redefined as a problem of green growth, TNCs are the natural answer to the environmental challenges: they are the global actors, not only economically but also politically, and they have the financial power to promote green growth. Once one has accepted green growth as the answer, it would only be logical to recognize the driving role of the TNCs and the subsidiary role of governments (e.g. by way of enforcing competition rules, of guaranteeing private environmental regulations, of guaranteeing intellectual property rights, and perhaps of attributing subsidies for innovation). Any other position would indeed be intellectually incoherent. Yet, most of the scholars, though they have accepted or even embraced the discourse of green growth as resulting from the process of international negotiations (see below), continue to think that governments, and not TNCs, should be in charge of green growth. This is for example the case when they propose a new international environmental organization, though the World Trade Organization would already be the logical liberal solution to global green growth (e.g. see Pardee Center Task Force Report 2011).

The Triumph of TNCs in Global Environmental Governance

In this section, I will show that the concept of green growth, as it is has come out of the Rio+20 Earth Summit (2012) is indeed the triumph of the TNCs or, rather, the result of their successful lobbying. In other words, during international negotiations since the 1970s, TNCs have managed to transform the environment, which initially was a threat, into a business growth opportunity. In retrospect, this transformation may well appear as an ex post rationalization of a much less planned process. Yet, the results are nevertheless there: the "limits to growth" have first been replaced by "sustainable development" and have now been transformed into "green growth." Concretely, such lobbying can be analyzed as a three-pronged approach or strategy, namely a strategy vis-à-vis the United Nations system, a strategy vis-à-vis non-state actors, especially non-governmental organizations (NGOs), and a strategy vis-à-vis nation-states.

To recall, the original United Nations Conference on the Human Environment in Stockholm in 1972 was a threat to the then emerging TNCs, which were not organized to face it. There was a conflict between the optimists in favor of development, mainly embodied by developing countries (and not by TNCs) and the pessimists or rather conservationists, embodied by the social movements of that time and some rising Northern NGOs. But one can say that already at that time the optimists somewhat had the upper hand, though with little active TNC support. TNCs became really active in the preparation for the follow-up UN Conference on Environment and Development (UNCED), to be held in 1992 in Rio. They used the preparatory process (Prepcoms) in a systematic way to introduce their positions, namely by actively promoting the concept of "sustainable development" as discussed above (e.g. see Chatterjee and Finger 1994). A second success, beyond having the concept of sustainable development widely accepted, is the isolation of the two most threatening issues which the concept of sustainable development was actually not able to tackle, namely the issue of climate change and the issue of biodiversity loss. Both were transferred to other arenas, namely respectively to a biodiversity and a climate change conventions building process (both of which led nowhere). A third success is the removal of TNCs as being a problem. This was done by, among other things, successful lobbying for the elimination of the UN Center on Transnational Corporations (UNCTC) (e.g. see Greer and Bruno 1997).

UNCTC was somewhat "replaced" by the TNCs' (self-)organization in the form of the World Business Council for Sustainable Development (WBCSD). Indeed, parallel to the dismantling of the UNCTC, and especially parallel to the preparation of the Earth Summit, this powerful new organization emerged (WBCSD 2006) as a result of an initiative taken by the International Chamber of Commerce (ICC): "On a warm Spring night in 1990 ... more than 140 business leaders, CEOs and diplomats dined ... to discuss how business might join the global conversation around spearheading economic progress while safeguarding the environment" (WBCSD 2006: 5). Among the participants was also a certain Maurice Strong (see below). Members of the WBCSD were all the big TNCs of that time, covering mining, oil, paper, chemical, energy, agriculture, water, automotive, telecom, aluminum, cement, steel, utilities, and other industries. Stephan Schmidheiny, a Swiss industrialist and president of the WBCSD, wrote its "manifesto," which came out just in time for the Rio 1992 Summit (e.g. see Schmidheiny 1992). Writing up the successful lobbying of the TNCs in the preparation of the Rio 1992 Summit would fill a book in itself and will have to be done later on. Nevertheless, the WBCSD and the Secretariat preparing UNCED were located at the same premises in Geneva (where the author of this chapter also worked at that time) and that the placement of Maurice Strong, a powerful friend of the WBCSD, as Secretary General of UNCED was in itself a success for the TNCs (see Strong's autobiography: Strong 2000).

After having successfully promoted the confusing concept of sustainable development (see section 1) in Rio in 1992, Rio+10, i.e., the so-called Johannesburg Summit of 2002, further cements the key role of the TNCs. TNCs now presented themselves as the most appropriate, if not the only, actors to be able to solve the environmental problems. Business, they said, had now taken seriously the message of the environmental crisis, i.e., had become "environmentally responsible," and now offered concrete solutions, namely in the form of green technologies and green market instruments. Also, the concept of sustainable development was being redefined in 2002 as "sustainable economic growth" (a precursor of "green growth"), which was said to be necessary so that society and business can pay for environmental mitigation efforts. In other words, development, which generates environmental destruction, must be so important that it can pay for repairing the destruction it has generated. Finally, Rio+20, recently held again in Rio de Janeiro, imposes the concept of "green growth" and definitely asserts the TNCs as *the* relevant environmental actors. It must also be noted that, besides climate change and biodiversity, natural resources have now also been eliminated from the international fora, and so population growth, social justice, and the loss of cultural diversity. All this leads to defining the environment as an almost technical problem of further economic growth, now called green growth. This is the very success of the TNCs by way of all these international conferences. The United Nations, and especially the UN conferences on the environment, have served as the main platform to achieve this success. But, as mentioned above, there were other parallel platforms, which were also instrumental in promoting TNCs and their views. The WBCSD has already been referred to, but one should also mention the World Industry Council on the Environment, as well as the so-called Global Compact, a platform convened by the then Secretary General Kofi Annan, where TNCs and the United Nations could strategize together. Needless to say that the Global Compact's "Rio+20 Corporate Sustainability

Forum," lasting five days, has become more important an event than the Rio+20 Summit itself.

A second, yet parallel approach or strategy of the TNCs pertains to *non-state actors*, especially NGOs. The process by which NGOs, notably big environmental NGOs such as the International Union for the Conservation of Nature (IUCN), but also the World Wide Fund for Nature (WWF), as well as big US NGOs, have gradually aligned with TNC arguments has already been well documented (Princen and Finger 1994). Indeed, after the Stockholm Conference of 1972 TNCs have gradually warmed up to the idea of collaborating with environmental NGOs to the point that, by now, many of these global NGOs are not only financed by the TNCs, but have even become spokespersons for the TNCs and their arguments (e.g. see Lyon 2010). Not surprisingly then, the original business organizations, such as the WBCSD, have recently decreased in importance. It is no exaggeration to say that the big environmental NGOs, notably IUCN and WWF, are today fully aligned with TNCs to the point that they actually do the preparatory work for the TNCs, namely in the areas of environmental standardization, production of environmental codes of conduct, and others more (see below). These are indeed areas where environmental NGOs are much more credible than TNCs ever could be.

The third approach or strategy of TNCs is vis-à-vis nation-states or governments. More than NGOs, nation-states actually turn out to be the most natural partners when it comes to transforming the environmental threat into an economic growth opportunity. Indeed, nation-states are naturally inclined towards economic growth, as nation-states are by their very nature "development agencies," albeit a development agency that is limited to their national territory. It is therefore easy (too easy actually; see below) for TNCs to convince governments to promote green growth by creating appropriate market conditions and suitable rules and by supporting their green innovation efforts financially. Suffice for TNCs to explain to governments that they are significant employers and that they can, by their location decisions and their investments, not only create jobs, but moreover help countries and governments gain competitive advantages in the global green economy. The example of so-called "clean technologies" is a good case in point. In other words, when it comes to promoting green growth, TNCs and governments are totally aligned. Such alignment of course again comes in handy in the international arena when promoting a global green economy.

From "Regulating" TNCs to "Regulating TNCs"

TNCs have successfully lobbied, mainly on the international arena, and positioned themselves as the relevant actors of green growth, a concept that the international organizations, environmental NGOs, and governments have embraced as the appropriate answer to (global) environmental problems. In doing so, the latter have also relegated themselves to a subsidiary or supporting role for TNCs, in line, by the way, with broad neo liberal market principles. In this section, I will discuss whether the TNCs are likely to live up to the challenge of delivering the green growth they are promising. This may well not be the case, as I will argue here, since TNCs may be tempted to abuse the powerful position they are increasingly in: rather than delivering the green growth they have been promising and lobbying for, TNCs may well be tempted to use the "environment" in order to seek competitive strategic advantages over one another. I will show that this could be done thanks to three "tools" that only TNCs have at their disposal, namely the control over global supply chains, the control of industry structure, and the control over innovation.

TNCs control their global supply chains. They also control a significant portion of global trade. TNCs therefore have it in their hands to promote an efficient and green global economy. They can – or cannot – produce their goods in these countries where the strictest environmental standards apply. They can – or cannot – impose the strictest environmental standards all along their supply chain and force their suppliers to comply. They have it in their hands to make governments oppose strict environmental standards (i.e., internalization measures for externalities) or, in the opposite, make governments impose strict environmental standards also to their competitors. Depending on their perceived competitive advantage and strategic positioning, they will do either (or a mix of both). For example, TNCs can derive a strong competitive advantage from strict rules codified in ISO 14000 standards and enforced by the World Trade Organization if they can meet them and their competitors cannot (Finger and Tamiotti 1999). Inversely, TNCs can derive competitive advantage from environmental dumping. In both cases, this is made possible by the power of the TNCs, especially their power over governments and international organizations. In short, the environment is, just like wages or access to financing, a source of competitive advantage among TNCs. It cannot be excluded that TNCs will use this tempting tool, now that they are well positioned to do so.

The same considerations apply to industry structure more generally: besides being able to derive a competitive advantage from greening – or not – the supply chain, TNCs can also derive competitive advantage in regard to market entry or foreclosure by way of environmental conditionalities. Again, governments and international organizations are instrumental in this matter: they can help set environmental standards in a way that may make market entry difficult if not impede it altogether or, on the other hand, in a way that allows for easy market entry. An example here is catalytic converters for cars or incandescent lightbulbs which can either favor the national car industry or instead promote imports. A similar consideration goes for substitutes, where governments can again favor or impede substitutes. An example here is the recognition, or not of the electronic signature, thus favoring, or not, e-substitution of mail. TNCs can significantly influence industry structure by virtue of their sheer power over governments. This can be important at least in countries with a strong domestic market, thus helping TNCs gain competitive advantage in a particular industry globally.

The third dimension where TNCs can use the "environment" for their own competitive advantage is state aid or subsidies: even though neoliberal economic theory generally considers state aid as favoring inefficiencies, TNCs especially, by virtue of their power and their innovation capacity, are certainly able to convince governments to subsidize green innovation projects or simply green products, sometimes also called "green stimulus." Indeed, in a green growth economy, government subsidies will now go to firms directly. TNCs may well be tempted to leverage such subsidies, even though they are market distorting and overall inefficient.

Controlling state aid for green innovation, environmental substitutes, green market entry and more generally the environmental dimensions of the supply chain could well be abused by TNCs for their own competitive advantages. Yet, if it appeared that TNCs were indeed using the "environment" to distort markets, to collect undue subsidies, to foreclose competitors, to create monopolies, to cartelize, and so on, rather than to promote green growth, this would seriously reduce their credibility. At the least, it would discredit their environmental efforts since the 1990s. It would also diminish the credibility of environmental NGOs, international organizations, and governments, which, over these years, have become the TNCs' partners. Of course, the situation would be even worse if green growth turned out *not* to be the answer to the global ecological crisis.

Conclusion

In this chapter I have shown how TNCs have successfully managed to change the overall discourse about the environment: from being a threat to their development, the environment has now not only become the opportunity for green growth, it has moreover legitimized TNCs as *the* actors for green growth. This has been achieved thanks to their active lobbying of the international organizations, especially the various United Nations' Conferences on Environment and Development, national governments, and NGOs. This development and fact should be seen as a challenge to the currently still prevailing governance theory I have presented in the introduction. As a matter of fact, governments and international organizations, no matter how legitimate and citizen-backed, no longer do regulate TNCs in environmental matters. Rather, TNCs are setting the rules of the game (by which they are subsequently officially regulated), international organizations offer the platform for this game, environmental NGOs do the preparatory work, and governments ease the process. In my opinion, governance theory is not reformable so as to accommodate this situation, even though academics – notably political scientists, political economists, lawyers, and other regulatory specialists – will still go on for a long time, given the institutionalization of their respective disciplines, but also given the fact that the (global environmental) governance discourse actually serves the TNCs. It indeed allows them to distract the attention from themselves, to direct the social movements' attention and activities towards the international political arena and governments more generally, and to shift the blame on politicians in case of lack of success or failure.

Increasingly the concept of "stakeholder" is being used in global environmental matters. For example, the Global Compact's Rio+20 Corporate Sustainability Forum, i.e. the joint UN-TNC partnership mentioned above, defines its participants as stakeholders, which can range from governments to businesses to cities to NGOs and many others more. Stakeholder theory may thus be a more realistic alternative: indeed, in this theory stakeholders are actors (i.e. governments, international organizations, unions, NGOs, local communities, media, etc.) which have a stake in a given business (firm) or business activity. Stakeholder theory contributes to identifying these business relevant actors (e.g. stakeholders), to defining the exact stakes these actors have in the business or the business activity (in our case environmental issues), and ultimately to managing them to the benefit of the firm. It places firms – i.e. TNCs – at the center, and not governments, as is the case with governance theory. While stakeholder theory certainly offers a more realistic description of the relationship between TNCs and all other actors, especially governments and international organizations, it still does not address the challenge I have identified in the last section of this chapter: indeed, once TNCs are the globally dominant actors in environmental (and other matters), how can they be prevented from using the "environment" for their own competitive advantage, rather than using their power and their resources for addressing the global ecological crisis?

Note

1   Climate change was not yet a topic at that time.

References

Adger, Neil, and Jordan, Andrew, eds. 2009. *Governing Sustainability*. Cambridge: Cambridge University Press.

Bardi, Ugo. 2011. *The Limits to Growth Revisited*. New York: Springer.

Bennett, Steven J. 1991. *Ecopreneuring*. New York: John Wiley and Sons.

Bennis, Warren, Parikh, Jagdish, and Lessem, Ronnie. 1994. *Beyond Leadership: Balancing Economics, Ethics and Ecology*. London: Blackwell.

Chatterjee, Pratap and Finger, Matthias. 1994. *The Earth Brokers. Power, Politics, and Development*. London: Routledge.

Commoner, Barry. 1971. *The Closing Circle: Nature, Man, and Technology*. New York: Alfred J. Knopf.

Cullet, Philippe. 2005. *Intellectual Property Protection and Sustainable Development*. New Delhi: LexisNexis Butterworths.

Cutler, Claire A., Haufler, Virginia, and Porter, Tony. 1999. *Private Authorities and International Affairs*. Albany: SUNY.

Delmas, Magali and Young, Oran. 2009. *Governance for the Environment: New Perspectives*. Cambridge: Cambridge University Press.

Dunning, John. 1993. *The Globalization of Business*. London: Routledge.

Finger, Matthias and Tamiotti, Ludivine. 1999. "New Global Regulatory Mechanisms and the Environment: The Emerging Linkage Between the WTO and the ISO." *IDS (Institute for Development Studies) Bulletin*, 30 (3): 8–15.

Freeman, R. Edward. 2010. *Strategic Management: A Stakeholder Approach*. Cambridge: Cambridge University Press.

Fuchs, Doris. 2007. *Business Power in Global Governance*. Boulder: Lynne Rienner.

Greer, Jed and Bruno, Kenny. 1997. *Greenwash: The Reality behind Corporate Environmentalism*. Kuala Lumpur: Third World Network.

Hall, Rodney Bruce and Biersteker, Thomas J., eds. 2002. *The Emergence of Private Authority in Global Governance*. Cambridge: Cambridge University Press.

Hanley, Nick, Shogren, Jason, and White, Ben. 1997. *Environmental Economics in Theory and Practice*. New York: Palgrave Macmillan.

Ietto-Gillies, Grazia. 2005. *Transnational Corporations and International Production*. Cheltenham: Edward Elgar.

Korten, David. 1995. *When Corporations Rule the World*. West Hartford: Kumarian Press.

Lanz, Rainer and Miroudot, Sébastien. 2011. *Intra-Firm Trade: Patterns, Determinants, and Policy Implications*. Paris: OECD.

Levy, David and Newell, Peter, eds. 2005. *The Business of Global Environmental Governance*. Cambridge: MIT Press.

Lyon, Thomas. 2010. *Good Cop/Bad Cop: Environmental NGOs and Their Strategies towards Business*. London: Earthscan.

Malone, Thomas and Roederer, Juan. 1985. *Global Change*. Cambridge MA: ICSU Press.

Marcuse, Herbert. 1964. *One-Dimensional Man: Studies in the Ideology of Advanced Industrial Society*. Boston: Beacon Press.

Meadows, Donella, Meadows, Dennis, Randers, Joergen, and Behrens, William. 1972. *The Limits to Growth*. New York: Universe Books.

Meadows, Donella, Randers, Joergen, and Meadows, Dennis. 2004. *Limits to Growth: The 30-Year Update*. London: Earthscan.

Mitriuc, Dan, Mitriuc, Valentin, and Diana Andrusca. 2011. *The Role of Transnational Corporations in Economic Globalization: Economy and Globalization*. Lambert Academic Publishing.

Pardee Center Task Force Report. 2011. *Beyond Rio+20: Governance for a Green Economy*. Boston University: Frederick S. Pardee Center for the Study of the Longer-Range Future.

Piasecki, Bruce W. 1995. *Corporate Environmental Strategy: The Avalanche of Change since Bhopal*. New York: John Wiley and Sons.

Prakash, Aseem. 2000. *Greening the Firm: The Politics of Corporate Environmentalism*. Cambridge: Cambridge University Press.

Princen, Thomas and Finger, Matthias. 1994. *Environmental NGOs in World Politics: Linking the Global and the Local*. London: Routledge.

Rifkin, Jeremy. 2011. *The Third Industrial Revolution: How Lateral Power Is Transforming Energy, the Economy and the World*. New York: Palgrave Macmillan.

Schmidheiny, Stephan. 1992. *Changing Course*. Cambridge, MA: MIT Press.

Stead, Jean Garner and Stead, W. Edward. 2009. *Management for a Small Planet*. New York: M.E. Sharpe.

Stern, Nicholas. 2009. *The Global Deal: Climate Change and the Creation of a New Era of Progress and Prosperity*. New York: Public Affairs Books.

Stopford, John, Strange, Susan, and Henley, John S. 1991. *Rival States, Rival Firms*. Cambridge: Cambridge University Press.

Strong, Maurice. 2000. *Where on Earth Are We Going?* New York: Texere.

Uetting, Peter and Clapp, Jennifer, eds. 2008. *Corporate Accountability and Sustainable Development*. Oxford: Oxford University Press.

UNCTAD. 1996. *Transnational Corporations and World Development*. London: ITBP.

WBCSD. 2006. *Catalyzing change: A Short History of the WBCSD*. Geneva: WBCSD.

Welford, Richard. 1996. *Corporate Environmental Management: Systems and Strategies*. London: Earthscan.

World Commission on Environment and Development. 1987. *Our Common Future*. Oxford: Oxford University Press.

Chapter 18

Global Companies, the Bretton Woods Institutions, and Global Inequality

Pamela Blackmon

Introduction

In order for global companies to be economically successful they must be able to export their goods. There are at least three interrelated entities that directly or indirectly support firms in this goal. First, the export of goods is generally supported by the domestic government in which they are located. This is because international trade is crucial to the viability of export industries and to the economic viability of most states today (Evans and Oye 2001). Second, national Export Credit Agencies (ECAs) are set up by governments in order to support exports to international markets by providing guarantees or insurance for the private-sector financing of the export contract (Gianturco 2001). Thus, global companies that are involved in international trade rely heavily on ECAs. One estimate is that ECAs finance about one out of every eight dollars of world trade (Gianturco 2001: 1). ECAs often operate to support exports to developing country markets in which commercial bank financing is unavailable or too expensive due to unacceptable political and economic risks that the export contract will not be paid (Stephens 1999). Political or sovereign risk is the risk of nonpayment on an export contract by the buyer's government. Commercial or non-sovereign risk is the risk of nonpayment on an export contract by a private buyer or commercial bank (Stephens 1999: 76, 102). The third entity that supports firms indirectly in their goal of continued high exports is the Bretton Woods Institutions of the International Monetary Fund (IMF) and the World Bank (Rieffel 2003).

The IMF, more specifically, helps firms in this regard because they consistently encourages (often through structural adjustment criteria) their member countries to continue with international trade even if the country is having balance-of-payments problems. In fact, the IMF was set up originally in 1945 with the goal of providing loans to countries having balance-of-payments difficulties so that they would not set

The Handbook of Global Companies, First Edition. Edited by John Mikler.
© 2013 John Wiley & Sons, Ltd. Published 2013 by John Wiley & Sons, Ltd.

up trade barriers or resort to beggar-thy-neighbor trade distorting policies (Crockett 1992; Blackmon 2008; 2010). The Bretton Woods Institutions also provide direct support to programs encouraging national and regional trade in developing countries. For example, the World Bank's Multilateral Investment Guarantee Agency (MIGA) was established in 1988 to "promote foreign direct investment in emerging market economies by offering political risk insurance (guarantees) to investors and lenders" (Gilman and Wang 2003: 11).

This chapter will provide evidence to illustrate that this triangular support for exports between governments, their national ECAs, and the Bretton Woods Institutions has resulted in worsening the debt situation of developing countries. To begin with, some of the developing country debt is comprised of loans and guarantees from export credit agencies whose activities are largely backed and guaranteed by the governments of those respective agencies (Birdsall, Williamson, and Deese 2002: 35; Rieffel 2003: 35). Indeed, in 1996, the IMF estimated that more than 24% of the indebtedness of developing and transition countries was held by ECAs (IMF 1998: 11). In 1999, about 50% of the debt of the Heavily Indebted Poor Countries (HIPCs) was owed to bilateral creditors (although some was concessional) but almost all of the 13% of private creditor debt was also backed by a sovereign guarantee of an ECA (Birdsall, Williamson, and Deese 2002: 8). The HIPC countries are a group of countries, most of them in sub-Saharan Africa, identified by the IMF and World Bank as being extremely poor and to be having the most difficulty in improving their external debt situation (Gamarra, Pollock, and Primo Braga 2009: 25). High debt levels are problematic for alleviating poverty in developing countries because research has shown that debt displaces social expenditure spending and that it specifically impacts health expenditure (Lora and Olivera 2006: 6). Much of this bilateral public-sector debt of developing countries is then rescheduled at various time periods through the Paris Club negotiations. The Paris Club is an informal group of creditor governments (there is no fixed membership) known as such because its representatives meet in Paris, France to reschedule the bilateral debts of countries with heavy debt burdens (Rieffel 1985; Stephens 1999). The problem is that most of these creditor countries are members of the Paris Club and thus have a "substantial" amount of control over the negotiations of debt that many of their ECAs extended to these debtor countries (Rieffel 2003: 85, 86; Callaghy 2010: 162).

For example, in most debt restructuring arrangements the debt has been consolidated among the "Paris Club" of creditor countries thus allowing for consolidation of the entire stock of debt (Gamarra, Pollock, and Primo Braga 2009: 12–13). Since structural adjustment policies devised by the IMF and World Bank are required by Paris Club creditors in order for loan re-structuring of the external debt of developing countries, what role do the IMF and World Bank play in assuring that these debts are repaid? Previous research has shown that the adjustment policies of the Fund and the Bank have worsened the poverty and inequality levels for many people in developing countries (Stewart 1995; Chossukovsky 1997; Wade 2004; Woods 2006). This debt restructuring process seems to perpetuate the debt cycle for developing countries since after old loans are restructured, they can then be eligible for new export credit loans. Specifically, this process is known as the "subordination strategy" in which old loans are subordinated to new credits in order to keep the flow of new credits in the form of guarantees or insurance for exports continuing, thus allowing many of these countries to continue to be eligible for additional export loans (Kuhn 1994: 24). These types of financing arrangements are an important way that large and small companies are able to export their goods abroad, but are the interests of these firms superseding what is best for the developing countries?

The purpose of this chapter is to examine how global companies' exports are facilitated by ECAs and to show how the interests of the IMF and its powerful member states converge in Paris Club debt rescheduling. The chapter will be organized as follows. First, the role of official ECAs in supporting financing to developing countries will be reviewed. This section will also explain the degree to which global companies rely on ECA financing in order to export their goods. Next, the share of the external debt of developing countries that is comprised of export credits will be reviewed. The third section will list specific firms that use ECAs including the types of projects that are financed, their costs, and the various markets for their exports. The fourth section of the chapter provides a case study of the rescheduling of Ecuador's debt in 2003 in order to illustrate the interplay of factors responsible for debt, re-scheduled debt, and new export credits.

Official Export Credit Agencies

One of the primary ways that firms are able to export their products to developing and transition countries is through trade financing provided by ECAs. The first governmental export credit agency was the Export Credits Guarantee Department (ECGD) of the United Kingdom, established in 1919 (Stephens 1999: 1). The US Export-Import Bank was established in 1933, and many more agencies were established after World War II and in the 1990s (Stephens 1999; Gianturco 2001). In fact, all member states of the OECD have ECAs, in addition to non-member states such as Brazil, Russia, India, and China (also known as the BRICs). Governments view the establishment of an ECA as a way to increase their country's exports, which has become even more important in the era of increasing globalized trade. In addition, governments can boast that they are creating jobs through the financing support provided by their ECAs (US Ex-Im Bank Annual Report 2004: 3). Firms benefit from ECA activity since these financial arrangements allow them to increase their business opportunities to regions that otherwise would have been lost due to unacceptable risk (Blackmon 2011).

ECA financing for developing and transition economies is deemed to be necessary by firms for two reasons. First, while these regions have the greatest potential for increased trade activity, they also entail greater risks of non-payment for exporting firms to do business in those countries. The second reason that ECA financing is necessary is because private-sector finance is either unavailable or too expensive especially for medium- or longer-term financing arrangements. Most ECA credit activity has been for medium-term financing for capital goods; and longer-term financing for investment and infrastructure related projects (Kuhn, Horvath, and Jarvis 1995: 5, 14). There is greater risk in insuring these projects of a longer-term nature such as large infrastructure and capital goods projects, investments of sunk capital in which losses would be difficult to recover (Moran 1999; 2006).

Export industries prefer ECA insurance because commercial banks covering the risks for these types of projects would charge much higher interest rates. Thus, exporters turn to ECAs when private-sector insurance is either more expensive or not available (Kuhn *et al.* 1995: 12, 14). Short-term trade credits (two years or less) are seen as less risky; thus they are more often covered by private finance. Short-term credits have also been exempted from debt rescheduling in the past, whereas longer-term debt has been subject to rescheduling (Cline 2005: 20).

ECAs operate by provide financing through direct lending, or through insurance, or guarantees of loans made through private-sector finance designed to reduce the risk of nonpayment on exports incurred by domestic export industries. The risk of nonpayment due to the buyer's government is under the category of political (or sovereign) risk that ECAs ensure against; specifically these are actions by a government that include civil war, acts of war, or preventing the transfer of payments. The second category of risk that ECAs ensure against is commercial (or non-sovereign) risk which is the risk of nonpayment by a private buyer, commercial bank, or public buyer; specifically insolvency, bankruptcy, or nonpayment (Stephens 1999: 76, 106). Official or governmental ECAs can insure against political and commercial risks; but only political risk covered under loans to a sovereign government would fall under the category of public or bilateral debt.

Bilateral debt in the context of the Paris Club is defined as "debt between an individual (normally public or sovereign) debtor and a sovereign creditor. Creditors are thus governments or export agencies, and the governments of the debtor countries bear responsibility for repayment of the rescheduled debts" (Stephens 1999: 72). According to the Paris Club website, the category of debt classified as bilateral debt includes "[c]laims granted by States (governments or their appropriate institutions, especially export credit agencies)" (Paris Club 2010). ECAs can be public-sector or government entities or they can be private-sector insurers supported by official guarantees. This chapter will focus on public or official debt but it should be kept in mind that if export credits were extended by a private entity, but guaranteed or assumed by a debtor government, that that debt would also qualify for a debt rescheduling agreement (Rieffel 1985: 2; Stephens 1999: 42).

There are a few explanations as to why such little attention is paid to ECAs and to the debt levels that developing and transition countries incur through their activities. First, not much is written about ECAs and their activity in trade finance in general. Gianturco (2001: 1) begins his book with the statement, "The 'unsung giants' of international finance are the world's export credit agencies (ECAs) – highly specialized financial institutions that currently cover about $800 billion of exports each year but rarely receive the attention of the press or of the average citizen." Second and related to the latter, there is little written about how trade finance is carried out as compared to private financing. Private financing of exports is more commonplace than official agency trade financing and the former had become more prevalent than public or government financing for developing countries especially during the 1990s when private finance was abundant (Borensztein, Yeyati, and Panizza 2006: 112). The following section provides an overview of the breakdown of debt by creditor from lower middle-income countries in order to illustrate the amount of debt held by ECAs.

The World Bank classifies total external debt stocks as the sum of public and publicly guaranteed debt; private non-guaranteed long-term debt; short-term debt and the use of IMF credit (Global Development Finance database). For the lower middle-income countries ($1,006 to $3,975 Gross National Income (GNI) per capita), high levels of external debt are comprised of public and publicly guaranteed debt which is defined as "long-term external obligations of public debtors, including the national government, political subdivisions (or an agency of either), and autonomous public bodies, and external obligations of private debtors that are guaranteed for repayment by a public entity." This debt indicator comprises some of the debt owed to public ECAs because it includes debt from the national government and the private debt that is guaranteed for repayment. This debt indicator is also the highest for the years 1980–2010 (in five-year intervals) when compared to bilateral concessional, multilateral, and multilateral concessional for the same timeframe (Global Development Finance database). The total external debt stocks for these countries using the previous data range was 3.6 trillion; the composition of public and publicly guaranteed debt was 2.4 trillion comprising almost 67% of total external debt stocks (Global Development Finance database). In addition, for this group of countries this debt indicator is much larger than the debt that is comprised of private nonguaranteed long-term debt (654 billion; about 17% of total external debt stocks) defined as "long-term external obligations of private debtors that are not guaranteed for repayment by a public entity." In other words, this is debt held by private creditors (banks) that is long term and not guaranteed by an ECA. The composition of short-term debt is defined as "debt that has an original maturity of one year or less. Available data permit no distinction between public and private nonguaranteed short-term debt." If the short-term debt is public, then it would be guaranteed by an ECA.

While there is no distinct debt indicator representing loans from official ECAs, the previous data illustrate that debt levels comprised of ECAs have represented a substantial part of the debt of developing economies. The following section details how global companies use export credit agencies to help them with their exports. The section will also illustrate how ECAs are involved in the extension of export credits to developing countries, how this debt is then rescheduled through the Paris Club, followed by the extension of new export credits from ECAs.

Firms That Use ECAs

Complete publicly available data on ECAs is extremely difficult to find. One US Ex-Im Bank official explained that European ECAs (Germany, France, Italy) want a high level of secrecy about their data and therefore make very few public documents available (Author interview, Ex-Im Bank official, May 7, 2012). Non-OECD ECAs operate with an even higher level of secrecy and they do not have to follow certain "Arrangement" rules on officially supported export credits since they are not part of the OECD (Moravcsik 1989; Blackmon 2012). The US Ex-Im Bank is set up differently in this aspect, in that as part of its charter, it is mandated to submit a report on the competitiveness of its export financing services annually to Congress (US Ex-Im Bank Competitiveness Reports, any year, introductory material). The ECAs of the United Kingdom (the ECGD) and Canada (EDC) provide some comparable firm-level data but much of the detailed data on business activity supported by ECAs contained in the US Ex-Im Bank Competitiveness Reports is not found in other ECA reports.

The US Ex-Im Bank also publishes annual reports that include data on virtually all of their activities. For example, there is data on the types of authorizations by market (country) and the amount of loans, guarantees, and insurance or exposure to each country. For each fiscal year, if a country receives new loans or new long-term guarantees, the amount is provided as well as information on the obligor, guarantor, and principal supplier (the firm) for the project. There is also information on "Paris Club Bilateral Agreements" including countries to which debt relief and/or debt rescheduling was provided. In FY 2004, the US Ex-Im Bank provided debt relief and/or debt rescheduling to 15 countries; in FY 2003 debt relief and/or debt rescheduling was provided to 13 countries (US Ex-Im Bank 2004 Annual Report, 42). Countries that had debt rescheduled in FY 2003 included Cote d'Ivoire ($26,715), DRC (Zaire) ($597,227), Indonesia ($259,329), Macedonia ($10,523), Pakistan ($220,053), and Yugoslavia ($274,014). Four of those six countries – DRC (Zaire), Indonesia, Pakistan, and Yugoslavia – also had debt rescheduled in FY 2004 (US Ex-Im Bank 2004 Annual Report, 42).

However, what is surprising is that some of the countries that had debt rescheduled in FY 2003 or FY 2004 also had new long-term guarantees, or new loans in FY 2004 and 2005 from the US Ex-Im Bank. Loan guarantees basically guarantee to the private lender that the Ex-Im Bank will pay the lender the outstanding principal and interest on the loan if the borrower defaults (US Ex-Im Bank Annual Report 2004: 35). This type of guarantee from an official creditor-country agency also means that the credit would be dealt with through Paris Club negotiations (Rieffel 1985: 2). This is problematic for these countries because it sets up a revolving door of rescheduled debt, new debt, and rescheduled debt again.

For example, Nigeria had $915,934,000 in debt rescheduled in FY 2004, yet benefited from a long-term guarantee in FY 2004 of over $18 million in order for Nortel Networks Inc. to provide Bourdex Telecommunications with telecommunications equipment (US Ex-Im Bank Annual Report 2004: 31). Nigeria also benefited from a long-term guarantee in FY 2005 of $13,488 in order for HSBC Bank PLC to authorize a credit increase for equipment supply and installation (US Ex-Im Bank Annual Report 2005: 31).[1] Pakistan had $220,053,000 in debt rescheduled in FY 2003, yet benefited from a long-term guarantee in FY 2004 of $3,772,737, in order to buy commercial aircraft from the Boeing Co.; Pakistan subsequently had $2,413,000 in debt rescheduled that same year (US Ex-Im Bank Annual Report 2004: 42). Quiport, a firm in Ecuador was provided a loan for $70 million from the US Ex-Im Bank so that the firm could have Caterpillar Inc. construct a new international airport in FY 2004 (US Ex-Im Bank Annual Report 2004: 28). Ecuador then had $2,591,000 debt rescheduled under Paris Club Bilateral Agreements in FY 2005 (US Ex-Im Bank Annual Report 2005: 42). New export credits or even loans in one case, are being extended by the US Ex-Im Bank seemingly without regard to the financial difficulties that these countries are having in paying off these debts. Global companies certainly seem to be benefiting from these export contracts, especially if it is the case that these exports would have been otherwise forgone without the US Ex-Im Bank financing. The following section will explain the terms of the export contract between US companies and the US Ex-Im Bank.

The listing of principal suppliers or firms in the Ex-Im Bank publications includes large multinational firms such as Boeing, General Electric, General Motors, Nortel,

Lucent Technologies, Caterpillar, Motorola Inc., and ABB Lummus Global. These represent very large well funded multinational firms although in its mandate the US Ex-Im Bank is only authorized to support US exports and/or provide funding to foreign entities in order for them to purchase US exports. There are various reasons as to why US firms use Ex-Im Bank financing. In general, firms turn to ECAs when private-sector finance is either unavailable or is too expensive. It is likely that for many firms the high cost of private-sector finance may make the export deal not worth the expense. Indeed, in a series of interviews that I conducted in 2003 with US business representatives that used US Ex-Im Bank financing for exports to two former Soviet Union republics, they stated categorically that Ex-Im Bank financing was the deciding factor in whether or not the business transaction would be concluded (Blackmon 2011: 84–88). That is not to say that country risk criteria were not factored into the business decision in some cases, but representatives were aware that the Ex-Im Bank conducts its own risk analysis and it was presumed that if the Ex-Im Bank were willing to guarantee the financing then the risks were acceptable. This is important because the US Ex-Im Bank will only provide guarantees or insurance for up to 85% of a privately financed loan contract; the firm has to supply 15% of the contract up front (Blackmon 2011: 86).

The 85% is also referred to as the domestic content of the export contract (the percentage that is manufactured in the United States). This also means that the firm can have the remaining portion of the export contract assembled or manufactured in the importing country; which can include painting equipment, assembling additional parts, etc. This option of having some of the assembly done in the importing country is attractive to the host government because it allows for employment of local workers, training programs, and certification of factories for parts assembly (Blackmon 2011: 86). By dollar value, large firms have received the most support from the US Ex-Im Bank, however smaller firms have benefited from a higher number of transactions from the US Ex-Im Bank (Ilias 2012: 2). The following section provides information on firms supported by other export credit agencies.

The United Kingdom's (UK's) ECA the Export Credits Guarantee Department (ECGD) participated in nine Paris Club agreements to reschedule debt in 2004–2005: Iraq, Nicaragua, Niger, Ethiopia, Senegal, Ghana, Madagascar, and Congo Republic (all but Iraq are HIPC countries) and Gabon (ECGD 2004–2005: 15). This section in the annual report notes that if the HIPC countries follow the HIPC Initiative and successfully reach the Completion Point, that they are no longer required to service their debts to ECGD, and that the debt is irrevocably written off. The HIPC Initiative was developed in 1996 and enhanced in 1999 by the IMF and the World Bank as a mechanism for countries in unsustainable debt situations to be provided bilateral and, for the first time, multilateral debt forgiveness on the condition that that money be re-directed into poverty alleviating initiatives (Blackmon 2008; 2010). Per ECGD policy, "(a)s long as they (the countries) remain on track with their IMF/World Bank supported programmes, the United Kingdom will agree to forgiveness of all their debt and the Department for International Development will pay ECGD on their behalf" (UK ECGD Annual Report 2004–2005: 15). However, one of the primary criticisms of the HIPC Initiative is that the HIPC countries were unlikely to be able to ever pay off this debt, and furthermore, that not much new money would then be directed toward poverty alleviating initiatives (Easterly 2001; Cohen 2001; Chauvin and Kraay 2005). Thus, in these cases, the debt is forgiven but there are no new resources directed at alleviating poverty from the debt owed to ECGD.

The list of exporters to which guarantees were issued by ECGD included large firms such as Airbus S.A.S. (by far the firm that received the highest level of support), Capital Valves Ltd, Kellogg Brown & Root Ltd, Rolls-Royce Plc., Motorola Ltd, and Guralp Systems Ltd (ECGD Annual Report 2004–2005: 16–17). Two other European Union (EU) ECAs, France (Coface) and Germany (Euler Hermes) also participate in support for Airbus and for other transactions. One specific transaction explained that ECGD, Coface, and Euler Hermes "cooperated with commercial lenders to support purchases of Global Standard for Mobile Communications for mobile phone equipment" from those three countries (the United Kingdom, France, and Germany) by Pakistan Mobile Communications Ltd. The United Kingdom's portion of this transaction was stated to be US$50 million (ECGD Annual Report 2004–2005: 23).

In 2005–2006 the ECGD participated in Paris Club agreements to reschedule debt with Zambia, Indonesia, and Nigeria. Zambia received its final debt treatment under HIPC meaning that all remaining debt was forgiven. It was also noted that Indonesian payments under the current bilateral debt agreements due in 2005 were deferred in order to provide relief from the 2004 tsunami (ECGD Annual Report 2005–2006: 15). However, this same document reported that Indonesia was also issued a guarantee for £4.6 million in support of exports from Greys Exports Ltd for an EODD System and Equipment Project (ECGD Annual Report 2005–2006: 16). In a subsequent ECGD Annual Report (2007–2008: 12) Indonesia was also issued a guarantee for £1.6 million in support of exports from Fernau Avionics Ltd for the purchase of radar equipment.

Ghana was previously involved in a Paris Club rescheduling in 2004–2005 with ECGD; however, in 2008–2009 the country was issued a guarantee for £18.7 million in support of exports from PW Ltd to support the Kotoka International Airport Extension (ECGD Annual Report 2008–2009: 12). In addition, Nigeria made its final payment to ECGD on April 26, 2006 per its agreement with its Paris Club creditors. Nigeria does not qualify for the HIPC Initiative because it is not an IDA-only country, having previously been provided loans from the IBRD and it has been argued that Nigeria is an oil rich member of OPEC and thus should not need the assistance of HIPC (Callaghy 2010: 173–177). However, ECGD or, more correctly, UK companies working with ECGD, wasted no time in working out three new export contracts with Nigeria to be guaranteed by ECGD. First, Airbus S.A.S. secured a guarantee and/or insurance policy (the table did not differentiate between the two) for £30.4 million, and Gentec Energy Plc. secured two separate Guarantees and/or Insurance Policies for a total of £21 million for gas-capture power plants (ECGD Annual Report 2008–2009: 12).

These examples have illustrated that export credits are being extended by the United Kingdom's ECGD to countries having previously requested debt rescheduling under a Paris Club agreement. It should be noted that these cases do have more of a time lag between Paris Club agreements and the extension of new export credits than did some of the cases with US Ex-Im Bank financing. As of June 2012, neither Ghana nor Nigeria had requested debt rescheduling from the Paris Club. However, both countries are still classified by the World Bank as lower middle-income

economies (as of 2012) and it is important to question whether the continued extension of these export credits, which add to the debt levels of these countries, is an
appropriate method to move these countries forward in their socio-economic development. The following section provides information on the Boeing Company and
Airbus as the two of the biggest beneficiaries of ECA supported financing from the
US Ex-Im Bank and the United Kingdom's ECGD, France's Coface, and Germany's
Euler Hermes.

The Boeing Company was one of the "featured companies" profiled in the 2005
Ex-Im Annual Report, which explained, "Boeing is one of the leading exporters in
the US ... and that in FY 2005, Ex-Im Bank helped to finance the export of 78
Boeing aircraft to 19 different airlines in 18 different countries" (US Ex-Im Bank
Annual Report 2005: 13). The firm profile also noted the competition that Boeing
faces in the international market from Airbus and its financing support from the
ECAs of the United Kingdom, Germany, and France, and that by guaranteeing the
loans of commercial banks to foreign-based airlines that purchase or lease Boeing
aircraft, Ex-Im Bank "levels the playing field" in its competition with Airbus as the
only two manufacturers of large commercial aircraft in the world (p. 13).

Information from ECGD on its support for Airbus is also detailed in various
reports. The 2005–2006 ECGD Annual Report noted that the value of guarantees
issued by Airbus deliveries increased to 44% of business issued (the previous percentage level was not provided) which was explained to be a "significant" part
of ECGD export support (ECGD 2005–2006 Annual Report: 6). The 2008/2009
ECGD annual report reported that the value of guarantees comprised of Airbus
deliveries increased to 72% of the business underwritten by ECGD and export credit
support from France, Germany, and the United Kingdom was reported to account
for 21% of the total deliveries of Airbus for 2008–2009 (UK ECGD Annual Report
2008–2009: 8). The following section examines how global companies use Canada's
export agency.

Canada's Export Credit Agency, the Export Development Corporation (EDC)
operates a little differently in that it both helps Canadian firms export abroad, and
provides financing to Canadian firms that may not necessarily be exporting abroad.
For example, in December 2009, EDC provided $Cdn5–15 million in financing
to the Canadian firm Motovan Corporation for the "Sale of various Canadian
goods and services" in which the country of transaction was listed as Canada
(Individual Transaction Information, https://www19.edc.ca/edcsecure/disclosure/
DisclosureView.aspx?yr=2009&lang=EN). In this and other examples, EDC was
guaranteeing payment to the firm, Motovan Corporation. So EDC acts more as a
commercial yet public ECA although it is not privatized like COFACE and Euler Hermes. Canadian exports comprise one of the highest levels of Gross Domestic Product
(GDP) of all the countries in the OECD, yet there are few banks that focus on the
trade financing needs of Canadian companies; EDC performs this task exclusively
(Gillespie 2001: 228–229).

The firms that EDC assists in exporting abroad include Yamana Gold Inc.
providing financing in the amount of $Cdn50–100 million in December 2009 to
Brazil for "General Corporate Purposes"; MacDonald Dettwiler and Associates
Ltd provided financing in the amount of $Cdn 250–500 million to Ukraine for
the sale of satellite equipment to Ukraine State Enterprise (Individual Transaction

Information, https://www19.edc.ca/edcsecure/disclosure/DisclosureView.aspx?yr=2009&lang=EN).

The transaction information provided by EDC also illustrates the way that global firms can use ECAs to their advantage based on their transnational status. Or more specifically, that they can take advantage of using ECAs in several host countries in order to support their export activity. For example, Nortel Networks Limited had two separate transactions in December 2009 for financing from EDC for the sale of telecommunications equipment to India; one transaction in the amount of $Cdn 5–15 million, and the other in the amount of $Cdn 15–25 million. Nortel Networks had previously benefited from long-term guarantees from the US Ex-Im Bank for the sale of telecommunications equipment to Nigeria. Ford Motor Company of Canada, Limited was also able to benefit from financing from EDC for the "support for future procurement of various Canadian goods and services" in the amount of $Cdn 100–250 million to "various countries" (Individual Transaction Information, https://www19.edc.ca/edcsecure/disclosure/DisclosureView.aspx?yr=2009&lang=EN). This is a problem in deciphering the country of transaction for some of the data from EDC in that it is not complete data. Specific information on these global companies that have been profiled in this chapter including their industry classification and their size (represented by sales and number of employees) is provided in Table 18.1.

Many of these firms had multiple company names or subsidiaries in many different countries, and some very large firms had many subsidiaries in the same country. For example, the Boeing Company with one location in the United States and an industry classification of "civil aircraft" was the information used in Table 18.1, however "Boeing Aerospace Operations Inc." also had a location in the United States but with an industry classification of "technical services" which was not used because the descriptive information provided for Boeing was for aircraft in the 2005 US Ex-Im Bank Annual Report. Therefore, in searching the Factiva database, I matched the industry classification with the project description listed in the report of the corresponding ECA. Boeing also had listings in Australia, Ireland, and Canada, just to name a few (Factiva database powered by Dow Jones Companies, accessed May 17, 2012). The previous information shows that global firms have used ECA financing in order to be able to export their goods to developing and/or lower middle income countries. The following section examines the relationship between the Paris Club debt rescheduling of official debt and the structural adjustment policies facilitated by the IMF and World Bank.

Debt Rescheduling, Structural Adjustment Policies, and New Debt

Thomas Callaghy (2010: 162) explains, "[f]rom very early on, the work of the Paris Club has been tightly linked to IMF-mandated economic reform efforts, which only intensified after the Third World debt crisis broke in 1982 and structural adjustment became a more generalized term." The fact that rescheduling of Paris Club debt is provided on the condition that economic reform programs are successfully continued with the IMF and the World Bank is deemed necessary for two interrelated reasons (Callaghy 2002: 15). First, from the viewpoint of the creditors, they want assurances that the required policy reforms will be followed, and going through the IMF is believed to be the best way to get these assurances (Rieffel 1985: 8). Indeed,

Table 18.1	ECA supported global companies.

Country of ECA	Company	Industry classification	Sales, US$ million	Employees
Canada	Nortel Networks Ltd	Telecommunications	620.00	30,329
Canada	Motovan Corporation	Motor vehicle parts	81.75	150
Canada	Yamana Gold Inc.	Gold ore/silver ore mining	2106.00	n.a.
Canada	MacDonald Dettwiler and Associates Ltd	Applications software	45.69	305
Canada	Ford Motor Company of Canada Ltd	Passenger cars	2780.00	13,200
France	Airbus Sas (only for France, listed as "Sas")	Civilian aircraft	38,763.00	5709
UK	Capital Valves Ltd	Machinery/industrial goods	28.75	11
UK	Kellogg Brown & Root Ltd	Technical services	1328.96	1164
UK	Rolls-Royce plc	Motor vehicle parts	16.70	950
UK	Motorola Solutions Ltd	Telecommunications equipment	877.17	1471
UK	Guralp Systems Ltd	Measuring/precision instruments	14.95	85
UK	Gentec Energy plc	Engines/turbines	51.16	19
USA	Nortel Networks Inc.	Telecommunications equipment	0.28	4
USA	Boeing Industry	Civilian aircraft	68,735.00	171,700
USA	Caterpillar Inc.	Construction machinery	60,138.00	125,099
USA	General Electric	Diversified holding companies	142,237.00	301,000

Source: Factiva database powered by Dow Jones Companies, accessed May 17, 2012.

according to the Paris Club website in order for a developing country to have its debt restructured, the country must have implemented reforms "necessary to restore their economic and financial situation. This means in practice that the country must have a current program with the IMF supported by a conditional arrangement" (http://www.clubdeparis.org/sections/services/faq/77-forum-aux-questions).

The second reason is more practical; the creditors want to negotiate to have assurances that at least some of the debt owed is paid, and then are more willing to have some debt rescheduled. For example, the 2004–2005 ECGD Annual Report noted that payments received under Paris Club arrangements for rescheduled debt and interest payments were £1.2 billion; amounts received in 2009–2010 were £152 million; 2010–2011 were £147 million (ECGD Annual Report 2004–2005: 15; ECGD Annual Report 2010–2011: 23). Information on amounts received from the US Ex-Im Bank and Canada's EDC under Paris Club arrangements for rescheduled debt and interest payments was not available. However, the Paris Club website provides extensive information on the countries under which debt is canceled, rescheduled and the terms of the IMF program. The following section will illustrate one such case in the rescheduling of Ecuador's debt in 2003 in which the United States and the United Kingdom (among others) participated in the reorganization of Ecuador's debt and then the US Ex-Im Bank (in 2004) and Canada's EDC (two transactions in 2011) subsequently provided trade financing to the country. Transaction information for EDC is only available going back to 2009.

Ecuador completed discussions for an Article IV Consultation with the IMF on March 7, 2003; prior to the rescheduling agreement concluded with the Paris Club on June 13, 2003 (IMF Country Report No. 03/90). In this consultation report, specifics on the debt rescheduling were discussed such as the fact that the rescheduling would be on a nonconcessional basis and that it would involve all bilateral creditors. The report noted that the IMF staff assumed that Paris Club creditors would provide about US$60 million in rescheduling (in fact they agreed to treat or reschedule principal maturities in the amount of US$81 million) (IMF Country Report No. 03/90, 19). Rieffel (1985: 8) calls this situation of differences in the specific amount of debt to be rescheduled a "tug-of-war" between the IMF and the creditors. He explains that before concluding the standby arrangement with the debtor country, the IMF would like to know how much debt relief is being planned by the creditors. However, the creditors want to see the IMF arrangement to determine the debt relief that they can offer based on the policy commitments and balance-of-payments projections that the IMF has made; thus the "tug-of-war."

One other interesting detail in the Article IV Consultation report is a reference made to the Paris Club and specific policy advice from the IMF for Ecuador to pay off Paris Club debt. The IMF staff noted that since Ecuador derives revenue from its export of oil and that subsequently, if oil prices were to be higher based on World Economic Outlook projections, then "Ecuador could use the extra revenue to amortize (payoff) later in the program period some of the amounts rescheduled, or deferred by the Paris Club" (pp. 19–20). In effect, the IMF was encouraging Ecuador to use extra revenue to pay off Paris Club creditors as opposed to using that revenue for other socio-economic purposes.

Ecuador's Stand-by Arrangement approved by the IMF on March 21, 2003 was also included as part of the document file from the Paris Club website. Much of the information in Stand-by Arrangements (SBAs) concluded with countries is standard, but a few objectives and policies will be pointed out in order to illustrate how the IMF through the SBA encourages developing countries to continue to incur more debt through continuation with international trade. First, there are stipulations listed that Ecuador must pursue for the period of the SBA, and for successfully following those objectives and policies "purchases" or tranches of money from the IMF are disbursed (IMF Country Report No. 03/90, 55). Specifics also note that purchases will not be made "if at any time during the period of the stand-by arrangement, Ecuador imposes or intensifies restrictions on the making of payments and transfers for current international transactions, or introduces or modifies multiple currency practices, or concludes bilateral payments agreements which are inconsistent with Article VIII, or imposes or intensifies import restrictions for balance of payments reasons" (IMF Country Report No. 03/90, 57–58). While the Stand-by Arrangement does not force Ecuador to incur more debt through ECA financing activity it certainly does not discourage it; and in fact the IMF encourages countries to engage in and be open to international trade under all circumstances. There are valid economic reasons that support this economic growth policy, but it is odd that some of the very countries that participate in the Paris Club debt cancellation and rescheduling arrangements with developing countries provide financing or guarantees to them in the future. For example, the United States and Canada were both listed as participants in the reorganization of Ecuador's debt in 2003, and the ECAs of both countries were involved in financing to Ecuador in subsequent years.

The US Ex-Im Bank's loan guarantee to Ecuador was discussed previously in the broader context of US Ex-Im Bank activity. To review, representatives of the US government were listed as a participant in the reorganization of Ecuador's debt with Paris Club creditors on June 13, 2003 (Paris Club 2003). On September 30, 2004, the US Ex-Im Bank then authorized a loan for about $70 million to Quiport, a firm in Ecuador, so that the firm could have Caterpillar Inc. participate in the construction of a new international airport (US Ex-Im Bank 2004 Annual Report 28).

Representatives of the Canadian government were also listed as a participant in the reorganization of Ecuador's debt with Paris Club creditors on June 13, 2003 (Paris Club 2003). Transaction information for EDC is only available from 2009 onward, but on April 30, 2011, EDC provided a guarantee in the range of $Cdn 1–5 million to Husky Injection Molding Systems Ltd for the sale of various Canadian goods and services to Ecuador. On August 3, 2011, EDC provided a guarantee in the range of less than $Cdn1 million to the Airborne Sensing Corporation for the sale of various Canadian goods and services to Ecuador (Individual Transaction Information, https://www19.edc.ca/edcsecure/disclosure/DisclosureView.aspx?yr=2009 &lang=EN).

In a comparative sense, the level of activity by the US Ex-Im Bank could be viewed as more problematic under these circumstances for two reasons. First, the Ex-Im Bank provided a direct loan, thus assuming full responsibility for the transaction minus the fee paid by Caterpillar Inc. Second, the Ex-Im Bank provided this loan the year after Ecuador had participated in rescheduling with the Paris Club. Clearly there seems to be some level of disconnect between a recognition that the government of Ecuador is having difficulty in servicing its debt and a decision to provide new loans that are in effect being guaranteed for repayment by the government of Ecuador.

Conclusion

Global companies use ECAs in a variety of ways to support the export of their goods abroad. The problems with this scenario arise when the export of goods are to developing countries that already have high levels of debt. The primacy of the interests of the entities supporting these exports is most visible when some of the developing country debt is owed to an ECA. In order to be able to reschedule this debt, or to have a portion of it forgiven through the Paris Club, the IMF dictates criteria or structural adjustment policies that the country must agree to follow in order to receive a balance-of-payments loan. The involvement of the IMF is a requirement by the creditor states in order for them to agree to reschedule and/or forgive some of this debt. In the case of Ecuador in 2003, the IMF advised the country to remain engaged in international trade and to use additional revenue to pay down its Paris Club debt. IMF policy in this regard is very much driven by appeasing its more powerful member states, which is a common critique of the overall policies of the institution. However, the problem with the IMF's involvement with Paris Club debt rescheduling is that those creditor states' ECAs are also responsible for much of the debt of those countries. Furthermore, ECAs are able to extend new loans or export credits to these same countries, often during the *same* year that the Paris Club agreement for rescheduling is concluded. Global companies (through their national ECAs) are able to continue exporting their goods to these countries, sales that otherwise would have been lost due to the lack of private-sector finance. However, these export credits or loans could possibly need to be rescheduled in the future, thereby perpetuating this debt cycle.

The US Ex-Im Bank, the United Kingdom's ECGD, and Canada's ECD were the ECAs profiled as participating in these processes. However, these ECAs also provide the most information on their financing activities, and in fact the US Ex-Im Bank provides the most information. It is highly doubtful that other ECAs do not behave in the same manner; information about their finance and lending activities is simply limited. Future research should follow the trends of ECA activity to ensure that developing countries are not repeatedly caught in this cycle of debt, rescheduling, additional loans, and more rescheduling.

Note

1   These tables do not provide data on the obligor or guarantor so it is not clear whether they were made under the sovereign (to a government) or commercial risk category. Since they are guaranteed by an official agency, and are long term, they can be rescheduled under Paris Club agreements (Rieffel 1985: 19).

References

Birdsall, Nancy, Williamson, John, and Deese, Brian. 2002. *Delivering on Debt Relief: From IMF Gold to a New Aid Architecture*. Washington, DC: Peterson Institute for International Economics.

Blackmon, Pamela. 2008. "Rethinking Poverty Through the Eyes of the International Monetary Fund and the World Bank." *International Studies Review*, 10: 179–202.

Blackmon, Pamela. 2010. "International Economic Institutions and Global Justice." In *The International Studies Encyclopedia*, ed. Robert Denemark, 4021–4034. Oxford: Wiley-Blackwell.

Blackmon, Pamela. 2011. *In the Shadow of Russia: Reform in Kazakhstan and Uzbekistan*. Michigan: Michigan State University Press.

Blackmon, Pamela. 2012. "The Role of Export-Credit Agencies in the 2008 Financial Crisis: Were They Used to Supplement Private Sector Finance and Sustain International Trade?" Paper presented at the Annual Meeting of the International Studies Association, San Francisco, April 1–4.

Borensztein, Eduardo, Yeyati, Eduardo Levy, and Panizza, Ugo. 2006. *Living with Debt: How to Limit the Risks of Sovereign Finance*. Washington, DC: Inter-American Development Bank.

Callaghy, Thomas. 2002. *Innovation in the Sovereign Debt Regime: From the Paris Club to Enhanced HIPC and Beyond*. Washington, DC: World Bank Operations Evaluation Department.

Callaghy, Thomas. 2010. "The Paris Club, Debt and Poverty Reduction: Evolving Patterns of Governance." In *Global Governance, Poverty and Inequality*, ed. Jennifer Clapp and Rorden Wilkinson, 162–184. London: Routledge.

Chauvin, N. and Kraay, Aart. 2005. What Has 100 Billion Dollars of Debt Relief Done for Low-Income Countries?, http://papers.ssrn.com/sol3/papers.cfm?abstract_id=818504. Accessed December 19, 2012.

Chossukovsky, Michael. 1997. *Globalisation of Poverty: Impacts of IMF and World Bank Reforms*. London: Zed Books.

Cline, William R. 2005. "Trade Finance and Financial Crises." In *Access to Trade Finance in Times of Crisis*, ed. Jian-Ye-Wang and Marcio Ronci, 19–23. Washington, DC: IMF.

Cohen, Daniel. 2001. "The HIPC Initiative: True and False Promises." *International Finance*, 4 (3): 363–380.

Crockett, A.D. 1992. "The International Monetary Fund in the 1990s." *Government and Opposition*, 27 (3): 267–282.

Easterly, William. 2001. "Think Again: Debt Relief." *Foreign Policy*, 127: 20–26.

Evans, Peter C. and Oye, Kenneth A. 2001. "International Competition: Conflict and Cooperation in Government Export Financing." In *The Ex-Im Bank in the 21st Century: A New Approach?*, ed. Gary Clyde Hufbauer and Rita M. Rodriguez, 113–158. Washington, DC: Institute for International Economics.

Gamarra, Boris, Pollock, Malvian, and Primo Braga, Carlos A. 2009. "Debt Relief to Low-Income Countries: A Retrospective." In *Debt Relief and Beyond: Lessons Learned and Challenges Ahead*, ed. Carlos A. Primo Braga and Dorte Doemland, 11–33. Paris: OECD.

Gianturco, Delio. 2001. *Export Credit Agencies: The Unsung Giants of International Trade and Finance*. Westpoint: Quorum Books.

Gillespie, A. Ian. 2001. "A Canadian Perspective." In *The Ex-Im Bank in the 21st Century: A New Approach?*, ed. Gary Clyde Hufbauer and Rita M. Rodriguez, 227–234. Washington, DC: Institute for International Economics.

Gilman, Martin G. and Wang, Jian-Ye. 2003. *Official Financing: Recent Developments and Issues*.Washington, DC: IMF.

Ilias, Shayerah. 2012. *Reauthorization of the Export-Import Bank: Issues and Policy Options for Congress*. Washington, DC: Congressional Research Service.

International Monetary Fund. 1998. *Official Financing for Developing Countries*. Washington, DC: IMF.

International Monetary Fund. 2003. *IMF Country Report No. 03/90, April 2003*. Washington, DC: IMF.

Kuhn, Michael. 1994. *Official Financing for Developing Countries: World Economic and Financial Surveys, International Monetary Fund*. Washington, DC: International Monetary Fund.

Kuhn, Michael, Horvath, Balaz, and Jarvis, Christoper J. 1995. *Officially Supported Export Credits: Recent Developments and Prospects*. Washington, DC: IMF.

Lora, Eduardo and Olivera, Mauricio. 2006. "Public Debt and Social Expenditure: Friends or Foes?" *Inter-American Development Bank Working Paper 563*. Washington, DC.

Moran, Theodore. 1999. *Foreign Direct Investment and Development: The New Policy Agenda for Developing Countries and Economies in Transition*. Washington, DC: Institute for International Economics.

Moran, Theodore. 2006. *Harnessing Foreign Direct Investment for Development: Policies for Developed and Developing Countries*. Washington, DC: Center for Global Development.

Moravcsik, Andrew M. 1989. "Disciplining Trade Finance: The OECD Export Credit Arrangement."*International Organization* 43 (1): 173–205.

OECD DAC Committee. 2010. DAC Statistical Reporting Directives. November 12.

Paris Club. 2003. The Paris Club Agrees to a Rescheduling of Ecuador's Debt, press release, http://www.clubdeparis.org/sections/communication/archives-2003/equateur4884/viewLanguage/en. Accessed May 18, 2012.

Paris Club. 2010. Classification, http://www.clubdeparis.org/sections/dette-traitee-en-club/categories-de-dette/definition-dettes. Accessed July 14, 2011.

Rieffel, Alexis. 1985. *The Role of the Paris Club in Managing Debt Problems*. Essays in International Finance, 161. Princeton: Princeton University Press.

Rieffel, Lex. 2003. *Restructuring Sovereign Debt: The Case for Ad Hoc Machinery*. Washington, DC: Brookings Institution Press.

Stephens, Malcolm. 1999. *The Changing Role of Export Credit Agencies*. Washington, DC: IMF.

Stewart, Frances. 1995. *Adjustment and Poverty: Options and Choices*. London: Routledge.

UK ECGD. Annual Report 2004–2005; 2005–2006; 2008–2009.

US Ex-Im Bank Annual Report. 2004; 2005. Washington, DC: US Ex-Im Bank.

Wade, Robert Hunter. 2004. "On the Causes of Increasing Inequality and World Poverty, or Why the Matthew Effect Prevails." *New Political Economy*, 9 (2): 163–188.

Woods, Ngaire. 2006. *The Globalizers: The IMF, the World Bank, and Their Borrowers*. Ithaca: Cornell University Press.

Chapter 19

Outsourcing Global Governance: Public-Private Voluntary Initiatives

Marianne Thissen-Smits and Patrick Bernhagen

Introduction

Every week, Chevron, one of the world's major oil producers, proclaims in *The Economist* that "the world needs more than oil" (Chevron 2012). In May 2003, the fast food chain McDonald's announced the creation of a Global Advisory Council on Healthy Lifestyles that should guide the company and its commitment to promote healthier lifestyles (CSRwire 2012). And the furniture giant IKEA claims that it is doing what it can "to help create a world where we take better care of the environment, the earth's resources, and each other" (IKEA 2012). These examples illustrate the extent to which it has become standard practice in recent years for firms to advertise their socially and environmentally responsible behavior and promote their ethical image. But beyond the mere propagation of wider social goals, many firms are actively developing codes of conduct and participating in voluntary initiatives of environmental and social responsibility developed by these actors. These initiatives have the potential to serve as vehicles of global governance, and they are therefore of great interest to states, international organizations (IOs), and non-business, non-governmental organizations (NGOs), who seek to enlist companies for their goals. This chapter examines these attempts at outsourcing global governance via voluntary initiatives joined by global companies and how these have evolved over the years. After introducing the concept of outsourcing global governance with the help of public–private voluntary initiatives (PPVIs), we identify the factors that make companies engage in them. Finally, we discuss the effectiveness of PPVIs for addressing global social and environmental problems.

The Handbook of Global Companies, First Edition. Edited by John Mikler.
© 2013 John Wiley & Sons, Ltd. Published 2013 by John Wiley & Sons, Ltd.

Voluntary Codes in Global Governance

In the process of globalization, the social and political power of large, globally active companies has grown. Due to relationships and networks between firms, control and ownership of the global economy is in the hands of a relatively small number of companies (Vitali, Glattfelder, and Battison 2011). Economic globalization has surpassed political globalization as there is no world government that is accountable to the people of every country (Stiglitz 2002). Nation states have limited control over global markets, so that there is an increasing interest in alternative institutions of "global governance." Defined by Rosenau (1995: 13) to "include systems of rule at all levels of human activity – from the family to the international organization – in which the pursuit of goals through the exercise of control has transnational repercussions," the concept of global governance implies a role for companies. As Kytle and Ruggie (2005) point out, global companies are "capable of making and implementing decisions at a pace that neither governments nor international agencies can match." Their global activity prompts other social actors to look for opportunities to build broader social capacity – "to help fill global governance gaps and compensate for governance failures" (Ruggie 2004: 514). As a result, global governance is increasingly outsourced to the private sector, which controls the necessary resources and expertise (Cutler, Haufler, and Porter 1999). For their part, companies have begun to actively join states, IOs, and NGOs in the influencing the process of global governance (Held *et al.* 1999).

Developing countries in need of foreign investment may ease regulations to attract business. They also frequently lack the capacity to enforce regulations. In other cases, social and environmental issues are simply not very salient for the rulers (Williams 2000; Sethi 2003). In these countries, companies are often expected, either by local or global actors, to take more responsibility for social issues. For this, they need guidelines to encourage ethical behavior and provide guidance – "rules of the road" – to function correctly (Cutler, Haufler, and Porter 1999: 9). Because international laws are both slow to develop and difficult to enforce, IOs, for their part, are looking to companies in the development and adaptation of voluntary codes of conduct, standards, and guidelines. In the words of Ruggie (2004: 503):

> TNCs have gone global and function in near real time, leaving behind the slower moving, state-mediated international world of arm's-length economic transactions and traditional international legal mechanisms, even as they depend on that world for their licenses to operate and to protect their property rights.

As global companies become bigger and more powerful and operate across various jurisdictions with different requirements, it becomes even more important that partnerships develop between NGOs, IOs, governments, and firms so that PPVIs are initiated and promoted.

Private voluntary initiatives and "non-state market driven" governance systems are central pillars of the effort to outsource global governance (Cashore, Auld, and Newsom 2004: 24). We can distinguish two types of codes which govern the social and environmental behavior of firms. Firstly, there are codes developed by companies or business associations to serve as a means of "self regulation" (Kolk and van

Tulder 2005). Companies engage in lobbying and other political activities to shape policy at the national or regional level or international agreements at the regional or global level (Rowlands 2001; Coen and Grant 2006; Hillman, Keim, and Schuler 2004). They increasingly complement their political strategies by creating guidelines or voluntary practices as means for addressing society's concerns, improving their reputation, and reducing the costs of, or even preventing, further public regulation (Sethi 2003; Post 2000; Baron 2010). Secondly, there are codes designed by governments, IOs, or NGOs to guide or restrict company behavior. NGOS and IOs in particular have become very active and are playing an increasingly important public role in governing the gaps that appear where local or global governance is lacking.

While many new public–private governance instruments have been developed to close the gap between political and economic development that results from the lack of a system of global governance (Haufler 2001), the idea of voluntary standards is not a mere reaction to globalization, nor is it new: Historically, firms have often preceded the state in regulating their activities (Vogel 2010: 70; Haufler 2001). Therefore, rather than a shift from public to private regulation, we seem to witness a change to a "more inclusive institutional area" where civil society organizations with moral authority and knowledge influence TNCs to promote a better society and accountability (Ruggie 2004: 503). In this view, the state and private interests are "partners in public-private governance arrangements" for addressing either state or market failure (Flohr *et al.* 2010: 7).

The growth of PPVIs occurred in two periods. In the 1970s, codes of conduct were developed mainly by international organizations. The first code of conduct designed for globally active companies was the OECD Guidelines for Multinational Enterprises. Adopted by the Organization for Economic Co-operation and Development (OECD) in 1976. The guidelines are "voluntary principles and standards for responsible business conduct in areas such as employment and industrial relations, human rights, environment, information disclosure, combating bribery, consumer interests, science and technology, competition, and taxation" (OECD 2011). Around the same time, the first private international code of conduct was developed to address apartheid in South Africa. Proposed in 1977 by Leon Sullivan for 12 American firms operating in South Africa (Sethi and Williams 2000; Sethi 2003). The OECD guidelines and other initial codes developed by the OECD as well as by the United Nations (UN) and its various agencies in the 1970s had little effect on corporate behavior. However, they laid the "groundwork" for later guidelines (Haufler 2001; Kolk and van Tulder 2005). The OECD Guidelines were reviewed several times, and in 2011 they were amended to include a chapter on human rights based on the Guiding Principles on Business and Human Rights implementing the United Nations "Protect, Respect and Remedy" framework proposed by UN Special Representative John Ruggie (OECD 2012). Presently, the OECD guidelines are regarded as the "world's most comprehensive international corporate responsibility instrument developed by governments" (Boucher 2010). Similarly, the Sullivan principles had a second wind in the late 1990s when they formed the core to a more general code: the Global Sullivan Principles on Social Responsibility. Their goals are to ensure that companies "respect the law" and are "responsible member(s) of society" (Leon H. Sullivan Foundation 2012).

In the 1990s, companies and NGOs began taking the lead in the development of voluntary codes (Kolk and van Tulder 2005). Industry is active in developing certification schemes, reporting systems, and management systems. On the eve of the Rio Earth summit in 1992, a number of large globally active companies formed a CEO-led association, the World Business Council for Sustainable Development (WBCSD). By March the WBCSD had 191 members from all regions of the world and offers various tools to help firms contribute to sustainable development (World Business Council for Sustainable Development 2012). The reporting or disclosure of social and environmental behavior is promoted by the Global Reporting Initiative (GRI), a nonprofit organization that facilitates sustainability reporting for currently over 3,500 organizations, including many globally active companies, in more than 60 countries (Global Reporting Initiative 2011). The GRI provides principles and guidelines for organizations to report and monitor their economic, social, and environmental performance (Brown, de Jong, and Lessidrenska 2009; Global Reporting Initiative 2011). The number of GRI reports registered in 2010 increased by 22%, where the percentage reporting from developing countries increased by 29% (Global Reporting Initiative 2011). This global reporting trend emphasizes how firms are increasingly eager to participate in initiatives on a global scale. The UN encourages participants in its Global Compact to use the GRI reporting framework to produce their annual Communication on Progress, turning this civil society initiative into a vehicle for the outsourcing of global governance.

Since the 1990s additional pressure has been put on business from institutional investors who have created socially responsible investment funds. These investors emphasize environmental, social, and corporate governance (ESG) issues, which are perceived to have an effect on the investment portfolios. Negative externalities, such as environmental damage, can affect shareholder value and reduce returns to investors. Accidents like the 2010 Deepwater Horizon disaster in the Gulf of Mexico provide vivid illustrations of this. As visibly unethical behavior may affect investment negatively and pressure from investors increases, companies take measures to address environmental or social risks. They provide information to organizations compiling lists such as the Dow Jones Sustainability Index (DJSI), the FTSE4Good, and the Carbon Disclosure Project (CDP) to help investors understand their economic, environmental, and social performance. These organizations have been important drivers for companies to disclose, as favorable listings on various sustainability indices provide reputational benefits. The Carbon Disclosure Project (CDP) is an investor-driven, voluntary initiative encouraging companies to report on greenhouse gas emissions and climate risks. The CDP has specific reporting guidelines with regard to climate change and over 3000 companies responded to a questionnaire sent out by CDP in 2011 (Carbon Disclosure Project 2012). In this area too, political organizations are driving the agenda. An example is the Principles of Responsible Investment, a UN-backed network of international investors. Over 915 investment institutions have signed the Principles by October 2011 (Principles for Responsible Investment 2011).

The UN now sees business as a "critical partner" in its efforts to solve global problems. During the 1999 World Economic Forum in Davos the then UN Secretary General Kofi Annan, challenged business leaders to "initiate a global compact of shared values and principles, which will give a human face to the global market" (United Nations 1999). This led to the establishment of the UN Global

Compact (UNGC) the following year. The UNGC contains ten principles relating to human rights, labor rights, care for the environment, and corruption. The two main objectives of the UNGC are to "mainstream the Global Compact's ten universally accepted principles" in business activities and "to catalyze business actions in support of broader UN goals, including the Millennium Development Goals" (Latham and Watkins 2009). Within half a decade, the UNGC has developed into "the world's largest corporate citizenship initiative" (United Nations 2006: 45). It currently has over 6000 participating companies from more than 130 countries. The UNGC and the OECD guidelines are based on a similar set of values. But while the OECD guidelines are government driven recommendations, the UNGC is primarily a means, provided by an IO, for companies to express their commitment to business ethics publicly (Murphy 2005: 300–400).

Globally active companies also subscribe to environmental management standards such as the ISO 14001 or the ISO 26 000 standard on social responsibility of the International Organization for Standardization (ISO). Though the ISO standards may be promoted by governments, they are developed through the ISO membership bodies with involvement of the private sector (Clapp 1998). Five years after the implementation of the ISO environmental standard there were already 22,500 certified firms (Perkins and Neumayer 2010). Other certification schemes have been driven primarily by non-governmental, non-profit organizations. For example, the forest stewardship council (FSC), a timber certification program, was initiated and led by environmental groups (Cashore, Auld, and Newsom 2004), while the Fair Trade certification was initiated by the Dutch ecumenical development agency Solidaridad (Fairtrade 2012). These standards or certifications schemes are important to companies as they are proof of their "good management" practices.

What Makes Companies Engage?

In the pursuit of profitability, companies can choose to become politically active in efforts to influence public policy-making and prevent adverse regulation (Grier, Munger, and Roberts 1994; Stigler 1971). States and other public institutions affect companies and the markets in which they operate by means of subsidies, taxation, regulation, and control of competition. There is growing recognition that firms are expanding their repertoire of political activity and combine different types of activity in an integrated non-market strategy (Baron 2010; Schuler, Rehbein, and Cramer 2002). In particular, the legitimacy that an organization can gain by participating in PPVIs can reduce the threat of adverse political activity. A survey of CEOs, carried out in 2010 by management consulting firm Accenture and the UNGC Office, found that 72% of the respondents identified "brand, trust and reputation" as one of the top three factors driving them to "take action on sustainability issues" (Accenture and United Nations Global Compact 2010: 20). This means that companies need to be able to show in public that they are good "corporate citizens" (Matten and Crane 2005). Signing codes of conduct or participating in voluntary initiatives on social and environmental behavior can be a means to achieve this task. With participation in PPVIs thus becoming part of a company's wider strategy to influence its non-market environment, the political and institutional context takes on a major explanatory role (Brammer and Pavelin 2006; Doh and Guay 2006). Researchers have begun to identify the political dimension of corporations in activities commonly referred to as CSR (Hillman and Hitt 1999; Matten and Crane 2005; Waddock 2008). A central concern is the considerable variation in the extent to which companies participate in global initiatives (Bennie, Bernhagen, and Mitchell 2007; Perez-Batres, Miller, and Pisani 2011): Why are some firms very active while others abstain altogether? This variation has been explained by reference to companies' individual characteristics, to the mobilization of normative biases within their home countries, to the behavior and success of countervailing interests, and to the wider institutional environment.

Characteristics of the Company

A first factor behind a company's decision to engage in PPVIs is its size. Its assets, sales, or workforce reflect a company's resources and market power as well as what it has at stake in economic and political conflict (Cowen, Ferreri, and Parker 1987; Hillman, Keim, and Schuler 2004: 839; Meek, Roberts, and Gray 1995). As larger firms have more to gain from political activity, they can be expected to invest more, and more often, in non-market strategies (Olson 1965). Large companies often operate globally and therefore are also more likely to participate in global initiatives. Analysis of the non-market behavior of the Forbes Global 2000 firms has shown that larger firms are significantly more likely to sign the UN Global Compact (Bennie, Bernhagen, and Mitchell 2007). Similarly, 84% of the GRI reports come from large companies, although reporting by small and medium-sized companies is increasing (Global Reporting Initiative 2011).

Secondly, differences in corporate governance systems may further explain some of the variation in uptake of global voluntary initiatives (Kolk and van Tulder 2005). Different forms of corporate governance place varying degrees of emphasis on shareholders and other key actors involved in the making of major decisions in the company. Some of these differences are along national lines: for example, American managers have more decision-making power than their counterparts in German or Japanese firms (Roe 1993). And companies' non-market activity may be driven by the top management team, whose personal preferences and ideas might affect how companies deal with their perceived social responsibilities (Ozer 2010).

Thirdly, companies' involvement in PPVIs is shaped by the nature of their sectoral activity. For example, firms in the *extractive sector* are exposed to a higher risk of conflict with external actors in the environmental and human rights areas. Their operations are often tied to certain geographical locations, limiting them in their choice of investment options. Natural resources such as oil, gas, and minerals are fixed and they are frequently located in politically difficult locations. For example, the largest proven oil reserves are found in countries with quite poor human rights records. For global companies active in these locations, reputation building and related non-market activities are important instruments for safeguarding their investments. These "resource-cursed" corporations seek opportunities to enhance their reputation and take counter-measures to increase their legitimacy. Public–private voluntary initiatives provide such opportunities. As a result, companies in the oil, gas, and mining sectors are significantly more likely to sign up to the UNGC than others (Bennie, Bernhagen, and Mitchell 2007).

Countervailing Actors

In pluralist societies, NGOs and organized labor enable citizens to mount "counter-vailing power" to the economic and political clout of companies (Galbraith 1954). A vital element of these countervailing forces is of particular importance in the transnational or global arena, where traditional governance structures are often ineffective. But while labor unions have struggled with globalization, NGOs have become formidable countervailing powers to the activities of global companies from the mid-1970s onward (Rugman and Doh 2008). International NGOs have become active in the development and implementation of environmental policies and govern-ments are increasingly relying on their services (Rowlands 2001). NGOs can confront global companies directly using voluntary codes or certification systems in a carrots and sticks approach, where carrots include enhanced reputation and market access while sticks can involve the "naming and shaming" (Vogel 2010: 74) of companies with questionable ethical conduct.

The reputational leverage of NGOs can easily be underestimated, and in some instances global companies have done so to their disadvantage. A prominent exam-ple is the case of Shell, which was targeted by Greenpeace for planning to sink an oil loading facility, the Brent Spar, in the North Atlantic. The decision to dispose of the platform in deepwater was based on engineering complexity, safety, and cost issues (Baron 2010: 109). Greenpeace occupied the Brent Spar platform for a period of three weeks after which the activists were removed. The David and Goliath tactic worked and Shell became seen as an example of "unresponsive and inconsider-ate big business" (Baron 2010: 110). Some £350,000 was spent by Greenpeace on media campaigns to win over public opinion. Public opinion about deep sea dis-posal changed, resulting in a boycott of Shell petrol stations in Germany, Denmark, and the Netherlands (Jordan 1998: 609). In the end, Shell agreed to dispose of the Brent Spar onshore. Quantitative analyses of public-private voluntary initiative sup-port the expectation that global companies react to the pressure of countervailing powers. Seeking to avoid such public relations disasters, firms tend to adapt to the normative context and the "mobilization of bias" (Schattschneider 1960) of their home countries (Bennie, Bernhagen, and Mitchell 2007). This makes firms located in countries with strong environmental movements more likely to participate in the UN Global Compact. As countervailing actors shift their political strategies from the national to the transnational level, the incentives for companies to participate in non-market activity at this level also increase. Recent studies by Bernhagen, Mitchell, and Thissen-Smits (2012) and Perez-Batres, Miller, and Pisani (2011) have found an association between labor and citizen group participation in the Global Compact and participation by companies, supporting the expectation that corporate involvement in PPVIs is influenced by the level of participation of these countervailing actors.

The Political-Economic Context

Companies' institutional environments shape their decisions to engage in non-market activities. North (1990: 97) defines institutions as "the humanly devised constraints that structure political, economic and social interactions. They consist of both infor-mal constraints (sanctions, taboos, customs, traditions and codes of conduct), and formal rules (constitutions, laws, property rights)." Many of the most effective institutions are located at the level of the nation state, and even globally active companies operate within existing, nationally distinct politico-economic systems.

The political regime plays a particularly important role in shaping companies' strategic environment and their decisions about participation in PPVIs. Liberal democracies provide opportunities for external pressure from the free organization of interests on diverse areas including environmental issues (Li and Reuveny 2006) and human rights concerns (Bueno de Mesquita *et al.* 2005; Davenport and Armstrong 2004). Relatively free flow of information means that citizens and consumers in democracies are better informed about the social and environmental externalities of corporations. As a result, companies from democratic countries are exposed to demands from a greater variety of external actors. In their efforts to engage with these actors, companies headquartered in democratic countries have increased incentives to participate in PPVIs in comparison to firms from non-democratic countries. Furthermore, the same pluralist features and participatory opportunities that empower non-business interests in democratic countries also enable companies to pursue a wider array of non-market strategies. In the area of environmental concerns, a lively universe of activist groups that put pressure on companies as well as lobbying governments for stricter environmental regulation and supporting international organizations' aim to solve global problems leads to higher environmental demands in democracies (Neumayer 2002; Payne 1995; Li and Reuveny 2006). By contrast autocratic regimes are more likely to neglect environmental problems, prevent activist groups from gaining attention, and censor the media that would otherwise notify the public of environmental or social problems (Neumayer 2002: Payne 1995; Li and Reuveny 2006). Democratic countries are also more likely to sign multilateral environmental agreements and participate in environmental intergovernmental organizations (Congleton 1992; Neumayer 2002). As a result, companies hailing from democratic countries should be under more pressure from the external actors in a strong civil society to sign and participate in voluntary agreements, including those at a global level.

However, the empirical evidence concerning the role of the political regime of the home country is mixed. Perkins and Neumayer (2010) find support for their expectation that democracy has a positive, conditioning influence on domestic receptivity to the spread of the UNGC across borders: transnational connectivity increases UNGC participation in democratic countries more than in nondemocratic ones. Berliner and Prakash's (2012) study suggests that any positive influence democratization may have on UNGC adoption would need several years to take effect. Analyzing all countries with at least 1 million inhabitants, Bernhagen, Mitchell, and Thissen-Smits (2012) find a positive relationship between democracy and companies' take-up of the UNGC once the full variation in political regimes that can be found in today's world is analyzed.

Differences in national capitalism might further help us understand variation in corporate engagement in PPVIs. Various attempts have been made to identify varieties of capitalism, but Hall and Soskice's (2001) is arguably the most established one by now.[1] These authors contrast liberal market economies (LME) with coordinated market economies (CME) regarding the degree to which they depend on market or strategic forms of coordination. In LMEs, "firms coordinate their activities primarily via hierarchies and competitive market arrangements" while in CMEs, "firms depend more heavily on non-market relationships to coordinate their relationships with other actors" (Hall and Soskice 2001: 8). Companies from CMEs in continental Europe and Japan are also more accustomed to taking responsibility for the concerns of employees and external actors. This should make them more likely to agree to long-term commitments in the areas of human rights, labor rights, and the environment (cf. Janney, Dess, and Forlani 2009). By contrast, companies from LMEs are more reliant on contractual relations while emphasizing "shareholder value." These companies are used to weaker trade unions and employment protection. They are also more likely to lobby for deregulation with the aim of allowing firms to coordinate activities mainly through the market and through litigation in courts. For these reasons, CME companies should be less likely to participate in PPVIs (cf. Kolk and van Tulder 2005).

Finally, the non-market behavior of global companies is affected by national regulation. European firms are given less discretion in the area of environmental risk than US companies, as environmental externalities are more stringently regulated. By contrast, in the US environmental management is considered a part of companies' social responsibility (Matten and Moon 2008). Similarly, labor regulation differs considerably across countries (Knoke *et al.* 1996), which is likely to affect companies' strategies in this area. Furthermore, different countries have different requirements concerning corporate reporting in areas of social or environmental responsibility. In Denmark, the Financial Statement Act was amended in 2009 to require reporting on corporate social responsibility. France has had a legal requirement since 1977 for companies with more than 300 employees to publish a social review (KPMG *et al.* 2010). Since 2003, the "Nouvelles Regulations Economiques" require companies with more than 300 employees to report their social and environmental as well as their financial performance. Thus, in their efforts to outsource global governance to private actors, IOs have allies in individual nation states. Even so, when companies operate across borders in less stringent jurisdictions, they are keen to show their commitment to universal standards in an effort to prevent any adverse pressure from external actors.

The Role of the Sponsoring Organization

Governmental and nongovernmental sponsors of PPVIs can pursue a variety of strategies to increase participation in these schemes as well as implementation of their contents and principles. The UNGC uses a system of Local Networks that are organized at the country level. By providing assistance to firms in fulfilling their UNGC commitments, these Local Networks can lower the cost of participation for individual companies. To retain their official status, the networks have to stage a UNGC related activity at least once a year. Beyond this minimally required level of activity, however, there is wide variation in the levels of Local Network activity observed in different countries. For 2009, many Local Networks reported no activity at all, while the Ukrainian network reported 36 activities in that year. Whelan (2010: 320) suggests a correlation between the activity of Local Networks and the corporate take-up rate, while Hamid and Johner (2010: 272) propose that the observed geographical variation in the percentage of UNGC participants "can mainly be explained by the strength of and efforts undertaken by Local Networks." Similarly, the 68% increase in GRI participants in Brazil between 2009 and 2010 can be attributed to the GRI network's proactive recruitment efforts which targeted companies with "letters of encouragement" to adopt GRI guidelines (Global Reporting Initiative 2011: 48). However, the relationship between company participation and local recruitment and support structures is not straightforward: It takes participation to support a network, and then the network is expected to boost corporate participation further. Controlling for this endogeneity of mobilizing network activity, Bernhagen, Mitchell, and Thissen-Smits (2012) have found no robust evidence for the expectation that Local Networks increase companies' take-up of the UNGC.

Does It Work?

A major criticism of voluntary codes of conduct formulated by international organizations is that they have no legal enforcement or monitoring mechanisms. Participating companies are not forced to implement the substance of the codes but rather pledge to abide by them to the extent that they perceive this to be in their interest (Murphy 2005: 389). Thus, the question remains to what extent companies' non-market strategies contribute to the global governance goals of the sponsoring organizations. Some commentators see voluntary codes as insufficient and ultimately incapable of solving global problems. Instead, it is feared that these programs enable companies to whitewash, or "greenwash," their reputation (Laufer 2003) while preventing more effective, public regulations from being developed and enacted (Haufler 2001). Participation in voluntary regimes is a "proactive" non-market strategy (Hillman and Hitt 1999). As a "buffering activity" (Meznar and Nigh 1995) it is aimed at shielding the company from the adverse effects of government activity. By contrast, many NGOs and activist groups would prefer tougher regulation and legal accountability instead of more PPVIs. Furthermore, Clapp (1998) fears that global voluntary initiatives may exacerbate a North–South divide, with the countries of the North imposing standards on developing countries in the South. For companies, this can lead to moral as well as strategic dilemmas: Is appropriate behavior determined by the countries' laws and customs or should companies behave in host countries as they do in their home country (Baron 2010: 752).

Supporters of self-regulation, for their part, have limited faith in state capacity to regulate business. They see voluntary agreements as an important part of a learning process within and among companies, supplementing or preceding regulation (Vogel 2010). In this view, voluntary codes help operationalize behavioral standards, communicate commitment to these standards to the outside world and produce common knowledge on compliance. In other words, they produce a platform where best practice can be exchanged, performance monitored, and socialization can be organized (Conzelmann and Wolf 2008).

Analyzing large, transnational garment companies, Kolk and van Tulder (2002) have found that codes are important, though not exclusive, tools for addressing child labor. However, while the footwear sector is now generally quite advanced in the implementation of codes, including its supply chains, the International Labor Organization (ILO) found the apparel and retail sectors lagging behind and appearing to treat CSR as a mainly symbolic exercise (Mamic 2003). Nonetheless, the ILO acknowledges that working conditions would not have improved in any of these sectors if there had not been pressure from external actors, facilitated by the existence of PPVIs (Mamic 2003). More generally, companies that participate in the UNGC are more likely than non-participants to have substantive human rights policies in place and to be regarded as sustainable corporations by external audiences (Bernhagen and Mitchell 2010). Similarly, while ISO standards are management systems rather than performance driven controls, research has shown that the environmental performance of certified companies is indeed better than that of others (Potoski and Prakash 2005). Thus, while voluntary initiatives may not solve global governance problems, progress is being made as programs are becoming more institutionalized (Haufler 2001; Kell and Levin 2003).

Why do companies not simply take the reputational benefits from participation in PPVIs while reneging on the potentially costly implementation? Legitimacy and reputation are important assets for companies, and codes that have been developed in cooperation with IOs and NGOs achieve high levels of legitimacy. But companies cannot assume their audiences to be naïve (Bernhagen and Mitchell 2010). To render their commitments credible they must be willing to take on material burdens and communicate these. ISO 14001 certification is a good example of this, which has been analyzed as a "club good" for which firms are willing to incur costs beyond what is required by law in order to reap reputational benefits (Prakash and Potoski 2007). The high profile of some PPVIs, the reputation of their sponsoring organizations, and a degree of visibility of social and environmental performance provides governmental and non-governmental actors with information that serves to pressure companies into implementing the substance of the voluntary schemes they enter. Large companies and those whose operations bring them in contact with precarious social, environmental, or human rights practices are often the first to be targeted in NGO campaigns, which in turn induces them to implement voluntary codes of conduct (Mamic 2003: 244). External monitoring might well improve implementation, but, on the whole, companies tend to do what they claim to do (Kolk 2004).

Some commentators have identified a trade-off between the ambitions of voluntary standards and their likelihood to achieve (some of) their goals. If voluntary initiatives ask too much, they may not accomplish what they aim to do, as was the case with the Sullivan Principles (Sethi and Williams 2000). Some certification schemes, such as the FSC, are strict, specific and have effective enforcement mechanisms and auditing requirements (Kolk and van Tulder 2005). However, in the case of the FSC this has also led to timber industries creating their own, weaker standards in some countries (Fuchs and Vogelmann 2008: 75). Similarly, if a globally active company imposes standards on local contractors in an effort to eliminate child labor, it may end up sending children to domestic employers with worse working conditions (Kapstein 2001; Vogel 2006; 2010). Furthermore, the financial burden of implementation is often incurred disproportionately by small firms or those in developing countries. And finally, the scope of many of the more successful voluntary standards, such as Fair Trade, is limited to particular sectors and has little effect in areas where many of the employees in the developing world are active: at home and in the informal sector. Thus, as other institutions can fail, so can voluntary initiatives, especially if some companies manage to free-ride on the efforts of others that take their obligations more seriously (Prakash and Potoski 2007).

Conclusion

Governments, business associations, IOs, NGOs, and investors develop PPVIs to address a lack of a central global political authority and an increasing recognition of a need for effective governance at the global level. In an attempt to meet social and political demands and improve their reputation and legitimacy, from the 1990s onward companies have increasingly engaged in this "nonstate, market-based variant of trading up" (Vogel 2010: 71) in the areas of environmental, labor, and social issues. Where companies used to aid development at a "micro level" by means of philanthropic activities, they are now expected to promote social progress more generally. For large, global companies, operating across countries with varying jurisdictions and different societal needs, and especially for those whose operations bring them into conflict with universally accepted social, environmental, and human rights standards, PPVIs have become a way to show commitment to social responsibility and a means to reduce the trust gap between them and society.

Despite the global nature of many of today's governance problems, many of the factors shaping companies' engagement in PPVIs can be found at the national level. Even if companies operate in the global market place, their origins and operational practices are still embedded in political, economic, and social systems at the level of the nation state: democratic regimes and the locally specific mobilization of bias can explain some of the variation in corporate engagement with PPVIs. Little is still known about the role played by regulatory regimes and different forms of capitalism. The countervailing power of national and international civil society seems to be a major force shaping global companies' decisions to engage in PPVIs. In doing so, NGOs have to rely on "credible information, expertise and moral authority" (Karns and Mingst 2004: 242). Equipped with these resources, they often act as foot soldiers of IOs' strategies of "outsourcing" global governance.

Voluntary codes are soft laws that lack enforcement and often have only weak monitoring mechanisms. While there is tentative evidence that global companies committing to these initiatives tend to put their money where their mouth is, there has been little systematic research on the effectiveness of these standards, particularly when firms operate across borders and in developing countries. Many of the host countries in which TNCs operate have lax regulatory regimes and limited enforcement capacities. Yet, many NGOs continue to push for the norms contained in these initiatives to be legally binding so that rather than committing to corporate *responsibility* companies are subject to corporate *accountability* (Clapp 2005). If, as some fear, companies really use CSR strategies to avert stricter regulation and accountability (Vogel 2008), then any achievements of global governance goals brought about by PPVIs may be more than undone by the setbacks that result from anti-regulatory lobbying facilitated by the very same PPVIs. Until this question is addressed in future research, we concur with Vogel's dictum on CSR more generally, that it may be the "second best alternative, but second best is better than nothing at all" (Vogel 2006: 163).

Note

1 For an overview, see Hancké (2009).

References

Accenture and United Nations Global Compact. 2010. *A New Era of Sustainability, UN Global Compact-Accenture CEO Study 2010*. New York: Accenture and United Nations.

Baron, David P. 2010. *Business and Its Environment*, 6th edn. London: Pearson.

Bennie, Lynn, Bernhagen, Patrick, and Mitchell, Neil J. 2007. "The Logic of Transnational Action: The Good Corporation and the Global Compact." *Political Studies*, 55: 733–753.

Berliner, Daniel and Prakash, Aseem. 2012. "From Norms to Programs: The United Nations Global Compact and Global Governance." *Regulation & Governance*, 6: 149–166.

Bernhagen, Patrick and Mitchell, Neil J. 2010. "The Private Provision of Public Goods: Corporate Commitments and the United Nations Global Compact." *International Studies Quarterly*, 54: 1175–1187.

Bernhagen, Patrick, Mitchell, Neil J., and Thissen-Smits, Marianne. 2012. "Corporate Citizens and the UN Global Compact: Explaining Cross-National Variations in Turnout." Second Annual Conference of the European Political Science Association, Berlin, June 21–23.

Boucher, Richard. 2010. OECD is Partner in UN Global Compact: Remarks by the OECD Deputy Secretary-General at the Ministerial Session of the UN Global Compact Leaders Summit 2010, http://www.oecd.org/document/17/0,3746,en_2649_34889_45593297_1_1_1_1,00.html. Accessed July 2, 2011.

Brammer, Stephen J. and Pavelin, Stephen. 2006. "Corporate Reputation and Social Performance: The Importance of Fit." *Journal of Management Studies*, 43: 435–455.

Brown, Halina S., de Jong, Martin, and Lessidrenska, Teodorina. 2009. "The Rise of the Global Reporting Initiative: A Case of Institutional Entrepreneurship." *Environmental Politics*, 18: 182–200.

Carbon Disclosure Project. 2012. Investor CDP, http://www.cdproject.net/en-US/Programmes/Pages/CDP-Investors.aspx#who. Accessed April 4.

Cashore, Benjamin William, Auld, Graeme, and Newsom, Deanna. 2004. *Governing through Markets*. New Haven: Yale University Press.

Chevron. 2012. "The World Needs More than Oil." *Advertisement in The Economist*, March 17–23.

Clapp, Jennifer. 1998. "The Privatization of Global Environmental Governance: ISO 14000 and the Developing World." *Global Governance*, 4 (3): 295–316.

Clapp, Jennifer. 2005. "Global Environmental Governance for Corporate Responsibility and Accountability." *Global Environmental Politics*, 5: 23–34.

Coen, David and Grant, Wyn. 2006. "Business and Government: Methods and Practice." In *Managing Business and Government Relations*, ed. David Coen and Wyn Grant, 13–31. Opladen: Barbara Budrich.

Congleton, Roger D. 1992. "Political Institutions and Pollution Control." *Review of Economics and Statistics*, 74: 412–421.

Conzelmann, Thomas and Wolf, Klaus D. 2008. "The Potential and Limits of Governance by Private Codes of Conduct." In *Transnational Private Governance and Its Limits*, ed. Jean-Christophe Graz and Andreas Nölke, 98–114. London: Routledge.

Cowen, Scott S., Ferreri, Linda B., and Parker, Lee D. 1987. "The Impact of Corporate Characteristics on Social Responsibility Disclosure: A Typology and Frequency-Based Analysis." *Accounting, Organizations and Society*, 12: 111–122.

CSRwire. 2012. McDonald's Announces Members of Global Advisory Council on Healthy Lifestyles, http://www.csrwire.com/press_releases/25189-McDonald-s-Announces-Members-of-Global-Advisory-Council-on-Healthy-Lifestyles. Accessed April 4.

Cutler, A. Claire, Haufler, Virginia, and Porter, Tony, eds. 1999. *Private Authority and International Affairs*. Albany: SUNY Press.

Davenport, Christian and Armstrong II, David A. 2004. "Democracy and the Violation of Human Rights: A Statistical Analysis from 1976 to 1996." *American Journal of Political Science*, 48: 538–554.

De Mesquita, Bruce B., Downs, George W., Smith, Alastair, and Cherif, Feryl M. 2005. "Thinking Inside the Box: A Closer Look at Democracy and Human Rights." *International Studies Quarterly*, 49: 439–457.

Doh, Jonathan P. and Guay, Terrence R. "Corporate Social Responsibility, Public Policy, and NGO Activism in Europe and the United States: An Institutional Stakeholder Perspective." *Journal of Management Studies*, 43: 47–73.

Fairtrade. 2012. Fairtrade Labeling International History, http://www.fairtrade.org.uk/what_is_fairtrade/history.aspx. Accessed April 4.

Flohr, Annegret, Rieth, Lothar, Schwindenhammer, Sandra, and Wolf, Klaus Dieter. 2010. *The Role of Business in Global Governance: Corporations as Norm Entrepreneurs.* Basingstoke: Palgrave Macmillan.

Fuchs, Doris and Vogelmann, Joris. 2008. "The Power of TNCs in Transnational Private Governance." In *Transnational Private Governance and Its Limits*, ed. Jean-Christophe Graz and Andreas Nölke, 71–83. London: Routledge.

Galbraith, John K. 1954. "Countervailing Power." *American Economic Review*, 44: 1–6.

Global Reporting Initiative. 2011. *A New Phase: The Growth of Sustainability Reporting, GRI's Year in Review 2010/2011.* Amsterdam.

Grier, Kevin B., Munger, Michael C., and Roberts, Brian E. 1994. "The Determinants of Industry Political Activity, 1978–1986." *American Political Science Review*, 88 (4): 911–926. JSTOR Stable URL: http://www.jstor.org/stable/2082716.

Hall, Peter A. and Soskice, David W. 2004; 2001. *Varieties of Capitalism: The Institutional Foundations of Comparative Advantage.* Oxford: Oxford University Press.

Hamid, Uzma and Johner, Oliver. 2010. "The United Nations Global Compact Communication on Progress Policy: Origins, Trends and Challenges." In *The United Nations Global Compact: Achievements, Trends and Challenges*, ed. Andreas Rasche and Georg Kell, 265–281. Cambridge: Cambridge University Press.

Hancké, Bob, ed. 2009. *Debating Varieties of Capitalism.* New York: Oxford University Press.

Haufler, Virginia. 2001. *A Public Role for the Private Sector: Industry Self-Regulation in a Global Economy.* Washington DC: Brookings Institution Press.

Held, David, McGrew, Anthony G., Goldblatt, David, and Perraton, Jonathon. 1999. *Global Transformations: Politics, Economics and Culture.* Cambridge: Polity Press.

Hillman, Amy J. and Hill, Michael A. 1999. "Corporate Political Strategy Formulation: A Model of Approach, Participation, and Strategy Decisions." *Academy of Management Review*, 24 (4): 825–842.

Hillman, Amy J., Keim, Gerald D., and Schuler, Douglas. 2004. "Corporate Political Activity: A Review and Research Agenda." *Journal of Management*, 30: 837–857.

IKEA. 2012. Responsibility beyond Home Furnishing, http://www.ikea.com/ms/en_GB/the_ikea_story/people_and_the_environment/index.html. Accessed April.

Janney, Jay J., Dess, Greg, and Forlani, Victor. 2009. "Glass Houses? Market Reactions to Firms Joining the UN Global Compact." *Journal of Business Ethics*, 90 (3): 407–423.

Jordan, Grant. 1998. "Indirect Causes and Effects in Policy Change: The Brent Spar Case." *Public Administration*, 76: 713–740.

Kapstein, Ethan B. 2001. "The Corporate Ethics Crusade." *Foreign Affairs*, 80: 105–119.

Karns, Margaret P. and Mingst, Karen A. 2004. *International Organizations: The Politics and Processes of Global Governance.* Boulder: Lynne Rienner.

Kell, George and Levin, David. 2003. "The Global Compact Network: An Historic Experiment in Learning and Action." *Business and Society Review*, 108: 151–181.

Knoke, David, Pappi, Franz U., Broadbent, Jeffery, and Tsujinaka, Yukata. 1996. *Comparing Policy Networks: Labor Politics in US, Germany, and Japan.* Cambridge: Cambridge University Press.

Kolk, Ans. 2004. "More than Words? An Analysis of Sustainability Reports." *New Academy Review*, 3: 59–75.

Kolk, Ans and van Tulder, Rob. 2002. "The Effectiveness of Self-Regulation: Corporate Codes of Conduct and Child Labour." *European Management Journal*, 20: 260–271.

Kolk, Ans and van Tulder, Rob. 2005. "Setting New Global Rules? TNCs and Codes of Conduct." *Transnational Corporations*, 14: 1–27.

KPMG, Unit for Corporate Governance in Africa, Global Reporting Initiative, UNEP. 2010. Carrots and Sticks: Promoting Transparency and Sustainability, an Update on Trends in Voluntary and Mandatory Approaches to Sustainability Reporting, https://www.globalreporting.org/resourcelibrary/Carrots-And-Sticks-Promoting-Transparency-And-Sustainability.pdf. Accessed December 20.

Kytle, Beth and Ruggie, John G. 2005. "Corporate Social Responsibility as Risk Management: A Model for Multinationals, Corporate Social Responsibility Initiative." *Working Paper*, 10; Cambridge, MA: John F. Kennedy School of Government, Harvard University.

Latham & Watkins LLP. 2009. The Importance of Voluntarism, http://www.unglobalcompact.org/docs/about_the_gc/Voluntarism_Importance.pdf. Accessed April 12.

Laufer, William S. 2003. "Social Accountability and Corporate Greenwashing." *Journal of Business Ethics*, 43: 253–261.

Leon H. Sullivan Foundation. 2012. Global Sullivan Principles, http://thesullivanfoundation.org/. Accessed April 5.

Li, Quan and Reuveny, Rafael. 2006. "Democracy and Environmental Degradation." *International Studies Quarterly*, 50: 935–956.

Mamic, Ivanka. 2003. *Business and Code of Conduct Implementation: How Firms Use Management Systems for Social Performance*. Geneva: International Labour Organization.

Matten, Dirk and Crane, Andrew. 2005. "Corporate Citizenship: Towards an Extended Theoretical Conceptualization." *Academy of Management Review*, 30: 166–179.

Matten, Dirk and Moon, Jeremy. 2008. "'Implicit' and 'Explicit' CSR: A Conceptual Framework for a Comparative Understanding of Corporate Social Responsibility." *Academy of Management Review*, 33: 404–424.

Meek, Gary K., Roberts, Clare B., and Gray, Sidney J. 1995. "Factors Influencing Voluntary Annual Report Disclosures by US, UK and Continental European Multinational Corporations." *Journal of International Business Studies*, 26: 555–572.

Meznar, Martin B. and Nigh, Douglass. 1995. "Buffer or Bridge? Environmental and Organizational Determinants of Public Affairs Activities in American Firms." *Academy of Management Journal*, 38: 975–976.

Murphy, Sean D. 2005. "Taking Multinational Corporate Codes of Conduct to the Next Level." *Columbia Journal of Transnational Law*, 43: 388–433.

Neumayer, Erik. 2002. "Do Democracies Exhibit Stronger International Environmental Commitment? A Cross-Country Analysis." *Journal of Peace Research*, 39: 139–164.

North, Douglas C. 1990. *Institutions, Institutional Change, and Economic Performance*. New York: Cambridge University Press.

OECD. 2011. Guideline for Multinational Enterprises, http://www.oecd.org/daf/internationalinvestment/guidelinesformultinationalenterprises/oecdguidelinesformultinationalenterprises.htm. Accessed July 2, 2012.

OECD. 2012. Consultation on the Guidelines for Multinational Enterprises and the UN "Protect, Respect and Remedy" Framework, http://www.oecd.org/daf/internationalinvestment/guidelinesformultinationalenterprises/consultationontheguidelinesformultinationalenterprisesandtheunprotectrespectandremedyframework.htm. Accessed May 12, 2012.

Olson, M. (1965/1971) *The Logic of Collective Action: Public Goods and the Theory of Groups*. Cambridge, MA: Harvard University Press.

Ozer, Mine. 2010. "Top Management Teams and Corporate Political Activity: Do Top Management Teams have Influence on Corporate Political Activity?" *Journal of Business Research*, 63: 1196–1201.

Payne, Rodger A. 1995. "Freedom and the Environment." *Journal of Democracy*, 6 (3): 41–55.

Perez Batres, Luis A., Miller, Van V., and Pisani, Michael J. 2011. "Institutionalizing Sustainability: An Empirical Study of Corporate Registration and Commitment to the United Nations Global Compact Guidelines." *Journal of Cleaner Production*, 19 (8): 843–851.

Perkins, Richard and Neumayer, Erik. 2010. "Geographic Variations in the Early Diffusion of Corporate Voluntary Standards: Comparing ISO14001 and the Global Compact." *Environment and Planning C: Government Policy*, 42: 347–365.

Post, James E. 2000. "Global Codes of Conduct: Activists, Lawyers, and Managers in Search of a Solution." In *Global Codes of Conduct: An Idea Whose Time Has Come*, ed. Oliver F. Williams, 113–116. Notre Dame: University of Notre Dame Press.

Potoski, Matthew and Prakash, Aseem. 2005. "Green Clubs and Voluntary Governance: ISO 14001 and Firms' Regulatory Compliance." *American Journal of Political Science*, 49 (2): 235–248.

Prakash, Aseem and Potoski, Matthew. 2007. "Collective Action through Voluntary Environmental Programs: A Club Theory Perspective." *Policy Studies Journal*, 35: 773–792.

Principles for Responsible Investment. 2011. An Investor Initiative in Partnership with UNEP Finance Initiative and the UN Global Compact, http://www.unpri.org/. Accessed April 4.

Roe, Mark, J. 1993. "Some Differences in Corporate Structure in Germany, Japan, and the United States." *Yale Law Journal*, 102: 1927–2003.

Rosenau, James N. 1995. "Governance in the Twenty-First Century." *Global Governance*, 1: 13–43.

Rowlands, Ian H. 2001. "Transnational Corporations and Global Environmental Politics." In *Non-State Actors in World Politics*, ed. Daphne Josselin and William Wallace, 133–149. Basingstoke: Palgrave.

Ruggie, John G. 2004. "Reconstituting the Global Public Domain: Issues, Actors, and Practices." *European Journal of International Relations*, 10 (4): 499–531.

Rugman, Ann M. and Doh, Jonathan P. 2008. *Multinationals and Development*. New Haven: Yale University Press.

Schattschneider, Elmer E. 1960. *The Semisovereign People: A Realist's View of Democracy in America*. New York: Holt.

Schuler, David A., Rehbein, Kathleen, and Cramer, Roxy D. 2002. "Pursuing Strategic Advantage through Political Means: A Multivariate Approach." *Academy of Management Journal*, 45: 659–672. JSTOR Stable URL: http://www.jstor.org/stable/3069303.

Sethi, S. Prakash and Williams, Oliver F. 2000. "Creating and Implementing Global Codes of Conduct: An Assessment of the Sullivan Principles as a Role Model for Developing International Codes of conduct: Lessons Learned and Unlearned." *Business and Society Review*, 105: 169–200.

Sethi, S. Prakash. 2003. *Setting Global Standards: Guidelines for Creating Codes of Conduct in Multinational Corporations*. Hoboken: J. Wiley.

Stigler, George J. 1971. "The Theory of Economic Regulation." *Bell Journal of Economics and Management Science*, 2: 3–21.

Stiglitz, Joseph E. 2002. *Globalization and Its Discontents*. London: Lane.

UNEP Finance Initiative and PRI. 2010. *Universal Ownership, Why Environmental Externalities Matter to Institutional Investors*. UNEP FI and PRI.

United Nations. 1999. Kofi Annan's Address to World Economic Forum in Davos. Davos (Switzerland), February 1, 1999, http://www.un.org/News/ossg/sg/stories/statments_search_full.asp?statID=22. Accessed April 4.

United Nations. 2006. "Report of the Secretary-General on the Work of the Organization." *Official Records Sixty-First Session*, Supplement 1 (A/61/1).

Vitali, Stefania, Glattfelder, James B., and Battiston, Stefano. 2011. "The Network of Global Corporate Control." *PLoS ONE*, 6 (10): e25995.

Vogel, David. 2006. *The Market for Virtue*. Washington, DC: Brookings Institution Press.

Vogel, David. 2008. "Private Global Business Regulation." *Annual Review of Political Science*, 11: 261–282.

Vogel, David. 2010. "The Private Regulation of Global Corporate Conduct." *Business and Society*, 49: 68–87.

Waddock, Sandra. 2008. "Building a New Institutional Infrastructure for Corporate Responsibility." *Academy of Management Perspectives*, 22 (3): 87–108.

Whelan, Nessa. 2010. "Building the Global Compact Local Network Model: History and Highlights." In *The United Nations Global Compact: Achievements, Trends and Challenges*, ed. Andreas Rasche and Georg Kell, 317–339. Cambridge: Cambridge University Press.

Williams, Olivier F. 2000. *Global Codes of Conduct: An Idea Whose Time Has Come*. Notre Dame: University of Notre Dame Press.

World Business Council for Sustainable Development. 2012. Membership, http://www.wbcsd.org/about/members.aspx. Accessed March 25.

Part V Global Companies and Society

The Handbook of Global Companies, First Edition. Edited by John Mikler.
© 2013 John Wiley & Sons, Ltd. Published 2013 by John Wiley & Sons, Ltd.

Chapter 20

Global Companies and Global Society

The Evolving Social Contract

Ann Florini

Introduction

The for-profit sector has always found it necessary to operate under some type of contract with society, whether implicit or explicit, and that social contract is always contested and under negotiation. Companies often have negative as well as positive impacts on the societies in which they are embedded, such as pollution, extraction of rents, or treatment of labor, and societies differ across space and time in their tolerance for those negative externalities. Moreover, business rarely thrives in a society that lacks certain public goods, such as a financial system to make cash and credit available, a legal system to ensure contracts are honored, and usually some sort of regulatory system. The costs for the provision of those public goods are borne at least in part by people who are not directly sharing the profits, and their willingness to bear those costs depends in part on their acceptance of the legitimacy of the private sector. As John Braithwaite and Peter Drahos (2000) show in their magisterial survey of the history of business regulation through the ages, much of the story of economic history is a story of the ever-changing nature of the social contract for business.

The social contract is complex enough when the "social" side is well-defined and circumscribed, as in a national polity that has a government that can at least in principle represent the interests of society and serve as a societal check on the power of business (even if government does not always actually do so). But the era of global economic integration has raised questions about whether national governments, either acting individually or attempting to cooperate with other governments, retain that capacity (Alexandroff 2008; Avant, Finnemore, and Sell 2010; Held and McGrew 2002; Jones, Pascual, and Stedman 2009; Ruggie 1993; Slaughter 2004). Such doubts have fostered efforts by a wide range of other social actors to find

The Handbook of Global Companies, First Edition. Edited by John Mikler.
© 2013 John Wiley & Sons, Ltd. Published 2013 by John Wiley & Sons, Ltd.

ways to regulate and shape the roles of business, and their efforts are increasingly facilitated by the information and communications revolution. Although clearly the global sphere does not have the relatively well defined society that exists at the national level, where at least most residents usually share the common definition of "citizen," it is reasonable to argue that there has been some degree of development of what might be called "global society" (Scholte 2005). This article explores the relationship between global companies and the nascent global society through the lens of the evolving social contract for global business.

When the current incarnation of economic globalization got underway in the 1960s and 1970s, it largely consisted of American corporations going overseas. Thus, the social contract under which US business then operated was the mental model available for those increasingly global companies. Within the United States, the traditional division of labor among the three sectors – private (business), public (government), and civil society – was assumed to be clear-cut. Business, usually in the form of corporations, would seek profits, and in so doing would provide wealth, jobs, goods, and services to society. Governments would regulate those corporations and would provide the public goods needed for society and business to flourish, including such public goods as contract enforcement, rules of the road, and property rights. Civil society groups would agitate for change in government regulations and attempt to broaden the definition of public goods that should be provided. Certainly there were disputes about the extent of corporate social responsibility, as we will see below, but in general these assumptions about the appropriate roles for the three sectors prevailed.

Globalization, privatization, and changing ideas about the roles of business and government have blurred these distinctions. In this new world, corporations increasingly deliver essential services and meet basic public needs in their areas of operation (and sometimes beyond), exert heavy influence over public policy, and find that their consumers and investors hold them directly accountable for their effects on the environment and on human rights. Intergovernmental organizations and transnational civil society networks demand to partner with global companies in pursuit of various definitions of the public interest. The notion of the social contract for business has always been contested, but now more hotly than ever. What now are the terms of the implicit "social contract" between business operating at a global scale, and society?

Before we turn to that question, some definitional caveats are needed. First, "global business" is not a well-defined concept. It includes both Western and the smaller but rapidly growing category of transnational non-Western-based firms, particularly those based in Asia. Within each category, further subdivision is needed according to the nature of the transnational ties of a given firm, whether those ties primarily involve sales and trade, supply chains, or major operations abroad (particularly for extractive industries). Different elements of the social contract may be more or less relevant for different types of global companies.

"Global society" has even less coherence as a concept. At the global level, there are two "societies" to consider. One is the society of states, which we will consider in its most organized form, the intergovernmental organization (IGO). The other is global civil society. Clearly, there is no single demarcated set of nongovernmental social ties that cross borders in ways that influence corporate licenses to operate. But a reasonably close approximation, for the purposes of this chapter, can be found in the NGO sector, via both formally constituted international NGOs (INGOs) and networks that bring together national and local civil society groups across borders in less formal ways. Global firms must interact with both IGOs and INGOs.

This chapter will begin by laying out the US roots of the always-contested nature of the social contract for business and how some older ideas about that social contract no longer make sense under conditions of globalization. It then assesses how and why the social contract has evolved through the interaction of global business and global society, with the latter conceptualized in two ways: transnational civil society networks as an example of social forces, and IGOs as proxy for the society of states. It concludes by exploring emerging questions that affect the social license to operate, such as the growing contestation over varieties of capitalism, the natural resource/environmental crisis, and new forms of social organization.

The American Models

Two publications from the same time in the United States point to the contested nature of the social contract for business. The first is a *New York Times Magazine* article by Milton Friedman (1970) that admirably summarized his views that the business of business is business – in other words, that the social contract requires of business only that it seek profits within the boundaries of the law. Friedman contended that the sole obligation of corporate managers is to do what shareholders want, which is assumed to be profit maximization.[1] Friedman also argued that the "best interests" of corporations, and therefore corporate shareholders, is the sole legitimate criterion for all managerial decision-making (beyond legal compliance). Friedman did allow a bit of wiggle room for "hypocritical window dressing" that may serve to attract employees and reduce sabotage, which implied that some thinking about the social contract might be useful, and customers and employees received passing mention as deserving some managerial responsibility – but since they are not owners, it is not clear on what basis Friedman extended that responsibility to them.

Friedman's argument included one key claim and one key omission. The claim was a strong assertion that government will take care of externalities, collective action problems, and public goods provision by taxing, spending, and regulating as needed to serve the public interest. The omission was to ignore corporate incentives and possibly disproportionate capacity to influence public policy, not least to free themselves from regulations and to win the legal right to externalize costs onto the rest of society. As we will see below, the claim, always questionable in a world of imperfect government, became far more problematic with globalization. And the omission became too glaring to ignore when massive multinational corporations engaged directly with emerging or less-developed countries.

With the temporary triumph of the neoliberal revolution in the 1980s and 1990s, such views began to be seen elsewhere in the world as representing an American consensus. But it is important to remember that in the 1970s Friedman was writing in response to a chorus of calls, including several by business leaders, for greater social responsibility on the part of American corporations. At the same time that Friedman's article appeared, a distinguished group of American business and academic leaders was coming to a very different conclusion about the nature of the social contract for business.

The Committee for Economic Development (CED), an American think-tank founded in 1942 whose 200 trustees are business and academic leaders, had been searching for a pragmatic middle ground between voices such as Friedman's at one extreme and calls for business to solve all of America's problems on the other. In 1971, after an intensive process engaging a wide range of those trustees, the CED issued its report on "Social Responsibilities of Business Corporations" (Committee for Economic Development 1971). This report is worth citing at length, as it took a much broader view of the social contract in ways that strikingly foreshadow current debates:

> Business functions by public consent, and its basic purpose is to serve constructively the needs of society – to the satisfaction of society. Historically, business has discharged this obligation mainly by supplying the needs and wants of people for goods and services, by providing jobs and purchasing power, and by producing most of the wealth of the nation... (Committee for Economic Development 1971: 11)

> [However,] the sluggishness of social progress is engendering rising criticism of *all* major institutions – government, schools, organized labor, the military, the church, as well as business. In this context, the large business corporation is undergoing the most searching public scrutiny since the 1930s about its role in American society... (p. 14, emphasis in original)

> Today it is clear that the terms of the contract between society and business are, in fact, changing in substantial and important ways. Business is being asked to assume broader responsibilities to society than ever before, and to serve a wider range of human values. Business enterprises, in effect, are being asked to contribute more to the quality of American life than just supplying quantities of goods and services. Inasmuch as business exists to serve society, its future will depend on the quality of management's response to the changing expectations of the public... (p. 16)

> *The great growth of corporations in size, market power, and impact on society has naturally brought with it a commensurate growth in responsibilities; in a democratic society, power sooner or later begets equivalent accountability.* (p. 21, emphasis in original)

As the report went into details, it cited approvingly a wide range of ways in which corporations could pursue "enlightened self-interest" via engagement in a broader range of activities than a pure profit focus would entail, from philanthropy to capacity building for government to internalization of environmental externalities. At one point, it foreshadowed what has since come to be known as "social enterprise":

> business must recognize that the pursuit of profit and the pursuit of social objectives can usually be made complementary. From the standpoint of business, profit can be earned by serving public needs for social improvements as well as for goods consumed privately... There are likely to be many areas of social improvement in which the prospects for profit do not meet prevailing corporate investment criteria. In such cases, corporations will need to reexamine the traditional concepts and measurements of profit in the newer context. This may well involve, among other things, a substantial diversion of resources away from private consumption into higher priority social improvements. (Committee for Economic Development 1971: 31–32)

As the consensus document makes clear, even within the United States views within the business and academic communities about the nature of the social contract for business have long been far more varied and nuanced than the simplistic slogan "the business of business is business" would suggest. This greater sophistication of views can also be found in US government policy and its role in protecting citizens from the untrammeled functioning of market forces. In that regard, another important precursor of current debates can be found in the academic literature of the early 1980s. In an article well known to all graduate students of international relations, John Ruggie (1983) introduced the notion of "embedded liberalism." Ruggie suggested that the post-World War II American-led liberal economic order differed fundamentally from its British predecessor. British liberalism was based on a widely shared norm that the purpose of state monetary policy should only be to maintain external stability via gold parity. In the 1920s and 1930s, that norm was breaking down, with the result that the design of the post-war economic order reflected a fundamentally different view of the appropriate role of state economic policy. The Bretton Woods, American-led version of the liberal order extended legitimacy to the notion of state economic intervention in pursuit of purely domestic goals such as full employment and domestic social stability (pp. 208, 215). This significant norm shift embodied the notion that citizens should not be vulnerable to international economic forces beyond their control and that governments should and could intervene to protect them. As we will see below, such thinking about the appropriate relationship between markets and societies has transferred into debates about global markets and global societies, featuring particularly in the United Nations' efforts to promote an improved global social contract for business.

The Globalization of Business and Society

The story of the globalization of business and the rise of global companies is well described elsewhere in this Handbook. A quick review of the statistics shows a rapid rise in the sheer numbers of transnational corporations with foreign affiliates. From some 35,000 parent transnational corporations with about 170,000 foreign affiliates at the beginning of the 1990s, the number jumped to 103,786 parents with 892,114 affiliates as of 2010 (UNCTAD 1992: 5; 2011). As global companies burgeoned and took on more direct roles in international governance, scholars began exploring in depth the emergence of what was termed "private authority" in the international system (Cutler, Haufler, and Porter 1999; Hall and Biersteker 2002; Buthe 2010). This literature generally addresses issues of business self-regulation.

It is less well known that the same trends of ever-cheaper transportation and communications technologies, along with the great opening up of the former Soviet bloc, China, and India, that have propelled the globalization of business have had similar if harder to measure impacts on global social ties. The impact of both formally constituted international NGOs (INGOs) and less formal transnational networks of civil society actors on international affairs became so pronounced that the 1990s saw the rise of a cottage industry of scholarly publications documenting such impacts in fields ranging from arms control to corruption to environmental protection (Keck and Sikkink 1998; Boli and Thomas 1999; Edwards and Gaventa 2001; Florini 2000; Gordenker and Weiss 1996; Kaldor 2003; Khagram, Riker, and Sikkink 2002; O'Brien et al. 2000; Risse-Kappen 1995; Smith, Chatfield, and Pagnucco 1997; Weiss and Gordenker 1996). For the most part, this literature focuses on interactions between transnational civil society networks and governments, IGOs, or international regimes, rather than global companies. A few significant international relations works have looked explicitly at the roles of global companies in setting international rules (Sell 2003; Strange 1996). The management and international business literature has also included significant attention to the interaction between businesses and NGOs, including some at the global level. A comprehensive survey of this literature argues that it can be divided among six principle themes: NGO activism; NGO–business partnerships; multi-sectoral partnerships; global governance and standardization; national-level governance; and company stakeholder management (Kourula and Laasonen 2010). Although many of these works from all of these disciplines address questions of governance, power, authority, and legitimacy, surprisingly few have explicitly addressed the question of the existing and evolving social contract under which global companies may operate.

The Evolution of the Global Social Contract

As a result of global economic and social integration, more and more of the business–society interaction has played out at a transnational rather than purely national level, involving transnational corporations, transnational civil society networks and organizations, and intergovernmental organizations. There is no simple way to categorize these interactions. As MacIntosh and Thomas (2002) point out, the NGOs that interact with business vary in their fundamental characteristics: their scope (from the very local to the global), the nature of the organization (from community group to business association to professional body), their structure, their focus (which can be virtually any topic, from service delivery to human rights to environmental protection), their activities, and their choices about how to engage with corporations and with IGOs. Thus, business-NGO interactions, unsurprisingly, can vary enormously.

The most visible of the interactions between global companies and global society have occurred in the form of NGO campaigns against individual businesses and against whole corporate sectors. Such campaigns are certainly not new – they date back at least to the late 1700s, when opponents of slavery in such organizations as the US-based Pennsylvania Society for Promoting the Abolition of Slavery and the British Society for Effecting the Abolition of the Slave Trade joined forces across the ocean, exchanging information and sharing tactics aimed at mobilizing popular pressure for antislavery legislation (Florini 2000). Starting in the 1970s and accelerating in ensuing decades, however, has been a trend toward much more transnational mobilization in such campaigns. As Spar and La Mure (2003) note, this is not surprising given the shift in power from states to corporations:

> In the earliest days of NGO activity, protestors targeted the obvious source of power: if they wanted to end slavery or child labor, for example, they pressured the governments that presided over, or at least permitted, such practices ... However, as corporations have gained prominence in the global economy, they have become more and more the direct target of activism – of boycotts, consumer protest, and shareholder rebellion ... These strategies make eminent sense. In places like Burma, Indonesia, and Sierra Leone, corporations such as The Gap or DeBeers can wield a disproportionate amount of economic influence, an influence made even larger in recent years by the

relative decline of both foreign aid and official lending. If economic influence can be translated into political pull, then the best way to change a country's laws or practice may well be through the corporations that invest there. (pp. 80, 81)

Such campaigns can have significant impact. Among the best known is the campaign that arose in protest of implementation of the Trade-Related Intellectual Property Rights (TRIPS) regime in the late 1990s. The TRIPS accord, negotiated at the behest of, and largely incorporating the terms preferred by, a number of large multinational corporations, particularly pharmaceuticals, stirred a firestorm of controversy when its stringent protections of intellectual property rights came into conflict with the needs of many countries for less expensive versions of patent-protected medicines to address such compelling medical emergencies as HIV/AIDS (Sell 2003). In what may be one of the most glaring public relations blunders of modern times, dozens of international drug companies filed suit in 1997 to prevent South African president Nelson Mandela from enforcing a law that would sidestep TRIPS protections for HIV/AIDS medicines. Suing Nelson Mandela in pursuit of greater profits and at the expense of dying poor people did not go over well in the court of global public opinion. After a global campaign involving Médecins Sans Frontières, Oxfam International, and many others, the global pharmaceutical corporations reversed course, dropping the lawsuit and joining a number of efforts to make medicines affordable in developing countries (Florini 2005).

Yet as Spar and La Mure (2003) demonstrate, in most cases the measurable financial threat from NGO activism is not at all clear to firms, yet nonetheless under some conditions the campaigns have considerable impact in changing the behavior of global business, while in others the campaigns seem not to matter much. When Nike, for example, faced activist and media pressures related to working conditions in the overseas factories that supplied it in the 1990s, it initially resisted calls for action, insisting it had no responsibility for those conditions. By 1998, however, the firm capitulated, and over the next few years became an active leader of efforts to improve working conditions in the apparel industry around the world. Swiss pharmaceutical giant Novartis, although it was not a producer of AIDS treatments and had not been targeted in the TRIPS campaign described above or in other significant NGO campaigns, nonetheless began a dialogue with NGOs and established a corporate social responsibility program, and launched a number of philanthropic ventures related to health in developing countries. The oil firm Unocal, in contrast, fended off years of intensive criticisms of its involvement in the Udana natural gas field in Burma, a country that only recently has begun to emerge from a status as an international pariah for its brutal record on human rights.

Spar and La Mure (2003) suggest that firms consider three variables in deciding how to respond when they are targeted: transaction costs, brand input, and competitive position (p. 84). Unocal faced high transactions costs for withdrawing from Burma, whereas Nike could relatively easily switch to other suppliers. Branding concerns did not apply to Unocal, which had divested its retail gas stations, whereas Nike was entirely dependent on retail consumer willingness to buy its products. Firms may seek to improve their competitive position in their industry by moving early to align themselves with NGO demands, as Novartis sought to differentiate itself from the rest of the pharmaceutical industry, then under widespread attack. But as Spar and

La Mure concede, not all can be explained by such commercial calculations. Even among large publicly traded corporations, there is a role for the personal convictions of top managers, who may choose to "do good" for its own sake.

Zadek (2006; 2010) describes corporations as moving through several stages of organizational learning as they find themselves pushed by global society to take on new forms of corporate responsibility thinking. Global companies often begin with a defensive response contesting the notion of any such responsibility or any implied wrongdoing. They then move to a "compliance" stage of going along with certain demands, such as signing up to codes of conduct. As corporations internalize new ways of thinking, management practices change, and ultimately "social responsibil-ity" steps may become part of corporate strategy. For a few, but only a few, such social responsibility goals may become the primary purpose of the corporation.

On the other side of the corporate–NGO relationship, there has been a strong and growing trend among NGOs to look for ways to partner with corporations – some-times at the same time as campaigning against them. Most strikingly, Greenpeace, better known for its spectacular stunts than for broad dialogue, took to joining meetings with corporate and governmental leaders on such key environmental issues as climate change. A 2012 *New York Times* account began as follows:

> The bearded South African in the red dashiki took a seat in the front row amid a sea of dark-suited executives at a side meeting of the United National climate change conference [in Durban, South Africa] in December [2011]. "Kumi, it's good to see you here," Bjorn Stigson, president of the World Business Council for Sustainable Development, told Kumi Naido, executive director of Greenpeace International. "I'd much rather have you inside the room here than outside protesting." At that moment, a group of Greenpeace activists under Mr. Naidoo's direction were outside the hotel picketing the business gathering. Seven were arrested and charged with trespassing; three were fined and deported. (Broder 2012)

On the part of both global companies and global society, there has been a demonstra-ble, if far from universal and often hotly contested, evolution toward a willingness to partner in the pursuit of social goals. Austin (2000) provides a helpful categorization of how such partnerships may evolve, as viewed in relatively conventional business terms. Often relationships between companies and NGOs begin as simple philan-thropy, generally characterized by low engagement on the part of the firm, with the philanthropy not central to the business mission, few resources invested, infre-quent interaction between the business executives and the social groups, all of which adds up to a low-cost and low-benefit relationship for the firm. As the relationship develops, it may become more transactional, with the firm gaining more benefits, possibly in the form of publicity and community goodwill. Finally, a meaningful and longer-lasting integrative partnership could bring about joint value creation. How-ever, as Austin noted in 2000, the "marketplace" for such alliances was then poorly developed, with a serious shortage of information about potential partners and few mechanisms for finding them.

Although the marketplace remains underdeveloped, significant progress has occurred since Austin wrote. One milestone was the World Summit on Sustainable Development, held in Johannesburg, South Africa, in 2002, which became known as the "Partnership Summit" for the large number of partnerships agreed among companies, governments, and NGOs (Cowe 2004). Such undertakings as the Extractive Industries Transparency Initiative got their start at Johannesburg, and many global companies and NGOs took their first steps toward new collaborations.

Global Companies and the Society of States: The Evolving Relationship with IGOs

The relationship between market forces more broadly and companies specifically and intergovernmental organizations dates back at least a century, to the founding of the International Labor Organization (ILO). The ILO's tripartite membership, unique among international organizations, brought together employers, governments, and labor unions as equal partners in setting labor standards – the West's attempt after Russia's Bolshevik revolution to ensure the future of capitalism. Thereafter, however, little happened on the IGO front for many decades.[2] In the 1970s, a series of scandals involving American multinational corporations operating in developing countries, such as ITT's interference in Chile's domestic elections (United States Senate 1975), triggered pushback from those developing countries via the intergovernmental organizations in which they had recently acquired majority voting power. Most significantly, the United Nations set up a Centre on Transnational Corporations and began negotiations aimed at developing standards to require corporations to respect national sovereignty and to disclose information about their operations (Haufler 2001: 16).

With the Reagan–Thatcher "neoliberal revolution" of the 1980s, however, the impetus for regulating transnational business via IGOs faltered. Driven partly by technology and partly by normative shifts, developing countries began to welcome the foreign investment and skills of global companies (Martin 1999; Yergin and Stanislaw 1998). Yet the "anti-globalization" protests of the 1990s sparked renewed concerns about the social contract within which global companies were operating (Florini 2003).

In response to such concerns, the United Nations returned to Ruggie's idea of "embedded liberalism" to consider how economic liberalism could be re-embedded in the increasingly integrated global economy.[3] In 1999, UN Secretary General Kofi Annan gave a speech to the World Economic Forum (WEF) annual meeting in Davos, Switzerland, an ideal site for reaching corporate leaders as the WEF's membership includes the world's thousand largest corporations. In it, he pleaded for what he called a global compact, essentially a new social contract "of shared values and principles, which will give a human face to the global market":

> Globalization is a fact of life. But I believe we have underestimated its fragility. The problem is this. The spread of markets outpaces the abilities of societies and their political systems to adjust to them, let alone to guide the course they take. History teaches us that such an imbalance between the economic, social and political worlds can never be sustained for very long . . .
>
> Let us remember that the global markets and the multilateral trading system we have today did not come about by accident. They are the result of enlightened policy choices made by governments since 1945. If we want to maintain them in the new century,

all of us – governments, corporations, nongovernmental organizations, international organizations – have to make the right choices now.

We have to choose between a global market driven by calculations of short-term profit, and one which has a human face. Between a world which condemns a quarter of the human race to starvation and squalor, and one which offers everyone at least a chance of prosperity, in a healthy environment. Between a selfish free-for-all in which we ignore the fate of the losers, and a future in which the strong and the successful accept their responsibilities, showing global vision and leadership. I am sure you will make the right choice.

The outcome of that stirring call to arms was strikingly different from the UN's previous venture into restructuring the social contract for business via the Center for Transnational Corporations. This time, the UN set up an entirely voluntary "Global Compact," a code of conduct with a difference. The Global Compact does not set specific standards for member companies to attain. Instead, it lays out ten principles in the arenas of human rights, labor standards, environmental protection, and anti-corruption, based on international agreements widely adopted by the world's governments. Member companies are required to report annually on their efforts to align their practices with those principles. The reporting requirement and discussions among the member companies and other Global Compact adherents (civil society groups and UN agencies) are intended to help the member companies learn how to make progress toward what is essentially global social contract.

In short, the Global Compact aims to re-embed liberal market functions on a voluntary basis in a social contract based on principles legitimized by governments for other purposes. It demonstrates clearly the shift in UN attitudes regarding global companies to one that seeks engagement (Therien and Pouliot 2006). Its efficacy in changing business practices is hotly disputed. Although it regularly expels member companies that fail to comply with its reporting requirements or for failing to report substantive progress toward the goals (it expelled its 3000th member company in February 2012), thus ensuring that the Compact is not merely a fig leaf, it is not designed to verify the companies' self-reported accomplishments. That leaves civil society activists skeptical about whether the terms of this new social contract are in fact being honored (Marx 2012).

Although it is the most ambitious attempt to date to design a social compact appropriate for the global era, the Global Compact is only one of many interactions between global companies and IGOs. As Bull, Boas, and McNeill (2004) show, the Global Compact is just one of multiple forms of cooperation underway between IGOs, particularly the United Nations, and global companies. These include policy dialogue (such as corporate participation in the UNAIDS governing board), advocacy partnerships (such as the NetAid initiative that brought together the UN Development Program and Cisco), information and learning partnerships (such as the Global Compact), and direct engagement in operations (such as the Refugee Registration Project of the UN High Commissioner for Refugees and Microsoft).[4]

This growing engagement results from multiple factors. One is clearly simple need for resources – cash-strapped IGOs have gone in search of funds and in-kind contributions. But the growing degree of partnership between global companies and IGOs could not have happened with the UN of the 1970s. Clearly, there has been an ideological shift within the UN's membership, from neo-Marxist to neoliberal, that has included a willingness to engage with global companies in lieu of trying to regulate them. Here, a crucial factor has been the practical and intellectual leadership of particular individuals, notably former Secretary General Kofi Annan, senior officials such as Mark Malloch Brown, John Ruggie, and UN Global Compact head Georg Kell, along with leaders in other IGOs such as Gro Harlem Brundtland at the World Health Organization. On the part of global companies, issue specific factors have impelled greater interest in collaborating with IGOs, such as the growing prevalence of HIV/AIDS among labor forces (Bull, Boas, and McNeill 2004).

Assessments of the implications of greater private-sector involvement with UN organization have been mixed. On the positive side, as Bull, Boas, and McNeill (2004) suggest, the partnerships bring greater flexibility and relevance to IGOs, in addition to resources. But these are instrumental considerations. Critics raise concerns about the explosion of public-private "funds," particularly in the health arena, that may challenge efforts to create more coherent programs. The Global Alliance for Vaccines and Immunization (GAVI), for example, has been criticized for focusing on vaccinating children – a particular concern of funder Bill Gates – at the expense of building robust and sustainable health systems with trained personnel able to respond to local priorities. Corporate involvement may also distort policy priorities, with the particular engagement of large pharmaceutical corporations following the TRIPS debacle a possible explanation of why there have been so many fragmented health initiatives. Partnerships between IGOs and global companies may also shift the balance of power among UN agencies in favor of those agencies whose mandates or operations happen to be of greatest corporate interest.

Many in transnational civil society remain suspicious of the relationship between global business and IGOs (and their most influential member states), seeing these relationships as means by which business shapes global rules to its own benefit in what is in effect privatization of the multilateral system. In 2006, for example, ActionAid, an international non-governmental federation of development organizations, released a report arguing that "[b]ig business's privileged access to policy-makers is contributing to global trade rules that undermine the fight against poverty" (p. 4). ActionAid (2006: 10) contended that in addition to common indirect means of influence on policy-makers such as financial contributions, media coverage, and wining and dining of policy-makers, global companies also have disproportionate influence on trade policy via such direct means as:

- face to face meetings with policy-makers;
- serving on government advisory committees;
- making presentations to policy-makers;
- sending letters, memos and emails to policy-makers;
- making formal submissions to government consultations;
- even serving on government delegations.

ActionAid argued that the outcome of such disproportionate corporate influence can be seen in such global trade rules as TRIPS and the Global Agreement on Trade in Services, which it contends have benefitted global companies at the expense of the global public interest.

Bull, Boas, and McNeill (2004), however, note that influence may be a two-way street. Although advocates for corporate–IGO partnerships usually focus on instrumental questions of efficiency and effective operations, and critics are concerned with the impact on the power, authority, and legitimacy of IGOs, Bull, Boas, and McNeill have a constructivist take, pointing out the potential positive impact, with IGOs becoming "an arena for encounters between different forces in which multilateral institutions become nodal points in complex *networks of governance*, rather than a system constituted mainly by state actors" (p. 493). The question of who influences whom with regard to ideas and framing is an empirical one that should be investigated, not asserted: "Authority and legitimacy are not fixed but flexible – subject to changing, malleable interpretations over time" (p. 494).

Conclusion

The current state of the global social contract is rather messy. The former neat distinction of the three sectors and their respective roles clearly no longer holds, and the notion of a social contract that allows business to seek profits by any legal means is not tenable, particularly given the degree to which business is now setting the rules that determine what is legal. But where does this leave us?

John Ruggie, who as both scholar and practitioner has played as large a role as anyone in both analyzing and shaping the evolving social contract for global companies, describes that evolution as follows. Ruggie's assessment begins with what he calls the accountability chapter, with attention to the accountability of global firms to the wide range of stakeholders affected by corporate decisions and actions. This chapter in the evolution of the global social contract includes the whole array of codes, reporting initiatives, certification schemes, and other proliferating experiments in transparency and accountability, driven primarily by NGOs, although with slowly increasing involvement from investors and governments – an important story, but one that may have run its course in terms of impelling change. Chapter two, in Ruggie's view, is social capacity-building, where he locates the Global Compact that he helped to establish, and which includes many of the operational partnerships described above. Chapter three, where little progress has yet been made, concerns the imbalance in the system of global rule-making, which "has increasingly privileged private capital over other social actors, and the spread of global markets over other social concerns – be they human rights, labor standards, or environmental principles" (Ruggie *et al.* 2004: 14). Such an imbalance is not socially sustainable, and managing these tensions would require finding ways to "marry world civic politics with global private governance" (p. 14).

Ruggie may be correct that Chapter one-type initiatives are unlikely to cumulate into adequate means of addressing the imbalances between global companies and global society, but they are also unlikely to fade away. Codes of conduct, disclosure standards, new business models, and investment standards are still largely experimental and it is probably too early to dismiss them altogether. Yet it is certainly true that they are piecemeal and uncoordinated efforts at best. Social capacity-building is certainly needed, but it is not clear what that capacity will then be able to accomplish in the absence of a more coherent and cohesive global governance system within which the social contract would apply. And it is certainly the case that a system of global rule-making that excessively privileges capital at the expense of societies is not one likely to satisfy society's concerns in the social contract.

Many questions remain to be addressed. One key question is: who will set the terms of a new global social contract? As we have seen, multiple dialogues are underway, both in the form of conversation and via the practice of partnerships, but little research has yet been done on the implications of those dialogues. Despite Bull, Boas, and McNeill's intriguing suggestion of the power of IGOs to influence global companies in the global public interest, little is yet known about which direction influence actually flows. Moreover, with the emergence of global companies from countries not previously strongly represented in these debates, such as China and India, the question of "who" will necessarily involve whole societies whose attitudes toward such questions have yet to be rigorously investigated.

A second question is: what will drive the terms of the new social contract? The global agenda of the next few decades is likely to be shaped by two very powerful trends. The first is what might be called the age of scarcity: the increasingly tight constraints on available water, arable land, climate "space," and other natural resources that previously were relatively available to global firms. On such key issues as climate, biodiversity loss, the imbalances in the nitrogen cycle, and other severely threatening global environmental threats, the utter failure of intergovernmental cooperation to rise to the scale of the challenges is likely to spur social demands on global companies to act – demands that current business models are ill designed to meet. The second is inequality, given the socially stressful trends toward concentration of wealth and income in most countries in an ever smaller elite, trends from which leaders of global companies have benefited. A stable social contract for business may entail quite significant changes in how rewards are allocated.

All this leaves us with a rich research agenda. In the growing array of partnerships, who is actually influencing whom? Can these partnerships move beyond service delivery to entail much deeper collaboration around the thorny issues on the global agenda? Will varieties of capitalism engage in the debate over the social contract in different ways, with shareholder-driven public companies responding differently from privately held global companies, not to mention the impact of globally active state-owned enterprises?

Even more important than these analytical puzzles is the basic normative question. What is the right model for a social contract for global companies and global business in the twenty-first century? While answers to that question will undoubtedly vary widely, the process of having the conversation is crucial. We must find ways to foster reasoned debate over a wide spectrum of actors. Without processes that can lead to the development of such a social contract, global companies are unlikely to enjoy the long-term stability that only such legitimacy can bring.

Notes

1   Among the many implicit assumptions of this argument is that most shareholders hold equities for a sufficiently long time that their interests are reasonably aligned with the longer-term interests of other stakeholders. In other words, Friedman does not consider the existence of shareholders who would be satisfied with company plans that would create very short-term spikes in share prices but would drive

the firm out of business shortly thereafter. In the era of hyperspeed traders, an era in which the average holding of SU equities is well under one year, short-term shareholders and long-term shareholders have very different interests, even defined solely in narrow profit terms. See Martin (2011).

2 The post-World War II Bretton Woods institutions were supposed to have a third partner, an International Trade Organization that among other things would have protected cross-border business investments and controlled restrictive business practices – but the US Congress refused to ratify the treaty creating the ITO (Jenkins 2001: 1–2).

3 Ruggie at the time was serving as Assistant Secretary General, on leave from Columbia University.

4 Bull, Boas, and McNeill include mobilization of private funds in support of multilateral programs, such as Ted Turner's $1 billion gift to create the UN Foundation in support of UN-related goals, or the Gates Foundation $750 million contribution to GAVI. However, these are gifts from individuals or foundations, not companies per se, and thus are not included in my analysis of the relationship between global companies and IGOs.

References

ActionAid. 2006. Under the Influence: Exposing Undue Influence over Policy-making at the WTO, http://www.actionaid.org.uk/doc_lib/174_6_under_the_influence_final.pdf. Accessed December 19, 2012.

Alexandroff, Alan S., ed. 2008. *Can the World Be Governed? Possibilities for Effective Multilateralism*. Waterloo, Canada: Center for International Governance Innovation and Wilfred Laurier University Press.

Austin, James. 2000. "Strategic Collaboration between Nonprofits and Businesses." *Nonprofit and Voluntary Sector Quarterly*, 29 (1, Supplement): 69–97.

Avant, Deborah D., Finnemore, Martha, and Sell, Susan K. eds. 2010. *Who Governs the Globe?* Cambridge: Cambridge University Press.

Boli, John and Thomas, G. 1999. *Constructing World Culture: International Nongovernmental Organizations Since 1975*. Stanford: Stanford University Press.

Braithwaite, John and Drahos, Peter. 2000. *Global Business Regulation*. Cambridge: Cambridge University Press.

Broder, John M. 2012. "Greenpeace Leader's Boardroom Presence." *New York Times*, reprinted in *Today*, January 22, 2012, p. 13.

Bull, Benedicte, Bøås, Morten, and McNeill, Desmond. 2004. "Private Sector Influence in the Multilateral System: A Changing Structure of World Governance?" *Global Governance*, 10: 481–498.

Buthe, Tim, ed. 2010. *Private Regulation in the Global Economy: Special Issue of Business and Society*, 3.

Committee for Economic Development. 1971. *Social Responsibilities of Business Corporations: A Statement on National Policy by the Research and Policy Committee of the Committee for Economic Development*. Washington, DC.

Cowe, Roger. 2004. Business/NGO Partnerships: What's the Payback?, *Ethical Corporation*, http://www.ethicalcorp.com/content.asp?ContentID=1921. Accessed December 19, 2012.

Cutler, Clair A., Haufler, Virginia, and Porter, Tony, eds. 1999. *Private Authority and International Affairs*. New York: SUNY.

Edwards, Michael and Gaventa, John, eds. 2001. *Global Citizen Action*. Boulder: Lynne Rienner.

Florini, Ann. 2003. "From Protest to Participation: The Role of Civil Society in Global Governance." In *Global Governance: An Architecture for the World Economy*, ed. Horst Siebert, 95–119. Berlin: Springer.

Florini, Ann. 2005. *The Coming Democracy: New Rules for Running a New World*. Washington, DC: Brookings Press.

Florini, Ann, ed. 2000. *The Third Force: The Rise of Transnational Civil Society*. Washington, DC: Japan Center for International Exchange and Carnegie Endowment for International Peace.

Friedman, Milton. 1970. "The Social Responsibility of Business is to Increase Its Profits," *The New York Times Magazine*, September 13.

Gordenker, Lynn and Weiss, Thomas G, eds. 1996. *NGOs, the UN, and Global Governance*. Boulder: Lynne Reiner.

Hall, Rodney Bruce and Biersteker, Thomas J., eds. 2002. *The Emergence of Private Authority in Global Governance*. Cambridge: Cambridge University Press.

Haufler, Virginia. 2001. *Public Roles for the Private Sector: Industry Self-Regulation in a Global Economy*. Washington, DC: Carnegie Endowment for International Peace.

Held, David and McGrew, Anthony, eds. 2002. *Governing Globalization: Power, Authority and Global Governance*. Cambridge: Polity Press.

Jenkins, Rhys. 2001. *Corporate Codes of Conduct: Self-Regulation in a Global Economy*. Programme Paper 2. Geneva: United Nations Research Institute for Social Development, Technology, Business, and Society Program.

Jones, Bruce, Pascual, Carlos, and Stedman, Stephen John. 2009. *Power & Responsibility: Building International Order in an Era of Transnational Threats*. Washington, DC: Brookings Institution Press.

Kaldor, M. 2003. "The Idea of Global Civil Society." *International Affairs*, 79: 583–593.

Keck, Margaret and Sikkink, Katherine. 1998. *Activist Beyond Borders: Advocacy Networks in International Politics*. Ithaca: Cornell University Press.

Khagram, Sanjeev, Riker, James, and Sikkink, Katherine, eds. 2002. *Restructuring World Politics: Transnational Social Movements, Networks, and Norms*. Minneapolis: University of Minnesota Press.

Kourula, Arno and Laasonen, Salla. 2010. "Nongovernmental Organizations in Business and Society, Management, and International Business Research: Review and Implications From 1998 to 2007." *Business & Society*, 49(35): 35–67.

Macintosh, Malcolm and Thomas, Ruth. 2002. Corporate Citizenship and the Evolving Relationship between Non-Governmental Organizations and Corporations, British–North American Committee, www.cdhowe.org/pdf/bnac_45.pdf. Accessed December 19, 2012.

Martin, Peter. 1999. "Multinationals Come into Their Own." *Financial Times Millennium Survey*, December 6, p. 16.

Martin, Roger L. 2011. *Fixing the Game: Bubbles, Crashes, and What Capitalism Can Learn from the NFL*. Boston: Harvard Business Review Press.

Marx, Eric. 2012. "Global Compact: Stripped of their Fig Leaves?" *Ethical Corporation*, posted online March 30.

O'Brien, Robert, Goetz, Anne Marie, Scholte, Jan Aart, and Williams, Marc. 2000. *Contesting Global Governance: Multilateral Economic Institutions and Global Social Movements*. Cambridge: Cambridge University Press.

Risse-Kappen, Thomas, ed. 1995. *Bringing Transnational Relations Back In: Non-State Actors, Domestic Structures and International Institutions*. Cambridge: Cambridge University Press.

Ruggie, John, 1983. "International Regimes, Transactions, and Change: Embedded Liberalism in the Postwar Economic Order." In *International Regimes*, ed. Stephen D. Krasner, 195–232. Ithaca: Cornell University Press.

Ruggie, John. ed. 1993. *Multilateralism Matters: The Theory and Praxis of an Institutional Form*. New York: Columbia University Press.

Ruggie, John, Kolb, Charles, O'Rourke, Dara, and Kuper, Andrew. 2004. The Impact of Corporations on Global Governance, Carnegie Council on Ethics and International Affairs and the Centre on International Cooperation, http://www.carnegiecouncil.org/resources/articles_papers_reports/5016.html. Accessed December 19, 2012.

Scholte, Jan Aart. 2005. *Globalization: A Critical Introduction*, 2nd edn. New York: Palgrave Macmillan.

Sell, Susan K. 2003. *Private Power, Public Law: The Globalization of Intellectual Property Rights*. Cambridge: Cambridge University Press.

Slaughter, Anne-Marie. 2004. *A New World Order*. Princeton: Princeton University Press.

Smith, Jackie, Chatfield, C., and Pagnucco, R., eds. 1997. *Transnational Social Movements and Global Politics: Solidarity beyond the State*. Syracuse: Syracuse University Press.

Spar, Debra L. and La Mure, Lane T. 2003. "The Power of Activism: Assessing the Impact of NGOs on Global Business." *California Management Review*, 45 (3): 78–101.

Strange, Susan. 1996. *The Retreat of the State: The Diffusion of Power in the World Economy*. Cambridge: Cambridge University Press.

Therien, Jean-Philippe and Pouliot, Vincent. 2006. "The Global Compact: Shifting the Politics of International Development?" *Global Governance*, 12: 55–75.

United Nations. 1999. Secretary-General Proposes Global Compact on Human Rights, Labour, Environment, in Address to World Economic Forum in Davos, http://www.un.org/News/Press/docs/1999/19990201.sgsm6881.html. Accessed December 19, 2012.

United Nations Conference on Trade and Development (UNCTAD). 1992. *World Investment Report 1992: Transnational Corporations as Engines of Growth*. New York: United Nations.

United Nations Conference on Trade and Development (UNCTAD). 2011. Web Table 34: Number of Parent Corporations and Foreign Affiliates, by Region and Economy, 2010, http://unctad.org/Sections/dite_dir/docs/WIR11_web%20tab%2034.pdf. Accessed May 24.

United States Senate Select Committee to Study Governmental Operations with Respect to Intelligence Activities. 1975. *Covert Action in Chile, 1963–1973. 94th Congress, 1st Session*. Washington, DC: US Government Printing Office.

Weiss, Thomas and Gordenker, Lynn, eds. 1996. *NGOs, the UN, and Global Governance*. Boulder: Lynne Reiner.

Yergin, Daniel and Stanislaw, Joseph. 1998. *The Commanding Heights: The Battle between Government and the Marketplace That Is Remaking the Modern World*. New York: Simon and Schuster.

Zadek, Simon. 2006. "The Logic of Collaborative Governance: Corporate Responsibility, Accountability, and the Social Contract." Corporate Social Responsibility Initiative, *Working Paper* 17. Cambridge, MA: John F. Kennedy School of Government, Harvard University, http://www.hks.harvard.edu/mrcbg/CSRI/publications/workingpaper_17_zadek.pdf. Accessed December 19, 2012.

Zadek, Simon. 2010. "Emerging Nations and Sustainability: Chimera or Leadership?" Corporate Social Responsibility Initiative. *Working Paper* 61, Cambridge, MA: Harvard Kennedy School.

Chapter 21

Global Companies as Social Actors

Constructing Private Business in Global Governance

Tanja Brühl and Matthias Hofferberth

Introduction

According to the narrative of global governance, the role of private actors in global policy has changed as processes of time and space compressions have diminished state capacities to govern. Global governance, so the argument goes, has become more complex as private actors themselves have become "global governors" (Avant, Finnemore, and Sell 2010). And indeed, today we can witness non-state actors increasingly participating in processes and arrangements of rule setting and implementation to fill governance gaps caused by globalization (Held *et al.* 1999: 281–282). This empirical observation is captured and well-documented in academia, which observes new forms of "private authority" (Cutler, Haufler, and Porter 1999), "private international regimes" (Cutler 2002), "private participation in governance" (Haufler 2006), and emerging "transnational private governance" (Graz and Nölke 2008).

Among the private actors integrated into governance arrangements, we find what is to many the quintessential expression of globalization: the global company (Kobrin 2008). Such companies are no longer considered as economic actors solely committed to their *share*holders, but also are assumed to bear responsibilities towards their wider group of *stake*holders (Zadek 2007: 131–147). Either in global partnerships like the *UN Global Compact* or in specific approaches, "the international community increasingly appears to view corporations as powerful partners in global governance" (Flohr *et al.* 2010: 7). In fact, the regulation *of* private business has changed to new forms of regulation *together with* or even *through* private business. Global companies are expected to embrace (more) social responsibility and become political actors, at least according to voices within the debate surrounding the concept of corporate social responsibility (CSR) (Scherer, Palazzo, and Baumann 2006: 508–510). Global

The Handbook of Global Companies, First Edition. Edited by John Mikler.
© 2013 John Wiley & Sons, Ltd. Published 2013 by John Wiley & Sons, Ltd.

governance, in a nutshell, is "moralizing the corporation," implying new corporate roles and responsibilities for global companies (Holzer 2010).

While we empirically share the notion of global governance becoming more complex and that of private (business) actors becoming involved, to us the debate on global companies in global governance tends to overemphasize the structural effects and impact of corporate participation and does not discuss the implications of participating for the enterprises. Only recently has private business "received attention within academic debates in international relations – at least as an actor in its own right" (Deitelhoff and Wolf 2010: 5). Introducing an alternative conceptualization of global companies as social actors whose very meanings are constituted in and through (inter-)action, we argue that global governance characterizes a changing frame of social expectations towards corporate actors and leaves these actors in conflict and uncertainty about their own roles. Thus, while we agree that the role of corporate actors is changing, we do not consider this as either a functional necessity or a moral imperative. Rather, we understand private business as a product of social interaction and therefore look at how global companies generate new meanings and how they are constructed in the light of social expectations beyond assumingly fixed interests and rationalized modes of action (Cutler 2008: 195).

Sharing the criticism on a "myopic view of business actors as simple profit seekers" (Kollman 2008: 397), we contend that corporate publications and documents reflect social expectations and are manifestations of the (re-)definition of what constitutes corporate actors and their appropriate scope of actions (Palan 2000: 15). Moreover, these "artefacts of meaning" are instructive in that regard that they can help us explain the prevailing gap between corporate rhetoric on the one hand and corporate implementation on the other (Brühl 2007). By analyzing the documents of global companies, one can gain access to the processes of (self-)construction of these actors and thereby reconstruct newly emerged meanings, which other actors and whose expectations they consider to be relevant, and how the company processes and deals with these expectations. As most corporate decisions today are cast in a situation where neither rationality nor profit is clearly defined (Sabel and Zeitlin 1997: 5–15), this perspective offers a more appropriate account of the changing role of global companies than those emphasizing the rational predisposition of global companies to maximize profit.

The purpose of this contribution is therefore to broaden the debate on global governance and global companies. While the corporate role is changing, it is intellectually worthwhile to reconstruct more carefully how new expectations contribute to this change and potentially cause conflict and crisis. Unsatisfying corporate contributions to global governance originate not only in strategic and rational profit-maximization but also indicate contradicting and discrepant expectations and responsibilities of global companies, leaving them in doubt and uncertainty how to mediate between them (Kobrin 2008). To support these argumentative claims, we offer at first a brief synthesis of the current global governance discourse on global companies. Secondly, the theoretical argument of global companies as social actors is elaborated and, thirdly, illustrated by (a) analyzing the reasoning of extractive companies engaging in CSR policy and (b) sketching the self-constructed role of Shell in the Nigerian crisis in the 1990s. Finally, we conclude by discussing how the insights into processes of constructing private business in global governance might help to better to integrate these actors into new modes of global policy.

Global Governance and Global Companies

Since the 1990s, a narrative of global governance has developed in International Relations (IR). According to this narrative, the role of business actors has changed in the last decades. They are no longer conceptualized only as economic actors, but also as political actors. In this section, we summarize the most important findings of the global governance discourse with regard to global companies. We focus on the mainstream discourse, which goes hand in hand with the notion of conceptualizing global governance as a change in governance modes which can be observed empirically. Thereby, global governance concepts that explicitly have normative claims are not considered.

Since the mid-1990s, the discourse on global governance has evolved in IR. The discourse itself conceptualizes the historic setting as a once-in-a-lifetime opportunity for establishing more effective governance systems. Accordingly, the global governance discourse has four different points of origin as reasons for its emergence (Avant, Finnemore, and Sell 2010: 4–6). Firstly, globalization has undermined the correspondence between social action and the territory enclosed by state borders (Held and McGrew 2002: 3) which is why effective governance solely by the state is not possible (Zürn 1992; 2002). In addition, the problems at hand have changed: Due to globalization, new transsovereign problems have emerged and existing ones have been aggravated (Rittberger *et al.* 2008: 2). Secondly, and closely related to globalization, the liberalization of markets has changed the interaction between state and non-state actors. World leaders of the 1980s who first embraced such policies such as Ronald Reagan and Margaret Thatcher therefore tremendously promoted the role of non-state actors (Cutler 2003: 19). Thirdly, new technologies have facilitated globalization processes by easing communication, population flows, and the interchange of ideas. The technological revolution has enabled non-state actors to gather and process information still more easily and rapidly. Accordingly, they are able to formulate more timely and persuasive political appraisals (Brühl and Rittberger 2001: 2). Fourthly, the end of the Cold War was seen by many actors as an opportunity for change. In the early to mid-1990s, the impression that new priorities could be set was dominant and a more peaceful and just world seemed possible. This is why many activists and non-state actors had begun to push for change.

All four factors have in common that according to them the room for non-state governance contributions has widened. This was generally perceived as a good development due to the common understanding that the more actors engaged in governance processes, the better the outcome would be. Differences between the various types of non-state actors, which encompass civil-society groups as well as business actors with sometimes opposing interests, were neglected. In addition, power asymmetries were not conceptualized (Barnett and Duvall 2005). This is remarkable, since IR had discussed the power of business actors controversially only some years before as global companies had become more active in the 1960s and 1970s than ever before. While there was some understanding of conflicting ideas between different types of private actors and a hands-on experience with changing power relations, mainstream global governance handled both types of private actors mostly equally.

Since the end of the 1990s, a common understanding regarding core concepts has evolved in the global governance discourse. Governance refers to the various institutionalized modes of social coordination which produce and implement binding rules or provide public goods (Mayntz 2008). Thereby, governance can be perceived as structure and process. The structure-dimension of governance refers to institutions and both state and non-state actors; the process-dimension pinpoints the modes of social coordination by which actors engage in rulemaking and implementation (Börzel and Risse 2010: 114). The global governance discourse distinguishes itself from former governance modes. Accordingly, global governance should not be confused with international governance, which was the dominant governance mode for many decades. After World War II, governance beyond the nation state, or international governance, was conceptualized as the output of a non-hierarchical network of mostly intergovernmental institutions which regulate the behavior of states and other international actors in different issue areas of world politics (Brühl and Rittberger 2001: 2). The "treaty based institutionalization" contributed to transforming the original stage of anarchy to sectoral governance functions (Wolf 2008: 229). This process was "more or less effective in civilizing the interaction among states" (Kobrin 2008: 253). Although non-state actors were active in global governance, they were not conceptualized as political actors. This is also true for business actors, whose activities were seen as economic, thus neglecting the political power they exercised (Kobrin 2008: 253).

In contrast to that, the global governance discourse assigns power to non-state actors. Due to the four factors mentioned above, the problem-solving capacity of international governance came under severe criticism. In fact, a "continual non-attainment of governance goals" was diagnosed (Brühl and Rittberger 2001: 20). According to the global governance discourse, the attainment of governance goals could be guaranteed only if non-hierarchical networks became more complex. This was demonstrated by the empirical research that took place. Global governance is therefore best characterized by an increased degree of complexity of governance beyond the state (Wolf 2008: 235). First and most important, a diffusion of actors can be observed: a variety of actors, both public and private as well as national and international, take part in the formulation and implementation of norms and rules. These actors interact on different levels, from the local to the global. "Non-hierarchical modes of coordination" have become even more important (Börzel and Risse 2010: 113) since they do not only refer to coordination between the same actors (states), but between different ones: there are many partnerships among states, NGOs, and global companies. As nation states continue to play an important role in global governance, global governance can be summarized as governance by, with, and without governments (Zürn 2002).

The inclusion of private (business) actors in international political governance structures is thus conceptualized as a new development. This does not mean that the global governance discourse denies that private actors have been active participants in world politics before. However, originally their role focused either on the input phase (such as agenda setting, norm generation, program development) *or* on the output phase (norm implementation, evaluation of policies) (Wolf 2008: 233). In contrast nowadays, private actors set standards, supply public goods, participate in international negotiations. They are even involved in the center of decision-making in public-private partnerships (Kobrin 2008: 255). Interestingly, the inclusion of private (business) in global governance is, due to its functionalist bias, hailed by the global governance discourse. Accordingly, private actors are able to deliver resources that are needed in order to properly deal with governance tasks. In other words, the basis for their inclusion "is typically drawn from their expertise, resources, and perceived efficacy" (Haufler 2010: 107). By providing resources, private (business) actors might contribute to the closing of existing governance gaps (Brühl and Rittberger 2001: 21–24). Especially business actors are conceptualized by the global governance discourse as being able to provide the necessary resources in terms of personnel, organizational capacity, and money that other actors lack. Thus, they could enhance the effectiveness of the implementation processes and contribute to the realization of governance goals (Kobrin 2008: 253).

Including business actors in governance systems indicates that they are no longer seen as originators of regulatory problems, but rather as problem solvers (Wolf 2008: 234). It is perceived as legitimate (and in fact welcomed by many) that business actors exercise political authority since they have experience, a historical practice or an implicit grant of power over states (Kobrin 2008: 253). From a more critical standpoint, it is important to investigate the regulatory potential and limits of these actors (Wolf 2008: 234). While the legitimacy and effectiveness of global governance in general has been discussed recently (Dingwerth 2007; Pattberg 2007), more research is needed on the role of business actors in global governance in particular. Up to now, the global governance literature focuses too much on structures and neglects (business) actors as it seems to "happen" without any actors involved. Thus, it is important to "think about who global 'governors' might be" (Avant, Finnemore, and Sell 2010: 1), what these governors constitute, and why they behave the way they do. In the following section, we contribute to answering these questions by sketching our understanding of global companies as social actors.

Global Companies as Social Actors

Since the mainstream global governance discourse neglects agency, conceptualizing global companies as social actors promises to offer different insights into processes of global companies constructing themselves in global governance. The starting point for this is an anti-foundationalist rejection of both a fixed "world out there" as well as the essentialization of social phenomena and the reduction of corporate agency to mere rational behavior. Drawing on a "relational sociology" outlined by Mustafa Emirbayer (1997) and introduced to IR by Jackson and Nexon (1999), social phenomena such as global companies do not possess a fixed substantial core. Although social scientists often (and sometimes for good reasons) "presume that entities precede interaction, or that entities are already entities before they enter into social relations with other entities" (Jackson and Nexon 1999: 293), such essentializations reduce agency as no choices remain for the actor. In fact, agency in this perspective depends solely on predefined attributes and fixed characteristics: it is not the actor but rather the "variables – attributes of entities – which do the acting" (Jackson and Nexon 1999: 294). The actor itself merely becomes the location where these attributes play out. Contrary to this, we consider actors to be social in that regard that their very meanings are constituted in and through action. Both the scope of appropriate and inappropriate actions as well as the choice between different options is constantly constituted in light of changing social expectations as the very attributes and characteristics of actors are constructed and thus subject to change.

Thereby, we reject the notion to conceptualize global companies as fixed entities. According to this conceptualization, corporate rationality and a strategic outlook on the world are the driving factors for corporate behavior. While this answers the question *how* a company acts, one has to add assumptions about corporate interests and aims to explain *why* a company acts in a specific way. Here, one would, for obvious reasons, rely on the idea of maximizing profit and shareholder value as the essential aims of corporate agency to answer the question *what* motivates a company.[1] Thus, in this perspective, global companies "have come to be understood as essentially rational actors whose expansionary behavior can be explained through the profit motive" (Amoore 2000: 184), or as Haufler (2010: 106) puts it more critically, "[c]orporations are often theorized in a simple way: they are the ultimate rational actors, driven by profits alone."

Such an actor image based on an essentialization in terms of its aims and a rationalization in terms of its mode of action (Cutler 2008: 195) can go a long way when explaining different manifestations of corporate behavior. One can explain why global companies participate in new global governance initiatives – evasion of stricter state regulation and civil society pressure as well as the beneficial effects this has for the corporate reputation (Haufler 2001: 20–27) – as well as why companies do not participate as they rationally and strategically only choose those initiatives from which they benefit. However, while there is an argumentative beauty in this parsimonious account of corporate behavior, to some extent contradictions and tautologies remain. In what follows, we argue that (a) the notion of corporate rationality is not sufficient to explain behavior, (b) especially in new and uncertain situations, as (c) the precise meaning of profit remains vague.

Firstly, if one starts from an essentialized corporate rationality, one basically argues like this: a company rationally maximizes profit because it *is* a company. As a company, however, it *has* to rationally maximize profit or it will not last as a company. Thus, corporate rationality is not only essentialized, it is also derived from a (teleo-)logical necessity and not reasoned for within a broader context of a theory of action. Such a tautological conceptualization does not suffice, neither for the enterprise to purposively act in light of uncertain and indeterminate economic situations (Zeitlin 2007) nor for the social scientist to explain such action (Beckert 2003). No matter how companies in different situations decide, their behavior can always be explained by referring to external and absolute corporate rationality. While in some cases it might be rational to join initiatives, in other examples it might also be rational not to do so. Thus, corporate behavior is solely explained by drawing on different definitions of corporate cost/benefit calculations.

Secondly, the parsimony of this perspective assumes that rationality as the decisive benchmark for corporate action is something which lies beyond the immediate act of decision. Although the notion of limited rationality creates some space for the opportunity of computing information incorrectly (Zürn 1992), in the end, each situation, no matter how problematic or new, is something that can be correctly assessed by the actor who then is able to optimally choose between clearly defined alternatives of action optimally. Strictly speaking, however, the only thing that rationality allows is the avoidance of previous mistakes and miscalculations in the future. It does not allow to ponder or demarcate different alternatives in order to reach a decision in a previously not experienced situation (Herborth 2004: 81–82). However, economic decision-making, precisely in an era of globalization and changing social expectations towards global companies, is mainly characterized by such situations. In fact, global companies more often than not find themselves in complex and uncertain decision situations, in which neither the choices between different courses nor their implications and consequences are obvious (Beckert 2003).

Thirdly, the maximization of profit marks a viable and indispensable yet at the same time contingent goal for corporate actors. It is thus not our purpose to question the constitutive effect of profit for private business since this very notion helps to distinguish companies from other (private) actors (Risse 2002: 256). However, as the "default option" for corporate behavior, it is "only loosely defined at any given moment and [therefore] constantly being redefined" (Sabel and Zeitlin 1997: 15). How it is precisely filled with meaning and translated into action in a specific situation is not determined but subject to and the result of contingency. Obviously, as discussed within the "theory of the firm" approach, there are other corporate goals such as increasing market shares or outrivaling competitors which play a role for how profit is maximized (Williamson 1981). On yet another level, one could also argue that social expectations have fundamentally changed the very notion of profit. Whether a company maximizes profit without any regard for human rights and environmental issues or whether a company increases profit without (or at least less) harming human rights and the environment depends on the social contexts the company operates in. As such, the vague and abstract notion of profit has been spelled out in different ways throughout the history of corporate activity and is therefore not sufficient as a fixed corporate aim to explain action (Palan 2000: 3–4).

While rejecting notions of external and absolute rationality as well as the idea that profit-maximization as an end is sufficient to explain corporate behavior, both of these assumptions still play a crucial role in the self-understanding of corporate actors. Put the other way around, companies are most likely to act as rational as possible "in the sense of pursuing their best alternatives" (Sabel and Zeitlin 1997: 6–7) and to maximize profit in that sense as it is temporarily defined by relevant others. Such "determinants of corporate action" are the result of socially held expectations and institutionalized responsibilities, both towards their own shareholders as well as other social actors. Those *routinely expect* nothing different from companies than "relentless competition and unforgiving market forces" (Cohen 2007: 30). Absolutizing these expectations to explain corporate behavior, however, remains problematic. Instead, as social actors, we conceptualize private business relying on (1) their primary sociality and (2) their situated creativity, as (3) both the situations they act in as well as the aims and intentions on which the act becomes contingent. The following sections will spell out each of these actor assumptions in relation to global companies in global governance.

The Primary Sociality of (Corporate) Action

As argued before, there is no such thing as an atomistic actor in the relationalist perspective. Actors are constituted only in relation to others and their social expectations. Essentially, it is their entanglement in intersubjective structures of meaning which allows them to make sense of experiences and enables them to assess and choose between different courses of action, thereby constituting them as actors in the first place (Joas 1997: 184–195). Sociality in this sense is the actor disposition to be able to access these structures of meanings. As they neither *exist within* nor *independently of* the actors and their interpretive performances, these structures of meanings are required to perform action. Primary sociality is thus a constitutive requirement for any action.[2] Consequently, individual will, beliefs, and goals, necessary preconditions to act, are not properties of individual agents but instead developed "coterminously within contexts" (Emirbayer and Mische 1998: 967). Very much like Granovetter (1985: 487) argued, "[a]ctors do not behave or decide as atoms outside a social context" as "[t]heir attempts at purposive action are instead embedded in concrete, ongoing systems of social relations."

The implication of this proposition is the negation of individual(-istic) means/end calculations. Rather, sociality *is* constitutive for individual action as boundaries of meanings are identified and (re-)defined in social interaction. The epistemological argument for this is the rejection of a separation between acting and thinking (Joas 1997: 145–148) – instead of assuming a dualist relation between mind and world, actors are always embedded in social contexts because of a mind-world monism. There is no such thing as individual, world-independent cognition before one acts. Simply because actions would be meaningless without the broader social context in which they are embedded, one cannot divorce cognition from action (Jackson 2011: 37–38). Ontologically speaking, global companies do not simply act rationally and maximize profit through cross-border economic activities because they *are* global companies. Rather, socially constituted actions (re-)stabilize the boundaries of what it means to be a global company at a specific point in time and space. To put it differently, only through interaction with relevant others are meanings and thus appropriate actions constructed and (re-)produced.

The Situated Creativity of (Corporate) Action

Primary sociality, however, does not negate situated creativity as the second dimension of action. Rather, precisely because of the indeterminate and fluid nature of social phenomena, action always "involves defining that which is as yet undefined, rather than simply making a different selection from a reservoir of situation components that are either already defined or have no need of definition" (Joas 1997: 133). Which structures of meaning the actor calls upon, how she assesses and defines the situation at hand based on these patterns of interpretation as well as how she incorporates and translates these into action by ascribing (potentially new) meaning to it depends to a great range on her imagination and inventiveness. Thus, action plays out in situations that are "always subject to reevaluation and reconstruction of the part of the reflective intelligence" (Emirbayer and Mische 1998: 967–968). Creativity, in other words, is a logical consequence following the social character of action as well as the inevitability not to act as one cannot flee from (inter-)action and constantly face situations in which one has to make decisions. Taken together, action is understood as the social yet creative "determination of indeterminacy" and thus depends on the social context as well as the situated interpretation of the actor within and of this context (Shalin 1986: 12).

To be sure, most of the situations an actor faces are already habitualized as routines have been developed or can be adapted from other contexts. However, no two situations are exactly the same and every now and then we stumble into "problematic situations" where we are in need of new beliefs to guide our actions as previous beliefs are fundamentally called into question. In such situations of crisis, creative intelligence becomes indispensable for restabilizing one's actions and interpretations to fit again with the newly experienced world (Hellmann 2010: 149–150). Creativity in this sense is a situated actor's disposition to continuously ensure her capacities to act (Jackson 2009: 657–658). Instead of simply choosing between different options based on pre-defined motives and intentions, creativity allows actors to deal with inevitable crisis by developing new motives and intentions. These motives and intentions creatively emerge *within* the process of (inter-)action and thus are necessarily non-teleological in nature (Joas 1997: 148–167).

Global companies just as individuals depend on such "interpretative acts by which [they] construct perceptions of rationality intersubjectively in the action process itself," simply because of the "complexity and novelty inherent in economic decision situations" (Beckert 2003: 770). In fact, more often than not global companies find themselves in situations "in which the rules and norms of socially acceptable decision making – the institutionalized environments of the corporation – are in flux" (Holzer 2010: 121). Global governance thus constitutes a fundamental crisis of corporate legitimacy. Understood as the dissolution of a clear separation between public and private, global companies not only face new expectations but are also confronted with the task to fundamentally reassess their own beliefs and world views (Deitelhoff and Wolf 2010: 7–9). This demanding task is virtually impossible without creatively developing new routines and beliefs to guide corporate action.

The Double Contingency of Situations and (Corporate) Aims

As action is thought of, it also becomes dynamic and processual and thus contingent as does the situation in which it is played out. Situations are contingent because they contain "a horizon of possibilities which in a crisis of action has to be rediscovered" (Joas 1997: 133). While the sum of individual situations retrospectively constitutes historical developments, each situation itself could have played out in different ways because of being indeterminate and mutable. This is very convincingly argued for and shown by the "historical alternatives approach" (Zeitlin 2007), which understands the development of private business as the result of single contingent situations and not as a determined process. At various stages in this process, developments could have taken a different direction and neither of the involved actors – states, business entities, or stakeholders – were solely in control of this development (Cohen 2007: 19–37).

Corresponding to the contingency of situations, agency and the aims of actors are contingent, too. With regard to this, we agree with Strauss (1993: 36) who states that "[c]ontingencies are likely to arise during a course of action" and not only bring about change in its duration and pace but also in its intent and purpose. As argued before, neither preferences nor intentions, neither goals nor motives are preceding an action. Rather, they are contingent upon it in that sense that they are realized and changed through action. To put it differently, contingent "ends arise and function within action" (Dewey 1922: 223). However, the contingent character of ends does not negate their constitutive role within the process of acting. Given the need to constantly act, preliminary and contingent goals structure action and guide decisions. We have already argued that related to global companies, the maximization of profit marks such contingent goals. How an actor translates this abstract notion into concrete action in a specific situation as well as how this notion is related to other corporate goals is subject to and the result of contingency following the social and thus fluid character of social phenomena as well as the fact that actors necessarily develop creative solutions and beliefs in new and problematic situations.

The Construction of Global Companies in Global Governance

Having outlined our theoretical foundation in more detail, we now discuss the implications and what we consider to be the advantages of our alternative actor image. Taken together, an actor image based on social primacy, situated creativity, and the double contingency of indeterminate situations and corporate dispositions within such situations allow for a more nuanced perspective on how exposure to and adoption of new social expectations construct global companies. This perspective, we believe, is better suited to access construction processes of global companies by which these actors develop and are ascribed with meanings. By posing the "very basic question about the social definition of a corporation" (Kobrin 2008: 267) and by looking at how corporate meanings are constructed, one can better understand why and how these actors act. Neither the result of rational strategies nor based on intrinsic ethics, it is the processes of how these actors themselves are constructed in light of social expectations which constitute their actions. In this perspective, corporate artefacts and documents become manifestations of the ongoing social, creative, and contingent attempt to situationally determine meanings and beliefs:

> Multinational enterprises are viewed no longer simply as instrumentalist advantage maximizing institutions, but as complex organizations which exceed their goals and functions, but in non-utilitarian ways. Their language, their scripts, their histories, their technostructures and artefacts matter; analysis of which reveals them to be trapped in their own evolutionary logic but also constantly at work to renew themselves (Palan 2000: 15).

Looking into these manifestations allows us to reconstruct what currently constitutes global companies and take into perspective the processes of constructing meanings for the otherwise unspecified concept of corporate agency. These processes of constructing corporate actors involve global companies as well as other actors. Especially the expectations of "relevant others" will be echoed within corporate construction processes.[3] Thus, our contributions offer an alternative perspective on the complex process of corporate meaning and preference generation. This allows us to understand global governance as a frame of new social expectations towards global companies. Apart from describing empirical processes, global governance, at least in a structural-functionalist reading, tends to underemphasize conflict und uncertainty as a result. Instead of becoming political actors deliberately and easily, global companies face discrepant expectations and are thereby engaged in an ambiguous and complex process in which indeterminacy prevails. We believe the following two empirical examples from our own research illustrate the argument well. While the first illustration shows that CSR can be understood as an expression of and answer to new social expectations, the second illustration indicates the difficulty and ambiguity of this process.

Illustration I: CSR Commitment as an Expression of New Social Expectations

As we have shown above, most authors researching global companies agree that the role of business is changing as processes of globalization increase and new forms of global governance emerge in different issue areas (Held *et al.* 1999; Cutler, Haufler, and Porter 1999; Hall and Biersteker 2002). At least for some, at the core of this lies the notion of corporate social responsibility. CSR emerged as a bundle of normative expectations which created new notions of appropriate behavior for private business actors with regard to social and environmental standards, human rights, and working conditions (Segerlund 2010). As an answer to the question why rational actors deliberately accept and engage in CSR, it is often argued that this is the *most rational* thing to do because further regulation can be avoided, a positive corporate reputation maintained and/or costs reduced (Cutler 2008: 205–210). We argue differently. Because of the social nature of global companies and because of the emergence of new social expectations expressed in the normative bundle of CSR, joining such initiatives becomes fundamentally important for the constitution of being a global company at the beginning of the twenty-first century. It is the *most appropriate* thing to do for companies. However, this does not automatically imply that CSR commitment is understood in the same terms nor that it will be effectively implemented and realized in corporate decision-making. In fact, we argue that the very notion of CSR itself depends on how global companies translate new social expectations within the process of constructing themselves.

Based on a constitutive understanding of language which does not represent but creates reality, being "exposed" to norms and their "constitutive process of identity formation" (Jepperson, Wendt, and Katzenstein 1996: 66) influences corporate definitions of what it means to be a successful company. In light of such new expectations being expressed in CSR, corporate interests and preferences need to be restated (Conzelmann and Wolf 2007: 162–163).[4] For example, contrary to the early stages of capitalism, the uncompromising exploitation of human beings and nature is no longer considered as appropriate behavior for private business. Put simply, it seems no longer to fit in the identity of any company to unethically exploit the environment (although some might still do secretly). Instead, ideas such as sustainable development and CSR have become socially held expectations and thus are – at least partially – implemented by many companies (Flohr *et al.* 2010: 165–166).

To illustrate this, we looked at the patterns of arguments used by global companies for their CSR commitment and analyzed what reasons private business actors gave for becoming involved in CSR (Hofferberth *et al.* 2011). To do so, we formed three categories. The arguments given by companies were related to a notion of calculating expected consequences, thereby reduce costs, increase profit, and reputation or generally improve the company's performance. These arguments would fit into the mainstream conceptualization of private business. Global companies, however, could also refer to a notion of appropriateness first introduced as a theoretical concept by March and Olsen (1989). Within this logic, aspects such as identity as well as social rules and expectations are fundamental for agents as they try to behave in socially acceptable ways and accordingly to their own identity and self-image. Obviously, both notions relate to different actor images. While the *homo sociologicus* acting upon a logic of appropriateness relates her action to what she sees as right and normatively accepted, the *homo economicus* calculates and maximizes returns drawing upon the logic of consequentialism. Therefore, the first category is linked to the rational notion of the *homo economicus* and the logic of consequentialism, while the second category comprises self-expectations and expectations by others as well as ethical arguments and thus draws on the notion of the *homo sociologicus*. An additional third category of statements using elements of both logics was introduced as it became obvious that most speeches drew on patterns of arguments related to both logics.

For three reasons we chose statements by extractive companies. Firstly, the sector is dominated by a small number of global companies which are huge in size and operate in many countries.[5] Secondly, the problems that are resulting from corporate cross-border activities in multiple countries are even more pressing for the extractive sector than for any other because of their "asset specificity." Extractive companies cannot simply leave conflict areas and choose to operate somewhere else due to the limited availability of resources. Thirdly, the regions where most extractive companies operate are defined as "areas of limited statehood" (Risse 2011) or post-conflict regions. In such areas, CSR becomes even more important as there are no governance structures to regulate corporate behavior.

All in all, a total number of 96 corporate representative speeches from companies such as *Chevron Texaco*, *Royal Dutch/Shell*, *BP*, and *Rio Tinto* among others held between 1996 and 2006 were collected from different initiatives such as the *UN Global Compact* and the *Extractive Industries Transparency Initiative* as well as specific interest groups such as the *World Business Council for Sustainable Development* and the *World Diamond Council*. Moreover, homepages of inter-corporate CSR workshops and those of the companies themselves were screened as well.[6] The speeches were analyzed by using a content analysis focusing on the corporate reasoning for CSR as each of the speeches were assigned to one of the three categories. In addition, the first two categories were further divided into seven sub-categories of argumentative patterns and corporate motivation for CSR. Table 21.1 summarizes these different sub-categories and shows keywords for each derived from a first pilot study.[7]

The content analysis shows a mixed picture. While 11 speeches highlighted the rational for taking part in CSR (11.5%), 10 speeches could be linked solely to appropriateness (10.4%). A total of 75 speeches drew on both logics (78.1%). Put differently, although using rational arguments related to expected consequences, a total of 88.5% of all speeches drew at the same time on arguments related to the

Table 21.1 Sub-categories for corporate participation in CSR and their keywords.

Sub-categories for the logic of expected consequences:

Name of sub-category	Keywords
economic success	*business advantage; good business reason*
corporate future	*long-term interests; sustainability; survival of company*
reputation	*trust; corporate image; reduction of damaging criticism*
improved political/social environment	*stable economies; political stability*
qualification/education of staff	*developing and retaining a diverse workforce*
security of staff	*take care of safety; medical care; reduce costs of accidents*
relations to host country	*build relationships of mutual advantage; local commitment*

Sub-categories for the logic of appropriateness:

Name of sub-category	Keywords
values and moral obligations	*core values; integrity; honesty; responsibility*
social expectations (ego & alter)	*our role; good corporate citizen; society's expectations*
norms & standards	*respect for human rights; business principles*
positive impact for host country	*contribute to sustainable development; improving lives*
respect for local cultures	*protect indigenous people; protect cultural heritage*
general humanitarian impact	*reduce human tragedy; improve conditions*
global benefits	*global poverty reduction; tackle important global issues*

logic of appropriateness. Nine out of ten speakers linked aspects such as business reasons, profit-maximizing, and means–end calculations rhetorically to appropriate behavior defined by CSR and its underlying social expectations. This demonstrates that private business actors are not (only) *rational* but (also) *social* actors. Instead of essentializing corporate rationality, their meanings were constructed in the context of social interaction. This initial finding from looking at different companies motivated us to analyze more closely one example of a construction process of an extractive global company in crisis. For reasons of accessibility, relevance, and global visibility, we decided to analyze Shell's self-constructed role in Nigeria in the humanitarian crisis of the 1990s.

Illustration II: The Unsuccessful Handling and Translation of New Expectations by Shell in the Nigerian Crisis in the 1990s

In today's Nigeria, the extractive industry of oil is essential for the national economy. Ever since huge oil reserves were discovered in the 1960s, the exploration and extraction of these became crucially important for the country. Today, because of the oil, Nigeria receives more inward FDIs than any other African country and most of these investments come from multinational oil companies (UNCTAD 2004: 41).

Among these companies, by courtesy of its pioneer access to the region, the Anglo-Dutch company of Shell has remained the largest oil enterprise in Nigeria and roughly accounts for almost half of Nigeria's oil production today. Since this production is mainly carried out in onshore facilities in the Niger Delta, no other company is as present in everyday life as the Nigerian subsidiary of Shell, the Shell Petroleum Development Company (SPDC).

At the same time, however, the Niger Delta remains "one of the world's most dangerous and difficult oil-producing areas" (Soares 2007: 252), best characterized as a complex nexus of various conflict causes and prone to violence. Among political issues such as regional struggles for (more) autonomy, the ongoing environmental degradation as well as the failure to improve living standards despite increasing oil production mark further causes for conflict (Zimmer 2010: 61–63). In addition, the "socio-graphic composition of the Niger Delta is equally complex, comprising, at least, 26 ethnic and language groups that are distributed across nine oil-producing states," which adds an ethnic dimension to the political, economic, and environmental conflicts (Omeje 2006: 32). Especially the question of how to distribute oil revenues among ethnic groups has become a highly contested issue and caused inter-ethnic strife for control of land containing oil wells.

These long-term conflicts erupted into a full-scale crisis situation in the early 1990s when corporate security was increasingly threatened by local militant groups. Shell did not engage in dialogue with these groups. Instead, it shut down some of its production and partly left the region. For those instances where the company remained, it relied more heavily on state security forces. These security provisions came in the form of regional "militarization, leading to repression, torture, looting, rape and extra-judicial killings" in the region (Omeje 2006: 142). In May 1994, Ken Saro-Wiwa and eight other activists were arrested and sentenced to death in what seemed to many a show trial by the military dictatorship government of Sani Abacha. Through global media coverage, the crisis as well as the protests quickly gained international attention. Culminating in the allegation of complicity in the executions, Shell was directly held responsible and accused for cooperating with a corrupt and inhumane dictator. It is in this context of both a manifest crisis in the everyday use of the term as well as in the pragmatist notion of crisis where no routines exist in which we analyzed meanings constructed by Shell.

In order to do so, we looked at corporate documents understood as temporary manifestations of contingent corporate meanings. Assuming that companies are the "result of a series of contests" between different actors (Amoore 2000: 184), these documents reflect corporate attempts to establish and justify new meanings and beliefs on which future action can be based. Although rhetorical in nature and published in order to present the enterprise in a positive light, these documents at the same time mark an "indispensable... source of information about the range and robustness of the constraints [Shell] faced and created" (Sabel and Zeitlin 1997: 15). In order to reconstruct these meanings established and expressed in social interaction, sequence analysis as a hermeneutic approach was used. This approach considers documents to be "protocols of social action" where underlying beliefs and meanings for action become manifest and by which change can be reconstructed.[8]

Across the documents, Shell predominantly defined its own role in economic terms. Whenever corporate activities in other areas such as community development or environmental activities were referred to, they were portrayed as additional contributions not constitutive for being an enterprise. Thus, across all documents, Shell was very hesitant to define new corporate responsibilities or engage in deliberative dialogue with civil society. At least in the early documents it was more important for Shell not to be responsible for the crisis than presenting the enterprise capable of action. Given that Shell became more involved in community development and other social activities in Nigeria, it is surprising that this involvement is not presented in the documents. According to Soares (2007: 249–250), the enterprise increased its social spending from $100.000 in 1991 to $69 million in 2002. However, this is almost not discussed in corporate publications. One can argue that despite engaging in social activities beyond the narrow definition of an economic actor, Shell is not willing to document this as new responsibilities might be derived from this. Its corporate measures therefore can be better understood as "damage limitations" and not so much as an expression of a changed corporate role in Nigeria.

However, by introducing and discussing new aspects such as corporate "humanitarian values" in the later documents, the company began to construct itself around the yet unanswered question of what "decent business" constitutes. Stating its own role in one document by arguing that "of course our major contribution remains to run a decent business there," the company at least created space for new dimensions of corporate meaning and responsibilities. At the same time, these "rhetorical frailties" showed that the company did not have a clear crisis management strategy. The way it referred to criticism dramatically changed from the first documents in 1995 to how the company constructs itself today. It seems that while constructing itself, the company constantly assessed and reassessed the situation. In fact, the enterprise appeared to be surprised, overwhelmed, and overtaxed by the expectations and persistence of civil society criticism and did not know how to react.

Within this crisis, one can see as a result how a multinational enterprise was effectively targeted by civil society which created a situation of justification for the company. Novel corporate meanings were constructed and succeeded in the public discourse. Thus, the enterprise had to incrementally adapt its own role in Nigeria which in turn increased the pressure on the enterprise to change its behavior. Although reluctant and in an indecisive way, Shell began to adapt and change its behavior very slowly, for example (although still very careful) by voicing criticism towards the Nigerian government. Such changes mark moments of corporate uncertainty in which routines no longer work. Due to that, new modes of actions are introduced to reassess corporate meanings. All in all, although experiencing the situation in Nigeria as a full-scale crisis and creatively and contingently generating new meanings, in the end Shell only adapted selectively to new expectations and did not comprehensively redefine its own role as a multinational enterprise in Nigeria. As such, the illustration has shown that while constructing itself as an actor in Nigeria, conflicts, uncertainty, and indeterminacy prevailed as the company was very reluctant (and overtaxed) to adhere to new roles expressed in the normative expectations of global governance.

Conclusion

In this chapter we have shown that mainstream global governance emerged as a new narrative in the 1990s. Within this narrative, global companies are often discussed in a structural-functionalist frame. Because of this frame, corporate actors are conceptualized by essentializing their preferences and interests as well as by rationalizing their modes of action. By drawing on a different theory of action, we have questioned this actor image and sketched out an alternative. Therein, global companies are not understood as fixed in their meanings but rather continuously and dynamically construct these in interaction with relevant others. These construction processes are marked by sociality, creativity as well as contingency. Assuming that global companies are exposed to new expectations, information, and pressure by different stakeholders on different levels, the first illustration showed that these expectations not only exist but are also integrated into corporate reasoning. CSR commitments are consequently an immediate expression of new social expectations articulated towards global companies. The second illustration then showed that these expectations are by no means translated easily into corporate identity and action. Instead, conflicts and ambiguities remain for actors previously constructed solely in economic terms, which now are expected to become involved in political issues.

Both the critique of mainstream global governance as well as the illustrations have shown that the optimism expressed in the functionalist argument that global companies will (or at least should) become political actors *because* they have the resources and capacities to solve governance gaps, remains unwarranted. While we consider corporate rhetoric to be important, we agree with others being more sceptical about the corporate potential and will to overcome the gap between rhetoric and corporate implementation at the same time (Wolf 2008). However, we offer an alternative explanation for this gap besides global companies rationally and strategically exploiting it at will. Contrary to this, corporate actors are confronted by ambiguous and conflicting demands and expectations. While the literature seems to be eager to frame them as political actors, in everyday corporate decision-making they experience more hesitancy and reluctance from their own shareholders and workers but also from their social environment. Put differently, global governance constitutes new expectations which are more difficult to relate to corporate action than assumed in the narrative of global companies becoming political actors.

In global policy terms, creating space for historical contingency as well as corporate creativity broadens the "debate about the range of strategic choices open to us in the present and future" on how to integrate global companies in global governance (Zeitlin 2007: 135). As suggested by Dewey a long time ago, imputing to corporate actors only risks to lose the means necessary to better conditions:

> That captains of industry are creative artists of a sort, and that industry absorbs an undue share of the creative activity of the present time cannot be denied. To impute to the leaders of industry and commerce simply an acquisitive motive is not merely to lack insight into their conduct, but it is to lose the clew to bettering conditions. (Dewey 1922: 146)

Thus, global governance initiatives need to be designed carefully and engage global companies precisely in their uncertainty about their roles and responsibilities. Instead of assuming that global companies accept political responsibilities, we should discuss both whether or not this is legitimate and how we can ensure comprehensive implementation of diverging expectations towards these actors. While the "definition of what it means to be a successful firm" (Kollmann 2008: 145) remains an open research question which depends on as many theoretical perspectives as possible to be answered convincingly, filling this definition with the notion of liability and obligations towards a broadly defined society remains a crucial task for global policy in the twenty-first century.

Notes

1   Depending on theoretical convenience, one might also add moral and ethical considerations as well as the status of being a political actor to the definitional core of global companies (see for example Scherer, Palazzo, and Baumann 2006). However, we consider this adding of new definitional aspects to global companies as a repetition of our argument: a new social environment creates new expectations which then creates new aspects for private business.

2   This argument obviously draws on ideas from American Pragmatism where beliefs are understood as "rules for action" (Hellmann 2010: 146–149). Following this, we suggest to think of these social structures as a diverse and ambiguous reservoir of collective beliefs and world views.

3   This basically constitutes our methodological argument why it is worthwhile to look into corporate communication: all relevant stakeholder and civil society positions will to some extent influence the company. In other words, we do not consider these documents to be corporate "cheap talk" or "public relation ploy" (Haufler 2001: 1). Instead, they constitute different reactions to different expectations and thereby reflect corporate meanings and beliefs how to (or how not to) accommodate new expectations.

4   There are numerous examples of the interlinkage between CSR and corporate identity. Almost every company analyzed referred to a specific CSR philosophy or individual code of conduct such as the "Chevron Way," http://www.chevron.com/about/chevronway, accessed July 23, 2012; BP's "Commitment to Integrity," http://www.bp.com/sectiongenericarticle.do?categoryId=9003494& contentId=7006600, accessed July 23, 2012; or the "Shell General Business Principles," http://www .shell.com/home/content/aboutshell/who_we_are/our_values/sgbp/ (accessed July 23, 2012) to name but a few.

5   Sorted by foreign assets, there were four companies from the extractive sector among the non-financial Top Ten companies of the world in 2001 (BP, Exxonmobil, Royal Dutch/Shell, and Total Fina Elf) (UNCTAD 2004: 41).

6   To increase the representative value of the speeches, a minimum of three speeches per company had to be found to take it into consideration. As the extractive sector is dominated by petroleum companies, these appear more often in the analysis than other companies extracting minerals or diamonds (e.g. de Beers).

7   Note that the keywords were derived from a pilot study including ten speeches and represent only illustrative examples ("Ankerbeispiele") of the categories. The coding process was not carried out by looking only for these keywords but instead the wider context in which single phrases were placed were taken into account and related to the categories.

8   This approach takes seriously the text as an expression of social reality which, in order to reconstruct this reality, needs to be read patiently and in its "own" language, sequence by sequence (Oevermann 2000). Sequence analysis is thus motivated by an open and anti-essential understanding of social action through which reality is situationally constituted. It is assumed that the words used in a text are not chosen arbitrarily but rather reflect structures of meanings and beliefs held by the author of the document.

References

Amoore, Louise. 2000. "International Political Economy and the 'Contested Firm'." *New Political Economy*, 5 (2): 183–204.

Avant, Deborah D., Finnemore, Martha, and Sell, Susan K. 2010. "Who Governs the Globe?" In *Who Governs the Globe?*, ed. Deborah D. Avant, Martha Finnemore, and Susan K. Sell, 1–31. Cambridge: Cambridge University Press.

Barnett, Michael and Duvall, Raymond, eds. 2005. *Power in Global Governance*. Cambridge: Cambridge University Press.

Beckert, Jens. 2003. "Economic Sociology and Embeddedness: How Shall We Conceptualize Economic Action?" *Journal of Economic Issues*, 37 (3): 769–787.

Börzel, Tanja A. and Risse, Thomas. 2010. "Governance without a State: Can It Work?" *Regulation & Governance*, 4 (2): 113–134.

Brühl, Tanja. 2007. "Public-Private Partnerships: Unlike Partners? Assessing New Forms of Regulation." In *Globalization: State of the Art and Perspectives*, ed. Stefan A. Schirm, 143–161. London: Routledge.

Brühl, Tanja and Rittberger, Volker. 2001. "From International to Global Governance: Actors, Collective Decision-Making, and the United Nations in the World of the Twenty-First Century." In *Global Governance and the United Nations system*, ed. Volker Rittberger, 1–47. Tokyo: United Nations University Press.

Cohen, Stephen D. 2007. *Multinational Corporations and Foreign Direct Investment: Avoiding Simplicity, Embracing Complexity*. Oxford: Oxford University Press.

Conzelmann, Thomas and Dieter Wolf, Klaus. 2007. "Doing Good While Doing Well? Potenzial und Grenzen grenzüberschreitender privatwirtschaftlicher Selbstregulierung." In *Macht und Ohnmacht internationaler Institutionen: Festschrift für Volker Rittberger*, ed. Andreas Hasenclever, Klaus Dieter Wolf, and Michael Zürn, 145–175. Frankfurt a.M.: Campus.

Cutler, Claire A. 2002. "Private International Regimes and Interfirm Cooperation." In *The Emergence of Private Authority in Global Governance*, ed. Rodney Bruce Hall and Thomas J. Biersteker, 23–40. Cambridge: Cambridge University Press.

Cutler, Claire A. 2003. *Private Power and Global Authority: Transnational Merchant Law in the Global Political Economy*. Cambridge: Cambridge University Press.

Cutler, Claire A. 2008. "Problematizing Corporate Social Responsibility under Conditions of Late Capitalism and Postmodernity." In *Authority in the Global Political Economy*, ed. Volker Rittberger and Martin Nettesheim, 189–217. Basingstoke: Palgrave Macmillan.

Cutler, Claire A., Haufler, Virginia, and Porter, Tony, eds. 1999. *Private Authority and International Affairs*. New York: SUNY.

Deitelhoff, Nicole and Dieter Wolf, Klaus. 2010. "Corporate Security Responsibility: Corporate Governance Contributions to Peace and Security in Zones of Conflict." In *Corporate Security Responsibility? Corporate Governance Contributions to Peace and Security in Zones of Conflict*, ed. Nicole Deitelhoff and Klaus Dieter Wolf, 1–25. New York: Palgrave Macmillan.

Dewey, John. 1922. *Human Nature and Conduct: An Introduction to Social Psychology*. New York: Henry Holt and Company.

Dingwerth, Klaus. 2007. *The New Transnationalism: Transnational Governance and Democratic Legitimacy*. Basingstoke: Palgrave Macmillan.

Emirbayer, Mustafa. 1997. "Manifesto for a Relational Sociology."*American Journal of Sociology*, 103 (2): 281–317.

Emirbayer, Mustafa and Mische, Ann. 1998. "What Is Agency?" *American Journal of Sociology*, 103 (4): 962–1023.

Flohr, Annegret, Rieth, Lothar, Schwindenhammer, Sandra, and Dieter Wolf, Klaus. 2010. *The Role of Business in Global Governance: Corporations as Norm Entrepreneurs*. Basingstoke: Palgrave Macmillan.

Granovetter, Mark. 1985. "Economic Action and Social Structure: The Problem of Embed-dedness." *American Journal of Sociology*, 91 (3): 481–510.

Graz, Jean-Christophe and Nölke, Andreas, eds. 2008. *Transnational Private Governance and Its Limits*. London: Routledge.

Hall, Rodney Bruce and Biersteker, Thomas J., eds. 2002. *The Emergence of Private Authority in Global Governance*. Cambridge: Cambridge University Press.

Haufler, Virginia. 2001. *A Public Role for the Private Sector: Industry Self-Regulation in a Global Economy*. Washington, DC: Carnegie Endowment for International Peace.

Haufler, Virginia. 2006. "Global Governance and the Private Sector." In *Global Corporate Power*, ed. Christopher May, 85–103. Boulder: Lynne Rienner Publishers.

Haufler, Virginia. 2010. "Corporations in Zones of Conflict: Issues, Actors, and Institutions." In *Who Governs the Globe?*, ed. Deborah D. Avant, Martha Finnemore, and Susan K. Sell, 102–130. Cambridge: Cambridge University Press.

Held, David, McGrew, Anthony, Goldblatt, David, and Perraton, Jonathan. 1999. *Global Transformations: Politics, Economics and Culture*. Stanford: Stanford University Press.

Held, David and McGrew, Anthony, eds. 2002. *Governing Globalization: Power, Authority and Global Governance*. Cambridge: Polity Press.

Hellmann, Gunther. 2010. "Pragmatismus." In *Handbuch der Internationalen Politik*, ed. Carlo Masala, Frank Sauer, and Andreas Wilhelm, 145–178. Wiesbaden: VS Verlag für Sozialwissenschaften.

Herborth, Benjamin. 2004. "Die via media als konstitutionstheoretische Einbahnstraße: Zur Entwicklung des Akteur-Struktur-Problems bei Alexander Wendt." *Zeitschrift für Internationale Beziehungen*, 11 (1): 62–87.

Hofferberth, Matthias, Brühl, Tanja, Burkhart, Eric, Fey, Marco, and Peltner, Anne. 2011. "Multinational Enterprises as 'Social Actors': Constructivist Explanations for Corporate Social Responsibility." *Global Society*, 25 (2): 205–226.

Holzer, Boris. 2010. *Moralizing the Corporation: Transnational Activism and Corporate Accountability*. Cheltenham: Edward Elgar.

Jackson, Patrick T. 2009. "Situated Creativity, or, the Cash Value of a Pragmatist Wager for IR." *International Studies Review*, 11 (3): 656–659.

Jackson, Patrick T. 2011. *The Conduct of Inquiry in International Relations*. New York: Routledge.

Jackson, Patrick T. and Nexon, Daniel H. 1999. "Relations Before States: Substance, Process and the Study of World Politics." *European Journal of International Relations*, 5 (3): 291–332.

Jepperson, Ronald L., Wendt, Alexander, and Katzenstein, Peter J. 1996. "Norms, Identity, and Culture in National Security." In *The Culture of National Security: Norms and Identity in Word Politics*, ed. Peter J. Katzenstein, 33–75. New York: Columbia University Press.

Joas, Hans. 1997. *The Creativity of Action*. Chicago: University of Chicago Press.

Kobrin, Stephen J. 2008. "Globalization, Transnational Corporations and the Future of Global Governance." In *Handbook on Global Corporate Citizenship*, ed. Andreas Georg Scherer, 249–272. Northampton: Edward Elgar.

Kollman, Kelly. 2008. "The Regulatory Power of Business Norms: A Call for a New Research Agenda." *International Studies Review*, 10 (3): 397–419.

March, James G. and Olsen, Johan P. 1989. *Rediscovering Institutions: The Organizational Basis of Politics*. New York: Free Press.

Mayntz, Renate. 2008. "Von der Steuerungstheorie zu Global Governance." In *Governance in einer sich wandelnden Welt*, ed. Gunnar Folke Schuppert and Michael Zürn, 43–61. PVS-Sonderheft 41.

Oevermann, Ulrich. 2000. "Die Methode der Fallrekonstruktion in der Grundlagenforschung sowie in der klinischen und pädagogischen Praxis." In *Die Fallrekonstruktion: Sinnverstehen in der sozialwissenschaftlichen Forschung*, ed. Klaus Kraimer, 58–156. Frankfurt a.M.: Suhrkamp.

Omeje, Kenneth. 2006. *High Stakes and Stakeholders: Oil Conflict and Security in Nigeria*. Aldershot: Ashgate.

Palan, Ronen. 2000. "New Trends in Global Political Economy." In *Global Political Economy: Contemporary Theories*, ed. Ronen Palan, 1–18. London: Routledge.

Pattberg, Philipp. 2007. *Private Institutions and Global Governance: The New Politics of Environmental Sustainability*. Cheltenham; Northampton, MA: Edward Elgar.

Risse, Thomas. 2002. "Transnational Actors and World Politics." In *Handbook of International Relations*, ed. Walter Carlsnaes, Thomas Risse, and Beth A. Simmons, 255–274. London: Sage.

Risse, Thomas. 2011. *Governance without a State? Policies and Politics in Areas of Limited Statehood*. New York: Columbia University Press.

Rittberger, Volker, Nettesheim, Martin, Huckel, Carmen, and Göbel, Thorsten. 2008. "Introduction: Changing Patterns of Authority." In *Authority in the Global Political Economy*, ed. Volker Rittberger and Martin Nettesheim, 1–9. Basingstoke: Palgrave Macmillan.

Sabel, Charles F. and Zeitlin, Jonathan. 1997. "Stories, Strategies, Structures: Rethinking Historical Alternatives to Mass Production." In *World of Possibilities: Flexibility and Mass Production in Western Industrialization*, ed. Charles F. Sabel and Jonathan Zeitlin, 1–33. Cambridge: Cambridge University Press.

Scherer, Andreas Georg, Palazzo, Guido, and Baumann, Dorothée. 2006. "Global Rules and Private Actors: Toward a New Role of the Transnational Corporation in Global Governance." *Business Ethics Quarterly*, 16 (4): 505–532.

Segerlund, Lisbeth. 2010. *Making Corporate Social Responsibility a Global Concern: Norm Construction in a Globalizing World*. Burlington: Ashgate.

Shalin, Dmitri N. 1986. "Pragmatism and Social Interactionism." *American Sociological Review*, 51 (1): 9–29.

Soares de Oliveira, Ricardo. 2007. *Oil and Politics in the Gulf of Guinea*. London: Hurst and Company.

Strauss, Anselm L. 1993. *Continual Permutations of Action*. New York: Walter de Gruyter.

UNCTAD. 2004. *Development and Globalization. Facts and Figures*. New York: United Nations Publications.

Williamson, Oliver E. 1981. "The Modern Corporation: Origins, Evolution, Attributes." *Journal of Economic Literature*, 19 (4): 1537–1568.

Wolf, Klaus Dieter. 2008. "Emerging Patterns of Global Governance: The New Interplay Between the State, Business and Civil Society." In *Handbook of Research on Global Corporate Citizenship*, ed. Andreas Georg Scherer and Guido Palazzo, 225–248. Cheltenham; Northampton: Edward Elgar.

Zadek, Simon. 2007. *The Civil Corporation: The New Economy of Corporate Citizenship*, 2nd edn. London: Earth Scan.

Zeitlin, Jonathan. 2007. "The Historical Alternatives Approach." In *The Oxford Handbook of Business History*, ed. Geoffrey Jones and Jonathan Zeitlin, 120–140. Oxford: Oxford University Press.

Zimmer, Melanie. 2010. "Oil Companies in Nigeria: Emerging Good Practice or Still Fueling Conflict?" In *Corporate Security Responsibility? Corporate Governance Contributions to Peace and Security in Zones of Conflict*, ed. Nicole Deitelhoff and Klaus Dieter Wolf, 58–84. New York: Palgrave.

Zürn, Michael. 1992. *Interessen und Institutionen in der internationalen Politik: Grundlegungen und Anwendungen des situationsstrukturellen Ansatzes*. Opladen: Leske & Budrich.

Zürn, Michael. 2002. "Societal Denationalization and Positive Governance." In *Towards a Global Polity: Future Trends and Prospects*, ed. Morten Ougaard and Richard Higgott, 78–104. London: Routledge.

Chapter 22

The Socially Embedded Corporation

Kate Macdonald

Introduction

The contemporary global political economy is cluttered with examples of global companies caught between a multiplicity of competing social expectations and demands. Take, for example, the prominent multinational company Unilever – a company that sells its products across 190 countries,[1] and prides itself on operating as a "multi-local" multinational company,[2] which is deeply integrated into the social fabric of each country in which it operates. The range of social actors and settings with which the company interacts bring a corresponding diversity of demands for the company to comply with and in some ways actively to support valued social processes and outcomes. For instance, in the United Kingdom and the Netherlands, where the company is headquartered, investors expect competitive returns and governments expect compliance with European standards on human rights, transparency, and environmental protection; customers around the world expect high quality and competitively priced goods, adapted for local needs and preferences; governments in countries from which many of the company's agricultural products are sourced expect the company's activities to contribute to processes of growth and development in their countries; and so the list of social demands goes on.

The channels through which these wide ranging social pressures are brought to bear on the company's decision-making processes are equally diverse. Such pressures are exerted (among other means) through formal corporate governance arrangements, concerted NGO and network-based campaigns, legal activism, routine forms of government administration and regulation, and broader processes of socialization through which attitudes and behaviors of company management are constituted. How global companies such as Unilever respond to these competing social pressures has significant consequences for the economic and social welfare of individuals

The Handbook of Global Companies, First Edition. Edited by John Mikler.
© 2013 John Wiley & Sons, Ltd. Published 2013 by John Wiley & Sons, Ltd.

and populations coming into contact with the company itself, their products, and their suppliers.

Reflecting on examples such as these, it becomes rapidly apparent that the central question confronting those with a theoretical and practical interest in the social and political activities of contemporary corporations is not simply *whether* they are "socially embedded" – that is, conditioned and constrained by the social relationships in which they participate. Manifestly they are. That is not to say that corporate activity cannot be "more" or "less" socially embedded. Certainly it is possible for companies to be "less" socially embedded, in the sense that their behavior is shaped predominantly by fundamental economic drivers underpinned by self-interest and structural forces of supply and demand, or "more" embedded, whereby such economic drivers are subordinated in significant ways to more contingent social norms and pressures (Polanyi 1944; Block 2003; Gemici 2007). Nevertheless, we can acknowledge such variation of degree, and still accept Karl Polanyi's contention that market activity is "always embedded" in the social in one way or another, however the balance of forces might play out in a particular context (Block 2003).

A more controversial and difficult question – on which this chapter focuses – asks *how* is global corporate activity socially embedded? This requires us to "unpack" processes of social embedding in both normative and empirical dimensions, highlighting the contestation that characterizes both channels of social influence over companies, and the normative values that sit behind these competing pressures. This exercise not only offers us a more fine-grained empirical picture of how social embedding operates. It also enables a much more overtly *political* account of social embedding than is commonly presented.

We begin with a conceptual introduction to some of the most influential ways in which the term "socially embedded" has come to be used in relation to economic activity in general, and global corporate activity in particular. To highlight both the plurality and the deep contestedness of social embedding processes, discussion then breaks down both the multiple normative agendas and then the multiple channels of social influence that compete to influence global corporate activity. We then reflect on the context-specific processes through which these influences interact to shape the widely varying activities, roles, and responsibilities taken on by contemporary global companies.

What Does It Mean for Companies to Be "Socially Embedded"?

The Concept

The term "embedded" is a highly elastic and arguably overused one. There is reasonably clear agreement on the basic sense in which the term "socially embedded" is usually applied to companies: that is, it highlights the ways in which companies are *conditioned and constrained by the social relationships in which they participate*.[3]

In one sense the usefulness of the concept of "embedding" lies precisely in this conceptual breadth, which can accommodate the extremely diverse range of social influences that shape corporate behavior. These influences come from an array of actors and institutions, including national and regional governments, local and global markets, and more diffuse complexes of territorially grounded social institutions. In order to retain this conceptual breadth, it is useful to deploy the concept of embedding as an expansive umbrella term, which gestures towards a range of social actors and institutions that are external to the organizational container of the company itself, but which contribute in significant ways to shaping corporate behavior.[4]

Nevertheless, if the term embeddedness is used carelessly, its breadth can obscure several important distinctions within both the concept and practice of social embedding. Existing analyses of embedding have dealt with these distinctions in different ways, varying most notably along three dimensions: the *level of analysis* they focus on (ranging from a broad macro-systemic focus to a narrower focus on actors, institutions, and networks); the economic *subjects* of social embedding they focus on (markets, economic policy regimes, or companies); and the way they balance *normative versus empirical* analysis. We discuss each of these briefly below. Although scholarly literature on the social embeddedness of economics is expansive, the concept is deeply associated in the minds of many with a key set of influential authors. The discussion below focuses on these key thinkers, but also makes reference to the broader traditions in which their writings are located.

Levels of Analysis

One way in which approaches to studying the social embedding of economic activity have varied is the differing levels of analysis through which processes of social embedding have been examined. Although such distinctions are usually blurred and often rather subtle, they can help us understand the varying scope and focus of writings on social embeddedness.

Some of the most influential writings on social embedding come from a prominent collection of economic sociologists and political economists whose analytic lens is fixed at a very broad, macro-sociological, and often deeply historicized level. Such theorists have tended to conceptualize social embedding as a pattern of social conditioning of economic activity prevalent during particular phases or forms of capitalism (Polanyi 1944; Jessop 2001). Understood in this way, the concept refers to a "background" complex of interlocking norms, practices, and institutions that exercise a conditioning or regulatory influence over those economic actors that comprise the core subject of investigation.

Foremost in most people's minds among theorists of this bent is Karl Polanyi, whose writings on the social embeddedness of markets have been extremely influential. Although his original focus was on social embedding at the national level, his ideas have enjoyed a revival in recent years, applied in adapted ways to a globalizing social and economic environment. Polanyi's (1944) famous account of social embeddedness certainly recognized the importance of transformative social agency, particularly in the form of large-scale social movements demanding that social values be re-asserted against the market, so to speak. Nevertheless, his analytical lens was focused at what we might loosely call a macro-sociological, historical-institutionalist level (Krippner and Alvarez 2007).

This approach can be contrasted to that of (Granovetter 1985), another influential economic sociologist writing on this subject, who has characterized embeddedness in *network* terms, focusing on how economic actors orient themselves to one another in the market. Many have suggested that the latter conception is too narrow, losing sight of the macro-institutional picture that Polanyi accentuated (Krippner and Alvarez 2007; Beckert 2009). Nevertheless, both institution- and network-based conceptualizations can be useful in complementary ways, highlighting, on the one hand, the rule/norm/script-governed nature of market activity, and on the other, its social-interactive character.

Economic Subjects of Embedding

Accounts of social embedding have also varied in notable ways with regard to the kinds of economic actors and processes whose "social embedding" is being theorized: the economic subjects of social embedding, in other words. In concrete terms, that is to say that some approaches have focused on the embedding of markets, others have focused on the embedding of economic policy regimes, and only a sub-set of these have explicitly focused on the embedding of (global) companies. Although this distinction is not always explicitly highlighted, the material channels of social embedding, as well as the normative principles with respect to which embedding occurs, usually differ importantly across different economic subjects. Because we are particularly interested in applying and adapting analyses of social embedding to global companies, this is an especially important distinction to tease apart in this chapter.

Polanyi's influential analysis was cast in terms of socially embedded "markets," and this is perhaps still the most common way in which the notion of socially embedded economies is conceptualized. Although all economic and social activity can be described as "embedded," the focus of Polanyi's analysis is specifically on market activity – that is, activity related to the exchange of commodities through a price-driven coordination mechanism. In this context, embeddedness has to do essentially with the constitutive institutions and networks of interaction that shape market activity. Many of the analytical tools developed to analyze socially embedded *markets* certainly translate to the analysis of socially embedded corporate activity, though the translation is imperfect. In particular, as we will see, Polanyi's macro-historical analysis of societal shifts first towards a "market society," and then back towards strengthened patterns of social embedding, require some adaptation before they can be applied to a fine-grained analysis of how processes of social embedding vary in relation to different kinds of companies, in distinct social contexts.

Economic policy regimes comprise another kind of economic institution whose social embedding has been widely analyzed. John Ruggie's influential writings on what he called "embedded liberalism" reflected a way of thinking about a *political* regime of social embeddedness (Ruggie 1982). Ruggie used this term to capture an interpretation of the national and international economic policy institutions established under the post-WWII "Bretton Woods" regime. He characterized these as a kind of grand "social bargain" through which liberal markets could be contained, socially legitimized and in turn rendered politically sustainable after a period of tumultuous change and conflict in the global order (Ruggie 1982; Ruggie (ed.) 2008; Abdelal and Ruggie 2009). This approach offers a useful example of how the concept of embedding can be applied with a narrower institutional focus than Polanyi's more epochal, society-wide view. Nevertheless, Ruggie's early focus on the design of (mainly) trade and macroeconomic policy institutions clearly concentrated on distinct normative and institutional agendas to those most relevant to the social embedding of global companies, on which we focus here.

More recently, Ruggie himself, together with a range of others, have worked to adapt earlier writings on social embedding to analysis of global companies, and the changing social expectations placed on them against a backdrop of social and economic globalization (Ruggie 2003; Utting 2005). Ruggie's early work on this theme focused on voluntary "global governance" initiatives such as the UN's Global Compact, assessing their contribution to embedding corporate activity in social norms. More recently Ruggie's work in his capacity as Special Representative to the United Nations on Business and Human Rights has expanded this focus to encompass a broader range of legal and quasi-judicial instruments, alongside voluntary mechanisms of social embedding (Ruggie 2008). Much of this work has however been positioned primarily within a human rights law framework, and has tended not to be articulated within the more sociological language of "embedding."

Normative versus Empirical Focus

To adapt broader traditions of social embedding to a more focused analysis of global companies, we require analytical tools of two kinds. First, we must analyze the distinctive *normative* demands that have been invoked by those making social claims on global companies. Second, we need a means of analyzing the distinct *sociological channels* through which global companies are socially embedded. Typically, analyses of embedding encompass both normative and empirical dimensions, though they tend to be mixed in together in rather ambiguous ways. Polanyi for example was making an empirical claim when he suggested that a more embedded market was one subjected to greater discipline by social institutions. But he was also making a moral claim about what he saw as an urgent need to impose this control, lest the free market ravage the society that gave birth to it.

Certainly, some writers on social embedding largely sidestep normative questions, focusing instead on detailed empirical analysis of the features and dynamics of contrasting political and economic institutions in which corporate behavior is constituted and constrained. The "varieties of capitalism" tradition of comparative political economy exemplifies this approach (Hall and Soskice 2001; Marshall, Mitchell, and Ramsay 2008; Mikler 2009), as do many studies of comparative corporate governance (Jacoby 2004). Nevertheless, much writing on social embedding is very explicit in viewing "social" interests or values as standing apart from, and often in some kind of normative tension with, economic and financial interests of a narrower kind. Those who use the language of social embedding therefore usually intend this to signal a normative commitment to the goal of disciplining the free market in the cause of *wider* public interests (Jessop 2001). As Sen puts it, the notion of social embedding is in this way fundamentally about how private relations of power operating through markets can be subordinated to "social values that we can defend ethically" (Sen 2009).

What such overtly normative conceptions of social embedding often downplay, however, is the *diversity* of social norms that are usually at work, competing for influence over corporate decisions in any given context. The social norms that drive the embedding of corporate behavior can be "social" – in the sense of conditioning and constraining more narrowly construed *economic* goals – without conforming to a distinctively "progressive" (leftist liberal) normative position of the kind often assumed. We can therefore deploy the concept of social embeddedness to explain *deviations* from "progressive" labor and social practices just as usefully we can apply it to explain progressive patterns of corporate behavioral change. Indeed, as we see below, processes of social embedding are almost always characterized by overt contestation surrounding the substance of the social norms in which corporate behavior is anchored.

To explore these contested dynamics of social embedding in greater depth, it is therefore useful to disentangle and examine in turn: first, the some of the competing social *norms* through which the embedding of global corporate activity occurs; and second, some of the multiple *institutional channels* through which competing social pressures on corporate behavior play out.

Competing Normative Demands on Global Companies

Typically, there is contestation concerning both the *basic purposes and values* that social institutions (in general) are expected to promote, and the appropriate *roles and responsibilities* of corporations (in particular) in advancing and protecting these values. To illustrate some of the ways such normative contests play out within processes of social embedding, it is instructive to examine a few examples of such conflict within economic sectors characterized by extensive global corporate activity.

One very clear example of such conflict arises within the supply chains of global manufacturing and retail companies, in which narrow economic goals commonly come into tension with broader social, developmental, and environmental concerns. Conflict of this kind confronts companies ranging from major clothing and sportswear retailers like Nike or Wal-Mart, electronics and IT brands like Apple, global agribusiness companies like Unilever or Nestlé, through to furniture retailers like IKEA. What all of these companies share in common is the sourcing and selling of their products across wide-ranging geographical and social spaces; this breadth is associated with a correspondingly expansive set of competing social demands. Labor and human rights activists protest about the threat of labor exploitation and so-called poverty wages; environmental and sometimes also indigenous activists demand an end to the encroachment of forests for large-scale agricultural plantations; consumers concerned about animal welfare demand products that are certified as protecting dolphins, or chickens, or migratory birds, or any of a host of other "social" or "ethical" causes with which they normatively identify. Such demands are not always contradictory. But more often than not, companies find themselves caught between a plurality of competing accounts of the "social" values that they ought to be actively promoting (or at least more passively respecting).

Conflicts of these kinds have often been particularly stark when global companies have become enmeshed in large-scale processes of economic and industrial development, as is commonly the case. Such processes are often accompanied by widespread social dislocation and change, in which routine processes of social contestation are often intensified. Such conflicts have been particularly heated in relation to natural resource-intensive sectors such as mining, agribusiness, and forestry (Human Rights Council 2008). In such cases, normative conflicts between concerns for environmental protection, the rights of indigenous people, protection of land tenure for subsistence farmers, and corporate-led economic development, have been intense and sometimes violent. Even a brief glance at the mining sector in PNG (Harper and Israel 1999; Filer and Imbun 2004), or the forestry and palm oil sectors in Indonesia (Colchester *et al.* 2006), for instance, reveals the intense conflicts between competing social values and interests that confront global companies operating in these sectors.

Not only do conflicts arise in relation to what *kinds* of social outcomes are valued, but also concerning *whose* concerns should be prioritized. For example, conflicts between societal groups in different geographical locations have played an important role in shaping the politics of social embedding for many global companies. In the garment sector, US retailers such as Wal-Mart are subject to ongoing social pressure for them to support the needs of low-income American consumers by maintaining their widely touted "always-low-prices" in American retail stores (Ortega 1999). The company has also been assailed with sustained campaigns to improve wages, working conditions, and social protections for American Wal-Mart employees. At the same time, "anti-sweatshop" activists have pressured Wal-Mart to invest increasing resources in strengthening working conditions and social protections for workers making Wal-Mart products in offshore factories.

Once again, while such demands are not always contradictory, there are some very clear examples where they do directly conflict. For example, consumer demands for low prices and up-to-date seasonal inventory in retail stores have been shown by a large body of empirical research to directly undermine demands for living wages and no forced overtime among factory workers (Ascoly 2003). Such conflicts highlight the fact that simply asking *whether* Wal-Mart's global operations are "socially embedded" would be missing the most important question of all: that is, in terms of *whose* social values, interests, and concerns does such embedding occur?

Such examples also highlight a further important dimension of normative conflict, concerning attribution of *responsibilities* for promoting valued social concerns. Frequently, companies acknowledge the inherent value of objectives such as environmental protection, regulation of labor conditions in factories, and so on, and yet argue that it is not the proper role of companies to take on the responsibility of regulating social standards of these kinds. Rather, so the argument goes, one of the reasons we now so extensively resource specialized political institutions in the form of national governments is precisely so they can take on such responsibilities for embedding the economy in social values, in an effective and democratic manner. To demand that companies should be "socially embedded" in any way that goes beyond compliance with the law would be to misunderstand this distinction between social values in general, and role-specific social responsibilities in particular. Milton Friedman's classic statement about the social responsibility of business being to increase their profits illustrates this view starkly (Friedman 1970).

In contrast, the view of many advocates of "corporate social responsibility" for issues of these kinds has been that serious and persistent "governance gaps" have emerged within national regulatory arrangements, thereby requiring companies (alongside non-state actors of other kinds) to take on direct responsibilities for supporting such social values, which under other circumstances might be left to governments to care for (Ruggie 2003). The emergence of a wide array of "private" governance schemes (discussed in more detail elsewhere in this volume) are often interpreted as evidence that such responsibilities are being increasingly accepted (Haufler 2003; Vogel 2005; Macdonald 2007b). Nevertheless, the appropriate *attribution of responsibility* to corporations for supporting social standards of valued kinds remains an important aspect of normative contestation in its own right.

Competing Channels of Social Influence over Global Companies

To understand how such processes of contestation have played out in practice, we need to bring into the picture some analysis of the multiple channels through which battles to influence corporate priorities and behavior unfold. Dominant traditions of thinking about social embedding have often conceptualized these channels of social influence through a very "macro"-level lens (as highlighted earlier). An important point this chapter seeks to emphasize is that this needs to be supplemented with a more fine-grained "micro" analysis of how such social forces are instantiated in particular cases. This requires that we bring competing social *actors* more squarely into the story, highlighting the ways in which their deliberate strategies of mobilization and claim-making interact with broader macro-sociological and historical processes in shaping the balance of social forces that come to bear on corporate behavior. Accordingly, the following analysis teases apart some of the multiple sources of social pressure – operating through various social actors and institutions and at multiple geographical levels – through which competing sources of leverage are exerted over the behavior of global companies, shaping the patterns of social embeddedness that emerge.

Macro-Social Influences

We begin by examining some of the more diffuse, macro-sociological processes through which values, identities, and expectations prevailing at a "whole-of-society" level filter through to influence the decisions and behavior of individual global companies.

Perhaps most obviously, the decisions of the corporate executives and managers situated at the heart of corporate command centers are influenced by diffuse processes of normative socialization, through which the perceptions, identities, and values of these individuals are constituted. Such socialization processes play a similarly important role in conditioning the decisions of individual employees, investors, consumers, business partners, and others who in turn influence corporate behavior (as discussed further below). Even without such individual actors making concerted efforts to steer company behavior towards "socially responsible" practices, broad shifts in social expectations can still play an important role in shaping corporate responsiveness to new issues. We can observe such diffuse processes of socialization at work by examining how corporate social responsibility agendas have evolved over time, often closely tracking broader shifts in social attitudes towards social issues of different kinds, whether these be concerns for "sweatshop" labor, climate change, corporate tax evasion, or other issues that have waxed and waned on public and corporate agendas over recent decades (Blowfield 1999; Blowfield and Frynas 2005).

Evidence of this kind is sometimes interpreted as suggesting that companies adopting unilateral programs of corporate responsibility, signing up to voluntary certification schemes such as Rainforest Alliance or Fairtrade, or joining Multi-Stakeholder schemes such as the Common Code for the Coffee Community or Roundtable for Sustainable Palm Oil, are doing this because they have now "got religion" in some authentic way. In other words, some suggest that rising social concern for issues such as environmental protection and global poverty has re-shaped values and identities among individual corporate managers and grassroots staff, leading the constitutive values, purposes and perceived "interests" of *companies* in turn to be re-wired, to place greater weight on social alongside economic objectives.

Most observers, however, continue to question the extent to which such fundamental re-wiring of the constitutive values and objectives of major corporations has occurred. Instead, many interpret observable shifts in corporate engagement with the social responsibility agenda as a reflection of companies' more instrumental concern for *social legitimation* (Kell and Ruggie 1999; Campbell 2000). Social legitimacy is important in part because it enables companies to access various social "resources" that they need to survive and prosper: legitimacy can enable them to evade intensified government regulation, draw on a willing and able workforce, attract consumers to buy the company's products, and so on. Even when prospective investors, consumers or employees of a global company do not deliberately set out to strategically influence companies through their conferral or withdrawal of "legitimacy," the decentralized choices they make as individual workers, investors, or consumers can often reflect these concerns, translating into potentially powerful forms of social influence.

One much cited story tells of the CEO of Nike at the time of intense, worldwide campaigns directed against Nike's "sweatshop" labor practices finally yielding to activist pressure and adopting a range of corporate responsibility programs in Nike supply chains, in part because of concern that employees were becoming embarrassed at dinner parties and among family and friends to admit that they worked for Nike (Schwartz 2000). This is a classic example of how the broader social de-legitimation of the company's activities filtered through to damage the company's economic interests, not only via damage to the brand from the consumer perspective, but also via the increased costs in recruiting and retaining high quality employees. Of course, as we will discuss further below, such processes of societal legitimation and de-legitimation are also often strategically mobilized and deployed. But the point here is that even when this is not the case, such diffuse, constitutive processes of socialization can play an important role in shaping corporate behavior.

Social Embedding via Market Mechanisms

Although prevailing social norms influence corporate behavior via these broad socialization processes, employees, customers, and investors also employ more overt and strategic methods of leveraging their market relationships with companies as a basis for a range of social demands.

One of the most direct and visible means through which market mechanisms have been used to promote "social" norms of corporate conduct is the development of "socially responsible" or "ethical" investment schemes. In essence, such initiatives appropriate conventional market channels of corporate governance as means of broader social influence. Many pension funds and other institutional investors have developed indexes through which the ethical character of publicly listed companies can be screened and rated, thereby enabling socially minded investors to prioritize or filter investment choices on these grounds (Sparkes 2001). Government investment agencies have also sometimes been used in this way. The Norwegian Government Pension Fund for example is overseen by an influential ethics committee which screens investments to identify those that are seen as posing an unacceptable risk of the Fund contributing to serious or systematic human rights violations, serious environmental damage, gross corruption, or other serious violations of fundamental ethical norms (Chesterman 2008). In addition to proscribing investment in companies involved in "intrinsically" unethical activities such as the manufacture of cluster weapons or anti-personnel land mines, a number of prominent companies in mainstream sectors (such as Wal-Mart and Freeport McMoRan Copper & Gold) have had investment withdrawn as a result of ethical concerns regarding their business operations. Such initiatives can influence corporate behavior not only via the threat of de-investment, but also via their broader impact on shifting agendas and discourses within investor, management, and business media circles towards a more detailed understanding and serious engagement with the social impacts of business activity.

Nevertheless, the increasing occurrence of "socially responsible" investment initiatives of these kinds has in no way diminished the pressure of mainstream investors for sustained corporate performance in economic and financial terms, generating significant tensions between the economic and (broader) social demands being placed on corporate management through such channels.

The exercise of social influence via market mechanisms has also been widely documented with reference to the role of so-called "ethical" or "socially responsible" consumers. Increased consumer awareness and changing expectations surrounding the social and environmental conditions of production of the goods they consume have led to a proliferation of "ethical labeling" schemes, across a range of economic sectors. To receive social certification of this kind, companies must certify their compliance with designated social or environmental standards. They can then use this label as a basis for marketing their products to "ethically" aware consumers. Prominent examples include the Fairtrade mark, Rainforest Alliance and the Forest Stewardship Council, all of which have been widely embraced by mainstream manufacturers and retailers ranging from McDonalds, to Cadbury's, and even notorious social laggards such as Wal-Mart (Macdonald and Marshall 2010). Such labels have been established in relation to a vast array of social causes, including organic food products, dolphin friendly tuna, free range eggs, migratory bird friendly coffee, and so on – this diversity clearly reflecting the range of conflicting "ethical" social concerns and demands to which companies are now subject.

In these examples too, there remain important tensions between consumer demands for "ethical" production methods, and for desirable "economic" qualities such as competitive pricing, and desired product characteristics (Boulstridge and Carrigan 2000; Auger and Devinney 2007). Despite the increasing popularity of social certification and responsible sourcing schemes of these kinds, companies continue to receive extremely "mixed messages" from consumers who say they want ethical products, but are often unwilling to sacrifice other price or quality characteristics in return.

Overt Social Mobilization

Strategic attempts to influence corporate behavior occur not only via market mechanisms, but also through more conventional strategies of social mobilization, familiar to scholars of contentious politics and social activism more broadly (Tarrow 1994; Keck and Sikkink 1998; Tarrow 2005). In analyzing strategic action of this kind, we can therefore draw usefully on a wider range of analytic tools than are typically applied to the topic of social embedding.

The most obvious examples in which strategic pressure of this kind has been brought to bear on global companies come from iconic corporate accountability campaigns such as those directed at Nestlé on the issue of breast-milk substitutes (Dobbing 1988), Shell on gas flaring (Friends of the Earth Nigeria and Climate Justice Programme 2005; Justice in Nigeria Now 2010), Nike, and a range of other garment and sportswear brands on the issue of "sweatshop" labor (Ballinger 2010), Starbucks in relation to its purchases of Fairtrade certified coffee (Macdonald 2007a), and so on. These tactics are typically grounded in recognition of the value to global companies of their brand reputation (largely because of implications for relationships with employees, investors, consumers and governments, as discussed above). On this foundation, activists then seek strategically to mobilize pressure via these multiple corporate relationships, through which their social legitimacy is secured or undermined.

Often, such market-based tactics are complemented by the mobilization of legal and political channels to intensify pressure for change. For example, social activists have creatively deployed private law mechanisms – usually designed for very different purposes – as means of pressuring companies to take social responsibilities seriously. For example, unfair competition and false advertising legislation has been used to try and hold companies accountable for claims made in their CSR marketing materials, such as in the Californian case *Kasky v. Nike*; 45 P 3d 243 (Cal, 2002)). A class action aiming to enforce codes of conduct also went before the Californian courts under California's Unfair Business Practices laws; this action claimed that Wal-Mart failed to meet their contractual duty and made false and misleading statements to the American public.[5]

Direct forms of overt social mobilization don't always occur in ways that are this strategic and coordinated. Communities in which business operations are located often wield significant forms of influence over companies simply by virtue of the corporate interest in securing social order and compliance at such sites. In part this is simply an illustration of the broader need for companies to secure social legitimacy – or the "social licence to operate," as it is sometimes called (Gunningham, Kagan, and Thornton 2006). In some cases, however, the costs of illegitimacy in the form of overt social conflict can be stark. Significant management time can be taken up managing costly processes to deal with community complaints and problems around sites such as mines (Jenkins 2004). Local conflicts become even more costly when they escalate into events such as strikes, road blockages, or in the most extreme cases, such as around mining operations in Bougainville, in Papua New Guinea, violent conflict that led to the shut-down of mining operations altogether in 1989 (Filer 1990).

Political Channels of Social Embedding

For Polanyi, Ruggie, and others, modern governments have always been recognized as central agents of social embedding. There is a vast array of political and sociological literature that tries to make sense of the mechanisms through which this government role can be discharged. Part III of this handbook addresses the role of the state in influencing global companies in greater depth. Here we simply sketch some of the most important political channels of social embedding – many of which interact importantly with the other social mechanisms surveyed above.

Governments use the full array of tools at their disposal to promote the embedding of corporate behavior within valued social norms. Most obviously, traditional "coercive" mechanisms continue to play an important role. These include constitutive vehicles like company law, which sometimes specify company director duties in relation to social and environmental responsibility alongside core financial responsibilities.[6] Many governments also make extensive use of direct forms of statutory or administrative regulation of social and environmental standards, and there are increasing moves towards requiring publicly listed companies to report on elements of their social and environmental performance.[7]

More indirectly, governments often play a role in providing oversight or "meta-regulation" of private standard-setting processes (2007), or participating directly in multi-stakeholder corporate responsibility schemes such as the Ethical Trading Initiative or Extractive Industry Transparency Initiative. They can also importantly shape corporate incentives by supporting ethical public procurement policies, or providing direct programmatic support for capacity building among businesses operating in sectors with complex social and environmental impacts.[8]

Although national governments play a central role in shaping policies of these kinds, government influence over corporate "rules of the game" can be exercised at all levels. For example, municipal governments in the United States and various European countries have played important roles in driving "ethical" procurement programs, such as Fair Trade purchasing programs in many European municipalities,[9] and "Sweatfree Purchasing" schemes adopted by many US counties and cities.[10] And in countries that have adopted significant decentralization programs, provincial governments often play important legislative and policy-making roles in relation to intensely contested issues such as land tenure and forestry regulation.

Beyond national borders, inter-governmental trade, investment, labor, and environmental rules exercise increasingly powerful influence over corporate behavior. Such international rules have been widely criticized for their tendency to proliferate voluntary (or otherwise poorly enforced) standards of corporate conduct in relation to social and environmental goals, while institutionalizing protections for the core economic interests of transnational businesses through "hard," legally binding mechanisms. The contrast between binding investor rights protections on one hand and largely voluntary standards of investor responsibility on the other has come under particularly intense criticism (Bachand and Rousseau 2003; Mann 2008).

A less visible but equally important channel through which government action influences transnational business activity is the influence of national government policy on corporate behavior *offshore*. There are some isolated examples where national governments have established social and environmental performance standards as conditions for provision of export credit, insurance, or private-sector development finance (Keenan 2008), or implemented explicitly extra-territorial regulations relating to egregious corporate practices such as bribery (Zerk 2010). In such cases, these interventions can provide important leverage for strengthened agendas of "corporate social responsibility." Conversely, national policies that encourage investors to move off-shore in pursuit of profits to be repatriated to the home country, without attendant social safeguards, generate dynamics of embedding that encourage and reward the de-prioritization of social norms of these kinds.

Interactions between Competing Social Forces

The above has sketched in highly schematic terms some of the most important sources of both normative contestation and social conflict that interact to shape the ways in which any given corporation will find itself socially embedded. There is a very large body of evidence indicating that the intensity of pressure to subordinate core corporate objectives to wider social goals varies significantly across different contexts, depending on variables such as the sector in which corporate activity occurs, geographical locations of production, investment and consumption, company-specific variables, and so on. Competing social pressures can also interact in highly path-dependent and contingent ways which can be very difficult to predict. To understand variation of this kind, we need to be attentive not only to shifting ideas and social power relations at the "whole-of-society" level, but also to the dynamics through which particular social groups are able to strategically mobilize social norms and social pressure to bring about change.

Conclusion

What then are the implications of all of this for how we make sense of the changing role of the corporation within a globalizing social, economic, and political order?

This chapter's account of contemporary corporate social embedding as highly pluralist and contested has important implications for how we understand the role of the contemporary corporation in global politics. First, it highlights the positioning of companies within an increasingly multi-level global political arena. As companies themselves increasingly carve up and spread out their operations over geographical, political, and social space, so too the dynamics of social and political contestation play out across multiple levels. Increasingly, companies are expected to participate in new systems of private and multi-stakeholder "governance beyond government" (analyzed in greater depth elsewhere in this volume); the terms of such arrangements are importantly shaped by the contested dynamics documented in this chapter.

More broadly, this picture of plural and contested social embedding resonates with widespread accounts of an increasingly plural global political order, in which large question marks hang over the evolution of global contests of value and power. This uncertainty sits uneasily with the tendency among many analysts to cast contemporary developments through the lens of a broader, secular trend towards *more* or *less* social embedding of some normatively specified kind. The evidence surveyed in this chapter does not support such a narrative with any clarity or confidence. In contrast, the social contest to set the terms within which corporations must operate is still very much in play, and the goal posts and terms of engagement continue to shift as distributions of norms and power in the global political economy fluctuate and evolve.

At stake in these deeply political contests are fundamental normative questions about what expectations society can legitimately place on business. Within the plural and dynamic environment of contemporary global politics, there are no clear answers to such questions, and the battles to determine whose answers will prevail remain intense. For companies such as Unilever, or the many others referred to in the examples presented above, there is no escaping the inherently political dynamics of social embedding. The clamor of contradictory local and global voices, demanding corporate responsiveness to a proliferation of social and environmental concerns, reflects clearly the multi-level, pluralist character of contemporary global politics. It is this messy, contested social order in which the contemporary socially embedded corporation is inescapably enmeshed.

Notes

1 www.unilever.com/aboutus; accessed August 2012.
2 http://www.unilever.com/images/Global%20Challenges%20Local%20Actions_tcm13-5100.pdf, accessed August 2012.
3 See for example a range of authors collected in a 2004 special issue of *Socio-Economic Review* addressing the topic of embeddedness (Krippner *et al.* 2004).
4 This view resonates with that of Granovetter (cited in Krippner *et al.* 2004): "For me [the concept of embedding] is just an announcement or a conceptual umbrella under which one should look into and think about what are the connections between economic activity and the social, the political, the institutional, the historical, the cultural elements that economic activity is mixed up with. So it is a sensitizing umbrella concept and that is how I have come to use it, because I think anything else will just get us into endless debates."
5 See www.laborrights.org, accessed December 19, 2012.
6 For a discussion of changes to Director Duties in the United Kingdom, see for example: http://corporate-responsibility.org/wp-content/uploads/2009/09/Companies_Bill_Supporter_Verdict_Long _Nov06.pdf, accessed August 2012.
7 See for example: http://ec.europa.eu/enterprise/policies/sustainable-business/corporate-social-respo nsibility/reporting-disclosure/index_en.htm and http://www.sec.gov/spotlight/dodd-frank/specco rpdisclosure.shtml, both accessed August 2012.
8 See for example: http://www.pm.gc.ca/eng/media.asp?category=1&featureId=6&pageId=26&id= 4435, accessed December 19, 2012.
9 See http://www.europarl.europa.eu/RegData/bibliotheque/briefing/2012/120334/LDM_BRI(2012) 120334_REV1_EN.pdf, accessed December 19, 2012.
10 See http://buysweatfree.org/about, accessed December 19, 2012.

References

Abdelal, R.E. and Ruggie, J.G. 2009. "The Principles of Embedded Liberalism: Social Legitimacy and Global Capitalism." In *New Perspectives on Regulation*, ed. D. Moss and J. Cisternino. Cambridge: Tobin Project.

Ascoly, N. 2003. Pricing in the Global Garment Industry, IRENE and Clean Clothes Campaign, http://www.cleanclothes.org/documents/03-05-pricingreport.pdf. Accessed December 19, 2012.

Auger, P. and Devinney, T.M. 2007. "Do What Consumers Say Matter? The Misalignment of Preferences with Unconstrained Ethical Intentions." *Journal of Business Ethics*, 76: 361–383.

Bachand, R. and Rousseau, S. 2003. *International Investment and Human Rights: Political and Legal Issues*. Ottawa: Rights & Democracy.

Ballinger, J. 2010. "The Threat Posed by 'Corporate Social Responsibility' to Trade Union Rights." In *Fair Trade, Corporate Accountability and Beyond: Experiments in Globalising Justice*, ed. K. Macdonald and S. Marshall, 223–244. Aldershot: Ashgate.

Beckert, J. 2009. "The Social Order of Markets." *Theory and Society*, 38 (3): 245–269.

Block, F. 2003. "Karl Polanyi and the Writing of The Great Transformation." *Theory and Society*, 32: 275–306.

Blowfield, M. 1999. "Ethical Trade: A Review of Developments and Issues." *Third World Quarterly*, 20 (4): 753–770.

Blowfield, M. and Frynas, G. 2005. "Setting New Agendas: Critical Perspectives on Corporate Social Responsibility in the Developing World." *International Affairs*, 81 (3): 499–513.

Boulstridge, E. and Carrigan, M. 2000. "Do Consumers Really Care about Corporate Responsibility? Highlighting the Attitude-Behaviour Gap." *Journal of Communication Management*, 4 (4): 355–368.

Campbell, D. 2000. "Legitimacy Theory or Managerial Reality Construction? Corporate Social Disclosure in Marks and Spencer PLC Corporate Reports 1969–1997." *Accounting Forum*, 24 (1): 80–100.

Chesterman, S. 2008. "The Turn to Ethics: Disinvestment from Multinational Corporations for Human Rights Violations – the case of Norway's Sovereign Wealth Fund." *New York University Public Law and Legal Theory Working Papers*, 23: 577–615.

Colchester, M., Jiwan, N., *et al.* 2006. *Promised Land Palm Oil and Land Acquisition in Indonesia: Implications for Local Communities and Indigenous Peoples*. Forest Peoples Program, Perkumpulan Sawit Watch, HuMA and the World Agroforestry Center.

Dobbing, J. 1988. *Infant Feeding: Anatomy of a Controversy*. Berlin: Springer-Verlag.

Filer, C. 1990. "The Bougainville Rebellion, the Mining Industry and the Process of Social Disintegration in Papua New Guinea." *Canberra Anthropology*, 13 (1): 1–39.

Filer, C. and Imbun, B. 2004. "A Short History of Mineral Development Policies in Papua New Guinea." *Working Paper*, 55, Resource Management in Asia Pacific Series, Research School of Pacific and Asian Studies, Australian National University.

Friedman, Milton. 1970. "The Social Responsibility of Business is to Increase Profits." *New York Times Magazine*, September 13.

Friends of the Earth Nigeria and Climate Justice Programme. 2005. *Gas Flaring in Nigeria: A Human Rights, Environmental and Economic Monstrosity*. Amsterdam: Friends of the Earth Nigeria/Climate Justice Programme.

Gemici, K. 2007. "Karl Polanyi and the Antinomies of Embeddedness." *Socio-Economic Review*, 6: 5–33.

Granovetter, M. 1985. "Economic Action and Social Structure: The Problem of Embeddedness." *American Journal of Sociology*, 91 (3): 481–510.

Gunningham, N., Kagan, R., and Thornton, D. 2006. "Social Licence and Environmental Protection: Why Businesses Go Beyond Compliance." *Law & Social Inquiry*, 29 (2): 307–341.

Hall, Peter and Soskice, David, eds. 2001. *Varieties of Capitalism: The Institutional Foundations of Comparative Advantage*. Oxford: Oxford University Press.

Harper, A. and Israel, M. 1999. "The Killing of the Fly: State-Corporate Victimisation in Papua New Guinea." *Working Paper*, 22, Resource Management in Asia Pacific Series, Research School of Pacific and Asian Studies, Australian National University.

Haufler, V. 2003. "New Forms of Governance: Certification Regimes as Social Regulations of the Global Market." In *Social and Political Dimensions of Forest Certification*, ed. E. Meidinger, C. Elliott, and G. Oesten, 237–248. Germany: Remagen-Oberwinter.

Human Rights Council (2008). *Promotion and Protection of All Human Rights, Civil, Political, Economic, Social and Cultural Rights, including the Right to Development; Protect, Respect and Remedy: A Framework for Business and Human Rights; Addendum 2: Survey of Scope and Patterns of Alleged Corporate-Related Human Rights Abuse*. Report of the Special Representative of the Secretary General on the Issue of Human Rights and Transnational Corporations and Other Business Enterprises, John Ruggie, Human Rights Council.

Jacoby, S. 2004. *The Embedded Corporation*. Princeton: Princeton University Press.

Jenkins, H. 2004. "Corporate Social Responsibility and the Mining Industry: Conflicts and Constructs." *Corporate Social Responsibility and Environmental Management*, 11 (1): 23–24.

Jessop, B. 2001. *The Social Embeddedness of the Economy and Its Implications for Economic Governance*, http://www2.cddc.vt.edu/digitalfordism/fordism_materials/jessop2.htm. Accessed December 19, 2012.

Justice in Nigeria Now. 2010. *Gas Flaring in Nigeria: An Overview, April 2010*. San Francisco: Justice in Nigeria Now.

Keck, M.E. and Sikkink, K. 1998. *Activists beyond Borders: Advocacy Networks in International Politics*. Ithaca: Cornell University Press.

Keenan, K. 2008. *Export Credit Agencies and the International Law of Human Rights*. Ottawa: Halifax Initiative.

Kell, G. and Ruggie, J.G. 1999. "Global Markets and Social Legitimacy: The Case of the Global Compact." *Transnational Corporations*, 8 (3): 101–120.

Krippner, G. and Alvarez, A. 2007. "Embeddedness and the Intellectual Projects of Economic Sociology." *Annual Review of Sociology*, 33: 219–240.

Krippner, G., Granovetter, M., Block, F., *et al*. 2004. "Polanyi Symposium: A Conversation on Embeddedness." *Socio-Economic Review*, 2: 109–135.

Macdonald, K. 2007a. "Globalising Justice within Coffee Supply Chains? Fair Trade, Starbucks and the Transformation of Supply Chain Governance." *Third World Quarterly, Special Issue on "Beyond CSR? Business, Poverty and Social Justice,"* 25 (7): 739–812.

Macdonald, K. 2007b. "Public Accountability within Transnational Supply Chains: A Global Agenda for Empowering Southern Workers?" In *Forging Global Accountabilities: Participation, Pluralism and Public Ethics*, ed. A. Ebrahim and E. Weisband, 252–279. Cambridge: Cambridge University Press.

Macdonald, K. and Marshall, S., eds. 2010. *Fair Trade, Corporate Accountability and Beyond: Experiments in Globalizing Justice*. London: Ashgate.

Mann, H. 2008. *International Investment Agreements, Business and Human Rights: Key Issues and Opportunities*. International Institute for Sustainable Development.

Marshall, S., Mitchell, R., and Ramsay, I., eds. 2008. *Varieties of Capitalism, Corporate Governance and Employees*. Melbourne: Melbourne University Press.

Mikler, J. 2009. *Greening the Car Industry: Varieties of Capitalism and Climate Change*. Cheltenham: Edward Elgar.

Ortega, B. 1999. *In Sam We Trust: The Untold Story of Sam Walton and Wal-Mart, the World's Most Powerful Retailer*. Philadelphia: Kogan Page.

Parker, C. 2007. "Meta-Regulating Corporate Governance: Legal Accountability for Corporate Social Responsibility." In *The New Corporate Accountability: Corporate Social Responsibility and the Law*, ed. D. McBarnet, A. Voiculescu, and T. Campbell, 207–239. Cambridge: Cambridge University Press.

Polanyi, K. 1944. *The Great Transformation: The Political and Economic Origins of Our Time*. Boston: Beacon Press.

Ruggie, J. 1982. "International Regimes, Transactions, and Change: Embedded Liberalism in Postwar Economic Order." *International Organization*, 36 (2): 370–415.

Ruggie, J.G. 2003. "Taking Embedded Liberalism Global: The Corporate Connection." In *Taming Globalization: Frontiers of Governance*, ed. D. Held and M. Koenig-Archibugi, 93–129. Cambridge: Polity Press.

Ruggie, J. 2008. "Protect, Respect and Remedy: A Framework for Business and Human Rights." *Innovations: Technology, Governance, Globalization*, 3 (2): 189–212.

Ruggie, J., ed. 2008. *Embedding Global Markets: An Enduring Challenge*. Aldershot: Ashgate.

Schwartz, P. 2000. "When Good Companies Do Bad Things." *Strategy & Leadership*, 28 (3): 4–11.

Sen, A. 2009. "Capitalism Beyond the Crisis." *New York Review of Books*, 56 (5): 26.

Sparkes, R. 2001. "Ethical Investment: Whose Ethics, Which Investment." *Business Ethics: A European Review*, 10 (3): 194–205.

Tarrow, S. 1994. *Power in Movement: Social Movements, Collective Action and Politics*. Cambridge: Cambridge University Press.

Tarrow, S. 2005. *The New Transnational Activism*. New York: Cambridge University Press.

UNRISD. 2002. Technology Business and Society Programme Paper Number 15. Geneva: UNRISD.

Utting, P. 2005. *Rethinking Business Regulation: From Self-Regulation to Social Control*. Technology Business and Society Programme Paper Number 15. Geneva: UNRISD.

Vogel, D. 2005. *The Market for Virtue: The Potential and Limits of Corporate Social Responsibility*. Washington, DC: Brookings Institution Press.

Zerk, J. 2010. "Extraterritorial Jurisdiction: Lessons for the Business and Human Rights Sphere from Six Regulatory Areas." *Working Paper*, 59, Harvard Corporate Social Responsibility Initiative.

Chapter 23

Ecological Modernization and Industrial Ecology

Frank Boons

Introduction

The international dimension of ecological problems has been recognized for at least forty years. Cross boundary issues such as acid rain and the pollution of international river basins were among the first of such issues. In the 1970s the depletion of the ozone layer marked the advent of truly global impacts on the earth's ecosystem (Benedick 1991). Changes in global climatic systems (of which the human origin is still contested by some) have brought the point home that the ecological impact of human activities, including the production and consumption of goods and services, extend to the global scale (Vitousek 1994; Biermann *et al.* 2010). At the same time, the relationship between global problems and local action is problematic. One example is the production of biofuels, which is promoted by several governments as a contribution to mitigating climate change, while it leads to substantial negative ecological impacts at the local level. Local communities may disregard such impacts because they focus on the economic gains they derive from it (Selfa 2010).

The global nature of ecological impact raises questions about the role of global companies, which in this chapter are defined as "an enterprise that engages in foreign direct investment and owns or controls value-adding activities in more than one country" (based on Dunning 1993: 3). Given their international scope of activities, they have been framed by governments and NGOs both as a source of global ecological problems as well as a potential solution (Hart 1997: Korten 2001). This view may be too simple though. The issue of resource scarcity provides an illustration of the complexities involved. The rapid economic growth of countries such as China, Brazil, India, and Russia since the mid-1990s has led to the increased scarcity of a number of resources, including several so-called rare earths (Hagelüken 2011). These countries have not only become important growth markets for international

The Handbook of Global Companies, First Edition. Edited by John Mikler.
© 2013 John Wiley & Sons, Ltd. Published 2013 by John Wiley & Sons, Ltd.

companies; they are also increasingly providing the workforce for production activities resulting in products that are shipped across the globe. As a result, there has been a multifaceted shift in terms of global resource flows, with global companies as important conduits. As a consequence, firms need to reassess their supply chains (Bell, Mollenkopf, and Thornton 2012).

In this chapter I will give an overview of academic work that has sought to unravel such complex issues. The basic question this work seeks to answer is: how do the activities of global companies contribute to (the reduction of) negative impacts on ecosystems?

It is not possible to provide a comprehensive overview of this work. Instead, the focus will be on strategies to deal with ecological impact that move beyond the boundary of the single firm. Such strategies build on more systemic perspectives on the relationship between business and the environment (Jennings and Zandbergen 1995). Such perspectives stress that the impact of human activities on natural ecosystems can only be addressed if actors take larger social systems as a basis for their activities. For firms this implies the adoption of inter-firm strategies and stakeholder dialogues. For a further underpinning of such strategies, I use the field of industrial ecology as a source of inspiration. This field seeks to analyze the material and energy flows in industrial societies in a systemic way, as is made clear in the following definition:

> Industrial ecology is the study of the flows of materials and energy in industrial and consumer activities, of the effects of these flows on the environment, and of the influences of economic, political regulatory and social factors on the flow, use and transformation of resources. (White 1994)

Industrial ecology thus combines the analysis of the physical flows, including their impact on ecosystems, the technologies employed to transform resources, and the social systems that create these flows and technologies (see Lifset and Boons 2012 for a recent overview). The systemic perspective draws attention to the boundary used by researchers as well as practitioners in analyzing and preventing ecological impact from industrial activities. In this chapter I will look at two of such boundaries: that of regional industrial clusters and global product chains. These two provide a useful parallel to the often used global–local dilemma posed to international companies. This should come as no surprise, as sustainable development has often been summarized with the maxim "Think globally, act locally." The two system boundaries each entail different strategies for dealing with ecological impact, and one of the questions this provokes is how these could be connected.

In the second section an influential theory is discussed on how ecological impact relates to economic development in advanced capitalist societies. This sets the stage for an exploration of the ways in which global companies can deal with their ecological impact. Drawing on the field of industrial ecology, the focus in the following section will be on two basic strategies: reducing the ecological impact of production facilities by engaging in by-product exchanges in geographically bounded clusters, and coordinating the activities along the value chain in which the firm is engaged. Finally, these insights are linked back to the global–local dilemma as it needs to be resolved by global companies in relation to their ecological impact.

Are We Witnessing Ecological Modernization?

The sociological work on the relationship between society and negative impact on ecosystems has produced several theories, of which ecological modernization theory has been particularly influential. This theory was developed by Huber (1982) and Spaargaren and Mol (1992) and starts from the central sociological thesis that Western societies are engaged in a continuous process of modernization. This process involves increasing rationalization in all societal spheres (economic, cultural, and political). The starting point of this theory is the hypothesis that an ecological rationality develops as part of the ongoing process of modernization (Dryzek 1987; Mol 1995). A central proposition of ecological modernization theory is that this process initially results in increasing ecological damage, as technology enables human beings to exploit the earth's resources with negative consequences that are difficult to foresee. But at some point, through further rationalization and industrialization, societies are able to counter this trend and decrease their level of ecological impact even when technological and economic development continue. While this leaves the basic capitalist structure of these societies intact, it involves changes in their coordinative structures, including shifts in state policies and the balance between state and market. In this respect, ecological modernization theory differs from other theories, such as the "treadmill of production," which hypothesizes that ecological degradation is inherent in capitalist economic systems (Schnaiberg 1980; Schnaiberg, Weinberg, and Pellow 2002). Whereas such theories imply that the reduction of ecological impact requires a radical transformation of most developed economies across the globe, ecological modernization predicts that such reduction will result from gradual improvements inherent in the further modernization of such societies.

Ecological modernization theory was initially corroborated by a finding that came to be known as the Environmental Kuznets Curve (EKC), which shows that initially, national economies combine low ecological impact with low per capita income, then witness an increase in both ecological impact and economic performance, and in a third stage continue to improve per capita income while reducing ecological impact (Selden and Song 1994; Shafik 1994).[1] Initially, empirical support for the EKC was found (Dasgupta et al. 2002; Kaufmann et al. 1998). Later on, it was established that, depending on structural features of the national economy at hand, different shapes of the curve occur (Azomahou et al. 2006; Richmond and Kaufmann 2006). In assessing such endogenous factors, it needs to be taken into account that the EKC assesses the relationship between economic and ecological performance at the level of national societies. Given the extensive international linkages between national economies, this system boundary significantly affects the analysis. As Suri and Chapman (1998) pointed out early on, the initially found shape of the EKC is likely to result from the effect of changing international economic relationships. The pollution haven effect is one example: as legislation on pollution in one country becomes stricter, international firms move their operations to countries where regulation is less strict. Another development which has affected the reduced ecological impact of economic activities in Western countries is the strategic move of many firms to outsource production activities to suppliers in China. While this may de facto increase the level of pollution throughout the product lifecycle (because of a less restrictive regulatory system), when assessing the ecological performance of western countries, it appears as reduced ecological impact of their economies.

Such phenomena need also to be taken into account when assessing ecological modernization theory, which also mostly has taken national societies as its unit of analysis. In doing so, Mol and Spaargaren (2005) have proposed to change the focus of environmental sociology towards flows. They draw on the work from Castells (1996) and Urry (2000; 2003), who identify that globalization has resulted in the increased importance of international flows of information (in terms of cultural transmission as well as web-facilitated data exchange). Castells points out that this has led to a relative decrease in the importance of characteristics of the locality where activities take place. His argument resonates with the idea of "footloose" global companies, who are disconnected from local practices. Urry's perspective allows for more complexity, but it aligns with Castells in analyzing the consequences of globalization in terms of the complexity of connections among material, financial, and informational flows. Mol and Spaargaren extend this "flow"-perspective to include environmental flows. This helps to overcome the limits of the national system boundary that provides a basis to much of the work on ecological modernization (Mol 2010). It provides the background for understanding both the social causes of increased environmental flows, as well as the way in which economic actors, governmental agencies, NGOs, and citizens respond to such flows at various places (Boons and Mendoza 2010; Widener 2009). Also, such responses are increasingly situated in the international "space of flows" as well, becoming part of international governance arrangements (Oosterveer 2007).

We may thus conclude that the ecological modernization hypothesis is as yet untested, as it has been conceptualized and tested mainly at the level of national societies. At the same time, research presented below indicates that there is at least some support for the gradualist position that over time, at least some global firms are starting to incorporate an ecological rationality in their activities.

International Companies and Ecological Impact: Organization and Material Flows

The level of national societies is not the only one where the ecological impact of economic activities can be assessed (Boons and Wagner 2009). At the level of the individual firm the impact of production processes and the costs of dealing with these can be assessed; also, the benefits related to preventing them from occurring at all may be analyzed. However, adopting this approach may lead to displacement of ecological impacts from one firm to another, as is the case when a firm decides to reduce its impact by substituting input A for input B; if the supplier producing A has a higher ecological impact than the supplier of input B, then a displacement of ecological impact takes place. For this reason, a system boundary that encompasses the lifecycle of a product (from raw material extraction to consumption to dealing with post-consumer waste) is generally thought to be more effective.

We can look at the ecological impact of global companies in two ways: from a materials flow perspective and from an organizational perspective. In terms of material flows, the activities of global companies directly or indirectly contribute to the development, production, and marketing of goods and services.

Depending on the characteristics of its products and services, these activities are more or less geographically dispersed. Such dispersion is an issue in itself, as transport is often a considerable contributor to ecological impact, as in the case of retailers who rely on foreign suppliers for food products (Sim *et al.* 2007). If we focus on production activities, it depends on product and market characteristics how close to customer markets these will be performed. Ecological impact in the supply chain is then a function of: (1) the impact of extracting raw materials, (2) the impact of logistic processes involved in transporting raw materials between various stages of production to the consumer as an end product, and (3) the impact of the production processes that constitute the transformation of raw materials into end products.[2]

In organizational terms, this means that we look at global companies as part of product chains. As product chains most often cross national boundaries, they are a useful system boundary when looking at the way in which global companies deal with their ecological impact (Boons, Baumann, and Hall 2012). However, within this system boundary the global company is confronted with conflicting demands.

First, global companies have local operations in different countries, and the local impact of these activities is monitored by local authorities and citizens. Global companies thus need to be sensitive to the legitimacy demands coming from these local contexts, which may differ substantially and may even be contradictory (Yang and Rivers 2009).

Second, global companies operate on national markets that each has distinct characteristics. Their products thus need to fulfill the requirements posed by national regulators and customers regarding their ecological performance. Global companies thus confront a differential set of demands not only in terms of production activities, but also in terms of their products. This has specific consequences for the way they organize themselves and their ecological strategy, as is evidenced in recent research in the automobile industry. While generally considered to be a global industry, companies like Toyota or Volkswagen develop distinct products for different geographical regions, and also display distinct ecological strategies. In addition, the national home base of these global companies affects this strategy considerably (Mikler 2009; Boons 2009). This is also apparent in the way in which global companies become engaged in nationally specific arrangements to deal with post-consumer waste (Orsato, Den Hond, and Clegg 2002). Here again, nationally distinct contexts in terms of consumer practices, logistic infrastructure, and regulatory approaches affect the activities of global companies.

Another demand with which global companies are confronted comes from the fact that within specific local contexts, the subsidiaries of global companies are often seen as powerful actors by local consumers, NGOs, and governmental agencies. This visibility and perceived power makes them vulnerable for local demands (Wheeler *et al.* 2001). Such vulnerability is enhanced by the fact that global companies may display different levels of conduct across their range of activities (Strike, Gao, and Bansal 2006). This invites criticism about the level of commitment they display in the local context regarding the reduction of ecological impact. Connected to such comparisons is the possibility that the activities that global companies display in other countries may become contested in their country of origin (Peng and Pleggenkuhle-Miles 2009).

Furthermore, given their international sphere of action, and their (perceived) power, global companies are often seen as potential contributors to change, either as networks of dissemination of new ideas or practices, or as instrumental in importing innovations into countries that lack the infrastructure to develop such innovations themselves (Moser 2001). This may include the development of collaborative relationships with suppliers to help develop practices with less ecological impact, as in the case of organic coffee (Boons 2009) or organic cotton (Goldbach, Seuring, and Back 2003).

Finally, global companies have an inherent drive to seek international economies of scope and scale as much as the characteristics of products and markets allow. This drive often translates into initiatives to standardize products, services, and management routines. While this provides tension with demands for responsiveness to local actors, markets, and regulations, it also provides an opportunity for standardization that contributes to reduction of ecological impact. Christmann (2004) has assessed such standardization, which can take the form of minimum criteria for environmental performance, standardization of environmental management routines, and standardization of environmental communication.

In the literature on international management and strategic decision-making Prahalad and Doz (1987) have put forward the global–local dilemma as a basic issue that needs to be solved by global companies. Such companies confront a pull towards international standardization alongside a pull for local responsiveness to adjust to local circumstances. The relative strength of both forces depends on various aspects, but dealing with ecological impact is among the issues where this dilemma comes to the fore. I will explore this dilemma by focusing on two strategies open to global companies in dealing with ecological impact: (1) *industrial symbiosis*, which involves closing material and energy loops in local industrial clusters, and (2) *strategizing in production and consumption systems*, which engages the global company in the (often global) governance of larger parts of the product chain to ensure improved ecological performance.

Going Local: Industrial Symbiosis

For many years firms have sought to reduce ecological impact through changing the technical process and the way in which this is organized within the boundary of a single production facility. Traditionally, this perspective has been facilitated, if not invited, by governmental agencies who seek to regulate the emissions of individual production units. Increasingly however, firms seek to improve their ecological performance through building regional clusters of by-product exchanges. Inevitably, each production process leads to some form of waste, as raw materials are transformed into end-products. By-products and waste streams, including excess heat from production processes, can often be used by other firms or households in close vicinity of production plants. If such options are implemented, they lead to increased efficiency of the production process, additional monetary benefits, and a decreased ecological impact. Thus, industrial symbiosis is based on a logic that parallels the ecological modernization thesis (Huber 2000; Gibbs 2003).

Realizing such benefits, however, is not straightforward. The study of the evolution of symbiotic clusters has led to a number of insights (Boons, Spekkink, and

Mouzakitis 2011) concerning the conditions that need to be met to facilitate the successful implementation of symbiotic exchanges.

First of all, symbiotic exchanges require geographical proximity. If the distance increases too much, costs of transportation dampen the economic benefits, or the resource itself disappears (as in case of transporting excess heat). The necessity of geographical proximity limits the potential for symbiotic exchanges, when the production processes that can make use of a certain by-product are not situated close by.

Secondly, symbiotic exchanges lead to increased coupling among production processes of different production facilities. As a consequence, there are spill-over risks of production stops and increased dependency on local suppliers. These are not problematic, but they require the installment of organizational arrangements to allow firms to manage such transaction risks (Stift 2011).

Thirdly, firms constituting a local cluster need to have accurate information about the quantity and quality of available waste streams. This requires some form of institutional capacity (Boons, Spekkink, and Mouzakitis 2011). Institutional capacity provides channels of communication and the trust which is required for the exchange of sensitive information.

The potential of industrial symbiosis for global companies is directly affected by each of these points. The point of geographical proximity means that industrial symbiosis adds weight to the "local" side of the dilemma sketched by Doz and Prahalad: it provides an additional demand for local responsiveness. The second point implies that symbiotic exchanges tie the local subsidiary to its geographic location because it requires more structural organizational engagement with other firms in that local cluster. The third point places a further demand by requiring that the subsidiary sheds some of its "footloose" character.

The above is more than just conjecture. Empirical research of symbiotic clusters has shown that the managers of production plants of global companies play a special role, and part of it is explained by the reluctance of their headquarters to give in to the "pull to localize" (Ashton 2008). At the same time, there are several cases where local subsidiaries of global companies play the role of "anchor tenant," that is, they are a central node in the local network that facilitates the emergence of a symbiotic cluster (Baas 2008; Spekkink 2012). This is a function of the advantageous position that such subsidiaries often hold within local clusters and the networks of regulation in which they are embedded.

Going Global: Strategizing in Production and Consumption Systems

At the strategic level, global companies make decisions on two important dimensions: the products and services that are delivered to customers, and the geographical positioning of markets and production activities. In making these decisions, they engage with geographically dispersed production and consumption systems (PCS) (Lebel and Lorek 2008). A production and consumption system consists of the economic actors (firms and consumers) involved in the production and consumption of a set of products and/or services and the material and energy flows they generate (Boons 2009: 15). The system thus encompasses the actors engaged in the lifecycle of a product as defined above. In addition, NGOs and governmental agencies that try to influence the activities of these economic actors are part of the PCS. The PCS is defined as a social system, but through resource extractions, transformations, and waste streams it is connected to natural ecosystems at several scale levels.

While from a local perspective global companies can be seen as powerful actors, within a PCS they are dependent on a large set of actors that are linked in four overlapping resource networks (Boons 2009). Such networks are a consequence of the fact that firms do not control all of the resources necessary for their goal attainment. As a result they need to engage in relationships with other organizations that control relevant resources. The way in which such relationships are managed is a function of the extent to which the focal organization depends on the other organization (Pfeffer and Salancik 1978). Dependency is high when a resource is central to the focal organization and cannot easily be replaced (for instance through accessing it from another supplier). When dependency is low, transactions can be coordinated through the market mechanism, while in relationships where the firm is highly dependent, it will engage in more intensive coordination mechanisms such as joint ventures, partnerships, or even resort to vertical integration. Thus, power asymmetries rather than efficiency is taken as the central variable determining types of coordination mechanisms.

This relevance of this focus on so-called resource dependencies becomes clear when we recognize that resources do not only concern physical inputs for production and finances, but also knowledge and legitimacy. The latter may be viewed as a resource (Dowling and Pfeffer 1975) and can be defined as the situation in which the activities of a firm "are desirable, proper, or appropriate within some socially constructed system of norms, values, beliefs, and definitions" (Suchman 1995: 574). Legitimacy is acquired and maintained by firms through interactions with governmental agencies and other organizations that formulate and monitor formal rules, as well as NGOs and the media who are able to influence the legitimacy of an organization through influencing public perceptions (Oliver 1991).

As a result of the necessity to obtain these physical and financial resources as well as legitimacy, firms are part of resource networks. In obtaining these resources, firms interact with other firms and stakeholders, and these often are related to one another, or to still other organizations (Harland 1996; Rowley 1997). In extending their efforts to reduce ecological impact beyond the organizational boundary, firms engage in relationships with other organizations that include not only supplying firms, but also competitors, NGOs, governmental agencies, and knowledge institutes. Thus, global companies operate in resource networks to acquire material and financial resources, knowledge, and legitimacy (Boons 2009). In order to deal with their ecological impact, they need to engage in supplier relationships whenever they want to substitute an unwanted input (such as hazardous substances or inputs that come from countries with questionable labor practices) or even develop a new product. They may also seek to improve the recyclability of their product after use, which requires them to engage with firms in the recycling and waste stages of the product lifecycle. Each of these options has consequences for the dependency position of the firm (Boons 2002).

Such innovations often require that the firm engages in networks of knowledge development and exchange, as they typically do not possess the capabilities to develop sustainable innovations singlehandedly (Weber and Hemmelskamp 2005).

Such exchanges entail risks of spillover and the creation of future dependencies because only those that participate in the innovative endeavor may be able to serve as future suppliers (Nooteboom 2000).

Finally, developing sustainable products requires that a firm engages in networks where legitimate definitions of sustainability are created. While in general it is often defined in terms of integrating social and ecological values with economic performance, this tells little about the exact specification of what this means for a specific firm. This specification is a social construction which is created in interaction between scientists, governmental agencies, NGOs, the media, and firms (Hannigan 1995). The growth in initiatives from firms to address the issue of global warming is an example of this process of social construction. During the 1990s there was growing concern about the human contribution to global warming due to CO_2 emissions. Firms like General Motors and Ford participated in an advocacy organization called the Global Climate Coalition, which sought to question this relationship (Levy and Rothenberg 2002). Over time, the IPCC assessed scientific studies and provided a legitimate basis for this relationship. Together with the wide attention attracted by Al Gore's movie, *An Inconvenient Truth*, this issue has become one of the major ecological impacts to consider for firms. At this moment, firms throughout the automotive industry see climate change as the major ecological issue with which they have to deal. This example illustrates not only how ecological issues are constructed over time, but also that firms actively engage in their shaping its definition.

Summarizing, global companies that seek to reduce their ecological impact need to deal with their globally extended production and consumption system. To succeed, they need to extend existing relationships and/or develop new resource networks in order to achieve their goals. Analyzing the role of global companies as embedded in such resource networks has a number of advantages.

Firstly, it enables an explanation of why firms respond differently to similar challenges. As Pulver (2007) shows, oil companies have responded differently to claims about climate change. She finds this to be a result of the fact that corporate decision-makers in different oil companies were embedded in different knowledge and rule setting resource networks. A similar case can be made for the divergent responses of global companies to the issue of climate change, which range from defensive lobbying to product innovation (Levy and Rothenberg 2002; Mikler 2009). Such differential responses lie to a great extent in the fact that firms are embedded in different resource networks, often as a result of their differential national origins and relative strength on certain national markets.

Secondly, analyzing such resource networks helps to uncover the precise ways in which actors influence each other across the product chain. This topic has been studied by economic geographers under the heading of commodity chain analysis (Gereffi 1999; Gereffi and Korzeniewicz 1994; Giuliani, Pietrobelli, and Rabellotti 2005; Humphrey and Schmitz 2002; Kaplinsky 2000; Morrison, Pietrobelli, and Rabellotti 2008), a term related to world systems theory (Hopkins and Wallerstein 1977). It combines geographical analysis with a focus on power asymmetry between the actors in the product chain, and over time it has enabled the analysis of complex relationships between firms and their suppliers (Gereffi, Humphrey, and Sturgeon 2005). Such analysis can be complemented with an assessment of the way in which ecological impacts and economic value are distributed across the product

chain (Clift and Wright 2000). Such an analysis may reveal that negative ecological impacts accumulate in early stages (resource extraction, growing and harvesting
produce), while monetary value and power predominantly accrue to actors in later
stages (final stages of production). This does not mean that actors in early stages are
powerless; an analysis of the palm oil product chain showed that growers in Colom-
bia are able to contribute to shaping the definition of what constitutes sustainability,
and are thus able to bring in their local ecological and economic concerns (Boons and
Mendoza 2010).

Thirdly, analyzing the resource networks in which international companies operate uncovers the way through which international arrangements allow them, as well
as NGOs and governmental agencies, to coordinate their activities across the globe.
Given the fact that most product chains cross national boundaries, and thus combine
different networks of rule setting national governmental policies are often insufficient for such coordination. As a result, there are several initiatives where firms
have developed schemes of self-governance, i.e. setting and monitoring rules relating
to the ecological impact of their products (Cashore 2002; Vogel 2008; Mayer and
Gereffi 2010). Examples include the Marine Stewardship Council (Lozano *et al.*
2010; Schouten and Glasbergen 2011) and the Forest Stewardship Council (FSC;
Pattberg 2005). The constitution of such arrangements may start with the extended
collaboration of one firm with its suppliers, as in the case of the Fair Trade standard
for coffee. At a later stage in the development, the firm may find it strategically
relevant to give up its role and let the standard transform into an independent private initiative, as in the case of Utz Certified Coffee (Boons 2009). In some markets,
several self-governing initiatives have emerged, and rather than leading to a winner-
takes-all situation, such standards continue to exist along side each other (Manning *et al.* 2012). This serves the function that suppliers of international companies
can develop their ecological performance in several steps, while gaining access to
international markets.

Access to international markets is also a major reason for supplying firms to engage
in international standards for environmental management practices. Such standards,
including ISO 14000 have diffused rapidly since the early 2000s, aided by pressure
from international companies towards their suppliers. Here resource networks acts
as a conduit for the global standardization of environmental practices. A question
that arises here is the extent to which such adoption is symbolic, i.e. the adoption
of ISO standards does not necessarily imply reduced ecological impact (Corbett and
Kirsch 2001; Raines 2002; Christmann and Taylor 2006).

Conclusion

In dealing with their ecological impact, global companies confront a challenge
that constitutes a complicated version of the local-global dichotomy advanced by
Prahalad and Doz (1987). The challenge consists of the requirement to simultaneously address three system boundaries. The first boundary is that of the *local
cluster* in which production activities are embedded. This cluster includes material
and energy flows among co-located firms and households, but it also includes the
communities and regulatory agencies from which legitimacy needs to be obtained.

Such clusters also extend to other actors, such as knowledge institutes to which the local subsidiaries may connect in efforts to reduce ecological impact.

The second boundary is that of the *global corporate organization*, where economies of scale and competitive advantage are assessed by top managers. As part of such assessments, decisions are made about geographical location of production activities, but also overarching decisions about how to source resource inputs for these activities. Also, this is the level where standardization of organizational practices for the management of environmental risks and impacts is pushed forward.

Finally, the system boundary of the *global production and consumption system* is relevant, of which there are usually several in a global company. This system boundary includes the internationally dispersed actors and activities related to the whole lifecycle of the product. From the perspective of the firm, it involves its upstream and downstream value chain. Here, the firm engages in more or less intensive relationships with (parts of) these value chains in order to reduce ecological impact. As presented above, this often includes the engagement in some form of self-governance arrangement.

Of course, simultaneously addressing the demands within each of these system boundaries is made easy within an international company because managers, workers, and activities are dispersed and have delineated autonomy. In routine cases, parallel processes thus take care of the coordination of actions within these boundaries. For emergent and strategic issues, such routines do not suffice. Then the relative weight of actors representing the local, global, or product chain boundaries becomes important. Such relative power explains how international companies can become captured by legitimacy concerns in one of the countries where it operates, or that potentially economic and ecologically beneficial symbiotic exchanges are thwarted by the concerns of managers concerned about production targets agreed upon with company headquarters.

While in practice the balance between local, global, and product chain demands needs to be found, in research the interplay between such demands has not yet been adequately studied. Instead, each boundary remains the province of a separate field of research (Boons, Baumann, and Hall 2012). The above suggests that a promising avenue for future research lies in connecting those inquiries: to link the study of decision-making in international companies with that of industrial symbiosis, and to analyze the way in which firms deal with conflicting demands resulting from attempts to decrease the ecological impact of a local cluster and a global product chain. It would also allow the analysis of conditions under which local subsidiaries of international companies are the linkages through which outside knowledge flows into the local cluster (Bathelt, Malmberg, and Maskell 2004). Such research may also provide an avenue for assessing the extent to which the ecological modernization thesis, in its revised form (Mol 2010; Jänicke 2008) still holds.

Notes

1 The name is derived from the Kuznets-curve, which predicts a likewise concave relationship between economic development and economic inequality among citizens of a country.
2 I leave aside here the impact that results from the use phase and post-consumer phase of the total lifecycle of a product as analyzed in life cycle analysis (Baumann and Tillman 2004).

References

Ashton, W. 2008. "Understanding the Organization of Industrial Ecosystems: Asocial Network Approach." *Journal of Industrial Ecology*, 12 (1): 34–51.

Azomahou, T., Laisney, F., and Nguyen, P. Van. 2006. "Economic Development and CO2 Emissions: A Nonparametric Panel Approach." *Journal of Public Economics*, 90: 1347–1363.

Baas, L. 2008. "Industrial Symbiosis in the Rotterdam Harbour and Industry Complex: Reflections on the Interconnection of the Techno-Sphere with the Social System." *Business Strategy and the Environment*, 17: 330–340.

Bathelt, H., Malmberg, A., and Maskell, P., 2004. "Clusters and Knowledge: Local Buzz, Global Pipelines and the Process of Knowledge Creation." *Progress in Human Geography*, 28 (1): 31–56.

Baumann, H. and Tillman, A. 2004. *The Hitch Hiker's Guide to LCA: An Orientation in Lifecycle Assessment Methodology and Application*. Lund: Studentlitteratur.

Bell, J. Autry, Mollenkopf, D., and Thornton, L. 2012. "A Natural Resource Scarcity Typology: Theoretical Foundations and Strategic Implications for Supply Chain Management." *Journal of Business Logistics*, 33 (2): 158–166.

Benedick, R. 1991. *Ozone Diplomacy: New Directions in Safeguarding the Planet*. Cambridge, MA: Harvard University Press.

Biermann, F., Betsill, M., Gupta, J., Kanie, N., Lebel, L., Liverman, D., Schroeder, H., Siebenhüner, B., and Zondervan, R. 2010. "Earth System Governance: A Research Framework." *International Environmental Agreements*,10: 277–298.

Boons, F. 2002. "Greening Products: A Framework for Product Chain Management." *Journal of Cleaner Production*, 10 (5): 495–506.

Boons, F. 2009. *Creating Ecological Value: An Evolutionary Approach to Business Firms and the Natural Environment*. Cheltenham: Edward Elgar.

Boons, F. and Wagner, M. 2009. "Assessing the Relationship between Economic and Ecological Performance: Distinguishing System Levels and the Role of Innovation." *Ecological Economics*, 68: 1908–1914.

Boons, F. and Mendoza, A., 2010. "Constructing Sustainable Palm Oil: How Actors Define Sustainability." *Journal of Cleaner Production*, 18 (16–17): 1686–1695.

Boons, F., Spekkink, W., and Mouzakitis, Y. 2011. "The Dynamics of Industrial Symbiosis: A Proposal for a Conceptual Framework." *Journal of Cleaner Production*, 19 (9–10): 905–911.

Boons, F., Baumann, H., and Hall, J. 2012. "Conceptualizing Sustainable Development and Global Supply Chains." *Ecological Economics*, doi:10.1016/j.ecolecon.2012.05.012.

Cashore, B. 2002. "Legitimacy and the Privatization of Environmental Governance: How Non-State Market-Driven (NSMD) Governance Systems Gain Rule-Making Authority."*Governance*, 15: 503–529.

Castells, M. 1996. *The Rise of the Network Society*. Oxford: Blackwell.

Christmann, P. 2004. "Multinational Companies and the Natural Environment: Determinants of Global Environmental Policy Standardization." *Academy of Management Journal*, 47 (5): 747–760.

Christmann, P. and Taylor, G. 2006. "Firm Self-Regulation through International Certifiable Standards: Determinants of Symbolic versus Substantive Implementation." *Journal of International Business Studies*, 37: 863–878.

Clift, R. and Wright, L. 2000. "Relationships between Environmental Impacts and Added Value along the Supply Chain." *Technol. Forecast. Soc. Change*, 65: 281–295.

Corbett, C. and Kirsch, D. 2001. "International Diffusion of ISO 14000 Certification." *Production and Operations Management*, 10 (3): 327–342.

Dasgupta, S., Laplante, B., Wang, H., and Wheeler, D. 2002. "Confronting the Environmental Kuznets Curve." *Journal of Economic Perspectives*, 16 (1): 147–168.

Dowling, J. and Pfeffer, J. (1975), "Organizational Legitimation." *Pacific Sociological Review*, 18 (1): 122–136.

Dryzek, John. 1987. *Rational Ecology: Environment and Political Economy*. Oxford: Blackwell.

Dunning, J. 1993. *Multinational Enterprises and the Global Economy*. Reading, MA: Addison Wesley.

Gereffi, G., 1999. "International Trade and Industrial Upgrading in the Apparel Commodity Chain." *Journal of International Economics*, 48: 37–70.

Gereffi, G. and Korzeniewicz, M., eds. 1994. *Commodity Chains and Global Capitalism*. Westport: Praeger.

Gereffi, G., Humphrey, J., and Sturgeon, T., 2005. "The Governance of Global Value Chains." *Review of International Political Economy*, 12 (1): 78–104.

Gibbs, D.C. 2003. "Trust and Networking in Interfirm Relations: The Case of Eco-Industrial Development." *Local Economy*, 18 (3): 222–236.

Giuliani, E., Pietrobelli, C., and Rabellotti, R., 2005. "Upgrading in Global Value Chains: Lessons from Latin American Clusters." *World Development*, 33: 549–573.

Goldbach, M., Seuring, S., and Back, S. 2003. "Co-ordinating Sustainable Cotton Chains for the Mass Market." *Greener Management International*, 43: 65–78.

Hagelüken, C. 2011. "Sustainable Resource Management in the Production Chain of Precious and Special Metals." *International Economics of Resource Efficiency*, 5: 357–369.

Hannigan, J. 1995. *Environmental Sociology: A Social Constructionist Perspective*. London: Routledge.

Harland, C. 1996. "Supply Chain Management: Relationships, Chains and Networks." *British Journal of Management*, 7 (1): s63–s80.

Hart, S. 1997. "Beyond Greening: Strategies for a Sustainable World." *Harvard Business Review*, 75 (1): 66–76.

Hopkins, T. and Wallerstein, I. 1977. "Patterns of Development of the Modern World System." *Review*, 1 (2): 111–145.

Huber, J. 1982. *Die verlorene Unschuld der Ökologie. Neue Technologien und superindustriellen Entwicklung*. Frankfurt am Main: Fisher Verlag.

Huber, J. 2000. "Towards Industrial Ecology: Sustainable Development as a Concept of Ecological Modernization." *Journal of Environmental Policy and Planning*, 2: 269–285.

Humphrey, J. and Schmitz, H. 2002. "How Does Insertion in Global Value Chains Affect Upgrading Industrial Clusters?" *Regional Studies*, 36: 1017–1027.

Jänicke, M. 2008. "Ecological Modernisation: New Perspectives." *Journal of Cleaner Production*, 16: 557–565.

Jennings, P. and Zandbergen, P. 1995. "Ecologically Sustainable Organizations: An Institutional Approach." *Academy of Management Review*, 20 (4): 1015–1052.

Kaplinsky, R. 2000. "Globalisation and Unequalisation: What Can Be Learned from Value Chain Analysis?" *Journal of Development Studies*, 37 (2): 117–146.

Kaufmann, R., Davidsdottir, B., Garnham, S., and Pauly, P., 1998. "The Determinants of Atmospheric SO2 Concentrations: Reconsidering the Environmental Kuznets Curve." *Ecol. Econ.*, 25: 209–220.

Korten, D. 2001. *When Corporations Rule the World*, 2nd edn. San Francisco: Berrett-Koehler.

Lebel, L. and Lorek, S. 2008. "Enabling Sustainable Production-Consumption Systems." *Annual Review of Environment and Resources*, 33: 241–275.

Levy, D. and Rothenberg, S. 2002. "Heterogeneity and Change in Environmental Strategy: Technological and Political Responses to Climate Change in the Global Automobile Industry." In *Organizations, Policy and the Natural Environment: Institutional and Strategic Perspectives*, ed. M. Ventresca and A. Hoffman, 173–193. Stanford: Stanford University Press.

Lifset, R. and Boons, F.A.A. 2012. "Industrial Ecology: Business Management in a Material World." In *The Oxford Handbook of Business and the Natural Environment*, ed. P. Bansal and A.J. Hoffman, 310–326. Oxford: Oxford University Press.

Lozano, J., Blanco, E., and Rey-Maquieira, J. 2010. "Can Ecolabels Survive in the Long Run? The Role of Initial Conditions." *Ecological Economics*, 69 (12): 2525–2534.

Manning, S., Boons, F.A.A., Hagen, O. von, and Reinecke, J. (2012). "National Contexts Matter: The Co-Evolution of Sustainability Standards in Global Value Chains." *Ecological Economics*, 83: 197–209.

Mayer, F. and Gereffi, G. 2010. "Regulation and Economic Globalization: Prospects and Limits of Private Governance." *Business and Politics*, 12 (11): 1–25.

Mikler, J. 2009. *Greening the Car Industry: Varieties of Capitalism and Climate Change*. Cheltenham: Edward Elgar.

Mol, A. 1995. *The Refinement of Production: Ecological Modernization Theory and the Chemical Industry*. Utrecht: International Books.

Mol, A. 2010. "Social Theories of Environmental Reform: Towards a Third Generation." In *Environmental Sociology: European Perspectives and Interdisciplinary Challenges*, ed. Matthias Gross and Harald Heinrichs. Dordrecht; New York: Springer.

Mol, A.P.J. and Spaargaren, G. 2005. "From Additions and Withdrawals to Environmental Flows: Reframing Debates in the Environmental Social Sciences." *Organization and Environment*, 18 (1): 91–107.

Morrison, A., Pietrobelli, C., and Rabellotti, R., 2008. "Global Value Chains and Technological Capabilities: A Framework to Study Learning and Innovation in Developing Countries." *Oxford Development Studies*, 36: 39–58.

Moser, T. 2001. "MNCs and Sustainable Business Practice: The Case of the Colombian and Peruvian Petroleum Industries." *World Development*, 29 (2): 291–309.

Nooteboom, B. 2000. "Learning by Interaction: Absorptive Capacity, Cognitive Distance and Governance." *Journal of Management & Governance*, 4 (1–2): 69–92.

Oliver, C. 1991. "Strategic Responses to Institutional Processes." *Academy of Management Review*, 16 (1): 145–179.

Oosterveer, P. 2007. *Global Governance of Food Production and Consumption*. Cheltenham: Edward Elgar.

Orsato, R., Den Hond, F., and Clegg, S. 2002. "The Political Ecology of Automobile Recycling in Europe." *Organization Studies*, 23 (4): 639–665.

Pattberg, P. 2005. "What Role for Private Rule-Making in Global Environmental Governance? Analyzing the Forest Stewardship Council (FSC)." *Int. Environ. Agreements*, 5: 175–189.

Pfeffer, J. and Salancik, G. 1978. *The External Control of Organizations: A Resource Dependency Perspective*. New York: Harper and Row.

Peng, M. and Pleggenkuhle-Miles, E. 2009. "Current Debates in Global Strategy." *International Journal of Management Reviews*, 11 (1): 51–68.

Prahalad, C. and Doz, Y. 1987. *The Multinational Mission*. New York: Free Press.

Pulver, S. 2007. "Making Sense of Corporate Environmentalism: An Environmental Contestation Approach to Analyzing the Causes and Consequences of the Climate Change Policy Split in the Oil Industry." *Organization and Environment*, 20 (1): 44–83.

Raines, S. 2002. "Implementing ISO 14001: An International Survey Assessing the Benefits of Certification." *Corporate Environmental Strategy*, 9 (1): 418–426.

Richmond, A. and Kaufmann, R., 2006. "Is There a Turning Point in the Relationship between Income and Energy Use and/or Carbon Emissions?" *Ecol. Econ.*, 56: 176–189.

Rowley, T. 1997. "Moving beyond Dyadic Ties: A Network Theory of Stakeholder Influences." *Academy of Management Review*, 22 (4): 887–910.

Schnaiberg, A. 1980. *The Environment: From Surplus to Scarcity*. Oxford: Oxford University Press.

Schnaiberg, A., Weinberg, A.S., and Pellow, D.N. 2002. "The Treadmill of Production and the Environmental State." In *The Environmental State under Pressure*, ed. A.P. J. Mol and F.H. Buttel, 15–32. London: JAI/Elsevier.

Schouten, G. and Glasbergen, P. 2011. "Creating Legitimacy in Global Private Governance: The Case of the Roundtable on Sustainable Palm Oil." *Ecological Economics*, 70 (11): 1891–1899.

Selden, T. and Song, D. 1994. "Environmental Quality and Development: Is There a Kuznets Curve for Air Pollution Emissions?" *J. Environ. Econ. Manage.*, 27: 147–162.

Selfa, T. 2010. "Global Benefits, Local Burdens? The Paradox of Governing Biofuels Production in Kansas and Iowa." *Renewable Agriculture and Food Systems*, 25 (2): 129–142.

Shafik, N. 1994. "Economic Development and Environmental Quality: An Econometric Analysis." *Oxf. Econ. Pap.*, 46: 757–773.

Sim, S., Barry, M., Clift, R., and Cowell, S. 2007. "The Relative Importance of Transport in Determining an Appropriate Sustainability Strategy for Food Sourcing: A Case Study of Fresh Produce Supply Chains." *Int. J. Life Cycle Assess.*, 12: 422–431.

Spaargaren, G. and Mol, A.P.J. 1992. "Sociology, Environment, and Modernity: Ecological Modernization as a Theory of Social Change." *Society Nat. Resources*, 5: 323–344.

Spekkink, W. 2012. "Institutional Capacity Building for Industrial Symbiosis in the Canal zone of Zeeland in The Netherlands: A Process Analysis." *Journal of Cleaner Production* (resubmit).

Stift, N. 2011. "Industrial Symbiosis and Transaction Costs." Masters thesis, Leiden and Delft University.

Strike, V., Gao, J., and Bansal, P. 2006. "Being Good While Being Bad: Social Responsibility and the International Diversification of US firms." *Journal of International Business Studies*, 37: 850–862.

Suchman, M. 1995. "Managing Legitimacy: Strategic and Institutional Approaches." *Academy of Management Review*, 20 (3): 571–610.

Suri, V. and Chapman, D. 1998. "Economic Growth, Trade and Energy: Implications for the Environmental Kuznets Curve." *Ecol. Econ.*, 25: 195–208.

Urry, J. 2000. *Sociology beyond Society*. London: Routledge.

Urry, J. 2003. *Global Complexity*. Cambridge: Polity.

Vitousek, Peter M. 1994. "Beyond Global Warming: Ecology and Global Change." *Ecology*, 75: 1861–1876.

Vogel, D. 2008. "Private Global Business Regulation." *Annual Review of Political Science*, 11: 261–282.

Weber, M. and Hemmelskamp, J., eds. 2005. *Towards Environmental Innovation Systems*. Berlin: Springer.

Wheeler, D., Rechtman, R., Fabig, H., and Boele, R. 2001. "Shell, Nigeria and the Ogoni: A Study in Unsustainable Development: III. Analysis and Implications of Royal Dutch/Shell Group Strategy." *Sustainable Development*, 9 (4): 177–196.

White, R. 1994. "Preface." In *The Greening of Industrial Ecosystems*, ed. B.R. Allenby and D. Richards. Washington, DC: National Academy Press.

Widener, P. 2009. "Global Links and Environmental Flows: Oil Disputes in Ecuador." *Global Environmental Politics*, 9 (1): 31–57.

Yang, X. and Rivers, C. 2009. "Antecedents of CSR Practices in MNCs' Subsidiaries: A Stakeholder and Institutional Perspective." *Journal of Business Ethics*, 86 (S2): 155–169.

Part VI   The Exercise and Limitations of Private Global Governance

The Handbook of Global Companies, First Edition. Edited by John Mikler.
© 2013 John Wiley & Sons, Ltd. Published 2013 by John Wiley & Sons, Ltd.

Chapter 24

Global Companies as Agents of Globalization

Shana M. Starobin

Introduction

Debates surrounding the process of globalization have long been preoccupied with the management of externalities borne out of transnational production – and, particularly, the magnitude and distribution of social costs firms impose on society and the environment as a result of their activities (Abbot and Snidal 2009; Mattli and Woods 2009; Coase 1960). Scholars, practitioners, and activists alike deliberated over the extent to which the liberalization of international trade would lead to a regulatory "race to the bottom," with relocating firms creating pollution havens in new jurisdictions with weaker regulations (Brunnermeier and Levinson 2004; Beghin and Potier 1997; Daly 1993; Bhagwati 1993). Others countered that globalization may have led to a "ratcheting up" of standards – a race to the middle or even the top (DeSombre 2006; Vogel and Kagan 2004; Garcia-Johnson 2000; Vogel 1995). The framing of a "race" to the bottom or top portrays a regulatory competition in which the rules of the race seem fixed by an exogenous set of disinterested actors, rather than one in which global companies are not only competitors among themselves but also – along with states and international organizations – contrivers of the rules of the game from the very beginning.

Consistent with a growing literature on private governance in transnational production systems, this chapter examines global companies not as disinterested passengers to a policy process exclusively driven by nation states but as rule-makers in their own right – using their structural, discursive, and market power to shape the proverbial rules of the road (Büthe and Mattli 2011; Abbot and Snidal 2009; Cutler, Haufler, and Porter 1999). By design, corporations possess a fundamental set of self-interested priorities – related to the corporation's obligation to generate profits for its shareholders – often at the expense of the public interest or broader considerations of social responsibility (Abbot and Snidal 2009: 59; Friedman 1970).

The Handbook of Global Companies, First Edition. Edited by John Mikler.
© 2013 John Wiley & Sons, Ltd. Published 2013 by John Wiley & Sons, Ltd.

To realize this goal, among other things, companies persevere in constant pursuit of uninhibited access to new markets and profit maximization.[1]

In many respects, global companies possess "go-it-alone power" (Abbot 2012; Abbot and Snidal 2009) – by virtue of their size, scope of involvement in international markets, and the resources they retain to mobilize towards the realization of their goals. If left unchecked by state boundaries, regulations, or other barriers to market entry, some global firms retain the capability to realize their interests and spread their influence to all corners of the globe. They can, and often do, act unilaterally, as through the independent creation of industry codes of conduct and other means of self-regulation (Abbot and Snidal 2009: 60). As Falkner (2009) points out, if we are indeed witnessing the "retreat of the state" (Strange 1996) and the corresponding rise of private authority, some corporations are positioned to avail themselves of oversight gaps in a seeming effort to "rule the world" (Korten 1995).

Contrasted against a more state-centric frame for globalization as a process in which non-state actors, like large multinational corporations, appear to take a more passive role (Cutler, Haufler, and Porter 1999; Strange 1996),[2] this chapter argues that global companies employ myriad strategies to actively advance the process of globalization. As "agents" of globalization, global companies, thus, can be viewed as pursuing a strategic agenda to further the opening up of borders to free trade and exchange of goods, communication, and culture; in doing so, they become key actors in regulation and governance – as their core strategies likewise require the sculpting of transnational regulations to match their interests. Drawing on examples from the agrifood sector (i.e. agriculture and food), I articulate six mechanisms by which global companies foster globalization, as follows.

First, navigating existing global trade rules, companies facilitate globalization by directly introducing products into new markets – effectively transforming local production, consumption, and demand for regulation. Second, as strategic political actors in their own right, global companies endeavor to influence public rule-making processes and public policy to serve their interests and achieve national and global rules more favorable to their agendas. Third, global companies act as private standard setters and rule makers, outside public and quasi-public forums (i.e. design industry codes of conduct and other voluntary rules that structure global production systems). Fourth, global companies are the importers and carriers of global standards, in some cases, introducing higher social or environmental standards in new locales and, at times, fostering a ratcheting up of standards. Fifth, through public-private partnerships (i.e. a government agency directly partnered with a business), global companies accelerate their access to new markets under the pretext of contributing to local social or economic development efforts. Sixth and finally, through private-private partnerships, global companies partner with foundations or non-governmental organizations (NGOs) to similarly bolster their presence in emerging markets while under the beneficent shadow of publicly oriented philanthropic entities.

Transformers of Consumption, Production, and Demand for Regulation

Navigating international trade rules and their domestic counterparts, global companies facilitate globalization by directly introducing their products into new markets, transforming local consumption, production, and, relatedly, the demand for regulation. Often in the absence of regulation, global companies create circumstances – *vis-à-vis* their entry into new markets – that invite (or incite) civil society reaction and engagement (Abbot 2012; Abbot and Snidal 2009). Firms thereby create an impetus for consumers, public interest advocates, and transnational activist networks to curb the activities of firms, especially where the products they introduce or their behavior has become implicated in harm to people or the environment (Tarrow 2005; O'Rourke 2004; Keck and Sikkink 1998). This in turn enables a regulatory response – engaging public and private authorities from local to global scales – that further shapes the character of transnational regulation.

In many respects, global firms have already succeeded in extending their reach into the farthest corners of the earth. Touted as a hallmark of globalization, McDonalds' golden arches are more known and identifiable as a symbol in some parts of the world than the Christian cross (Schlosser 2001). Coca-Cola has found its way into even the most remote villages of the global south; paradoxically, communities lacking access to basic public services like clean, potable drinking water, healthcare, and education are visited regularly by Coca-Cola's delivery trucks. [3]

In the agrifood sector, processed food manufacturers, the fast-food restaurant industry, and large retailers and groceries like Wal-Mart represent international brands well known to end-consumers, which have become some of the most visible firms augmenting their presence in markets worldwide (Clapp and Fuchs 2009). Yet they are not the only global firms involved in the large-scale industrial production of food; manufacturers of agricultural inputs – from seeds, fertilizer, and pesticides to tractors and heavy machinery – also play a key role, especially agro-biotechnology firms, like Cargill, Monsanto, and Syngenta (Schurman and Munro 2010; Falkner 2009; Shiva, Emani, and Jafri 1999).

These global firms shape the preferences of would-be consumers, at times long before state or international regulatory efforts have caught up to intervene. On their way to cultivating viable international markets for their products, multinational firms have garnered criticism from affected local communities and civil society more broadly: for fostering consumer dependency on their processed foodstuffs (Holt-Gimenez and Patel 2009); for encouraging small-holder farmer dependency on capital-intensive production inputs – such as genetically modified "improved" seed, chemical fertilizers, pesticides, and machinery (Shiva, Emani, and Jafri 1999; Brunch 1982); and for other introduced social and environmental externalities imposed on local people and the environment, including labor abuses (Bartley 2003) and pollution (O'Rourke 2004).

In one infamous case, the Nestlé corporation's successful advertising campaigns in developing countries persuaded poor women to abandon the traditional practice of breast-feeding in favor of the manufactured alternative – infant formula (Keck and Sikkink 1998). This led to dire consequences – with a causal link eventually being established between high mortality rates among infants consuming Nestlé's product. Significant damage had already been done long before causal evidence of the product's harm could be established and transnational advocacy networks could launch a widespread and visible boycott of the company's products. Only then did international institutions, like the World Health Organization (WHO) take action to regulate Nestlé's behavior (through the passage of the 1981 WHO Code of Marketing for Breast-Milk Substitutes). [4]

More recently, the emerging effects of globalization – and the unregulated activities of global companies – can be witnessed on the farms and in the fields of small farmers around the globe. Small farmers, long accustomed to saving seeds from one harvest to the next, find themselves having to invest their limited resources or liquefy assets to purchase seeds (Shiva 1999). The new genetically modified (GM) varieties developed by agro-biotech firms are "terminal" seeds – preventing farmers from replanting them from one season to the next. In India and elsewhere around the globe, farmers often secure loans to purchase these seeds – along with pesticides and chemical fertilizers – only to find themselves unable to repay them after a poor harvest. In other cases, farmers inadvertently growing the GM seed without permission (or purchase) risk being sued by these companies for violating the firms' intellectual property rights. Most tragically, as a result of crop failures and indebtedness, the rate of suicide among small farmers in India has reached astronomic levels – with more than 200,000 farmers reportedly taking their lives since 1997 (Shiva 2009).

Similarly, global companies behaving badly when relocating to new jurisdictions or outsourcing their production to other manufacturers face social regulation, including reputational sanctions from consumer watchdog organizations and an increasingly connected and aware audience of global consumers (Vogel 2005; O'Rourke 2004). In addition to being the target of consumer boycotts and campaigns for its purported contribution to the global obesity epidemic, Coca-Cola has been sharply criticized for its over-exploitation of limited water supplies in developing countries, including contaminating critical sources of ground water in India (Gardiner 2011).

Yet, as Falkner (2009: 232) notes, not all global companies are alike and interfirm differences, business conflict, and issue-area specificity affect the extent to which some global companies – despite their power – can shape market outcomes according to their will. International commodity chains are structured to integrate transnational production among a diverse group of actors, performing a variety of activities related to the production, distribution, and sale of goods often across multiple jurisdictional boundaries (Gereffi and Korzeniewicz 1994). While some multinational firms may share a common interest in dominating their business sector, interests do not always align across issue areas. Depending on where companies are situated within the structure of a global value chain, multinational firms embedded within buyer-driven networks (Gereffi 1994) assert structural power in ways distinct from those firms more embedded within producer-driven networks (Falkner 2009).

In the agrifood sector, retailers in buyer-driven commodity chains, like Wal-Mart and Tesco, play a powerful role in transforming global value chains for agricultural products – placing increasing demands on producers for uniformity, quality, consistency, and standardization (Fuchs and Kalfagianni 2010). At the same time, within producer-driven networks, agro-biotechnology firms like Monsanto play a key role in the manufacture and distribution of inputs to agricultural production – especially seeds. Yet, by virtue of their location in buyer versus producer driven commodity chains, Wal-Mart and Monsanto are positioned differently to influence activities within supply chains as well as public and private regulations around certain issue areas (Falkner 2009).

Moreover, a firm's location along global commodity chains in turn affects the openings for activists and advocacy organizations to assert their influence in the policy process – in turn shaping firm responses and the broader regulatory agenda.

As Schurman and Munro (2010: xxi) note, "the commodity chain for food offers activists a number of distinct 'choke points' at which they can potentially debilitate the industry." In the case of activist efforts launched against the introduction of Genetically Modified Organisms (GMOs) into new markets, those actors most susceptible to the demands of anti-GMO activists were those "supermarkets and food manufacturers located in countries where citizens were extremely sensitive to the safety and quality of their food and to the environmental consequences of producing it" (Schurman and Munro 2010: xxi). In contrast, those agricultural biotechnology firms directly involved in manufacturing the GM seed were less susceptible to activist influence and the threat of reputational damages consumer campaigns sought to inflict on their corporate targets.

Influencers of Public Rule-Making Processes

As strategic political actors in their own right, global companies endeavor to influence public rule-making processes and public policy to serve their interests and achieve regulatory rules more favorable to their agendas. Firms may hold a self-interested and instrumental relationship with governments – at times allied, adversarial, or indifferent – depending on the firm's necessity at a given moment in time (Sell 1999: 172). Multinational firms insert themselves (and assert their power and influence) in public rule-making processes for a number of reasons: to remove barriers to trade, to achieve regulatory harmonization, or to stake out claims to protect their future comparative advantage in new markets (Smythe 2009). One way they do this is by amplifying their participation, and that of relevant business associations, in expert committees affiliated with public institutions like the World Trade Organization (WTO). At the international level, global companies may be involved as participants in the formulation of public regulations around a given issue area – serving as observers to standard-setting and expert advisory committees, like the Codex Alimentarius Commission (Smythe 2009; Büthe 2009).[5] In this role, firms may seek to influence the positions adopted by countries directly engaged in international negotiations around key issue areas pertinent to firm interests – such as intellectual property rights (Sell 2009; 1999) and GMOs (Smythe 2009).

As Susan Sell (1999: 172) aptly surmises in her analysis on the influence of global companies in shaping the ultimate international agreement on intellectual property rights – Trade Related Aspects of Intellectual Property (TRIPs) accord: "Twelve corporations made public law for the world." In negotiating for global rules around intellectual property, it served the interests of a small-subset of US firms – eight of which were among the top exporting companies in the United States – to interact with the US government extensively in an effort to shape the preferences and position of the United States in international trade negotiations, ostensibly to enhance America's overall global competitiveness during uncertain times. In reality, these global companies were primarily focused on their own interests in assuring global trade rules would safeguard their exclusive rights in markets otherwise lacking domestic intellectual property protections.

Similarly, despite widespread consumer concern and scientific debate about the potential risks associated with the production and consumption of genetically modified organisms (GMOs) – coupled with heightened public demands for transparency in the labeling of foods more broadly – the Codex Alimentarius Commission refrained from articulating a clear position on the mandatory labeling of GM foods (Smythe 2009). As Smythe (2009) notes, the absence of a clear position by the Codex on GMO labeling provides evidence of the instrumental power held by global companies; the preferences of large agribusinesses like Monsanto were evident in the rules (or lack thereof).

Firms, moreover, endeavor to influence the policies adopted by individual countries to encourage convergence among global and domestic rules – which facilitates market entry and reduces compliance costs for those firms operating across multiple jurisdictional boundaries (Büthe and Mattli 2011).[6] Global companies endeavoring to operate in multiple countries face the ongoing challenge of navigating a multilayered, complex web of regulations across multiple issue areas – from health and safety to quality and the environment – with the potential for substantive differences across countries and even within one country – from national, to sub-national and local levels. Harmonization of rules within and across countries (convergence) serves the interests of multinational firms, which seek to reduce their overall compliance costs (Vogel 2012; Büthe and Mattli 2011). Yet, harmonization may not well serve the interests of other subsets of firms and domestic stakeholders who might actually face increasing compliance costs should domestic standards (or private industry standards) suddenly shift to a different set of rules (Büthe and Mattli 2011).

In addition, international rules – especially if uncontested in global forums – readily become embedded in national and local standards and regulatory policy. Though these standards are purportedly recommended for "voluntary adoption" when developed at the international level,[7] in practice, such voluntary international standards, like the Good Agricultural Practices (G.A.P.) promulgated by GLOBALG.A.P,[8] can become the de facto norm in domestic settings as well (Fuchs et al. 2009). This risks pushing out competing alternative standards deemed more consistent with the preferences of domestic stakeholders, including small to medium enterprises, local retailers, small farmers, or civil society more broadly.

Private Standard Setters and Rule Makers

As architects in shaping the rules that govern global production systems, multinational firms go beyond ensuring that international agreements and national policies align with their preferences. Outside public and quasi-public forums, global companies further globalization by acting as private standard setters and rule makers – engaging in the design of retail standards, voluntary codes of conduct and certification schemes. These private rules include product and process standards for maintaining food safety and quality in agriculture (Fuchs et al. 2009; Coglianese et al. 2009), environmentally sustainable management of fisheries (Constance and Bonanno 2000) and "organic" farms (DeLind 2000), as well as fair wages for small farmers in developing countries (Bacon 2005), and adherence to religious dietary laws (Starobin and Weinthal 2010).

Such increasing participation of firms in regulation and standard setting – signaling the rise of private authority in global governance – continues to invite the question: are these private regulators devising regulatory alternatives as complements or substitutes to governance by an unwilling or incapable state? Early discussions of this emergence of "private authority" debated whether the expanding role of non-state actors within global decision-making processes – such as treaty formation and rule-making within international institutions like the World Trade Organization (WTO) necessarily indicated a lessening role, if not an outright decline, of state authority (Cutler, Haufler, and Porter 1999; Strange 1996). As Abbot and Snidal (2009: 87) surmise, "when it comes to regulating the externalities of transnational production, the state is far from the only game in town, and may no longer be the most important game in town." Indeed, private governance schemes have emerged at times in parallel to (or in the absence of) state-led and international efforts (Cashore, Auld, and Newsom 2004).

Various theories – and terms – have been offered to explain emerging private governance schemes as well as how they interact with their public counterparts. Cashore, Auld, and Newsom (2004: 4) enlist the terminology of "non-state market-driven" governance to distinguish the characteristic of these new institutions as deriving their rule-making authority and legitimacy not from the state but from the market and companies operating in global supply chains, which determine for themselves whether to opt-in to private schemes and comply with their associated rules and procedures. Abbot and Snidal (2009) propose the "governance triangle" as a visual illustration of the interrelationship among institutions engaging in "regulatory standard setting" (RSS) – which involves direct participation by states, firms, and NGOs. Bartley (2011) proposes not a term but a conception of the intersection of public and private standards as the "layering" of rules within transnational governance; examining community rights in sustainable forestry standards and freedom of association in fair labor standards in Indonesia, he illustrates how public and private standards both compete with and complement one another in private regulation.

Yet, how exactly private regulatory schemes interact and comingle with existing public forms of governance remains an area ripe for exploration – especially within a range of issue areas from finance to safety, labor, and the environment (Falkner 2003). Those schemes which have received the greatest scholarly attention have, up until now, been those initiated by larger organizations from the global north, those that focus exclusively around a single commodity (i.e. coffee) or issue area (i.e., labor), and those which happen to offer data more readily available for analysis.[9]

Some private governance efforts led by non-state actors – including but not limited to global companies – do appear to fill a regulatory void. Firms may devise their own industry codes and attempt to pursue "beyond compliance" behavior in an effort to "preempt mandatory regulation, litigation, or some other action that depends on state authority" (Abbot and Snidal 2009: 88). As Abbot and Snidal (2009: 60) point out, while the state may not appear as the central actor in private governance, the threat of state action as through the imposition of strict regulations can induce firms to pursue self-regulation and to design codes with substantive rules more friendly to business.

Alternatively, some companies might choose to self-regulate and pursue voluntary process or product certification (as by opting to label their products) not only in anticipation of future government action but also as a potential market opportunity. In this respect, the adoption of beyond compliance practices may help firms to cultivate niche markets for their products. The US-based company Land O'Lakes decided to place negative labels on its products in an effort to create a new niche market for hormone free milk (Runge and Jackson 2000). Independent of US law at the time, Land O'Lakes provided information through its voluntary product labels to inform consumers that its milk, butter, and other dairy products were free from recombinant bovine growth hormone (rBGH), moreover noting that the scientific research showed no significant difference in impacts to cows or humans. Independent of rules within the United States at the time, the company acted alone in labeling its own products in alignment with rules already established in Europe and elsewhere (Starobin 2012; Runge and Jackson 2000).

Global companies may pursue the creation of private governance initiatives for pragmatic reasons – to improve upon the purported inefficiency and lack of technical expertise exhibited by public actors engaged in standard-setting (Fuchs, Kalfagianni, and Arentsen 2009: 38). Firms may, moreover, seek to fill an oversight gap in key areas and make up for what has not been achieved in the public policy process. Large multinational retailers – like Wal-Mart and Tesco – formulate their own voluntary codes of conduct and standards, either individually or collectively, which they then pass along to suppliers in "buyer-driven" commodity chains. As noted by Fuchs *et al.* (2009: 35), these standards are most often created collectively among the major retailers, thereby enhancing firms' overall structural power and, moreover, prompting participation and compliance from their suppliers.

Yet given the ever increasing market share of retail companies like Wal-Mart, the standards they create inevitably establish the choice architecture for suppliers (and producers further down the line). With few market choices available to them, suppliers (and eventually the farmers supplying them) can choose to accept these standards or not. In essence, there are profound asymmetries of participation and limited representation in the creation of retail standards, with consumer buy-in or considerations regarding impacts to developing country suppliers and producers only an afterthought (Fuchs *et al.* 2009: 38). Moreover, as Fuchs *et al.* (2009) point out, the private agrifood retailers' creation of their own set of private standards is curious, given the long existence of a clear public forum for standard-setting around issues like food safety and quality (the Codex Alimentarius Commission, established in 1962), raising the question: are they pursuing this in order to pursue "sufficient protection" for consumers or rather merely in anticipation of more stringent regulation from public authorities?

Carriers of Global Standards

Global companies are often the importers and carriers of global standards, in some cases introducing higher social or environmental standards in new locales, potentially fostering a ratcheting up of standards in emerging markets and jurisdictions with weaker standards (Vogel and Kagan 2004; Garcia-Johnson 2000; Vogel 1995). In the wake of the passage of new global trade rules in the 1990s, politicians, scholars, and activists alike contended regarding the extent to which opening new avenues for global trade and allowing for increasing mobility of capital and firms would inevitably lead to a regulatory race to the bottom (Daly 1993). Some feared that firms would not only relocate to jurisdictions with lower labor costs but, moreover, with lower social and environmental standards – reducing firms' overall compliance costs.

Yet some scholars have demonstrated that relocating global companies might have incentives to actually improve standards in the areas of health, safety, and the environment in both home and host countries (Prakash and Potoski 2006; Garcia-Johnson 2000). Indeed, as transnational actors, global companies cross multiple socio-economic and political jurisdictions in their pursuit of more attractive and cost-effective locations to site production facilities and new markets for their products. These firms often bring with them aspects of their organizational identity – including informal aspects of organizational culture, institutions, and norms – as well as formal rules and codes of behavior institutionalized within the company. In some cases, these rules and codes are endogenous to an individual company; in other cases, companies have adopted formal codes and private standards shared across a given industry or sector and they carry these standards along with them to new locales. Thus, global companies may be key agents involved in the export and import of particular sets of standards (Vogel 2012; Garcia-Johnson 2000).

These global companies – along with other civil society actors – could further be viewed as responsible for the exportation of whole new ideologies, as a result of trade liberalization, with the potential to change the relations between industry and stakeholders in developing states (Garcia-Johnson 2000: 11). In her investigation of chemical companies in Mexico and Brazil that exported the Responsible Care voluntary industry program, Garcia-Johnson (2000) argues that "as free trade emerges globally, multinational corporations will gain in incentives to privately promote corporate, voluntarist environmentalism" (Garcia-Johnson 2000, 10).[10] Consistent with the notion that trade might enhance social and environmental outcomes, multi-national corporations have three main reasons to seek the spread of ideologies like environmentalism: the threat of competitive disadvantage; new opportunities to gain competitive advantage; and avoidance of government intervention (i.e. by making strides to go beyond compliance, companies avoid attracting unwanted, negative attention). Furthermore, given public and state perceptions of environmental harm that might exist at the industry level, global companies leading the way in environmental practices might have the incentive to improve the practices of other industry members that could indirectly damage their reputation (Garcia-Johnson 2000: 108).

Moreover, viewing environmentalism as an ideology, Garcia-Johnson suggests that civil society actors can additionally access new avenues to export their ideology – with prospects for adoption to the extent that these ideas fit with local practices. This is also consistent with the notion that trade may open up new avenues for transnational networks of activists working across borders to share information, build new relationships, and effectively pressure global companies from new directions to improve their social and environmental performance (Tarrow 2005; O'Rourke 2004: Keck and Sikkink 1998).

Public-Private Partnerships

Through public-private partnerships, global companies accelerate their access to new markets, at times under the pretext of contributing to local social, economic development, or environmental efforts. A government agency may partner with a global company to tackle some social, economic, or environmental problem or attempt to supply a missing or undersupplied public good. Global companies – by virtue of their size, scale, and ready access to capital, which can exceed that available in government coffers – can augment scarce public resources for development projects or new initiatives, and pragmatically help advance public policy goals that have otherwise eluded politicians, policy-makers, or development agencies alone. In other cases, global companies may partner and provide assistance by providing in-kind donations of their product directly to programs or communities presumably in need.

Rising in popularity as a tool in global governance, public-private partnerships are purported to supply governance that is both effective and legitimate across a variety of issue areas (Bäckstrand 2008: 74; Börzel and Risse 2005).[11] Bäckstrand (2008) conceives of these partnerships as networks, identifying three main types: public-private (hybrid), governmental, and private-private. In the realm of international climate policy, for example, some three hundred multi-stakeholder partnerships were launched at the 2002 World Summit on Sustainable Development (WSSD) (Bäckstrand 2008: 74).

While on the face of it, corporate-government partnerships signpost a celebrated "win-win" for private and public interests alike, closer examination might suggest otherwise. Some proclaimed acts of corporate social responsibility (CSR) and presumed altruism may conceal corporations' pure strategic interest in skirting requisite policy processes in the service of accessing new markets and in concentrating power and influence over government and market actors alike.

Private-Private Partnerships

Through "private-private partnerships" – the little studied sibling of the more ubiquitous "public-private partnerships" – global companies partner with private foundations or NGOs to bolster their presence in emerging markets while under the beneficent shadow of public interest oriented philanthropic entities. Despite their non-profit status and pursuit of activities often framed as the public interest, private philanthropies – similar to other NGOs – are private organizations (Anheier and Daly 2005). Like other such non-state actors and organizations, including global companies, whose legitimacy and authority are scrutinized in the literature on global private governance (Cashore *et al.* 2004), philanthropic foundations similarly operate behind closed doors and out of the public eye (Frumkin 1998). Their organizational decisions are determined by private stakeholders – including a board of directors – with no requisite de jure accountability to a voting public (or even the targets of their grants and initiatives).

Moreover, there is no global, public overseeing body charged with the authority and responsibility for monitoring their actions. In effect, by partnering with a non-profit organization or foundation, companies are able to more readily bypass public rule-making processes and escape attention from watchdog groups monitoring their presence, especially surrounding contentious issues, like the introduction of potentially harmful products into new markets.

The term "private-private partnerships" has been employed previously in some contexts as a framework for increasing access to capital among struggling non-profit entities, like hospitals. As of yet, however, private-private partnerships have yet to be widely examined in the context of private governance within global production systems. While she includes "private-private partnerships" among her types of networked governance, Bäckstrand (2008) suggests that they do not represent "new modes of governance" given the limited nature of "public-private interaction." Rather Bäckstrand (2008: 95) views them as a form of "self-regulation among private actors, either business-to-business or civil society networks," with the primary functions being advocacy and implementation. The primary mechanisms of accountability in private-private partnerships are market and reputational accountability – requiring voluntary information disclosure to enable monitoring and enforcement (Bäckstrand 2008: 97).

Moving further than Bäckstrand (2008), I view private-private partnerships as having implications for regulations – if not themselves explicitly regulatory in nature – in that they may drive regulations in directions more favorable to the preferences of global company partners – irrespective of public debates or domestic preferences around a given issue area. For example, the Gates Foundation – one of the largest philanthropic foundations in the world – invested significant funds in Monsanto in 2010 and has since partnered with the agribusiness giant in an effort to transform agricultural production across Africa (Holt-Gimenez 2010). The Gates Foundation's rationale for encouraging the adoption of "improved" seeds (i.e. GMOs) is consistent with that of Monsanto. While this private-private partnership purports to be an effort aimed at promoting poverty alleviation and food security, this approach fundamentally propagates industrial agriculture and green revolution strategies aligned with Monsanto's business interests of expanding into one of the largest emerging markets for agricultural development in the world (Holt-Gimenez and Patel 2009). Irrespective of whether key domestic stakeholders, like small farmers, view the presence of "improved seeds" in their market as desirable or whether public authorities anticipate a need to regulate them (Shiva 1999), the size and scope of a private–private partnership between a large foundation like Gates and a massive global company like Monsanto makes the proliferation of GMOs seemingly inevitable in emerging markets that have yet to regulate them.

Conclusion

As this chapter demonstrates, global companies act as "agents" of globalization by asserting their influence as central actors in global, regional, and national policy processes – pursuing a strategic agenda that strives to open up global borders to free trade and exchange of goods, communication, and culture. In so doing, they become key actors in regulation and governance – as their core strategies necessitate sculpting the substantive rules of transnational regulation to match their interests and pursuing exclusive partnerships to achieve their goals. Yet they do this often at the expense of other competing interests, especially those of civil society stakeholders who continue to lack a crucial voice in the policy process.

In global agrifood governance in particular, those that stand to be the most disadvantaged by corporate-interest-driven (as opposed to public-interest driven) policies are often small-holder producers, subsistence farmers, and the rural poor in the global south. These groups already face increasingly high barriers to entry in global and domestic markets, and their participation in policy processes – often in association with NGOs intending to represent their interests – is negligible at best. Their perspectives become further marginalized when global firms unilaterally craft private standards or build partnerships behind closed doors – without substantial consultation and input from those individuals and communities most likely to bear the social, environmental, and economic costs of firm decisions.

If indeed private interests now dominate the formulation and exercise of regulation from international to domestic levels, they supplant the preferences, if not also the rights, of impacted stakeholders not currently represented in public and private policy forums – those whose lives and livelihoods may be at stake as a result of the unregulated and free flow of products, like GM seeds, stemming from globalization. Alternative regulatory architectures are possible – governance schemes that better recognize and address the needs of the most disadvantaged members of society and account for potential impacts to local food security and environmental sustainability. Yet these alternatives can only emerge when the power and authority of global firms is fully understood and recognized, and when civil society participants are empowered to challenge corporate preferences in the crafting of transnational regulation.

Notes

1   This is not to suggest that firms simply view all regulation as universally bad. As Abbot and Snidal (2009: 60) point out, firms are most concerned with the content of regulation and its particular impact around substantive issues. In some cases, firms actually prefer more stringent regulations; firms that have already attained compliance with higher social and environmental standards may seek to level the playing field and impose higher costs on lagging competitors. See also Mattli and Woods (2009) and Prakash and Potoski (2006).

2   Within the international relations literature, a new focus by some scholars on private authority represented a departure from the exclusive focus on the state as the primary actor of interest in international affairs (Cutler, Haufler, and Porter 1999). Governance, rule-making, and regulatory oversight – long deemed activities within the exclusive realm of the state – garnered attention of scholars reconsidering the particular role that non-state actors – business, international organizations, and advocacy groups – might play in these realms as well. For a thorough discussion of private regulation in the global economy, see Büthe (2010).

3   In the United States and internationally, McDonald's and Coca-Cola have been criticized for their social, environmental, and health impacts separately and together. Recently, McDonald's and Coca-Cola have been implicated as targets in campaigns by Corporate Accountability International for opposing New York City's pending regulations on drink-cup sizes at New York eateries. See http://www.stopcorporateabuse.org/blog/mcdonald%E2%80%99s-and-coca-cola-%E2%80%93-unhealthy-alliance, accessed December 19, 2012.

4   To view the 1981 WHO Code of Marketing for Breast-Milk Substitutes, see http://www.who.int/nutrition/publications/code_english.pdf, accessed December 19, 2012.

5   A joint body of the Food and Agriculture Organization (FAO) and the World Health Organization (WHO), the Codex Alimentarius Commission was founded in 1962 with the mandate of developing and harmonizing food standards in order to both protect consumer health and guarantee fair practices in the food trade. See Smythe (2009) for an extensive discussion on corporate influence in the Codex's rule-making process around mandatory labeling of foods containing genetically modified organisms (GMOs). See also Büthe (2009).

6   Various factors will affect the ultimate magnitude and distribution of costs borne by firms when either public or private authorities modify existing rules or switch to altogether new sets of technical standards (Büthe and Mattli 2011). Exporting agricultural firms, moreover, may see changes to domestic standards, such as the permitting of new GM crop varieties in US markets, as limiting their ability

to compete in global markets. Monsanto abandoned its efforts to promote the commercialization of Round-Up-Ready wheat among US growers, as many American growers deemed it unfeasible since their main target export markets already had adopted stringent restrictions on GMOs and would be unlikely to permit these new products into their markets (Falkner 2009).

7   Büthe and Mattli (2011: 6) indicate that the use of international standards in place of domestic ones is a non-trivial commitment made by governments, with substantial economic implications.

8   GLOBALG.A.P. is an NGO which sets voluntary standards for the certification of agricultural goods produced internationally according to Good Agricultural Practice (GAP). See Fuchs, Kalfagianni, and Arentsen (2009).

9   Among programs initiated by companies or private organizations, the Responsible Care Program as well as ISO 14001 have received a great deal of scholarly attention. See Garcia-Johnson (2000); Prakash and Potoski (2006). Among schemes initiated by NGOs based in the global north, the Forest Stewardship Council (FSC) and Fair Trade (especially for coffee) have been studied to a greater extent as compared to emerging schemes initiated in the global south. On private forest certifications, see Bartley (2003) and Cashore, Auld, and Newsom (2004). On Fair Trade and Organic certifications, particularly for coffee, see Bray, Sanchez, and Murphy (2002); Gonzalez and Nigh (2005); and Bacon *et al.* (2008).

10 On the Responsible Care Program, see also Prakash (2000). On the role of firms in promulgating voluntary environmental stewardship in general, see Prakash and Potoski (2006).

11 On the role of transnational public-private partnerships in international relations, see also Schäfer-hoff, Campe, and Kaan (2009).

References

Abbott, K.W. (2012). "Engaging the Public and the Private in Global Sustainability Governance." *International Affairs*, 88 (3): 543–564.

Abbott, Kenneth W. and Snidal, Duncan. 2009. "The Governance Triangle: Regulatory Standards Institutions and the Shadow of the State." In *The Politics of Global Regulation*, ed. Walter Mattli and Ngaire Woods, 44–88. Princeton: Princeton University Press.

Anheier, Helmut and Daly, Siobhan. 2005. "Philanthropic Foundations: A New Global Force." In *Global Civil Society 2004/5*, ed. Helmut Anheier, Mary Kaldor, and Marlies Glasius. London: Sage.

Bäckstrand, Karin. 2008. "Accountability of Networked Climate Governance: The Rise of Transnational Climate Partnerships." *Global Environmental Politics*, 8: 74–102.

Bacon, C. 2005. "Confronting the Coffee Crisis: Can Fair Trade, Organic, and Specialty Coffees Reduce Small-Scale Farmer Vulnerability in Northern Nicaragua?" *World Development*, 33: 497–511.

Bacon, C., Mendez, V.E., Gliessman, S.R., Goodman, D., and Fox, J.A., eds. 2008. *Confronting the Coffee Crisis: Fair Trade, Sustainable Livelihoods and Ecosystems in Mexico and Central America*. Cambridge, MA: MIT Press.

Bartley, Tim. 2003. "Certifying Forests and Factories: States, Social Movements, and the Rise of Private Regulation in the Apparel and Forest Products Fields." *Politics and Society*, 31: 433–464.

Bartley, Tim. 2011. "Transnational Governance as the Layering of Rules: Intersections of Public and Private Standards." *Theoretical Inquiries in Law*, 12: 517–542.

Beghin, J. and Potier, M. 1997. "Effects of Trade Liberalization on the Environment in the Manufacturing Sector." *World Economy* 20: 435–456.

Bhagwati, Jagdish. 1993. "The Case for Free Trade." *Scientific American*, 269 (5): 41–49.

Börzel, Tanja A. and Risse, Thomas. 2005. "Public-Private Partnerships: Effective and Legitimate Tools of International Governance?" In *Complex Sovereignty: On the Reconstitution of Political Authority in the 21st Century*, ed. Edgar Grande and Louis W. Pauly, 195–216. Toronto: University of Toronto Press.

Bray, D.B., Sanchez, J.L.P., and Murphy, E.C. 2002. "Social Dimensions of Organic Coffee Production in Mexico: Lessons for Eco-labeling Initiatives." *Society & Natural Resources*, 15: 429–446.

Brunch, Roland. 1982. *Two Ears of Corn: A Guide to People-Centered Agricultural Improvement*. Oklahoma City: World Neighbors.

Brunnermeier, S.B. and Levinson, A. 2004. "Examining the Evidence on Environmental Regulation and Industry Location." *Journal of Environment and Development*, 13: 6–41.

Büthe, Tim. 2009. "The Politics of Food Safety in the Age of Global Trade: The Codex Alimentarius Commission in the SPS-Agreement of the WTO." In *Import Safety: Regulatory Governance in the Global Economy*, ed. Cary Coglianese, Adam M. Finkel, and David Zaring, 88–109. Philadelphia: University of Pennsylvania Press.

Büthe, Tim. 2010. "Private Regulation in the Global Economy: A (P)Review." *Business and Politics*, 12. DOI: 10.2202/1469-3569.1328.

Büthe, Tim and Mattli, Walter. 2011. *The New Global Rulers: The Privatization of Regulation in the World Economy*. Princeton: Princeton University Press.

Cashore, Ben, Auld, Graeme, and Newsom, Deanna. 2004. *Governing through Markets: Forest Certification and the Emergence of Non-state Authority*. New Haven: Yale University Press.

Clapp, Jennifer and Fuchs, Doris. 2009. *Corporate Power in Global Agrifood Governance*. Cambridge, MA: MIT Press.

Coase, R.H. 1960. "The Problem of Social Cost." *Journal of Law and Economics*, 3: 1–44.

Coglianese, Cary, Finkel, Adam M., and Zaring, David. 2009. *Import Safety: Regulatory Governance in the Global Economy*. Philadelphia: University of Pennsylvania Press.

Constance, Douglas H. and Bonnano, Alessandro. 2000. "Regulating the Global Fisheries: The World Wildlife Fund, Unilever, and the Marine Stewardship Council." *Agriculture and Human Values*, 17: 125–139, http://www.springerlink.com/content/q4472l45n1101j14/fulltext.pdf. Accessed December 19, 2012.

Cutler, A. Claire, Haufler, Virginia, and Porter, Tony. eds. 1999. *Private Authority and International Affairs*. Albany: State University of New York Press.

Daly, Herman. 1993. "The Perils of Free Trade." *Scientific American*, 269 (5): 50–57.

DeLind, Laura B. 2000. "Transforming Organic Agriculture into Industrial Organic Products: Reconsidering National Organic Standards." *Human Organization*, 59: 198–208.

DeSombre, E.R. 2006. *Flagging Standards: Globalization and Environmental, Safety, and Labor Regulations at Sea*. Cambridge, MA: MIT Press.

Falkner, Robert. 2009. "The Troubled Birth of the 'Biotech Century': Global Corporate Power and Its Limits." In *Corporate Power in Global Agrifood Governance*, ed. Jennifer Clapp and Doris Fuchs, 225. Boston: MIT Press.

Falkner, Robert. 2003. "Private Environmental Governance and International Relations: Exploring the Links." *Global Environmental Politics*, 3: 72–87.

Friedman, Milton. 1970. "The Social Responsibility of Business Is to Increase Its Profits." *New York Times Magazine*, September 13.

Frumkin, Peter. 1998. "The Long Recoil from Regulation: Private Philanthropic Foundations and the Tax Reform Act of 1969." *American Review of Public Administration*, 28: 266–286.

Fuchs, Doris and Kalfagianni, Agni. 2010. "The Causes and Consequences of Private Food Governance." *Business and Politics*, 12. DOI: 10.2202/1469-3569.1319.

Fuchs, Doris, Kalfagianni, Agni, and Arentsen, Maarten. 2009. "Retail Power, Private Standards and Sustainability in the Global Food System." In *Corporate Power in Global Agrifood Governance*, ed. Jennifer Clapp and Doris Fuchs, 29–59. Boston: MIT Press.

Garcia-Johnson, Ronie. 2000. *Exporting Environmentalism: U.S. Multinational Chemical Corporations in Brazil and Mexico*. Cambridge, MA: MIT Press.

Gardiner, Beth. 2011. Beverage Industry Works to Cap Its Water Use. *New York Times*, March 21, http://www.nytimes.com/2011/03/22/business/energy-environment/22iht-rbog-beverage-22.html?_r=0. Accessed December 19, 2012.

Gereffi, Gary. 1994. "The Organization of Buyer-Driven Global Commodity Chains: How U.S. Retailers Shape Overseas Production Networks." In *Commodity Chains and Global Capitalism*, ed. Gary Gereffi and Miguel Korzeniewicz, 95–122. Westport: Praeger.

Gereffi, Gary and Korzeniewicz, Miguel, eds. 1994. *Commodity Chains and Global Capitalism*. Westport: Praeger.

Gonzalez, A and Nigh, R. (2005). "Smallholder Participation and Certification of Organic Products in Mexico." *Journal of Rural Studies*, 21: 449–460.

Holt-Gimenez, Eric. 2010. Monsanto in Gates' Clothing? The Emperor's New GMOs. *Huffington Post*, August 26, http://www.huffingtonpost.com/eric-holt-gimenez/monsanto-in-gates-clothin_b_696182.html. Accessed December 19, 2012.

Holt-Gimenez, Eric and Patel, Raj. 2009. *Food Rebellions!: Crisis and Hunger for Justice*. Cape Town: Pambazuka Press; Oakland: Food First Books; Boston: Grassroots International.

Keck, Margaret E. and Sikkink, K. 1998. *Activists Beyond Borders: Advocacy Networks in International Politics*. Ithaca: Cornell University Press.

Korten, David C. 1995. *When Corporations Rule the World*. London: Earthscan.

Mattli, Walter and Woods, Ngaire. 2009. "In Whose Benefit? Explaining Regulatory Change in Global Politics." In *The Politics of Global Regulation*, ed. Walter Mattli and Ngaire Woods, 1–43. Princeton: Princeton University Press.

O'Rourke, Dara. 2004. *Community Driven Regulation: Balancing Development and the Environment in Vietnam*. Cambridge, MA: MIT Press.

Prakash, Aseem. 2000. "Responsible Care: An Assessment." *Business and Society*, 39: 183–209. DOI: 10.1177/000765030003900204.

Prakash, Aseem and Potoski, Matthew. 2006. *The Voluntary Environmentalists*. Cambridge: Cambridge University Press.

Runge, C.F. and Jackson, L.A. 2000. "Negative Labeling of Genetically Modified Organisms (GMOs): The Experience of rBST." *AgBioForum*, 3: 58–62, http://www.agbioforum.org. Accessed December 19, 2012.

Schäferhoff, Marco, Campe, Sabine, and Kaan, Christopher. 2009. "Transnational Public-Private Partnerships in International Relations: Making Sense of Concepts, Research Frameworks, and Results." *International Studies Review*, 11: 451–474.

Schlosser, Eric. 2001. *Fast Food Nation: The Dark Side of the All-American Meal*. New York: Houghton Mifflin.

Schurman, Rachel and Munro, William A. 2010. *Fighting for the Future of Food: Activists versus Agribusiness in the Struggle over Biotechnology*. Minneapolis: University of Minnesota Press.

Sell, Susan K. 1999. "Multinational Corporations as Agents of Change: The Globalization of Intellectual Property Rights." In *Private Authority and International Affairs*, ed. A. Claire Cutler, Virginia Haufler, and Tony Porter, 169–197. Albany: SUNY.

Sell, Susan K. 2009. "Corporations, Seeds, and Intellectual Property Rights Governance." In *Corporate Power in Global Agrifood Governance*, ed. Jennifer Clapp and Doris Fuchs, 187–223. Boston: MIT Press.

Shiva, Vandana. 2009. From Seeds of Suicide to Seeds of Hope: Why Are Indian Farmers Committing Suicide and How Can We Stop This Tragedy? *Huffington Post*, April 28, http://www.huffingtonpost.com/vandana-shiva/from-seeds-of-suicide-to_b_192419.html. Accessed December 19, 2012.

Shiva, Vandana, Emani, Ashok, and Jafri, Afsar H. 1999. "Globalisation and Threat to Seed Security: Case of Transgenic Cotton Trials in India." *Economic and Political Weekly*, 34: 601–613.

Smythe, Elizabeth. 2009. "In Whose Interests? Transparency and Accountability in the Global Governance of Food: Agri-Business, the Codex Alimentarius and the World Trade

Organization." In *Corporate Power in Global Agrifood Governance*, ed. Jennifer Clapp and Doris Fuchs, 93–123. Boston: MIT Press.

Starobin, Shana. 2012. "Tackling Information Problems in Agrifood Governance: The Role of Eco-labels and Third Party Certification Schemes." In *Environmental Leadership: A Reference Handbook*, ed. Deborah Rigling Gallagher, 635–643. Newbury Park: Sage.

Starobin, Shana and Weinthal, Erika. 2010. "The Search for Credible Information in Social and Environmental Global Governance: The Kosher Label." *Business and Politics*, 12. DOI: 10.2202/1469-3569.1322.

Strange, Susan. 1996. *The Retreat of the State: The Diffusion of Power in the World Economy*. New York: Cambridge University Press.

Tarrow, Sidney G. 2005. *The New Transnational Activism*. New York: Cambridge University Press.

Vogel, D. 1995. *Trading Up: Consumer and Environmental Regulation in a Global Economy*. Cambridge, MA: Harvard University Press.

Vogel, D. 2005. *The Market for Virtue: The Potential and Limits of Corporate Social Responsibility*. Washington, DC: Brookings Institution Press.

Vogel, D. 2012. *The Politics of Precaution: Regulating Health, Safety, and Environmental Risks in Europe and the United States*. Princeton: Princeton University Press.

Vogel, D. and Kagan, R.A. 2004. *Dynamics of Regulatory Change: How Globalization Affects National Regulatory Policies*, 4th edn. Berkeley: University of California Press.

Chapter 25

The Greening of Capitalism

John A. Mathews

Introduction

There is a global green transition under way, denied only by those with a vested interest in doing so. The evidence is abundant and occurs in several different settings – from international treaty negotiations over mitigation of anthropogenic global warming, through various national "green growth" strategies (linked to developmentalism) and to claims by global companies themselves that they are pursuing "corporate and social responsibility" strategies with an emphasis on greening their practices (e.g. see Stern 2009).

Global companies are both drivers of this shift, or transition, as well as the primary actors in having to accommodate to its many demands. The insights of Porter and van der Linde (1995) on the convergence of competitiveness with adherence to more stringent environmental standards, remain as valid as ever. The relationship between the competitiveness of global companies and their impact on the environment has conventionally been viewed as one involving trade-offs, with competitiveness calling for lower costs and less stringent standards, and the environment being seen to demand higher-cost renewable and recycling alternatives. Despite the widespread discussion triggered by the intervention of Porter and van der Linde (1995), where they claimed that stricter environmental standards would also engender more innovative and competitive companies, the "trade-off" mentality remains dominant. It is still the case that the relationship between competitiveness and environmental standards is viewed in a static framework, where firms are driven to make least-cost choices – and environmental regulation is then inevitably seen as a cost add-on. In a dynamic framework where the two issues interact places the choices in a fresh light, where a decision to go beyond existing standards in the name of green corporate and social responsibility may be viewed as a contributor to competitiveness.

The Handbook of Global Companies, First Edition. Edited by John Mikler.
© 2013 John Wiley & Sons, Ltd. Published 2013 by John Wiley & Sons, Ltd.

The striking feature of the greening of global companies' strategies is that the initiative, both from companies themselves as well as the regulatory and administrative settings in which the strategies are formulated, appears to be shifting to the East. Specifically, China is emerging as a clear leader in the race to build renewable energy industries and advance the resource efficiency technology frontier – against all scholarly expectations and certainly those of the US political leaders themselves. This is a puzzle of enormous scope, whose resolution constitutes one of the most challenging issues in the social sciences today.[1]

In this chapter I offer a resolution of this paradox, drawing on three fundamental lines of research and argument, each associated with an original and path-breaking thinker of the twentieth century. The argument is *neo-Schumpeterian*, in that it turns on the capacity of leading firms to drive change, subject to the institutional incentives and barriers created by the prevailing techno-economic paradigm. The latest such shift may be identified with the surge of investment in renewable energies and low-carbon technologies. The argument is *Olsonian* in that it emphasizes the capacity of vested interests to take political and economic steps to block or delay changes unleashed by the emergent shift of techno-economic paradigm in favor of a greening of industries and their lead companies. And the argument is *Gerschenkronian* in that it emphasizes the changing patterns of industrialization promoted by late-comers, in particular China and to some extent India, which now taking advantage of their latecomer opportunities to catch up with the advanced countries (see Schumpeter 1939; Olson 1982; and Gerschenkron 1962, together with the extensive secondary literatures).

In terms of greening of capitalism, the firms in these countries are actually in the lead, given their capacity to absorb technologies already developed by western firms for ushering in renewable energies but left unused or obstructed in the west by Olsonian vested interests. It is the latecomers like China that have the most pressing need for green growth strategies, given the terrible environmental catastrophes they are suffering, and which have moreover the state capacity to do something about such problems. China's current 12th Five-Year Plan provides as close a template as one is likely to find on greening an industrial economy, while China has now been joined by South Korea as another East Asian practitioner of green growth industrial strategy. This is providing the institutional and competitive setting within which all firms are now forced to operate.

Global Companies as Principal Beneficiaries of Business as Usual

Global companies have been the principal beneficiaries of a "Business as Usual" (BAU) model of industrial expansion, with its reliance on low-cost fossil fuels and resource extraction. The entire industrial system established since the Industrial Revolution in Britain, which spread through Europe and the United States and then into Japan, and is now going global and lifting billions of people out of poverty in China, India, Brazil, and elsewhere, is predicated on a common material and energetic foundation. This system is basically one of securing power through tapping into the cornucopia of fossil fuels, together with exploiting ever-growing supplies of materials and commodities from an apparently inexhaustible sink, called Nature (Friedrichs 2011; for a discussion of the implications see Mathews 2011a).

BAU is utilized as the benchmark in energy pathways studies; it implies no change in current practices, and hence no change in underlying rules and institutions. But we know that the current set of rules that we call industrial capitalism is remorselessly driving the system to collapse through destroying its own resource base. Over and above calls to action that amount to prohibitions and grand gestures, changes in underlying rules are increasingly being canvassed (e.g. see contributions under the rubric "ecological modernization" such as Mol and Sonnenfeld 2000). In the energy markets, renewable energies are acquiring momentum through logistic industrial dynamics; in resources and commodity markets, recirculation is being favored; and in financial markets, green bonds (or climate bonds) are widely discussed. It is the connections between these shifts, already under way, that provide the "system rebooting," that promise to spell the end of Business as Usual, and lead to the greening of capitalism.

The current shift involved in the greening of capitalism will be triggered not so much by a global response to a series of interlinked ecological crises and peaking of resource flows, culminating in global warming – since it is clear that fossil fueled industrial inertia is blocking such a process – but more by national-level "green growth" strategies, as found for example in China and Korea. China in particular has amazed the world with its astonishing growth rates, averaging close to 10% per year for 30 years (and so creating a 12-fold expansion of the economy in that time) – but these have depended on a doubling and tripling of its energy system, initially fueled by coal and oil, leading to China's global scramble for resources. The Chinese leadership understand very well that this global resource race will probably lead to wars, or even to war with the United States itself – over disputed oil claims in central Asia, for example. As China is following a "peace first" development strategy, it is induced to invent a new growth model based on resource efficiency (circular economy) and renewable energies, financed by eco-efficient investments. And the evidence is accumulating that China is indeed inventing such a model; in the words of Hu Angang (Hu 2006a and b), a green development model is becoming "the inevitable choice for China." Korea likewise is banking on a new "green growth" strategy to not only take it off a fossil-fueled trajectory, with all the problems this entails, but to create the industrial platforms for the future (e.g. see Mathews 2012; for a note of caution see Zysman and Huberty 2011).

The Fossil Fuel Cornucopia

When people in the west started burning fossil fuels on a fairly large scale (starting in Britain in mid-eighteenth century) there were 160 million inhabitants in Europe (790 million people in the world). Europe grew to 200 million by 1800, then doubled again to 400 million by 1900. This was the first time in world history that a large population could double in size without destroying its own environment.

How did Europe do it? There were three ways in which Europe escaped the Malthusian trap (e.g. see Clark 2007).[2] The first was by expanding its access to resources worldwide – so escaping the trap of domestic resources, particularly food resources. The second was by switching from organic energy sources to fossil fuel sources (starting with coal) which created a vast "subterranean forest" of fuel reserves (Sieferle 1982; 2001).[3] The third was by employing a set of institutions and rules that had never been tried as a whole before on such a large scale – the rules and institutions that we call capitalism.

The kind of capitalism that quickly took over the world was an expansionist, acquisitive, and ruthless kind of economic system that employed rational calculation in place of moral or community values and practices.[4] It regarded nature as an objectified entity to be plundered at will (and likewise regarded nature as a limitless sink where waste could be disposed). It sought to turn existing products and practices, with their community links and associations, into commodities that could be bought and sold – starting with manufactured products, then encompassing services such as insurance, freight handling, stock jobbing, and extending eventually to health and education. And it regarded labor as likewise a commodity to be bought and sold, in extreme cases in the form of slavery and child labor. Above all it recognized no limits to its expansion, given its access to fossil fuels and the cornucopia they generated. For all its faults, this was an incredibly successful system that liberated those who enjoyed its benefits from manual labor, from famine, and from what Marx called the "idiocy of rural life." It effected what Polanyi (2001[1944]) called, with good reason, the Great Transformation.[5]

The BAU Paradigm Now Running up against Limits

Successful as this industrial system has been, it has to come up against limits, and these were starting to be felt with alarming severity in the first decade of the twenty-first century. The market for fossil fuel energy was coming up against "peak" issues as reserves were declining and competition for remaining resources grew more intense.[6] The market for resources was becoming more competitive and contested, and the impact of their extraction, throughput and dumping was starting to put enormous strains on the capacity of the system, particularly in China.[7] The market for finance was suffering from over-reach and bubble-formation, and investment in pursuit of energy and resources, and activities based on them, was starting to look more and more precarious. The whole system was starting to look non-sustainable, threatening its own resource base and the biodiversity of the planet (see Costanza 2007; and Steffen *et al.* 2007 for an early warning on this theme).

This is the situation we face now, as the process of globalization of industrial capitalism continues, but with increasing resource toll and diminishing prospects for longevity in its current wasteful form. This is "Business as Usual." It is not capitalism itself that is the problem, but the industrial scale of the form of capitalism that has taken over the world, exhausting fisheries, industrializing agriculture and livestock as commodity production, denuding forests, and expanding cities over the face of the planet. The pollution problems have moved from being local and regional to global, led by the global warming that is now linked, incontrovertibly, with the burning of fossil fuels. The wanton discarding of products, together with the materials from which they are made, is creating uncontrollable landfill problems. The financial bubbles generated by ever more creative innovation in financial instruments have taken their toll of investment in productive activity.

Global Companies Feel Pressures to Green Their Strategies

As the pressures to green the industrial model are being felt, global companies will likewise turn out to be the principal drivers of the changes involved, either voluntarily or under duress. Capitalist corporations now face the bill for their years of neglect under the BAU paradigm. As thousands of freshly minted corporations from China, India *et al.* play the same game harder and better, the onus is now on corporations as never before to lift their game and frame a new mode of strategizing. This goes well beyond the timid efforts made so far in terms of individual corporations' initiatives to foster "corporate and social responsibility" (CSR).

Global companies are widely viewed as drivers of the global business system, setting the competitive standards that other companies need to meet. But they do so in conditions not of their own making. Global companies have to operate in a regulatory environment that shapes their choices, and increasingly in an environment that drives their adoption of a broader conception of their profit derivation, from one based narrowly on costs to one where many issues formerly counted as externalities come into the business equation. Ultimately it is at the level of firms themselves that we must look for changes in business behavior that offer less threat to the planet, and to the survival of our industrial civilization.

Let us take the case of industrial agriculture as an immediate case in point – "industrial agriculture" with intensive reliance on fossil fuel inputs in the form of fertilizers, herbicides, pesticides, mechanization of planting and harvesting, loss of biodiversity, extensive soil spoliation, lowering of water tables, and all the other threats that stand as a grave reminder of the inadequacies of the BAU model. Here there is extensive scope for new kinds of businesses to emerge that look for profit in ways that do not extend and perpetuate these processes – in the form of new value chains that operate expressly without chemical inputs or outputs; in the form of new farmer cooperatives that adopt organic methods and sell direct to consumers via farmers' markets. These might be small beginnings, but they signal the reality of an alternative to the BAU industrial model.

An even more radical break, however, is entirely feasible, such as through extensive mariculture using seaweeds, known for decades in Japan as highly nutritious foodstuffs and sources of food ingredients that can be grown in coastal and continental shelf areas with zero chemical and fossil fuel inputs. The sea-plants grow entirely from the nutrients found in the sea and from sunshine. What is needed to set this alternative food and feedstuffs model into motion is corporations committed to both profits and to the new model itself as a means of earning profits. Our civilization's reaping of harvests from the sea is as yet at a very early stage, yet potentially sea-plants could provide food and feedstuffs for a global population with zero chemical inputs, no reliance on rainfall, no reduction in water tables, no soil loss or erosion, and direct benefits from solar inputs via photosynthesis (e.g. see Neori *et al.* 2004). The possibilities for business to take the initiative in such a recasting of food production from agriculture to mariculture does not have to wait for a carbon tax to be imposed on industrial farmers or for a ban to be placed on use of chemical fertilizers; it can be initiated by corporations themselves in profit-seeking entrepreneurial initiatives.

Thus the changes to be unleashed by corporations are limited only by their own imaginations. But corporations cannot do the job on their own, through their own individual efforts. States need to set the rules of the game, as applying to all firms, and provide both inducements for the new and ways to undo the inertia of "carbon lock-in" (Unruh 2000). They can only accomplish such far-reaching changes through collective action, involving entire value chains and clusters. Yet this is not implausible; it is, after all, how capitalism works, and what has made it such a formidable global system.

Capitalism Will Be Greened Not by Companies Acting Alone but via Blocs, Transvections

Capitalism will be greened not one company at a time (via purported corporate social responsibility) but by entire value chains and clusters moving to green their resources, activities, and products. Let us take a capitalist perspective on the emergence of a green economy. The new "green shoots" can be expected to propagate themselves through the entire economy via inter-firm linkages and value chains, particularly in clusters and eco-industrial parks (EIPs). As one firm seeks advantage through claiming a commitment to reducing its carbon footprint, and insists on similar commitments from its suppliers, who in turn will insist on such commitments from their suppliers, so the new green standards will propagate via competitive emulation. Kaldor (1970) used the term "circular and cumulative causation" to characterize the way that a modern sector could be established, for example in a particular region. Now we can resort to the same terminology to describe the emergence and propagation of a green sector within the modern capitalist economy. Kaldor (1970) was at pains to point to the fact that what drove such propagation was the search for increasing returns, which are achieved as more and more firms become interconnected. Again we can pose the search for increasing returns as the driver of firms' green initiatives – and thus as a solution to whether the green economy can grow while maintaining a constant resource base.

A printing firm, for example, may seek competitive advantage as a low-carbon operation, insisting that its paper suppliers adhere to international standards certifying that papers are not sourced from old-growth forests, or certifying that all paper is sourced from recycled materials; and likewise with its suppliers of printing plates and inks, insisting that they too meet standards of reduced resource impact that will propagate through the economy. Or take the global automotive industry, where there have been extensive greening initiatives adopted (such as improvements in fuel economy of internal combustion engines) while at the same time the most dogged resistance to any change in the BAU status quo is also evident. As argued persuasively by Mikler (2009), the global automotive industry is greening not just through tighter regulations and standards (although they are important) but above all by the micro-decisions of thousands of firms supplying components and parts in vast supply chains of which the major brands – Toyota, Ford, BMW *et al.* – are the flagships. They steer these supply chains and clusters, often in surprisingly rapid and dramatic fashion – as in the swing towards electric vehicles and hybrids, and away from conventional internal combustion engines. The end-point of these processes is found in consumer behavior – but there is little doubt that the means of causation are to be found in the decisions of the firms themselves, co-located as they are in larger aggregates of firms that share in an ever-growing profit pool.

The Propagation of Green Shoots

The green economy can be expected to grow and propagate within the womb of the fossil fuel economy, through interfirm connections. Small islands will start and they will then make connections with other firms and with each other, always through insistence on reducing resource and carbon intensity in their transactions. In this way the islands will link up to form archipelagos and eventually come to dominate the entire economy. Connections will be made between firms that are not necessarily close to each other, forming "virtual" eco-industrial parks. A vivid illustration would be provided by the ancient game of GO, where the players start with isolated stones and build up structures through interconnections (adjacent stones) and then eventually join them up so that they reinforce each other.

The new system that is emerging can be expected to come to fruition first in China and India and then in the rest of the world by mid-twenty-first century. It is in China that the principle of a Circular Economy has been adopted as a national development goal, emphasizing multiple eco-linkages between firms as the wastes of one firm become the inputs for another firm. As these linkages propagate, they generate circular flows of resources and materials, in emulation of the great flows of materials through the natural world. In this way the green economy will become more of a *biomimetic economy*.

The green economy will continue to emphasize growth, but it will be intensive growth, based on increasing returns, rather than extensive growth based on expansion of throughput. It will generate growth in terms of value creation but not in terms of resource and energy throughput. Companies will continue to grow, through innovation and entrepreneurial initiative – although not in ways that have the effect of expanding resource use or fossil fuel dependence.

It was the American economist Allyn Young (1928), in his Address to the British Association, who boldly posed the issue of increasing returns as the *central question* to be addressed in economic analysis of the modern industrial system. In place of seeing the genesis of increasing returns as a marginal issue, to be dealt with alongside externalities as something quaint and uncommon, Young grasped that increasing returns are central to the way that mass production industries go about building the market for their products. On the strength of the expanded market they are able to invest in specialized capital equipment, and as the market further expands they are able to make use of specialized value chains of intermediate suppliers, sometimes aggregated altogether in industrial clusters. Young saw this as the central issue, the focus of analysis. Now the framework of increasing returns generated through circular and cumulative causation may be viewed as the means of propagation of the capitalist green economy within the matrix of the old, fossil fuel economy. It will be the *growth in demand for green products*, and the preparedness of capitalist firms to make investments in production systems to meet the anticipated demand, that will enable the green sector to outgrow the old, fossil fuel sector. Indeed Kaldor coined the happy expression "chain reaction" for such a process – again in a way that is exactly applicable to the growth of firms within the green economy, multiplying the opportunities for interaction amongst themselves as their interconnections grow.

So we may anticipate the appearance of new green sectors, either as completely new creations (such as extensive mariculture utilizing sea-plants) or as adaptations and green extensions of existing sectors (as in the greening of the automotive sector or the printing sector by corporate decisions), and their growth and propagation through a *chain reaction* of processes that spread the green profits meme throughout the entire economy.

Indeed this is essentially what drives the capitalist system itself, and makes it so successful. It is, in spite of all the talk of competition, essentially a cooperative system of profit-sharing. Let me explain. One company secures a contract to supply 10,000 widgets – based on its demonstrated expertise and capacity to fulfil such orders in the past. But in order to fulfill the contract, it must purchase inputs – products, materials, components, perhaps subsystems, as well as intermediate specialized services – which it then coordinates in response to its specific contract. In order to make its own profit, it is forced to make profit opportunities for other firms. And each of the firms it engages likewise seeks supplies of inputs – goods, materials, or services – from other companies – and so on, along the entire length of the value chain. Each of these value-creating chains (supply chains, or what Alderson called transvections) is in fact a profit-sharing chain, where the companies cooperate in meeting final demand by sharing out the profits along the value-creating process.

It was the marketing theorist Wroe Alderson who first formulated the idea of the *transvection*, as encompassing all the sequence of value-adding steps that lead to an end-product being placed in the hands of a consumer. He saw each of these steps as involving transactions, but perceived the need for a name for the sequence of steps as a whole – to wit, transvection. It is a powerful idea, for (as I argue) the success of capitalism depends on such transvections distributing profits to all the firms involved in the sequence of steps that encompass the value-adding chain (Alderson and Martin 1965).[8] By contrast, the notion of "supply chain" is a much more narrow concept that expands on the original notion of procurement.

The point is that this concept efficiently captures the idea that every product produced under capitalist conditions is the end-result of a series or chain of transformations, each one of which adds value (or is a source of profit) and where self-interest guides the formation and coordination of the sequence, rather than control by fiat or some authoritarian arrangement.

We may pose the greening of capitalism in this setting, where firms will pursue their own profit interests, along with other firms in a transvection, in order to meet some perceived need. In order to trigger or catalyze the process, various forms of state intervention have been devised (falling short of authoritarian orders) which stimulate market expansion or consumer interest, or help to create a market in the first place through public procurement or military procurement.

In fact we have a very clear model for such interconnections, to bring out the power of their connectivity – and that is the brain. Intelligence resides in the degree to which neurons are able to fashion multiple connections with each other – just as value created by increasing returns resides in multiple interconnections generated by firms doing business with each other. Real green economies will work through the interconnections between firms and through the way that such interconnections become clustered or aggregated in space.

We see this process in the formation of eco-industrial parks and their drive to create interconnections with each other, drawing more and more firms into their ambit and measuring their progress in reducing energy- and resource-intensity. In the eco-industrial park of Suzhou, in China, there are multiple interconnections forming, with firms sharing some inputs and sharing some outputs, thus reducing overall resource intensity. The park was opened in 1994 as a cooperative development between Singapore and China, and after a rocky start it is now flourishing, having attracted more than 2400 foreign-invested firms, as well as local entrepreneurial firms, in sectors encompassing electronics, semiconductors, biotechnology, information technology (IT), biopharmaceuticals, and healthcare. The park's municipal managers deliberately follow a "value chain completion" strategy in attracting new firms, identifying gaps in the existing value chains and seeking to fill them with new firms. Overall the firms in the park are notching up environmental performance standards that are vastly superior to those found in China generally.[9] In 2008, Suzhou and its sister industrial park, Suzhou New and Hi-tech Industrial Development Zone, were both recognized as two of the first three approved EIPs in China. And there are many others moving in the same direction in China, such as Tianjin Economic Development Area with its ambitious eco-development plans (e.g. see Mathews and Tan 2011).

The emergent green blocs will propagate via capitalist corporate profit-seeking, as capitalist corporations adapt to the new situation created by new incentives to green their strategies (e.g. consumer demand, industry associations), market creation incentives (e.g. market mandates and public procurement), and outright coercion (as in more stringent regulations, such as vehicle fuel efficiency standards). The insight from Porter and van der Linde, that more stringent environmental standards actually enhance efficiency and thereby competitiveness, has stood the test and is actually most visibly at work in China.

The fundamental aspect of the transition to the new paradigm is to utilize reduced cost to drive rapid diffusion. Diffusion of renewable energies (REs) and low-carbon, low-waste technologies is held back while their costs exceed fossil-fueled technologies and carbon-intensive products and processes. But as grid parity is approached, fundamental policies are needed to drive diffusion faster – to bring on the "rapid adoption" phase of the logistic curve even faster. This is where market mandates and direct support policies such as feed-in tariffs as well as government procurement play a significant role. Abundant experience indicates how these kinds of government policies can work to speed up the process of diffusion.

A Neo-Schumpeterian Framework of Techno-Economic Paradigm Shifts

The current shift in techno-economic paradigm towards REs is certainly not the first such transition. Indeed since the Industrial Revolution there have been five such shifts – the first, the IR itself, associated with steam and mechanization, and introducing a new mode of organizing production, namely the factory. The second, in the 1830s and 1840s, was driven by the spread of even larger steam engines and its application to transport, via the railroad, together with iron and coal. The third, ushered in in the 1870s and 1880s, was associated with steel, electrification, and the application of steam to sea transport, via steamships. This ushered in the twentieth century, with all its aspects of modernization such as skyscrapers (a product of steel, electric power for elevators, and imagination). The fourth was the era of oil, internal combustion engines, and mass production – together with the spread of road networks, suburbanization, and mass consumption. Then in the 1980s and 1990s came the fifth such techno-economic paradigm (TEP) shift, this time driven by IT and ICT, and bringing in its wake new decentralized organizational principles and modes of organization (such as networking, outsourcing, business process outsourcing, and global value chain) culminating in the Internet.[10]

Now in the 2010s we have the beginnings of the sixth such TEP, this time driven by RE as the new "lead factor" which will be taken up across the economy and create new entrepreneurial possibilities and new business models as firms drive the diffusion of REs into more and more novel applications.[11]

Governments can play a powerful role in promoting a new techno-economic surge of investment simply by stating a target for substitution. This is now widely practised – as in China's targets for electric power to be generated from renewable sources, or Germany's RE targets announced in 2011, or EU targets. Simply by making such a statement, and backing it with policies to make it credible, governments can reduce the risk and uncertainty associated with investing in the new sector. Governments can also play a powerful role in driving the changes by utilizing the tool of public (and military) procurement. All of this is evident in the case of the green transition.

The process of the greening of capitalism can be illustrated in any number of examples, but space permits the mention of just one aspect, which combines all three perspectives – neo-Schumpeterian, Olsonian, and Gerschenkronian. It is the adoption of national Green Growth (GG) strategies, in China itself through the twelfth Five Year Plan (FYP) but also in other East Asian countries, particularly South Korea.

China's GG Strategy Followed by Korea's GG Strategy

China presents a contradictory face to the world. On the one hand there is the China that is bounding ahead at unprecedented rates of growth (averaging close to 9% per year since the 1980s) but poisoning its own environment and population in the process. It is underpinning its surge in manufacturing since acceding to the WTO in 2001 with a surge in energy production and consumption by industry, mostly sourced from coal, and the emissions from these processes are fouling the air in China's cities as well as boosting greenhouse gas emission levels, raising the threat of global warming. This is the "black China."

On the other hand there is the China that is developing "green industry" initiatives in greater depth and seriousness than any other country on the planet, growing its renewable energy industries faster than its coal-consuming fossil fuel sector, and building a new pattern of growth that "internalizes" sustainability goals – attracting the admiration of observers around the world. In the wind power sector for example, China doubled the size of its industry each year from 2005 to 2010, and has now become the world's largest market for wind power devices, as well as the world's largest producer of the equipment (turbines, gears, blades) needed for wind power. This is the "green China" (e.g. see Stern 2010; Mathews 2011b).

The12th Five Year Plan, covering the years from 2011 to 2015, sets out the comprehensive goals for China's economic development for the next five years, as approved by the National People's Congress in March 2011. Successive Five Year Plans document the evolving nature of China's economy and its management by the Chinese Communist Party – emphasizing the power of the Chinese state to implement the plans, as well as its search for legitimacy through raising incomes and prosperity via such achievements. The 12th FYP is distinctive in laying out a new, more balanced vision for the Chinese economy (rather than focusing just on growth in GDP), and in laying the foundations for a new, less energy- and resource-intensive pattern of growth and the building of a green economy.

The principal feature of the twelfth FYP is its "rebalancing" of the China economy. The full-bore emphasis on manufactured exports and breakneck growth, evident in the 10th and 11th FYPs issued since China acceded to the WTO in 2001, has now been moderated. The target growth rate for the next five years is "only" 7% per year, which implies some slack from previous high-speed growth to build social sustainability, rebalance the regions and provide the infrastructure such as energy and transport systems needed in coming years. There is a new emphasis in the 12th FYP on building China's domestic consumption as a new engine of development; the plan expresses this as a shift from manufacturing exports to combined development of manufacturing and services, consumption, and production.[12] There is a continuing emphasis on urbanization, which is expected to tip beyond 50% during the current FYP, and is increasing at a rate of 0.9% per year. Consider the implications of this: China has emerged from being a largely rural, peasant country in the twentieth century, to an urban economy by the beginning of the twenty-first century, reaching 60% urbanization by 2020, 70% by 2030 or thereabouts and 80% by mid-century, powered by migration from the countryside – making China one of the most urbanized countries in the world. China's leadership recognizes that cities nurture modernization, industrial upgrading, and innovation, and are home to industrial clusters which are now seen as the principal vehicle for China's further industrial development.

But an even more far-reaching shift is evident in the 12th FYP in the form of its "internalization" of sustainability goals and the building of a new "green" economy in the womb of the "old" fossil-fuel driven economy. This internalization means that China is now actively creating a new pattern of growth, based on lower levels of resource intensity, greater reliance on renewable energies, explicit commitment to resource recirculation (the "Circular Economy") and pricing of inputs to reflect their ecological significance.[13] The emphasis on "green industry" in the 12th FYP is complemented by an emphasis on "green cities" and "green buildings" which signal again how closely the urbanization evolution in China is linked to the emergence of a new, "green" development and growth pattern.

The 12th FYP takes the next step, and brings the focus on to "seven emerging and strategic industries" which are designed to take China's industrial development on to a new trajectory, based on innovation and indigenous technological development, earmarking them for special promotion over the next five years (following the classic East Asian development model). The plan laid out a target that production value-added from these seven emerging and strategic industries should reach 8% of GDP by 2015.[14] No less than three of the targeted seven industries involve aspects of the green energy industrial revolution – the building of new industries producing energy efficiency improvements, new energy sources, and new systems of transport that can be powered by renewable energy. In addition, the bioindustries to be developed will include bioenergy sources (biomass for electric power and biofuels) while the high-end manufacturing developments will include the Internet of Things, through which products will be tagged with their resource history and thereby contribute to the creation of a Circular Economy in China.

Investment in the seven strategic industries is earmarked to be RMB 10 trillion over the next five years, and clearly the green energy sector will be allocated a major proportion of this huge expenditure. This is why logistic industrial dynamics can be expected to drive uptake of renewable energies in China – as an effect of cumulative investment and the momentum created by these investments. China stands alone in the major industrial countries as being able to follow up the designation of desirable industrial directions with targeting of substantial investment funds. This is likely to prove to be a powerful competitive weapon for Chinese industry in the twenty-first century.

The case of China's promotion of electric vehicles provides the most vivid illustration of this process at work. As a latecomer to the automotive industry, China was concerned to promote technology transfer as fast as possible. This it did through a variety of well-known and recognized strategies – foreign direct investment by major Japanese, European, and American producers, with incentives being offered in terms of accessing the Chinese market, in return for commitments to transfer technology and build local supply chains. Modularity undoubtedly played an important role – just as modularity and standardization played an important role in the development of the US automotive industry. The result has been a rapid build-up in China's share of global production, rising from a global share of just 4% in 2001, when China joined the WTO, to close on 25% today (Wang and Xiao 2011; see also Wang and Kimble 2011). China has thus invaded the global automotive industry in the space of a decade – and is now set to leapfrog the entire industry to dominate in electric vehicles, both two-wheeled and four-wheeled varieties.

Three Perspectives

Three perspectives are therefore of value in providing insight into these processes. The first is Schumpeterian, with its emphasis on the restless character of the capitalist system, and its possibility of generating new business models through entrepreneurial initiative that drives creative destruction. Without creative destruction there would be stagnation – as there was for long stretches of time prior to industrialization. Now as industrialization diffuses worldwide, the process of creative destruction is proceeding at hitherto unprecedented rates, creating enormous resistance on the part of vested interests. In particular, the promotion of China's and Korea's GG strategies sets in motion a powerful broom that is clearing the global industrial system of firms that are "locked-in" to the carbon economy. The key to seeing the green sector of the economy expand, and to weakening the political opposition from traditional energy firms, is to build and strengthen the capitalist entrepreneurial sector that sees its future in such a sector. This is precisely what was achieved in the case of the EEG (Renewable Energy Law) in Germany, as the Feed-in Tariff system created new entrepreneurial opportunities for promoters of renewable energy projects – effectively splitting the economic opposition to renewables. Likewise in China, the twin Renewable Energy Law and Circular Economy Law achieved a similar result, opening up "economic space" for entrepreneurial opportunities that previous energy orthodoxy had suppressed.[15]

There is a complementary and opposing process, which is the Olsonian perspective on institutional inertia and blockage, which open democratic societies tend to foster. There is a process of institutional rigidity and regulatory capture, through which companies tied to the fossil fuel economy seek to utilize all the means at their disposal to frustrate the efforts of the greening firms. They do so through lobbying (usually successfully) for continued payment of subsidies to reduce drilling and exploration costs, for example, as well as frustrating passage of legislative changes (such as enactment of carbon taxes) and slowing international recognition of the problem. This is a process that the political scientist Mancur Olson saw as one that is fundamental to an open economy where business interests are free to organize politically and influence regulatory outcomes and implementation in their short-term interests (on Olsonian obstruction, see Moe 2009; 2010).

Finally there is the Gerschenkronian perspective of the latecomer and the potential advantages of coming late to the industrial game – as China, India *et al.* are doing now. China provides a telling example of such a latecomer country, enjoying manifold advantages such as tapping into the accumulated knowledge store of the advanced countries, and in particular RE and RE technologies, and formulating smart strategies that are powering its entry into and rapid assumption of leadership in many of the RE industries.

Conclusion

In this chapter it has been argued that the green shoots of a sustainable industrial model will grow through propagation via value chains within the matrix of the incumbent system, driven by profit-seeking firms working together in blocs, value chains, and what Alderson called transvections. The chapter has discussed the major features of the adjustments under way, and the potential for Olsonian obstruction by vested interests to delay the needed transition away from Business as Usual.

These are all encouraging trends in the greening of capitalist dynamics via the initiatives being taken by global corporations and their associated blocs, value chains, clusters, and transvections. But nothing is determined, and it may turn out that Olsonian resistance will overwhelm neo-Schumpeterian industrial dynamics and entrepreneurship, even with the powerful impetus provided by Chinese and Indian firms seizing Gerschenkronian latecomer advantages. The future remains, as always, open.

Notes

1 On the tensions in the global economy created by China's rise, see for example Spence (2011); for a Chinese perspective, see Hu (2011).

2 He provides an authoritative account of the Malthusian trap that has constrained growth in incomes for most of recorded history. But he proposes a bizarre theory of genetic changes underpinning Britain's industrial breakthrough.

3 Sieferle provides an illuminating account of the struggle by industrial entrepreneurs to find ways to substitute for wood or charcoal by coal in Britain in the seventeenth century, in advance of the later series of famous innovations such as the Boulton and Watt steam engine or the power loom.

4 The German sociologists/economic historians Max Weber and Werner Sombart, writing at the turn of the nineteenth and twentieth centuries, provided a penetrating critique of the rationalist underpinnings of capitalism.

5 His great book still repays close reading, even if his claims for the recent emergence of markets have been disproved.

6 On the peaking of oil supplies, see Deffeyes (2001) for a clear introduction.

7 Economy (2005) provides a vivid description of the terrible environmental toll taken by China's breakneck industrial growth.

8 In this, his last paper expounding the idea, the words used are: "A transvection is ... the outcome of a series of transactions ... [It] includes the complete sequence of exchanges, but it also includes the various transformations which take place along the way" (Alderson and Martin 1965: 118).

9 For example, firms in Suzhou achieve levels of chemical oxygen demand and sulphur dioxide emissions that are 1/18 and 1/40 of China's national averages, and its energy consumption levels to only 0.36 tonnes of standard coal equivalent per 10,000 RMB. See the official Suzhou website: http://www.sipac.gov.cn/english/zhuanti/jg60n/gjlnbtsj/, accessed December 19, 2012.

10 On techno-economic paradigm shifts, see Freeman and Perez (1988) and more extensively Freeman and Louçã (2001); for a recent application to the greening of capitalism, see Altenburg and Pegels (2012).

11 For a spectral analysis of K-waves in the global economy, see Korotayev and Tsirel (2011).

12 This is the aspect of the twelfth FYP focused on by many commentators, such as Stephen Roach, "China's Turning Point" (February 24, 2011) at the Project Syndicate blog: http://www.project-syndicate.org/commentary/roach2/English, accessed December 19, 2012.

13 This feature of China's twelfth FYP has so far attracted less commentary. One exception is Nobel prize winner Michael Spence, in his Project Syndicate blog posting "Asia's New Growth Model" (June 1, 2011): http://www.project-syndicate.org/commentary/spence23/English, accessed December 19, 2012.

14 The seven strategic industries are: energy-saving and environmental protection – e.g. recycling (circular economy); next-generation IT – next-gen communications, TV/internet networks, etc; bio-industries – biopharmaceuticals, bio-agriculture, bio-manufacturing; high-end assembly and manufacturing industries – aerospace, rail and transport, ocean engineering, smart manufacturing; new energy sources – nuclear, solar, wind, biomass, smart power grids; new materials – advanced structures, high-performance composites, rare earths; and new energy-powered cars – electric vehicles, urban charging infrastructure.

15 Hermann Scheer (2007) put the matter very clearly: "This [building of renewable energy opportunities] opens the way for a split in the 'economy,' a fracture in the business community that is a necessary precondition for any breakthrough to renewable energy. It is a fracture between those business interests that are or feel themselves to be dependent (for better or worse) on the traditional energy business and those that recognize or pursue their future opportunities in the shift to renewable energy ... These interest conflicts come to light through the creation of a 'critical mass,' in other words, through a growing number of renewable energy businesses inside Germany that are already earning annual sales of more than 10 billion Euros" (2007: 276).

References

Alderson, W. and Martin, M.W. 1965. "Toward a Formal Theory of Transactions and Transvections." *Journal of Marketing Research*, 2 (2): 117–127.

Altenburg, T. and Pegels, A. 2012. "Sustainability-Oriented Innovation Systems: Managing the Green Transformation." *Innovation and Development*, 2 (1): 5–22.

Clark, G. 2007. *A Farewell to Alms: A Brief Economic History of the World*. Princeton: Princeton University Press.

Costanza, R. 2007. "Avoiding System of Failure: An Upgraded Version of Capitalism Is Needed to Protect the World's Resources." *Nature*, 446 (April 4): 613–614.

Deffeyes, K. 2001. *Hubbert's Peak: The Impending World Oil Shortage*. Princeton: Princeton University Press.

Economy, E. 2005. *The River Runs Black: The Environmental Challenges to China's Future*. Ithaca: Cornell University Press.

Freeman, C. and Perez, C. 1988. "Structural Crises of Adjustment: Business Cycles and Investment Behaviour." In *Technical Change and Economic Theory*, ed. G. Dosi *et al.* London: Frances Pinter.

Freeman, C. and Louçã, F. 2001. *As Time Goes By: From the Industrial Revolutions to the Information Revolution*. Oxford: Oxford University Press.

Friedrichs, J. 2011. "Peak Energy and Climate Change: The Double-Bind of Post-Normal Science." *Futures*, 43: 469–477.

Gerschenkron, A. 1962. *Economic Backwardness in Historical Perspective*. Cambridge, MA: Harvard University Press.

Hu, Angang. 2006a. Green Development: The Inevitable Choice for China (Part 1), *China Dialogue*, http://www.chinadialogue.net/article/show/single/en/134. Accessed December 19, 2012.

Hu, Angang. 2006b. Green Development: The Inevitable Choice for China (Part 2), *China Dialogue*, http://www.chinadialogue.net/article/show/single/en/135-Green-development-the-inevitable-choice-for-China-part-two-. Accessed December 19, 2012.

Hu, Angang. 2011. *China in 2020: A New Type of Superpower*. Washington, DC: Brookings Institution.

Kaldor, N. 1970. "The Case for Regional Policies." *Scottish Journal of Political Economy*, 17: 337–348.

Korotayev, A.V. and Tsirel, S.V. 2011. "A Spectral Analysis of World GDP Dynamics: Kondratieff Waves, Kuznets Swings, Juglar and Kitchin Cycles in Global Economic Development, and the 2008-2009 Economic Crisis." *Structure and Dynamics*, 4 (1), e-journal, http://escholarship.org/uc/item/9jv108xp. Accessed December 19, 2012.

Mathews, J.A. 2011a. "Naturalizing Capitalism: The Next Great Transformation." *Futures*, 43: 868–879.

Mathews, J.A. 2011b. "China's Energy Industrial Revolution." *l'Industria*, 32 (2): 307–326.

Mathews, J.A. 2012. "Green Growth Strategies: Korean Initiatives." *Futures*, 44 (8): 761–769.

Mathews, J.A. and Kidney, S. 2010. "Climate Bonds: Mobilizing Private Financing for Carbon Management." *Carbon Management*, 1 (1): 9–13.

Mathews, J.A. and Tan, H. 2011. "Progress towards a Circular Economy in China: The Drivers (and Inhibitors) of Eco-industrial Initiative." *Journal of Industrial Ecology*, 15 (3): 435–457.

Mikler, J. 2009. *Greening the Car Industry: Varieties of Capitalism and Climate Change*. Cheltenham: Edward Elgar.

Moe, E. 2009. "Mancur Olson and Structural Economic Change: Vested Interests and the Industrial Rise and Fall of the Great Powers." *Review of International Political Economy*, 16 (2): 202–230.

Moe, E. 2010. "Energy, Industry and Politics: Energy, Vested Interests, and Long-Term Economic Growth and Development." *Energy*, 35: 1730–1740.

Mol, P.J. and Sonnenfeld, D.A. 2000. "Ecological Modernisation around the World: An Introduction." *Environmental Politics*, 9 (1): 1–14.

Neori, A., Chopin, T., Troell, M., Buschmann, A.H., Kraemer, G.P., Halling, C., Shpigel, M., and Yarish, C. 2004. "Integrated Aquaculture: Rationale, Evolution, and State of the Art Emphasizing Seaweed Biofiltration in Modern Mariculture." *Aquaculture*, 231: 361–391.

Olson, M. 1982. *The Rise and Decline of Nations*. New Haven: Yale University Press.

Polanyi, K. 1944 (1957; 2001). *The Great Transformation: The Political and Economic Origins of Our Time* (Foreword Joseph E. Stiglitz; Introduction Fred Block). Boston: Beacon Press.

Porter, M.A. and van der Linde, C. 1995. "Toward a New Conception of the Competitiveness–Environment Relationship." *Journal of Economic Perspectives*, 9 (4): 97–108.

Scheer, H. 2007. *Energy Autonomy*. London: Earthscan; Routledge.

Schumpeter, J.A. 1939. *Business Cycles* (2 vols). Philadelphia: Porcupine Press.

Sieferle, R.P. 2001; 1982. *The Subterranean Forest: Energy Systems and the Industrial Revolution*. Cambridge: White Horse Press.

Spence, M. 2011. *The Next Convergence: The Future of Economic Growth in a Multispeed World*. New York: Farrar, Straus & Giroux.

Steffen, W., Crutzen, P.J., and McNeill, J.R. 2007. "The Anthropocene: Are Humans Now Overwhelming the Great Forces of Nature?" *Ambio*, 36 (8): 614–621.

Stern, N. 2009. *A Blueprint for a Safer Planet: How to Manage Climate Change and Create a New Era of Progress and Prosperity*. London: Bodley Head.

Stern, N. 2010. China's Growth, China's Cities, and the New Global Low-Carbon Industrial Revolution. *Working Paper*. Centre for Climate Change Economics and Policy/Grantham Research Institute on Climate Change and the Environment, http://www.cccep.ac.uk/Publications/Policy/docs/PPStern_China-industrial-rev_Nov10.pdf. Accessed December 19, 2012.

Unruh, G. 2000. "Understanding Carbon Lock-In." *Energy Policy*, 28: 817–830.

Wang, H. and Kimble, C. 2011. "Leapfrogging to Electric Vehicles: Patterns and Scenarios for China's Automobile Industry." *International Journal of Automotive Technology and Management*, 11 (4): 312–325.

Wang, H. and Xiao, J. 2011. "Delivering Discontinuous Innovation through Modularity: The Case of the Chinese Electric Vehicle Industry." *Proceedings ICMET Conference, 2011*.

Young, A.A. 1928. "Increasing Returns and Economic Progress. *Economic Journal*, 38 (152): 527–542.

Zysman, J. and Huberty, M., eds. 2011. Green Growth: From Religion to Reality, Berkeley, Berkeley Roundtable on the International Economy (BRIE), http://brie.berkeley.edu/publications/From-Religion-to-Reality.pdf. Accessed December 19, 2012.

Chapter 26

Global Companies and the Private Regulation of Global Labor Standards

Luc Fransen

Introduction

This chapter analyzes what contribution the private labor standard-setting makes to the global governance of labor standards as a specific global social policy issue. It discusses the role of global companies in the emergence of private labor standards and the major indicators of its effectiveness: the institutional design of standards; the business demand for standards; and impact of standard-setting efforts at farm and factory sites. It uses data and empirical examples from the apparel, footwear, multi-product retail, consumer electronics, coffee\tea\cocoa, and fresh produce sectors of industry. The general argument is that private standard-setting offers mixed results in terms of protecting or advancing worker rights. Although the effectiveness of standards varies slightly across sectors, the economic conditions of production in most sectors, the national-institutional features discouraging worker organization in most countries, and the uneven engagement of global industry players with private regulation offer a too unfavorable opportunity structure for private standards to deliver results. The chapter then discusses three trends that will shape private standard effectiveness in the near future: the rise to economic and political power of the BRICS and in particular China, the consequences of slowing economic growth in Europe and Northern America, and the evolution of governmental and intergovernmental governance. These trends signify that the privatization of labor standards regulation interacts with a changing balance of power in the global political economy.

The Emergence of Private Labor Standards

Private labor standard-setting is a response to the co-existence of three phenomena: the contemporary global organization of production, a neoliberal international

The Handbook of Global Companies, First Edition. Edited by John Mikler.
© 2013 John Wiley & Sons, Ltd. Published 2013 by John Wiley & Sons, Ltd.

regulatory framework, and increased societal pressure on multinational companies (Bartley 2003). These three phenomena and their inter-linkages are discussed in turn, followed by a discussion of why businesses participate in private standard-setting, instead of developing Corporate Social Responsibility policies for labor standards individually.

For mass consumer goods, the organization of production has become geographically dispersed and functionally disintegrated. Transnational production chains have come into existence that connect formally independent companies, running from North America and Europe into Central and South America, Eastern Europe, and South and Southeast Asia. Labor-intensive manufacturing increasingly takes place in regions of the world characterized by relatively low wage levels and an abundant non-skilled labor supply. Next to that, agricultural commodities and raw materials for production are sourced from developing countries in Africa, Latin America, and Asia. Studies point to an overall asymmetry in power relations, advantaging Northern buyer firms *vis-à-vis* Southern supplier firms in these chains. Analysts note a deflationary pressure running downward through mass manufacturing chains, while in agricultural commodities prices are volatile (Dicken 2006; Kaplinsky and Morris 2001).

Consumer goods brands and retailers rely on a large, differentiated set of suppliers who regularly receive large orders with tight deadlines. Studies emphasize that specific industrial characteristics could stimulate excessive overtime, abuse, and suppression of labor representation. For instance, labor abuse has been identified in the clothing chain in small informal workplaces in India, often involving sewing work by whole families, including children (Ascoly and Finney 2005). In China, factories supplying global brands have been known to apply harsh quasi-military management techniques in order to push workers towards higher production levels (Ngai 2005). In agricultural commodities, large retailers increasingly choose their products through spot market interactions with a large pool of suppliers (Gereffi *et al.* 2005). In many Latin American, Asian, and African plants producing tea, coffee, cocoa, and fresh produce, working conditions are determined by low wages and short-term contracts (Raynolds and Long 2007). Mass consumer good production and agricultural production are thus a manifestation of a fragmented and unequal form of global economic integration, which potentially puts workers in a vulnerable position. What is the role of public regulation with regard to this issue?

Regulating globally organized production has been subject to discussion since the rise of the multinational corporation in the 1960s. The coalition of actors willing to regulate multinationals dissolved, however, during and after the economic crises of the 1970s. Developing countries shifted their attention to a strategy of export-orientation, while in Europe and the United States notions of de-regulation and freedom for markets gained prominence. This is understood as the basis of the *neoliberal* perspective on global production: global (rather than domestic) markets are the source of growth on the domestic level, and trade across borders is therefore the key to development (Harvey 2005). Barriers to world trade should therefore be reduced.

Increasingly, national regimes in the Global South follow this recipe and labor regulation has subsequently been affected. States with governments as different in political character as China, Indonesia, and Mexico nowadays have legal frameworks that ostensibly protect workers' rights. But low standard working conditions persist in export industries (and elsewhere) because of a lack of enforcement of these legal frameworks. Government policy priorities do not leave much room for a sensibility for the worker's plight. In some countries, the shift towards export orientation has been paralleled by legal adjustments reducing worker rights (Kocer 2007). Public attention has at times focused on the deplorable working circumstances in export production regions (Klein 1999).

On the intergovernmental level, the neoliberal regulatory framework is supported by UN policies that favor international voluntary action by businesses over binding rules for economic transactions. At the World Trade Organization, discussions about social clauses have failed due to especially Southern governmental and non-state actor opposition (Bartley 2003: 449–451; Van Roozendaal 2002).

These failures mean that pressures for labor standard enforcement are redirected away from governmental and intergovernmental bodies of decision-making. Instead, Northern multinational corporations immersed in transnational production chains more often come under pressure once they are revealed to have sourced from supplier factories, plants, and farms where labor abuse take place. Pressure is exercised by activist networks, unions, developmental NGOs, consumer movements, and share-holder movements in North America and Western Europe (Bartley 2003; Merk 2007). Most of these groups have ties with worker organizations in producer countries. Individually or collectively, activist organizations campaign for worker rights in the Global South, using multinational corporations (and their brands) as levers. Amplified by reports in the global media, they increase sensitivity among the consumer audience in Europe and Northern America for global justice issues. Public campaigns are followed up by face-to-face interactions with firm representatives that are sometimes contentious, often more cooperative (Fransen 2012a). Supported by Northern governments, the option of voluntary action by firms on labor issues then takes shape and evolves through further business-activist interactions.

Private labor standard-setting is a particular category in the wider realm of voluntary corporate activities to manage social and environmental consequences of doing business. Arguably globalization, neoliberalism, and societal pressure have similarly stimulated other aspects of Corporate Social Responsibility (CSR), such as sustainability reporting, socially responsible investment, and philanthropy. Within the universe of CSR practices, private labor standard-setting takes a special place because it organizes corporate commitment to ethical standards in the form of *rules*, in *sector-wide* approaches, with mechanisms for *external review* of compliance.

Firms work together on labor standard-setting because, first, for many production chains, they do not have the power to individually enforce standards on their suppliers, being only one of a larger group of buyers. This makes cooperation between buyers a necessary precondition (Merk 2007). Second, concerns about free-riding on other firm's efforts, or uneven reputational benefits of developing CSR activities, may lead firms to prefer collective action among firms instead of on their own (Prakash and Potoski 2007). Third, some scholars note the possible benefit of information exchange and learning between participants in private regulatory organizations, leading to improved practices of enforcing labor standards (Ruggie and Kell 1999). Furthermore, an increasing amount of firms view credible review mechanisms as provided by private standard-setting organizations as necessary tools in voluntary business regulation, in order to prevent allegations of window-dressing (Prakash and Potoski 2007).

The privatization of labor standard regulation signifies that in the contemporary global economy, many governments (and intergovernmental organizations) are not fulfilling the role implicit in the development of labor law: as a corrector of a power deficit between capital owners and laborers (Bakels 1973). At the same time, the emergence of transnational private labor standards across borders also signifies a progressive harmonization of aspirations towards worker rights across borders (Hassel 2008). Because of this it is worthwhile to study to what extent private labor standard-setting as an alternative institution for advancing worker rights holds promise.

The Effectiveness of Private Labor Standard-Setting

This section discusses different approaches to gauging the current effectiveness of private standard organizations. In turn, it will discuss the institutional design of, the business demand for and the impact of standards.

Institutional Design

Nowadays, we can identify private standard organizations in various sectors that focus on labor standards enforcement in supply chains as core or one of the core issues to be regulated. Table 26.1 shows some famous examples. These organizations vary in their approaches to regulation. Below four types of variation are discussed that all impact potential effectiveness.

First, the participation of various stakeholder groups and the way responsibilities in governance are organized, matters, and leads to a distinction between so-called multi-stakeholder-governed private standards and business-driven standards. Multi-stakeholder-governed programs contain three values that other governance-models lack: inclusiveness, expertise-based effectiveness and procedural fairness (Quack 2010: 7).

First, programs developed and governed by a variety of stakeholder groups allow parties relevant to a specific issue to have a say in matters, thus increasing legitimacy of decision-making (Boström 2006). Second, governance with groups of various backgrounds can be justified with reference to notions of "learning" between, among and inside organizations with different sets of expertise, improving decision-making and policy (Börzel and Risse 2005). And third, when companies work with NGO (and/or trade union) representatives in programs, they engage critics of business behavior in business attempts at improvements, thus letting them perform the function of watchdog (Jenkins, 2002; Utting 2001).

Within the clothing and forestry sectors, multi-stakeholder-governed standard-setters such as the Ethical Trading Initiative, Social Accountability International, Forest Stewardship Council, and Fair Labor Association nowadays compete with business-driven organizations such as the Business Social Compliance Initiative and the Program on Endorsement of Forest Certification. In sectors like toys and electronics, business-driven organizations such as the Electronics Industry Citizenship Coalition and the International Council of Toy Industries dominate the

Table 26.1 Overview of private standard organizations.

Products	Issue to be regulated	Predominant geographic scope	Examples of private standard organizations	Examples of business participants	Examples of CSO governance participants
Forestry products	Deforestation; fair and safe working conditions	Global	Forest Stewardship Council (FSC); Program for Endorsement of Forest Certification schemes (PEFC)	Kingfisher; Faber-Castell; AC Timber	World Wildlife Fund; ICCO
Clothing	Labor abuse	Global	Fair Labor Association (FLA); Fair Wear Foundation (FWF)	Nike; Liz Claiborne; Adidas	Global Garments Union (ITGLWF); Clean Clothes Campaign
Fresh produce	Environmental degradation; labor abuse; equitable trade relations	Africa; Latin America	Ethical Trading Initiative (ETI); Social Accountability International (SAI); Business Social Compliance Initiative (BSCI)	Marks & Spencer; Sainsbury's; ALDI	International Trade Union Confederation (ITUC)
Coffee	Environmental degradation; labor abuse	Africa; Latin America; South East Asia	Utz; Rainforest Alliance; ETI	Nestlé; Kraft; Sara Lee	Oxfam; Global Food Union (IUF)

Source: Adapted from Fransen (2012b).

standard-setting market. Most of these organizations do develop some systems to engage stakeholder groups in discussion (Fransen 2012b; Egels-Zanden and Wahlqvist 2007), but less systematically than multi-stakeholder-initiatives, which calls into question their inclusiveness, and the quality of review of business performance in these organizations.

Beyond the governance model, three more specific elements of standard-setting can be identified that predict effectiveness: standard content, monitoring, and compliance measures.

Labor standards in private regulation vary according to their comprehensiveness, the degrees to which they are discretionary and specific, and to what extent they reference existing labor standards (Fransen 2012a; cf. O'Rourke 2006). The scope of the different labor standards applied is quite similar: directed at issues such as freedom of association and right to collective bargaining, health and safety, forced labor and child labor, and discrimination. Three major differences distinguish the private regulatory organizations. First, they differ in terms of the public arrangements to which the standards relate as a reference for the substance of worker rights. Most analyzed organizations use ILO core conventions and UN conventions as the standards to adhere to. But a few standards, such as the Worldwide Responsible Accredited Production program, refer to national and local laws. For most developing countries this means less protection of worker's positions than in the case of actual implementation of international standards. Second, a contentious issue is the "living wage": the possibility for the workers to receive wages for their working hours that enable subsistence. Initiatives like Social Accountability International and Fair Wear Foundation include the promise of a "living wage," while for instance Fair Labor Association does not. Finally, there is variation in the degree to which some of the standard requirements are aspirational or obligatory for participants.

In terms of monitoring, most private standards rely on external monitoring by commercial professional auditors of companies such as Intertek, TUV, and SGS, which are accredited by the private standard organizations themselves (Fransen and Kolk 2007). These auditors visit factories, check the books, interview managers, and arrange for interviews with workers. A minority of private regulatory organizations work with not-for-profit audit teams and investigators (Fair Wear Foundation and the Worker Rights Consortium). Others leave the option of not-for-profit auditing open to companies (notably Social Accountability International and Ethical Trading Initiative) but see most of their business participants opting for the commercial audit option.

In the 2000s, academic and policy discussion about the quality of private labor monitoring increased, focused on working conditions in mass consumer goods manufacturing (O'Rourke 2002; Clean Clothes Campaign 2005; Merk 2007; Esbenshade 2004). In general, commercial audits were found wanting in quality: auditors were simply not up to the task of investigating working conditions. Second, observers held that the auditors were not trusted by workers, which is why workers did not disclose sensitive information to them. Third, activists questioned commercial relations between supplier factories and audit firms, which might lead to conflicts of interest. In addition, contracts between suppliers and audit firms made it very difficult to investigate violations in factories, since the outcomes of labor standard audits were kept confidential under those contracts. It is difficult to gauge to what extent the quality of audits, and the interactions between auditors, brands/retailers, and suppliers have evolved since the mid-2000s. In any event, the features of commercial audits understood by some policy observers and activist to form structural impediments to effective monitoring, persist for most private standard organizations up until today.

Private standards also vary with regard to their compliance and enforcement policies. Variation can be found in terms of what standard organizations ask from business participants, and what they offer, in terms of policy instruments to improve enforcement, and in terms of external signifiers of business compliance. In mass consumer goods manufacturing, across the board, the ambitions of private standard-setters about the scope of suppliers covered, and the improvements required in factories have been toned down over the years. It is now becoming clear that certifying a company's complete supply chain is difficult, if not impossible, and that certification does not always mean sustained care for worker rights in factories. The barriers to a certification model have to do with the structure of the supply chain and the location of manufacturing, as impact studies on the ground, to be discussed below, evidence (Frenkel 2001; Locke *et al.* 2009).

Some organizations such as Ethical Trading Initiative and Business Social Compliance Initiative have therefore never sought to certify companies, suppliers or products for labor standard. Others who initially did plan to certify, have largely abandoned this ambition, including Fair Wear Foundation and Fair Labor Association. Staff of these organizations saw that progress towards verifiable compliance with labor standards was too slow with their first generation of business members. These organizations instead now emphasize a model of continuous improvement, in which they gauge the firm's commitment to increase monitoring efforts and contribute to solutions in cases of grievances and malcompliance at suppliers. In some cases, businesses are allowed to prioritize specific parts of their supply chain for monitoring, so as to target core parts of manufacturing supply, or factories in more challenging countries. Clothing retailer H&M for instance focuses on China with regard to its commitments to the Fair Labor Association (Fransen 2012a: 143–147).

In agricultural commodities, the certification of economic units for labor standard enforcement is much more widespread. As one of the requirements for certification, next to equitable trade transactions (in the case of Fair Trade) and environmental obligations (in the case of Rainforest Alliance and Utz), labor standards are certified of small farms and larger plants supplying to European and American markets (Kolk 2011). For most smallholders, there is hardly an employer–employee relationship, but for most larger plants, there is a significant workforce to which standards apply, also bringing with it challenges with regard to worker organization and collective bargaining. Large business supporters of these standards can choose to increase their buying of these certified products, or commit themselves to a percentage of certified products to be bought.

Business Demand

Private standard-setters promote standards, but if businesses do not adopt them, working conditions in transnational production chains will hardly be impacted. Because of this, academics also theorize about a relationship between stringency of private standards on the one hand and the likelihood of businesses adopting them on the other (Prakash and Potoski 2007). Aseem Prakash and Matt Potoski propose that too stringent standard-setting does not attract that many companies, because it is too costly, but too lenient regulation is not popular either because it may induce accusations of window dressing. Such reasoning is based on rational-choice assumptions about business behavior. Empirical analysis of business motivations to join private regulatory organizations in part confirms this dynamic, but also points to other important factors (Bartley 2009; Fransen and Burgoon 2012a; Marx 2008).

First, the crucial factor motivating firms to join private standard organizations is societal pressure and its possible consequences for the firm. Businesses involved in mass consumer good manufacturing join in particular multi-stakeholder governed and more stringent regulatory organizations to appease critical stakeholder groups, such as labor activists, developmental NGOs, and unions (Fransen and Burgoon 2012a; Marx 2008). Second, and very much related, large brands and high street brands and retailers such as Nike, Levi's, and Marks & Spencer are more likely to join more stringent and multi-stakeholder governed regulatory organizations (Bartley 2009). In Western countries, these businesses have most to fear from societal pressure through activist campaigns. Activists seek out large and wellknown firms. Similarly, these visible firms are more likely to receive critical questions from consumers. Meanwhile, at the point of production, in developing countries, these businesses still interact with their suppliers about manufacturing and product requirements. Labor standard regulation requirements may add on to these interactions. Mass retailers and companies competing on price, such as Aldi and Karstadt, form the reverse image to brands. At the point of consumption they have less to fear from a critical consumer audience, while at the point of production their interaction with suppliers is limited and most often mediated by trade agents. This makes it less likely that these firms will invest in interventions in factories that are, both in the geographic and managerial sense, remote (Fransen and Burgoon 2012a).

In agricultural commodity chains the picture is somewhat different, due in part to the predominance of farm and plant certification as a regulatory model. This changes the issue for businesses, so that instead of "what standard should we adopt for our supply chain?" the question becomes "to what extent do we certify what parts of our supply chain, using which standards?" In deciding on this matter to some extent similar dynamics are at play as in manufactured goods, regarding the importance of societal pressure, brand reputation, and position in the production chain. Famous brands and retailers like Nestlé and Starbucks are more likely to receive criticism for their buying practices than smaller and cost-competing firms (Kolk 2011). But because, unlike manufactured consumer goods, agricultural products can have a label signifying certification according to sustainability standards (including labor), there is also a direct role for consumer choice in business strategies. Businesses can thus develop a diverse standard portfolio, monitoring parts of their supply chain using their own code of conduct, certifying a small amount of commodities with Fair Trade, and another part using Utz or Rainforest standards. In this way they actively cater to specific consumer audiences.

What do these dynamics bring about in terms of overall industry uptake of private labor standards? For an answer we again distinguish between manufacturing and agricultural chains. For the business uptake of clothing, sportswear, electronics, toys, and other manufactured goods in retail stores, not all standard-setters communicate consistently about business participation. Moreover, suppliers overlap for many companies, and lack of industry figures do not allow us to express the participation in private labor standards as a percentage of a sector. However, we can make a calculated rough estimation based on information available.

We see that over 1000 buying firms such as brands and retailers participate in private standard-setting in the clothing chain, sportswear chain, and multi-product retail chains, while close to 800 of such firms regulate toys, and over 60 brand and technology firms regulate IT-electronics chains. From these figures it is reasonable to assume that tens of thousands of suppliers in developing countries are subject to labor standard monitoring. In addition, private labor regulation is not confined to the prime figures in the industry. Regulating labor standards is not only the business of Sony, Nike, Mattel, and Liz Claiborne, but also of Lenovo, Mizuno, Golden Bear Products, and Gsus. A majority of firms participating in private standard-setting adopt standards that are not multi-stakeholder-governed and less stringent than existing multi-stakeholder-governed organizations. Geographically, most participating firms have head offices in Europe, followed by firms with American head offices. Participation from Latin American, Asian, and African firms is noted but rare.[1] Business uptake of this type of private standard-setting is therefore uneven: in terms of who is participating and who is not participating, in terms of stringency of standards adopted and degree of oversight by non-profit organizations, and in geographic terms.

In agricultural chains, overlapping suppliers also decrease the actual scope of certificates for sustainably grown coffee, cocoa, tea, and fresh produce. Overall, more precise figures are available than in consumer goods sectors. In 2011, 16% of coffee was produced conforming to sustainability standards, the majority of which take into account labor (TCC 2012). Tea and cocoa rank lower in their sustainability effort, with similar standard organizations, but lower impact in terms of certification of produced commodities, 7.7% over 2009 for tea produced and 1.2% for cocoa sold respectively. However, both in tea and cocoa, big players have committed to scaling up certification in their supply chain in the coming years. In fresh produce, bananas are the most commonly certified commodity, with over 20% of bananas exported certified for social and environmental criteria in 2009 (Hainmuller *et al.* 2011; Potts *et al.* 2010; TCC 2012).

One final issue with regard to business demand of private standards is the consequence of private regulatory competition. Among others, the clothing, sportswear, tea, cocoa and coffee sector, different private standard organizations compete for business support. Speculations about possible races to the bottom or to the top in terms of standard quality abound (Elliott and Freeman 2003; Sabel *et al.* 2000), but more important is that this competition has direct negative consequences for the current effectiveness of standard-setting (Fransen 2011). It leads to the following challenges: contradictory implementation efforts at factories, plants, and farms; higher cost of certification for producers that often have to implement different standards using different policies; confusion among businesses and consumers about the meaning of programs, certificates, and labels; and increased costs for supporting organizations such as NGOs and government agencies that subsidize private regulatory organizations. Despite calls for harmonization and policy efforts in the direction of coordination among regulators, in all mentioned competitive sectors fragmentation of the private regulatory effort persists up until today (Fransen 2011; Kolk 2011; TCC 2012).

Impacts and Economic and Local Contexts

Increasingly, academic and policy studies focus on the impact of private standards at factories, plants, and farms (ETI 2006; Locke *et al.* 2007; Kamau *et al.* 2010). In combination with knowledge of the difference between standards and the patterns of business uptake, impact studies crucially contribute to our understanding of standard effectiveness.

In general, we can distinguish two types of research efforts. First, studies track the workings of one particular standard, using the institutional support from standard-setters and firms (ETI 2006; Frenkel 2001; Locke *et al.* 2007; 2009; 2010; Kamau *et al.* 2010). Second, studies investigate particular geographic zones, analyzing productive practices that are subject to different standards (COSA 2008; Kocer and Fransen 2009; Rodriguez-Garavito 2005; Ruben and Zuniga 2010).

Overall, the results of studies are more encouraging for private standards in agricultural production than for those focused on mass consumer goods production. Studies in the former category show progress in labor standards enforcement, while studies of the latter form a long shopping list of contextual factors that enable or constrain working conditions improvement. Most of the factors enabling working conditions improvement are often not in place at factory sites sourcing to American and European brands and retailers. Improvements in factories are therefore visible with regard to health and safety and ruling out of child labor, but not with regard to wages, freedom of association, and collective bargaining (ETI 2006; Kocer and Fransen 2009).

In keeping with the general thread of this handbook, we can review these contextual factors that affect the success of private labor standard-setting in light of decision-making within global businesses. Most of all, firms' sourcing decisions affect the impact that private labor regulation has. First, firms' decision to source from countries with political cultures and legal frameworks hostile to trade unions and Freedom of Association complicate the enforcement of labor standards (Merk 2008). While private standards include rights to collective bargaining and worker organization, actual worker organization is very challenging in a country with a contentious democratic culture like Turkey, very difficult in a fractured society like Bangladesh, and effectively illegal in an authoritarian society like China.

Second, the work of Richard Locke and colleagues (2007; 2009; 2010) reflects the importance of business to business relations. Buyer firms' decision to create long- or short-term relations with suppliers affects private labor regulation. In general, short-term contracts hardly allow for sustained social improvements at factory sites. In addition, firms' decision to order with short time horizons and low prices negatively affects labor standards enforcement by private regulation, leading supplier management to distrust the labor standards imposed on them. Next to that, the decision to either keep suppliers at a distance or interact more closely with them affects labor-standards enforcement. Frequent interaction between buyer and supplier encourages learning about management of production that may streamline productive practices and release some of the pressure on workers to increase output in ineffective and socially harmful ways. Finally, firms' decision to develop a larger or smaller supplier network affects labor standard enforcement. With a more fragmented supply chain, a firm's economic leverage towards suppliers decreases and enforcement of labor standards as provisioned by their private regulatory organization of choice becomes more difficult.

Tellingly, most of these factors pertaining to current international business strategy are currently not within the regulatory scope of most private standards. Private standard organization staff may *encourage* long-term relationships with suppliers among its participating firms, or the design of a smaller supplier base, but most organizations have not *standardized* these policies as requirements (Fransen 2012a: 143–147).

The Future of Private Labor Standard-Setting

A set of political-economic trends will in the future affect business strategies with regard to private labor standard-setting. Three of them will shortly be discussed below: the rise of China, slowing economic growth in Europe and North America, and developments in intergovernmental and national public governance.

The Rise of China

Analysts of international political and economic developments have concerned themselves for the last couple of years with the degree and consequences of the economic growth of China, Brazil, Russia, India, China, and South Africa (Khanna 2009). In this section we focus on China, given its size, its importance for mass consumer goods production, and its indirect impact on labor standards across the globe. However, some of the implications discussed also go for other so-called BRICS-countries. The growth in the economic and political power of China may have three sorts of immediate implications for the field of private labor standard-setting in particular: for the organization of production chains, the organization and impact of private standards, and the labor conditions themselves.

In transnational production chains, some Chinese firms take on more complex, technologically intensive, and higher value added functions, or increasingly concentrate horizontal and vertical supplier functions (Merk 2008). In addition, some firms develop branding functions. Increased supplier power through concentration means that the current form of private standard-setting is in need of revision, since it relies on the idea that buying firms could force labor standards on their suppliers by coordination of their buying power. This may in the near future become harder. In the near future, we may therefore expect different kinds of interaction between Western buyers and Chinese suppliers, new Chinese standard-setting efforts, and possibly increased participation of Chinese firms in private standard organizations.

The Chinese government in 2006 revised its labor law, aimed at strengthening worker positions. Although a lack of enforcement of this law means that many workers do not profit, there are also concerns in the industry about its inflationary effects. Moreover, literature on Chinese Industrial Relations marks a rise in strikes and rebellion against factory management in China's border provinces and rising wages (He 2012).

Sourcing patterns are sensitive to shifts in labor costs, and buyers could place increasing orders in countries like Cambodia and Bangladesh where labor costs are decidedly lower than in China (that is, if these buyers are willing to swallow relatively lower level infrastructure). Rising wages and stalling supply of migrant workers in China's border provinces can also stimulate Chinese suppliers and trade agents to look for new export zones in China's mainland. The significance for private labor standard-setting is that the global wage-depressing effect of the scaling up of Chinese export-manufacturing, could be lessening in the future.

Meanwhile, a growing Asian consumer goods market also increases sourcing options for suppliers. Mass consumer goods manufacturer managers can decide to dedicate their goods to Asian, rather than Western markets. Ultimately, the choice may be between connecting to Western-destined production chains where various private standards (environment, labor) come into play, or to Eastern-destined production chains where, up until now, private standard pressures seem less intense. This also means that Western buying companies' influence on Eastern suppliers lessens (Kocer and Fransen 2009).

In short, the rise of China, chief among the BRICS countries, may affect production chains organization, consumer demand, working conditions, and the organization of private standards, and therefore deserves careful further study.

The Implications of Slower Economic Growth

Since the 2008 financial crisis, both Northern America and Europe have gone through a prolonged period of slowing economic development, affecting economic and political conditions far beyond their continents. We established that the growth of private labor standards relates to increased societal pressure on corporations in these continents. It is therefore worthwhile to shortly discuss what are the implications of less economic growth for private standard-setting.

David Vogel (2005) questions the existence of a so-called *Market for Virtue* of ethically minded consumers that can sustain private regulations. Some scholars claim that consumer demand for fair and sustainable production may be influenced by the business cycle. Such demand will not last in times of economic hardship (see for instance Govekar *et al.* 2002). Added to this cyclical scenario, specific challenges await European and American consumer audiences in the coming years. Economic "catch-up" growth in Asia, Latin America, and Eastern Europe means rising demand for natural resources and food. Particular resources with a finite supply (especially gas and oil) are becoming increasingly scarce. Because of this many food and non-food consumer products have become substantially more expensive in recent years. Will consumer pressure for social and environmentally sound production persist, grow, or decline given these challenges? One may question whether consumer concern with higher prices competes with consumer sensitivity to ethical issues. If it does and the sombre forecasts about price developments are right, notions of fairness with regard to affordable prices might then negatively affect other notions of fairness that deal with global solidarity issues.

For private labor standards in agricultural chains, the rise in food prices (if it is persistent and not due to speculation) may bring some good news. Higher prices for agricultural commodities entail the promise of higher profit for agricultural producers. Whether workers actually share in the benefit is of course dependent on developments in power relations in the production chain and in worker–management relations.

Gay Seidman (2007) establishes that most politically significant consumer action for ethical trade was organized by intermediate groups (church groups, unions) and did not result from a mass of individual consumer decisions. Economic downturn can also affect these intermediate promoters of private labor standard-setting. First, many trade union organizations, activist networks, and developmental NGOs rely to a large extent on government funds, which are likely to decrease in the coming years (Fransen and Burgoon 2012b). Second, such organizations may equally face a drop in private funding, with citizens and businesses reordering their priorities.

Finally, the jury is out whether slower growth in Europe and the US leads to a downturn in terms of business commitment to private labor standards. Participation in private standard-setting and certification of products has steadily risen in the past crisis years.[2] This signifies that slower growth may not affect the possible success of private labor standards. At the same time, anecdotes about cuts in budgets of CSR departments are ripe. We may therefore hypothesize that while the crisis does not lead firms to return from promises they have made, firms may currently invest less in standards, meaning that the pace of implementation could slow down.

With government budget cuts a reality for the coming years, the question is also whether the private standards phenomenon will become more pervasive. After all, governments may choose to cut public oversight of rules within their jurisdiction to balance their budgets and encourage private parties to take over. A first example of this trend is the Dutch initiative *FairProduce* which certifies fresh produce from the Netherlands for the Dutch market, according to Dutch labor standards.[3] This initiative is supported by the Dutch government, which recognizes that its monitoring of agricultural working circumstances is inefficient. Will labor standards within the EU and in North America become more privatized?

Evolutions in Governmental and Intergovernmental Governance

The issue of *private* labor standards is on the table in the absence of enforced public labor regulation. Reviewing contemporary governmental and intergovernmental policies, two impacts on labor regulation can be identified: first, the degree to which public labor regulation may become more or less enforced and make private regulation redundant; second, the degree to which public policies may interact to make for more or less effective public-private enforcement of labor standards. While a cursory overview shows that the first impact is unlikely, the second one deserves more attention, focusing on the issues of developing country governments, trade, and CSR policy.

Notable is first the development of private tools by developing country governments that seem to mimic the efforts of Western private labor regulators. Chinese product quality authorities have, for instance, launched a private labor standard certificate program CSC9000T in 2006, and invited Chinese factories (both export and home market focused) to seek certification. The Thai government initiated a similar program for its industries (Fransen, 2012a: 185). One may infer from this that certain export country governments are moving to *publicly* support labor standards, through *private* means and on a *voluntary* basis. Another pressing question is how public monitoring of labor standards interacts with private efforts (Seidman 2007). Matthew Amengual (2010) for instance concludes on the basis of case studies in the Dominican Republic that private standard-setting efforts could in turn affect the quality and focus of public monitoring efforts. While national regimes hostile to worker rights may not experiment with making these interactions effective, it could be that in countries with poor governments, these interactions could be improved from both sides.

Trade policy is relevant for labor policy, first, since it influences the organization of production across borders. Second, trade agreements may include labor conditions provisions, and can determine the degree to which trading country governments take into consideration worker rights. This may enhance or diminish the significance of private labor standards. At the World Trade Organization negotiation table, the debate on the social clause as a possible route towards the advancement of labor standards has ended, given opposition from Southern governments that aimed to protect their export strategies. The question for the future is how strongly its member states will uphold the rules agreed to under the WTO and how far its agenda of free trade can be realized further. Any future fall-out between a group of producing countries and a group of buying countries leading to a cycle of protectionist retaliation might affect various production chains. This would have repercussions for private standards too.

The deadlock at the WTO has raised the significance of bi-lateral and regional agreements. In particular the United States and the European Union have social clauses in their Generalized System of Preferences (GSP) which aim to offer more beneficial terms of trade to developing countries that ratify labor conventions. The jury is out on whether such a clause actually improves working conditions, but it does offer a route for complaints on lack of compliance beyond the nation state (Nolan-Garcia 2010).

Meanwhile, the ILO has assisted in labor standards programs based on bilateral treaties. The Better Factories program that was introduced in the clothing industry of Cambodia has been extended to Better Work pilot projects in Jordan, Vietnam, and Lesotho. Such programs offer the hope of regionally concentrated improvements in working conditions through interactions between bilateral policy favoring compliance with labor standards, ILO cooperation, and private support from for profit and non-profit organizations. Catering to small developing countries that otherwise would probably lose out to Chinese suppliers, Better Work aims to create a market for virtue for buying firms on a national level. Specialists meanwhile warn against too much optimism regarding the fruits of such projects (Oka 2010).

In terms of CSR policies of intergovernmental organizations, developments in the United Nations and EU are worth a closer look. Within the UN, since the early 2000s, the discussion of standards for multinationals has been the responsibility of John Gerrard Ruggie, special secretary to business at the UN. Ruggie first supported the UN Global Compact, a loose assembly of businesses and societal actors geared towards setting exemplary best practice. Recently he finished a proposal for the division of responsibilities between states, IGOs, businesses, and civil society regarding human rights issues, under the banner "Protect, respect and remedy." The final draft is striking for his lack of mentioning of private standard organizations as institutions for embedding voluntary practice, the absence of a defined role for civil society organizations in the process of business human rights policy development and progress, and the lack of specificity of proposed soft-law standards (Melish and Meidinger 2011). This effectively reduces the impact of Ruggie's effort on private labor standards.

The EU's policy towards CSR and private regulation, which evolved through rounds of consultation with both business and societal stakeholder groups, has since the early 2000s been lax, focusing on voluntary business activity, without criteria for what is appropriate, nor legislation for businesses (Kinderman 2012). However, with the switch in Commission appointments in 2010, the recent plans for governing CSR are more stringent, proposing legislation for mandatory sustainability reporting, together with a host of soft-law approaches for both national and regional advance of good practices. Further academic inquiry can establish how both UN and EU efforts will interact with existing private labor standards.

Conclusion

This chapter has argued that private labor standards have emerged as a response to the global re-organization of production, a neoliberal regulatory framework, and increased societal pressure on global companies. While viewed as a trend in the global economy that marks the retreat of governments as possible allies in the advance of worker rights, it raises the question whether workers find new allies in terms of private standard organizations and their supporters, among which most notably global companies. The chapter has therefore highlighted the results of ongoing research with regard to different indicators of private standard effectiveness. Private labor standards vary in stringency and in the inclusiveness of governance models. Their uptake by businesses has been significant, but in mass consumer goods production focused standard organizations, most firms support standards without civil society overview, and apply less stringent standards.

On the ground, private standard efforts have only led to marginal increases of worker rights and labor power. While its positive effects are visible in some agricultural chains, its effectiveness in mass manufacturing is dependent on a large set of conditions that are not present in most relevant sectors. Despite its evolution into an institutionally settled ingredient of business regulatory activity, private regulation therefore currently does not effectively enforce labor standards.

Any future attempts to include global corporate strategy as a progressive factor in the efforts at raising labor standards will therefore likely focus on better inter-mixing of public and private regulation, on the local, national, regional, and international level. These attempts ideally would also reckon with opportunities and constraints due to shifts in power between big players in the global economy, as signified in this chapter.

Notes

1 Own research, April 2012, based on measurement of business participation in private regulatory organizations using policy documentation of the websites of the Better Sugar Cane Initiative, Business Social Compliance Initiative, Common Code for the Coffee Community, Electronics Industry

Citizenship Coalition, the Ethical Trading Initiative(s) in the United Kingdom and Scandinavia, Fair Labor Association, Fair Wear Foundation, Initiative Clause Sociale, Made-By, Responsible Jewellery Council, Social Accountability International's Corporate Involvement Program.

2   Also based on own research, see previous note.

3   See http://www.fairproduce.nl/, accessed March 23, 2012.

References

Amengual, Matthew. 2010. "Complementary Labor Regulation: The Uncoordinated Combination of State and Private Regulators in the Dominican Republic." *World Development*, 38 (3): 405–414.

Ascoly, Nina and Finney, Chantal. 2005. "The Shifting Patterns of Women's Work." In *Made by Women*, ed. Clean Clothes Campaign, 56–65. Amsterdam: CCC.

Bakels, H.L. 1973. *Arbeidswetgeving*. Deventer: Kluwer.

Bartley, Tim. 2003. "Certifying Forests and Factories: States, Social Movements, and the Rise of Private Regulation in the Apparel and Forest Products Fields." *Politics & Society*, 31 (3): 433–464.

Bartley, Tim. 2009. "Standards for Sweatshops: The Power and Limits of the Club Approach to Voluntary Labor Standards." In *Voluntary Programs: A Club Theory Perspective*, ed. Matt Potoski and Aseem Prakash, 107–131. Cambridge: MIT Press.

Börzel, Tanja A. and Risse, Thomas. 2005. "Public-Private Partnerships: Effective and Legitimate Tools of Transnational Governance." In *Complex Sovereignty: Reconstituting Political Authority in the 21st Century*, ed. E. Grande and Louis W. Pauly, 195–216. Toronto: University of Toronto.

Boström, Magnus. 2006. "Regulatory Credibility and Authority Through Inclusiveness: Standardization Organizations in Cases of Eco-Labeling." *Organization*, 13 (3): 345–367.

Clean Clothes Campaign (CCC). (2005). *Looking for a Quick Fix. How Weak Social Auditing is Keeping Workers in Sweatshops*. Amsterdam: CCC.

COSA. 2008. Seeking Sustainability: COSA Preliminary Analysis of Sustainability Initiatives in the Coffee Sector, http://papers.ssrn.com/sol3/papers.cfm?abstract_id=1338582. Accessed February 23, 2012.

Dicken, Peter. 2006. *Global Shift: Reshaping the Global Economic Map in the 21st Century*. London: Sage.

Egels-Zanden, Niklas and Wahlqvist, Evelina. 2007. "Post-Partnership Strategies for Defining Corporate Responsibility: The Business Social Compliance Initiative." *Journal of Business Ethics*, 70: 175–189.

Elliott, Kimberley Ann and Freeman, Richard B. 2003. *Can Labor Standards Improve Under Globalization?* Washington, DC: Institute for International Economics.

Esbenshade, Jill. 2004. *Monitoring Sweatshops: Workers, Consumers, and the Global Apparel Industry*. Philadelphia: Temple University Press.

Ethical Trading Initiative (ETI) (2006). *The ETI Code of Labor Practice: Do Workers Really Benefit?*, http://etiskhandel.no/Artikler/2317.html?l=en. Accessed December 11, 2012.

Fransen, Luc. 2011. "Why Do Private Governance Organizations Not Converge? A Political-Institutional Analysis of Transnational Labour Standards Regulation." *Governance*, 24 (2): 359–387.

Fransen, Luc. 2012a. *Corporate Social Responsibility and Global Labor Standards: Firms and Activists in the Making of Private Regulation*. New York: Routledge.

Fransen, Luc. 2012b. "Multi-Stakeholder Governance and Voluntary Programme Interactions: Legitimation Politics in the Institutional Design of Corporate Social Responsibility." *Socio-Economic Review*, 10: 163–192.

Fransen, Luc and Kolk, Ans. 2007. "Global Rule-Setting for Business: A Critical Analysis of Multi-Stakeholder Standards." *Organization*, 14 (5): 667–684.

Fransen, Luc, and Burgoon, Brian. 2012a. "A Market for Worker Rights: Explaining Business Preferences for International Private Labour Regulation." *Review of International Political Economy*, 19 (2): 236–266.

Fransen, Luc and Burgoon, Brian. 2012b. "Global Labor Standards Advocacy by European Civil Society Organizations: Trends and Developments." Presented at the International Studies Association annual conference, San Diego, April 1.

Frenkel, Stephen J. 2001. "Globalization, Athletic Footwear Commodity Chains and Employment Relations in China." *Organization Studies*, 22 (4): 531–562.

Gereffi, Gary, Humphrey, John, and Sturgeon, Timothy. 2005. "The Governance of Global Value Chains." *Review of International Political Economy*, 12 (1): 78–104.

Govekar, Michele A., Govekar, Paul L., and Rishi, Meenakshi. 2002. "The Effect of Macro-Economic Shocks on Corporate Philanthropy." *Journal of Economics and Politics*, 15(1): 1–11.

Hainmueller, Jens, Hiscox, Michael J., and Tampe, Maja. 2011. Productivity in Cocoa Farming in Ghana, October, http://www.people.fas.harvard.edu/~hiscox/papers.html. Accessed November 23, 2011.

Harvey, David. 2005. *A Brief History of Neo-Liberalism*. Oxford: Oxford University Press.

Hassel, Anke. 2008. "The Evolution of a Global Labor Governance Regime." *Governance*, 21 (2): 231–251.

He, Gaochao. 2012. "The Making of a Tipping Point: Changing of Labor Regime in Guang Dong, China." Paper presented at Global Worker Rights Workshop, Penn State University, March 30.

Jenkins, Rhys. 2002. "The Political Economy of Codes of Conduct." In *Corporate Responsibility & Labor Rights: Codes of Conduct in the Global Economy*, ed. Rhys Jenkins, Ruth Pearson, and Gill Seyfang, 13–30. London: Earthscan.

Kamau, Mercy, Mose, Lawrence, Fort, Ricardo, and Ruben, Ruerd. 2010. The Impact of Certification on Smallholder Coffee Farmers in Kenya: The Case of Utz Program, http://www.tegemeo.org/documents/work/WP47-The-Impact-of-Certification-on-Smallholder-Coffee-Farmers-in-Kenya-The-case-of-UTZ-program.pdf. Accessed March 26, 2011.

Kaplinsky, Raphael and Morris, Mike. 2001. A Handbook for Value Chain Research, http://www.srp-guinee.org/download/valuechain-handbook.pdf. Accessed December 11, 2012.

Khanna, Parag. 2009. *The Second World: Empires and Influence in the New Global Order*. New York: Random House.

Kinderman, Daniel. 2012. "The Neoliberal Politics of EU-Level Corporate Social Responsibility, 1995–2012." Presented at the International Studies Association annual conference, San Diego, April 1.

Klein, Naomi. 2000. *No Logo*. New York: Harper Collins.

Kocer, Ruya Gokhan. 2007. "Trade Unions at Whose Service? Coercive Partnerships and Partnership in Coercion in Turkey's Metal Sector." *Industrielle Beziehungen*, 14 (3): 245–269.

Kocer, Ruya Gokhan and Fransen, Luc. 2009. "Codes of Conduct and the Promise of a Change of Climate in Worker Organization." *European Journal of Industrial Relations*, 15 (3): 237–256.

Kolk, Ans. 2011. "Mainstreaming Sustainable Coffee." *Sustainable Development*, doi: 10.1002/sd.507.

Locke, Richard and Romis, Monica. 2010. "The Promise and Perils of Private Voluntary Regulation: Labour Standards and Work Organization in Two Mexican Factories." *Review of International Political Economy*, 17 (1): 45–74.

Locke, Richard, Kochan, Thomas, Romis, Monica, and Qin, Fei. 2007. "Beyond Corporate Codes of Conduct: Work Organization and Labor Standards at Nike's Suppliers." *International Labor Review*, 146 (1–2): 21–37.

Locke, Richard, Amengual, Matthew, and Mangla, Akshay. 2009. "Virtue Out of Necessity? Compliance, Commitment, and The Improvement of Labor Conditions in Global Supply Chains." *Politics & Society*, 37 (3): 319–351.

Marx, Axel. 2008. "Limits to Non-State Market Regulation: A Qualitative Comparative Analysis of the International Sport Footwear Industry and the Fair Labor Association." *Regulation and Governance*, 2 (2): 253–273.

Melish, Tara J. and Meidinger, Errol. 2011. "Protect, Respect, Remedy and Participate: 'New Governance' Lessons for the Ruggie Framework." In *Business and Human Rights at a Crossroads: The Legacy of John Ruggie*, ed. Radu Mares. Leiden: Martinus Nijhoff.

Merk, Jeroen. 2007. "The Private Regulation of Labor Standards: The Case of the Apparel and Footwear Industries." In *The Limits of Transnational Private Governance*, ed. Jean-Christophe Graz and Andreas Nölke, 115–125. London: Routledge.

Merk, Jeroen. 2008. "Restructuring and Conflict in the Global Athletic Footwear Industry: Nike, Yue Yuen and Labor Codes Of Conduct." In *Global Economy Contested: Power and Conflict Across the International Division of Labor*, ed. Marcus Taylor, 79–97. New York: Routledge.

Ngai, Pun. 2005. *Made in China: Subject, Power and Resistance in a Global Workplace*. Durham: Duke University Press.

Nolan-Garcia, Kimberley. 2010. "Enforcement By Design: The Legalization of Labor Rights Mechanisms in US Trade Policy." *Working Paper*. Centro de Investigacion y Docencia Economicas.

Oka, Chikoka. 2010. "Accounting for the Gaps in Labour Standard Compliance: The Role of Reputation-Conscious Buyers in the Cambodian Garment Industry." *European Journal of Development Research*, 22: 59–78.

O'Rourke, Dara. 2002. "Monitoring the Monitors: A Critique of PwC Labor Monitoring." In *Corporate Responsibility & Labor Rights: Codes of Conduct in the Global Economy*, ed. Rhys Jenkins, Ruth Pearson, and Gill Seyfang, 196–209. London: Earthscan.

O'Rourke, Dara. 2006. "Multi-Stakeholder Regulation: Privatizing or Socializing Global Labor Standards?" *World Development*, 34 (5): 899–918.

Potts, Jason, van der Meer, Jessica, and Daitchman, Jaclyn. 2010. The State of Sustainability Initiatives Review 2010: Sustainability and Transparency, http://www.iisd.org/pdf/2010/ssi_sustainability_review_2010.pdf. Accessed November 26, 2011.

Prakash, Aseem and Potoski, Matt. 2007. "Collective Action through Voluntary Environmental Programs: A Club Theory Perspective." *Policy Studies Journal*, 35 (4): 773–792.

Quack, Sigrid. 2010. "Law, Expertise and Legitimacy in Transnational Economic Governance: An Introduction." *Socio-Economic Review*, 8: 3–16.

Raynolds, Laura and Long, Michael. 2007. "Fair \ Alternative Trade: Historical and Empirical Dimensions." In *Fair Trade: The Challenges of Transforming Globalization*, ed. Laura Raynolds, Douglas Murray, and John Wilkinson, 15–29. London: Routledge.

Rodriguez-Garavito, Cesar A. 2005. "Global Governance and Labor Rights: Codes of Conduct and Anti-Sweatshop Struggles in Global Apparel Factories in Mexico and Guatemala." *Politics and Society*, 33: 203–233.

Ruben, Ruerd and Zuniga, Guillermo. 2010. "How Standards Compete: Comparative Impact of Coffee Certification Schemes in Northern Nicaragua." *Supply Chain Management: An International Journal*, 16 (2): 98–109.

Ruggie, John Gerrard and Kell, Georg. 1999. Global Markets and Social Legitimacy: The Case of the Global Compact, www.csmworld.org. Accessed March 15, 2003.

Sabel, Charles, O' Rourke, Dara, and Fung, Archon. 2000. Ratcheting Labor Standards: Regulation for Continuous Improvement in the Global Workplace, http://www2.law.columbia.edu. Accessed February 15, 2005.

Seidman, Gay. 2007. *Beyond the Boycott: Labor Rights, Human Rights, and Transnational Activism*. New York: Russell Sage Foundation.

TCC. 2012. The Tropical Commodity Coalition: Tea, Coffee, Cocoa, http://www. teacoffeecocoa.org/. Accessed March 16.

Utting, Peter. 2001. Regulating Business via Multi-Stakeholder Initiatives: A Preliminary Assessment, http://www.people.fas.harvard.edu/~hiscox/Utting.pdf. Accessed December 19, 2012. Accessed December 11, 2012.

Van Roozendaal, Gerda. 2002. *Trade Unions and Global Governance: The Debate on a Trade Clause*. London; New York: Continuum.

Vogel, David. 2005. *The Market for Virtue: The Potential and Limits of Corporate Social Responsibility*. Washington, DC: Brookings Institution Press.

Chapter 27

Global Private Governance

Explaining Initiatives in the Global Mining Sector

Hevina S. Dashwood

Introduction

At the start of the new millennium, it was considered news when students of global governance learned that there is a large and growing array of global private governance initiatives. Variously referred to as global private regimes, non-state market-based governance, industry self-regulation and/or corporate social responsibility (CSR), these private (non-state-based) initiatives have acquired considerable importance in the delivery of public goods at the local, national, regional, and global levels.

It is broadly understood that the phenomenon of global private governance is a product of globalization and the expanding transnational scope of corporate activities. Debates as to whether states find their regulatory capacity constrained through corporate control and a "new constitutionalism" (Gill 2002) or whether there has been a voluntary devolution of political authority on the part of states to other, non-state actors (Hall and Biersteker 2002; Grande and Pauly 2005), remain unresolved. It is often assumed that global companies are the most powerful actors, whether in negotiating global trade and investment rules or in negotiating the terms of their investments in developing countries with weak bargaining tools. Contrary to what might be expected, global companies are not necessarily the most powerful actors, and their economic power does not always translate into political power. The transnational activities of global companies, coupled with the transnational nature of complex problems such as environmental degradation, have produced "governance gaps" that states are unable to resolve on their own. Global companies need to be understood and studied as political actors in their own right (Avant, Finnemore, and Sell 2010; Fuchs 2007).

The Handbook of Global Companies, First Edition. Edited by John Mikler.
© 2013 John Wiley & Sons, Ltd. Published 2013 by John Wiley & Sons, Ltd.

In order to assess the potential benefits and drawbacks of private global governance, it is necessary to understand what is driving these activities. Motivations for private global governance are likely to vary from industry to industry, and from company to company. Broadly speaking, private companies will be induced to provide public goods if doing so will translate into private benefits for the company and/or industry as a whole (Prakash 2000). In addition to instrumental reasons, it is argued that global companies operate in a global normative framework, and are influenced by normative understandings of appropriate behavior (Dashwood 2011; Dashwood 2012). These normative understandings influence the standards that private companies establish for themselves and industry as a whole.

Since the 1990s, there has been an explosion of global private governance initiatives. Rather than attempt to account for them all, this chapter will provide an explanation for CSR adoption and industry-wide self-regulation in the global mining industry. Case studies of three major Canadian mining companies will be drawn upon as empirical evidence to support the arguments developed in this chapter. The companies, Noranda (now Xstrata), Placer Dome (now Barrick Gold) and Barrick Gold, were/are major players in the global mining industry. The core business activities of Noranda included zinc, copper, aluminum, and smelting, while Placer Dome and Barrick Gold concentrate primarily in gold mining.

This chapter argues that, contrary to the "race to the bottom" thesis, the forces of globalization and ensuing governance gaps have induced mining companies to collaborate to improve their environmental and social performance. Global companies play an important and necessary role in addressing governance gaps, from the global down to the local levels. Global companies pursue political strategies for a variety of reasons: to influence public policy, to stave off regulation, and/or to substitute for the lack of regulation. These strategies can be broadly typified as unilateral, where individual companies adopt CSR policies and practices, and collaborative, where companies initiate national and global industry-wide self-regulation. Companies engage with a wide range of global institutions to influence public policy, including international organizations, non-governmental organizations (NGOs), and industry associations. In doing so, global companies are in turn influenced by global normative developments that shape the industry standards adopted.

The next section will develop a conceptual and methodological framework for explaining unilateral CSR adoption and global collaborative private governance initiatives. A brief overview of the major developments in the global mining industry will then be provided, before applying the theoretical framework to an explanation of the strategies adopted to address reputational challenges confronting the global mining industry. Incentives to adopt voluntary unilateral initiatives on the part of individual companies will be examined, before turning to industry self-regulation through collaborative initiatives. The final section will summarize the key findings, and discuss their theoretical relevance.

Theoretical and Methodological Approach

It is argued that in order to understand/explain the processes and influences driving global private governance initiatives, and the forms they take, it is necessary to draw on theories from a range of disciplines. Institutional approaches provide a critical part of the explanation for why firms develop global private governance initiatives, and the processes by which they come about. A three-level institutional analysis is proposed, combining rational choice, historical, and "new" institutional approaches. Institutional analysis is coupled with insights from international relations theory on norms dissemination and the means by which particular self-regulatory practices become institutionalized (for detailed explication, see Dashwood 2012).

Consistent with institutional approaches, firms are understood to be embedded in a larger social environment beyond the marketplace, which induces them to conform to societal norms. As argued by Campbell (2006), institutional context has an important and even determining impact on firms' proclivity to address their environmental and social responsibilities. Institutions refer to governments, organizations, regulations, and political processes, but also have a broader understanding. Drawing on March and Olsen (1999), an "institution" is defined as a "relatively stable collection of practices and rules defining appropriate behavior for specific groups of actors in specific situations" (306), a definition that is similar in meaning to the understanding of norms employed within the constructivist literature in international relations theory (Finnemore 1996; Keck and Sikkink 1998).

In order to fully understand why and under what conditions firms seek to become more socially responsible, it is necessary to combine institutionalist and constructivist approaches (Campbell 2007). Rational choice institutionalism seeks to understand how institutions mediate or structure the choices made by rational actors (Hall and Taylor 1996). Rational choice institutionalism assumes that firms are instrumental actors which are motivated by the self-interested desire to maximize profits and shareholder value, as dictated by the institution of the competitive marketplace. Consistent with the rational choice approach, stakeholder theory argues that firms will factor in the interests of stakeholders. Stakeholder theory extends the realm of actors to whom firms are responsible, to include local communities affected by a firm's operations, the natural environment, NGOs, governments (all levels), the media, and industry associations (Donaldson and Preston 1995; Jacobs and Getz 1995; Sagebien and Lindsay 2011).

Historical institutionalism is concerned with how structure conditions responses to external constraints (Hall and Taylor 1996). Historical institutional approaches are useful here, because they emphasize the temporal ordering and timing of key developments (Thelen 1999: 388), and trace the unfolding of processes over time (p. 400). The concept of "critical junctures" found in historical institutional approaches helps to explain the coming together of external pressures that would bring about significant change in policy and practices, and induce industry to accept its social and environmental responsibilities. Critical junctures, "interaction effects between distinct causal sequences that become joined at particular points in time" (Pierson 2004), advance understanding about how changes in the external environment reach a critical threshold, thereby triggering significant change in institutionalized practices (Thelen 1999).

Institutional approaches in organization theory, including "new" institutionalism, point to structural dynamics that induce firms to mimic each other and adopt similar institutional forms (Powell and DiMaggio 1991). New institutionalism observes a tendency towards "isomorphism," where striking similarities in institutional forms, procedures, or symbols have been observed across organizational fields and nations (DiMaggio and Powell 1983; Powell and DiMaggio 1991; Scott and Meyer 1994).

The problem with institutional approaches that emphasize (or reify) structure, is that they tend not to be able to account for change in firm (or state) behavior, and minimize the role of agency, or choice, in influencing firm behavior (Hirsch and Lounsbury 1997). To understand this variation, dynamics internal to the firm (micro level) need to be factored into explanations of isomorphic outcomes (Heugens and Lander 2009). As noted by Crossan, Lane, and White (1999) and Cooksey (2003), individual policy entrepreneurs play a critical role in fostering a change of attitudes and practices (see also Flohr et al. 2010). Research employing this approach looks beyond external pressures and path dependency, in order to account for the variation in firms' responses (Halme 2002; Howard-Grenville 2006). Approaches that factor in agency, and dynamics internal to the firm (micro level), need to be factored into explanations of isomorphic outcomes (Heugens and Lander 2009).

Constructivist approaches in international relations theory draw our attention to evolving social norms at the global (or macro) level, and help to explain the process of norms dissemination at the global level, as well as how norms are internalized at the level of the firm (micro level). Global norms that reflect a global consensus on such matters as fundamental human rights or environmental preservation, once institutionalized in multilateral treaties, international organizations, and global industry associations, influence global companies. Global companies, even though profit-maximizing entities, are responsive to global normative developments (Dashwood 2007; Flohr et al. 2010). There is increasing recognition in international relations theorizing that not only states but also NGOs and multinational corporations play a role in shaping global norms (Flohr et al. 2010; Florini 2000). By integrating insights from institutional approaches, and constructivist accounts from international relations theory, this paper takes a multi-disciplinary approach by building on existing theory in order to provide a better explanation of the influences on unilateral CSR adoption and private global governance through industry self-regulation.

Major Developments in the Global Mining Industry

Significant structural changes in the global mining industry since the late 1980s have influenced unilateral and collaborative CSR adoption on the part of global mining companies. There have been substantial geographic shifts in exploration and development, away from traditional locations in the United States, Canada, and Australia, towards South America, the Asia-Pacific region, and Africa (Clark 1997). These developments were facilitated by the opening up of new investment opportunities in the developing world, brought about by the privatization of state-owned mining companies and changes to and/or enactments of mining laws designed to attract foreign direct investment (FDI). At the same time, major mining companies with headquarters in the advanced industrialized economies of Canada, the United States, Australia, the United Kingdom, and Japan encountered increased restrictions on their activities due to the strengthening of existing environmental regulation, and the introduction of new, stricter regulations.

The mining industry has benefited from increased demand in emerging economies such as India, China, and Brazil, leading to acceleration in the exploration and development of new mines in the 1990s. The strong demand from these countries for metals needed in the appliances, automobiles, and beverages industries, as well as for metals used in computers and cell phones, drove major mining companies' global expansion, and in the 2000s, prompted further structural changes through record levels of merger and acquisition activity. In addition to increased demand for iron ore, copper, zinc, silver, cobalt, nickel, lead, tin, and aluminum, the 2008 global financial crisis has ensured continued strong demand for gold, with record price increases.

Tightening environmental restrictions in developed countries might lead one to infer that major mining companies were attracted to developing countries because of lax or non-existent environmental regulation (the "race to the bottom" argument). It is argued here that major mining companies sought to strengthen CSR standards precisely because of regulatory deficiencies that produced governance gaps (see also Borzel and Risse 2010). As will be explained below, expansion into developing countries was coupled with growing public awareness and concern for environmental damage caused by mining. Serious environmental disasters brought damage to the entire industry, not just poor performers, inducing major mining companies to adopt unilateral CSR initiatives and to collaborate to promote industry-wide self-regulation.

Overview of Global Collaborative Initiatives

In 1991, major mining companies around the world established the International Council on Mining and the Environment (ICME), in order to address a range of challenges facing their industry. In the face of a growing and ever louder crescendo of opposition to mining, a number of CEOs of major mining companies launched in 1999 the Global Mining Initiative (GMI). The GMI's first major initiative was to conduct a two year study on the contribution of mining to sustainable development; the Mining Metals and Sustainable Development (MMSD) project (MMSD 2002). The other key initiative was to create in 2001 the International Council of Mining and Metals (ICMM), which replaced the ICME. Through the ICMM, sustainable development has been actively promoted as a means for mining companies to frame their CSR policies, and as the normative framework guiding initiatives to improve their performance.

Efforts to improve the industry's reputation through voluntary mechanisms can be seen to be a strategic response to external pressures and constraints. The unevenness in regulatory environments in many parts of the developing world where mining companies now operate pointed to the need for more effective efforts at industry-wide collaboration at the global level. The damage to mining's reputation due to negative publicity over major disasters and controversies and the external pressures experienced by mining companies from the advanced industrialized economies form the key elements of influences on the political strategies of major mining companies. By the mid-1990s, mining companies found their access to land, markets, and finance increasingly restricted.

Evidence from the Global Mining Industry

By the mid-2000s, most major mining companies with global operations had converged around the global norm of sustainable development as a means to frame their CSR policies and practices. Nevertheless, the process of arriving at this convergence reveals different responses in terms of the timing and degree of commitment to sustainable development on the part of major mining companies both between and within countries. In the early 1990s, a small number of mining and metals companies from the advanced industrialized countries began reporting on their environmental policies and practices (Yakovleva 2005). In all such countries, there were early movers and late movers in terms of the uptake and disclosure of CSR policies and practices (Dashwood 2012). As has been found in research on other industries, some companies are leaders in terms of their CSR policies and practices, while others are laggards (Campbell 2006: 926; Gunningham, Kagan, and Thornton 2003). By extension, not all mining companies were leaders in moving forward with global collaborative private governance initiatives. The three-level institutional analysis, when combined with constructivist insights, provides a complete explanation for unilateral CSR adoption and collaborative efforts at industry self-regulation.

Rational Choice Institutionalism

Rational choice institutionalism draws attention to the domestic institutional context that influenced the incentive structures of major mining companies. The institutional context in developed countries such as Canada, Australia, the United States, the United Kingdom, and Japan, where most major mining companies are headquartered, exerted pressure on mining companies to internalize the environmental and social costs of their operations (Jenkins and Yakovleva 2006). This pressure can be traced to the introduction of environmental and health and safety regulations in the 1970s, the tightening of these regulations in the 1990s, and the rising expectations of voting publics in these countries. The timing and nature of environmental regulations in these countries share common elements in terms of regulatory instruments (Yakovleva 2005).

The institutional context in developing countries is also salient to the explanation of CSR adoption and global collaboration in the mining industry. Regulatory deficiencies in developing countries, widespread poverty, and weak or non-existent protection for the rights of people in local communities affected by mining produced serious environmental and social challenges for mining companies investing there (Borzel and Risse 2010; Dashwood and Puplampu 2010). During the Cold War, mining companies might have negotiated with authoritarian regimes to deal with attendant opposition to their operations. With the end of the Cold War, and advent of political liberalization in many developing countries, NGO scrutiny and local community opposition made this strategy unviable for mining companies with long-term investments. The fact that companies must locate where the ore is, and lack mobility, make them vulnerable to community opposition. The need for a "social license to operate" (Gunningham *et al.* 2003) influenced CSR adoption on the part of mining companies operating in developing countries. As such, institutional context in both the advanced industrialized economies and developing countries where mining companies expanded their operations influenced unilateral CSR adoption.

Historical Institutionalism: The Critical Juncture

An important part of the explanation for CSR adoption and global collaboration is that mining companies were facing a crisis in the mid to late 1990s. Consistent with historical institutionalism, it is argued that the mining industry had reached a "critical juncture" as a number of distinct yet interrelated developments came together at this time to produce a crisis for the mining industry. The industry as a whole suffered from a bad image due to widely publicized mining accidents in the 1990s. The serious negative social impacts that can arise from mining led to protracted NGO activism against the industry. Coupled with these developments were changes to international environmental treaty law and the advent of "green conditionalities" attached to financing. The coming together of these developments negatively affected the mining industry's access to land, finance, and markets (see Dashwood 2012 for detailed explication).

New Institutionalism

Rational choice institutionalism expects that mining companies would respond in the same way to these broadly similar risks and constraints. "New" institutionalism in organization theory expects that firms will adopt similar institutional forms, and through isomorphic pressures, converge around similar practices and normative understandings. At one level, this has indeed occurred in the mining industry, as the overwhelming majority of major (and mid-tier) mining companies frame their CSR policies around the norm of sustainable development. However, mining companies did not all respond in similar ways, as some were early movers in terms of CSR adoption, and some were late movers. Furthermore, some, but not all major mining companies assumed a leadership role in promoting industry-wide self-regulation, through which the norm of sustainable development came to be accepted. Institutional approaches in organization theory can account for both isomorphic pressures within the industry (acceptance of the norm of sustainable development, similar internal organization changes, etc.), but also variation in terms of the timing and nature of individual mining companies' responses. As noted earlier, dynamics internal to the firm need to be factored into the explanation, to shed light on the thinking informing managerial actions and the role of managerial discretion. Analysis of individual firm responses is necessary to explain variation, which is provided in the next section through case study analysis of Noranda, Placer Dome, and Barrick Gold (the next section draws from Dashwood 2012).

Explanation of Unilateral CSR Adoption: Noranda, Placer Dome, and Barrick

Noranda

The influences on unilateral CSR adoption at Noranda, Placer Dome, and Barrick illustrate the explanatory relevance of the three-level institutional approach and highlight the variation as well as similarities in their response to external pressures to improve their environmental and social performance. As the first major mining company to begin issuing stand-alone CSR reports in 1990, and having instituted CSR policies and practices in the 1980s, Noranda was an early mover in CSR adoption (Dashwood 2012). Noranda's early mover status can be explained in part by a series of environmental disasters, which sensitized management to potential vulnerabilities for the company.

One influential development was the derailment in November 1979 of a large freight train carrying various chemicals in Mississauga, a city 20 kilometers from

Toronto. The train exploded because one of the tank cars carried propane, and a mass evacuation was ordered because some tank cars carried chlorine (other cars carried styrene and toluene). The evacuation of 218,000 people from the surrounding area made it the largest peacetime operation in North America until the New Orleans evacuation after Hurricane Katrina (Slack 2009). As a company that handles, produces, and transports dangerous chemicals, the resultant public outrage and questions about the safe transport of dangerous chemicals led Noranda management to adopt CSR policies and management systems.

The second significant incident was the chemical accident in 1984 in Bhopal, India, when a chemical spill at one of Union Carbide's plants led to thousands of deaths. Bhopal was the trigger that set in motion a major review and reform of Noranda's management systems. A third development which influenced thinking in Noranda was the 1989 Exxon Valdez oil spill. Exxon incurred huge costs as a result of the oil spill. As of 2008, Exxon had paid US\$3.4 billion in remediation, fines, compensation, and other costs (Anderson, Gold, and Bravin 2008: B10). The message brought home to senior management was that Noranda should seek to avoid such economic and legal risks, a clear business case for CSR adoption.

Placer Dome

Placer Dome can also be considered to be an early mover in CSR adoption relative to the industry as a whole. As had been the case with Noranda, the experience of operating mines in remote parts of Canada provided vital lessons that were incorporated into the development of Placer Dome's CSR policies. Institutional context in Placer Dome's Asia Pacific operations was also a very important influence on the company's approach to CSR. Leadership was crucial in projecting learnings from operational challenges in different locales into specific policies and practices. Management recognized that practices appropriate in one developing country location might not be completely transferable to other locations due to variation in local community dynamics. It was the responsibility of mine managers to institute specific practices relevant to their operational challenges.

When it began to seriously examine its CSR in the early 1990s, global developments, specifically the growing global consensus around the norm of sustainable development, influenced Placer Dome's approach to CSR. With headquarters in British Columbia, home of Greenpeace, management at Placer Dome witnessed first hand the growing strength and influence of the global environmental movement. The global momentum behind sustainable development informed the evolution of Placer Dome's CSR policies and practices, pointing to the importance of timing in influencing CSR adoption. The combination of internal leadership, receptiveness to global normative developments, and learning from experiences in specific institutional settings explains why Placer Dome was an early mover in CSR adoption framed around the norm of sustainable development.

Barrick Gold

Until the late 1990s, the majority of Barrick's operations were in the United States, with a small number of Canadian mines. As was the case in Canada, stricter regulations governing exploration, strong opposition to new mining projects, and no-go areas set aside for environmental preservation limited opportunities for expanding operations in the United States. The disaster at the Summitville mine (1991) in Colorado, involving a Canadian company, was an important development that drew public attention to continued irresponsibility on the part of the mining industry. In response to these developments, Barrick moved early to address its environmental responsibilities, with the creation of the VP, Environment position in 1995.

A key difference between Barrick and the other two companies is that it did not expand beyond North America until the late 1990s. Barrick sought to replicate its approach to community relations at its flagship Goldstrike mines in developing countries, with poor results. It took management a few years to start to seriously address the social side of its operations, by which time the stakeholder terrain was much more complex and (arguably) difficult than had been the case with Noranda and Placer Dome. Barrick expanded rapidly in the mid-2000s, and with the acquisition of Placer Dome in 2006, became the world's largest gold producer. As such, Barrick has come to be specifically targeted by NGOs critical of mining.

In the mid-2000s, Barrick implemented substantial internal organizational change and policy innovation across the full range of CSR. Leadership played an important role in influencing the timing of these transformative changes, but it is also the case that, by the mid-2000s, many global CSR standards affecting mining had become institutionalized through the ICMM and other institutions such as the International Finance Corporation (IFC). Evolving global CSR/sustainable development standards/norms have had a significant influence on Barrick's policies and practices. By the mid-2000s, collaborative efforts at industry self-regulation, such as through the ICMM, meant that major mining companies had to report according to a range of indicators in order to maintain/gain credibility with external stakeholders. In the mid-2000s, Barrick rapidly expanded its membership in a range of global voluntary programs. Until the decision to join the ICMM in 2006, Barrick, more so than Noranda and Placer Dome, had to adopt CSR standards already established by early movers such as Noranda and Placer Dome.

Explanation of Collaborative Global Private Governance Initiatives

Institutional approaches that focus on internal firm dynamics and the role of leadership help to explain why Noranda and Placer Dome were early movers and leaders in industry-wide self-regulation. Noranda and Placer Dome were very active both unilaterally and collaboratively in shaping global public policy affecting mining and minerals. Senior managers' proactive approach to external challenges influenced their thinking on the need to play a leadership role in promoting global collaboration to improve the industry's reputation. With the exception of its role in the development of the International Cyanide Management Code (ICMC), a standard specific to its gold business, Barrick did not become engaged in industry-wide collaboration until the mid-2000s. Indeed, Barrick pulled out of the ICMM in early 2002, rejoining in 2006 after the acquisition of Placer Dome.

Influences on Global Collaboration

By the early 1990s, Placer Dome, Noranda, and other leading mining companies recognized that the mining industry would need to coordinate its efforts at the global level, especially for the purposes of engaging with and influencing public policy in international organizations. Strategies employed by the industry to coordinate initiatives to influence public policy include consensus-building through multistakeholder engagement, international networking with other countries' industry associations and governments, international organizations and global environmental NGOs, and the promotion of voluntary agreements at the national and global levels. These strategies are similar to what individual mining companies were undertaking unilaterally and through national mining associations, especially the Mining Association of Canada (MAC) and the Australian Minerals Council (AMC) (Fonseca 2010; Sanchez 1998: 524–528).

The creation of the ICME in 1991 represented the mining industry's first effort to coordinate its activities at the global level. The ICME was established in part to coordinate the efforts of various national mining associations and to provide an institutional setting at the global level through which the mining industry's interests could be represented and strategic alliances with other resource-producing countries fostered. As a major player in the global mining industry, Canadian mining companies had a strong interest in global collaboration to provide an industry relationship with multilateral organizations that were involved in the global development of standards and regulations affecting mining. It is no coincidence, then, that the initial impetus behind the decision to launch a global industry association for mining came from Canada, specifically MAC, with key backing from Noranda.

Throughout the mid-1990s, the ICME gave high priority to market access issues. A key focus of activity was directed at the Basel Convention on the Control of Transboundary Movements of Hazardous Wastes and Their Disposal, which was negotiated to address concerns about the growing traffic and dumping of hazardous wastes into developing countries. In 1995, Basel Convention negotiators decided to ban the export of hazardous wastes (including those intended for recycling) from developed to developing countries (Decision 111/1). Given the inclusion of many metals in the Convention list of hazardous waste, the mining industry was greatly concerned about the effects on the metals recycling trade (ICME 1998: 3).

Although the ICME performed effectively within its mandate, it became apparent by the late 1990s that it was unable to counter the reputational crisis the industry was facing. The ICME was set up to address issues of a scientific/technical nature and was not well-equipped to address reputational issues. The communications function was to promote broad principles, rather than concrete standards for the industry. The ICME was primarily focused on influencing policy development affecting mining, through engagement with multilateral organizations such as the OECD and UNEP. The ICMM has focused less on policy and more on developing self-regulatory initiatives with a view to improving the industry's reputation (Dashwood 2012).

In December 1998, CEOs from nine major mining companies came to the view that a bold new initiative was needed to turn things around, leading to the launch of the Global Mining Initiative (GMI). Mining CEOs recognized that the industry was in danger of being "legislated out of business," and that it was necessary to re-position the mining industry (Dashwood 2012). Some more forward-thinking CEOs recognized that the industry had little credibility in the eyes of governments, NGOs, and international agencies and were cognizant of the fact that the industry's critics maintained control of the communications agenda (Cooney 2008). These CEOs perceived that the global mining industry was facing a crisis, and were concerned about the perceived loss of control of the global public policy agenda.

Under the leadership of Sir Robert Wilson, at that time CEO of Rio Tinto, the original group of companies included Noranda, Placer Dome, Anglo American, Western Mining Company (WMC), Codelco, BHP, (BHP subsequently merged with Billiton in 2001), Phelps Dodge (which pulled out in October 2002), and Newmont. Some of these companies were members of the Mining and Minerals Working Group of the WBCSD (for details, see ICMM 2005). The WBCSD was the organization of choice to spearhead the GMI. As Sir Robert Wilson noted, "I would say that the WBCSD has a voice and authority which is remarkably free of the taint of being a lobby group and is listened to seriously by governments, inter-governmental agencies and NGOs, as well as by industry" (WBCSD 2004).

From the initial meeting of the GMI in December 1998, the 2002 World Summit on Sustainable Development was top of mind, and the industry needed to prepare a position piece. The mining industry felt that at the Rio conference in 1992, mining had been mentioned only as a problem, because government representation had been by Environment Ministries (Dashwood 2012). Of further concern to mining companies was that NGOs were increasingly involved not just in setting the environmental agenda, but participating in decision-making in global fora, as became clear at Rio and in key organizations such as the World Bank. CEOs hoped to influence the agenda at the World Summit, and anticipated the need to have an industry position on sustainable development. In May 1999, to move forward on this task, members of the GMI launched the Mining, Minerals and Sustainable Development Project (MMSD).

The MMSD was a major program of participatory analysis and research whose key objective was to advance understanding about how the mining and mineral sector's contribution to sustainable development at the global, national, regional, and local levels could be maximized (Dashwood 2005; Sethi 2005). In late 2001, it was decided that the ICME be transformed into the International Council on Mining and Metals (ICMM), so as to provide a more effective organizational architecture that would strengthen industry representation, promote a more ambitious mandate than had been pursued by the ICME, and support the industry transition to sustainable development (McPhail 2008). (Politics were also a factor, as the ICME was headquartered in Ottawa, and the new ICMM is headquartered in London, headquarters of the spearheading company, Rio Tinto.) Significantly, the ICMM was granted a larger mandate to promote change than had been the case with the ICME (Dashwood 2012). Furthermore, the creation of the ICMM was meant to ensure that policy recommendations flowing from the MMSD would actually be acted upon.

In addition to the need to represent industry at the World Summit, the second immediate task of the ICMM was to provide representation for the mining industry at the World Bank's Extractive Industry Review (EIR) process (EIR: www.eir.com). The EIR was the direct result of pressure from some NGOs and governments, which felt that the GMI/MMSD had been too industry centric and that too much had been conceded to mining at the 2002 World Summit (Dashwood 2012). The mining industry was very concerned about the EIR process, fearing it was losing the agenda to NGOs. As a multistakeholder process, it was considered risky to treat governments as merely stakeholders, which were perceived by the mining industry to be largely absent in the decision-making process. The EIR was of particular concern, as some NGOs with representation (such as Greenpeace) were of the view that the Bank should not be lending to the extractive industry at all if prior and informed consent of the local communities affected by the operations had not been attained (Dashwood 2012). The fear that NGOs could indirectly influence regulations through their advocacy of tougher international standards for mining (Walde 2005) served as another incentive to form the ICMM.

The most important initiative launched by the ICMM is the Sustainable Development Framework (ICMM 2003). The ICMM defines sustainable development as "investments [that are] financially profitable, technically appropriate, environmentally sound and socially responsible" (ICMM 2003). Mining companies must adhere to the Sustainable Development Framework as a condition of membership.

The second major initiative of the ICMM is to establish reporting mechanisms for the mining sector, against which mining companies can report on their environmental, social, and economic performance (ICMM 2003). Although criticized for a variety of reasons, the GRI emerged as one of the foremost global standards for reporting on environmental and social performance (Fonseca 2010). In 2000, the GRI was revised to incorporate "sustainability" indicators ("G2") and in 2005, the third revised version was published ("G3") (GRI 2006). The ICMM worked with the GRI to prepare a separate mining and metals supplement, and to develop reporting indicators relevant to the mining industry, which was accomplished in 2005 (GRI 2007). The Mining and Metals Sector Supplement (MMSS) of the GRI was adopted by the ICMM in 2005 so as to provide a set of common indicators that could be uniformly applied across the industry (GRI 2006).

The third element of the Sustainable Development Framework is the commitment to independent third party assurance. Third party assurance is a condition of membership in the ICMM, but the problem has been finding a credible, independent assurance process recognized as legitimate by external stakeholders (a problem widely noted in the literature as applicable to all industries) (Fonseca 2010). To address this problem, the ICMM developed a pilot assurance procedure, based on AccountAbility's AA1000 standard and the global accounting industry's International Standard for Assurance Engagement (ISAE) ISAE3000 standard.

The AA1000AS standard was chosen for external verification of reports because it incorporates principles that are considered more inclusive and responsive to stakeholders' concerns (AccountAbility 2008; Fonseca 2010). Starting with reports published in 2010 for the 2009 reporting year, member companies are required to provide external assurance on both their commitment to the Sustainable Development Framework principles, as well as reporting in accordance with GRI guidelines (McPhail 2008). The mining industry is at the forefront of industry in reducing the information asymmetries inherent in industry reports to external stakeholders (Fonseca 2010). In a context where repairing reputation is a key motivating factor for ICMM members, the ICMM has been compelled to introduce increasingly stringent conditions of membership, culminating with the verifiable external independent assurance initiative.

At the global level, there are now a set of global voluntary standards that represent accepted practice for adherence to sustainable development in the industry. In addition to the Sustainable Development Framework and GRI Mining and Metals Sector Supplement developed under the auspices of the ICMM, a number of other initiatives developed outside the ICMM have acquired wide acceptance. Virtually all members of the ICMM have started to have their sites certified under ISO 14,001, an indication of the status of that environmental management standard as an accepted norm of business practice for major mining companies.

Other initiatives developed outside the ICMM have seen some up-take amongst members of the ICMM. The IFC Performance Standards (2006, revised 2011), for example, were the result of multi-stakeholder consultations with government, industry, and NGOs in the aftermath of the World Bank's Extractive Industry Review (EIR). Although not "voluntary" in the strict sense, some companies are adopting the Performance Standards as corporate policy, regardless of whether or not they have a particular project being financed by the Bank. Private financial institutions, through the Equator Principles, also uphold the Performance Standards. The Extractive Industry Transparency Initiative (EITI) is another example of a tri-partite initiative involving government, NGOs, and extractive companies. Once again, although "voluntary," once a government decides to join the EITI, mining companies must report the royalties paid to government. The Voluntary Principles on Security and Human Rights incorporates a tri-partite governance structure, and has become an important indicator of a company's ability to manage its human rights challenges, and respect human rights at its operations. The International Cyanide Management Code (ICMC) is voluntary, but involves a third party audit to certify compliance with Code requirements. Respect for human rights is the most recent normative development, as reflected in global consensus around the "Ruggie Framework" (Ruggie 2008).

Explaining Variation in Response to External Pressures

Why did some companies take on a leadership role in promoting industry-wide collaboration? As already noted, Noranda and Placer Dome had extensive external relations with a wide range of stakeholders, including governments, NGOs, international organizations, and national and global industry associations (this discussion draws from Dashwood 2012). Senior management recognized the need to manage external relations effectively, and to be able to keep abreast of evolving thinking on CSR, and to respond to issues as they emerged. Both companies saw the advantage of being proactive, rather than reactive, to shifting societal norms. Placer Dome sought to construct alliances with other institutions that have credibility around the world, such as international financial institutions, bilateral aid agencies, NGOs focused on economic development, social, and environmental issues, and with local communities. Such a strategy would not only improve the company's reputation through association with legitimate agencies, but allow it to continually acquire information and learn about emerging issues and shifting societal expectations. These extensive external engagements pre-disposed these companies to be leaders in promoting global collaboration towards industry self-regulation.

Barrick's approach to global collaboration can be contrasted with that of Placer Dome and Noranda. These companies' status as major mining companies, and the global scope of their operations, provided a strong incentive for them to address reputational issues through global collaboration. In Barrick's case, the lack of a global profile in the late 1990s/early 2000s and what at the time was still a modest position within the industry in terms of production, meant the incentives to participate in a global collaborative industry-wide effort were not as strong. Barrick assumed a leadership role in developing the International Cyanide Management Code (ICMC), an initiative specific to its business of gold mining, but stepped back from industry-wide collaboration after the ICME was replaced by the ICMM. Barrick joined the ICMM during the initial transition process, and then pulled out shortly thereafter (as did Inco, Codelco, and Phelps Dodge). Barrick was concerned about being involved in a venture where the ICMM's priorities were not deemed directly relevant to the company, and where there was likely to be little traction for the resources to be expended. Barrick was undergoing internal transition in 2001, having just merged with Homestake mining company, and did not want its limited resources to be spread too thin.

Having stepped away from the ICMM, what influenced Barrick's decision to re-join the organization? Although the immediate impetus behind Barrick's re-joining the ICMM was the membership inherited from Placer Dome, there are a variety of factors that influenced the decision. A major factor was the change in staffing and management at Barrick as it enhanced its organizational competency around CSR. The appointment of Greg Wilkins as CEO in 2003 served as a catalyst for formalizing existing CSR activities, implementing organizational change, and adopting new CSR initiatives. Those within Barrick who might have resisted joining came to recognize the case for re-joining the ICMM. Membership in the ICMM provided the potential for cross-fertilization of best practices, where Barrick could learn from its peers, rather than re-inventing the wheel when entering new jurisdictions. At the same time, Barrick wanted to contribute to the ongoing development of standards and add its expertise based on the experience acquired from its own operations.

As a relative newcomer in terms of engaging in industry collaboration through the ICMM, Barrick was more of a "taker" of voluntary standards developed by the industry (with the exception of the International Cyanide Management Code). Dynamics internal to the firm are clearly relevant in explaining the company's change of heart, but Barrick management has also had to align its policies with leading global CSR standards applicable to mining as well as to growing public expectations. As such, once private governance standards are institutionalized globally, through the processes outlined above, isomorphic pressures become more important. Barrick's need to align its CSR with global industry standards, and to participate directly in global industry collaboration, demonstrates the importance of both structure and agency, as well as timing, in explanations of unilateral CSR adoption and global collaboration.

Conclusion

This chapter has demonstrated that global mining companies have employed a range of unilateral and collaborative strategies in order to respond to the reputational crisis they encountered. In the process of executing these strategies, major mining companies sought to influence, and were influenced by, participation in international organizations, through engagement with NGOs and with other stakeholders.

Efforts to improve the industry's reputation through voluntary mechanisms can be seen to be a strategic response to external pressures and constraints. The unevenness in regulatory environments in many parts of the developing world where mining companies now operate pointed to the need for more effective efforts at industry-wide collaboration at the global level. Rational choice institutionalism advances the explanation of why it was mining companies from the advanced industrialized economies which began to adopt unilateral CSR policies and promote collaborative initiatives in the 1990s. The damage to mining's reputation due to negative publicity over major disasters and controversies and the external pressures experienced by mining companies from the advanced industrialized economies form the key elements of the critical juncture faced by the mining industry in the mid to late 1990s. By the mid-1990s, mining companies found their access to land, markets, and finance increasingly restricted. The critical juncture faced by the industry set the stage for new initiatives to address the industry's reputational problems. Institutional approaches in organization theory shed light on the convergence that occurred around the global norm of sustainable development, as well as the thinking informing managerial actions and the role of managerial discretion.

The critical juncture faced by the industry set the stage for new initiatives to address the industry's reputational problems. Still, it was not a foregone conclusion that mining companies would take action; the willingness of some major mining companies to assume a leadership role explains the major push from the late 1990s. What was critical was the perception on the part of some company CEOs that the industry had reached a crisis, which induced leading companies to step outside the ICME process by launching the GMI. The growing global presence of major mining companies put the spotlight on social and environmental performance in developing countries with weak regulatory frameworks. The industry recognized the need to address and minimize externalities associated with its operations in responding to NGO pressure and public concerns.

The variation in firm responses to common external pressures confirms the salience of managerial discretion and leadership, and the need to look at dynamics internal to the firm. Using the examples of Noranda, Placer Dome, and Barrick, this chapter explains how managers interpret pressures in their external environment in order to understand the differences in response and strategy. Ultimately, isomorphic pressures brought Barrick in line with other major mining companies, as evidenced by management's decision to re-join the ICMM and by extension, accept the ICMM's Sustainable Development Framework. Social structural determinants are therefore important, but are not a sufficient part of the explanation for Barrick's actions. Pressure from an increasingly complex stakeholder terrain contributed to a shift in attitudes discernible within the mining industry as a whole regarding acceptance of environmental and social responsibilities, together with evidence of responsiveness to the global norm of sustainable development.

This chapter has shown that expansion into developing countries did not lead to a race to the bottom. Major mining companies, facing serious reputational problems, and vulnerable to withdrawal of local community support for their operations, were motivated to collaborate to improve the performance of the industry as a whole. The hope was that good performers could be differentiated from bad performers, and that the bad behavior of a few would not negatively affect the industry as a whole. In this regard, the establishment of ever-stricter standards for the global mining industry continues to be a work in progress.

Although there may be features unique to the mining industry, the importance of institutional context in explaining the influences on global private governance initiatives would suggest that explanations of why and how global companies collaborate globally should be grounded in institutional analysis. The three-level institutional approach elaborated in this chapter provides a potential framework for explaining the how and why of industry collaboration to develop standards that meet global companies' economic, environmental, and social responsibilities. When blended with constructivist insights on the dissemination of global norms, a more complete explanation can be provided that incorporates the extent to which global companies respond to global normative developments.

References

AccountAbility 2008. *AA1000 Assurance Standard 2008*. London: AccountAbility.

Anderson, Mark H., Gold, Russell, and Bravin, Jess. 2008. "Supreme Court Rules Exxon Valdez Payout." *Globe and Mail: Report on Business*, June 26. Toronto: B10.

Avant, D., Finnemore, M., and Sell, S. 2010. *Who Governs the Globe?* Cambridge: Cambridge University Press.

Borzel, Tanja and Risse, Thomas. 2010. "Governance Without a State: Can It Work?" *Regulation & Governance*, 4: 113–134.

Campbell, John L. 2006. "Institutional Analysis and the Paradox of Corporate Social Responsibility." *American Behavioural Scientist*, 49 (7): 925–938.

Campbell, John L. 2007. "Why Would Corporations Behave in Socially Responsible Ways? An Institutional Theory of Corporate Social Responsibility." *Academy of Management Review*, 32 (3): 946–967.

Clark, Allen L. 1997. "Emerging Challenges and Opportunities for the Minerals Industry in the 21st Century." Fifth Annual Asia-Pacific Mining Congress, Jakarta.

Cooksey, Ray W. 2003. "'Learnership' in Complex Organisational Textures." *Leadership and Organizational Development Journal*, 24 (4): 201–214.

Cooney, Jim. 2008. "Sustainable Mining and the Oil Sands." Paper presented at the Alberta Environment Conference, Calgary.

Crossan, Mary, Lane, Henry, and White, Roderick. 1999. "An Organizational Learning Framework: From Intuition to Institution." *Academy of Management Review*, 24 (3): 522–537.

Dashwood, Hevina S. 2005, "Canadian Mining Companies and the Shaping of Global Norms of Corporate Social Responsibility." *International Journal*, 60 (4): 977–998.

Dashwood, Hevina S. 2007. "Canadian Mining Companies and Corporate Social Responsibility: Weighing the Impact of Global Norms." *Canadian Journal of Political Science*, 40 (1): 129–156.

Dashwood, Hevina S. 2011. "Sustainable Development Norms and Self-Regulation in the Mining Sector." In *Corporate Social Responsibility and Governance Ecosystems: Emerging Patterns in the Stakeholder Relationships of Canadian Mining Companies Operating in Latin America*, ed. Julia Sagebien and Nicole Marie Lindsay, 31–46. New York: Palgrave Macmillan.

Dashwood, Hevina S. 2012. *The Rise of Global Corporate Social Responsibility: Mining and the Spread of Global Norms*. Cambridge: Cambridge University Press.

Dashwood, Hevina S. and Puplampu, B.B. 2010, "Corporate Social Responsibility and Canadian Mining Companies in the Developing World: The Role of Organizational Leadership and Learning." *Canadian Journal of Development Studies*, 30: 175–196.

DiMaggio, Paul and Powell, Walter. 1983. "The Iron Cage Revisited: Institutional Isomorphism and Collective Rationality in Organizational Fields." *American Sociological Review*, 48: 147–160.

Donaldson, Thomas and Preston, Lee E. 1995. "The Stakeholder Theory of the Corporation: Concepts, Evidence and Implications." *Academy of Management Review*, 20 (1): 65–91.

Finnemore, Martha. 1996. *National Interests in International Society*. Ithaca: Cornell University Press.

Flohr, Annegret, Rieth, Lothar, Schwindenhammer, Sandra, and Wolf, Klaus Dieter. 2010. *The Role of Business in Global Governance: Corporations as Norm-Entrepreneurs*. New York: Palgrave Macmillan.

Florini, Ann, ed. 2000. *The Third Force: The Rise of International Civil Society*. Washington, DC: Japan Center for International Exchange and Carnegie Endowment for International Peace.

Fonseca, Alberto. 2010. "How Credible Are Mining Corporations' Sustainability Reports? A Critical Analysis of External Assurance under the Requirements of the International Council on Mining and Metals." *Corporate Social Responsibility and Environmental Management*, 17: 355–370.

Fuchs, Doris. 2007. *Business Power in Global Governance*. Boulder: Lynne Rienner.

Gill, Stephen. 2002. "Constitutionalizing Inequality and the Clash of Globalizations." *International Studies Review*, Summer: 47–65.

Global Reporting Initiative (GRI). 2006. *Sustainability Reporting Guidelines: Version 3.0*. Amsterdam: Global Reporting Initiative.

Global Reporting Initiative (GRI). 2007. Mining and Metals Sector Supplement, Amsterdam: Global Reporting Initiative, www.globalreporting.org. Accessed June 10, 2010.

Grande, Edgar and Pauly, Louis W. 2005. *Complex Sovereignty: Reconstituting Political Authority in the Twenty-first Century*. Toronto: University of Toronto Press.

Gunningham, Neil, Kagan, Robert A., and Thornton, Dorothy. 2003. *Shades of Green: Business, Regulation, and Environment*. Stanford: Stanford University Press.

Hall, Peter and Taylor, Rosemary. 1996. "Political Science and the Three New Institutionalisms." *Political Studies*, 44: 936–957.

Hall, Rodney Bruce and Biersteker, Thomas J. 2002. *The Emergence of Private Authority in Global Governance*. Cambridge: Cambridge University Press.

Halme, Minna. 2002. "Corporate Environmental Paradigms in Shift: Learning During the Course of Action at UPM-Kajaani." *Journal of Management Studies*, 39 (8): 1087–1109.

Heugens, Pursey and Lander, Michel. 2009. "Structure! Agency! (and Other Quarrels): A Meta-Analysis of Institutional Theories of Organization." *Academy of Management Journal*, 52 (1): 61–85.

Hirsh, Paul and Lounsbury, Michael. 1997. "Ending the Family Quarrel: Toward a Reconciliation of 'Old' and 'New' Institutionalisms." *American Behavioral Scientist*, 40: 406–418.

Howard-Grenville, Jennifer A. 2006. "Inside the 'Black Box': How Organizational Culture and Subcultures Inform Interpretations and Actions on Environmental Issues." *Organization and Environment*, 19 (1): 46–73.

International Council on Metals and the Environment (ICME).1998. *ICME Newsletter*, 6, 2.

International Council on Mining and Metals (ICMM). 2003. About ICMM: Work Programme, www.icmm.com/our-work. Accessed December 9, 2012.

International Finance Corporation (IFC). 2006. Performance Standards on Social and Environmental Sustainability, IFC, www.ifc.org/wps/wcm/connect/topics_ext_content/ifc_exte rnal_corporate_site/ifc+sustainabillity/publications/publications_handbook_pps. Accessed December 9, 2012.

Jacobs, David and Getz, Kathleen. 1995. "Dialogue on the Stakeholder Theory of the Corporation: Concepts, Evidence, and Implications." *Academy of Management Review*, 20 (4): 793–795.

Jenkins, Heledd and Yakovleva, Natalia. 2006. "Corporate Social Responsibility in the Mining Industry: Exploring Trends in Social and Environmental Disclosure." *Journal of Cleaner Production*, 14: 271–284.

Keck, Margaret E. and Sikkink, Kathryn. 1998. *Activists Beyond Borders: Advocacy Networks in International Politics*. Ithaca; London: Cornell University Press.

March, James and Olsen, Johan. 1999. "The Institutional Dynamics of International Political Orders." In *Exploration and Contestation in the Study of World Politics*, ed. Peter Katzenstein, Robert Keohane, and Stephen Krasner. Cambridge, MA: MIT Press.

McPhail, Kathryn. 2008. "Contributing to Sustainable Development through Multistakeholder Processes: Practical Steps to Avoid the 'Resource Curse'." *Corporate Governance*, 8 (4): 471–481.

MMSD (Mining, Minerals and Sustainable Development). 2002. Breaking New Ground: Mining, Minerals and Sustainable Development, London, International Institute for Environment and Development (updated December 6), http://www.iied.org/mmsd-final-report. Accessed December 9, 2012.

Pierson, Paul. 2004. *Politics in Time: History, Institutions, and Social Analysis*. Princeton; Oxford: Princeton University Press.

Powell, Walter and DiMaggio, Paul, eds. 1991. *The New Institutionalism in Organizational Analysis*. Chicago: Chicago University Press.

Prakash, Aseem. 2000. *Greening the Firm: The Politics of Corporate Environmentalism*. Cambridge: Cambridge University Press.

Ruggie, John Gerard. 2008. Protect, Respect and Remedy: A Framework for Business and Human Rights. Report of the Special Representative of the Secretary-General (SRSG) On the Issue of Human Rights and Transnational Corporations and Other Business Enterprises, UN Doc. A/HRC/8/5, www.unhcr.org/refworld/docid/484d2d5f2.html. Accessed February 10, 2010.

Sagebien, Julia and Lindsay, Nicole Marie, eds. 2011. *Corporate Social Responsibility and Governance Ecosystems: Emerging Patterns in the Stakeholder Relationships of Canadian Mining Companies Operating in Latin America*. New York: Palgrave Macmillan.

Sanchez, Luis E. 1998. "Industry Response to the Challenge of Sustainability: The Case of the Canadian Nonferrous Mining Sector." *Environmental Management*, 22 (4): 521–531.

Scott, Richard W. and Meyer, John W., eds. 1994. *Institutional Environment and Organizations: Structural Complexity and Individualism*. Thousand Oaks: Sage.

Sethi, S. Prakash. 2005. "The Effectiveness of Industry-Based Codes in Serving Public Interest: The Case of the International Council on Mining and Metals." *Transnational Corporations*, 14 (3): 55–99.

Slack, Julie. 2009. Derailment Changed our History, November 10, www.mississauga.com/news/article/161133-train-derailment-changed-our-history. Accessed October 3, 2011.

Thelen, Kathleen. 1999. "Historical Institutionalism in Comparative Politics." *American Review of Political Science*, 2: 369–404.

Walde, Thomas. 2005. "International Standards: A Professional Challenge for Natural Resources and Energy Lawyers." In *International and Comparative Mineral Law and Policy: Trends and Prospects*, ed. Elizabeth Bastida, Thomas Walde, and Janeth Warden-Fernandez, 219–247. The Hague: Kluwer.

World Business Council for Sustainable Development (WBCSD). 2004. Interview with Sir Robert Wilson, Geneva, September 2, www.wbcsd.org/plugins/DocSearch/detailsasp?type=DocDet&objectid=N2EwNg. Accessed May 16, 2012.

Yakovleva, Natalia. 2005. *Corporate Social Responsibility in the Mining Industries*. Aldershot; Burlington: Ashgate.

Chapter 28

Will Business Save the World?[1]

Simon Zadek

Introduction

Tomorrow's history will judge whether companies will prove to be the troubled but all-important titans of our age, or more like a flotilla of Titanics, grand projects floating us off on our last, fateful journey. Separating these competing futures is whether a new generation of businesses can invert today's logic in internalizing costs as a systemic means of creating value.

Societies through the ages have collapsed because their elites, acting in pursuit of power and privilege, have been able to protect themselves for too long against the negative impact of their own actions (Acemoglu and Robinson 2012; Diamond 2006). Business exemplifies this pattern in prospering by externalizing the costs of their gains onto others despite clear evidence that the effects are degenerative and unsustainable (IPCC 2007). This is not a matter of malevolence or misdemeanor. Our business leaders are doing what is expected of them, to externalize costs since the law does not dictate otherwise, and in fact demands such practice as a fiduciary responsibility (Zadek *et al.* 2005). Beyond the law, it just makes good financial sense for individual businesses to remove from their profit and loss accounts social and environmental costs that do not generate adequate value, placing them firmly on societies' balance sheets to cope with the consequences.

Positively, there are signs of such an inversion for some externalities, driven by an assortment of price, policy, and regulatory signals as well as some measure of customer preferences. And there are exceptional companies that lead the charge of sustainability, companies that attempt to reinvent themselves according to the principles of "true cost."[2] The business benefits, from brand to cost efficiencies, employee motivation, and refocused innovation and product development, are often real and on occasion material. Yet such exemplary cases remain small-scale and

The Handbook of Global Companies, First Edition. Edited by John Mikler.
© 2013 John Wiley & Sons, Ltd. Published 2013 by John Wiley & Sons, Ltd.

ad hoc. There are few instances to date of such leadership radically reshaping the value creation equation of an entire sector or even market segment.

Negatively, are the headwinds of vested business and associated political interests that seek to prevent a transition away from today's profitable and politically palatable status quo towards a more sustainable pathway (Greenpeace 2011). Needless to say, highly profitable externalization is often a source of damage and destabilization, from the impacts of soda drink on the incidence of obesity and diabetes to the climatic effects of coal-fired energy generation. The simple fact is that tens of trillions of dollars are invested in carbon-intensive or otherwise damaging business models. It is understandable that investors and businesses alike are keen to avoid such assets becoming "stranded" due to regulatory or other changes in their operating environment. Understandable but not acceptable, argued Sir Nicholas Stern in a highly critical article of the financial community in the *Financial Times* during the global climate negotiations in Durban, South Africa, in December 2011. Investor behavior cannot be tolerated; he argued, that pricing carbon at zero in their analysis and investment decision is effectively betting on an increase in global temperatures in exchange for higher short-term financial rewards that puts our collective future in doubt.

Our challenge is one of systemic change, and addressing it effectively is proving to be tough going. Optimists and pessimists battle over the meaning of the historical evidence and tomorrow's potential. Yet in seeking to convince, most simply miss the point. Just as there are inspiring examples of directionally positive change, there are predatory institutions run by mean-spirited leaders. Amplifying the good and blunting destructive behavior can make a difference, but only at the margin. The unrelenting rise in bribery and corruption across the world is endemic, and attempts to dampen it through building "islands of integrity" have frankly failed. Overconsumption, similarly, is the aggregation of billions of daily, individual acts – yet as Vice President Al Gore pointed out at the acceptance speech of his Nobel Prize for his contribution to the climate agenda, no one seriously believes that unsustainable consumption can be effectively combated by engaging each person, one by one in a process of grassroots re-education (WEF 2012a).

The Civil Corporation Revisited

Business is a major vector of change, or its lack thereof, although it is only one piece of the puzzle alongside an increasingly complex array of actors. Businesses' growing power, and so potential to make a difference, one way or another, has catalyzed a generation of reflection, theory, and practice. Corporate responsibility, business and sustainability, and business in society are just three of the array of labels and movements under which such reflection has evocatively interacted with active experimentation (Schmidheiny 1992; Zadek 2007). Driven principally by mid-North Atlantic values, interests, and institutions, this flurry of innovation has spread across the globe, framed by the potential of securing a peaceful pathway of transformation of business to forms that secure, if not champion, sustainability.

Business will of course neither save the world nor destroy it (Korten 1995). This is altogether the wrong lens through which to examine the situation. We should try to understand, rather, how best to shape a political economy that can help us survive, and hopefully more than survive, through this century and beyond. To that end, the question arises as to *what kind of business institutions* are needed to serve our collective interests? And closely associated to this question, to ensure that any principled declarations on the first bear some relationship to our historic context and likely pathway, is the question of *whether we are on track in generating such business institutions?*

My own understanding of these questions and their companion answers has evolved since the early 2000s. The opening lines of *The Civil Corporation*, finalized in early 2000, focused on specific businesses degrees of freedom to act, and enabling capabilities:

> Judging and ultimately guiding corporate performance requires an examination of whether a business is *doing what it can do* given its range of external options and internal competencies. Internally, this concerns the formal, explicit policies and processes, organizational cultures and values, and patterns of leadership. Externally, this is a question of the multitude of business drivers, from direct, short-term market pressures through to longer-term strategic challenges and opportunities.
>
> A business's contribution to sustainable development therefore needs to be understood in terms of its viable options and what it makes of them. Internal and external factors together create a spectrum of possibilities at any point in time – that define a corporation's practical scope for making decisions between viable choices. Whether and how a corporation acts within its degrees of freedom must be the test of responsibility, and indeed the basis on which management decisions are framed.
>
> These are the fundamentals of the *civil corporation*. A corporation that is said to be civil is understood here as one that takes full advantage of opportunities for learning and action in building social and environmental objectives into its core business by effectively developing its internal values and competencies. (Zadek 2001)[3]

Reflecting five years later in a new introductory chapter to the second edition of the same book, my argument focused more on the tougher issue of accountability as compared to the softer processes of engagement and collaboration, and the linkages between business accountability and the broader political economy:

> Extending accountabilities of business place it and the state increasingly on a par with each other in key respects. We see a convergence in their legitimacies despite their very different historical foundations, one in security, mediation and political representation and the other through their production of material needs and returns to finance capital. Such a convergence is accelerated by several factors, including the declining legitimacy of traditional electoral routes to the politics of representation, the emerging political empowerment of citizens through their roles in markets, notably as owners of capital, and the growing prevalence and visibility of complex partnerships involving public and private actors tasked to deliver public and indeed private goods. (Zadek 2007)

Today, some further years on, my tone has become perhaps more urgent and my message more propositional than reflective. Yet my focus on accountability and engagement has remained, as has my interest in the connections between business and political governance and accountability:

> A "public fiduciary" would replace the current, narrow focus of corporate governance of optimizing solely in favor of financial stakeholders. The dominant corporate governance model for publicly listed companies, broadly the Anglo-Saxon approach, would be overturned in favor of a pluralistic approach where corporate directors' fiduciary responsibility required them to address financial and broader sustainability outcomes ... Governance innovations in the investment community under this more disrupted scenario would mirror those of the wider business community. (Zadek 2012b)

This chapter builds on this evolution in arguing that we are entering a new phase of the debate and practice on the role of business in society. After decades in the political and economic wilderness, the matter of the role of the state, and the ownership and associated governance of business in pursuit of public as well as private purpose is once again moving center stage. In the West and its intellectual allies, the shift is tentative, battling against an entrenched neoliberal posture regarding the efficiency and sanctity of private capital and the profit motive. Elsewhere, practice is in a sense more advanced, emboldened by a shift in the global terms of trade in favor of commodities, the politically powerful exemplar of China's dominant state-owned enterprises, and the growing power of sovereign wealth funds and other state-controlled investment vehicles.

The challenge and opportunity for those concerned with sustainable development and therein the role of business, is to engage with and seek to shape this historic shift, rather than assuming its transience and irrelevance through backward-facing analyses and presumptive conclusions.

Coming in from the Cold

Sustainability has come in from the cold after decades of wandering on the edges of civil society, informed scientific evidence and the odd, in fact decidedly odd, business (Zadek et al. 1997). Economics, as a corollary to this development, has become an increasingly integral part of the sustainability debate. This is evident in the report of the UN Secretary General's High-Level Panel on Global Sustainability, co-chaired by South African President Jacob Zuma and Finnish President Tarja Halonen (UN 2012).[4] Launched in early 2012 as an appetizer to the UN Rio+20 event, the Panel's clear message concerned the need to get the economics right if we are to secure a sustainable pathway, highlighting in particular the need for financial market reform.

Translating this renewed focus on the economics into action has, however, proved challenging at every level. There is no better example of this than the current contestation of the "green growth" agenda, portrayed by many public intellectuals and political leaders from emerging nations as presaging another cycle of economic hegemony of the north over the south (BASIC Expert Group 2011; SID 2012).[5] Such challenges, whilst often posed polemically, clearly have some merit. Unequal starting points in terms of technological, institutional, and financial endowments will certainly contribute in generating unequal outcomes in any systemic transition to a greener economic pathway. The unwillingness of developed nations to substantively share the burden of such a transition has all but frozen the multilateral agenda and associated international institutions. The combination of claims of historic culpability, the painful implications of the user-pays principle, the economic hang-over being experienced in Europe and the United States, and the driving challenge of a burgeoning global middle class laying claim to their material rights, makes for a toxic context by any measure (Zadek 2011b).

That said, a growing global debate towards sustainability has been far more than rhetoric. Investment in clean energy reached a new record of US$260 billion in 2011, almost five times the total of US$53.6 billion in 2004 (Bloomberg New Energy Finance 2011).[6] Planned Chinese investment in green over its 12th Five Year Plan (to 2015)[7] is expected to include US$450 billion on environmental protection, US$457 billion on renewable energy and a further US$600 billion on smart grids.[8] At the enterprise level, companies like General Electric, Nike, and Nestlé are pushing the envelope on value chain design, technologies, products and services, citizen interface, and policy engagement. Companies like Nike have managed effectively to turn around their compliance challenges of the 1990s to become widely acknowledged sustainability leaders (Zadek 2004). General Electric has converted its profile from one resisting any engagement in the clean-up of the highly polluted Hudson River into one exemplified by its "ecomagination" portfolio of low-carbon, energy-efficient products. Nestlé has overcome the negative impacts of being the target of the world's longest running anti-corporate campaign because of its alleged mis-marketing of baby milk to become a global corporate leader in advancing improved nutrition and better water management practices.

Sustainability, furthermore, is no longer, if it ever was, just the business of incumbent companies (WEF 2012b; Zadek 2010). The "Global 100" is a reputable sustainability rating of the world's largest companies, with each year's selection drawn from a global sample of about 3500 stocks.[9] In 2005, its first year, the index counted just three companies outside of Europe and North America, all Japanese. The most recent Global 100, however, included 24 companies with headquarters outside of the North Atlantic zone of which 9 were from Brazil, India, Singapore, South Africa, and South Korea. Of the Dow Jones Sustainability Index's 19 "super sectors" analysis, 4 out of the 19 companies were from home countries outside of Europe and North America.

Sustainability and competitiveness, furthermore, is increasingly a matter for nations as well as companies. Innovative work since the early 2000s on "Responsible Competitiveness" provided the world's first quantitative measure of nations' progress in embedding sustainability at the heart of their competitiveness strategies and practices (Zadek et al. 2003; Zadek 2006a). More recently, the World Economic Forum has augmented its annual Global Competitiveness Index – the most authoritative international ranking of nations' competitiveness – nations' management of natural and social wealth. Seven new quantifiable variables: health, primary education, social cohesion, environmental policy, resource efficiency, management of renewable resources, and environmental degradation were added into a methodology already packed with data on more traditional measures of economic health (WEF 2011).[10]

The impact on national rankings of introducing these new measures as drivers of long-term competitiveness has been in many instances dramatic. Some of the traditional winners in competitiveness rankings remain on top, notably the Nordic countries and Switzerland, celebrated for their progress in de-coupling growth from natural resource use and carbon emissions. Other long-time leaders such as the United States have fallen down the rankings because of perceived risks to their long-term competitiveness associated with their extensive environmental footprints, weak investment in public infrastructure, and weak records of investment in human capital. Some newly emerging, economic powerhouses, notably China and India, have dropped when such factors, including institutional robustness and measures of corruption, have been taken into account. Other countries, notably Brazil, have been placed higher on the Sustainable Competitiveness Index when these factors have been taken into account as compared with their standard competitiveness ranking.

Stuck in the Valley of Death

Start-up companies have the "Valley of Death" as the most dangerous moment in their development. This is the moment between proof of concept and the beginning of mass production and significant sales. It is the place where most dreams perish in the face of conservative capital markets that doubt an entrepreneur's abilities to beat the competition (Zadek 2011c).

Sustainability has reached its own valley of death. After two decades of intense activities, we have excellent data on the nature and scale of the problem, an abundance of cases of successful experiments, and the growing attention of political and business leaders. Yet we cannot leverage our insights, resources, and passion to contain our production of carbon, manage the scarcity of water, or dampen the speculative fluctuations in the price and availability of basic foodstuffs. De-materialized products, rentalized markets, renewable power, and sustainability standards are amongst the social innovations that have provided inspiration and advances in offering consumers greener choices. Yet whilst our call to arms has been for transformation, we are, in practice, celebrating incremental changes in the spirit of increasingly desperate optimism.

The real challenge is not just to move in the right direction. Rather, the challenge is to move quickly enough to scale in changing direction so as to materially affect large-scale outcomes. Today's reality is that eco-services continue to be dramatically over-exploited. Furthermore, there are no signs of this changing quickly enough to prevent many eco-systems from collapse, from the extinction of all-important bee populations to extreme water scarcity becoming the norm for not millions but billions of people. A report by the United Nations Principles for Responsible Investment estimates that annual environmental costs from global human activity already amounted to US$6.6 trillion in 2008, equivalent to 11% of global GDP.[11] UNICEF estimates that 22,000 children die each day of avoidable diseases, one every four seconds, roughly the time it took to read this sentence.[12]

Scale is something today we know a lot about – in selling mobile phones, going to war, watching the World Cup, or in catalyzing fundamentalism in its many forms. Our US$70 trillion global economy is powered by US$210 trillion of financial assets; over five billion mobile phones are in circulation with penetration rates rising by 35%

each year; and over a period of just two weeks in August 2008, 4.7 billion people (70% of the world's population) tuned in to watch the Beijing Olympics on television. Business, the world's most fashionable vehicle of change over recent decades across richer nations, can in quick time sell billions of packets of crisps, tens of millions of cars, and millions of handguns. If the price is right, businesses can innovate, produce, and deliver, and citizens will turn out en masse and do the right thing, namely buy.

But the logic of the business community has, to date, limited its ability to deliver sustainability-aligned products and services at scale. Today's backward-facing markets, in the main, only reward companies for doing the right thing on the margin. The World Economic Forum's Global Sustainable Competitiveness Index confirms the common sense view that healthy, competitive economies in this century require an effective management of social and natural wealth. Unfortunately, these new measures of sustainable competitiveness are not describing what *is* the case today, but which countries would be more competitive *if* sanity prevails. Bangladesh today has amongst the world's most competitive apparel exporters, in the main by paying their workforce remarkably little, and co-opting the government into marginalizing, often violently, unions and civil society organizations seeking to advance labor rights. South Africa's mining industry, still a mainstay of the economy, remains competitive thanks to cheap energy produced by especially low quality coal. And the Nordic countries and Switzerland achieve their high sustainability status by excluding off-shored pollution. It is estimated that almost one quarter of China's carbon emissions are associated with its exports, particularly to Europe and North America (Pan and Forgach 2011).

Even for the optimist, "more" is not enough (Zadek 2008). The need to achieve speed-to-scale forces us to reject today's trajectory as a gradualist pathway *at best*. We need to revisit, and if necessary reinvent, the matter of change drivers.

The Life and Times of Civil Regulation

Much has been written about the drivers of modern-day "corporate responsibility," with most lists including changes in information technology, relative proportions of intangible over intangible assets of major corporations, the new demands on the legitimacy of business in the face of privatization, the collapse of the Soviet Union, and the advent of globalization. Most lists, however, at least in recent times, have been topped by the role of civil society.

Civil society has always sought to influence markets and re-shape their impact (Edwards 2011; GACCC 2011; Zadek 2011a). Contemporary experience should be appreciated in that context, but it must also be explored for its specific forms and outcomes. Since the late 1980s, the landscape of civil society engagement with business has been transformed. There are many more, and more diverse, civil society actors, and more extensive and intimate engagement between what historically were oppositional forces. Civil society strategies and tactics to affect the drivers of change have in this context become more diverse, and more complicated, from traditional public pressure through to stewardship partnerships, and processes of active co-design with business, and even co-investment and co-production of innovative products and processes with potential for more benign societal impacts.

The modern phenomenon of "civil regulation," civil society acting to change market rules through direct pressure rather than the traditional route of lobbying for statutory changes, was born out of a particular moment in corporate development and broader political history (Zadek 2007). Neoliberal economic policies implemented during the 1980s undermined the social contract between business and Western societies, a fragmentation that was reinforced because the feared counter-point of the Soviet Union could no longer be invoked. At the same time, a rapid shift in the locus of economic value from production up the value chain towards the brand, marked out a period of remarkable success for Northern-based corporations across global markets. This in turn was driven in particular by the ethos of privatization that opened markets up and at the same time further fractured the underlying social contract that was mediated by the State. Simultaneously, the rise of the Internet and the capacity of relatively resource-poor civil society organizations to mobilize media-friendly action was matched by the emergence of the first generation of multinational NGOs such as Oxfam and the World Wide Fund for Nature, which mirrored the rise of their corporate counterparts as had labor unions in the early development of industrial capitalism (Sogge 1996).

Civil regulation, and so the modern advance of "corporate responsibility," has largely relied on corporations' sense of brand vulnerability, correlated closely to oligopolistic markets, an ironic empirical turn for theorists focused hitherto on the downsides to consumers of highly concentrated markets (Zadek 2000). Intangible assets represented just 5% of the market capitalization of the FTSE250 in 1978 but had risen to 72% by 2005, an extraordinary shift that left benefiting corporations struggling to understand and manage these quixotic assets (Interbrand 2006). As a result, businesses over this period increasingly yielded to civil society demands. Campaigning was founded on several iconic cases, including Shell's reversal of its decision to sink the Brent Spar Oil Platform in the North Sea in the face of a media-savvy Greenpeace campaign, and the anti-Nike sweatshop campaigns that, to some, demonstrated all that was wrong with globalization and capitalism in general (Zadek 2004). In some instances, real damage was done by these actions, reinforcing the view for a time that campaigns of almost any form were a potentially lethal force. In most instances, fearful corporations did not wait to find out if civil campaigns would translate materially into market responses and asset valuations.

Over the years, the cut and thrust world of civil regulation has in many spheres matured into a more organized social contract between business and civil society. The World Wide Fund for Nature exemplifies this development, leading the way in creating global partnerships with individual corporations, including high-profile agreements with, for example, the Coca Cola Company and the French cement giant, Lafarge. Labor activists have joined with their erstwhile corporate targets in forming international, multi-company initiatives such as the Ethical Trading Initiative and the Fair Labor Association. Human rights activists and anti-corruption groups have joined forces with mining companies in the Extractive Industries Transparency Initiative and the Voluntary Principles on Security and Human Rights. And health activists sit together with the world's largest pharmaceutical companies through the Global Alliance for Vaccines Initiative (GAVI) and other multi-billion dollar partnerships designed to deliver health services to poor communities.

Today, there are hundreds of initiatives that together have created a "soft governance web," spread across every market and issue from nanotechnology to fish (Zadek 2006b). These initiatives have sought to reshape markets by blending voluntary rules for business to follow, public and private finance, and the combined competencies of civil society, business, and government in delivering innovative designs and implementation practices. Some of these initiatives have achieved significant market penetration. The Marine Stewardship Council, for example, covers 10% of the global wild fish catch, and the Equator Principles cover more than 80% of cross-border project investments. Such collaborative ventures have influenced the broader political narrative about public policy and international development.

Civil society has and does transform how business is done, of that there is no doubt. Just as black South Africans boycotted white businesses during Apartheid, so Chinese consumers vilified and abandoned French-owned shops, at least temporarily, when French President Sarkozy met with the Dalai Lama in December 2008. Nestlé, Nike, McDonald's, and Shell have joined a long list of global businesses that have visibly yielded to the perceived threat of damage to their cherished brand values created by targeted campaigns by community groups, environmental and human rights organizations, and labor unions. Such actions have clearly made a difference. Greater corporate transparency, new codes of conduct, a mainstream profession of social auditing that was considered exotic in the 1990s, and collaboratively developed standards on everything from sustainable forestry to Internet privacy have shaped corporate practices and improved the lot of workers in global supply chains, communities located around mining operations, indigenous groups protecting their bio-homes, and endangered species from whales to tree frogs. It is no longer possible to be a Western mainstream consumer brand to not commit to labor and environmental standards down one's global supply chain, just as it would be tough for any major Western financial institution funding major infrastructure projects not to sign up to the Equator Principles.

These new forms of collaborative governance, at least in their initial formulation, have succeeded in overcoming old impasses and embedding improved practices amongst market leaders. Yet it has rarely generated the level of transformational change required to address the challenges at stake. The Marine Stewardship Council is rightly proud that its certification covers 10% of the world's wild fish catch, but would be the first to agree that global fish stocks continue to plummet. Many anti-corruption initiatives have emerged, similarly, under pressure from civil society, governments, and sometimes business itself, including the Extractive Industry Transparency Initiative, the World Economic Forum-sponsored Partnership Against Corruption Initiative, and initiatives driven by single institutions such as Transparency International and the Soros-backed Revenue Watch Institute. But corruption continues unabated, and most measures suggest a steady increase. In Nigeria alone, hundreds of billions of dollars in oil revenues since the 1960s have been stolen.

Civil regulation has achieved a great deal in moving leading market players to adopt improved social and environmental practices. Yet after more than two decades of action by a more globalized, more professionalized, and more technologically empowered civil society, one must conclude that the scale of ambition has not been met by the scale of impact (Zadek 2006b). More profoundly, the underlying basis on which profit is largely made, through the externalizing of costs onto the shoulders of others, has changed very little. After all this global action on business accountability, the financial sector was still able to impose history's largest-ever exercise in "taxation without representation" during the crisis of 2009, destroying trillions of dollars of wealth in the process, accumulating trillions more in public debt, and putting tens of millions of people out of work. Yet despite the weight of public anger that resulted from the financial crisis, there has been an extraordinary accountability failure in bringing those responsible to book, and scant regulation to prevent a recurrence of unseemly rent taking in the context of asymmetrical risks.

Corporate capture of the political and regulatory process in many countries prevents such excesses being penalized, let alone the underlying dynamics been subjected to serious scrutiny and change. One recent report concluded that the financial sector in the United States invested more than US$5 billion in political influence purchasing in Washington since the early 2000s, a pattern confirmed in recent research published by the International Monetary Fund. A global climate deal, similarly, was not forged in Copenhagen in 2010, mostly as a result of the actions of several thousand corporate lobbyists in Washington, DC, who successfully buried what might have been the last opportunity for concerted action on climate management, in exchange for a few additional percentage points in share values and short-term profits.

Civil regulation in its diverse forms has been a major driver in contemporary shifts in how business has dealt with social and environmental externalities. Several decades into this experience, however, whilst seeing the real and positive effects, one must conclude that large-scale shifts have not been forthcoming, let alone systemic changes in the nature of economy and business. The weaknesses in the Occupy movement, now painfully apparent, illustrate the challenges in civil society action at scale to address scale. Whilst continued civil action is to be encouraged, therefore, there is a need to seek alternative change drivers.

Towards an Extensive Accountability

Businesses' embrace of sustainability is often framed as a matter of the need for "more" accountability. Surely, the argument runs, if the problem is too many negative externalities, then more accountability will address this problem – make them pay, whether in cash or legal liabilities – and like Pavlov's dog, they will come to heal and mend their ways. The challenge, however, is not so simple. One view, perhaps perversely on the surface, is that there is *inadequate* effective accountability to traditional accountability holders, particularly investors. Core to the argument is that the ultimate beneficiaries of shareholdings are citizens whose interests extend to the wider impacts of business (Davis *et al.* 2006). The failure of these interests to influence business behavior, by this argument, lies in the demonstrable passivity of these citizens in the face of powerful, rent-taking, intermediaries, notably fund managers (Zadek *et al.* 2005). Better informed and suitably empowered beneficiaries of business investments would, so the argument runs, insist on reforming the behavior of investees, i.e. companies that create negative externalities.

Opposing this view is the argument that businesses' traditional accountability holders, investors, are much too empowered for our common good. After all, publicly listed companies do not externalize negative costs because they are not accountable to their shareholders, but precisely because they are all-too focused on maximizing financial returns to these particular accountability holders. The way forward, according to this argument, is to weaken the power of financial investors in favor of other stakeholder interests. Reinforcing this argument is the evidence that short-termism has come to be an endemic flaw in capital markets, biasing fund managers' behavior towards competitive trading rather than investing in the underlying economic assets (Haldane 2011). Paul Polman, Unilever's Chief Executive, is, for example, one of a growing number of business leaders who have moved their companies away from quarterly reporting, citing short-termism as having a destructive impact on the ability to invest for the long term (Graham *et al.* 2005). Yet the level of corporate capture of the political process does not allow for such a broadening of accountability to be achieved through better regulation. What is needed, so the argument runs, is a more pluralistic set of accountabilities embedded in corporate governance arrangements.

Contested here are the relative merits of intensive and extensive accountability (Donahue and Zeckhauser 2005; Zadek 2006b). Intensive accountability provides a narrower basis for any organization to determine its performance model, and so its approach to its governance. If accountability is intensively focused on financial investors, the performance model, subject to the law, then concerns the maximization of risk-adjusted financial returns, and the governing process must ensure that the organization acts on behalf of financial investors by effectively implementing the associated performance model. If on the other hand the basis of accountability is more extensive, such as in the case of many public interest organizations, then the performance model is more complex in having to address multiple objectives. Governance is therefore also more extensively focused, with a mission-aligned approach that might require balancing the interests of many stakeholders with diverse interests.

"Corporate responsibility" in its modern form has been predicated on the intensive accountability of most businesses, especially publicly listed companies, to shareholders with a predominantly financial interest. In its modern form this approach is associated with the failure in the 1970s and 1980s of advocates of renewed economic nationalization or a shift in international corporate governance towards more pluralistic accountability structures. Tony Blair, after all, was successful in having the critical clause in the British Labour Party Constitution calling for the common ownership of the economy removed in 1995, two years before being elected to office,[13] as did Nelson Mandela in the equivalent commitment by the ANC to turn its face on nationalization before South Africa's first post-Apartheid elections in 1994.[14] Instead, a more technical trench warfare has been taking place focused on definitions of materiality, public disclosure, and the rights of minority shareholders that has significantly increased accountability to non-financial shareholders in some countries, despite the resilience of the underlying Anglo-Saxon model of a narrowly defined fiduciary responsibility to financial capital.

This incremental, tactical approach to squeezing the last ounce of public good out of the Anglo-Saxon model of corporate governance may come to be seen as a side-skirmish, or at least as an appetizer to more fundamental shifts that may accompany the growing importance of emerging economy businesses and governments. Core to this shift is the extensive role of the State in the ownership of economic assets in these countries. Today state-owned oil and natural gas companies, such as Saudi Aramco, Petróleos de Venezuela, and China National Petroleum Corp., own 73% of the world's oil reserves and 68% of its natural gas.[15] Similarly, in 2008, state-owned share of global mining production value amounts to about 24% (Raw Materials Group 2011). According to the Inter-American Development Bank, the percentage of state ownership in the banking industry globally by the mid-1990s is over 40%. The BRIC countries – Brazil, Russia, India, and China – contain nearly three billion of the world's seven billion people, or 40% of the global population. The BRICs all make heavy use of public sector banks, which compose about 75% of the banks in India, 69% or more in China, 45% in Brazil, and 60% in Russia.[16]

International consensus remains that state-owned enterprises are necessarily poor performers, both in financial and broader sustainability terms. Yet the evidence is mixed. It is the case, certainly, that publicly listed majors do outperform their equivalent Chinese state-owned competitors. But the comparison is generally unbalanced. Rio Tinto for example, has been a global mining operation since the middle of the nineteenth century, whereas Chinalco is a far more recent entrant onto the world's stage. Furthermore, a dip into the global mining company's not-so-distant past reveals behavior that matches the worst of that of the new, state-owned players. Exemplary experiences of state-owned enterprises, notably in the cases of Norway, Chile, and Botswana, are generally dismissed by opponents of state-ownership as arising under exceptional circumstances. Yet in the world's fastest growing and most competitive market, China, such conventional wisdoms are being challenged. Cheryl Automotives, a state-owned enterprise, is now fifth in the hotly contested Chinese automotive market. Shanghai Electric is challenging global leaders such as Japan's Mitsubishi and Marubeni in bidding to build new coal-fired power plants around Asia. China's two state-owned shipbuilding giants, China Shipbuilding Industry Corporation and China State Shipbuilding Corporation, are expanding rapidly and beginning to catch up with their Korean and Japanese competitors in terms of technology (Dyer and McGregor 2008).

Classical state ownership of enterprises is, however, only one of several routes through which public interest is being asserted in the matter of business through ownership and governance. Sovereign wealth funds, especially those of China and the Middle East, are rapidly growing in number and size, broadly expected to grow in assets under management from their current level of US$4 trillion to more than US$7 trillion over the course of this decade, powered by a combination of high commodity prices and concentrated trade surpluses. Whilst still representing only a modest fraction of the overall size of today's global capital markets, these funds punch well above their weight during this current period of unstable capital markets, recapitalization seeking companies and countries, and under-priced assets. Recent moves by the Norwegian and Qatari state-owned funds to block the merger of Xstrata and Glencore illustrates what is likely to be a major trend in financial markets going forward, the power of the state. National and regional development banks are another source of state-controlled investment, and are increasingly active in international markets, including increasingly the huge, state-owned development banks in emerging economies, such as the China Development Bank and Brazil's BNDES.

At a smaller scale, but with significant potential, is the emerging debate and practice of extended social enterprises in developed economies, notably the United States. "Corporation 2020," a US-based initiative, exemplifies this trend, having gathered leading practitioners from around the world in a large-scale co-design exercise focused on modeling the corporations needed for a sustainable future.[17] A parallel but aligned initiative, again in the United States, has been the enactment of legislation to allow companies to register as "B" Corporations that establishes fiduciary arrangements enabling and encouraging multiple accountability holders and interests to be considered in the process of corporate governance.[18] With 500 business registered under this regulatory framework worth an annual US$3 billion in revenues, this experiment is clearly still small change. Yet both Corporation 2020 and the B Corporation approach are indications of what the United States does best, experimenting in possible futures.

Last but not least is the emerging practice of governing public-private partnerships. Diverse in their forms, functions, and scope, what they hold in common is a mandate to address a blend of private and public interests. This common feature has in turn driven a generation of experiments in how best to govern such blended and at times conflicting interests. Over time, some of these partnerships have become effectively permanent features of our institutional landscape, including many of the larger global health partnerships such as the Global Fund[19] and GAVI,[20] and the growing number of global sustainability standards initiatives stewarded by partnerships, such as the Forest Stewardship Council and the Extractive Industries Transparency Initiative (Litovsky *et al.* 2007; Potts *et al.* 2010). Whilst rarely if ever conceived of as experiments in new forms of corporate governance, there is no doubt that in practice these partnership governance experiences provide one of the richest sources of data on how blended interest institutions can in practice be governed (Zadek and Radovich 2006).

Towards a Public Fiduciary

Business in society is an unfolding experience, responsive to many historic factors, coincidences, unintended consequences, and unexpected innovations and sources of inspiration and leadership. Today's historic context includes, first and foremost, the consequences of a century of cheap, under-priced eco-system services, and since the middle of the twentieth century an era of an unprecedented combination of cheap capital and cheap labor. As we tiptoe into this century, we face the "end of cheap," not least with the prospect of another three billion consuming middle class by 2030 and a further three to five billion people rightly aspiring to equal rights to the environment and material well-being. This, with the addition of the actual and expected impacts of climate change, and the painful foretaste of water scarcities to come, has driven the environment into center stage as a forcing mechanism to rebuild our business community and the political economies within which they exist.

Alongside this disciplining context is an equally seismic shift in global leadership. Obviously, China and other major emerging economies top the ranks of tomorrow's likely leading nations, together with a small number of other resource rich nations from Mongolia to Canada. Less obvious at this stage is what their leadership might bring with it. Positively, the signs are that China in particular will embrace the environmental dimensions of the sustainability agenda, both for survivalist reasons, and to provide an enabling moral narrative to its global rise to power (Keely and Zheng 2012; Zadek *et al.* 2013). Unclear, but beyond the scope of this paper, are the implications for the broader political economy, and specifically for the fate of core procedural aspects of European-style democracy. Less grand, but crucially important nevertheless, is the re-emergence of the "developmental state" as an economic actor, first and foremost with renewed interest in economic and industrial planning and as part of that, as described above, an enlarged role in the ownership and guidance of strategic enterprises.

This context provides the stage on which the role of business in society is being reinvented. The recent, specific evolution of "corporate responsibility" can only be understood, and its implications reasonably considered, with this context in mind. That is, this evolution has been until now an embedded feature of the rise of neoliberalism in the West combined with the growing importance of intangible assets and an internet-empowered civil society. Going forward, however, its future trajectory will be greatly informed by the economic consequences of environmental boundaries, notably flourishing commodity prices, and the leadership of new nations with very different political economies and in particular views of the role of the state in economic affairs.

Taken together, these factors speak to a shift in our understanding and practice of the fiduciary framing of corporate behavior. In today's corporate world, a fiduciary duty is a legal or ethical relationship of confidence or trust regarding the management of money or property between two or more parties (UNEP 2009). Most commonly, this duty exists between two parties, the principal or intended beneficiary in the relationship, and the fiduciary or agent that acts on the principal's behalf. Framed in these terms, our dilemma regarding business in society is when the principal does not have the capacity to exercise effective oversight over the fiduciary. Today, this is understood to be in exceptional circumstances where the principal is for example a child or disabled or in some other way deemed "unable to act effectively on her or his own behalf." In such instances, there is in many countries the provision in law to allow for a "public fiduciary," essentially a public official or agency appointed to serve as guardian, conservator, or personal representative for those individuals or estates with no one else willing or capable of serving.

A public fiduciary is, then, a helpful frame for understanding the shift from an intensive to a more extensive basis of accountability baked into the fiduciary rules and processes, rather than only the broader legal limitations to the pursuit of financial gains. Asserting the imperative for establishing a public fiduciary is the governing equivalence of demanding that negative social and environmental externalities be internalized into the strategic purpose of the business. The governance of the evolution of business in society can therefore be framed in terms of *"the need to build a 'public fiduciary' to represent those voices not able to represent themselves, notably natural capital and today's excluded communities and future generations."*

There is perhaps no greater sacrilege in the world of corporate governance than to propose the politicization of the governing process. Indeed, many if not most civil society activists in the area of corporate accountability would likewise opt for a reassertion of "the state as gamekeeper and the business as poacher" approach rather than seek to institutionalize a broader fiduciary goal for business. Yet the facts do get in the way of such conservatism, irrespective of its merits. Civil regulation has advanced to some degree a de facto development of extensive accountability. These developments, although broadly positive, are however increasingly and problematically at odds with the de jure rules of the game that dictate an intensive focus on shareholders. Argued here is that the second wave of corporate responsibility, largely driven from emerging nations will, unintentionally and using different mechanisms, further deepen extensive accountability in the practice of corporate governance. Crucially, they will take us to the next stage in realigning the formal rules of corporate governance with such a development.

Framed thus, whilst there is an interesting debate to be had as to whether this is a good direction to pursue, there is a critically important debate as to how best to shape a directional shift which is already in motion. Certainly, there is a mixed and often disappointing historical record of nationalized companies. And there is little doubt that political and bureaucratic, discretionary intrusion into the affairs of state-owned and controlled enterprises can have poor outcomes by almost any measure. Furthermore, the possible negative implications of a stronger, developmental state on the political space for civil society to act are very real, and arguably already apparent from China to Russia, and from South Africa to Brazil, raising the likelihood of real trade-offs in the power and influence of different candidates for steward of the public fiduciary (Zadek, 2011a). There is, not to put too fine a point on it, no *a priori* argument that supports the case that state intervention in the economy necessarily improves economic, let alone social and environmental outcomes.

That said, there is also evidence of good and indeed excellent practice in both state-owned enterprises, and more broadly in enterprises with significant state control. Furthermore, experiments such as B Corporation and new forms of partnership governance all point to the potential for us living through the early stages of a paradigm shift. More than anything else, what is pushing this is the problem of today's capital markets, the need for a radical change in asset allocation for the public good, and the apparent limits as to what can be achieved by the bullying and seduction of private enterprise into a wider consideration of its impact on society. Certainly some progress has and can continue to be made in establishing policies and regulations that internalize businesses' negative externalities, but in practice such progress is severely constrained by the lack of autonomy of the state in the face of aggressive corporate and other special interest lobbying.

Conclusion

Today's business community is simply unable to deliver the required level of public goods from its historically embedded means of creating private value. The challenge, to reiterate this key point, is not "to make progress," but to make it rapidly and at scale, something that today's arrangements make difficult, if not impossible. This community will be our collective Titanic unless we change the rules of the game. Three decades of contemporary "corporate responsibility" have made a difference, as are surging commodity prices and other regulatory and civil pressures. But it has not been enough, and is unlikely to be so on current trajectories. Macro-forces of history, only apparently disconnected from the matter of business in society, may catalyze us to a new and more productive pathway, or else may prove unhelpful in repeating at scale mistakes of the past. Business may yet adapt, or be adapted, to a radically different set of needs and pressures, and carry us forward on its shoulders as Titans.

What will be the balance between these opposing forces and implications is not a matter of theory, but of practice. Furthermore, past practice can only partially inform us as to what might happen, let alone what is possible or desirable. As always, the systematization of knowledge to inform decision-making is challenging at the leading edge of change. What is possible, however, is to consider the limits of what is and can be achieved with the current array of actors, tools and indeed values. With this in mind, it becomes possible to enlarge our understanding of today's historical context of the changing role of business in society, and in particular the role of new and newly empowered actors, and the implications for the modalities and pathways that are likely to be central going forward.

Notes

1 This chapter is an adapted version of Zadek (2012a), "Titans or Titanic: Towards a Public Fiduciary," published in a 2012 Special Issue of the *Professional and Business Ethics Journal*, 31 (2): 207–230, released at the Annual Symposium of the European Academy of Business in Society in July 2012.

2 http://www.trucost.com/, accessed December 19, 2012.

3 Italics in original text.

4 http://www.un.org/gsp/, accessed December 19, 2012.

5 http://www.unrisd.org/80256B3C005BCCF9/search/C3584FE61B5EAD60C12579BF004D3B40?OpenDocument, accessed December 19, 2012.

6 http://www.newenergyfinance.com/, accessed December 19, 2012.

7 http://en.wikipedia.org/wiki/Five-year_plans_of_the_People%27s_Republic_of_China#Twelfth_Guideline_.282011.E2.80.932015.29, accessed December 19, 2012.

8 http://www.huffingtonpost.co.uk/intelligence-squared/londons-policy-on-climate_1_b_1019007.html, accessed December 19, 2012.

9 http://www.global100.org/, accessed December 19, 2012.

10 http://www.weforum.org/content/pages/sustainable-competitiveness, accessed December 19, 2012.

11 http://www.trucost.com/news/100/putting-a-price-on-global-environmental-damage, accessed December 19, 2012.

12 http://www.globalissues.org/article/715/today-21000-children-died-around-the-world, accessed December 19, 2012.

13 http://en.wikipedia.org/wiki/Clause_IV, accessed December 19, 2012.

14 http://en.wikipedia.org/wiki/Nelson_Mandela, accessed December 19, 2012.

15 http://energyseminar.stanford.edu/node/403, accessed December 19, 2012.

16 http://the-tap.blogspot.com/2012/03/state-owned-banks-create-better.html, accessed December 19, 2012.

17 http://www.corporation2020.org/, accessed December 19, 2012.

18 http://www.bcorporation.net/, accessed December 19, 2012.

19 http://www.theglobalfund.org/en/, accessed December 19, 2012.

20 http://www.gavialliance.org/, accessed December 19, 2012.

References

Acemoglu, Darin and Robinson, James. 2012. *Why Nations Fail: The Origins of Power, Prosperity and Power*. London: Profile Books.

Basic Expert Group. 2011. *Equitable Access to Sustainable Development: Contribution to the Body of Scientific Knowledge*. Beijing; Cape Town; Mumbai: Basic.

Bloomberg New Energy Finance. 2011. *Who's Winning the Clean Energy Race*. New York: Bloomberg.

Collier, Paul. 2011. *The Plundered Planet: How to Reconcile Prosperity with Nature*. London: Penguin Books.

Davis, Stephen, Lukomnik, Jon, and Pitt-Watson, David. 2006. *The New Capitalists: How Citizen Investors Are Reshaping the Corporate Agenda*. Boston: Harvard Business School.

Diamond, Jared. 2006. *Collapse: How Societies Choose to Fail or Succeed*. London: Penguin Books.

Donahue, J.D. and Zeckhauser, R. 2005. "The Anatomy of Collaborative Governance." In *The Oxford Handbook of Public Policy*, ed. Michael Moran, Martin Rein, and Robert E. Goodin, 496–525. Oxford: Oxford University Press.

Dyer, Geoff and McGregor, Richard. 2008. "China's Champions: Why State Ownership is no Longer Proving a Dead Hand." *Financial Times*, March 16.

Edwards, Michael. 2010. *Small Change: Why Business Won't Save the World*. San Francisco: Berrett-Koehler.

Edwards, Michael, ed. 2011. *The Oxford Handbook of Civil Society*. Oxford: Oxford University Press.

German Advisory Council on Climate Change. 2011. *World in Transition: A Social Contract for Sustainability*. Berlin: WBGU.

Graham, J., Harvey, C., and Rajgopal, S. 2005. "The Economic Implications of Corporate Financial Reporting." *Journal of Accounting and Economics*, 40: 3–73.

Greenpeace. 2011. *Who Is Holding Us Back*. Amsterdam: Greenpeace International.

Haldane, Andrew. 2011. "The Short Long." Speech by Andrew G Haldane, Executive Director, Financial Stability, and Richard Davies at the 29th Société Universitaire Européene de Recherches Financières Colloquium, New Paradigms in Money and Finance?, Brussels.

Interbrand. 2006. *Brand Value Management*. London: Interbrand.

Intergovernmental Panel on Climate Change. 2007. *Climate Change 2007: Synthesis Report*. New York: IPCC.

Keeley, James and Yisheng, Zheng, eds. 2012. *Green China: Chinese Insights on Environment and Development*. London: International Institute for Environment and Development.

Korten, David. 1995. *When Corporations Rule the World*. London: Earthscan.

Litovsky, Alejandro, Rochlin, Steven, Zadek, Simon, and Levy, Brian. 2007. *Investing in Standards for Sustainable Development: The Role of International Development Agencies in Supporting Collaborative Standards Initiatives*. London: AccountAbility.

Pan, Jiahua and Forgach, John, eds. 2011. *Investment, Trade, and Environment: A Report by the CCICED Task Force on Investment, Trade, and Environment*. Beijing: CCICED.

Potts, Jason, van der Meer, Jessica, and Daitchman, Jaclyn. 2010. *The State of Sustainability Initiatives Review 2010: Sustainability and Transparency*. Winnepeg: International Institute of Sustainable Development.

Raw Materials Group. 2011. *Overview of State Ownership in the Global Minerals Industry*. Washington, DC: World Bank.

Schmidheiny, Stephen. 1992. *Changing Course: A Global Business Perspective on Development and the Environment*. Boston: MIT Press.

Society for International Development. 2012. "Greening the Economy." *Development*, Special Issue 51 (1) (in association with UNRISD).

Sogge, David. 1996. *Compassion & Calculation: The Business of Private Foreign Aid*. London: Pluto Press.

United Nations. 2012. *Resilient People, Resilient Planet: A Future Worth Choosing*. Report of the UN Secretary General's High Level Panel on Global Sustainability. New York: United Nations.

UNEP. 2009. *Fiduciary Responsibility: Legal and Practical Aspects of Integrating Environ-mental, Social and Governance Issues into Institutional Investment*. Paris: United Nations Environment Programme Finance Initiative.

World Economic Forum. 2011. *Global Competitiveness Report 2011–2012*. Geneva: World Economic Forum.

World Economic Forum. 2012a. *More With Less: Scaling Sustainable Consumption with Resource Efficiency*. Geneva: World Economic Forum with Accenture.

World Economic Forum. 2012b. *Emerging Best Practices of Chinese Globalizers*. Geneva: World Economic Forum with Boston Consulting Group.

Zadek, Simon. 2000. *Ethical Futures*. London: New Economics Foundation.

Zadek, Simon. 2001. *The Civil Corporation*. London: Earthscan.

Zadek, Simon. 2004. "Paths to Corporate Responsibility." *Harvard Business Review*, December.

Zadek, Simon. 2006a. "Corporate Responsibility and Competitiveness at the Macro Level." *Corporate Governance*, 6 (4): 334–348.

Zadek, Simon. 2006b. "The Logic of Collaborative Governance: Corporate Responsibility, Accountability, and the Social Contract." *Working Paper*, 17, Corporate Social Responsibility Initiative, Cambridge, MA: Harvard Kennedy School.

Zadek, Simon. 2007. *The Civil Corporation*, 2nd edn. London: Earthscan.

Zadek, Simon. 2008. "More Is Not Enough." In *Shaping Up: Scaling Up Voluntary Standards*: 8–10. Bonn: Federal Ministry for Economic Co-operation and Development.

Zadek, Simon. 2010. "Emerging Nations and Sustainability: Chimera or Leadership?" *Politeia*, 26 (98). ISSN 1128-2401: 153–167.

Zadek, Simon. 2011a. "Civil Society and Market Transformation." In *The Oxford Handbook of Civil Society*, ed. Michael Edwards. Oxford: Oxford University Press.

Zadek, Simon. 2011b. "Beyond Climate Finance: From Accountability to Productivity in Addressing the Climate Challenge." *Climate Policy*, 11 (3): 1058–1068.

Zadek, Simon. 2011c. Civil Society and the Valley of Death, *Guardian Online*, September 15, http://www.guardian.co.uk/sustainable-business/blog/civil-society-sustainable-behaviour-valley-of-death. Accessed 3 September 2011.

Zadek, Simon. 2012a. "Titans or Titanic: Towards a Public Fiduciary," *Professional and Business Ethics Journal*, 31 (2): 207–230.

Zadek, Simon. 2012b. "Catalyzing a Public Fiduciary: Corporate Reporting Futures." In *Making Investment Grade: The Future of Corporate Reporting*. Cape Town: UNEP in association with Deloitte and the Centre for Corporate Governance in Africa at the University of Stellenbosch Business School.

Zadek, Simon, Pruzan, Peter, and Evans, Richard, eds. 1997. *Building Corporate Accountability: Emerging Practices in Social and Ethical Accounting and Auditing*. London: Earthscan.

Zadek, Simon, Sapapathy, John, Døssing, Helle, and Swift, Tracey. 2003. *Responsible Competitiveness: Corporate Responsibility Clusters in Action*. London: Copenhagen Centre and AccountAbility.

Zadek, Simon, Merme, Mira, and Samans, Rick. 2005. *Mainstreaming Responsible Investment*. Geneva: World Economic Forum.

Zadek, Simon and Radovich, Sasha. 2006. "Governing Collaborative Governance: Enhancing Development Outcomes by Improving Partnership Governance and Accountability." *Working Paper*, 23, Corporate Social Responsibility Initiative, Cambridge, MA: Harvard Kennedy School.

Zadek, Simon, Forstater, Maya, and Yu, Kelly. 2013, forthcoming. "The Political Economy of Responsible Business in China." *Journal of Current Chinese Affairs*.

Index

Note: "n." after a page reference indicates the number of a note on that page.

The Handbook of Global Companies, First Edition. Edited by John Mikler.
© 2013 John Wiley & Sons, Ltd. Published 2013 by John Wiley & Sons, Ltd.